CHEMICAL DEPENDENCY

CHEMICAL DEPENDENCY
A Systems Approach

C. AARON McNEECE
Florida State University

DIANA M. DiNITTO
University of Texas at Austin

PRENTICE HALL, ENGLEWOOD CLIFFS, NEW JERSEY 07632

Library of Congress Cataloging-in-Publication Data

McNeece, Carl Aaron.
    Chemical dependency : a systems approach / C. Aaron McNeece, Diana
M. DiNitto.
        p.   cm.
    Includes bibliographical references and index.
    ISBN 0-13-859299-3
    1. Substance abuse.   I. DiNitto, Diana M.   II. Title.
HV4998.M46 1994
362.29'18--dc20   93-31569
                                                          CIP

Photographs on pages 2, 20, 32, 41, 67, 99, 146, 163, 199,
214, 240, 292, 312, 349, and 396 are by Sherrill McNeece.
Photograph on page 364 is by C. Aaron McNeece.

©1994 by Prentice-Hall, Inc.
A Paramount Communications Company
Englewood Cliffs, New Jersey 07632

Printed in the United States of America
10 9 8 7 6 5 4 3 2

ISBN   0-13-859299-3

In memory of
Nadine McNeece
1914–1992
C.A.M.

For the DiNitto and Salvatore families
D.M.D.

CONTENTS

*Except where indicated, all chapters were written by C. Aaron McNeece and Diana M. DiNitto.

4 THE PHYSIOLOGICAL AND BEHAVIORAL CONSEQUENCES OF ALCOHOL AND DRUG ABUSE 41

II *Intervention, Prevention, and Public Policy*

5 SCREENING, DIAGNOSIS, ASSESSMENT, AND REFERRAL 67

III   *Chemical Dependency in Special Populations*

IV   Summary and Conclusions

PREFACE

Both authors of this text have taught courses such as "alcoholism and alcohol abuse," "drug abuse, addiction, and treatment" and "chemical dependency" for a number of years. We also have several years of experience working with chemically dependent clients in detox centers, halfway houses, outpatient services, juvenile training schools, adult prisons, and probation and parole programs. Both authors have additional experience in volunteer organizations, research efforts, and policymaking bodies regarding drug and alcohol abuse. The other contributors to this book also have valuable experience working with chemically dependent clients. This volume grew out of our desire to make available a single textbook providing a comprehensive, systems-based examination of the subject of alcohol and drug abuse, as well as the associated problems, policies, and programs. We have attempted to include all the essential components that social workers and other human service professionals would need to understand to work effectively with chemically dependent clients within the policy system that provides treatment and other services.

While we believe that this volume contains "state of the art" information regarding theory and practice with chemically dependent persons, it is in no way intended to serve as a substitute for competent, professional help for anyone with a substance abuse problem.

Part One of this text, Chapters 1 through 4, deals with theories, models, and definitions of abuse and dependency. We have tried to be as comprehensive as possible, and, therefore, we have included *all* those theories that have any credence within the scientific and professional communities. Our current level of scientific understanding does not provide definitive answers to such questions as "What *causes* chemical dependency?" We caution the reader that many practicing professionals adhere to particular etiological models with an ideological fervor. Although our biases may shine through the veneer of scientific objectivity in places, we have tried to present as balanced a perspective as possible. Thus we really do believe that alcoholism *is* a disease when discussing consequences such as pancreatitis and cardiomyopathy. There are other times when we find it more useful to view drug dependency as an addiction or an addictive behavior rather than a disease. If there seems to be some uncertainty here in the adoption of the "best" model, it reflects the state of knowledge in this field.

Part Two of our text concerns intervention, broadly defined. Chapter 5 describes the common processes of screening, diagnosis, and referral. Common treatment approaches and their effectiveness are examined in Chapter 6. Chapter 7 presents prevention theories and describes current programs designed to prevent abuse or dependency. Chapter 8 of this part takes a *macro* approach to intervention, dealing with public policies regarding the manufacture, distribution, and use of psychoactive substances, as well as the social, economic, and political consequences of chemical dependency. Both the financing of treatment and the problem of drug-related crime are also covered in this chapter.

Part Three is devoted to special populations: children, families, ethnic groups, gay men and lesbians, dually diagnosed clients, older drug and alcohol abusers, and women. We apply some of the etiological theories described earlier in the text in attempting to explain the differential use of addictive substances by various groups, and we discuss some of the special problems that occur in these populations because of alcohol or drug use. In examining these populations, we try to link them to the larger systems and other subsystems in which they are connected—the community, the state, the church, the political system, the professions, the network of treatment agencies, et cetera. Chapter 10 takes a careful look at family systems theory, and Chapter 9 examines children within the context of both family and larger systems. Chapters 11 and 12 describe the special problems of substance abuse among ethnic minorities and in the gay and lesbian community. Chapter 13 examines dually-diagnosed clients; Chapter 14 looks at chemical dependency among the elderly. Gender issues and chemical dependency are covered in Chapter 15.

The final part summarizes major current issues, such as the decriminalization of some currently proscribed substances, and indicates some areas where our research efforts should be directed. Chapter 16 also examines the trends in service provision for chemically dependent clients, especially third-party coverage and managed care.

All the material contained in this text has been tested on students in our classes. Many thanks to them for a number of valuable suggestions. We also want to thank our families and Craig Deere for providing the caring environment that allowed this book to be written. A special note of thanks goes to Sherri McNeece for several of the photographs. Diana especially thanks Kelly Larson for her assistance in preparing the drafts of the manuscript. Thanks also to Louise Warren and Jane Kretzschmar for their helpful comments on some of the chapters; to Niaz Murtaza, Charles Austin, and Nancy Sonntag for their assistance with library research; and to Kathryn Webber, Laura Flora, and Phyllis Bassole for their help in completing this project.

1

THEORIES, MODELS, AND DEFINITIONS

Perhaps the most difficult thing for the student of chemical dependency to understand is why one person can drink socially for a lifetime and never develop a "drinking problem," while another person may become addicted to alcohol after a very short period of social drinking; why most teenagers experiment with illicit drugs or are only occasional users, while some of their peers will become quickly and perhaps fatally addicted. The complexity of this process is why we devote the first four chapters to theories, models, and definitions.

Chapter 1 covers the most common definitions of terms such as drug use, drug abuse, addiction, dependency, alcoholism, problem drinking, and so on. At the heart of these different definitions is the ongoing dispute about whether alcoholism is an addiction, a disease, a behavioral disorder, or something else. In addition, this chapter defines the major classes of drugs and examines the epidemiology of alcohol and drug use.

We take a closer look at the major etiological theories in Chapter 2, including psychologic, biologic, and cultural theories, as well as a moral model. A multicausal model of drug use is examined, in an attempt to link together all the major factors that are thought to influence drug use.

Chapter 3 presents a "user's view" of the process of becoming addicted, while Chapter 4 discusses the physiological and behavioral consequences of alcohol and drug abuse. In both these chapters, we attempt to break down some of the more common myths and stereotypes regarding addiction and "addicts."

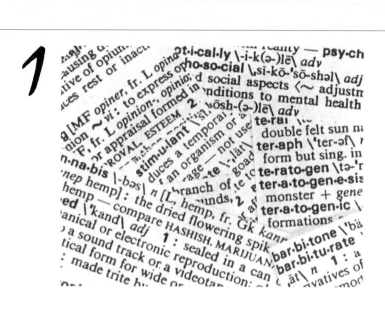

Definitions and epidemiology of alcoholism and drug addiction

In 1990 the estimated per capita consumption of alcoholic beverages by adults in the United States was 39.5 gallons. This is equal to a per capita consumption of 34.4 gallons of beer, 2.9 gallons of wine, and 2.2 gallons of distilled spirits.[1] "Heavy drinkers," about 10 percent of the drinking population, account for half this consumption. (Heavy drinkers are defined in the present context as those who consume 1 ounce or more of pure alcohol daily; moderate drinkers consume 0.22–0.99 ounce; light drinkers, less than 0.22 ounce daily.)[2] It is little wonder that there are 18 million "problem drinkers" and alcoholics in the United States. Neither is it surprising that half of all accidental deaths, suicides,

and homicides are alcohol related.[3] What is surprising is that despite the pervasiveness of health, social, and economic problems associated with the use of alcohol, we have yet to agree just what alcoholism really is. Is it a disease, a behavior problem, an addiction, or something completely different?

In recent years we have become much more concerned with the presence of other types of "drugs" in our society. It was estimated that by the early 1980s, 20 million Americans were spending $18 billion on cocaine.[4] By 1979, 60.4 percent of all high school seniors were estimated to have used marijuana, and by 1985, 17.3 percent had used cocaine.[5] Approximately half a million

Americans were dependent on heroin, and worldwide production of opium poppies reached 1,573 metric tons in 1984.[6] Generally our attention to other drugs has been focused on illicit mood-altering substances, but there is growing concern with the use of prescription drugs (such as Valium and Darvon), over-the-counter (OTC) drugs, and drugs that have only slight mood-altering properties, but that present substantial health risks (such as tobacco). There are other substances that might not ordinarily be considered as "drugs"—inhalants and solvents (toluene, paint thinner, glue, etc.) and naturally occurring plants such as mushrooms, morning glory, and yage. Perhaps it might be more technically appropriate to speak of *substances* rather than *drugs*. On the other hand, the reasons that people generally use or abuse a particular substance are related to the specific drug contained in that substance. Tobacco is smoked because of its nicotine; khat is chewed because it contains cathinone; mushrooms are eaten for their psilocybin. Our primary focus in this book is with the most commonly used psychoactive drugs—those which alter mood, cognition, and/or behavior—whether obtained through legal or illegal means.

DEFINITIONS AND MYTHS

Alcohol is a chemical compound that, when ingested, has the pharmacological property of altering the functioning of the nervous system. Alcohol, along with barbiturates and benzodiazepines, belongs to a class of chemicals called *central nervous system (CNS) depressants*. These drugs are used medically in the induction of anesthesia and the reduction of anxiety. They are often referred to as sedative-hypnotics. There are actually several different types of alcohol, but the two most common types are *methyl alcohol* or *methanol* (the type we use as fuel for our cars) and *ethyl alcohol* or *ethanol* (the type we drink). Alcoholic beverages generally consist of ethyl alcohol (C_3H_7OH), by-products of fermentation known as congeners, colorings, flavorings, and water.[7] Beverage alcohol has been used

by almost every known culture. Since any type of sugary fluid will ferment when exposed to omnipresent yeast spores, spontaneous fermentation is a common occurrence, and alcohol is a readily available pharmacological substance.

Technically, *cannabis* is also a CNS depressant, but it is usually treated separately in texts such as this because of the magnitude of the problems associated with it. Americans spent approximately $44 billion for marijuana in 1984. Between 30,000 and 60,000 tons of marijuana were imported in that year, and perhaps another 4,000 tons were produced domestically.[8]

CNS stimulants are drugs which in small doses produce an increased sense of alertness and energy, elevated mood, and decreased appetite. Included in this group are caffeine, cocaine, amphetamines, methamphetamines, and amphetamine-like substances such as Ritalin and Preludin.

Opiates are substances such as heroin, morphine, and codeine—opiods, synthetic morphinelike substances such as pethidine, methadone, and dipipanone. Small doses will produce an effect similar to that of the CNS depressants, but with somewhat less impairment of the motor and intellectual processes.[9]

Hallucinogens have the capacity to induce altered perception, thought, and feeling. Lysergic acid diethylamide (LSD), mescaline, and "magic mushrooms" with the ingredient psilocybin all produce these effects. Volatile solvents such as gasoline, benzene, and trichlorethylene can also produce effects similar to CNS depressants and hallucinogens when their vapor is inhaled.[10]

Disease, Addiction, or Behavioral Disorder?

The major definitional issue concerning chemical dependency is whether it is a bad habit, a disease, or a form of moral turpitude. It has been described as a product of the genes, the culture, the devil, and the body. Disagreements persist among professional groups as well as the public at large. The various definitions of addiction are frequently driven by political motives, ideology, personal interest, and professional training. We will have much more to say about the nature of addiction throughout this chapter. The major reason for our concern is that appropriate and effective treatment of addiction must be predicated on a reasonably accurate description of the etiology of the phenomenon. We cannot effectively diagnose or treat that we cannot define. The best that we can do is deal with the outward symptoms of the problem.

The reader may have noticed terms in the body of literature on chemical dependency that have not been precisely defined: terms such as *alcoholism, addiction, use, misuse, abuse, dependency,* and *problem drinking.* These terms are more often used as descriptions of a state of affairs rather than explanations, and there is considerable variation in the meaning attached to each term by different writers. We will do the best we can in the following pages to define these terms. However, we will still have to live with some ambiguity. "Problems" and "abuse" frequently exist only in the eye of the beholder.

We are also concerned that when the term "disease" is used in a metaphorical sense, it may actually make treatment more problematic, especially when the metaphoric aspect is forgotten—as it usually is. Over the years poverty, pornography, obesity, family violence, and rock music have all been portrayed as diseases. It is doubtful that the disease label has helped to facilitate a "cure" for any of these conditions.

Alcoholism and drug addiction also are frequently regarded as a "family disease." The implication is that chemical dependency impacts the family *system.* We will discuss this idea at some length in Chapter 10. Whether it is a disease or not, there is little doubt that it dramatically affects not only the family, but all other systems of which the family is a subsystem, or with which families interact.

Alcoholism is one of those peculiar phenomena for which every layperson usually has his or her own working definition, and many laypersons think an alcoholic is "anyone who drinks more than I do." The layperson's defi-nition of *alcoholism* usually does not differentiate *alcohol abuse* and *alcohol dependence.* Professionals working in this field do need to make these distinctions, and perhaps even finer ones. One astute observer has commented that it makes about as much sense to treat all alcoholics alike as to treat all persons having a rash in the same way. Imagine visiting the "rash ward" at your local hospital!

Contemporary scholars of alcoholism owe much to the earlier contributions of Jellinek and Bowman, who insisted that there were important differences between chronic alcoholism and alcohol addiction. The former covered all physical and psychological changes resulting from the prolonged use of alcoholic beverages. The latter was a disorder characterized by an urgent craving for alcohol.[11] According to their model, chronic alcoholism could exist without addiction, and addiction could occur without chronic alcoholism. Jellinek is usually identified as the most important researcher in making the disease concept of alcoholism scientifically respectable, but he also identified five separate types of alcoholism, thus demonstrating that the disease model was not a clear or unitary concept.[12]

According to Jellinek, *Alpha* alcoholics use alcohol to relieve physical or emotional pain more frequently and in greater amounts than are allowed under normal social rules. *Beta* alcoholics drink heavily and experience a variety of health and social problems because of their drinking, but they are not addicted to alcohol. *Gamma* alcoholics are characterized by loss of control over the amount consumed and by increased tissue tolerance to alcohol, adaptive cell metabolism, withdrawal symptoms, and craving. *Delta* alcoholics are similar to the gamma type, but they do not lose control over the amount consumed though they cannot abstain from continuous use of alcohol. *Epsilon* alcoholics are similar to gammas, but are "binge" or periodic drinkers.[13]

It should be noted that Jellinek's research was based on a questionnaire designed by members of Alcoholics Anonymous, distributed in the AA magazine *The Grapevine* and completed by only ninety-eight AA members. It could be very misleading to assume that all alcoholics would fall into the same patterns as these AA members.[14] In his book *The Disease Concept of Alcoholism,* Jellinek also noted that a disease is "simply anything the medical profession agrees to call a disease."

The World Health Organization (WHO) defines alcoholism as "a chronic behavioral disorder manifested by repeated drinking of alcoholic beverages in excess of the dietary and social uses of the community and to the extent that it interferes with the drinker's health or his social or economic functioning."[15] This definition, stressing cultural deviance and damage to the drinker, avoids the "alcoholism as a disease" controversy. The WHO also distinguished between alcohol addicts and symptomatic drinkers. The latter group are similar to Jellinek's Beta alcoholics.[16] The WHO committee on alcohol-related disabilities subsequently published a report endorsing the use of the term *alcohol dependence syndrome.* The use of this term suggests that a number of clinical phenomena occur with sufficient frequency to constitute a recognizable pattern, but the different elements are not always expected to appear with the same magnitude or frequency. The essential features of alcohol dependence syndrome are (1) regularity in the repertoire of drinking behavior, (2) emphasis on drink-seeking behavior, (3) increased tolerance to alcohol, (4) repeated withdrawal symptoms, (5) repeated relief or avoidance of withdrawal symptoms by further drinking, (6) subjective awareness of a compulsion to drink, and (7) reinstatement of the syndrome after periods of abstinence.[17]

A committee of medical authorities commissioned by the National Council on Alcoholism and Drug Dependence (NCADD) developed a set of guidelines to facilitate the diagnosis and evaluation of alcohol dependence at multiple levels. The criteria that were developed consist of eighty-six symptoms grouped into three major diagnostic levels, with each level divided into separate tracks based on physiologic symptoms, behavior, and attitudes.[18] An experimental evaluation of the use of these criteria on 120 male alcoholics concluded that thirty-eight items

did not differentiate between alcoholics and nonalcoholics and that only four items explained 90 percent of the variance between the two groups. These items were gross tremor, regressive defense mechanisms, morning drinking, and blackouts.[19]

As we mentioned earlier, a major issue in defining chemical dependency is whether or not it is a *disease.* As you might expect, those persons with medical training who work in this field tend to define both alcoholism and drug addiction as diseases; persons with other types of backgrounds are not so sure. This is not always the case, however. Vaillant points out quite clearly that members of the medical community are not united in their conceptualization of alcoholism. About 85 percent of general practitioners agree that alcoholism is a disease, while only 50 percent of medical school faculty consider alcoholism (or coronary thrombosis, hypertension, and epilepsy) to be a disease.[20] Pattison, Sobell, and Sobell feel that alcoholism is a collection of various symptoms and behaviors related to the inappropriate use of alcohol with harmful consequences.[21] In other words, describing a person as an alcoholic is no more useful than is describing someone as having a rash. They argue that there is no single factor that explicitly defines and delineates alcoholism and that there is not a clear dichotomy between alcoholics and nonalcoholics. Furthermore, the sequence of appearance of adverse symptoms associated with drinking is highly variable, and there is no conclusive evidence to support the existence of a specific biologic process that predisposes a person toward alcoholism. Their most controversial assertion, however, is that for many "alcoholics," alcohol problems are reversible. In other words, some alcoholics may safely return to social drinking. This clearly puts them at odds with the majority of alcoholism professionals as well as Alcoholics Anonymous, which regards alcoholism as an incurable illness that can be treated only through total abstinence.[22]

Criteria developed by the American Psychiatric Association in its *Diagnostic and Statistical Manual (DSM-III-R)* distinguishes between psychoactive substance *dependence* and psychoactive substance *abuse*. The *DSM-III-R* also avoids use of terms such as illness or disease. It includes two major sets of diagnoses related to chemical dependency. One is "Psychoactive Substance-Induced Organic Mental Disorders," which includes the problems associated with intoxication, withdrawal, dementia, and so on (i.e., the direct acute or chronic effects of such substances on the central nervous system).[23] The other is "Psychoactive Substance Abuse Disorders," which includes both abuse and dependence or "maladaptive behavior associated with more or less regular use of the substances."[24] (The current *DSM-III-R* standards are compared with the changes proposed for the *DSM-IV* and for the *International Classification of Diseases, 10th Revision [ICD-10]*, in Chapter 5.)

Dependence is defined by any three or more of these criteria:

1. substance often taken in larger amounts or over a longer period of time than the person intended;
2. persistent desire or one or more unsuccessful efforts to cut down or control substance use;
3. a great deal of time spent in activities necessary to get the substance or recover from its effects;
4. frequent intoxication or withdrawal symptoms when expected to fulfill major role obligations at work, school, or home;
5. important social, occupational, or recreational activities given up or reduced because of substance abuse;
6. continued substance use despite knowledge of having a persistent or recurrent social, psychological, or physical problem that is caused or exacerbated by the use of the substance;
7. marked tolerance: need for markedly increased amounts of the substance;
8. characteristic withdrawal symptoms; *and*
9. substance often taken to relieve or avoid withdrawal symptoms

Psychoactive substance *abuse* is defined (where the criteria for dependence have not been met) as:

1. continued use despite knowledge of having a persistent or recurrent social, occupational, psychological, or physical problem that is caused

or exacerbated by use of the psychoactive substance, *or*

2. recurrent use in situations in which use is physically hazardous, *and*
3. some symptoms of the disturbance have persisted for at least one month, or have occurred repeatedly over a longer period of time.

Not all use of a drug should be classified as *abuse* or *dependence*. If a person is using a drug without harming himself or herself or others, then it is simply drug *use*. The differentiation between use and abuse has important implications. If one has no moral or religious objections, drug use per se would not seem to be a bad thing. However, if the user is damaging himself or herself or others, drug use becomes *abuse*. (The reader should remember that our society has legalized the use of two major drugs, alcohol and tobacco, even though both frequently lead to abuse and dependence.)

If chemical dependency is a disease, is it a physical, emotional, or mental disease? How does one "catch" or "get" it? Is it transmitted by certain genes? Is there a physiological pathology that leads to alcoholism? There is a vast literature devoted to these and similar questions, but it is likely to be more confusing than enlightening to most readers, and this issue is unlikely to be resolved in the near future. Some of the most interesting and convincing evidence for the disease model comes from the studies of genetically identical (monozygotic) twins.

Kaij studied 174 male twin pairs in Sweden and discovered a 54 percent concordance for alcoholism in one-egg twins versus a 28 percent concordance for alcoholism in two-egg twins. Since both types of twins were raised within the same social environment, it is assumed that any differences in rates of concordance between the two types of twins are the result of genetic factors.[25] On the other hand, a recent longitudinal study of children of alcoholics found a much weaker relationship between their drinking and their parents' drinking problems.[26] This issue is unlikely to be resolved in the near future.

There is no doubt that cirrhosis, pancreatitis, Korsakoff's psychosis, or any other such *effects* that are a result of excessive drinking can properly and indisputably be called diseases. However, these are diseases that *result* from drinking; the debate concerns the etiology of alcoholism, and that is where we turn our attention in the subsequent sections of this chapter as well as Chapter 2.

Is there an identifiable *disease* called alcoholism that causes a person to engage in excessive and inappropriate drinking? As important a question as this would seem to be, some contemporary scholars of alcoholism see this debate as a rather futile and useless waste of energy. Levin argues that any behavior as dysfunctional and self-destructive as alcoholism is a disease, regardless of etiology. "For an organism to destroy itself is pathological, regardless of the source of the pathology."[27]

The same arguments concerning the disease concept of alcoholism are found in the literature on addiction to other drugs as well. Psychiatrists hold many different opinions about the relationship between drug abuse and disease/mental illness. The most consistent opinion is that several different forms of physical disease or mental illness may *result* from drug abuse.[28]

The World Health Organization describes *drug dependence syndrome* with dimensions very similar to those already used for alcohol dependence:

- A subjective awareness of a compulsion to use a drug or drugs usually during attempts to stop or moderate drug use
- A desire to stop drug use in the face of continued use
- A relatively stereotyped drug-taking habit and a narrowing of repertoire of drug-seeking behavior
- Evidence of neuroadaption
- Use of the drug to relieve or avoid withdrawal symptoms
- The salience of drug-seeking behavior over other priorities
- Rapid reinstatement of the syndrome after a period of abstinence[29]

Drug dependence is not described as an "all-or-nothing" condition, but one that exists in varying degrees. There is no attempt to weigh or prioritize the syndrome components, and not all of them need to be present for a person to be labeled "drug dependent."

As with alcoholism, proponents of the disease model of drug addiction can neither demonstrate a clear etiology for addiction nor predict its course or symptoms with any accuracy. It even has been suggested that the disease model is an elaborate and sinister hoax.[30] An important reason for labeling alcoholism and drug addiction as a disease is that it seems to reduce or alleviate the guilt or stigma associated with addiction and to make medical resources available for treatment. The recent decriminalization of alcoholism was undoubtedly related to the acceptance of the disease model. While most people view these events as improvements, one must allow the possibility that the disease model may also serve as an impediment to *scientific* research and to effective treatment. As we will see later, in Chapter 6, our track record in providing effective treatment to chemically addicted clients is not impressive.

EPIDEMIOLOGY

Alcohol

There is evidence that alcohol use was widespread by the Neolithic Age. Stone pots dating from the old Stone Age in Clairvoux, Switzerland, have been discovered that once contained beer or wine. Ancient civilizations of the Near East, India, and China made copious use of alcohol. Myths frequently depicted alcohol as a gift from the gods. Some societies worshipped specific gods of wine: Osiris (Egypt), Dionysius (Greece), and Bacchus (Rome). Priests frequently used alcohol as a part of religious rituals.[31]

Alcohol spread from ritual use to convivial use, and before long, it was a regular part of meals. Assyrians received a daily allotment of bread and barley beer from their masters. Bread and wine were used by the Hebrews after a successful battle. By the Middle Ages alcohol was an important staple in the diet and was used to celebrate births, marriages, coronations, diplomatic exchanges, and the signing of treaties.

Beverage alcohol came to the New World with the explorers and colonists. The *Mayflower* landed at Plymouth Rock because, according to the ship's log, "We could not now take time for further search or consideration, our victuals having been much spent, especially our bere. . . ."[32] Spanish missionaries brought grapevines to America and were making wine in California before the United States was a nation. The Dutch opened the first distillery on Staten Island in 1640. Jamaican rum became the most popular drink in America under British rule, with New England bankers financing the slave trade that was used to produce the molasses needed to make rum. After the American Revolution, rum was eventually superseded by sour-mash bourbon whiskey.[33]

Drinking in America was largely a family affair until the beginning of the nineteenth century. With increasing immigration, industrialization, and greater social freedom, alcohol use (and abuse) became more open and more destructive. The opening of the American West brought the saloon into prominence, with the frontier hero gulping his drinks with his foot on the bar rail.[34]

During the 1820s the founders of the Temperance Movement sought to make Americans into a clean, sober, godly, and decorous people whose values and life-styles would reflect the moral leadership of New England federalism. In the next few decades abstinence became a symbol of middle-class membership and a way to distinguish the ambitious and aspiring from the ne'er-do-well, the Catholic immigrant from the native Protestant, gradually losing its association with the New England upper classes and becoming democratized. By the 1850s, Temperance was allied with Abolition and Nativism to form a trio of major movements.[35]

Threatened by increasing urbanization, political defeats in both the North and the South, and a steady flow of Catholic immigrants, the Populist wing of the Temperance Movement adopted a theme of coercive reform. With the development of the Anti-Saloon League in 1896, it pitted the traditional rural Protestant society against urban Catholicism and industrialism, culminating in 1919 in that "grand experiment" that we know as Prohibition. Since the repeal of the Eighteenth Amendment in 1933, the Temperance Movement generally has been fighting a losing battle. "Dry" counties or precincts have become rare, and not even Protestant churches and the respectable, upper middle-class citizens can safely be counted on to support abstinence.

Estimating the prevalence of alcohol abuse, problem drinking, or whatever else we may choose to call it is very difficult. The first and most obvious difficulty is that there really is no widely accepted definition of just what kind of drinking behavior constitutes a problem. Next, as all experienced researchers know, the choice of investigative method may be the overriding factor in arriving at an estimate of this phenomenon. It is widely assumed that most respondents underreport their actual alcohol consumption, either because they do not know or remember how much they drink or because they fear that their admitted use may seem excessive.

The first national survey of the prevalence of drinking problems was conducted in 1967,[36] and three other nationwide surveys were completed within the next decade.[37] Using Plaut's definition of *problem drinking* as "repetitive use of beverage alcohol causing physical, psychological, or social harm to the drinker or to others,"[38] 15 percent of the men and 4 percent of the women in the samples were judged to have a problem with alcohol. Another interpretation of the data viewed 43 percent of the men and 21 percent of the women as having experienced some degree of problem drinking at some time within the preceding three years.[39] A more recent study reported that 16 percent of males and 6 percent of female drinkers disclosed personal problems associated with alcohol use.[40]

Using the DSM-III-R criteria, Grant and colleagues used the National Health Interview Survey (NHIS) to estimate an alcohol dependence rate within the preceding year of 8.63 percent in the general population, with white males aged 30 to 45 having the highest rate (26.14 percent). For nonwhite males, the rate was 9.29 percent; for nonwhite females, 2.50 percent. The rate for all men was 13.35 percent, and for all women it was 4.36 percent. The rate for white women was slightly higher, at 4.68 percent.[41]

Another approach is to study morbidity and mortality statistics related to the use of alcohol. Jellinek was one of the first researchers to devise a formula specifying a relationship between liver cirrhosis mortality and alcoholism. Using this approach, Lelbach estimated the proportion of cirrhosis deaths attributed to alcoholism to be 12 percent in Asia, 42 percent in Europe, and 66 percent in the United States.[42]

The 1979 national survey[43] indicates that alcohol problems and heavy drinking are more common among young males. There are more abstainers among older people and women, and married people tend to drink less than single, divorced, or separated persons. A later survey that focused on women's drinking patterns confirmed that women had fewer drinking-related problems and fewer dependence symptoms than did men, but it also found higher levels of problem consequences for women who were heavier drinkers.[44] Heavy drinking and adverse consequences were also higher among younger women and among those with depression or a history of obstetric and gynecologic problems.

Problem drinking rates are higher for African Americans than for whites. More than twice as many African Americans as whites report binge drinking and health problems related to drinking. On the other hand, far fewer African American than white women reported alcohol-related problems, and the proportion of abstainers is greater among African Americans than whites.[45]

Surveys of high school students also reveal a higher abstention rate for African-American teenagers than for whites, and *four* times as many heavy drinkers among white youngsters. While 16 percent of white youth consumed at least five drinks at least once per week, only 4 percent of African-American teenagers drank that heavily.[46]

A survey of Hispanic drinkers by Caetano revealed a high abstention rate among women (47 percent) and a high rate of "heavy" drinking among men (36 percent). Among Hispanics, Mexican Americans had the highest rates of both abstention and heavy drinking. There were higher rates of heavy drinking among Hispanics born in the United States to foreign-born parents compared to foreign-born Hispanic drinkers.[47] (As we will see in Chapter 11, the cultural stress experienced by immigrant groups is frequently associated with heavy drinking.)

Native Americans appear to be particularly susceptible to alcohol-related problems. American Indian men between the ages of 25 and 44 have the highest rates of alcohol consumption of any ethnic group. Accidents, liver cirrhosis, homicide, and suicide are among the leading causes of death for American Indians, and most of these are thought to be alcohol related. For example, it is estimated that 20 percent of all deaths are from accidents, and 75 percent of the accidents are alcohol related.[48]

Although there are significant differences in consumption patterns among Asian Americans, both male and female Asian Americans drink significantly less than Caucasians, African Americans, Hispanics, or American Indians.[49] A study of native Hawaiians, Japanese, Filipinos, and Chinese living in Hawaii found fewer Asian Americans in alcohol treatment programs and lower rates of cirrhosis among Asian Americans than Caucasians.[50] On the other hand, a recent study by Helzer and colleagues discovered a high rate of alcoholism among Korean males.[51]

Among other ethnic groups, Americans of Italian descent seem to have both lower abstention and lower problem drinking rates. Americans of British and German stock have intermediate rates, while Irish Americans have high rates of problem drinking.[52] Fundamentalist Protestants are more likely to be abstainers, but those who drink tend to do so more heavily. Catholics, "liberal" Protestants, and persons with no religious affiliation are less likely to abstain and more likely to be heavy drinkers. Jews have low rates of abstention as well as low rates of problem drinking.[53]

TABLE 1.1   Percentage Reporting Alcohol Use in the Past Year, by Age Group and Demographic Characteristics, 1990

Demographic Characteristic	Age Group (years)				
	12–17	18–25	26–34	≥35	Total
Total	41.0	80.2	78.8	62.5	66.0
Sex					
Male	40.8	86.0	83.1	68.5	71.0
Female	41.1	74.6	74.7	57.2	61.5
Race/Ethnicity[1]					
White	45.6	82.7	81.2	64.3	68.3
Black	24.7	74.4	72.7	50.3	55.6
Hispanic	37.9	74.4	75.3	62.8	64.5
Population Density					
Large metro	42.6	82.0	82.6	68.3	70.9
Small metro	40.4	83.6	80.0	65.9	68.4
Nonmetro	38.9	71.1	69.2	46.1	53.1
Region					
Northeast	41.2	82.8	83.4	74.7	74.1
North Central	42.6	86.6	83.8	66.8	70.9
South	40.2	74.6	72.2	48.8	56.3
West	40.0	79.3	80.2	67.7	69.1
Adult Education[2]					
Less than high school	N/A	70.2	75.4	44.2	52.4
High school graduate	N/A	79.3	75.5	61.3	67.7
Some college	N/A	86.4	81.9	76.7	80.1
College graduate	N/A	86.8	83.9	76.2	79.1
Current Employment[3]					
Full time	N/A	87.2	82.5	72.7	77.8
Part time	N/A	76.8	70.6	77.8	76.2
Unemployed	N/A	75.9	82.1	49.2	65.3
Other[4]	N/A	67.5	64.3	47.4	50.9

N/A – Not applicable.

[1] The category "other" for race/ethnicity is not included.

[2] Data on adult education are not applicable for persons aged 12 to 17. Total refers to persons aged 18 and older (unweighted $N = 7,082$).

[3] Data on current employment are not applicable for persons aged 12 to 17. Total refers to persons aged 18 and older (unweighted $N = 7,082$).

[4] Retired, disabled, homemaker, student, or "other."

Source: National Institute on Drug Abuse, *National Household Survey on Drug Abuse, 1990* (Washington, DC: U.S. Government Printing Office, 1991).

Alcohol consumption is also related to age, education, and location of residence, although the reasons are not clear (see Table 1.1). Some researchers attribute age variations in consumption to physiological changes that occur with aging such as a decrease in tolerance to alcohol.[54] Persons who begin to abuse alcohol earlier in life and continue into old age (early-onset drinkers) account for about two-thirds of elderly problem drinkers. Late-onset drinkers usually seem to begin drinking in response to late-life stresses such as the death of a spouse, retirement, or poor health.[55] Variations due to residence and education may be largely "cultural." These variables will be discussed in the next chapter.

Although two-thirds of the adult population drink, actual consumption of alcohol is very unevenly distributed. The 10 percent of drinkers who drink the most heavily account for half of all alcohol consumed, with the other half accounted for by the 90 percent who are infrequent, light, or moderate drinkers.[56] Ledermann has proposed a logarithmic model of alcohol consumption in which a large number of people drink relatively small amounts of alcohol, and a smaller proportion of the population drink larger amounts—accounting for more than their fair share of both alcohol consumption and alcohol problems.[57]

Among young adults 19 to 28 years of age, almost three-fourths had used alcohol within the past 30 days, over one-third had *five* or more drinks in a row during the past two weeks, and 6.1 percent admitted to daily use, according to a 1988 survey by the University of Michigan's Institute for Social Research.[58] There are twice as many heavy drinkers and daily drinkers among young males than young females.[59] The proportion of alcohol users in this ongoing study has changed very little in the past few years.

There are also some wide regional variations in alcohol consumption, with the largest proportion of abstainers in the South and the largest proportion of drinkers in the North and West (see Table 1.2). When urbanization, ancestry, and education are held constant, regional differences in alcohol consumption disappear, however.[60] This suggests that differences in alcohol consumption among geographic regions occurred mainly because of their different sociodemographic compositions.

Marijuana and the Hallucinogens

Marijuana was a legal drug and was grown as a cash crop in parts of the United States until its use and possession was prohibited by federal law in 1937. (It is still an important, but *illicit,* cash crop in many states today.) It was probably brought into Texas and California by Mexican immigrants in the early part of this century. Marijuana smoking was commonly accepted in many Mexican communities as a relaxant, a remedy for headaches, and a mild euphoriant. Cultivation of the plant was a major industry in the area around Mexico City and in several of the provinces. It

quickly spread to border towns like Laredo, El Paso, and Nogales. A direct railroad link between Mexico City and San Antonio facilitated marijuana trade between those cities, and for a while a druggist in Floresville, Texas, established a mail-order marijuana business with customers in Texas, Arizona, New Mexico, Kansas, and Colorado.[61]

Its use spread quickly to New Orleans where it was popular among African-American jazz musicians by the early 1920s.[62] They carried it with them as they immigrated to the urban centers of the north. Anecdotal accounts of its history indicate that marijuana was soon adopted by many "deviant" groups: professional criminals, prostitutes, and so on. In the 1960s it became one of the symbols of the "hippie" movement.[63] Very little hard data exist regarding its use until the mid-1970s, however.

Cannabis is generally regarded as the most commonly used illicit drug. During the 1970s, 16 million Americans used marijuana at least once per month, of whom about 4 million were between 12 and 17 years of age and 8.5 million were in the 18- to 25-year-old age group.[64] Marijuana use seems to have peaked between 1979 and 1981, with more than 10 percent of high school seniors being daily users. By 1986 daily use by this group had dropped to 4 percent.[65] By 1988 it had dropped further to 3.3 percent (4.5 percent for males and 2.2 percent for females).[66] By 1991, daily use by seniors was only 2.0 percent.[67] A 1988 estimate by the National Institute of Mental Health (NIMH) puts the total proportion of U.S. population who had *ever* used marijuana at 29.5 percent. This rate was the highest for the 26- to 34-year-old age group (66.4 percent), and it was only slightly higher for males than for females. Only a quarter of the population 35 and older had used this drug.[68] Among high school seniors in the class of 1991, 36.7 percent had used marijuana during their lifetime.[69]

Hallucinogens such as LSD, mescaline, psilocybin, and phencyclidine (PCP or "angel dust") provide the user with effects which are primarily psychological, such as sensory distortion, synesthesia (perceived overlapping of

TABLE 1.2   Percentage Reporting Alcohol Use in the Lifetime, by Age Group and Demographic Characteristics, 1990

Demographic Characteristic	Age Group (years)				
	12–17	18–25	26–34	≥35	Total
Total	48.2	88.2	92.0	85.0	83.2
Sex					
Male	49.5	91.9	94.4	92.3	88.1
Female	46.9	84.7	89.8	78.7	78.7
Race/Ethnicity[1]					
White	52.1	90.9	94.2	86.0	85.2
Black	32.7	81.5	85.4	83.4	76.6
Hispanic	47.8	81.0	90.7	81.0	78.6
Population Density					
Large metro	49.1	88.6	93.7	89.0	86.1
Small metro	49.0	91.6	92.9	85.5	84.2
Nonmetro	45.8	82.3	87.3	77.0	76.2
Region					
Northeast	46.8	86.8	89.6	88.6	84.6
North Central	48.3	91.6	96.0	91.5	87.9
South	48.2	86.3	89.4	76.6	77.7
West	49.6	88.7	93.8	88.6	85.8
Adult Education[2]					
Less than high school	N/A	81.3	88.8	77.4	79.6
High school graduate	N/A	87.4	91.4	84.2	86.4
Some college	N/A	93.4	94.4	93.3	93.6
College graduate	N/A	91.5	93.0	89.5	90.6
Current Employment[3]					
Full time	N/A	92.9	93.8	91.5	92.4
Part time	N/A	86.2	91.7	90.3	89.4
Unemployed	N/A	84.9	88.1	83.1	84.8
Other[4]	N/A	79.9	84.2	76.2	77.3

N/A – Not applicable.

[1] The category "other" for race/ethnicity is not included.

[2] Data on adult education are not applicable for persons aged 12 to 17. Total refers to persons aged 18 and older (unweighted *N* = 7,082).

[3] Data on current employment are not applicable for persons aged 12 to 17. Total refers to persons aged 18 and older (unweighted *N* = 7,082).

[4] Retired, disabled, homemaker, student, or "other."

Source: National Institute on Drug Abuse, *National Household Survey on Drug Abuse, 1990* (Washington, DC: U.S. Government Printing Office, 1991).

the senses), and a heightened sense of awareness and self-consciousness.[70] With the exception of some American Indians' traditional use of peyote, the use of these "psychedelics" is a relatively recent phenomenon. Like marijuana, "acid" and "mushrooms" are closely connected to the "hippie" subculture of the 1960s and 1970s.

There are few reliable statistics on the use of these drugs, but they are thought to be used mostly by younger persons. With the exception of PCP, hospital emergency room admissions related to hallucinogens have become much less frequent in recent years.[71] According to the Institute for Social Research's most recent study, 10.0 percent of the class of 1991 had used a hallucinogen during their lifetime. The most common hallucinogen used was LSD, with PCP a distant second.[72]

Nicotine

The only known natural source of nicotine is tobacco, a plant cultivated in temperate climates all over the world. The origin of *nicotiana tabacum* was America, and it is thought that the first and only users of the drug at the time of the European discovery of the New World were the aboriginal peoples of North and South America. A stone carving in an ancient Mayan temple depicts a priest smoking what appears to be a cigar. Columbus was greeted at San Salvador in 1492 with a gift of dried tobacco leaves.

Native Americans smoked or chewed the tobacco leaf. The practice of smoking soon spread to Europe (along with "snuffing"), but chewing was confined largely to America. Early proponents of tobacco use hailed its medicinal qualities, but almost from the beginning there were vigorous antismoking movements. The Roman Catholic church forbade smoking in churches on pain of excommunication; Muslim countries defined tobacco as an intoxicant and held that its use was contrary to the Koran; Dr. Benjamin Rush, founder of the Temperance Union, claimed that the use of tobacco created a desire for "strong drink."[73]

Early smoking was practiced by burning the tobacco in pipes or reeds, or by wrapping it in the form of a cigar. The discovery of a low-nicotine, sweet flue-cured tobacco in North Carolina in the midnineteenth century led to the popularity of cigarette smoking. By the 1880s machines were mass producing millions of cigarettes per day, and cigarettes still constitute the bulk of tobacco usage throughout the world.[74]

Most textbooks of this type do not deal with tobacco as an addictive substance. We think that it deserves special attention for several reasons. First, it is the second most commonly used legal drug, with about 50 million Americans smoking cigarettes on a daily basis. Second, it is a powerfully addicting substance, rivaling alcohol and heroin in the strength of its addictive powers.

- Former drug addicts and alcoholics who have been surveyed consider that it is harder to give up tobacco than heroin or alcohol.

- Only 10 to 15 percent of the people alive today who have ever used heroin are still addicted, whereas more than 66 percent of those still living who have ever smoked cigarettes are current daily smokers.
- According to one study, 85 percent of teenagers who smoked more than one cigarette became regular users.[75]

Third, tobacco constitutes more of a health risk than any of the other drugs—legal or illegal. Approximately 390,000 persons died in 1989 as a result of tobacco use—more than deaths from all other drugs combined, including alcohol! Approximately *37 million* Americans who are currently smoking tobacco will die premature deaths as a result.[76] Worldwide there are 2.5 million deaths attributed to cigarette smoking each year.[77]

Fourth, while smoking among the general adult population has recently declined, cigarette smoking among women and teenagers is increasing. Among high school seniors, females were smoking as much as males by 1977. Since 1988 smoking rates for female seniors has been slightly higher than for males.[78] Among the class of 1991, 10.7 percent were smoking one-half pack of cigarettes or more per day.[79] This trend is particularly disturbing when one realizes that cigarette smoking is one of the best predictors of other drug use.[80]

Finally, nicotine addiction that results from tobacco smoking is actually *promoted* by a very rich, active, and politically well-connected lobby. In some communities in North Carolina and Kentucky, it is considered almost un-American to oppose smoking. This makes the task of prevention and treatment even more difficult in dealing with this drug.

Cocaine

Cocaine is another drug that made its way into the United States from Latin America, but with a very different history from that of marijuana. Coca leaves have been found in burial middens in Peru that date back to 2500 B.C. Under the Incas, coca became sacred and was used primarily by priests and nobility for special ceremonies. Widespread daily use of the coca leaf did not appear until the Spanish conquest, when they used it to pay for labor in the gold and silver mines in the Andes. They also discovered that the Indians could work harder and longer and required less food if they were given coca.[81]

Samples of the plant were sent to Europe in 1749, but the anesthetic effects of cocaine were discovered in 1862. By 1884 it was in widespread use as a local anesthetic for the eye. In 1885 Freud delivered a lecture based on his observations of the effects of cocaine on mood and behavior.[82] The use of cocaine was a common theme in the literature of the day, with such popular heroes as Arthur Connan Doyle's Sherlock Holmes favoring a "seven percent solution." (Holmes once mysteriously disappeared for three years and returned to his Baker Street residence cured of his cocaine addiction.)

In addition to its legitimate medical uses, cocaine was an ingredient in patent medicines and beverages such as Coca-Cola until the passage of the Harrison Tax Act of 1914. Coca-Cola now uses only the decocainized coca leaves as a flavoring agent.[83]

The "rediscovery" and reintroduction of cocaine to modern American culture is sometimes attributed to the rock musicians of the 1960s. Until recent years the form of cocaine generally available for illicit use in the United States was the white, bitter-tasting, crystalline powder of cocaine hydrochloride. It could be smoked or injected, but was most commonly "snorted" (ingested intranasally). More recently, another more dangerous form of cocaine, "crack," is made by cooking the powder with baking soda to remove its impurities. The resulting product is smoked and provides a much more rapid and intense "high."[84] Unfortunately, most statistics on cocaine use have only recently distinguished cocaine powder and crack cocaine.

The number of people who had used cocaine rose dramatically from 5.4 million in 1974 to 21.6 million in 1982.[85] In 1976, 9 percent of high school seniors had tried cocaine; in 1985, it was 17.3 percent. Fortunately, by 1991 it had dropped to 7.8 percent.[86] In the 1988 National Household Survey on Drug Abuse, cocaine use appeared to be more common among 26- to 34-year-old males, especially those living in the western United States. Within this group almost 40 percent had ever used cocaine, and 3.1 percent had used it within the past month. The same report estimates that between 1.5 million and 2.5 million Americans are *frequent* users of cocaine.[87] According to a recent survey, 1.7 percent all persons 26 to 34 years old had used cocaine within the last month.[88] The proportion of persons who had ever used cocaine was estimated to be 11.3 percent, with an additional 1.4 percent having used "crack" during their lifetime.[89]

Other Stimulants and Sedatives

In general, amphetamines have an effect similar to cocaine, but with a slower and less dramatic action. Amphetamine is a synthetic stimulant synthesized in 1927 as a replacement for ephedrine, a common ingredient in asthma, cold, and hay fever remedies. Drinamyl, for many years the most widely prescribed drug for symptoms of anxiety and depression, was a combination of amphetamine and barbiturates. Amphetamines were widely used in World War II on both sides for keeping the troops alert and overcoming fatigue. During the 1960s many people unknowingly became addicted to a "Benzedrine inhaler" sold without a prescription for the treatment of colds, allergies, and sinusitis. Until new rules were adopted by the Food and Drug Administration in 1970, many others became addicted while using amphetamine-based "diet pills."[90] Amphetamines were also widely used in the 1960s and 1970s in both amateur and professional sports. One report in 1978 revealed that seventy-five of eighty-seven professional football players interviewed admitted using "speed."[91]

"Ice," a particularly strong and dangerous form of amphetamine, recently appeared in Hawaii and California and is rapidly spreading to other parts of the country. Although the data are largely anecdotal at this point, "ice" seems to be responsible for an alarmingly high number of hospital emergency room admissions.[92] No separate national statistics of use are kept for this particular drug.

The most commonly used stimulant, caffeine, is found in coffee, tea, and certain soft drinks. Although withdrawal effects are not uncommon, caffeine does not ordinarily present a threat to health or an impairment of functioning. For this reason we will not devote much space to it in this text. Methylphenidate (Ritalin) is still widely sought after by narcotic addicts maintained on methadone injections, since methadone has no antagonist effect on amphetamines. Statistics on its use are not available, but it does not seem to constitute a serious problem.[93] (Ritalin is a drug commonly prescribed to control hyperactivity in children.)

The nonmedical use of stimulant drugs seems be higher in the West, especially among 26- to 34-year-old males (22.1 percent). The highest rate of current use (within the past month) is among 18- to 25-year-old males (4.5 percent). Regional patterns of stimulant use vary greatly, and female users outnumber males in both the West and the Northeast.[94] Among young adults (19- to 30-year-olds), however, rates of stimulant use for females (2.7 percent) within the past month is slightly higher than that for males (2.6 percent).[95] Amphetamines became widely abused during the time that they were prescribed as diet pills.

Sedative drugs, those which may induce sleep, are usually divided into two categories: the barbiturates and the nonbarbiturates. Since their synthesis in 1903, over two thousand different types of barbiturates have been developed. They are used medically as sedatives, short-term anesthetics, anticonvulsants, and to treat psychiatric problems. Nonbarbiturate sedatives such as methaqualone were developed as a safer alternative to barbiturates. They were originally believed to be much safer than barbiturates, but soon proved to be equally dangerous. Marketed in Britain as Mandrax and in the United States as Quaalude, Sopor, and several other names, it soon became a popular drug among polydrug users, especially for "mixing" with alcohol.[96] Unfortunately, alcohol and Quaaludes were frequently a lethal combination. Many readers will remember the tragic case of Karen Ann Quinlan (see Chapter 4). The overall past-month use rate of sedatives in the United States in 1988 was 0.7 percent for males and 0.8 percent for females.[97]

Valium is one of the benzodiazepine minor tranquilizers and, during the 1970s, was the most frequently prescribed legal drug in the United States. Drugs such as Valium came into popular use because, according to Hollister, "The benzodiazepines are virtually suicide proof. Massive overdoses have been taken with very little difficulty in managing patients and with no fatalities in the absence of other drugs."[98] Although statistics on Valium abuse are spotty and unreliable, we do know that about 75 percent of all prescriptions written for this drug were by nonpsychiatrists and that the typical legal user was female. During the 1970s Valium came to be a sort of folk medicine in the drug subculture to treat complications of illicit use of other drugs. "Speedfreaks" as well as methadone and LSD users were widely known to maintain their "stash" of Valium.[99] The past-month use rate of tranquilizers by young adults in 1989 was 4.0 percent for males and 4.5 percent for females.[100]

Narcotics

Opium, morphine, codeine, and heroin are the major drugs included in this category. They are derived from the variety of poppy known as *papaver somniferum*. Under federal law, cocaine is classified as a "narcotic," but it is actually a stimulant. Narcotics have the effect of *depressing* the activity of the brain and the central nervous system.

The earliest reference to opium is a Sumerian idiogram dated about 4000 B.C., referring to it as "joy plant." Hippocrates and Pliny both recommended the use of opium for a number of conditions. Since it was not banned in Muslim countries, Arab traders carried it from the Middle East to India, China, and finally Europe. By the early sixteenth century, it was prescribed by physi-

.

7. Jerome D. Levin, *Alcoholism: A Bio-psycho-social Approach* (New York: Hemisphere, 1989), p. 5.

8. U.S. House of Representatives, *Annual Report for the Year 1984.*

9. Duncan Raistrick and Robin Davidson, *Alcoholism and Drug Addiction* (New York: Churchill Livingstone, 1985), p. 9.

10. Ibid., p. 11.

11. Karl M. Bowman and Elvin Morton Jellinek, "Alcohol Addiction and Chronic Alcoholism," *Quarterly Journal of Studies on Alcohol,* Vol. 2 (1941).

12. Elvin Morton Jellinek, *The Disease Concept of Alcoholism* (Highland Park, NJ: Hillhouse Press, 1960).

13. Ibid.

14. William A. McKim, *Drugs and Behavior: An Introduction to Behavioral Pharmacology* (Englewood Cliffs, NJ: Prentice Hall, 1991), p. 105.

15. Mark Keller, "Alcoholism: Nature and Extent of the Problem," *Annals of the American Academy of Political and Social Science,* Vol. 315 (1958), pp. 1–11.

16. World Health Organization, Expert Committee on Mental Health: "Report on the First Session of the Alcoholism Subcommittee," WHO Technical Reporting Service, No. 48 (Geneva: WHO, August 1952).

17. Wallace Mandell, "Types and Phases of Alcohol Dependence Illness," in M. Galanter (ed.), *Recent Developments in Alcoholism,* Volume 1 (New York: Plenum Press, 1983).

18. National Council on Alcoholism, "Criteria for the Diagnosis of Alcoholism," *American Journal of Psychiatry,* Vol. 129, No. 2 (August 1972).

19. Carol Ringer et al., "The N.C.A. Criteria for the Diagnosis of Alcoholism," *Journal of Studies on Alcohol,* Vol. 38 (1977).

20. George E. Vaillant, *The Natural History of Alcoholism* (Cambridge, MA: Harvard University Press, 1983), p. 15.

21. E. Mansell Pattison, Mark B. Sobell, and Linda C. Sobell, *Emerging Concepts of Alcohol Dependence* (New York: Springer, 1977).

22. Joan Curlee-Salisbury, "Perspectives on Alcoholics Anonymous," in Nada J. Estes and M. Edith Heinemann (eds.), *Alcoholism: Development, Consequences, and Interventions,* 3rd ed. (St. Louis, MO: C. V. Mosby, 1986).

23. American Psychiatric Association, *Diagnostic and Statistical Manual of Mental Disorders,* 3rd ed., rev. (Washington, DC: APA, 1987), pp. 165–185.

24. Ibid.

25. Lennart Kaij, *Alcoholism in Twins* (Stockholm: Almqvist and Wiksell, 1960).

26. Ernest Harburg, Wayne DiFranceisco, Daniel W. Webster, Llian Gleiberman, and Anthony Schork, "Familial Transmission of Alcohol Use: II. Imitation of and Aversion to Parent Drinking (1960) by Adult Offspring (1977)—Tecumseh, Michigan," *Journal of Studies on Alcohol,* Vol. 51, No. 3 (1990), pp. 245–256.

27. Levin, *Alcoholism,* p. 63.

28. Raistrick and Davidson, *Alcoholism and Drug Addiction.*

29. WHO Memorandum 1981, *Bulletin of the World Health Organization, 59,* pp. 225–242.

30. Jara Krivanek, *Addictions* (Winchester, MA: Allen & Unwin, 1988), pp. 31–38.

31. Levin, *Alcoholism.*

32. Jean Kinney and Gwen Leaton, *Loosening the Grip: A Handbook of Alcohol Information* (St. Louis, MO: Times Mirror/Mosby, 1987), p. 5.

33. W. J. Rorabaugh, *The Alcohol Republic: An American Tradition* (New York: Oxford University Press, 1979).

34. Kinney and Leaton, *Loosening the Grip,* p. 13.

35. Joseph R. Gusfield, "Symbolic Crusade: Status Politics and the American Temperance Movement," in Maureen E. Kelleher, Bruce K. MacMurray, and Thomas M. Shapiro, *Drugs and Society: A Critical Reader, 2nd ed.* (Dubuque, IA: Kendall/Hunt, 1988).

36. Don Calahan, *Problem Drinkers* (San Francisco: Jossey-Bass, 1970).

37. Don Calahan and R. Roizen, "Changes in Drinking Problems in a National Sample of Men," paper presented at a meeting of the Alcohol and Drug Problems Association, San Francisco, 1974.

38. T. F. Plaut, *Alcohol Problems: A Report to the Nation by the Cooperative Commission on the Study of Alcoholism* (New York: Oxford University Press, 1967).

39. Don Calahan and Ira H. Cisin, "Epidemiological and Social Factors Associated with Drinking Problems," in Ralph E. Tarter and A. Arthur Sugerman (eds.), *Alcoholism* (Reading, MA: Addison-Wesley, 1976), p. 541.

40. Henry Malin, R. Wilson, G. Williams, and S. Aitken, "1983 Alcohol/Health Practices Supplement," *Alcohol Health & Research World,* Vol. 8 (1986), pp. 56–57.

41. Bridget F. Grant, Thomas C. Harford, Patricia Chou, Roger Pickering, Deborah A. Dawson, Frederick S. Stinson, and John Noble, "Prevalence of DSM-III-R Alcohol Abuse and Dependence: United States, 1988," *Alcohol Health & Research World,* Vol. 15, No. 1 (1991), pp. 91–96.

42. Werner K. Lelbach, "Cirrhosis in the Alcoholic and Its Relation to the Volume of Alcohol Abuse," *Annals of the New York Academy of Science,* Vol. 252 (1975), pp. 85–105.

43. Walter B. Clark and L. Midanik, "Alcohol Use and Alcohol Problems Among U.S. Adults: Results of the 1979 National Survey," in *Alcohol Consumption and Related Problems,* National Institute on Alcohol Abuse and Alcoholism, Alcohol and Health Monograph No. 1 (Washington, DC: U.S. Government Printing Office, 1982), pp. 3–52.

44. Sharon C. Wilsnack, Richard W. Wilsnack, and Albert D. Klassen, "Drinking and Drinking Problems Among Women in a U.S. National Survey," *Alcohol Health & Research World,* Vol. 9 (1985), pp. 3–13.

45. Denise Herd, "A Review of Drinking Patterns and Alcohol Problems Among U.S. Blacks," in National Institute on Alcohol Abuse and Alcoholism (NIAAA), *Alcohol Use Among U.S. Ethnic Minorities,* Research Monograph No. 18 (Washington, DC: U.S. Government Printing Office, 1987).

46. Charles Lowman, Thomas C. Harford, and Charles T. Kaelber, "Alcohol Use Among Black Senior High School Students," *Alcohol Health & Research World,* Vol. 7 (1983), pp. 37–46.

47. Raul Caetano, "Drinking Patterns and Alcohol Problems in a National Sample of U.S. Hispanics," in NIAAA, *Alcohol Use Among U.S. Ethnic Minorities.*

48. Barbara W. Lex, "Alcohol Problems in Special Populations," in J. H. Mendelson and N. K. Mello (eds.), *The Diagnosis and Treatment of Alcoholism* (New York: McGraw-Hill, 1985), pp. 89–187.

49. Arthur L. Klatsky, Abraham B. Siegelaub, Cynthia Landy, and Gary D. Friedman, "Racial Patterns of Alcoholic Beverage Use," *Alcoholism: Clinical and Experimental Research,* Vol. 7 (1983), pp. 372–377.

50. Frank M. Ahern, "Alcohol Use and Abuse Among Four Ethnic Groups in Hawaii," in NIAAA, *Alcohol Use Among U.S. Ethnic Minorities.*

51. John E. Helzer, J. Gloriosa Canino, Eng-kung Yeh, and Roger C. Bland, "Alcoholism: North America and Asia: A Comparison of Population Surveys with the Diagnostic Interview Schedule," *Archives of General Psychiatry,* Vol. 47, No. 4 (April 1990), pp. 313–319.

52. Estes and Heinemann, *Alcoholism,* p. 45.

53. Charles R. Snyder, "Culture and Jewish Sobriety: The Ingroup-Outgroup Factor," in David J. Pittman and Charles R. Snyder (eds.), *Society, Culture, and Drinking Patterns* (New York: John Wiley and Sons, 1967).

54. Robert Straus, "Alcohol Problems Among the Elderly: The Need for a Biobehavioral Perspective," in G. Maddox, L. N. Robins, and N. Rosenberg (eds.), *Nature and Extent of Alcohol Problems Among the Elderly,* National Institute on Alcohol Abuse and Alcoholism, Research Monograph No. 14 (Washington, DC: U.S. Government Printing Office, 1984), pp. 9–28.

55. M. Williams, "Alcohol and the Elderly: An Overview," *Alcohol Health & Research World,* Vol. 8 (1984), pp. 3–9.

56. Henry J. Malin, J. Coakley, C. Kaelber, N. Munch, and W. Holland, "An Epidemiologic Perspective on Alcohol Use and Abuse in the United States," in National Institute on Alcohol Abuse and Alcoholism, *Alcohol Consumption and Related Problems* (Washington, DC: U.S. Government Printing Office, 1982), pp. 99–153.

57. Alcohol Education Centre, *The Ledermann Curve: Report of Symposium* (London: The Centre, 1977).

58. Lloyd D. Johnston, Patrick M. O'Malley, and Jerald G. Bachman, *Drug Use, Drinking, and Smoking: National Survey Results from High School, College, and Young Adults Population,* U.S. Department of Health and Human Services, Public Health Service, Alcohol, Drug Abuse, and Mental Health Administration, (Washington, DC: National Institute on Drug Abuse, 1989), pp. 209–210.

59. Ibid., p. 176.

60. John W. Welte and Marcia Russell, "Regional Variations in the Consumption of Alcohol in the U.S.A.," *Drug and Alcohol Dependence,* Vol. 10 (1982), pp. 243–249.

61. Richard J. Bonnie and Charles Whitebread II, "The Alien Weed," in Kelleher, MacMurray, and Shapiro, *Drugs and Society,* pp. 256–267.

62. Erich Goode, *Marijuana* (New York: Atherton Press, 1969), p. 7.

63. Maureen E. Kelleher, Bruce K. MacMurray, and Thomas M. Shapirof (eds.), *Drugs and Society: A Critical Reader* (Dubuque, IA: Kendall/Hunt, 1988), p. 249.

64. Executive Office of the President, *Drug Use, Patterns, Consequences, and the Federal Response: A Policy Review,* Office of Drug Abuse Policy, March 1978.

65. Lloyd D. Johnston, Patrick M. O'Malley, and Jerald G. Bachman, *National Trends in Drug Use and Related Factors Among American High School Students and Young Adults, 1975–1986* (Washington, DC: U.S. Government Printing Office, 1987).

66. Johnston et al., *Drug Use,* p. 176, 210.

67. National Institute on Drug Abuse (NIDA), *Monitoring the Future* (Washington, DC: U.S. Government Printing Office, 1991).

68. National Institute on Drug Abuse, *National Household Survey on Drug Abuse: 1988 Population Estimates,* Division of Epidemiology and Prevention Research (Washington, DC: U.S. Government Printing Office, 1989), p. 27.

69. NIDA, *Monitoring the Future.*

70. Kelleher, *Drugs and Society,* p. 247.

71. Sidney Cohen, *The Substance Abuse Problems* (New York: Haworth Press, 1981), p. 173.

72. NIDA, *Monitoring the Future.*

73. McKim, *Drugs and Behavior,* pp. 160–164.

74. J. E. Brooks, *The Mighty Leaf: Tobacco Through the Centuries* (Boston: Little, Brown, 1952).

75. Gwenda Blair, "Why Dick Can't Stop Smoking," in Kelleher, *Drugs and Society,* pp. 223–230.

76. Ibid.

77. Kelleher, *Drugs and Society,* p. 221.

78. Johnston et al., *Drug Use,* p. 81.

79. NIDA, *Monitoring the Future, 1991.*

80. Nada J. Estes and M. Edith Heinemann, "Issues in Identification of Alcoholism," in Estes and Heinemann (eds.), *Alcoholism,* pp. 317–333.

81. McKim, *Drugs and Behavior,* pp. 202–204.

82. Norman Imlah, *Addiction: Substance Abuse and Dependency.* (Wimslow, England: Sigma Press, 1989), pp. 56–67.

83. Cohen, *The Substance Abuse Problems,* p. 173.

84. Imlah, *Addiction,* p. 58.

85. Edgar H. Adams and Jack Durell, "Cocaine: A Growing Public Health Problem," in John Grabowski (ed.), *Cocaine: Pharmacology, Effects, and Treatment of Abuse,* National Institute on Drug Abuse Research Monograph 50 (Rockville, MD: National Institute on Drug Abuse, 1984).

86. NIDA, *Monitoring the Future.*

87. NIDA, *National Household Survey on Drug Abuse: 1988 Population Estimates,* p. 94.

88. National Institute on Drug Abuse (NIDA), *National Household Survey on Drug Abuse, 1990* (Washington, DC: U.S. Government Printing Office, 1991).

89. Ibid.

90. Imlah, *Addiction,* p. 59.

91. G. Rankin Cooter, "Amphetamine Use: Physical Activity and Sport," in Kelleher, *Drugs and Society,* p. 329.

92. Michael A. Lerner, "The Fire of `Ice,'" *Newsweek,* November 27, 1989, pp. 37–40.

93. Imlah, *Addiction,* p. 63.

94. NIDA, *National Household Survey,* 1990, p. 63.

95. Johnston et al., *Drug Use,* 1990, p. 178.

96. Cohen, *The Substance Abuse Problems,* p. 125.

97. Johnston et al., *Drug Use,* p. 178.

98. Leo E. Hollister, *Clinical Use of Psychotherapeutic Drugs* (Springfield, IL: Charles C Thomas, 1973), pp. 129–131.

99. Cohen, *The Substance Abuse Problems,* pp. 130–134.

100. Johnston et al., *Drug Use,* p. 178.

101. McKim, *Drugs and Behavior,* pp. 228–231.

102. David F. Musto, *The American Disease: Narcotics in Nineteenth-Century America* (New Haven, CT: Yale University Press, 1973).

103. McKim, *Drugs and Behavior,* pp. 228–231.

104. A. Wilker, *Opiod Dependence* (New York: Plenum Press, 1980).

105. Don C. Des Jarlais and Samuel R. Friedman, "HIV Infections Among IV Drug Users," in Kelleher, *Drugs and Society,* pp. 311–326.

106. Tam Stewart, *The Heroin Users* (London: Pandora Press, 1987).

107. Jara Krivanek, *Heroin: Myths and Realities* (Winchester, MA: Allen & Unwin, 1988).

108. NIDA, *National Household Survey,* p. 102.

109. Johnston et al., *Drug Use,* p. 177.

2

The etiology of addiction

ETIOLOGICAL THEORIES

There are at least as many explanatory theories as there are definitions of addiction. We will focus on three broad categories (psychologic theories, sociocultural theories, and biologic theories), and we will also discuss some alternative explanations. These theories are not mutually exclusive, and divisions sometimes seem quite arbitrary. None are presented as the "correct" way of explaining this phenomenon. We do have preferences, and we lean more toward certain models than others, but no single theory adequately describes the etiology of alcoholism. Before turning to those theories, however, we will briefly review

the "moral" model of addiction. Although generally discredited by modern scholars, the legacy of our history of treating alcoholism and drug addiction as sin or moral weakness still has a pronounced effect on public policies regarding alcohol and drug use.

The Moral Model

Widespread condemnation of the use of alcohol developed in England after the infamous "gin epidemic" of the early eighteenth century. After the monarchy was restored in 1660, distilleries were licensed, and the popularity of gin spread like an epidemic. Between 1684 and 1727 the consumption of distilled spirits creased over 700 percent, not counting large quantities of rum and brandy that were smuggled into the country to escape high tariffs![1] Opposition to drinking became so strong in some circles that by 1742 Parliament banned the distillation of grain altogether for several years.

Both the British propensity toward strong drink and moral-based temperance movements found homes in America. In the late eighteenth century Dr. Benjamin Rush, an American physician, wrote widely about the dangerous physical, social, and moral effects of alcohol. State and locally based temperance movements met with mixed success for the next hundred years. Summarizing the popular moral model of the temperance movement, one writer argued that temperance was preferable to drink because it was cheaper, it was healthier, and it could provide a sense of righteousness that taverns could not. Temperance also appealed to the ethics of capitalism and the new materialistic philosophy that dominated our developing industry. "Men who chased dollars naturally disapproved of liquor, because a drinking man poured his money down his throat dissipating and destroying wealth for selfish, nonproductive ends."[2]

During this same period, a religious revival was sweeping America, and total abstinence provided a symbolic way to express conversion and faith, and alcohol also provided a target for religious zeal. The movement was not content to rely on the force of moral suasion in drying up the country, however. Eleven states and two territories enacted prohibition laws, and a national prohibition party was founded. This campaign eventually culminated in the "noble experiment" of national prohibition in 1917.[3]

Until quite recently it was (and perhaps still *is* in some communities) common to arrest intoxicated persons and place them in the local jail's "drunk tank." Even though the use of alcohol has largely been decriminalized, similar attitudes and similar treatment of illicit drug users are widespread today. How else can we account for the tremendous increases in arrests and incarceration for drug-related crimes? Drug users are still perceived by a large segment of the public as morally weak, "evil" persons. Therefore, the proper response is jail or imprisonment. As we will see in a later chapter, this approach to alcohol and drug abuse has simply not worked.

Psychologic Theories

There are actually several different psychologic theories of alcoholism and drug addiction. Psychological models define addiction as an individual phenomenon but do not necessarily exclude or minimize social factors or other elements in the development of an addiction.

Psychodynamic Theories. Psychodynamic theories are more difficult than most other psychologic theories to substantiate because they deal with concepts that are difficult to operationalize and with events that may have occurred many years before the onset of addiction. Although Freud never devoted a single paper to the subject of alcoholism, his disciples were not the least bit reluctant to apply psychoanalytic theories to alcohol addiction. The earliest explanations linked alcoholism with the "primal addiction" of masturbation.[4] Most later explanations linked alcoholism to ego deficiencies, with alcohol used to attain a sense of security. This theory assumes that the alcoholic's parental environment and constitution cause the individual to be inadequate in forming attachments.[5] Alcohol abuse has also been explained by psychoanalytic theorists as an expression of hostility and homosexuality. Still others view alcoholics as self-destructive, narcissistic, or orally fixated.[6] Psychoanalytic theory has even blamed the development of alcoholism on the failure of mothers to provide milk![7]

A major problem with these theories is that experiences such as early childhood deprivation are not specific to alcoholism or addiction to other drugs. In fact, they are commonly reported by nonaddicted adults with a variety of other psychological problems. Perhaps the most serious shortcoming is in the psychodynamic theories' implications for the treatment of alcoholism or drug addiction. Many counselors warn that a nondirective approach that focuses on the patient's development of insight into their problems neglects the addictive power of alcohol or other drugs.[8]

Learning Theories. Learning or reinforcement theory assumes that alcohol or drug use results in a decrease in psychological states such as anxiety, stress, or tension, thus positively reinforcing the user. This learned response continues until physical dependence develops, at which time the aversion of withdrawal symptoms becomes a prime motivation for drug use.[9] Other rewards for drug use could be the approval of peers or a perceived improvement in social interactions.[10]

Although social drinkers and alcoholics both report using alcohol to "relax," tests of actual tension-reducing effects of alcohol have yielded quite different results. Scientific observations of persons using alcohol actually show them to become *more* depressed, anxious, and nervous.[11]

There is a considerable amount of evidence to support that part of learning theory related to alcohol use and physiological aversion. Abrupt cessation of drinking will lead to unpleasant symptoms of withdrawal.[12] For the social drinker, the symptoms may amount to what we call a "hangover." For the alcoholic, withdrawal could lead to trembling, shaking, hallucinations, and grand mal seizures. Similarly, for the heroin addict, abrupt withdrawal may lead to severe flu-like symptoms. The ten-cup-per-day coffee drinker may become anxious or agitated and lethargic, and develop a headache. In each case, the addict quickly learns that these symptoms may be avoided by resuming use of the drug.

An interesting view of becoming a heroin addict is provided by Krivanek.[13] Dependencies which involve drug use follow the same basic principles of learning theory as all other dependencies. Krivanek views drug dependence as a psychological phenomenon that can vary in intensity from a "mild involvement" to an addiction that seriously restricts the actor's other behaviors. "The dependent behavior is maintained by the degree of reinforcement it provides, and this in turn depends on the actor's perception of his or her need hierarchy and the likelihood that this course of action will meet the most important needs better than other available options."[14] This is similar to the idea of alcoholism as a continuum, proposed by Pattison, Sobell, and Sobell: "An individual's use of alcohol can be considered as a point on a continuum from nonuse, to nonproblem drinking, to various degrees of deleterious drinking."[15]

Learning theory is helpful in treatment planning because it addresses the adaptive consequences of drinking, and behavioral approaches to treatment have incorporated learning theory into a treatment framework based on the premise that what has been learned can be unlearned.[16] Learning theory is also quite adaptable to the *systems* view, which we will follow throughout this book.

Personality Theories. These theories, which frequently overlap the psychodynamic theories, assume that certain personality traits predispose an individual to drug use. An individual with an "alcoholic personality" is often described as dependent, immature, and impulsive.[17] Other personality theorists have described alcoholics as highly emotional, immature in interpersonal relationships, having low frustration tolerance, being unable to express anger adequately, and confused in their sex role orientation.[18] After reviewing these personality theories Keller summarized them in "Keller's law": *The investigation of any trait in alcoholics will show that they have either more or less of it.*[19] However, the many scales that have been developed in an attempt to identify alcoholic personalities have failed to distinguish consistently the personality traits of alcoholics from those of nonalcoholics. One of the subscales of the Minnesota Multiphasic Personality Inventory (MMPI) does differentiate alcoholics from the general population, but it may actually detect only the *results* of years of alcohol abuse, not underlying personality problems.[20]

There is some evidence that individuals with an antisocial personality (as defined in the DSM-III-R) have a higher incidence of alcoholism than the general population. There is no evidence that this personality disorder *caused* the alcoholism, but these individuals were more disposed to develop alcohol problems because of their antisocial personality. Apart from this relatively rare occurrence of the antisocial personality, alcoholics have not been found to exhibit a specific cluster of personality traits.[21] Vaillant argues persuasively in his book[22] that personality (as well as psychological) factors are, at most, of minimal consequence as a cause of alcoholism.

There have been similar attempts to link a constellation of certain personality traits to drug addiction[23] as well as alcoholism. A consensus seems to have evolved that personality traits are not of much importance in explaining drug dependence, and most of those who work in this field agree that anyone can become dependent irrespective of personality attributes.[24] A table in a recent book lists *ninety-four personality characteristics* that have been attributed to drug addicts by various theorists.[25] These include "poor self-image" as well "grandiose self-image," "ego inflation" and "ego contraction," "self-centered" and "externalization," "pleasure-seekers" and "pleasure-avoiders," and several dozen other contradictory pairs.

A recent report to the National Academy of Sciences concludes that there is no single set of psychological characteristics that embraces all addictions. However there are, according to the report, "significant personality factors that can contribute to addiction." These factors are:

- Impulsive behavior, difficulty in delaying gratification, an antisocial personality, and a disposition toward sensation seeking.
- A high value on nonconformity combined with a weak commitment to the goals for achievement valued by the society.
- A sense of social alienation and a general tolerance for deviance.
- A sense of heightened stress. (This may help explain why adolescence and other stressful

transition periods are often associated with severe drug and alcohol problems.)[26]

Biologic Theories

Biophysiological and genetic theories assume that addicts are constitutionally predisposed to develop a dependence on alcohol or drugs. These theories encourage a medical model of addiction. Their advocates apply disease terminology and generally place responsibility for the treatment of addicts in the hands of physicians, nurses, and other medical personnel. In reality, the medical model is generally practiced only during the detoxification phase. After that, physicians may be in charge of signing the paperwork, but few are directly involved in further treatment.

Genetic Theories. Genetic factors have never been established as a definite cause of alcoholism, but the statistical associations between genetic factors and alcohol abuse are very strong. A great volume of research has been amassed in this area over the last several decades, and much of the evidence points toward alcoholism as an inherited trait. It has been observed that (1) alcoholism occurs more frequently in some families than in others,[27] (2) concurrent alcoholism rates are higher in monozygotic twin pairs (53.5 percent) than in dizygotic pairs (28.3 percent),[28] (3) animal strains can be bred which have a preference for alcohol,[29] and (4) adopted children more closely resemble their biological parents than their adoptive parents in their use of alcohol.[30]

One study of 862 men and 913 women who had been adopted early in life by nonrelatives identified two types of alcoholism.[31] Type I, or milieu-limited, alcoholism is found in both sexes and is associated with alcoholism in either biological parent, but an environmental factor—low occupational status of the adoptive father—also had to be present as a condition for alcoholism to occur in the offspring. Type II, also known as male-limited, alcoholism is more severe but accounts for fewer cases. It is found only in men, and it does not appear to be affected by environmental factors.

Some genetic theorists speculate that an inherited metabolic defect may interact with environmental elements and eventually lead to alcoholism. This genetotrophic theory posits an impaired production of enzymes within the body.[32] Others hypothesize that inherited genetic traits result in a deficiency of vitamins (usually of the vitamin B complex), which leads to a craving for alcohol as well as cellular or metabolic changes.[33] It is important to remember that despite the impressive statistical relationships in these studies implying a genetic link, no specific genetic marker that predisposes one toward alcoholism has ever been isolated. The first biological marker "discovered" for alcoholism was thought to be color blindness, but a few years later it was demonstrated that the color blindness was actually a result of severe alcohol abuse.[34] Several other genetic discoveries have met a similar fate. A recent workshop on genetic and biological markers in drug and alcohol abuse suggested promising areas for genetic research, such as polymorphisms in gene products and DNA polymorphisms.[35] A more recent study reports that the so-called dopamine D_2 receptor gene, which affects the capacity of cells to absorb dopamine, was present in 77 percent of the brains of alcoholics and only 28 percent of nonalcoholics.[36]

In 1990 the front page of *The New York Times* hailed the discovery of gene claimed to be directly linked to alcoholism. Two years later this so-called alcoholism gene, formally known as the dopamine D_2 receptor gene, has become the focus of a bitter controversy. Kenneth Blum and Ernest P. Noble insist that their finding has been amply documented by subsequent research, and they are taking steps to market a test for genetic susceptibility to alcoholism. Blum suggests that the test could be given to job applicants, children, and perhaps even fetuses.

In Blum and Noble's experiments, the D_2 gene was shown to have at least two variants, or alleles, called A1 and A2. They found the A1 allele in the genetic material of 69 percent of the alcoholics studied, compared to only 20 percent of the controls. They theorize that A1 carriers may use alcohol or other drugs excessively to compensate for a reduced ability to absorb pleasure-inducing dopamine.

On the other side are skeptics such as geneticists Kenneth K. Kidd and C. Robert Cloninger. Both contend that Blum and Noble's claim has been contradicted by other studies and "is almost certainly invalid." Annabel M. Bolos and Joel Gelernter also found the incidences of the A1 allele among alcoholics not significantly higher than among controls.[37]

Brain Dysfunction Theories. Some scientists believe that the mode of inheritance in alcoholism may be a neurochemical deficiency that manifests itself in childhood as minimal brain damage. Alcoholic parents have children who more frequently exhibit symptoms of minimal brain dysfunction.[38] Others have reported more symptoms of childhood hyperactivity in children of alcoholics than in other children.[39]

Biochemical Theories. Two popular theories in recent years are that alcoholics have abnormalities in sugar metabolism[40] or a "allergic reaction" to alcohol or congeners.[41] The problem with the former theory is that abnormalities in metabolism are just as likely to develop as a *result* of years of alcohol abuse. It would require experimental studies of "pre-alcoholics" to isolate metabolic imbalances as a cause of alcoholism. It also stretches the meaning of "allergy" well beyond the normal use of the term. Allergies usually result in a pathology of one or more organs (such as a skin rash), not a *behavior* such as loss of control over drinking. No other substance is known to have such an "allergic" effect.

One of the more interesting biochemical theories is that alcohol may produce morphine-like substances such as tetrahydroisoquinolines in the brains of certain users, which are responsible for the development of an alcohol addiction.[42] A similar theory is that as alcohol is metabolized within the body, acetaldehyde reacts with serotonin to form salsolinol, an addicting chemical commonly found in the urine of alcoholics.[43]

A difficulty with all these biologic theories lies in the failure of the research to establish cause and effect. Factors that are frequently cited as possible biologic causes of alcoholism could just as easily be viewed as the *result* of long years of heavy drinking. Nevertheless, these theories do indicate some interesting and perhaps promising areas for future research.

Sociocultural Theories

As we mentioned earlier, almost every known culture has discovered the use of beverage alcohol. The ways in which different societies encourage, permit, or regulate the use of alcohol varies considerably, however. For the most part, sociocultural theories have been generated by observations of differences or similarities between cultural groups or subgroups. Sociocultural theorists are prone to attribute differences in drinking practices, "problem" drinking, or alcoholism to "environmental factors."

According to Goode, the social context of drug use strongly influences, perhaps even *determines* "four central aspects of drug *reality*.[44] These are *drug definitions, drug effects, drug-related behavior,* and *the drug experience*. The sociocultural perspective stands in direct opposition to what is called the *chemicalistic fallacy*— the view that drug A causes behavior X.

Because no object or event has meaning in the abstract, all these central aspects must be interpreted in light of social phenomena surrounding drug use. For example, morphine and heroin are not very different pharmacologically and biochemically. Yet heroin is regarded as a "dangerous drug" with no therapeutic value, while morphine is defined primarily as a medicine. Definitions are shaped by the social milieu surrounding the use of each substance.

Persons using morphine as an illegal street drug experience a "rush" or a "high" generally unknown to patients using the same drug in a hospital setting. Psychedelic drugs, such as peyote, which are taken for religious purposes (as in the Native American church) do not typically result in religious or mystical experiences when taken simply to "get high." Drugs, according to Goode, only *potentiate* certain kinds of experiences. They do not *produce* them. It is important that we distinguish between drug *effects* and the drug *experience*. Many changes may take place in the body when a chemical is ingested, not all of which are noted and classified by the user. A drug may have a more or less automatic effect of dilating the pupils, causing ataxia or amblyopia, and so on, but the experience is subject to the cognitive system of the user's mind. A person must be attuned to certain drug effects to interpret them, categorize them, and place them within appropriate experiential and conceptual realms.[45] Our propensity to use drugs, the way we behave when we use drugs, and our definitions of abuse and addiction are all influenced by our sociocultural systems. Why else would we define heroin and LSD as "dangerous" drugs, while almost never perceiving social drinkers and smokers as "drug users"?

Supracultural Theories. The pioneering work of Bales provides some general hypotheses regarding the relationships among culture, social organization, and the use of alcohol.[46] He proposed that a culture that produces guilt, suppressed aggression, and sexual tension and condones the use of alcohol to relieve those tensions is likely to have a high rate of alcoholism. Bales also believed that collective attitudes toward alcohol use dramatically influence rates of alcoholism. He classified these attitudes as favoring: (1) abstinence, (2) ritual use connected with religious practices, (3) convivial drinking in a social setting, and (4) utilitarian drinking—drinking for personal, self-interested reasons. The utilitarian attitude, especially in a culture that induces much inner tension, is the most likely to lead to problem drinking, while the other three mitigate against alcohol problems.

Also important in Bales's theory is the degree to which a society offers alternatives to alcohol use for the release of tension and for providing a substitute means of satisfaction. A social system with a strong emphasis on upward economic or social mobility will excessively frustrate an individual who has no available means of achieving success. In such a system, high rates of alcohol use would be expected.[47] Unfortunately, few alternatives to alcohol or drugs seem to exist in most modern societies. In traditional societies, such as the hill tribes of Malaysia, a shaman may assist tribesmen in achieving a trancelike state in which endorphin levels are altered.[48]

Also at the supracultural level, Bacon theorized that alcoholism is likely to be a problem in a society that combines a lack of indulgence of children with demanding attitudes toward achievement and negative attitudes regarding dependent behavior in adults.[49] Another important factor in sociocultural theories is the degree of societal consensus regarding alcohol use. In cultures where there is little agreement regarding drinking limits and customs, a higher rate of alcoholism is expected.[50] Cultural ambivalence regarding alcohol use results in weak social controls, allowing the drinker to avoid being labeled as a deviant.

Culture-Specific Theories.   Levin describes two examples of cultural contrast in attitudes toward drinking: the contrast between French and Italian drinking practices and the contrast between Irish and Jewish drinking practices.[51] There are many similarities between the French and Italian cultures; both are heavily Catholic, and both produce and consume large quantities of alcohol. The French, however, drink both wine and spirits, both with meals and without, both with and away from the family. The French do not strongly disapprove of drunkenness, and they consider it bad manners to refuse a drink. On the other hand, the Italians drink mostly with meals and mostly with family, and they usually drink wine. They strongly disapprove of drunkenness, and they do not pressure people into drinking. As one might expect, France has one of the highest rates of alcoholism in the world, while Italy's rate was only *one-fifth* as great. (Italy, which had the second highest rate of wine consumption in the world in 1952, consumed only *half* of what was consumed in France.[52]) The strong sanctions against drunkenness and the social control imposed by learning to drink

low-proof alcoholic beverages in moderation seems to have something to do with the lower rate of Italian alcoholism.

In a similar fashion, studies of Irish and Jewish drinking practices draw some sharp contrasts. While the Irish have a high proportion of both abstainers and problem drinkers, Jews have a low proportion of both.[53] While the Irish drink largely outside the home in pubs, Jews drink largely in the home with the family and on ceremonial occasions. The Irish excuse drunkenness as "a good man's fault," while Jews condemn it as something culturally alien. Bales found Irish drinking to be largely convivial on the surface, but purely utilitarian drinking was a frequent and tolerated pattern. Jewish drinking, on the other hand, was mostly ceremonial.[54] Again, it is no surprise that the Irish alcoholism rate is one of the highest in the world, while the Jewish rate is one of the lowest.

Subcultural Theories.   There also have been many investigations of sociological and environmental causes of alcoholism at the subcultural level. Within the same culture, a great diversity in alcoholism rates has been related to age, sex, ethnicity, socioeconomic class, religion, and family background.[55] One of the landmark studies of social variables at this level was conducted two decades ago by Cahalan.[56] He determined that social environment determines to a large extent whether an individual will drink or not, and that social-psychological variables also determine the level of drinking. In becoming a problem drinker, variables such as age, sex, ethnicity, and social position influence the probability that a person will learn to drink as a dominant response. Labeling the person as a "heavy drinker" then reinforces the probability of that response.

These processes do not occur in isolation from other factors, of course, such as the process of physical addiction.

Goode,[57] Laurie,[58] Imlah,[59] and many others have examined the sociocultural context of drug addiction and found there to be many similarities to alcoholism. A major difference is in the "outcast" nature of certain illicit drug users such as heroin addicts. Users of illegal drugs such as heroin may be more socially isolated than alcoholics because of their addiction. Also, certain types of drug addiction seem to thrive within specific subcultures. Heroin addiction is a persistent problem among jazz musicians. Inner-city youth frequently "huff" spray paint or sniff glue. With three feet of hose and an empty can, Native American youth on certain reservations will always be able to get high on gasoline fumes.

The impact of gender on drug use presents an interesting perspective on sociocultural theories. One could use either a culture-specific or subcultural model in explaining the differences between male and female drug-related behaviors in the United States. Historically, female drinking has been less accepted than male drinking in this country, and being intoxicated is clearly more disapproved for women than for men.[60] These double standards may account for the much lower rate of problem drinking noted among women. Social pressure and social stigma may result in less problem drinking by women as a *subgroup* of the larger American culture.

We must recognize that this phenomenon may be culture specific, however. An early cross-cultural study of sex differences in drinking found that in many societies men and women do not differ greatly with regard to various aspects of drinking.[61] The fact that men seem to drink more and to have more problems because of alcohol in some cultures and not in others fits into a supracultural model of drug use. The degree of female problem drinking appears to be related to cultural norms regarding the overall status of women within different societies. We should bear in mind that the vast majority of the research on alcohol and drug abuse has been conducted on men *only*. We have only recently begun to examine systematically gender-related issues in this area.

Alternative Explanations

Herbert Fingarette sees alcoholism as "neither sin nor disease."[62] Instead, he views it as a "life-style." According to Fingarette, proponents of the disease model describe alcoholism as a disease characterized by loss of control over drinking. Recovery is possible only if one voluntarily seeks and enters treatment and voluntarily abstains from drinking. Only then can one be "cured." Cured from what? From a disease that makes voluntary abstention impossible and makes drinking uncontrollable! This, says Fingarette, is an amazing contradiction.[63]

His alternative explanation views the "persistent heavy drinking of the alcoholic as a central activity" of the individual's way of life. Each of us develops our own unique way of life, which consists of a number of *central* activities. Some persons will adopt parenting as a central activity while others will place sex, physical thrills, or their career at the center. Why have some people chosen drinking as a central feature? Fingarette says that there is no "general answer," but that the explanation lies not only in motives but also in the person's cultural background, life circumstances, special life crises, or physical abnormalities. No single item will be *the* reason.

Fingarette believes that it is no harder for the alcoholic to *choose* to stop drinking than it is for the rest of us to abandon activities central to our way of life. "We should see the alcoholic, not as a sick and defective human being, but as a human being whose way of life is self-destructive. The difficulty we face is stubborn human nature, not disease."[64]

In a similar fashion, Peele has examined the evidence on addiction and concluded that "we have disarmed ourselves in combatting the precipitous growth of addictions by discounting the role of values in creating and preventing addiction and by systematically overlooking the immorality of addictive misbehavior."[65] This is not a revival of the "addiction as sin" model, but an argument that addicts and alcoholics do differ from other persons in the ways in which they prioritize their values. This fits comfortably with the World Health Organization definitions of both alcohol and drug dependence.

In his book, *Junky*, noted author (and addict) William S. Burroughs attempted to

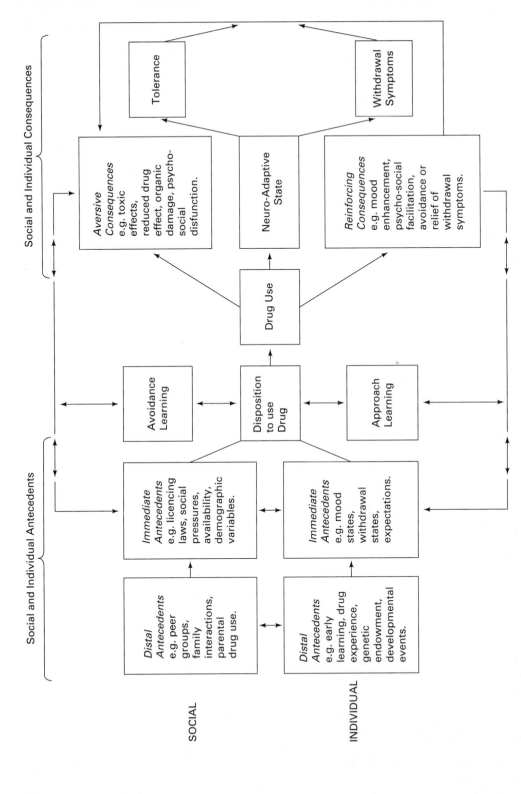

FIGURE 2.1 A model of drug use.
Source: Duncan Raistrick and Robin Davidson, *Alcoholism and Drug Addiction* (New York: Churchill Livingstone, 1985).

answer the question: "Why does a person become a drug addict?"

The answer is that he usually does not intend to become an addict. You don't wake up one morning and decide to be a drug addict. . . . You become a narcotics addict because you do not have strong motivations in any other direction. Junk wins by default. I tried it as a matter of curiosity. I drifted along taking shots when I could score. I ended up hooked. Most addicts I have talked to report a similar experience.[66]

A Multicausal Model

Which of these etiological models or explanations of drug abuse is "correct"? All are probably helpful, at least in a heuristic sense, but no single model or theory adequately explains the phenomenon of dependency or addiction. A significant advance in the study of chemical dependency is the realization that it is probably not a unitary disorder. Pattison and Kaufman made a strong case for a multivariate model of alcoholism a decade ago.[67] Even though there may be similar behavioral topography in all addicted individuals, the etiology and motivation for drug use may differ widely. Available evidence points strongly to the possibility that addiction may be manifest through different mechanisms. Therefore, a model such as the one in Figure 2.1 may be helpful in understanding this phenomenon.

For some individuals a genetic predisposition or physiological dysfunction is a necessary condition for drug use, drug abuse, and subsequent addiction. On the other hand, some persons with disturbances in their personal development or interpersonal orientation but with no known genetic predisposition or biochemical aberration may become addicted to a drug. This debate over which model is really "best" is valuable only in the sense that it leads us to see the utility in an interdisciplinary, multicausal model.

This model is similar to the *public health model*, promoted in recent years by health care and other human service professionals. This model conceptualizes the problem of chemical dependency in terms of an interaction among three factors: the agent, the host, and the environment. In most public health areas the agent is an organism (e.g., a virus), but in this case, it is ethanol. The second factor is the host, the chemically dependent person, including the person's genetic composition, cognitive structure, expectations about drug experiences, and personality. The last factor consists of the social, cultural, political, and economic variables that affect the use of alcohol or drugs, and the resulting consequences. The public health approach involves the examination of the complex interaction of the multitude of variables affecting the agent, the host, and the environment.[68]

SUMMARY

The most obvious fact about alcohol or drug addiction is that we have no single theory that explains this phenomenon. Some persons may be more genetically predisposed than others to become addicted. Other persons are more prone to addiction because of their social environment—peer pressure, role models in the family, societal values, and so on. Still others may have one or more personality traits that make them more likely to use or abuse alcohol or drugs. Once use begins, physiological processes such as withdrawal and tolerance make the individual even more prone to continue use.

ENDNOTES

1. William A. McKim, *Drugs and Behavior: An Introduction to Behavioral Pharmacology*, 2nd ed. (Englewood Cliffs, NJ: Prentice Hall, 1991), p. 87.

2. William J. Rorabaugh, *The Alcoholic Republic* (New York: Oxford University Press, 1979), p. 204.

3. McKim, *Drugs and Behavior*, p. 89.

4. Marie Bonaparte, Anna Freud, and Ernst Kris (eds.), *The Origins of Psychoanalysis; Letters to Fliess* (New York: Basic Books, 1954), letter no. 79.

5. B. Chordokoff, "Alcoholism and Ego Function," *Quarterly Journal of Studies on Alcohol*, Vol. 25 (1964), pp. 292–299.

6. Marc A. Schuckit, "Etiological Theories on Alcoholism," in Nada J. Estes and M. Edith Heinemann (eds.), *Alcoholism: Development, Consequences, and Interventions,* 3rd ed. (St. Louis, MO: C. V. Mosby, 1986), pp. 15–30.

7. Karl Menninger, *The Vital Balance* (New York: Viking Press, 1963).

8. Anne L. Cunynghame, "Some Issues in Successful Alcoholism Treatment," in David Cook, Christine Fewell, and John Riolo (eds.), *Social Work Treatment of Alcohol Problems* (New Brunswick, NJ: Rutgers Center of Alcohol Studies, 1983), pp. 49–59.

9. Ralph E. Tarter and Dorothea U. Schneider, "Models and Theories of Alcoholism," in Ralph E. Tarter and A. Arthur Sugarmen (eds.), *Alcoholism: Interdisciplinary Approaches to an Enduring Problem.* (Reading, MA: Addison-Wesley, 1976).

10. P. E. Nathan and S. A. Lisman, "Behavioral and Motivational Patterns of Chronic Alcoholics," in Tarter and Sugerman, *Alcoholism,* pp. 479–522.

11. J. S. Tamerin and J. Mendelon, "Alcoholics' Expectancies and Recall of Experiences During Intoxication," *American Journal of Psychiatry,* Vol. 126 (1970), pp. 1697–1704.

12. Tarter and Schneider, "Models and Theories of Alcoholism."

13. Java Krivanek, *Addictions* (Sydney: Allen & Unwin, 1989).

14. Ibid., p. 96.

15. E. Mansell Pattison, Mark B. Sobell, and Linda C. Sobell, *Emerging Concepts of Alcohol Dependence* (New York: Springer, 1977), p. 191.

16. Albert Bandura, *Principles of Behavior Modification* (New York: Holt, Rinehart and Winston, 1969).

17. Schuckit, "Etiological Theories on Alcoholism."

18. P. Catanzaro, "Psychiatric Aspects of Alcoholism," in D. J. Pittman (ed.), *Alcoholism* (New York: Harper & Row, 1967).

19. Mark Keller, "The Oddities of Alcoholics," *Quarterly Journal of Studies on Alcohol,* Vol. 33 (1972), pp. 1147–1148.

20. Craig MacAndrew, "On the Possibility of the Psychometric Detection of Persons Who Are Prone to the Abuse of Alcohol and Other Substances," *Journal of Addictive Behaviors,* Vol. 4 (1979), pp. 11–20.

21. M. Sherfey, "Psychopathology and Character Structure in Chronic Alcoholism," in W. O. Diethelm (ed.), *The Etiology of Chronic Alcoholism* (Springfield, IL: Charles C Thomas, 1955).

22. George E. Valliant, *The Natural History of Alcoholism: Causes, Patterns and Paths to Recovery* (Cambridge, MA: Harvard University Press, 1983).

23. Michael R. Gossop and Sybil Eysenck, "A Further Investigation into the Personality of Drug Addicts in Treatment," *British Journal of Addiction,* Vol. 75 (1980), pp. 305–311.

24. Duncan Raistrick and Robin Davidson, *Alcoholism and Drug Addiction* (New York: Churchill Livingstone, 1985), p. 21.

25. Stanley Einstein, *The Drug User: Personality Factors, Issues, and Theories* (New York: Plenum Press, 1983), pp. 9–11.

26. "The Addictive Personality: Common Traits Are Found," Sec. Y, *The New York Times,* January 18, 1983, pp. 11 and 15.

27. N. A. Cotton, "The Familial Incidence of Alcoholism," *Journal of Studies on Alcohol,* Vol. 40 (1979), pp. 89–116.

28. Lennart Kaij, *Alcoholism in Twins: Studies on the Etiology and Sequels of Abuse of Alcohol* (Stockholm: Almquist & Wiskell, 1960).

29. R. A. Meisch, "Animal Studies of Alcohol Intake," *British Journal of Psychiatry,* Vol. 141 (1982), pp. 113–130.

30. Donald W. Goodwin, Shirley Hill, Barbara Powell, and Jorge Viamontes, "Effect of Alcohol on Short-Term Memory in Alcoholics," *British Journal of Psychiatry,* Vol. 122 (1973), pp. 93–94.

31. Michael Boham, C. Robert Cloninger, Anne-Liis von Knorring, and Soren Sigvardsson, "An Adoption Study of Somatoform Disorders. III. Cross-fostering Analysis and Genetic Relationship to Alcoholism and Criminality," *Archives of General Psychiatry,* Vol. 41 (1984), pp. 872–878.

32. Roger J. Williams, *Alcoholism: The Nutritional Approach* (Austin: University of Texas Press, 1959).

33. Tarter and Schneider, "Models and Theories of Alcoholism," p. 84.

34. A. Valera, L. Rivera, J. Mardones, and R. Cruz-Coke, "Color Vision Defects in Non-alcoholic Relatives of Alcoholic Patients," *British Journal of the Addictions,* Vol. 64 (1969), pp. 67–71.

35. Warren W. Nichols, "Genetic and Biological Markers in Drug Abuse and Alcoholism: A Summary," in National Institute on Drug Abuse, Research Monograph Series No. 66, *Genetic and Biological Markers in Drug Abuse and Alcoholism* (Washington, DC: U.S. Government Printing Office, 1986), pp. 1–4.

36. Kenneth Blum, Ernest Noble, Peter Sheridan, Anne Montgomery, Terry Ritchie, Pudur Jagadeeswaran, Harou Nogami, Arthur Briggs, and Jay Cohen, "Allelic Association of Human Dopamine D$_2$ Receptor Gene in Alcoholism," *Journal of the American Medical Association,* Vol. 263 (1990), pp. 2055–2060.

37. John Horgan, "D$_2$ or not D$_2$," *Scientific American,* Vol. 266, No. 4 (April 1992), pp. 29–32.

38. Dennis Cantwell, "Psychiatric Illness in the Families of Hyperactive Children," *Archives of General Psychiatry,* Vol. 27 (1972), pp. 414–417.

39. Tarter and Schneider, "Models and Theories of Alcoholism," p. 85.

40. Frank Lundquist, "Influence of Ethanol on Carbohydrate Metabolism," *Quarterly Journal of Studies on Alcohol,* Vol. 32 (1971), pp. 1–12.

41. Richard Mackarness, "The Allergic Factor in Alcoholism," *International Journal of Social Psychiatry,* Vol. 18 (1972), pp. 194–200.

42. Floyd E. Bloom, "A Summary of Workshop Discussions," in F. Bloom et al. (eds.), *Beta-carbolines and Tetrahydroisoquinolines* (New York: Alan R. Liss, 1982).

43. Michael A. Collins et al., "Dopamine-Related Tetrahydroisoquinolines: Significant Urinary Excretions by Alcoholics After Alcohol Consumption," *Science,* Vol. 206 (1979), pp. 1184–1186.

44. Erich Goode, *Drugs in American Society* (New York: Alfred A. Knopf, 1972), p. 3.

45. Ibid., p. 8.

46. Robert F. Bales, "Cultural Differences in Rates of Alcoholism," *Quarterly Journal of Studies on Alcohol,* Vol. 6 (1946), pp. 480–499.

47. Tarter and Schneider, "Models and Theories of Alcoholism."

48. Carol Laderman, "Trances That Heal: Rites, Rituals, and Brain Chemicals," in William B. Rucker and Marian E. Rucker, *Drugs, Society and Behavior, 87/88* (Guilford, CT: Dushkin, 1987), pp. 233–235.

49. Margaret K. Bacon, "The Dependency-Conflict Hypothesis and the Frequency of Drunkenness," *Quarterly Journal of Studies on Alcohol,* Vol. 35 (1974), pp. 863–876.

50. Harrison Trice, *Alcoholism in America* (New York: McGraw-Hill, 1966).

51. Jerome D. Levin, *Alcoholism: A Bio-psycho-social Approach* (New York: Hemisphere, 1989), p. 59.

52. Jean Kinney and Gwen Leaton, *Loosening the Grip: A Handbook of Alcohol Information* (St. Louis, MO: C. V. Mosby, 1987), p. 85.

53. Levin, *Alcoholism,* p. 59.

54. Bales, "Cultural Differences in Rates of Alcoholism."

55. Tarter and Schneider, "Models and Theories of Alcoholism," p. 95.

56. D. Cahalan, *Problem Drinkers: A National Survey* (San Francisco: Jossey-Bass, 1970).

57. E. Goode, *Drugs in American Society,* 2nd ed. (New York: Alfred A. Knopf, 1984).

58. P. Laurie, *Drugs* (New York: Penguin Books, 1971).

59. N. Imlah, *Drugs in Modern Society* (Princeton, NJ: Averbach Publishers, 1971).

60. Edith S. Gomberg, "Women with Alcohol Problems," in Estes and Heinemann, *Alcoholism,* pp. 241–256.

61. Irving L. Child, Margaret K. Bacon, and Harry Barry, "A Cross-cultural Study of Drinking: III. Sex Differences," *Quarterly Journal of Studies on Alcohol,* Vol. 3 (1965), pp. 49–61.

62. Herbert Fingarette, "Alcoholism: Neither Sin Nor Disease," *The Center Magazine* (March/April 1985), pp. 56–63.

63. Ibid.

64. Ibid., p. 63.

65. Stanton Peele (ed.), *Visions of Addiction: Major Contemporary Perspectives on Addiction and Alcoholism* (Lexington, MA: D. C. Heath, 1988), p. 224.

66. William S. Burroughs, *Junky* (New York: Penguin Books, 1953), p. xv. Originally published as *Junkie* under the pen name of William Lee by Ace Books, 1953.

67. E. Mansell Pattison and Edward Kaufman, "The Alcoholism Syndrome: Definitions and Models," in Pattison and Kaufman (eds.), *Encyclopedic Handbook of Alcoholism* (New York: Gardner Press, 1982), p. 13.

68. Reid K. Hester and Nancy Sheehy, "The Grand Unification Theory of Alcohol Abuse: It's Time to Stop Fighting Each Other and Start Working Together," in Ruth C. Engs (ed.), *Controversies in the Addictions Field,* Volume I (Dubuque, IA: Kendall/Hunt, 1990), pp. 2–9.

3

Becoming addicted

Almost everyone has an easy answer to the question, "Why do people use drugs?" According to Tam Stewart, heroin addicts use junk the first time because they are curious. Heroin has a mystique. It is used by pop stars, writers, and "glamorous people."[1] And they like its effect. For those who find daily life to be fairly humdrum, heroin can be the ultimate filler of gaps—it can substitute for career, religion, romance, or virtually anything else. "If heroin gets there first, everything else takes second place and finally goes by the board."[2] As William S. Burroughs indicated in *Junky,* "Junk wins by default. I tried it as a matter of curiosity. I drifted along taking shots when I could score. I ended up

hooked."[3] This notion of *drift* is a recurrent theme in theories of addiction.

People begin using cocaine for *some* of the same reasons. According to one therapist, his clients provided these excuses for using cocaine:

> "The mystical reputation aroused my curiosity."
> "It's available and being offered all the time."
> "It gave me a sense of well-being, like I was worth something."
> "It felt good to be a part of a group."
> "It was a great way to escape."[4]

One of the major differences between heroin and cocaine is that cocaine has much less stigma attached to it. In fact, it seems to be as commonly accepted as alcohol or to-bacco in *some* circles. Middle-class "yuppies" planning a party may be just as embarrassed by forgetting to pick up some "coke" for the guests as by forgetting the hors d'oeuvres. People who refuse to "snort" a line frequently are shunned by friends who do use the drug. Pressure thus becomes much more intense for a person to use cocaine.

Most models of addiction assume that an addiction is an "addictive disease."[5] As such, it continues to exist whether or not the ad-dicted person continues to use the drug. Even if a person who has the disease is absti-nent for a long period of time, the symptoms of addiction will appear again from renewed contact with the drug. The disease model of addiction rests on three primary assump-tions: predisposition to use a drug, loss of control over use, and progression.[6] Vernon Johnson put it somewhat differently in saying that "The most significant characteristics of the disease (*alcoholism*) are that it is primary, progressive, chronic, and fatal."[7] There are others, of course, who question the validity of this model.

The most commonly used (and abused) psychoactive drug, of course, is alcohol. The route to alcohol addiction does vary some-what from that taken by "junkies," "coke-heads," and "speed freaks." Alcohol is a *legal* drug, and its use is so pervasive in our culture that many people do not ever seriously con-sider *not* using it. Also, the great majority of persons who drink alcohol use it on a fairly regular basis with no apparent negative con-sequences. These factors lead us to consider alcohol to be a relatively harmless drug. Con-sider the remarks of the mother of one teenager who discovered that her son was drinking almost on a daily basis: "Thank God it was only alcohol! We were worried that he had gotten involved with the 'wrong crowd' at school and was taking drugs."

Because alcohol is still the most widely abused drug, and because there are many sim-ilarities in the addiction process for all drugs, we will begin by describing some widely used models of the stages of alcoholism. After criti-cally examining these models, we will look at similarities and differences between alco-holism and other types of addiction.

THE STAGES OF ALCOHOLISM

Similar to the heroin addicts described ear-lier by Burroughs, most alcoholics probably "drift" into alcoholism in the sense that very few of them begin drinking with the inten-tion of becoming alcoholic. In many of the models described in this chapter, the journey from experimental drinking to social drink-ing to addiction (or dependence) generally takes place over the course of several years. AA meetings are full of middle-aged persons who considered themselves to be "social drinkers" for twenty or thirty years before rec-ognizing that they had a "drinking problem."

One of the first attempts to describe the "natural history" of alcoholism is found in Jellinek's study of 2,000 male members of Alcoholics Anonymous.[8] He characterized al-coholism as an insidious disease that pro-gresses through well-defined phases, each with symptoms that develop in the majority of persons in an additive, orderly fashion. In Jellinek's model, the drinker progresses through four distinct stages: (1) prealcoholic symptomatic phase, (2) prodromal phase, (3) crucial phase, and (4) chronic phase.[9] (See Figure 3.1.)

In the *prealcoholic symptomatic phase,* drink-ing is associated with rewarding relief from tension or stress, something almost all drink-ers engage in occasionally. The person who is more predisposed toward alcoholism (whether by chromosomes, culture, or other factors) will tend to increase the frequency of "relief drinking" over a period of time. At the same time, the drinker develops a physical toler-ance to alcohol, so that increasingly larger amounts are needed to bring the same degree of relief from stress or tension.

The onset of blackouts marks the begin-ning of the *prodromal* phase. These are peri-ods of amnesia not associated with the loss of consciousness. The drinker may seem to be acting "normally," but later has no recall of those events which occurred while in a

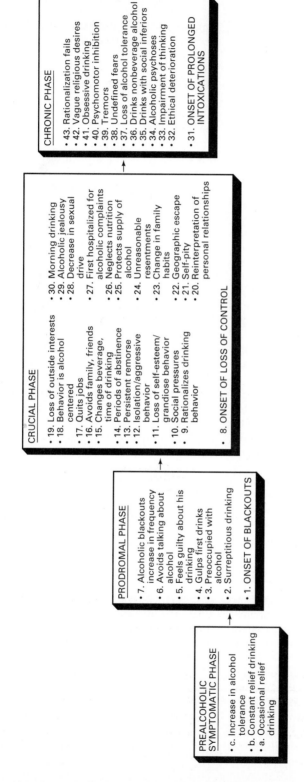

PREALCOHOLIC
SYMPTOMATIC PHASE

- c. Increase in alcohol tolerance
- b. Constant relief drinking
- a. Occasional relief drinking

PRODROMAL PHASE

- 7. Alcoholic blackouts increase in frequency
- 6. Avoids talking about alcohol
- 5. Feels guilty about his drinking
- 4. Gulps first drinks
- 3. Preoccupied with alcohol
- 2. Surreptitious drinking

- 1. ONSET OF BLACKOUTS

CRUCIAL PHASE

- 19. Loss of outside interests
- 18. Behavior is alcohol centered
- 17. Quits jobs
- 16. Avoids family, friends
- 15. Changes beverage, time of drinking
- 14. Periods of abstinence
- 13. Persistent remorse
- 12. Isolation/aggressive behavior
- 11. Loss of self-esteem/grandiose behavior
- 10. Social pressures
- 9. Rationalizes drinking behavior

- 30. Morning drinking
- 29. Alcoholic jealousy
- 28. Decrease in sexual drive
- 27. First hospitalized for alcoholic complaints
- 26. Neglects nutrition
- 25. Protects supply of alcohol
- 24. Unreasonable resentments
- 23. Change in family habits
- 22. Geographic escape
- 21. Self-pity
- 20. Reinterpretation of personal relationships

- 8. ONSET OF LOSS OF CONTROL

CHRONIC PHASE

- 43. Rationalization fails
- 42. Vague religious desires
- 41. Obsessive drinking
- 40. Psychomotor inhibition
- 39. Tremors
- 38. Undefined fears
- 37. Loss of alcohol tolerance
- 36. Drinks nonbeverage alcohol
- 35. Drinks with social inferiors
- 34. Alcoholic psychoses
- 33. Impairment of thinking
- 32. Ethical deterioration

- 31. ONSET OF PROLONGED INTOXICATIONS

PREPATHOGENIC PERIOD

PERIOD OF PATHOGENESIS

FIGURE 3.1 The natural history of alcoholism according to Jellinek's model based on male members of AA. Interactions between the host, environment, and agent influence the degree of exposure to alcohol, the response to this exposure, and the likelihood and consequences of further exposures. In some individuals this leads to alcoholism through a series of well-defined phases, as shown in the boxes.
Source: Nada J. Estes and M. Edith Heinemann (eds.), *Alcoholism: Development, Consequences, and Interventions*, 3rd ed. (St. Louis, MO: C. V. Mosby, 1986), p. 33.

blackout. This phase is also characterized by an increase in the need for alcohol (and attempts to hide the need for alcohol), surreptitious drinking, and increasing guilt.

The *crucial* phase's primary hallmark is the loss of control over drinking, as evidenced by the inability to abstain from drinking or the inability to stop once started. During this stage, the drinker often will drink during the morning, will experience behavior problems in relation to employment and social life, and will frequently seek to avoid family and friends.

The final or *chronic* phase finds the drinker intoxicated for several days at a time. Drinking becomes obsessive, and both serious physical and emotional problems are evident. According to Jellinek's original model, this is where the alcoholic "hits bottom." While this work was a pioneering effort in the field of alcoholism research, one must remember that Jellinek's sample were (1) all AA members, (2) all in the latter stages of alcoholism, and (3) all males.

This traditional view of alcohol addiction was supported by many other prominent scholars, however. Marty Mann described alcoholism as a "progressive disease, which, if left untreated, grows more virulent year by year."[10] Others seem to have conveniently ignored available scientific evidence in making assertions such as "the true alcoholic is no more able to metabolize ethanol than a diabetic can handle sugar."[11] Others concluded that alcoholism is the result of an "allergy" and that "One does not become an alcoholic: One is *born* an alcoholic."[12]

George E. Vaillant was involved in one of the most comprehensive studies of alcoholism.[13] Two samples were observed over a forty-year period, and a third group was observed for eight years. Among the sample of 110 core-city alcohol abusers, Vaillant identified four patterns: (1) progressive alcoholism, (2) return to asymptomatic drinking, (3) stable abstinence, and (4) atypical, nonprogressive alcoholism. While this study generally supports the developmental or progressive nature of Jellinek's model, it is important to note that Vaillant's study observed both reversibility and nonprogressive alcoholism among a substan-

tial proportion of subjects. Over the period of the study, 18 of the 110 subjects returned to social or asymptomatic drinking.

The traditional concept of the nature and progress of addiction to alcohol was also challenged by Pattison, Sobell, and Sobell. Perhaps the major difference in their view of alcohol *dependence* (a more precise, less value-laden term than addiction) are found in the following two assertions:

- The development of alcohol problems follows variable patterns over time and does not necessarily proceed inexorably to severe final stages.
- Recovery from alcohol dependence bears no necessary relation to abstinence, although such a concurrence is frequently the case.[14]

Thus a controversy was launched that continues today. Not only did Pattison, Sobell, and Sobell *not* believe in the disease model, but they also felt that alcohol dependence could be reversed. They pointed to some evidence that certain "alcoholics" had been able to return to social drinking. They also felt that the unproven assumptions that formed the basis for the traditional concept of alcoholism as a disease had been an *impediment* to proper treatment.

THE COURSE OF COCAINE ADDICTION

Other models of drug abuse/addiction reduce the stages to three—early, middle, and late. Washton's model of cocaine addiction describes it as a chronic disease that grows progressively worse if it is not treated. (*Chronic* indicates that cocaine addiction is never a single acute attack but is marked by a permanent condition, with a continued vulnerability to recurring symptoms.)[15]

According to Washton, cocaine addiction is progressive and predictable in its course.[16] "The disease of cocaine addiction is chronic, never reverses, and grows progressively more severe if left untreated." (See Table 3.1.) In the *early* stage of addiction, the user's brain chemistry is altered, withdrawal from normal

TABLE 3.1   The course of cocaine addiction

EARLY STAGE
Brain chemistry altered
Addictive thinking begins
Obsessive thoughts
Compulsive urges
Conditioned cravings
Life-style changes
Withdrawal from normal activities
Subtle physical and psychological consequences
(jitters, irritability, mood swings, etc.)

MIDDLE STAGE
Loss of control
Cravings
Inability to stop despite consequences
Denial
Increasing isolation
Increasing physical and psychological consequences—
paranoia, panic, seizures, etc.
Impaired work/school performance

LATE STAGE
Failure of efforts to stop
Severe financial problems
Severe work/school dysfunction
Plummeting self-esteem
Severe relationship problems
Chronic severe depression
Cocaine psychosis
Death

Source: Arnold M. Washton, *Cocaine Addiction: Treatment, Recovery, and Relapse Prevention* (New York: W. W. Norton, 1989), p. 56.

activities is usually observed, and mood swings occur with increasing frequency.

The *middle* stage of addiction is characterized by loss of control over cocaine use, impaired school or work performance, and denial of the problem. ("I'm not an addict; I just use the stuff a lot!") One can see that this is roughly comparable to the "crucial phase" in Jellinek's model of alcoholism. The *late* stage of addiction brings serious behavioral and emotional problems to the user, and it can terminate in severe depression, cocaine psychosis, and death.

BECOMING A HEROIN ADDICT

As we have mentioned several times earlier, a recurrent theme in heroin addiction is the notion of "drift." In a 1970 study of addicted inmates in California, Duster asked whether or not they consciously decided to become addicts. The overwhelming majority knew that heroin was addicting, illegal, and dangerous and could be fatal. They also replied that they neither intended nor believed that they would become addicts when they first began using the drug. The principal ingredient in becoming addicted was the addict's belief in the indestructibility of the self.[17] Two other essential ingredients were the normalcy of the first experience with heroin and the experience itself.

For most addicts, the first venture was an unplanned event. They happened to be in the "right place" at the "right time," and heroin was available, offered, and accepted. Most users found the first experience fairly neutral, with its duration relatively short and its after-effects minimal. Reasons for the second use are generally as "normal" and as social as for the first. The preaddict gradually slips into a level of use where dependence develops.[18]

Physical dependence has less of a relationship to heroin addiction than is commonly thought. According to some models, physical dependence has no *direct* relationship to addiction.[19] Becoming physically dependent on heroin requires that the drug be taken at intervals short enough to maintain a minimal level in the body constantly. Given the variable purity of heroin "on the street," between one and two months of daily usage or "two weeks of very heavy daily usage" is required to become physically dependent.[20] The "one shot and you're hooked" message that was popular in school drug prevention programs in the 1940s and 1950s was clearly a myth—at least from a physiological standpoint.

One of the more puzzling aspects of heroin addiction is that fewer than half the addicts who have been on the streets for more than a year will have used it daily for that entire period.[21] Addicts frequently withdraw on their own in order to reduce their tolerance, serve a jail or prison sentence, or simply give themselves a rest. One researcher also estimates that 25 to 40 percent of street addicts may have never used heroin with sufficient frequency or in high enough dosages to have developed a true physical dependence. Yet they consider themselves to be "addicted" to heroin, even during periods of abstinence.[22]

An interesting early systems theory approach to heroin addiction was developed by Lindesmith.[23] In this theory the development of addiction assumes physical dependence, but there are two additional requirements. In order to be addicted, one must have a "craving," defined as "an intense desire and conscious striving for the drug." The positive or euphoric effects of heroin are discounted as being unimportant in this theory. Craving is fixed by "negative rather than positive reinforcement, by relief and avoidance of discomfort and pain rather than by positive pleasure."[24] It is the *interpretation* of the withdrawal experience that is of paramount importance. If it is interpreted as an inevitable physiological process, then no connection is drawn between withdrawal and the consequences of drug use, and people do not become addicts. On the other hand, if withdrawal is interpreted as evidence of a *need* for the drug, addiction does occur.

Either of these interpretations, according to Lindesmith, is imposed upon the addict by the social environment and the interaction of the addict with other people, especially other addicts. The heroin user, "when he uses the symbols which society provides him, also assumes the attitudes appropriate to those symbols when he applies them to himself."[25] In other words, the individual's milieu tells whether the heroin user is an addict or not. Being defined by the social environment as an addict and accepting that definition results in becoming an addict.

Having joined the fraternity of those who have been hooked, he feels a continuing bond that unites him with others who have had the experience and a communication barrier with others who have not had it. It is in this sense that addiction may be called incurable.[26]

There are others who argue that we are mistaken in behaving as though dependence is a property of drugs. According to Stanton Peele, dependence is caused neither by drugs nor by their chemical properties. Instead, it has more to do with the experience of an individual using a drug under a specific set of circumstances. Addiction is not "a physical mystery, but rather an organic outgrowth of a person's relationship to the world."[27] What a person experiences from taking a drug is determined in large part by expectations, which are a product of the social environment. Before the heroin user takes that first "hit," he or she will have acquired certain folklore of the community regarding its effects. The relationship between heroin's pharmacological effect and physiological changes is relatively unimportant to the nature of the user's subjective experience. This subjective experience, according to some theories, is the most important aspect of the process of becoming addicted.[28] As we mentioned earlier (Figure 2.1), a person's potential for addiction is a function of susceptibility and exposure. Once the addiction develops, it will continue as long as the activity (drug taking) provides more positive rewards than other available options.

MARIJUANA ADDICTION

Unlike the drugs already discussed, the addictive potential of cannabis is still being debated. A decade ago many people assumed that the debate had been settled and that smoking marijuana would *not* lead to dependence or addiction.[29] Others argued that cannabis (as well as cocaine) produced only "psychic dependence" and little or no physical dependence.[30] In light of more recent studies, there is evidence that this conclusion was not warranted.[31] In fact many older studies also concluded that cannabis was addictive. Soueif's report on Egyptian hashish users,[32] Chopra's study of Indian "hemp habituation,"[33] and Scher's analysis of American marijuana use[34] all strongly suggest symptoms of dependence. The common symptom was an inability to discontinue using the drug, despite an expressed desire to do so. Experimental studies have also produced withdrawal symptoms (appetite and sleep disturbances, irritability, aggression, tremors, photophobia, etc.) in monkeys[35] and human[36] subjects.

We mentioned earlier that not everyone relies on the ability of a drug to produce withdrawal symptoms as a definition of addiction. According to Nahas, drug dependence results from "the reproducible interaction between an individual and a pleasure-inducing biologically active molecule."[37] The common denominator of all drug dependence is the reinforcement resulting from reward associated with past individual drug interaction and the subsequent increasing desire for repeated reinforcement.[38] Using either this criterion or the development of tolerance and withdrawal, it is obvious that the popular classification of cannabis as a "soft" drug was greatly misleading.

In an in-depth study of 150 "heavy" users of marijuana, Hendin and coworkers discovered that they all had begun regular, daily use of the drug within two to five years after smoking their first "joints."[39] The average age for beginning such regular use was about 20. The majority of the group stated that much of their social life revolved around marijuana, smoking it at their homes, and friends' homes and at parties. While three-fourths reported that most or all of their friends were regular users, 89 percent also said that they regularly used marijuana while alone. Their most common reasons for smoking marijuana were:

- To get pleasure, feel good, get high (99 percent)
- To relax, relieve tension (97 percent)
- To use with friends, enjoy effects (88 percent)
- To overcome depression (61 percent)[40]

A sample of this group selected for more intensive study consistently revealed substituting a sensory illusion of life gained by smoking marijuana for the boredom, fear, and "lifelessness" which they perceived surrounding them. Daily heavy marijuana use for these persons was closely related to adaptive difficulties in personal relationships and/or work. To the extent that they were aware of their difficulties, they saw marijuana as an escape from them. None of them considered marijuana to be the *cause* of their difficulties.[41]

Marijuana maintained these individuals in a troubled adaptation, reinforcing their tendency not to look at, understand, or attempt to master their difficulties. It served to detach them from their problems and allowed them to regard even serious difficulties as unimportant. Marijuana provided a buffer zone of sensation that functioned as a barrier against self-awareness and closeness to others.[42]

According to Nahas, modern neurophysiology and psychopharmacology support the idea that "soma and psyche are inextricably interwoven."[43] Therefore, a classification of dependence-producing drugs should be based on markers that reflect the biochemical alterations that they induce, primarily in the central nervous system. He suggests the following approach:

1. They produce reversible symptoms of neuropsychological or neurobehavioral toxicity. The effects of such drugs on neurotransmitters in the brain and on specialized function of the limbic structure produce neuropsychological and behavioral anomalies such as adverse effects on arousal, awareness, and psychological and psychomotor performance. These symptoms dissipate when the pharmacological action of the drug has ended.

2. They produce a primary pleasurable reward. Their pleasant effects are associated with the ability to dissipate unpleasant feelings, decrease anxiety, and produce detachment from the world. They are also capable of altering sensory perceptions. Their pleasurable sensations are concurrent with neuropsychological toxicity.

3. They act as "powerful reinforcers" inducing a craving for the drug and causing the user to have a major involvement in securing its use. There is a high tendency toward relapse after continuing use of the drug.

4. Tolerance is associated with frequent use and is closely linked to drug dependence. This is a drug-related adaptive process that allows the brain to function in the presence of xenobiotic substances.

5. Abrupt interruption of long-term use leads to an abstinence syndrome which may be mild or

severe, depending on the drug. Withdrawal symptoms may occur independently of tolerance and should not be considered as the major reinforcement for continuing drug use.

6. The long-term use of addictive drugs has been associated with somatic changes and, ultimately, an increased incidence of mental or physical illness.[44]

SUMMARY

In this chapter we have reviewed some similarities and differences between various theories of addiction, and we once more returned to examine the disease model of addiction. Some recurring ideas found in most of these models are (1) the progressive nature of addiction (from early, to middle, and then to late stages or phases), (2) the notion of "drift" from being a casual user to becoming an addict, (3) the development of tolerance and the presence of withdrawal symptoms, and (4) the distinction between physiological or physical dependence and psychological or "psychic" dependence.

Some researchers have used the psychic/physical dependence dichotomy to argue that drugs such as cocaine, cannabis, and nicotine are not truly addictive because cessation of their use is not accompanied by a full-blown withdrawal syndrome of the opiate type. Further claims have been made that the use of cocaine and cannabis could be promptly and readily terminated if the user only exerts enough "psychic" will. These claims, as well as artificial distinctions between mind and body, have become somewhat less defensible with the recent dramatic increase in "crack" addiction, an addiction that seems less amenable to treatment than alcoholism or heroin addiction.

Although some somatic changes have been reported for cannabis users, we cannot expect an accurate human pathology of this drug to be written before the end of the century. By that time, unfortunately, we will probably be concerned with the addictive potential and somatic effects of drugs yet to be discovered or manufactured. The damaging physical effects of drugs such as alcohol, cocaine, and heroin will be documented in the next chapter.

ENDNOTES

1. Tam Stewart, *The Heroin Users* (London: Pandora, 1987), p. 6.

2. Ibid.

3. William S. Burroughs, *Junky* (New York: Penguin Books, 1977), p. xv; originally published as *Junkie* under the pen name of William Lee, by Ace Books, 1953).

4. Joanne Baum, *One Step over the Line: A No-Nonsense Guide to Recognizing and Treating Cocaine Dependency* (New York: Harper & Row, 1985), pp. 25–42.

5. Arnold M. Washton, *Cocaine Addiction: Treatment, Recovery, and Relapse Prevention* (New York: W. W. Norton, 1989), p. 55.

6. Jara Krivanek, *Heroin: Myths and Realities* (Sydney: Allen & Unwin, 1988), p. 202.

7. Vernon E. Johnson, *I'll Quit Tomorrow* (New York: Harper & Row, 1973), p. 1.

8. Elvin M. Jellinek, "Phases of Alcohol Addiction," *Quarterly Journal of Studies of Alcohol,* Vol. 13 (1952), pp. 673–684.

9. Elvin M. Jellinek, *The Disease Concept of Alcoholism* (New Haven, CT: Hillhouse Press, 1960).

10. Marty Mann, *New Primer on Alcoholism,* 2nd ed. (New York: Holt, Rinehart and Winston, 1968), p. 3.

11. William Madsen, *The American Alcoholic: The Nature-Nurture Controversies in Alcoholic Research and Therapy* (Springfield, IL: Charles C Thomas, 1974), p. 94.

12. Joseph Kessel, *The Road Back, A Report on Alcoholics Anonymous* (New York: Alfred A. Knopf, 1962), p. 128.

13. George E. Vaillant, *Natural History of Alcoholism* (Cambridge, MA: Harvard University Press, 1983).

14. E. Mansell Pattison, Mark B. Sobell, and Linda C. Sobell, *Emerging Concepts of Alcohol Dependence* (New York: Springer, 1977), pp. 4–5.

15. Washton, *Cocaine Addiction,* p. 55.

16. Ibid.

17. T. Duster, *The Legislation of Morality* (New York: The Free Press, 1970).

18. Jara Krivanek, *Addictions* (Sydney: Allen & Unwin, 1989), p. 86.

19. Ibid.

20. Tom Field, *Escaping the Dragon* (London: Allen & Unwin, 1985), p. 53.

21. B. D. Johnson, "Once an Addict, Seldom an Addict," *Contemporary Drug Problems,* Vol. 7, No. 1 (1978), pp. 48–49.

22. Edward Senay, *Drugs, Society, and Behavior* (Guilford, CT: Dushkin, 1986).

23. Alfred R. Lindesmith, *Addiction and Opiates* (Chicago: Aldine, 1968).

24. Ibid., p. 95.

25. Ibid., pp. 192–193.

26. Ibid., p. 52.

27. Stanton Peele, in B. Hafen and B. Peterson, *Medicines and Drugs,* 2nd ed. (Philadelphia: Lea & Febiger, 1978), p. 167.

28. Krivanek, *Addictions,* pp. 85–105.

29. J. Griffin-Edwards, "Cannabis and the Question of Dependence," in *Report of the Expert Group on the Effects of Cannabis Use* (London: The Advisory Council on the Misuse of Drugs, 1982).

30. Erich Goode, *Drugs in American Society* (New York: Alfred A. Knopf, 1972), pp. 57–58.

31. Gabriel G. Nahas, *Marijuana in Science and Medicine* (New York: Raven Press, 1984), p. 208.

32. M. I. Soueif, "The Use of Cannabis in Egypt: A Behavioral Study," *Bulletin of Narcotics,* Vol. 4 (1971), pp. 17–18.

33. G. S. Chopra, "Man and Marijuana," *International Journal of Addiction,* Vol. 4 (1969), p. 215.

34. Jordan M. Scher, "The Marijuana Habit," *Journal of the American Medical Association,* Vol. 214 (1970), p. 1120.

35. S. Kaymakcalan, "Tolerance to and Dependence on Cannabis," *Bulletin of Narcotics,* Vol. 25 (1973), pp. 39–47.

36. Reese T. Jones and Neal Benowitz, "The 30-Day Trip: Clinical Studies of Cannabis Tolerance and Dependence," in M. C. Braude and S. Szara (eds.), *Pharmacology of Marijuana* (New York: Raven Press, 1976), pp. 627–641.

37. Nahas, *Marijuana in Science and Medicine,* p. 208.

38. M. H. Seever, "Drug Dependence and Drug Abuse, A World Problem," *Pharmacologist,* Vol. 12 (1970), pp. 172–181.

39. Herbert Hendin et al., *Living High: Daily Marijuana Use Among Adults* (New York: Human Sciences Press, 1987), p. 38.

40. Ibid., p. 42.

41. Ibid., pp. 170–172.

42. Ibid., pp. 171–172.

43. Nahas, *Marijuana,* p. 211.

44. Ibid., pp. 211–212.

4

The physiological and behavioral consequences of alcohol and drug abuse

In this chapter we will discuss the major physiological and behavioral consequences of alcohol and drug abuse. We will spare you the more technical details on such disorders as keukopoiesis and thrombopoiesis, which are of somewhat greater interest to the medical professions, but we will outline the more common consequences. Any professional person who has the responsibility of assisting clients with alcohol and drug problems must be able to recognize common symptoms and make appropriate referrals. In fact, it will undoubtedly be advantageous to the practicing social worker or other human service professional to be capable of deciphering a physician's report on an alcoholic or drug-abusing client. We will attempt to keep the medical terminology to a minimum, but it is essential to understand such terms as cardiomyopathy, hepatic dysfunction, and Korsakoff's psychosis.

Certain classes of drugs, such as CNS depressants, will have common effects on the users' behavior. Individual CNS depressants often will have very different physiological effects, however. In some cases the same drug will have different physiological effects, depending on the particular method of ingestion. Cocaine "snorters" may have very different physical problems than those who inject the same drug with a hypodermic needle. In fact, it is frequently observed that some addicts who inject drugs often seem to be more addicted to the process of "shooting up" than to the effects of a particular drug.

We will pay somewhat more attention to the effects of alcohol in the following pages, since it is the most widely used of all the drugs covered here. Because of its long history, we also know somewhat more about the consequences of alcohol abuse. Very little is known about the long-term consequences of abusing some of the newer drugs such as "ice."

THE EFFECTS OF ALCOHOL

Ethyl alcohol is almost exclusively ingested in the form of a potable beverage. (In relatively rare instances it is used for medical reasons and may be administered intravenously by a physician.) One of the most dangerous and widely used drugs throughout the world, it has the potential for causing deleterious effects on every part of the digestive system as well as every major organ in the human body.

THE METABOLIZATION OF ALCOHOL

As soon as alcohol is ingested, the body begins to eliminate or metabolize it, primarily through oxidation. Until recently it was thought that approximately 95 percent of all alcohol was eliminated through oxidation and 5 percent through bodily processes such as respiration, urination, and perspiration. It was recently discovered that much of the alcohol that is consumed in small doses is actually metabolized in the stomach.[1] Gastric metabolism acts as a barrier to toxicity with moderate doses of alcohol.

The major organ that metabolizes larger amounts of alcohol is the liver. Small amounts are also eliminated in the feces, and nursing mothers release some alcohol in their milk. The initial step is the conversion of alcohol to acetaldehyde by the enzyme, alcohol dehydrogenase (ADH). Next the acetaldehyde is converted by another liver enzyme to an active acetate that is further broken down into hydrogen, oxygen, and water. The metabolism of alcohol results in significant changes in the ratio of important chemicals within the liver cells, changes that affect the rate of the metabolism.

Depending on the mass of functioning liver that is available, the average adult can oxidize from 10 to 15 grams of alcohol per hour. (This is approximately the amount of pure ethanol in one "drink.") An average person could therefore consume about one drink per hour without accumulating alcohol in the body. However, there is tremendous variation in individual rates of metabolism, depending on such factors as other contents of the stomach at the time of ingestion, the body's proportion of fat, and the proportion of healthy versus cirrhotic liver tissue. Alcohol is approximately thirty times more soluble in water than in fat, a fact that accounts for the some of the gender and body weight differences in the rate of metabolism.[2] For example, women tend to metabolize alcohol at a slower rate than men because of the higher ratio of fat to water content in their bodies.

It is common knowledge that the experienced drinker may show some resistance to the effects of alcohol, a phenomenon known as *tolerance*. Such an individual requires larger and larger doses of alcohol in order to reach a "high" or desired state of intoxication. This phenomenon is one of the most reliable physical signs of alcoholism, and it may occur because of (1) altered distribution and/or metabolism of the alcohol, leading to lower concentrations at the receptor site; (2) altered receptor sensitivity to alcohol; and (3) the development of alternative pathways for bypassing the receptor system.[3] Heavy use of alcohol may lead to increased rates of ethanol oxidation up to 100 percent.[4]

INTOXICATION

The exact mechanism by which alcohol produces its effects on the central nervous system is not known. It is not thought to be like a narcotic, which binds specific receptor systems in certain areas of the brain. It appears that although the actions on specific cells are quite selective, alcohol has a very nonspecific effect on the physiochemical systems that regulate the functions of neurons.[5] The five basic effects of alcohol on the CNS are (1) euphoria, (2) removal of inhibitions, (3) impairment of vision, (4) muscular incoordination, and (5) lengthened reaction time.[6]

Intoxication and alcoholism are two completely different concepts. Intoxication will occur whenever alcohol is ingested. In small amounts it may produce euphoria and a decrease in inhibitions; at a blood-alcohol concentration (BAC) of 0.10 percent, ataxia and dysarthria generally occur.[7] Between 0.2 percent and 0.25 percent many people cannot sit or stand upright without support. The average person may fall into a coma when the BAC is between 0.3 percent and 0.4 percent, and death normally occurs beyond the 0.5 percent level.[8] These averages may be misleading, however, because of the development of *tolerance* in the chronic user. There have been persons arrested for driving under the influence (DUI) with blood-alcohol levels (BALs) of 0.4 percent—when the "average" drinker would be in a coma. There also have been reports of persons surviving a BAL of more than 0.7 percent.

WITHDRAWAL

The earliest and most common effects of alcohol withdrawal are anxiety, anorexia, insomnia, and tremor. In the early stages of withdrawal, a person will also be irritable and easily startled and have a subjective feeling of distress sometimes described as internal shaking. These symptoms peak within twenty-four to thirty-six hours and then rapidly disappear. The pulse rate is typically elevated during withdrawal and may reach 120 to 140 beats per minute.

Some persons going through withdrawal will experience alcoholic hallucinosis, a generally benign state that is not associated with paranoia or panic. Delirium tremens is the most severe state of withdrawal, characterized by marked tremor, anxiety, insomnia, anorexia, paranoia, and disorientation. The symptoms peak about three days after withdrawal, but may persist for two or three weeks. It may also be accompanied by fever, tachypnea, hyperpnea, diarrhea, diaphoresis, and vomiting. Tachycardia is almost always present.[9]

Grand mal convulsive seizures may also occur during withdrawal, but not usually as a part of delirium tremens. Anticonvulsant therapy should be used with any patient with a past history of seizures. Seizures occurring after more than two weeks of abstinence suggest a dependency on CNS depressants other than alcohol.[10]

THE DIGESTIVE SYSTEM

As we mentioned earlier, practically every part of the body is adversely affected by the use of alcohol. Cancer occurs with alarming frequency in the mouth, tongue, pharynx, esophagus, stomach, intestines, liver, and pancreas of alcoholics.[11] Alcoholics are also susceptible to inflammation of the esophageal mucosa. This may be caused by increased acid production induced by drinking alcohol, impaired esophageal peristalsis, the direct toxic effects of alcohol on the mucosa, and frequent vomiting.[12] A laceration of the gastroesophageal junction (known as the Mallory-Weiss syndrome) frequently results from alcohol-induced gastritis.[13] Rupture of the lower esophagus, Boerhaave's syndrome, is sometimes caused by vigorous vomiting, coughing, or seizures. This condition is fatal if not promptly treated.[14]

Another common outcome of heavy alcohol use is inflammation of the mucosal lining of the stomach, or *erosive gastritis*. If this condition is severe enough, it may also produce gastric ulcers. Erosive gastritis may be associated with nausea, vomiting, and distention. Occasionally, it may result in upper intestinal bleeding, a potentially life-threatening situation.[15]

One of the most common symptoms experienced by alcoholics is diarrhea. This condition may be caused either by the direct toxic effects of alcohol on the small intestine or by alcohol-related nutritional deficiencies that affect the functioning of the small intestine, most notably a folic acid deficiency.[16] Even moderate amounts of alcohol may cause blisters in the small intestine.[17] A much more serious problem, colon cancer, is also higher than normal among alcoholics.[18]

Alcohol can cause a number of changes in the liver: fatty liver, alcoholic hepatitis, and cirrhosis being the most common. In the United States cirrhosis is the ninth leading cause of death, and alcohol abuse is the major cause of cirrhosis.[19] A French study showed that as few as three drinks a day for men and one and one-half drinks a day for women could lead to cirrhosis,[20] a condition for which there is only a 50 percent survival rate after five years.[21]

Alcohol consumption can also lead to both acute and chronic pancreatitis. Acute pancreatitis is manifested by upper abdominal pain, nausea, and vomiting. In addition to these symptoms, chronic pancreatitis may be associated with malnutrition, weight loss, diarrhea, and foul-smelling, bulky stools. The chronic condition is so painful that victims often become addicted to analgesics or narcotics.[22] The exact causal mechanism is not clear, but alcohol is thought to have a direct, toxic effect on the pancreas, in addition to causing simultaneously an increase in pancreatic stimulation and obstructing the flow of pancreatic juice to the duodenum.[23] Acute pancreatitis is generally self-limiting, and most persons will recover within a few days. Chronic pancreatitis, on the other hand, is thought to be irreversible. Abstinence may reduce the pain, but the inflammation and scarring process continues.[24]

THE CARDIOVASCULAR SYSTEM

In normal, healthy persons alcohol causes an increase in the heart rate as well as lessened stroke power. In other words the heart simply functions less efficiently as a pump.[25] In normal subjects alcohol also decreases resistance to blood flow throughout the body, resulting in a reduction in blood pressure.[26] Other studies have found a strong relationship between alcohol use and elevated blood pressure among drinkers with hypertension.[27] Acute alcohol consumption causes dysfunctional changes in heart tissue, even in young, healthy adults.[28] In many chronic alcoholics there is a form of cardiomyopathy that is characterized by an actual wasting away of the heart muscle.[29]

Congestive heart failure associated with alcoholic cardiomyopathy, diseases involving thromboses (blood clots obstructing blood vessels), and low platelet counts are additional cardiovascular problems encountered in alcoholics. Among men, the average alcoholic has almost *twice* the chance of death from atherosclerotic and degenerative heart disease, compared to nonalcoholics. Women alcoholics are more than *four* times as likely to die from these diseases as nonalcoholics.[30]

THE ENDOCRINE AND REPRODUCTIVE SYSTEMS

Again, alcohol has both direct and indirect effects on the endocrine and reproductive systems. The spreading of endocrine effects is due in part to the organization of the endocrine glands into functional hierarchies called axes. Every endocrine axis has numerous feedback controls, and changes in one component may affect other components on that axis.[31]

The most common effects of alcohol on the hypothalamic-pituitary-thyroid (H-P-T) axis are a modest decrease in the levels of the hormone thyroxine and a marked decrease in the level of triiodothyronine. These changes are associated with serious liver disease, primarily through an inhibition of liver oxygen consumption.[32]

Alcohol also has serious consequences on the hypothalamic-pituitary-gonadal (H-P-G) axis in men, impairing the reproductive function and altering physiology.[33] These consequences include testicular atrophy, abnormal morphology of sperm cells, an increase in estrogen levels, and a decrease in testosterone. The relationship between liver disease and sexual dysfunction is extremely complex, but it widely recognized that alcoholics with cirrhosis are more likely than not to be sexually impotent.[34] Noncirrhotic alcoholics are also likely to lose sexual function for other reasons, such as a decrease in testosterone or psychological impairment.

In women alcohol-induced endocrinal failure is likely to result in early menopause, heavy menstrual flow, menstrual discomfort, infertility, and a higher frequency of obstetric and gynecologic problems. In both sexes heavy alcohol consumption is associated with the loss of secondary sex characteristics. Men may develop female hair patterns and gynecomastia (breast enlargement).[35] Another major health problem associated with alcohol use is fetal alcohol syndrome or fetal alcohol effects. Because of the severity and prevalence of the consequences of maternal drug abuse on the newborn, we have a separate section on this problem later in this chapter.

THE NEUROLOGIC SYSTEM

Excessive use of alcohol is known to lead to acute and chronic brain damage, as well as peripheral nerve dysfunction. The neuronal membrane is the location where the biochemical effects of alcohol on the central nervous system begin. Alcohol is believed to disrupt normal membrane function by penetrating into the membrane, expanding its volume, and disordering the lipid components. These changes can have profound effects on neurotransmission, the electrical signaling that occurs within and between neurons. This happens because the neurons are no longer capable of transmitting the ions through the neuronal membranes. The overall consequence is a disruption of the flow of information within the brain.[36]

Autopsy studies of alcoholic patients have found both cerebral and cortical atrophy to be quite common. In addition to being atrophied, the brains of alcoholics also have significant cell loss in many regions.[37] Computerized axial tomography (CAT) scans have also revealed that alcoholics have larger brain cavities, wider grooves on the brain's surface, and wider fissures.[38] The exact mechanism by which alcohol damages the brain is not known. One theory is that alcohol triggers a CNS antigen that leads to an autoimmune response that produces brain damage.[39] Another is that higher concentrations of alcohol in the blood leads to occlusion of vessels in the brain. The ensuing edema and hemorrhaging are responsible for the damage to brain tissue.[40] Still another is that brain damage is produced by alcohol-induced interference with protein synthesis.[41]

There are also a number of other secondary factors that may lead to brain damage in alcoholics. Oxygen deprivation related to such things as coma with hypoventilation or vomiting and aspiration of gastric contents can be responsible for such damage. Alcoholic hypoglycemia may also cause blood glucose levels to fall to dangerous levels. Brain cells (which have no capacity for regeneration) cannot function for long periods of time without both glucose and oxygen. In chronic alcoholics nutritional deficiencies may cause brain damage. Both Wernicke's syndrome and Korsakoff's psychosis are associated with thiamine deficiency. (Thiamine is a primary link in the production of energy for brain cells.)[42]

Common Neurologic Disorders

Acute brain syndrome is marked by a rapid onset and a high degree of reversibility. It is manifested simply as acute intoxication or hallucinosis. Chronic brain syndrome is characterized by a generally slow onset and is usually irreversible. Some of the symptoms of both acute and chronic brain syndrome are a decrease in complex intellectual functioning, alteration in memory, impaired judgment, and shallowness of affect.[43] Alcoholics with chronic brain syndrome suffer from recent memory loss, confusion, disorientation (for time, place, and person), and difficulty in concentration.[44] These symptoms may be preceded by months or even years of other symptoms such as fatigue, listlessness, loss of interest, depression, and anxiety or agitation. Unless the brain damage is halted, the person's speech will become monosyllabic and motor controls will fail. Eventually he or she will be unable to manage even the basic tasks, such as eating or dressing, and sphincter control will fail.[45]

One of the common diseases associated with chronic alcoholism is Wernicke's syndrome. The typical victim is a 40- to 60-year-old chronic alcoholic who becomes easily confused or excited. This person has already experienced peripheral neuropathy and diplopia, the first major clues to the disease. As mentioned earlier, this disease is related to thiamine deficiency, and thiamine replacement is the accepted therapy. With prompt treatment, the prognosis for recovery is generally good.[46]

Korsakoff's psychosis is frequently encountered in patients who are clearing from Wernicke's syndrome. These two conditions are so frequently found together that they are often described simply as the Wernicke-Korsakoff syndrome. The typical victim is a chronic alcoholic, often one with so severe a recent memory deficit that he may not be able to remember simple material for even a few moments. The Korsakoff's syndrome patient may show relatively normal retention of nonverbal information however, such as "Jimmie G.," described by Oliver Sacks in his fascinating book of "clinical tales."[47] The patient was 49 years old in 1975. He believed that he was still 19 years old and could remember the names of the different submarines on which he had served in World War II, as well as their missions, where he was stationed, and the names of shipmates. He remembered Morse code, was still fluent in touch typing, and could do complex mathematics (including algebra) in his head. On the other hand, after a brief conversation with Dr. Sacks, the doctor left the room for two minutes, reentered the room, and Jimmie did not recognize him. On one occasion Dr. Sacks laid out his watch, tie, and glasses on the desk, covered them, and asked Jimmie to remember them. "Then after a minute's chat, I asked him what I had put under the cover. He remembered none of them—or indeed that I had even asked him to remember."[48]

Alcoholic pellagra is the result of a thiamine deficiency characterized by a clouding of consciousness, rigidity, and uncontrolled sucking and grasping reflexes. Other symptoms associated with pellagra in nonalcoholics (dementia, dermatitis, and diarrhea) usually do not occur in alcoholics, because of the rapid onset of the disease.[49]

Peripheral neuropathy can also occur in alcoholics who do not have Wernicke-Korsakoff's syndrome. Hospital reports indicate that alcoholic peripheral neuropathy is more common than all other forms of peripheral neuropathy combined.[50] Problems occur first in the feet, the most distal parts of the longest peripheral nerves. First symptoms are usually burning, tingling, or prickling sensations, along with pain in the calf muscles or feet. Discomfort and numbness begins in the feet and gradually works up the legs, and muscle weakness and wasting occur as the process continues. A treatment consisting of abstinence, a nutritious diet, and supplementary vitamin B will usually allow most patients to recover.[51]

ALCOHOL AND OTHER DISORDERS

Alcohol use is a common cause of malnutrition, partly because alcoholic beverages are often substituted for other, more nutritional food, and partly because alcohol disrupts the body's ability to absorb and properly utilize some vitamins.[52] In one study, *all* forty-one patients with alcoholic liver disease were also found to suffer from thiamine deficiency.[53] Long-term alcohol intake commonly results in deficiencies in fiber, protein, calcium, iron, vitamins A and C, and thiamine.[54]

Persons who have not eaten within the past day may experience a drop in blood sugar and hypoglycemia, with a potential for coma and death. Insulin-dependent diabetics are extremely vulnerable to both hypoglycemia and ketoacidosis.[55] Alcohol consumption has also been associated with a reduction in bone mass and with osteoporosis in men.[56]

Chronic alcohol abuse is associated with higher susceptibility to several different types of infectious diseases, due to a suppression of the body's immune system, including tuberculosis, pneumonia, peritonitis, and hepatitis B. Equally disturbing is the fact that alcoholics are at a much higher risk for almost every form of cancer—from the mouth to the rectum! In fact, about one-fourth of all cancer of directly exposed tissue (lip, oral cavity, pharynx, stomach, etc.) is attributed to the effects of alcohol.[57]

From a medical perspective, almost nothing good can be said about the effects of alcohol on the human body. There is some rather inconclusive evidence that persons who are moderate drinkers may have slightly lower risks of atherosclerosis and coronary heart disease.[58] This may be because alcohol has some small effect on serum high-density lipoprotein (HDL cholesterol). Experts in cardiology are recommending against the use of alcohol, however. Even if moderate alcohol intake does provide this benefit, it is far outweighed by other health risks, and it makes more sense to control cholesterol levels by choosing a healthy diet.

THE EFFECTS OF CANNABIS

Compared to alcohol, the purely physiological effects of marijuana and hashish use are relatively few. However, there is still much controversy concerning the scientific evidence on the consequences of using this drug. Most of the proven health risks associated with cannabis come from the common method of ingesting the drug—smoking. The effect of the smoke creates a tendency toward bronchitis, rhinopharyngitis, sinusitis, and asthma.[59] Since marijuana smoke also contains carcinogens, regular users are also exposed to an increased risk of lung cancer. Just as in tobacco smoking, there is also an increased risk of heart disease.[60]

A person smoking marijuana will experience a reddening of the eyes (inflammation of the conjunctiva of the eye from the irritant effect of the smoke), slight tachycardia, and a dryness of the mouth. For a long time it was commonly accepted that dilation of the pupils was a common side effect of marijuana smoking, but that notion has been discredited. Blood sugar levels also seem to be unaffected by marijuana, despite the long-standing impact of this drug on subjective feelings of hunger ("munchies").[61]

No conclusive evidence exits supporting damage to other organs related to marijuana usage.[62] One of the major problems in conducting research in this area, however, is that it is difficult to isolate the effects of marijuana *alone,* apart from other drugs, since marijuana users commonly use other illicit drugs as well as alcohol and tobacco.

There is some evidence (which has been contradicted by other studies) of chromosomal[63] and genetic[64] damage associated with chronic marijuana use. It has long been suspected that heavy marijuana use may result in suppression of the immune system, and recent studies have confirmed this.[65] Reduced sperm counts and diminished ovulation have also been found among regular users.[66] Mixed results have resulted from studies of brain damage. Several studies have found brain atrophy in regular marijuana users, while others have found no evidence of atrophy.[67]

In experimental animals marijuana has proven injurious to all phases of gonadal and reproductive functions, through the direct action of the drug on the hypothalamo-pituitary axis as well as the gonads. In male nonhuman primates cannabis produces decreased testicular size and spermatogenesis. In females it disrupts ovarian cycles and ovulation.[68]

Cannabis generally produces a state of euphoria in which inhibitions are relaxed and thoughts appear to come more rapidly and to be more profound than normal thoughts. Users often report feeling an exaggerated sense of ability, despite a loss of critical faculties and distorted timing. The primary personality change for regular users has been called the "amotivational syndrome." The user loses ambition, becomes passive and apathetic, becomes increasingly introspective and disinterested in anything outside their dreamy fantasies.[69]

The psychological effects of cannabis have been studied and reported since the second century, when the use of hashish was reported by a Chinese investigator, Pen-Ts'ao Ching, to produce mental illness.[70] Hashish use was also associated with a certain form of psychosis among the followers (called assassins) of an eleventh-century Moslem leader. Jacques-Joseph Moreau, an officer in Napoleon's army, reported on the similarities between cannabis intoxication and mental illness in 1845. He lists eight "cardinal symptoms":

Unexplainable feeling of bliss, happiness

Excitement dissociation of ideas

Errors of time and space appreciation

Development of the sense of hearing, the influence of music

Fixed ideas (delusions)

Damage to the emotions

Irresistible impulses

Illusions, hallucinations[71]

While there may be some debate regarding whether a true cannabis psychosis exists, there is no doubt that its use has resulted in temporal disintegration and delusional-like ideation, panic reactions, dysphoric reactions (disorientation, immobility, acute panic, heavy sedation), problems with memory, and inability to follow or to maintain a conversation. Regular use also has been associated with acute brain syndrome and delirium, characterized by confusion prostration, disorientation, derealization, and sometimes auditory or visual hallucinations.[72]

THE EFFECTS OF STIMULANTS

Cocaine

Until recently, the most common method for ingesting cocaine in North America was the insufflation of refined coca paste, cocaine hydrochloride (otherwise known as "coke" or "snow"). This drug is also injected (alone or in combination with heroin) intravenously or intramuscularly. In other parts of the world users prefer to chew coca leaves or to smoke coca paste.[73] In the United States the most popular method seems to be smoking a form of solidified cocaine which has been treated with baking soda, known as "crack." This form is also known as "freebase" cocaine, since it is the cocaine alkaloid that has been chemically separated from cocaine hydrochloride. Crack or freebase is more suitable for smoking because more of the cocaine in the freebase form volatizes without decomposing.[74] Different methods of ingestion are frequently associated with different types of physiological problems.

Overdoses from smoking, inhaling, or injecting cocaine may be fatal, a result of ventricular fibrillation, cardiac arrest, apnoea, or hyperthermia. Heavy use may also result in extreme hypertension, cerebrovascular bleeding, stroke, and elliptiform fits.[75] Heart failure is a risk even among young, otherwise healthy persons who use cocaine. Chronic use also affects the vision. Users may experience "snow lights," patches or flashes of white light darting in and out of their field of vision. Others may report fuzzy or double vision.

Cocaine's behavioral effects do not differ much from those produced by amphetamines; their duration is simply much shorter.[76] The quality and intensity of the cocaine-induced "high" vary markedly from one user to the next, depending on the mood, personality, and expectations of the user and the setting and circumstances under which the drug is taken. The acute positive state generally is characterized by euphoria, feelings of increased energy and confidence, mental alertness, and sexual arousal. With continued use tolerance develops, making it more difficult to achieve a satisfactory "high" and bringing rebound effects which are dysphoric. When not high, the user feels anxious, confused, depressed, and often paranoid.

Ironically, only a decade ago common wisdom held that cocaine was not an addictive substance. Now it is regarded as being both physically and psychologically addictive, as well as one of the most dangerous of all addictive drugs. While withdrawal from cocaine does not produce physical symptoms as severe as some other drugs, its psychological hold on the user is one of the strongest. There are also considerable physical risks associated

TABLE 4.1   Medical Complications from Cocaine

I. Overdose or Toxic Reactions
  a. Rapid and/or irregular heartbeat (tachycardia, arrhythmia)
  b. Cardiac arrest (heart attack, ventricle fibrillation)
  c. Cerebral hemorrhage (stroke)
  d. Brain seizure (convulsion with loss of consciousness)
  e. Respiratory failure (suffocation)
  f. Hyperthermia (heat stroke due to elevated body temperature)

II. Complications Associated with Route of Administration
Intranasal
  a. Nasal sores, bleeding, congestion, and discharge
  b. Sinus congestion and headaches
  c. Perforation of the nasal septum

Freebase Smoking
  a. Chest congestion, wheezing, and black phelgm
  b. Chronic coughing
  c. Lung damage
  d. Burns of the lips, mouth, tongue, and throat
  e. Hoarseness

Intravenous
  a. Infections at injection sites
  b. Systemic infections (hepatitis, endocarditis, septicemia)
  c. AIDS

III. Complications from Cocaine Use During Pregnancy
  a. Premature separation of the placenta, spontaneous abortion
  b. Neurobehavioral deficits in the fetus
  c. Malformation of the fetus
  d. Premature birth, stillbirth, and/or low birth weight

Source: Arnold M. Washton, *Cocaine Addiction* (New York: W. W. Norton Company, 1989), p. 29.

with prolonged use or overdosing.[77] (See Table 4.1.)

Although regarded by some to be an aphrodisiac, continued cocaine use generally produces sexual dysfunction. Men suffer from a reduced sexual drive and erectile and ejaculatory functions, while women experience a reduction in sexual desire and lose the ability to produce vaginal lubrication. Weight loss, insomnia, and hallucinations ("cocaine bugs") are also frequently reported.[78]

Since cocaine enters the blood relatively quickly from mucous membranes, the nose is a favorite site for the ingestion or "snorting" of cocaine hydrochloride. The habit of snorting or sniffing cocaine eventually causes a perforation of the nasal septum, and users are sometimes referred to as "sniffy."[79] When the nasal membrane is beginning to be damaged, the user will appear to have either a stuffy or runny nose, and the mucous will be very watery. As the condition becomes more severe, the user will have difficulty breathing. Eventually, breathing through the nose becomes impossible, and the wall dividing the halves of the nose will disintegrate.

The effects of ingesting cocaine take about three minutes to reach the brain by snorting. "Freebasing" or smoking "crack" can deliver the same effects in about six seconds.[80] This form of administration can produce minor lung irritations, sore chest and neck, swollen glands, and a raspy voice. The "high" produced from smoking crack lasts from two to five minutes and ends as abruptly as it began. After the "crash" the user is irritable, anxious, and depressed and has increasingly severe cravings for more of the drug. Reports from addicts indicate that addiction occurs *much* more quickly from the use of crack than through any other form of cocaine use.[81]

Intravenous injection of cocaine hydrochloride in a water solution delivers a euphoric feeling almost as quickly as smoking crack—about fourteen seconds.[82] Some cocaine users prefer injecting a mixture of cocaine and heroin, a combination known as a "speedball." (The heroin is said to dampen the unpleasant jitteriness and crash from cocaine.) Taken together these two drugs sometimes completely halt the user's respiration or cause brain seizures. In one community two-thirds of cocaine-related deaths were attributed to the injection of speedballs.[83] The danger of cocaine overdoses cannot be overemphasized. Deaths from cocaine or cocaine/heroin combinations have exceeded heroin overdoses at least since 1983.[84]

There are many other risks associated with any type of intravenous drug use—such as hepatitis or HIV infection. Although the new user may begin by scrupulously maintaining sterile "works" (needles and syringes), the chronic user seldom exercises such care. One former user tells about "a day when I drove all the way across Liverpool to borrow a worn-out works from an addict who had recently had syphilis."[85] Since bacteria and viruses don't impede the addict's high, they are generally disregarded.

Finally, there is the problem of "cocaine babies." A much greater incidence of miscarriages, low-birth-weight infants, premature deliveries, and birth defects have been found to be associated with cocaine use during pregnancy.[86] As these children mature, they have a high incidence of learning disabilities and health problems. Early reports indicate that they are also much more likely to be physically abused by their parents.[87]

AMPHETAMINES

Amphetamines are one of the most preferred drugs of "normal" Americans—students cramming for exams, truck drivers working twenty-four-hour days, and athletes competing for national or international records. Millions of persons have legally used amphetamines for anxiety, depression, and obesity. As we mentioned earlier, millions of soldiers were given amphetamines in World War II to enhance combat performance. German Panzer troops used the drug to eliminate fatigue and maintain physical endurance. Because of the aggressive and violent behavior frequently noted in chronic users, some historians believe that many German atrocities were linked to the use of amphetamines.[88] Ten years after the war ended, 200,000 cases of amphetamine psychosis, one of the most extreme side effects of this drug, were reported in Japan.[89] As late as 1969 the U.S. armed forces were still purchasing massive amounts of amphetamine, with the Navy dispensing 21.1 pills per person per year, followed by the Air Force (17.5) and the Army (13.8).[90]

Low dosages of this drug will normally produce (1) a heightened competence in motor skills and mental acuity, (2) increased alertness, (3) a feeling of increased energy, (4) a stimulation of the need for motor activity (particularly walking or talking), (5) a feeling

TABLE 4.2   Physical Effects of Amphetamine

Increased blood pressure	Dry mouth
Increased heart rate	Headache
Increased body temperature	Nausea
Irregular heart beats	Vomiting
Increased breathing rates	Blurred vision
Damage to blood vessels	Increased blood sugar
Dilation of the pupils of the eyes	Sores and abcessess on the Skin (from intravenous use)
Increased use of energy	Decreased pain sensitivity
Weight loss	Salivation (at high doses)

Source: Scott E. Lukas (ed.), *The Encyclopedia of Psychoactive Drugs: Amphetamines* (New York: Chelsea House, 1985), p. 49.

of euphoria, (6) increased heartbeat, (7) an inhibition of appetite, (8) constriction of the blood vessels, (9) a dryness of the mouth, and (10) a feeling of confidence and even grandeur.[91] Other physical effects are noted in Table 4.2.

Amphetamines are usually taken orally by new users in dosages of 50 to 150 milligrams (mg) daily. Addicts soon discover that "highs" are obtained faster by snorting or injecting the drug. During a "speed run" a "speed-freak" may inject as much as 1,000 mg in one dose and up to 5,000 mg during a twenty-four-hour period. During a run, users will be disinclined to either eat or sleep and may lose 10 pounds or more during a week. Some users prefer the "balling" technique, in which a form known as "crank" is instilled into the vagina prior to intercourse. Low dosages of amphetamine may slightly enhance sexual performance, but higher dosages consistently disrupt sexual function.[92] Orgasm and ejaculation are either delayed or impossible to achieve while using large doses of speed.[93]

After "crashing," the user may experience marked depression, apathy, a variety of aches and pains, and a ravenous appetite. The user may be so exhausted that he will sleep for long periods. Some users will begin another speed run as soon as they feel that they are beginning to crash. It is not unusual for some users to inject amphetamines in combination with other drugs such as sedatives or heroin. (While the original "speedball" was cocaine and heroin, the "poor man's speedball" is methamphetamine and heroin.)[94]

Chronic amphetamine use may lead to cerebral hemorrhages, tachycardia, hypertension, cardia arrhythmias, and liver damage. Combining amphetamine use with drinking alcohol has a multiplicative effect which puts the user at a high risk for heart failure.[95] The anorexia produced by chronic use coupled with the high caloric intake required to sustain unusually high levels of motor activity often results in malnutrition. Paranoia inevitably comes with heavy and continued use. Violent behavior, including suicide, may come during or at the end of a "run."[96]

As with other drugs, repeated use of amphetamines leads to addiction, tolerance, and the need for increasingly large doses. During the initial phase of withdrawal, the user may sleep almost continuously for up to three days. This is usually followed by a state of depression lasting up to two weeks. During this time the individual may be irritable and apathetic and experience episodes of anxiety, extreme fear, and obsessions. Sleep disturbances may occur for the next several months. An additional problem for amphetamine users is that they frequently begin using alcohol, barbiturates, or other depressants in order to mitigate the stimulation effects of amphetamine. This is particularly dangerous because of the possibility of drug interaction effects.[97]

Chronic users develop amphetamine toxicity which is manifested in physical, mental, and behavioral symptoms. General health and personal hygiene deteriorate, and intravenous users may show track marks, infections, and abscesses. Behavioral signs include nervousness, irritability, and restlessness due to the constant overstimulation induced by the drug. This may lead to stereotypic compulsive behavior such as taking an object apart and putting it back together again. They may pace back and forth across a room, and conversation is quite repetitive. The most extreme form of this toxicity is a state of paranoia called amphetamine psychosis. The individual becomes suspicious of everyone, is physically exhausted, and will appear to be quite confused. Delusions or hallucinations

may occur, and violent, aggressive behavior is frequently noted. The paranoia of an amphetamine addict may be identical to that observed in schizophrenia.[98]

A unique feature of amphetamine psychosis is the occurrence of tactile hallucinations. The individual may feel that he has worms or lice on his body (similar to "cocaine bugs"). Constant picking or scratching often results in sores and abrasions. Some users have even used knives or razor blades to remove the imagined organisms from their skin.

Another particular feature of amphetamine psychosis is the speed (no pun intended!) with which it can occur. Recent studies have shown that it can be induced in human volunteers, who were carefully screened to ensure they did not have a previous history of psychosis, in approximately four days.[99]

MDMA

One of the more popular "designer drugs" of the 1980s was MDMA (3,4-methylenedioxymethamphetamine), more commonly known as "Ecstasy," "XTC," or "Adam." A designer drug is generally defined as a substance tailor-made for specific selected effects. It also usually involves the process of chemically engineering existing controlled substances to create a drug that is not currently illegal.[100] MDMA was created to replace its cousin (3,4-methylenedioxyamphetamine), which was a Schedule I drug under the 1970 Controlled Substances Act. It was sold openly, especially in bars in the Dallas, Texas, area until it also became a controlled substance in 1985.[101]

MDMA is described as an aphrodisiac, a "party drug," and a "yuppie psychedelic." It is generally taken orally in doses of 100 to 150 mg. A mild euphoria may appear between twenty and sixty minutes later, and the "rush" may last from a few minutes to a half hour. The rush levels off to a plateau lasting two to three hours. Users report being in an altered state of consciousness but still in control, having expanded mental perspective and insight into personal problems or patterns.[102] Researchers have noted that the drug tends to enhance the pleasure of touching but interferes with erection in men and inhibits orgasm in both men and women.[103] MDMA produces a distinct hangover with pronounced negative side effects on the second day after use, including sore jaw muscles (from teeth grinding), drowsiness, muscle aches, depression, and difficulty concentrating. Users seem to develop a tolerance quickly to the positive effects of the drug, but not to its negative effects.[104]

There has been recent concern that a large enough dose of MDMA can destroy serotonergic nerve terminals in the brain, thereby disrupting sleep, changing mood, causing sexual dysfunction, and creating hypersensitivity to aversive stimuli.[105] There is also some evidence that MDMA may suppress the immune system, with regular users experiencing more sore throats, colds, influenza, and herpes outbreaks.[106]

Crystal Methamphetamine

"Crystal meth" or "ice" recently has become one of the most popular drugs in Asia and has overtaken cocaine and marijuana as the most commonly used illicit drug in Hawaii.[107] The basic ingredients for this drug can be obtained from almost any chemical company; $100 worth of ingredients will produce a pound of "ice" in its most highly refined form—worth anywhere from $15,000 to $32,000 on the street.[108] The drug's popularity is growing so quickly because of the enormous profits, because it can be easily manufactured, and because the "high" from smoking ice lasts eight to twenty-four hours, compared to the fifteen-minute high from crack.[109]

Ice produces feelings of euphoria followed by severe depression, just as crack does, but the high lasts much longer, and the "crash" is much worse. Addicts call the sensation from smoking ice "amping" for the amplified euphoria it provides them.[110] Ice users may also experience symptoms of acute psychosis that are not normally associated with crack use. Severe paranoia, hallucinations, delusions, and incoherent speech may also make ice addicts indistinguishable from paranoid schizophrenics. Extremely violent and aggressive

behavior is common among addicts. One director of a crisis response team in Honolulu reported that "Every person on ice I have seen has to be in restraints."[111]

Other symptoms associated with use of this drug are weight loss, insomnia, irregular heartbeat, convulsions, and body temperatures that can reach 108 degrees—frequently resulting in kidney failure. Devastating effects have been noticed in children born to mothers using ice: they tend to be asocial and incapable of bonding. Some have tremors and cry for twenty-four hours without stopping. Nurses report that the problems of "ice babies" are much more severe than the problems of babies born addicted to cocaine.[112]

Crystalline methamphetamine is such a new drug to America that very little research has been conducted on its physiological or psychological effects. Nothing is available on the effectiveness of treatment for this addiction.

THE EFFECTS OF SEDATIVES

One of the greatest problems associated with abusing either barbiturate or nonbarbiturate sedatives is the danger of overdose. While some drugs, such as cannabis and amphetamines, have very large "safety zones," an overdose of only one or two seconal or methaqualone pills may cause death. This danger is even further heightened when the sedative is used in combination with alcohol. In the mid-1970s there were over ten thousand hospital admissions and two thousand deaths per year attributed to sedative overdoses, many of them in combination with alcohol.[113] Barbiturates are also the most frequent chemical agent used in committing suicide.[114]

Barbiturate intoxication is quite similar to alcohol intoxication: speech is slurred, thinking is confused, and movements are uncoordinated with a staggering gait. Addicts fall frequently, suffering many injuries and bruises. Barbiturates shift sleep patterns, and many users experience nightmarish, sleep-disrupting dreams upon withdrawal. Many return to using barbiturates or other sedatives in order to deal with insomnia. Barbiturates also depress the

Who Was Karen Ann Quinlan?

"The last thing we want to do is put Karen Ann Quinlan on trial," says county prosecutor Collester. "It makes no difference whether she was the Virgin Mary or Mary Magdalene," agrees attorney Coburn, who was appointed by the court to defend Karen's interests. But in court, Karen's parents have based their arguments on the belief that she would have wanted them to remove the machine prolonging her life—and that argument has thrust the question of what Karen was like, what she thought and how she lived, to the very heart of this tragic case.

Enigma

In spite of the probing investigations of the police, press and physicians, however, Karen Ann Quinlan remains something of an enigma. Adopted at the age of four weeks from a hospital for unwed mothers, she lived until last fall in Julia and Joseph Quinlans' New Jersey home, a two-story frame house with a white Madonna on the lawn. Her activities and ambitions seem to have been the ordinary stuff of middle-class suburbia. She was an average student at local parochial schools, principals and teachers recall nothing remarkable about her. A bit of a tomboy, she was avidly interested in sports, and at one time held a job as a gas station attendant and assistant mechanic.

In August 1974, shortly after she was laid off from her job as a technician at a ceramics factory, Karen moved out of the Quinlan household to live with a friend in an apartment miles away. After that, the accounts of her life-style start to vary tremendously. For one thing, she appears to have lost touch with her old friends from school and started running with a wholly new crowd. Her roommate Robin Croft scoffs at reports that they lived a drug and drink ridden life, saying that they only occasionally "tied one on" and that Karen "might have taken a few pills for a high, but she wasn't into drugs." But Thomas R. French, a young Morris County resident who was with Karen the last few days of her active life, tells a different story. French describes her as "self-destructive, popping whatever pills she could get her hands on" and often drinking to excess.

Tragedy

On the night of April 14, Karen accompanied French and several other friends to Falconer's, a roadside tavern in nearby Lake Lackawanna, where they were to celebrate a friend's birthday. According to French, they prefaced the trip to the tavern with several gin-and-tonics. French says he had seen Karen "popping pills" earlier in the day. He reports that Karen "started to nod out" after only one drink at the bar, so he drove her home. By the time they got there, Karen had passed out entirely. A few minutes later he realized she had stopped breathing and began to give her mouth-to-mouth resuscitation. His friends called an ambulance and Karen was carried off, unconscious, to the hospital, never to wake again.

Part of the Quinlans' argument for withdrawing Karen's life support rests on their claim that Karen had made it quite clear that she was horrified at the idea of being kept alive by mechanical means. Last week in court, Julia Quinlan described three separate occasions when Karen had said she would rather die than be kept alive by machines. Lori A. Gaffney, an 18-year-old friend, testified that Karen had told her she "would not want to be kept alive by such extraordinary means—under any circumstances." Miss Gaffney reports that Karen was particularly distressed after the father of a close friend, Nanette Foit, succumbed slowly and painfully to cancer.

"If anyone can make the decision to cut off treatment for an incompetent patient," says Dr. Robert Veatch, a specialist in medical ethics at New York's Institute of Society, Ethics and the Life Sciences, "it must be the person who best knows what she would want for herself." In Karen Ann Quinlan's case, it is not clear who knew her best during the last jumbled weeks of her active life. But her parents who knew her longest and are convinced that the Karen who lived with them was the real one, are convinced beyond doubt that they know what she would choose.

Source: Merrill Sheils and Susan Agrest, "Who Was Karen Ann Quinlan?" *Newsweek,* Vol. 86 (October 29, 1975), p. 60.

respiratory center, and apnea is a common danger to users with marginal pulmonary reserves. A more common problem is the effect of barbiturates on other drugs. Drugs such as phenobarbital induce liver enzymes that causes other drugs to be more rapidly degraded. This can reduce the effectiveness of anticoagulants, or it can speed the effect of drugs such as alcohol. With other drugs, it is simply impossible to predict the effect of the interaction.[115]

Withdrawal from barbiturates can be especially dangerous, much more so than heroin withdrawal. No one who has been using barbiturates over a long period of time should be withdrawn suddenly, and anyone who has taken addictive quantities should withdraw in a hospital. A delirium tremens–like condition occurs within twenty-four hours in a majority of cases. Three-fourths of persons going through abrupt withdrawal will experience major epileptic convulsions between the sixth and eighth day. Without close medical supervision, death is a distinct danger—frequently from exhaustion or pneumonia.[116]

Nonbarbiturate sedatives such as methaqualone (Quaaludes) may produce many of the same respiratory problems as the barbiturates. Other effects of methaqualone may include nausea, weakness, indigestion, numbness and tingling, and rashes. Withdrawal may resemble the symptoms of alcohol or sedative withdrawal, including delirium and convulsions.[117]

THE EFFECTS OF NARCOTICS

True narcotic drugs (which do *not* include marijuana and cocaine) depress the activity of the brain and the central nervous system. Their chief use in medicine is the relief of pain and the inducement of sleep.[118] They may be divided into two groups: (1) opium and opium derivatives and (2) synthetic substances that produce effects similar to opiates.

Opiates (opium, heroin, morphine, dilaudid, laudanum, paregoric, and codeine) are derived from the opium poppy. The poppy produces a white, milky substance that dries in contact with air. When further dried into a powder, this substance becomes opium. Morphine is the major alkaloid of opium. Heroin is a synthetic derivative of opium produced by exposing morphine to acetic acid. Codeine is a separate alkaloid found in opium. Raw opium contains about 10 percent morphine, and heroin is derived from morphine on roughly a 1-to-5 ratio.[119]

Opium is generally smoked, while the preferred method of administration for morphine and heroin is injection. Heroin may also be taken orally, "snorted," or smoked.[120] Among American soldiers in Southeast Asia, smoking was the most commonly used method of ingesting heroin.[121] Regular heroin users who "shoot" (inject) the drug have a characteristic slate-colored line along the veins into which they have been injecting. Frequent injection destroys superficial veins, and it becomes increasingly difficult to find healthy veins. Addicts will inject in sites such as the groin, the temples, and the penis. Gangrene, blood clots, AIDS, hepatitis, and venereal diseases are a common risk among addicts who share needles without paying adequate attention to cleaning their "works."[122]

Heroin reaches the brain from the bloodstream and is transformed into morphine. Heroin actually has minimal central nervous system effects per se, and it is only after being changed through hydrolysis to 6-mono-acetyl-morphine (MAM) and then to morphine that the major CNS effects are produced. Heroin is preferred to morphine by addicts, since it has an analgesic effect two to four times greater.[123] The effect of an injection is described by a former self-described "junky":

The rush is so hard to describe. It's like waiting for a distant thunderstorm to move overhead. A strange foreboding. A bizarre, awesome calm. It's in your blood, moving towards your brain, relentlessly; unstoppable, inevitable. A feeling starts to grow like a rumble from the horizon. The feeling swells, surging, soaring, crashing, screaming to a devastating crescendo. The gear [heroin] smashes against the top of your skull with the power of an uncapped oil well. You won't be able to bear the intense ecstasy. It is all too much. Your body may fall apart. The rock that is your head shatters harmlessly into a million sparkling, tinkling smithereens. They tumble at a thousand miles an hour straight back down over your body, warming, insulating, tingling, denying all pain, fear, and sadness. You are stoned, you are high. You are above and below reality and law.[124]

Morphine and heroin are cleared within six hours, and their subjective effects last four to five hours. With a large dose the new user "nods out" or enters a dream state moments after an injection. As with other drugs, tolerance develops to a degree that the addict ends up taking the drug simply to avoid the consequences of withdrawal, and increasingly larger doses have to be taken to accomplish this.[125] Other more purely physiological effects also are produced on the body. All opiates act on the gastrointestinal tract, resulting in dehydration of the feces and constipation in the majority of addicts. Contraction of the pupils is also obvious during chronic use.[126] Other major physical problems are common in addicts.

THE DIGESTIVE SYSTEM

Both peptic and duodenal ulcers are common in heroin addicts. Obstruction of the intestinal tract and hemorrhoids are also fre-

quently associated with their chronic constipation problems.[127]

THE ENDOCRINE SYSTEM

Morphine and heroin have been demonstrated to decrease the production of hormones and gonadotrophin.[128] Diabetes and hypoglycemic conditions are also frequently found in opiate addicts.[129]

INTEGUMENT

As mentioned earlier, the "tracks" seen on the bodies of heroin addicts are the result of repeated injections of heroin into the veins. These tracks are most often noticed on the sclerosed veins of the forearms, hands, and feet, but may occur anywhere on the body—including the dorsal vein of the penis, and external jugular and sublingual veins.[130] Dark pigmentation may also occur as a result of heating the tip of the "spike" with a match flame in order to "sterilize" it. The resulting carbon accumulation is deposited under the skin during injection.[131]

Abscesses and lesions of the skin frequently result from the practice of "skin-popping" (subcutaneous injection). These are usually found on the thighs and back. Another type of lesion commonly found on addicts is a "rosette" of cigarette burns on the chest resulting from "nodding out" while having a lighted cigarette in the mouth. Tattoos are also frequently found on heroin addicts, usually over the site of tracks they wish to conceal.[132]

GENITOURINARY SYSTEM

There is some evidence of an increased risk of both venereal disease and renal disease associated with heroin addiction, but these problems are not the direct result of the action of the drug. These diseases occur because of the contamination of the heroin or an addict's "works."[133]

OTHER PROBLEMS

Perhaps the greatest risk facing the heroin or morphine addict is the possibility of an overdose. Drugs such as this bought illegally on the street are always cut with some other substance such as quinine, domestic cleaning compounds, or even brick dust![134] It is impossible for the addict to know what the strength of his "gear" is, and there is not a large margin of safety for intravenous injection. Death from overdose is a constant risk.

As we mentioned earlier, tolerance develops rapidly, especially for the intravenous user. Many addicts purposefully go through withdrawal from time to time in order to reduce their tolerance. A substantial number of overdoses occur when addicts who have abstained for a period of time return to taking their usual dosage. Death or coma can also result from the combined use of opiates with either alcohol or barbiturates. The additive effect of these drugs may depress respiration to life-threatening levels.[135]

THE EFFECTS OF HALLUCINOGENS

The main property of a hallucinogen is to create an alteration of normal perceptions or to induce abnormal perceptions. These types of drugs are called psychotomimetic, but they also came to be known as "psychedelic" drugs in the "hippie" culture of the 1960s.[136] The term psychedelic is also applied to the philosophy of that particular generation of the drug culture, generally in a positive manner. This philosophy is that "man is a creature who has been lied to and blinded by the propaganda socialized into him from infancy."[137] The essential function served by psychedelic drugs, according to this line of thought, is to strip away the impediments that block a direct confrontation with reality and allow the user to see things clearly. Under the influence of mescaline, Aldous Huxley described the awesome "isness" of his trousers, his bookshelf, and the legs of a chair. "This is how things really are; how things really are."[138]

A much different point of view is summed up in the term, "hallucinogen." It brings forth images of something illusory—a deception, a fallacy, or perhaps the ravings of a madman or hallucination of someone in imminent need of treatment. Actually, a true hallucination (a perception without an object) is relatively rare during a drug experience. Much more common is a *distortion* of perception.[139] There is nothing mystical about the action of LSD; it is that of a toxic chemical that disrupts the brain's normal process. It is no more mystical than the hallucinations of an alcoholic, the delusions of a schizophrenic, or the dreams of an opium eater.

Hallucinogens do not cause the physical dependence of alcohol or opiates, and do not have the psychological compulsion of drugs like cocaine, although a psychological need to repeat the experience of "tripping" is common. In the true sense these are not drugs of dependence, but they are substances that can as easily result in disaster on the first as on each subsequent use.[140]

The most commonly used hallucinogens are LSD, mescaline (the main alkaloid of the peyote cactus), psilocybin (from a mushroom that flourishes in Mexico), and fly agaric (*amanita muscaria,* a common toadstool). LSD is the strongest of these, having a strength approximately two hundred times that of psilocybin and four thousand times that of mescaline! There are other synthetic hallucinogens such as 2,5-dimethoxy-4-methyl amphetamine (commonly known as STP, for serenity, tranquility, and peace) that have effects in common with both LSD and amphetamines.[141]

D-lysergic acid diethylamide 25 (LSD or "acid") is one of the most commonly used hallucinogens. It is usually taken orally via a pill, capsule, or "paper." During the 1960s it was commonly taken in a sugar cube impregnated with the chemical, but this method is not generally used today. In some areas LSD is still taken by placing a small amount in an eye dropper and depositing it on the eyes. So small a quantity as 25 micrograms (μg) is psychoactive for most people.[142] (An aspirin table is approximately 300,000 μg.)

A "trip" on LSD may last between five and twelve hours, although reactions may last for days, and "flashbacks" may occur indefinitely. During the trip, the user will experience distortions of the senses, especially vision. Loss of a sense of space and distance and the relationship of self to these dimensions is common. The user may describe colors, smells, and sounds as though they are being experienced for the first time. These experiences range from extremely pleasant to nightmarish.[143] A commonly reported effect is called eidetic imagery, or "eyeball movies," in which the user (with the eyes closed) "sees" physical objects, usually in motion, as sharply as if he were watching a movie. These images are abstract and usually lacking in any dramatic content, and they usually represent repetitions of a pattern or design—such as moving wallpaper—but with the patterns constantly changing.[144]

One of the most common hazards of LSD use is related to the distortion of visual perception. Users frequently fall through windows above ground level, later explaining that they thought they had left through the front door or a ground-level window. Normal physical changes that occur with use are related to overstimulation of the sympathetic nervous system. These include trembling, sweating, dilated pupils, goose bumps, changes in blood pressure and pulse rate, nausea, and bowel problems.[145] Asthma attacks are sometimes precipitated by LSD in the predisposed individual. Loss of appetite is also common. Convulsions occur rather infrequently, but depression may occur either during or immediately after a "trip."[146] A special hazard is the "flashback" phenomenon, especially when it occurs when victims are in a sit-

uation where they are at risk to themselves or others—such as driving an automobile. The accompanying boxed illustration points out these dangers.

THE EFFECTS OF INHALANTS

Most of the inhalants commonly abused today are solvents such as aerosols, paint, gasoline, lacquer thinner, airplane glue, lighter fluid, and trichloroethylene. Most of the users who sniff or "huff" these substances are under the age of 15, possibly because they are so much more easily available to children. Glue sniffers will typically empty the contents of a tube into the bottom of a paper bag, hold the bag tightly over the mouth (or mouth and nose), and inhale the vapors until the desired effect is reached. Liquid materials may be inhaled directly from a container or from saturated cloth.[147]

Most materials used in sniffing contain volatile or gaseous substances which are primarily generalized central nervous system depressants. The immediate effects may range from somnolence and dizziness to delusions of unusual strength or supernatural abilities (such as the ability to fly). Visual and auditory hallucinations similar to those associated with the hallucinogens are frequently noted. Other symptoms are slurred speech, ataxia, impaired judgment, and feelings of euphoria.[148] Excessive or prolonged sniffing of high vapor concentrations will ultimately lead to loss of consciousness. Too much solvent can also cause paralysis of the breathing center and death. Other sniffers may die

---

Robert was a 16-year-old student who had experimented with LSD, but who hadn't used the drug for almost a year. He was driving home from his part-time job one night (which involved about two miles of heavy traffic on an interstate highway) when he began seeing "large, yellow butterflies flying across the highway." He stopped his vehicle, got out, and "tried to catch one." There were no butterflies, of course. What he was actually trying to catch were the headlights of passing cars and trucks. Fortunately, a police officer stopped and took him into custody before he was hurt.

Tallahassee, Florida Police Department

from ventricular fibrillation induced by central respiratory depression. Deaths have also resulted from damage to the liver, kidneys, and bone marrow among chronic sniffers. Occasional deaths from asphyxiation also result from the practice of inhaling a solvent in a closed space or with one's head in a plastic bag.[149]

Amyl nitrite was introduced into medicine over a century ago when it was found to relieve angina pectoris by dilating coronary arteries and temporarily improving the perfusion and oxygenation of heart muscle.[150] It also has the effect of expanding the meningeal arteries over the surface of the brain and producing feelings of suffusion and fullness in the head. The action of amyl nitrite on the brain results in a subjective experience of time being slowed down, and it is this perception that began a modest amount of recreational use of the drug during the 1930s. Taken just before climax, it may extend the sensation of orgasm.

Although some use by heterosexual men and women has been reported, amyl nitrite is more popular as an orgasm expander among homosexual men. Originally available in a capsule or pearl that was crushed and inhaled (called "snappers" or "poppers"), it was later sold in aerosol form (either as amyl or isobutyl nitrite) under trade names such as Locker Room, Aroma of Men, Kick, Bullet, Jac, and Rush, ostensibly as room deodorizers![151]

Other symptoms accompanying use of this drug are nausea, dizziness, mild sensory intensification, a diminution of ego controls, and an increase in aggressive behavior. A drop in blood pressure and an increase in the heart rate are usually noted. Pulsating headaches also are frequently mentioned by regular users.[152] Some researchers believe that butyl nitrite depresses the body's immune system and weakens its ability to fight the AIDS virus.[153] The Centers for Disease Control in Atlanta cites evidence that Kaposi's sarcoma is much more common among AIDS victims who use "poppers" than among AIDS victims who do not use them. Other research indicates that 87 percent of the 290 compounds in

the nitrite family have proven to be carcinogenic in tests of laboratory animals.[154]

DRUG EFFECTS ON OFFSPRING

Offspring may be damaged by drug use by either parent, although the greater risks are generally associated with maternal drug use.[155] Female drug use may affect offspring when it happens prior to conception, during gestation, and following birth—if the baby is breast fed. The most severe consequence of drugs taken by a pregnant woman is prenatal or perinatal death. Many of the causes of drug-related prenatal death are not well understood, and they may not be noticed if it occurs early in pregnancy. The most commonly identified teratogenic drug is alcohol, but opiates, barbiturates, benzodiazepines, amphetamines, cocaine, tobacco, and marijuana are also frequently implicated in birth defects, pre- and postnatal growth deficiency, and cognitive development.[156]

Alcohol

Although the specific effects of maternal alcohol use on the fetus was not officially recognized and given a label until 1973, alcohol has been suspected as a teratogenic agent at least since biblical times. Judges 13:7 provides the injunction, "Behold thou shalt conceive and bear a son: now drink no wine or strong drink." Other early societies also recognized the danger of alcohol on offspring.[157] It was not until 1973, however, that Jones and co-workers[158] described the children born to chronic alcoholic mothers as having fetal alcohol syndrome (FAS). These children were characterized by prenatal and postnatal growth deficiency, a pattern of physical abnormalities (including short palpebral fissures, epicanthic folds, ear anomalies, and cardiac defects), and mental retardation. In a subsequent review of 245 cases, Clarren and Smith described the three primary characteristics of FAS as growth deficiency, characteristic facial dysmorphology, and central nervous system damage. Cardiac defects occur in 30 to 40 percent of FAS children.[159]

The incidence of FAS varies considerably among various subpopulations, but there is little doubt that the teratogenic effects of alcohol are dose related. One study concluded that between 11 and 13 percent of pregnant women who drink two to three drinks per day will give birth to children with FAS.[160] Careful studies conducted in Göteborg, Sweden, and Roubaix, France, found the rate of FAS to be 1 in 690 births. The rate in Seattle, Washington, is 1 in 750 births, and studies conducted on Indian reservations in the Southwest United States indicate a rate of 1 in 100 births.[161]

Children born with FAS are usually not grossly malformed, but they do have a particular cluster of facial characteristics which, along with their small stature and slender build, give them a readily identifiable appearance. Mental handicaps are the most debilitating aspect of FAS, with victims having an average IQ of 65.[162] FAS is one of the few types of mental retardation that is entirely preventable. Since there is no specific treatment for FAS, and its effects are permanent, the primary focus must remain on prevention. No safe level of drinking by pregnant women has ever been established.[163] The only way to eliminate the risk of FAS is to be abstinent during pregnancy.

Opiates

Although it has been difficult to separate the effects of opiates from other factors associated with the living conditions and general life-styles of opiate users, studies indicate that the offspring of heroin-dependent mothers tend to be low in birth weight, more frequently premature, and often suffer from perinatal complications and a range of abnormalities.[164] Neonatal narcotic withdrawal is a common problem of offspring exposed to opiates *in utero*. Hypoxia, hyperactivity, and fetal death have also been noted.[165]

Tobacco

Spontaneous abortion is much higher in pregnant women who smoke than in non-smokers. Smoking can induce malformations sufficiently severe to cause fetal death at an early stage of pregnancy. Fetuses that do survive are 10 to 15 percent lighter at birth than are those born to nonsmokers.[166] The combination of both smoking and drinking entails a much higher risk to the fetus and its postnatal development.[167]

Amphetamines and Cocaine

A wide range of abnormalities has been associated with maternal amphetamine and cocaine administration, although research on their teratogenic effects is still in its early stages. Among the consequences of maternal use of these stimulants are spontaneous abortion, low birth weight, cleft palate, urogenital anomalies, and an increase in excitability.[168] When a pregnant woman uses crack, it results in a constriction of the blood vessels and a decrease in the flow of oxygen and nutrients to the fetus. Many cocaine-exposed babies suffer physiological and neurological malformations, including deformed hearts, lungs, digestive systems, and limbs. Others may suffer a fatal stroke while still in the womb.[169]

Other Drugs

There is some evidence that maternal *barbiturate* use may result in both morphological and behavioral impairment. This is especially disturbing since many people have to use this drug to keep their epilepsy under control. *Benzodiazepine* use (especially diazepam) by pregnant women is reported to have caused a number of birth defects, including cleft palate. High levels of maternal *caffeine* use may result in higher rates of spontaneous abortion and certain congenital abnormalities. *Hallucinogens* such as LSD are capable of inducing chromosomal damage, but this does not seem to occur at normal human dosage levels. Structural abnormalities, especially of the limbs, have been more frequent in the offspring of LSD users. *Marijuana* also has been observed to induce chromosomal damage at high doses, but there is little evidence that this occurs at normal dosage levels. In animal studies, behavioral differences have been noted in the offspring of marijuana-treated mothers. There is little reliable evidence on the maternal effects of *inhalants.*[170]

SUMMARY

In this chapter we have described the most commonly observed physiological and behavioral consequences of alcohol and drug abuse. *The reader must bear in mind that individuals vary markedly in their reactions to specific doses of particular drugs, and the same reaction cannot be expected even within the same individual over a period of time.* The development of tolerance and chemically induced trauma to organs such as the brain make predictions of behavior somewhat more problematic than the physiological consequences. Except for alcohol, the effects of most drugs on the offspring of users are just beginning to be adequately studied.

ENDNOTES

1. Risto J. K. Julkunen, Carlo DiPadova, and Charles S. Lieber, "First Pass Metabolism of Ethanol: A Gastrointestinal Barrier Against the Systemic Toxicity of Ethanol," *Life Sciences,* Vol. 37 (1985), pp. 567–573.

2. Ted Loomis, "The Pharmacology of Alcohol," in Nada J. Estes and M. Edith Heinemann (eds.), *Alcoholism: Development, Consequences, and Interventions,* 3rd ed. (St. Louis: C. V. Mosby, 1986), pp. 93–102.

3. Ibid., p. 99.

4. Sujata Tewari and Virginia G. Carson, "Biochemistry of Alcohol and Alcohol Metabolism," in E. Mansell Pattison and Edward Kaufman (eds.), *Encyclopedic Handbook of Alcoholism* (New York: Gardner Press, 1982), pp. 83–104.

5. Loomis, "The Pharmacology of Alcohol," p. 101.

6. Robert B. Forney and Rolla N. Harger, "The Alcohols," in Joseph R. DiPalma (ed.), *Drill's Pharmacology in Medicine,* 4th ed. (New York: McGraw-Hill, 1971).

7. Frank A. Seixas, "The Course of Alcoholism," in Estes and Heinemann, *Alcoholism,* pp. 67–77.

8. Loomis, "The Pharmacology of Alcohol," p. 100.

9. Roger H. Butz, "Intoxication and Withdrawal," in Estes and Heinemann, *Alcoholism,* pp. 103–109.

10. C. Brown, "The Alcohol Withdrawal Syndrome," *Annals of Emergency Medicine,* Vol. 11 (1982), p. 276.

11. U.S. Department of Health and Human Services, *Fifth Special Report to the U.S. Congress on Alcohol and Health* (Washington, DC: U.S. Government Printing Office, December 1983).

12. L. Frederick Fenster, "Alcohol and Disorders of the Gastrointestinal System," in Estes and Heinemann, *Alcoholism,* pp. 145–152.

13. C. Michael Knauer, "Mallory-Weiss Syndrome: Characteristics of 75 Mallory-Weiss Lacerations in 528 Patients with Upper Gastrointestinal Hemorrhage," *Gastroenterology,* Vol. 71 (1976), p. 71.

14. R. J. Derbes and R. E. Mitchell, "Rupture of the Esophagus," *Surgery,* Vol. 39 (1956), p. 688.

15. U.S. Department of Health and Human Services (USDHHS), *Sixth Special Report to the U.S. Congress on Alcohol and Health* (Washington, DC: U.S. Government Printing Office, January 1987), p. 60.

16. John A. Hermos, "Mucosa of the Small Intestine in Folate-Deficient Alcoholics," *Annals of Internal Medicine,* Vol. 76 (1972), p. 957.

17. M. S. Millan, G. P. Morris, Ivan T. Beck, and J. T. Henson, "Villous Damage Induced by Suction Biopsy and by Acute Ethanol Intake in Normal Human Small Intestine," *Digestive Diseases and Sciences,* Vol. 25 (1980), pp. 513–525.

18. Charles S. Lieber, Helmut K. Seitz, Anthony J. Garro, and Theresa M. Worner, "Alcohol-Related Diseases and Carcinogenesis," *Cancer Research,* Vol. 39 (1979), pp. 2863–2886.

19. B. F. Grant, J. Noble, and Henry J. Malin, "Decline in Liver Cirrhosis Mortality and Components of Change: United States, 1973–1983," *Alcohol Health & Research World,* Vol. 10 (1986), pp. 66–69.

20. G. Pequignot and J. J. Tuyns, "Compared Toxicity of Ethanol on Various Organs," in C. Stock and H. Sarles (eds.), *Alcohol and the Gastrointestinal Tract* (Paris: INSERM, 1980), pp. 17–32.

21. E. Mezey, "Alcoholic Liver Disease," in H. Popper and F. Schaffner (eds.), *Progress in Liver Diseases,* Volume III (New York: Grune & Stratton, 1982), pp. 555–572.

22. L. Frederick Fenser, "Alcohol and Disorders of the Gastrointestinal System," in Estes and Heinemann, *Alcoholism,* pp. 145–152.

23. H. Kalant, "Alcohol, Pancreatic Secretion, and Pancreatitis," *Gastroenterology* Vol. 56 (1969), p. 380.

24. R. W. Ammann et al., "Course and Outcome of Chronic Pancreatitis: Longitudinal Study of a Mixed Medical-Surgical Series of 245 Patients," *Gastroenterology* Vol. 86 (1984), p. 820.

25. Konstanty Markiewi and Marian Cholewa, "The Effect of Alcohol on the Circulatory System Adaptation to Physical Effort," *Journal of Studies on Alcohol,* Vol. 43 (1982), pp. 812–823.

26. H. S. Friedman, S. A. Geller, and C. S. Lieber, "The Effect of Alcohol on the Heart, Skeletal, and Smooth Muscles," in L. H. Smight, Jr. (ed.), *Medical Disorders of Alcoholism, Pathogenesis, and Treatment,* Volume XXII in *Major Problems in Internal Medicine* (Philadelphia: W. B. Saunders, 1982), pp. 436–479.

27. J. F. Potter and D. G. Beevers, "Pressor Effect of Alcohol in Hypertension," *Lancet,* Vol. I (1984), pp. 119–122.

28. Roberto M. Lang, Kenneth M. Borow, Alexander Neumann, and Ted Feldman, "Adverse Cardia Effects of Acute Alcohol Ingestion in Young Adults," *Annals of Internal Medicine,* Vol. 102 (1985), pp. 742–747.

29. USDHHS, *Sixth Special Report,* p. 63.

30. Wolfgang Schmidt and Jan deLint, "Causes of Death in Alcoholics," *Quarterly Journal of Studies on Alcohol,* Vol. 33 (1972), pp. 171–185.

31. George Fink, "Feedback Actions of Target Hormones on Hypothalamus and Pituitary with Special Reference to Gonadal Steroids," *Annual Review of Physiology,* Vol. 41 (1979), pp. 571–585.

32. Y. Israel, P. G. Walfish, H. Orrego, S. Blake, and H. Kalant, "Thyroid Hormones in Alcoholic Liver Disease," *Gastroenterology,* Vol. 76 (1979), pp. 116–122.

33. Theodore J. Cicero, "Neuroendocrinological Effects of Alcohol," *Annual Review of Medicine,* Vol. 32 (1981), pp. 123–142.

34. C. M. Cornely, R. R. Schade, D. H. Van Thiel, and J. S. Gavaler, "Chronic Advanced Liver Disease and Impotence: Cause and Effect?" *Hepatology,* Vol. 4 (1984), pp. 1227–1230.

35. USDHHS, *Sixth Special Report,* pp. 66–68.

36. Walter A. Hunt, *Alcohol and Biological Membranes* (New York: Guilford Press, 1985).

37. B. Porjesz and Henri Begleiter, "Brain Dysfunction and Alcohol," in Benjamin Kissin and Henri Begleiter (eds.), *The Biology of Alcoholism, Volume VII of The Pathogenesis of Alcoholism: Biological Factors* (New York: Plenum Press, 1983), pp. 415–483.

38. M. A. Ron, "The Alcoholic Brain: CT Scan and Psychological Findings," *Psychological Medicine, Monograph Supplement No. 3* (Cambridge: Cambridge University Press, 1983).

39. John R. Tkach and Hokama Yoshitsugi, "Autoimmunity in Chronic Brain Syndrome," *Archives of General Psychiatry,* Vol. 23 (1970), pp. 61–64.

40. H. A. Moskow, R. C. Pennington, and M. H. Knisely, "Alcohol, Sludge, and Hypoxic Areas of Nervous System, Liver and Heart," *Microvascular Research,* Vol. I (1968), pp. 174–185.

41. S. Tewari and E. P. Noble, "Ethanol and Brain Protein Synthesis," *Brain Research,* Vol. 26 (1971), pp. 469–474.

42. James W. Smith, "Neurologic Disorders in Alcoholism," in Estes and Heinemann, *Alcoholism,* pp. 153–175.

43. Ronald D. Page, "Cerebral Dysfunction Associated With Alcohol Consumption," *Substance Alcohol Actions/Misuse,* Vol. 4, No. 6 (1983), pp. 405–421.

44. William R. Miller and J. Orr, "Nature and Sequence of Neuropsychological Deficits in Alcoholics," *Journal of Studies on Alcohol,* Vol. 41 (1980), pp. 325–337.

45. Smith, "Neurologic Disorders," p. 155.

46. Ibid.

47. Oliver Sacks, *The Man Who Mistook His Wife for a Hat* (New York: Summit Books, 1985).

48. Ibid., p. 25.

49. Norman Jolliffe et al., "Nicotinic Acid Deficiency Encephalopathy," *Journal of the American Medical Association,* Vol. 114 (1940) pp. 307–312.

50. Hiram H. Merritt, *A Textbook of Neurology, 6th ed.* (Philadelphia: Lea & Febiger, 1979).

51. Smith, "Neurologic Disorders," p. 163.

52. Charles S. Lieber, "Alcohol-Nutrition Interaction: 1984 Update," *Alcohol,* Vol. 1, No. 2 (1984), pp. 151–157.

53. Ranjit K. Majumdar et al., "Blood Vitamin Status (B1, B2, B6, Folic Acid and B12) in Patients with Alcoholic Liver Disease," *International Journal for Vitamin and Nutrition Research,* Vol. 5 (1982), pp. 266–271.

54. Virginia N. Hillers and L. K. Massey, "Interrelationships of Moderate and High Alcohol Consumption with Diet and Health Status," *American Journal of Clinical Nutrition,* Vol. 41 (1985), pp. 356–362.

55. Ronald A. Arky, "Alcohol Use and the Diabetic Patient," *Alcohol Health and Research World,* Vol. 8 (1984), pp. 8–13.

56. Daniel D. Bikle et al., "Bone Disease in Alcohol Abuse," *Annals of Internal Medicine,* Vol. 103 (1985), pp. 42–48.

57. USDHHS, *Sixth Special Report,* p. 6.

58. Elizabeth R. Gonzales, "Unresolved Issue: Do Drinkers Have Less Coronary Heart Disease?" *Journal of the American Medical Association,* Vol. 242 (1979), pp. 2745–2746.

59. Forest S. Tennant, Merle Prele, Thomas J. Pendergast, and Paul Ventry, "Medical Manifestations Associated with Hashish," *Journal of the American Medical Association,* 216 (1971), pp. 1965–69.

60. Norman Imlah, *Addiction: Substance Abuse and Dependency* (Winslow, England: Sigma Press, 1989), p. 87.

61. Erich Goode, *Drugs in American Society* (New York: Alfred A. Knopf, 1972), p. 55.

62. Sidney Cohen, *The Substance Abuse Problems* (New York: Haworth Press, 1981), p. 9.

63. White, *Drug Dependence,* p. 232.

64. Ibid., p. 220.

65. R. Weber, "Immunologic Effects of Drugs of Abuse," in *Problems of Drug Dependence, 1988: Proceedings of the 50th Annual Scientific Meeting, The Committee on Problems of Drug Dependence, Inc.,* DHHS Publication No. (ADM) 89–1605 (Washington, DC: U.S. Government Printing Office, 1988), pp. 99–104.

66. Imlah, *Addiction,* p. 88.

67. Cohen, *The Substance Abuse Problems,* p. 20.

68. Gabriel G. Nahas, *Marihuana in Science and Medicine* (New York: Raven Press, 1984), p. 215.

69. Imlah, *Addictions,* pp. 88–90.

70. Nahas, *Marihuana,* pp. 263–305.

71. Jacques Joseph Moreau, *Du Hashisch et de l'Alienation Mentale* (Paris: Librarie de Fortin, Masson, 1845; English edition: Raven Press, New York, 1972).

72. Nahas, *Marihuana,* pp. 280–285.

73. Awani Arif (ed.), *Adverse Health Consequences of Cocaine Abuse* (Geneva: World Health Organization, 1987).

74. Kirk J. Brower and M. Douglas Anglin, "Adolescent Cocaine Use: Epidemiology, Risk Factors, and Prevention," *Journal of Drug Education,* Vol. 17 (1987), pp. 163–180.

75. Arif, *Adverse Health Consequences,* p. 21.

76. Hoffman, *Handbook,* p. 242.

77. Arnold M. Washton, *Cocaine Addiction* (New York: W. W. Norton, 1989).

78. Cohen, *The Substance Abuse Problems,* pp. 75–78.

79. Imlah, *Addiction,* pp. 59–60.

80. Joanne Baumm, *One Step over the Line: A No-Nonsense Guide to Recognizing and Treating Cocaine Dependency* (San Francisco: Harper & Row, 1985), p. 67.

81. Arnold M. Washton, *Cocaine Addiction: Treatment, Recovery, and Relapse Prevention* (New York: W. W. Norton, 1989), p. 15.

82. Baum, *One Step over the Line,* p. 67.

83. Washton, *Cocaine Addiction,* p. 17.

84. Baum, *One Step over the Line,* p. 71.

85. Tam Stewart, *The Heroin Users* (London: Pandora Press, 1987), p. 25.

86. Susan Livesay, Saundra Ehrlich, Lynn Ryan, and Lorretta Finnegan, "Cocaine and Pregnancy: Maternal and Infant Outcome," in *Problems of Drug Dependence,* 1988, p. 328.

87. Douglas J. Besharov, "The Children of Crack: Will We Protect Them?" *Public Welfare,* (Fall, 1989), pp. 6–11.

88. Scott E. Lukas (ed.), *The Encyclopedia of Psychoactive Drugs: Amphetamines* (New York: Chelsea House, 1985), p. 21.

89. Imlah, *Addictions,* pp. 59–61.

90. Lukas, *Amphetamines,* p. 29.

91. I. R. Innes and M. Nickerson, "Amphetamine and Methamphetamine," in L. S. Goodman and A. Gilman (eds.), *The Pharmacological Basis of Therapeutics,* 3rd ed. (New York: Macmillan, 1970), pp. 501–507.

92. Lukas, *Amphetamines,* p. 43.

93. Cohen, *The Substance Abuse Problems,* p. 147.

94. Ibid., p. 148.

95. Stephen T. Higgins et al., "Behavioral and Cardiovascular Effects of Alcohol and d-Amphetamine Combinations in Normal Volunteers," *Problems of Drug Dependence,* 1988, pp. 35–36.

96. Imlah, *Addictions,* pp. 59–61.

97. Lukas, *Amphetamines,* pp. 54–55.

98. Ibid., pp. 57–58.

99. Ibid., pp. 58–60.

100. Jerome Beck and Patricia A. Morgan, "Designer Drug Confusion: A Focus on MDMA," *Journal of Drug Education,* Vol. 16 (1986), pp. 287–302.

101. "The Trouble with Ecstasy," *Life,* September 1985, pp. 88–94.

102. Beck and Morgan, "Designer Drug Confusion," pp. 292–295.

103. Jerome Beck, "The Popularization and Resultant Implications of a Recently Controlled Psychoactive

Substance," *Contemporary Drug Problems,* Vol. 13 (1986), p. 1.

104. Deborah M. Barnes, "New Data Intensify the Agony over Ecstasy," *Science,* Vol. 239 (1988), pp. 864–866.

105. C. Schuster, Statement to Congressional Subcommittee on Bills Relating to Designer Drugs, May 1, 1986.

106. Beck, "The Popularization and Implications."

107. Michael A. Lerner, "The Fire of 'Ice,'" *Newsweek,* November 27, 1989, pp. 37–40.

108. Jane Gross, "Speed's Gain in Use Could Rival Crack, Drug Experts Warn," *The New York Times,* November 27, 1988, Sec. 1, p. 1.

109. Katherine Bishop, "Fear Grows over Effects of a New Smokable Drug," *The New York Times,* September 16, 1989, Sec. 1, p. 1.

110. Lerner, "The Fire of 'Ice,'" p. 40.

111. Bishop, "Fear Grows," p. 8.

112. Lerner, "The Fire of 'Ice,'" p. 40.

113. Imlah, *Addiction,* pp. 64–69.

114. Cohen, *The Substance Abuse Problems,* p. 120.

115. Ibid., p. 120–121.

116. Imlah, *Addiction,* p. 66.

117. Cohen, *The Substance Abuse Problems,* p. 127–128.

118. Imlah, *Addiction,* p. 40.

119. Erich Goode, *Drugs in American Society* (New York: Alfred A. Knopf, 1972), p. 161.

120. Jerome J. Platt and Christina Labate, *Heroin Addiction* (New York: John Wiley and Sons, 1976), p. 48.

121. Barry J. Rosenbaum, "Heroin: Influence of Method of Use," *New England Journal of Medicine,* Vol. 285 (1971), pp. 299–300.

122. Imlah, *Addiction,* p. 45.

123. Platt and Labate, *Heroin Addiction,* pp. 51–52.

124. Tam Stewart, *The Heroin Users* (London: Pandora Press, 1987), p. 29.

125. Imlah, *Addiction,* p. 45.

126. Krivanek, *Heroin,* pp. 68–70.

127. Platt and Labate, *Heroin Addiction,* p. 91.

128. Anna J. Eisenman, H. F. Fraser, and Janus W. Brooks, "Urinary Excretion and Plasma Levels of 17-Hydroxycorticosteroids During a Cycle of Addiction to Morphine," *Journal of Pharmacology and Experimental Therapeutics,* Vol. 132 (1961), pp. 226–231.

129. Joseph D. Sapira, "The Narcotic Addict as a Medical Patient," *American Journal of Medicine,* Vol. 45 (1968), pp. 555–558.

130. F. G. Hofmann, *A Handbook on Drug and Alcohol Abuse* (New York: Oxford, 1975).

131. M. M. Baden, "Pathology of the Addictive States," in Ralph W. Richter (ed.), *Medical Aspects of Drug Abuse* (Hagerstown, MD: Harper & Row, 1975), pp. 189–211.

132. Sapira, "The Narcotic Addict."

133. Platt and Labate, *Heroin Addiction,* pp. 92–93.

134. Imlah, *Addictions,* p. 45.

135. Krivanek, *Heroin,* p. 83.

136. Imlah, *Addiction,* p. 95.

137. Goode, *Drugs in American Society,* p. 97.

138. Aldous Huxley, *The Doors of Perception and Heaven and Hell* (New York: Harper & Row, 1963), p. 34.

139. Imlah, *Addiction,* p. 95.

140. Ibid., p. 99.

141. Ibid., p. 102.

142. Goode, *Drugs in Modern Society,* p. 99.

143. Imlah, *Addiction,* p. 99.

144. Goode, *Drugs in American Society,* pp. 101–102.

145. Imlah, *Addiction,* p. 99.

146. Cohen, *The Substance Abuse Problems,* pp. 210–213.

147. Hofmann, *Handbook,* p. 132–135.

148. Ibid., p. 135.

149. Cohen, *The Substance Abuse Problems,* p. 49.

150. Ibid., p. 51.

151. Ibid., p. 52.

152. W. L. Dewey et al., "Some Behavioral and Toxicological Effects of Amyl Nitrite," *Research Communications in Chemical Pathology and Pharmacology,* Vol. 5 (1973), p. 889.

153. Jan P. Vandenbroucke and Veronique P. A. M. Pardoel, "An Autopsy of Epidemiologic Methods: The Case of 'Poppers' in the Early Epidemic of the Acquired Immunodeficiency Syndrome (AIDS)," *American Journal of Epidemiology,* Vol. 129, No. 3 (March 1989), pp. 455–457.

154. *Miami Herald,* "Trendy Chemical, AIDS Tie Feared," October 12, 1986, Sec. G, p. 14.

155. J. Joffe, "Influence of Drug Exposure of the Father on Perinatal Outcome," *Clinics in Perinatology,* Vol. 6 (1979), pp. 21–36.

156. White, *Drug Dependence,* pp. 227–232.

157. Ann Pytkowicz Streissguth, "Fetal Alcohol Syndrome: An Overview and Implications for Patient Management," in Estes and Heinemann, *Alcoholism,* pp. 195–206.

158. K. L. Jones and D. W. Smith, "Recognition of the Fetal Alcohol Syndrome in Early Infancy," *Lancet,* Vol. 2 (1973), pp. 999–1001.

159. S. K. Clarren and D. W. Smith, "Fetal Alcohol Syndrome," *New England Journal of Medicine,* Vol. 298 (1978), pp. 1063–1067.

160. J. W. Hanson, A. P. Streissguth, and D. W. Smith, "The Effects of Moderate Alcohol Consumption During Pregnancy on Fetal Growth and Morphogenesis," *Journal of Pediatrics,* Vol. 92 (1978), pp. 457–460.

161. Streissguth, p. 196.

162. A. P. Streissguth, C. S. Herman, and D. W. Smith, "Intelligence, Behavior, and Dysmorphogenesis in the Fetal Alcohol Syndrome: A Report on 20 Patients," *Journal of Pediatrics,* Vol. 92 (1978), pp. 363–367.

163. Ruth E. Little, John M. Graham, and Herman H. Samson, "Fetal Alcohol Effects in Humans and Animals," in Barry Stimmel (ed.), *The Effects of Maternal Alcohol and Drug Abuse on the Newborn* (New York: Haworth Press, 1982), pp. 103–125.

164. White, *Drug Dependence,* p. 230.

165. Mary Jeanne Kreek, "Opiod Disposition and Effects During Chronic Exposure in the Perinatal Period in Man," in Stimmel, *Effects of Maternal Alcohol and Drug Abuse,* pp. 21–53.

166. White, *Drug Dependence,* p. 231.

167. Little et al., "Fetal Alcohol Effects," p. 112.

168. White, *Drug Dependence,* p. 231.

169. Besharov, "Children of Crack," p. 7.

170. White, *Drug Dependence,* pp. 229–232.

II

INTERVENTION, PREVENTION, AND PUBLIC POLICY

Part One of this book covered many topics: definitions of chemical abuse and dependency; physiological, behavioral, psychological, social, and cultural aspects of chemical abuse and dependency; and the myriad etiological theories that have been offered to explain alcohol and drug problems. It also introduced the reader to the scope of substance abuse problems and to the processes and consequences of addiction. These chapters provide the foundation necessary to move on to Part Two, which presents the systems for preventing and treating chemical abuse and dependency.

In Chapter 5 the reader is introduced to the first steps in assisting individuals who are chemical abusers or who are chemically dependent. These steps are screening, diagnosis, assessment, and referral to appropriate resources. Some commonly used screening instruments and diagnostic tools are described and issues in their use and interpretation are discussed. Helping clients address denial of substance abuse problems and resistance to treatment are also included as are matters of confidentiality and the referral process.

Chapter 6 presents the components of the chemical dependency treatment system, including detoxification, intensive treatment, residential services, outpatient services, pharmacotherapy, education, aftercare, and maintenance. Self-help resources for those with alcohol and other drug problems are also discussed. Research on the effectiveness of each of the treatment components and on other aspects of effectiveness such as length of treatment and client-treatment matching is also presented. Finally, the two-tier system of treatment is examined: the private tier, serving clients with money or health insurance, and the public tier, serving mostly poor clients.

We begin to look at the system for regulating or controlling alcohol and drugs in Chapter 7, focusing on prevention. Primary, secondary, and tertiary models of prevention are discussed, but the chapter is organized around five major categories of prevention efforts: public information and education, service measures, technologic measures, legislative and regulatory measures, and economic measures. The effectiveness of prevention efforts, including the popular D.A.R.E. programs, is also examined.

In Chapter 8 we consider most of the other aspects of regulating drugs and their consequences. In doing so, we discuss the assumptions underlying governmental regulation as well as the major techniques for governmental control: prohibition, taxes and price controls, insurance and liability laws, and control over distribution. Other topics include minimum-age for purchase laws, DUI laws, the drugs-crime connection, and the merits of legalization or decriminalization of illicit drugs.

At the end of Part Two, the reader should have a good overview of the intervention system. From there, we will move directly into the problems of chemical abuse and dependency in several special populations.

5

Screening, diagnosis, assessment, and referral

This chapter presents a systems or biopsychosocial approach to determining whether an individual has a chemical abuse or dependency problem. The first steps in this approach are screening and diagnosis. The chapter also considers the extension of this process, called assessment, to examine the client's needs further. A thorough assessment is needed to develop a long-range treatment plan and to make referrals to appropriate resources.

Some individuals with alcohol or drug problems experience medical emergencies (intentional overdoses, accidental alcohol or drug poisoning, pancreatitis, delirium tremens, seizures, and so forth) that require immediate attention. Social workers, psychologists, and other human service professionals should know what these emergencies are, but these problems can be diagnosed and treated only by qualified medical personnel. The focus of this chapter is primarily on the work of helping professionals once such medical crises have been resolved or when a client is seen by a helping professional earlier in the addiction process, before these medical complications arise.

We begin by discussing screening, which can be defined as the use of brief instruments or other tools to determine the likelihood that an individual has a chemical abuse or chemical dependency problem. In practice, much screening is informal and is not done with structured or standardized instruments. For example, after reviewing a parolee's "rap" sheet containing repeated alcohol- or drug-related arrests, a parole officer may feel that is all the screening necessary for referring the client to a chemical dependency treatment program or insisting on participation in a self-help group as a condition of parole.

Diagnosis, discussed in the following section, is the confirmation of a chemical abuse or dependency problem, often using more than one source of information. For example, results of a screening instrument may be combined with a client interview or social history and perhaps an interview with others (referred to as collaterals) who know the client well. A medical examination including laboratory tests is often a part of this diagnostic process. Previous medical, psychological or psychiatric, criminal, school, or other records and consultation with other professionals might also be used.

Assessment is sometimes used synonymously with the term diagnosis, but we use it to mean an in-depth consideration of the client's chemical abuse or dependency problems as they have affected his or her psychological well-being, social circumstances (including interpersonal relationships), financial status, employment or education, health, and so forth. This process also includes consideration of the individual's strengths. Going beyond a confirmatory diagnosis, this type of multidimensional or biopsychosocial assessment provides the basis for treatment planning.[1]

The cornerstones of good screening, diagnosis, and assessment in the chemical dependency field are knowledge of alcohol and drug abuse and dependency and interviewing skills, including the ability to establish some level of rapport with clients in a relatively brief period. Denial is a pervasive issue in work with clients who have alcohol and drug problems, and helping professionals must frequently work with clients and their significant others to reduce defensiveness and resistance. The assurance of confidentiality in treatment and research settings can increase the validity of clients' reports of their

alcohol and drug problem,[2] but the extent to which confidentiality can be guaranteed varies and should be represented fairly to the client. Denial and confidentiality also warrant attention in this chapter.

In addition to chemical dependency treatment, clients often need the services of other agencies. The final section of this chapter discusses the process of referring clients to other services, including self-help groups.

SCREENING

Screening for alcohol and drug problems is done in many types of settings in addition to chemical dependency programs, such as in health facilities, mental health programs, and correctional facilities. Some of the many screening instruments available are the CAGE (defined shortly), the Michigan Alcoholism Screening Test (MAST), the Alcohol Use Disorders Identification Test (AUDIT), the Drug Abuse Screening Test (DAST), and the Substance Abuse Subtle Screening Inventory (SASSI). Before these instruments are administered, there is usually some interaction between the client and the treatment professional in order to explain the purpose of the screening, to put the client at ease, to encourage honest responses, and to answer questions the client might have about the procedure.

The CAGE, developed by Ewing and Rouse, is the briefest of the instruments discussed here.[3] It consists of four questions asked directly to the patient:

1. Have you ever felt you should **C**ut down on your drinking?
2. Have people **A**nnoyed you by criticizing your drinking?
3. Have you ever felt bad or **G**uilty about your drinking?
4. Have you ever had a drink first thing in the morning to steady your nerves or get rid of a hangover (**E**ye opener)?

The letters in bold typeface in each question make up the acronym that serves as the instrument's name; the letters also serve as a mnemonic device so that the instrument is easily committed to memory. A positive response to one or more of the questions indicates the need to explore problems the patient or client may be experiencing with the use of alcohol. This tool has been used by physicians and others who have a need to screen patients or clients quickly for possible alcohol problems. It is easily used in many types of settings. The CAGE is reported to be quite effective in correctly identifying those with alcohol problems.[4]

Since the CAGE inquires only about alcohol, Sciacca has also suggested asking about drugs in each of the four questions.[5] Sciacca, who has worked extensively with clients dually diagnosed with both substance abuse and mental illness, also recommends further screening in cases where individuals answer no to all questions, but their behavior or other information indicates that these answers may not be accurate.

A second widely used screening instrument for alcohol problems is the Michigan Alcoholism Screening Test, often referred to as the MAST.[6] It has been shown to have good validity and reliability.[7] The twenty-five item MAST and its scoring instructions are found in Table 5.1. The instrument is usually self-administered (i.e., the client is asked to read and complete it). As with most screening instruments, clarifying clients' responses can be helpful. For example, drinkers married to teetotalers may respond positively to question 3 about relatives' worries or complaints even if their drinking is not problematic, or an individual with ties to a religious group which prohibits drinking may respond positively to question 5 about guilt regardless of how much he or she drinks. In question 8, it is possible that an individual has attended an Alcoholics Anonymous meeting, perhaps with a friend who is a member, rather than because of his or her own drinking problem. Two shorter versions of the MAST are also available. One, called the Short MAST or the SMAST, contains thirteen questions.[8] The other is called the Brief MAST; it contains ten questions.[9] The shorter versions are often used with slower readers. These instruments

may also be tape recorded or read to the client or patient by the person administering the test. The MAST has been used as a screening tool in many settings such as in programs for those convicted of driving while intoxicated (DWI).

The Alcohol Use Disorders Identification Test (AUDIT) is a screening instrument developed by the World Health Organization (WHO) for use by primary health care providers.[10] The main instrument contains ten items, three on the quantity and frequency of drinking, three on alcohol dependence, and four on alcohol-caused problems. It can be administered by a variety of helping professionals. The WHO developed a second tool, the "Clinical Screening Instrument" for use when a patient may not be candid about alcohol use and related problems or when additional information is needed. The Clinical Screening Instrument, which must be conducted by health care professionals, contains two questions about traumatic injuries, five items pertaining to a clinical health examination, and a blood test called the serum GGT. The AUDIT has been used in a variety of countries and is available in English, Spanish, Slavic, Norwegian, Swahili, and Romanian. Since drinking preferences and customs vary among cultures, these factors must be taken into account when using the first three questions on the main instrument concerning quantity and frequency of drinking. There are separate scoring instructions for the main instrument and the Clinical Screening Instrument.

Some instruments assess for drug problems in addition to alcohol problems, such as the Drug Abuse Screening Test (DAST).[11] The DAST was patterned after the MAST. Like the CAGE, MAST, and the AUDIT main instrument, it relies on the client's or patient's self-report. A twenty-eight- and a twenty-item version of the DAST reportedly have high internal reliability.

The Substance Abuse Subtle Screening Inventory (SASSI), another instrument completed by the client, is found in Table 5.2.[12] The SASSI differs from many instru-

TABLE 5.1   Michigan Alcoholism Screening Test

Points	Question	Yes	No
	0. Do you enjoy a drink now and then?	____	____
(2)	*1. Do you feel you are a normal drinker? (By normal we mean you drink less than or as much as most other people.)	____	____
(2)	2. Have you ever awakened the morning after some drinking the night before and found that you could not remember a part of the evening?	____	____
(1)	3. Does your wife, husband, a parent, or other near relative ever worry or complain about your drinking?	____	____
(2)	*4. Can you stop drinking without a struggle after one or two drinks?	____	____
(1)	5. Do you ever feel guilty about your drinking?	____	____
(2)	*6. Do friends or relatives think you are a normal drinker?	____	____
(2)	*7. Are you able to stop drinking when you want to?	____	____
(5)	8. Have you ever attended a meeting of Alcoholics Anonymous (AA)?	____	____
(1)	9. Have you gotten into physical fights when drinking?	____	____
(2)	10. Has your drinking ever created problems between you and your wife, husband, a parent, or other relative?	____	____
(2)	11. Has your wife, husband (or other family members) ever gone to anyone for help about your drinking?	____	____
(2)	12. Have your ever lost friends because of your drinking?	____	____
(2)	13. Have you ever gotten into trouble at work or school because of drinking?	____	____
(2)	14. Have you ever lost a job because of drinking?	____	____
(2)	15. Have you ever neglected your obligations, your family, or your work for two or more days in a row because you were drinking?	____	____
(1)	16. Do you drink before noon fairly often?	____	____
(2)	17. Have you ever been told you have liver trouble? Cirrhosis?	____	____
(2)	**18. After heavy drinking have you ever had delirium tremens (DT's) or severe shaking, or heard voices or seen things that really weren't there?	____	____
(5)	19. Have you ever gone to anyone for help about your drinking?	____	____
(5)	20. Have you ever been in a hospital because of drinking?	____	____
(2)	21. Have you ever been a patient in a psychiatric hospital or on a psychiatric ward of a general hospital where drinking was part of the problem that resulted in hospitalization?	____	____
(2)	22. Have your ever been seen at a psychiatric or mental health clinic or gone to any doctor, social worker, or clergyman for help with any emotional problem, where drinking was part of the problem?	____	____
(2)	***23. Have you ever been arrested for drunk driving, driving while intoxicated, or driving under the influence of alcoholic beverages? (IF YES, How many times? ____)	____	____
(2)	***24. Have you ever been arrested, or taken into custody, even for a few hours, because of other drunk behavior? (IF YES, How many times? ____)	____	____

*Alcoholic response is negative.

**Five points for delirium tremens.

***Two points for each arrest.

NOTE: Programs using this scoring system find it very sensitive at the five point level and it tends to find more people alcoholic than anticipated. However, it is a screening test and should be sensitive at its lower levels.

SCORING SYSTEM: In general, five points or more would place the subject in an "alcoholic" category. Four points would be suggestive of alcoholism, three points or fewer would indicate the subject was not alcoholic.

Source: Dan J. Lettieri, Jack E. Nelson, and Mollie A. Sayers (eds.), *Alcohol Treatment Assessment Research Instruments,* Treatment Handbook Series 2 (Rockville, MD: National Institute on Alcohol Abuse and Alcoholism, 1985).

TABLE 5.2 The Substance Abuse Subtle Screening Inventory

SASSI

If a statement tends to be TRUE for you, fill in the square in the column headed T; that is,
If a statement tends to be FALSE for you, fill in the square in the column headed F; that is,
Please try to answer all questions.

Fill in this way.

Not like this.

T F

T F
- PEOPLE GENERALLY LIKE TO HELP OTHERS. *
- I USUALLY "GO ALONG" AND DO WHAT OTHERS ARE DOING.
- AT LEAST ONE OF MY PARENTS WAS OFTEN DEPRESSED, UNHAPPY OR INSECURE WHEN I WAS A CHILD.
- I HAVE NEVER BEEN IN TROUBLE WITH THE POLICE.
- I WAS ALWAYS WELL BEHAVED IN SCHOOL.
- MY TROUBLES ARE NOT ALL MY FAULT. *
- I HAVE NOT LIVED THE WAY I SHOULD.
- I CAN BE FRIENDLY WITH PEOPLE WHO DO MANY WRONG THINGS.
- I DO NOT LIKE TO SIT AND DAYDREAM.
- SOMETIMES I HAVE A HARD TIME SITTING STILL.
- AT TIMES I FEEL WORN OUT FOR NO SPECIAL REASON. *
- I BELIEVE EVERYTHING IS TURNING OUT JUST THE WAY THE BIBLE SAID IT WOULD.
- MY FATHER USUALLY IGNORED ME WHEN I WAS A CHILD.
- I HAVE HAD DAYS, WEEKS, OR MONTHS WHEN I COULDN'T GET MUCH DONE BECAUSE I JUST WASN'T UP TO IT.
- I AM VERY RESPECTFUL OF AUTHORITY.
- I LIKE TO OBEY THE LAW. *
- I HAVE BEEN TEMPTED TO LEAVE HOME. *
- I OFTEN FEEL THAT STRANGERS LOOK AT ME WITH DISAPPROVAL.
- FREQUENTLY I FEEL NAUSEATED. *
- I HAVE AVOIDED PEOPLE I DID NOT WISH TO SPEAK TO.
- SOME CROOKS ARE SO CLEVER I HOPE THEY GET AWAY WITH WHAT THEY HAVE DONE.
- MY SCHOOL TEACHERS HAD SOME PROBLEMS WITH ME.
- I HAVE NEVER DONE ANYTHING DANGEROUS JUST FOR FUN.
- I HAVE SOMETIMES DRUNK TOO MUCH. *
- MUCH OF MY LIFE IS UNINTERESTING. *
- SOMETIMES I WISH I COULD CONTROL MYSELF BETTER. *
- SOMETIMES I AM NO GOOD FOR ANYTHING AT ALL. *

T F
- I BREAK MORE LAWS THAN MANY PEOPLE. *
- IF SOME FRIENDS AND I WERE IN TROUBLE TOGETHER, I WOULD RATHER TAKE THE WHOLE BLAME THAN TELL ON THEM.
- PORNOGRAPHY AND OBSCENITY HAVE BECOME SERIOUS PROBLEMS AND MUST BE CURBED.
- I THINK THERE IS SOMETHING WRONG WITH MY MEMORY. *
- I HAVE SOMETIMES BEEN TEMPTED TO HIT PEOPLE. *
- I ALWAYS FEEL SURE OF MYSELF.
- I HAVE NEVER BROKEN A MAJOR LAW. *
- THERE HAVE BEEN TIMES WHEN I HAVE DONE THINGS I COULDN'T REMEMBER LATER.
- I THINK CAREFULLY ABOUT ALL MY ACTIONS. *
- I HAVE USED ALCOHOL OR "POT" TOO MUCH OR TOO OFTEN.
- I KNOW WHO IS TO BLAME FOR MOST OF MY TROUBLES.
- I GUESS I KNOW SOME PRETTY UNDESIRABLE TYPES. *
- MOST PEOPLE WOULD LIE TO GET WHAT THEY WANT.
- I HAVE RARELY BEEN PUNISHED. *
- I SMOKE CIGARETTES REGULARLY.
- AT TIMES I HAVE BEEN SO FULL OF PEP THAT I FELT I DIDN'T NEED SLEEP FOR DAYS AT A TIME.
- I HAVE SOMETIMES SAT ABOUT WHEN I SHOULD HAVE BEEN WORKING. *
- I AM OFTEN RESENTFUL.
- I TAKE ALL MY RESPONSIBILITIES SERIOUSLY. *
- AT LEAST ONCE A WEEK I USE SOME NON-PRESCRIPTION STOMACH AIDS (PEPTO-BISMOL, ROLAIDS, ETC.)
- I AM RARELY AT A LOSS FOR WORDS. *
- I AM USUALLY HAPPY. *
- I AM A RESTLESS PERSON.
- I HAVE NEGLECTED OBLIGATIONS TO FAMILY OR WORK BECAUSE OF DRINKING OR USING DRUGS.
- I HAVE HAD A DRINK FIRST THING IN THE MORNING TO STEADY MY NERVES OR GET RID OF A HANGOVER.

Name _____ Age _____ Sex _____ Marital Status _____ Date _____

Occupation _____ Last school grade completed _____

*These items are taken from the Psychological Screening Inventory.
Copyright 1968 by Richard I. Lanyon, Ph.D. and are used here by permission.

101492F

71

ments available in the field, because only four of its fifty-two "subtle" true or false items inquire directly about alcohol or drug abuse (one of these concerns cigarettes). The reverse side of the SASSI form contains another set of questions (formerly called the Risk Prediction Scales[13]) that do inquire directly about alcohol and other drug abuse. Using both sets of questions can increase the effectiveness of this screening procedure. Administration of the subtle true or false items before the more obvious alcohol- and drug-related questions may help to minimize client defensiveness. Since the denial common among many persons with chemical dependency problems may result in failure to provide accurate information on face-valid, self-report measures, there has been interest in less obtrusive measures of substance abuse and dependency like the SASSI. The SASSI includes a set of decision rules to determine if the respondent fits the profile of a chemically dependent individual. There are also guidelines to determine if an individual may be a chemical abuser. Separate profiles are used to score results for men and women. In addition to screening for alcohol and drug abuse problems, the SASSI's subscales may have other value to human service professionals. For example, one subscale indicates the client's level of defensiveness and also shows promise as a method of screening for potential suicides, an issue that often arises with chemically dependent individuals. There is a version of the SASSI for use with adolescents. The SASSI is available as a paper-and-pencil test and on computer disk.

The screening instruments discussed thus far are generally reported to have good validity and reliability by their authors, and there is evidence from others of their utility. Other factors to recommend them are that they are easy to administer and take from one to fifteen minutes to complete (depending on the instrument). Except for the AUDIT's Clinical Screening Instrument, they can be administered and scored by most human service professionals who need relatively minimal, special training in their use.

Another device included under the category of screening tools is the MacAndrew Alcoholism Scale.[14] It is a subscale of the well-known Minnesota Multiphasic Personality Inventory (MMPI), which is often used by psychologists to detect a wide range of mental disorders. It is unobtrusive and has been used for nearly three decades. Special training and approval are required to interpret the MMPI.

We have presented information on just a few of the instruments that may be useful to human service professionals in screening for substance abuse and dependency. Additional discussion of these and other instruments used primarily with adults is found in Lettieri et al.[15] and National Institute on Alcohol Abuse and Alcoholism.[16] In doing screenings and assessments, treatment providers often use instruments to detect other problems the client may be experiencing such as depression, suicidal ideation, or other mental problems.

CAN WE BELIEVE ALCOHOLICS AND ADDICTS?

In our section on screening, we mentioned the terms validity and reliability.[17] These are basic concepts in research and measurement in the social sciences. An instrument is reliable if it produces the same results with the same person at different times and under different circumstances. For example, if we administer the MAST or the SASSI to a client today during a visit to an outpatient clinic, we would expect the same or very similar results if we administered it to them next week at their home. If an instrument does not consistently produce the same results, it is not very reliable.

Validity refers to whether an instrument measures what we want it to measure. In this case, we want to be sure we are using an instrument that will detect problems with alcohol or drugs, not some other concept such as bipolar disorder or antisocial personality disorder. We may also be interested in these problems, but we clearly want to know which instruments should be used to screen for each of these problems.

An instrument can be reliable but not valid. For example, an instrument may consistently or reliably measure the same concept over and over, but it may not be the concept in which we are interested. To be valid, however, an instrument must be reliable. If an instrument fails to consistently measure the same concept, it is not valid, because we cannot be sure it is measuring what we want it to measure.

Also of concern is that the instrument have sensitivity and specificity.[18] Sensitivity refers to the instrument's ability to identify correctly those with substance abuse problems (called true positives). We want to avoid instruments which are likely to classify an individual as a substance abuser when they do not have such a problem (false positives). We also try to select instruments that have high specificity; they maximize the likelihood that persons that do not have substance abuse problems will be correctly classified (true negatives), and they minimize the likelihood that persons who have substance abuse problems will be misclassified as not having such a problem (false negatives).

Obviously, chemical dependency professionals want to select reliable and valid instruments with good sensitivity and specificity. Of prime concern is whether or not the instrument elicits accurate information from the client, that is, information that reflects the client's true situation. We are concerned about this not only in screening and assessment but also in other situations such as measuring client's progress during and after treatment and in evaluating the effectiveness of chemical dependency treatment programs. Factors such as the client's ability to recall past behaviors or events can affect accurate reporting. Questions which are ambiguous or poorly worded also present a problem.

We also want to be sure that the instrument has been validated on the populations of interest to us. Many instruments have been validated on men. They may be of less utility in assessing the problems of women (see

Chapter 15). Another issue is whether the instrument has been tested with various ethnic groups. Language is a particular concern here. Terms commonly used by one ethnic group may have no meaning or a different meaning for other ethnic groups. Some efforts have been made to develop instruments that are ethnic sensitive (see Chapter 11). Instruments that are valid across ethnic groups are particularly useful. Language can also be a problem when an instrument is used with individuals from different age cohorts since words can take on different meanings over time. Some instruments are designed specifically for use with adolescents, others with adults. The types of questions asked differ depending on the client's age. For example, an adult may be asked about job and family responsibilities while a child or adolescent may be asked about school.

Many of the instruments we have discussed so far rely on the client's self-report. Many of them are also face valid, because they clearly ask clients about their alcohol or drug use. When we use a face-valid instrument, what confidence do we have that clients are telling the truth about their behavior? When asked about the amount of alcohol or drugs they consume or whether they have had an alcohol-related blackout or lost a job due to drug use, clients can easily lie, but are they likely to do this?

Based on research designed specifically to determine the reliability and validity of clients' self-reports, many think that we can have confidence in them.[19] Most of these studies have correlated clients' self-reports with information from other sources such as collateral contacts and laboratory (medical) tests and have found good agreement among them. Fuller agrees that the balance of evidence favors their usefulness.[20] He also notes that some studies raise serious enough questions that self-reports should be used in combination with other evidence to gain the most accurate picture of the client's problems and functioning. Skinner has described the situations or conditions which influence the validity of clients' self-reports.[21] These factors include whether the client is detoxified and psychologically stable at the time of the assessment, the rapport established by the interviewer with the interviewee, the clarity of the questions asked, whether the client knows that his or her responses will be corroborated with other sources of information, and the degree of confidentiality which can be promised to the individual.

Hesselbrock and her colleagues have also suggested that the "demand characteristics of the situation" affect the accuracy of client self-reports.[22] For example, if clients have little to lose from reporting problem behaviors accurately, they are likely to do so. In many situations in which alcohol- and drug-dependent clients are found, such as criminal justice or child welfare settings, this is not the case. A diagnosis of chemical abuse or dependency can have serious consequences for the client. In these cases, it may be particularly important for the clinician to utilize additional sources of information to obtain a complete picture of the individual's alcohol and drug use and any related problem.

There has been an interest in the use of unobtrusive, that is, nonface-valid instruments, such as the MacAndrew scale and the SASSI, in situations where demand characteristics might inhibit clients from giving accurate responses to face-valid questions. However, even when unobtrusive measures are used, ethical, professional conduct generally requires that the client be told the purpose of the screening or assessment in which they are participating.

DIAGNOSIS

Once screening has been done, it is necessary to determine if there is sufficient evidence to confirm a diagnosis of chemical abuse or dependency. Ideally, diagnosis is accompanied by a multidimensional, biopsychosocial assessment, which includes not only an in-depth understanding of the client's alcohol- and drug-related problems, but also of the client's strengths, support systems, and other factors that may help promote recovery.

The history of attempts to reach agreement on the criteria needed to define and diagnose alcohol and drug problems has been recounted by various authors.[23] Within the last few decades considerable progress has been made in helping clinicians and researchers grapple with these issues. An important step was the work of the Criteria Committee of the National Council on Alcoholism (NCA), now the National Council on Alcoholism and Drug Dependence, Inc. (NCADD), which published "Criteria for the Diagnosis of Alcoholism" in 1972.[24] The committee unanimously defined the disease of alcoholism as "a pathological dependence on ethanol (alcohol)" and divided its criteria into two tracks and three diagnostic levels. Major and minor diagnostic criteria were also provided. Track I is Physiological and Clinical, and Track II is Behavioral, Psychological, and Attitudinal. Diagnostic level 1 indicates definite criteria of alcoholism, diagnostic level 2 indicates probable criteria, and level 3, possible criteria. This classification schema shows a variety of indicators of alcoholism such as withdrawal symptoms, alcohol-related illnesses, and social, vocational, and legal problems. Although the committee believed that any of the major criteria could be grounds for diagnosing alcoholism, it did not provide precise rules for determining the extent of the major and minor criteria necessary to make a diagnosis of alcoholism.[25] We reproduce the major criteria in Table 5.3 because of their value in delineating many of the medical, social, and psychological problems experienced by those with alcohol disorders that should be recognized by human service professionals.

The criteria of the American Psychiatric Association (APA) and the World Health Organization (WHO) are the most widely used diagnostic tools in the field today.[26] In the last three decades the APA has revised its criteria several times. The 1987 edition of the *Diagnostic and Statistical Manual of Mental Disorders* (*DSM-III-R*) delineates the current APA criteria for diagnosing psychoactive substance use disorders,[27] and changes for the DSM-IV are nearly complete. In addition to these alcohol and drug disorders, the *DSM-III-R*

TABLE 5.3   Criteria for the Diagnosis of Alcoholism, National Council on Alcoholism and Drug Dependence*

Major Criteria

Criterion	Diagnostic Level
TRACK I. PHYSIOLOGICAL AND CLINICAL	
A. Physiological Dependency	
1. Physiological dependence as manifested by evidence of a *withdrawal syndrome* (1), when the intake of alcohol is interrupted or decreased without substitution of other sedation.[1] It must be remembered that overuse of other sedative drugs can produce a similar withdrawal state, which should be differentiated from withdrawal from alcohol.	
a. Gross tremor (differentiated from other causes of tremor)	1
b. Hallucinosis (differentiated from schizophrenic hallucinations or other psychoses)	1
c. Withdrawal seizures (differentiated from epilepsy and other seizure disorders)	1
d. Delirium tremens. Usually starts between the first and third day after withdrawal and minimally includes tremors, disorientation, and hallucinations (1)	1
2. Evidence of *tolerance* to the effects of alcohol. (There may be decrease in previously high levels of tolerance late in the course.) Although the degree of tolerance to alcohol in no way matches the degree of tolerance to other drugs, the behavioral effects of a given amount of alcohol vary greatly between alcoholic and nonalcoholic subjects.	
a. A blood alcohol level of more than 150 mg without gross evidence of intoxication	1
b. The consumption of one fith of a gallon of whiskey or an equivalent amount of wine or beer daily, for more than 1 day, by a 180-lb individual	1
3. Alcoholic "blackout" periods. (Differential diagnosis from purely psychological fugue states and psychomotor seizures)	2
B. Clinical: Major Alcohol-Associated Illnesses	
Alcoholism can be assumed to exist if major alcohol-associated illnesses develop in a person who drinks regularly. In such individuals evidence of physiological and psychological dependence should be searched for.	
Fatty degeneration in absence of other known cause	2
Alcoholic hepatitis	1
Laennec's cirrhosis	2
Pancreatitis in the absence of cholelithiasis	2
Chronic gastritis	3
Hematological disorders:	
Anemia—hypochromic, normocytic, macrocytic, hemolytic and stomatocytosis, low folic acid	3
Clotting disorders—prothrombin elevation or thrombocytopenia	3
Wernicke-Korsakoff syndrome	2
Alcoholic cerebellar degeneration	1
Cerebral degeneration in absence of Alzheimer's disease or arteriosclerosis	2
Central pontine myelinolysis ⎫ diagnosis only possible postmortem Marchiafava-Bignami's disease ⎭	2
Peripheral neuropathy (*see* also beriberi)	2
Toxic amblyopia	3
Alcohol myopathy	2
Alcoholic cardiomyopathy	2
Beriberi	3
Pellagra	3

TRACK II. BEHAVIORAL, PSYCHOLOGICAL, AND ATTITUDINAL
   All chronic conditions of psychological dependence occur in dynamic equi-

TABLE 5.3   *(Continued)*

Major Criteria

Criterion	Diagnostic Level
librium with intrapsychic and interpersonal consequences. In alcoholism, similarly, there are varied effects on character and family. Like other chronic relapsing diseases, alcoholism produces vocational, social, and physical impairments. Therefore, the implications of these disruptions must be evaluated and related to the individual and his pattern of alcoholism. The following behavior patterns show psychological dependence on alcohol in alcoholism.	
1. Drinking despite strong medical contraindication known to patient	1
2. Drinking despite strong, identified social contraindication (job loss for intoxication, marriage disruption because of drinking, arrest for intoxication, driving while intoxicated)	1
3. Patient's subjective complaint of loss of control of alcohol consumption	2

[1] Some authorities term this "pharmacological addiction."

Source: National Council on Alcoholism (now the National Council on Alcoholism and Drug Dependence, Inc.), Criteria Committee, "Criteria for the Diagnosis of Alcoholism," published simultaneously in *American Journal of Psychiatry,* Vol. 129 (1972), pp. 127–135, and *Annals of Internal Medicine,* Vol. 77 (1972), pp. 249–258. Copyright 1972, the American Psychiatric Association. Reprinted by permission.

provides a standard set of criteria that professionals use to diagnose a wide range of mental problems. Table 5.4 contains a portion of the *DSM-III-R*'s description of cocaine abuse and dependence. The *DSM-III-R* diagnoses are often used by professionals to request third-party (insurance) payments for treating mental health problems, including chemical abuse and dependency. Interview protocols are available to assist in applying the *DSM-III-R* diagnostic criteria such as the Diagnostic Interview Schedule (DIS)-III-R which is a structured interview and the Structured Clinical Interview for DSM-III-R (SCID).[28]

The WHO has also been a leader in the development of diagnostic criteria for alcoholism since the early 1950s.[29] One of its most notable early consultants was E. M. Jellinek. Currently in use is the WHO's tenth edition of the *International Classification of Diseases (ICD-10)*. While the APA and the WHO have not achieved full consensus on their diagnostic criteria for alcohol disorders, there is hope that this might emerge.[30] Such a consensus would help to standardize definitions of alcohol problems for treatment and research purposes. A comparison of the cur-

rent *DSM-III-R* criteria for alcohol dependence and alcohol abuse, the *DSM-IV* draft criteria, and the *ICD-10* criteria is found in Table 5.5.

An historical controversy in the field of alcoholism centers on whether identifying and treating the underlying causes of alcoholism (such as fear of latent homosexuality or unmet needs for oral gratification) would result in remission of alcohol abuse. This approach has not proven satisfactory for two reasons. First, science has yet to discover the exact etiologies of substance disorders, and second, even if the underlying causes were known, substance abuse often becomes a problem in its own right. Our discussion of diagnosis generally refers to substance abuse or dependence as a major or primary problem presented by the client, requiring specific treatment. The reader may have also encountered the term "secondary" diagnosis. In 1972, the Criteria Committee of the NCA wrote that:

Reactive, secondary, or symptomatic alcohol use should be separated from other forms of alcoholism. Alcohol as a psychoactive drug may be used for varying periods of time to mask or alleviate psychiatric symptoms. This may often mimic a

TABLE 5.4 Abbreviated Description of Cocaine Abuse and Dependence

Patterns of use. Cocaine abuse and dependence are associated with two different patterns of use: episodic and chronic daily, or almost daily, use. In episodic use, the cocaine use tends to be separated by two or more days of nonuse, for example, it may be used on weekends and once or twice during the week. "Bingeing" is a common form of episodic use consisting of compressed time periods of continuous high-dose use, for example, consumption of several grams or more of cocaine during a single 48-hour period. Bingeing is most commonly associated with cocaine smoking and intravenous use. Binges tend to terminate only when the user collapses from physical exhaustion or when cocaine supplies are depleted. Binges are generally followed by an extremely intense and unpleasant "crash" requiring at least two or more days of recuperation. In some cases the "crash" may extend into cocaine withdrawal lasting several days.

Chronic daily, or almost daily, use may be at high or low doses. Use may be throughout the course of a day or be restricted to certain hours, for example, only during working hours or only during the evening. In this pattern there are usually no wide fluctuations in the amount of cocaine used on successive days, but there is often a general increase in doses used over time.

Associated features. Often the user of cocaine also abuses or is dependent on alcohol or a sedative, hypnotic, or anxiolytic, which is taken in an attempt to alleviate the unpleasant aftereffects of cocaine intoxication.

Psychological and behavioral changes associated with cocaine abuse and dependence include depression, irritability, anhedonia, anergia, and social isolation. Sexual dysfunction, paranoid ideation, attentional disturbances, and memory problems may also occur.

Course. Cocaine smoking and intravenous administration of cocaine tend to engender rapid progression from infrequent cocaine use to cocaine abuse or dependence, often within only a few weeks or months. Intranasal administration of cocaine tends to result in more gradual progression to cocaine abuse or dependence, which may not be clearly evident for months or years following initial use.

Cocaine abuse and dependence are usually associated with a progressive tolerance of the desirable effects of the substance, which leads to use of increasing doses. With continuing use there is a progressive diminution in pleasurable effects and a corresponding increase in dysphoric effects. Eventually, a point is reached at which the person still craves the cocaine despite the absence of substance-induced euphoria because of tolerance, and an accumulation of unpleasant adverse effects caused by the continued drug taking. Continuing use of cocaine appears to be driven by persistent craving and urges for the substance rather than attempts to avoid or alleviate withdrawal symptoms (as is typically seen in opioid dependence).

Source: American Psychiatric Association, *Diagnostic and Statistical Manual of Mental Disorders,* 3rd ed., rev. (Washington, D.C.: The Association, 1987), pp. 178–179.

prodromal [early] stage of alcoholism and is difficult to differentiate from it. If the other criteria of alcoholism are not present, this diagnosis must be given. A clear relationship between the psychiatric symptom or event must be present; the period of heavy alcohol use should clearly not antedate the precipitating situational event (for example, an object loss). The patient may require treatment as for alcoholism, in addition to treatment for the precipitating psychiatric event.[31]

It may even be that excessive alcohol or drug use that developed following a trau-

matic event, such as loss of a loved one, may remit without specialized substance abuse treatment once an adjustment is made to the new life circumstance. But this is different from the situation in which alcohol or drug use itself has become a problem for the individual. Take, for example, the case of an individual who blames his diagnosis of alcohol dependence on a divorce that occurred ten years ago. While it may be true that his drinking escalated at that time, the alcoholism itself has become a problem, requiring it to

TABLE 5.5 Comparison of the Diagnostic Criteria for Alcohol Dependence and Alcohol Abuse or Harmful Use in Three Diagnostic Schemes: The ICD–10,[1] DSM–III–R,[2] and Proposed DSM–IV[3]

Comparison of Criteria for Alcohol Dependence		
ICD–10	*DSM–III–R*	*DSM–IV*
Symptoms		
Essential: Drinking or a desire to drink; the subjective awareness of compulsion to use is most common during attempts to stop or control drinking.		
At least three of the following:	At least three of the following:	A maladaptive pattern of alcohol use leading to clinically significant impairment or distress, as manifested by three or more of the following:
(1) Evidence of tolerance to the effects of alcohol.	(1) Need for increased amounts of alcohol (at least 50%) to achieve intoxication or desired effect, or markedly diminished effect with continued use of the same amount of alcohol.	(1) Tolerance defined as (a) the need for markedly increased amounts of alcohol to achieve intoxication or desired effect or (b) markedly diminished effect with continued use of the same amount of alcohol.
(2) A psychological withdrawal state (characteristic alcohol withdrawal syndrome or drinking to relieve or avoid withdrawal symptoms).	(2) Characteristic withdrawal symptoms for alcohol. (3) Alcohol often taken to relieve or avoid withdrawal symptoms.	(2) Withdrawal, as manifested by (a) the characteristic alcohol withdrawal syndrome or (b) alcohol or a closely related substance taken to relieve or avoid withdrawal symptoms.
(3) Difficulties in controlling drinking behavior in terms of onset, termination, or levels of use.	(4) Persistent desire or one or more successful efforts to cut down or control drinking.	(3) Unsuccessful efforts or a persistent desire to cut down or control drinking.
	(5) Drinking in larger amounts or over a longer period than intended.	(4) Drinking in larger amounts or over a longer period than intended.
(4) Progressive neglect of alternative pleasures or interests because of drinking, increased amount of time to obtain or to drink alcohol, or to recover from its effects.	(6) Important social, occupational, or recreational activities given up or reduced because of drinking.	(5) Important social, occupational, or recreational activities given up or reduced because of drinking.

TABLE 5.5   *(Continued)*

| Comparison of Criteria for Alcohol Dependence | | |
| *ICD–10* | *DSM–III–R* | *DSM–IV* |

	Symptoms	
	(7) Frequent intoxication or withdrawal symptoms when expected to fulfill major role obligations or when drinking is physically hazardous.	
(5) Persisting in drinking despite clear evidence of harmful consequences which may be physical, psychological, or cognitive.	(8) Continued drinking despite knowledge of a persistent or recurring social, psychological, or physical problem caused or exacerbated by alcohol use.	(6) Continued drinking despite knowledge of a persistent or recurring physical or psychological problem caused or exacerbated by alcohol use.
	(9) A great deal of time spent in activities necessary to obtain alcohol, to drink, or to recover from its effects.	(7) A great deal of time spent in activities necessary to obtain alcohol, to drink, or to recover from its effects.
(6) A strong desire or compulsion to drink. Also a consideration: a narrowing of the repertoire of drinking patterns (e.g., drinking in the same way, regardless of social constraints that determine appropriate drinking behavior.		

Duration Criteria for Alcohol Dependence		
At least three of the above criteria have been met during previous year.	Some symptoms have persisted for at least 1 month or have occurred repeatedly over a longer period.	Three or more symptoms have occurred at any time during the same 12 month period.
		Criteria for Subtyping Dependence
		With physiological dependence. Evidence of tolerance or withdrawal (i.e., symptoms 1 or 2 above are present).
		Without physiological dependence. No evidence of tolerance or withdrawal (i.e., neither symptom 1 nor 2 is present).

TABLE 5.5 *(Continued)*

<table>
<tr><th colspan="3">Comparison of Criteria for Alcohol Dependence</th></tr>
<tr><th>ICD–10</th><th>DSM–III–R</th><th>DSM–IV Draft</th></tr>
<tr><td colspan="3" align="center">Course Modifiers for Alcohol Dependence</td></tr>
<tr>
<td>Currently abstinent.</td>
<td>*In partial remission.* During the past 6 months, some use of alcohol and some symptoms of dependence.</td>
<td>*Early remission.*
(a) *Early full remission.* No criteria for abuse or dependence met in last 1 to 12 months.</td>
</tr>
<tr>
<td>Currently abstinent, but in a protected environment.</td>
<td>*In full remission.* During the past 6 months, either no use of alcohol, or use of alcohol and no symptoms of dependence.</td>
<td>(b) *Early partial remission.* Full criteria for dependence not met in last 1 to 12 months, but at least one criterion for abuse or dependence met, intermittently or continuously.</td>
</tr>
<tr>
<td>Currently on clinically supervised maintenance or replacement regime.</td>
<td></td>
<td></td>
</tr>
<tr>
<td>Currently abstinent, but receiving aversive or blocking drugs (e.g., disulfiram).</td>
<td></td>
<td>*Sustained remission.*
Twelve months of early remission have passed.
(a) *Sustained full remission.* No criterion for abuse or dependence met at any time in past twelve months or longer.</td>
</tr>
<tr>
<td>Currently drinking.</td>
<td></td>
<td></td>
</tr>
<tr>
<td>Continuous drinking.</td>
<td></td>
<td>(b) *Sustained partial remission.* Full criteria for dependence not met in past 12 months or longer, but at least one criterion for abuse or dependence met, intermittently or continuously.</td>
</tr>
<tr>
<td>Episodic drinking.</td>
<td></td>
<td></td>
</tr>
<tr>
<td></td>
<td></td>
<td>If applicable:
On antagonist therapy. In a controlled environment.</td>
</tr>
<tr><td colspan="3" align="center">Severity Modifiers for Alcohol Dependence</td></tr>
<tr>
<td align="center">No modifiers</td>
<td>*Mild.* Few, if any, symptoms in excess of those required to make the diagnosis. The symptoms result in no more than mild impairment in occupational functioning, social activities, or relationships with others.</td>
<td>*Mild.* Few, if any, symptoms in excess of those required to make the diagnosis. The symptoms result in no more than mild impairment in social or occupational functioning.</td>
</tr>
<tr>
<td></td>
<td>*Moderate.* Symptoms or functional impairment between mild and severe.</td>
<td>*Moderate.* Symptoms or functional impairment between mild and severe.</td>
</tr>
<tr>
<td></td>
<td>*Severe.* Many symptoms in excess of those required to make the diagnosis. The symptoms markedly interfere with occupational functioning, social activities, or relationships with others.</td>
<td>*Severe.* Many symptoms in excess of those required to make the diagnosis, or several symptoms that are particularly severe, or the symptoms result in marked impairment in social or occupational functioning.</td>
</tr>
<tr><td colspan="3" align="center">Comparison of Criteria for ICD-10 Harmful Use of Alcohol and for DSM-III-R and DSM-IV Alcohol Abuse</td></tr>
<tr>
<td>Clear evidence that a pattern of alcohol use was responsible for:</td>
<td>A maladaptive pattern of alcohol use indicated by at least one of the following:</td>
<td>A maladaptive pattern of alcohol use leading to clinically significant impairment or distress, as manifested by one three or more of the following:</td>
</tr>
</table>

TABLE 5.5 *(Continued)*

Comparison of Criteria for Alcohol Dependence

ICD–10	*DSM–III–R*	*DSM–IV Draft*

Comparison of Criteria for ICD-10 Harmful Use of Alcohol and for DSM-III-R and DSM-IV Alcohol Abuse

ICD–10	*DSM–III–R*	*DSM–IV Draft*
(1) Actual physical damage to the user. or (2) Actual mental damage to the user.	(1) Continued drinking despite knowledge of having a persistent or recurring social, occupational, psychological, or physical problem that is caused or exacerbated by alcohol use. (2) Recurring drinking in situations in which it is physically hazardous.	(1) Recurrent drinking resulting in inability to fulfill major role obligations at work, school, or home. (2) Recurring drinking in situations in which it is physically hazardous (e.g., driving an automobile). (3) Continued alcohol use despite recurrent or persistent social or interpersonal problems caused or exacerbated by the effects of alcohol (e.g., arguments, physical fights). (4) Recurrent alcohol-related legal problems (e.g., arrests for alcohol-related disorderly conduct).

Duration Criteria for Harmful Use and Alcohol Abuse

ICD–10	*DSM–III–R*	*DSM–IV Draft*
None.	Some symptoms have persisted for at least 1 month or have occurred repeatedly over a longer period.	One or more symptoms have occurred at any time during the same 12 month period.

Exclusionary Criteria Related to Alcohol Dependence

ICD–10	*DSM–III–R*	*DSM–IV Draft*
Does not presently meet criteria for alcohol dependence, a psychotic disorder, or other drug- or alcohol-related disorder.	Never met criteria for alcohol dependence.	Never met criteria for alcohol dependence.

Severity Modifiers for Harmful Use or Abuse

ICD–10	*DSM–III–R*	*DSM–IV Draft*
No modifiers.	No modifiers.	*Mild, moderate,* or *severe* as described above for alcohol dependence.

[1] World Health Organization, *The ICD-10 Classification of Mental and Behavioural Disorders, Clinical Descriptions and Diagnostic Guidelines* (Geneva, WHO, 1992).

[2] American Psychiatric Association, *Diagnostic and Statistical Manual of Mental Disorders,* 3rd ed., rev. (Washington, DC: The Association, 1987).

[3] American Psychiatric Association, Task Force on DSM-IV, *DSM-IV Draft Criteria* (Washington, DC: The Association, March 1 1993). Reprinted with permission from the *DSM-IV Draft Criteria (3/1/93)*. Copyright 1993 American Psychiatric Association.

Source: Adapted from Bridget F. Grant and Leland H. Towle, "A Comparison of Diagnostic Criteria, DSM-III-R, Proposed DSM-IV, and Proposed ICD-10," *Alcohol Health and Research World,* Vol. 15, No. 4 (1991), pp. 284–292.

be addressed as such. Exploring the issues that caused the client to fixate on his divorce may also be helpful at some point, but this alone is unlikely to resolve his years of alcohol problems. Treatment must first focus on arresting the alcohol dependence.

Today we find that a substantial number of persons with mental disorders also have diagnoses of alcohol or drug disorders. While their drinking or drug use may have been precipitated by the desire to relieve symptoms of mental disorders (hallucinations, anxiety, etc.), many of them require treatment for substance abuse as well as treatment for mental illness. In fact, the subject of dual or multiple diagnoses has become of such importance that we devote Chapter 13 to it. Severe mental disorders include psychotic disorders such as schizophrenia and schizoaffective disorder as well as mood disorders such as bipolar disorder, major depression, and anxiety disorders. Other types of mental disorders that also commonly appear in conjunction with psychoactive substance abuse disorders include borderline, antisocial, dependent, and other personality disorders. In the case of a person who first experiences a severe mental disorder and later psychoactive substance abuse or dependence, the convention has been to call the mental disorder the primary diagnosis and substance abuse or dependence the secondary diagnosis. It is also quite possible for a substance disorder to predate a severe mental disorder, in which case the substance disorder would technically be called the primary diagnosis and the mental disorder, the secondary diagnosis. However, listing one diagnosis as primary and another as secondary does not necessarily mean that one is more serious than, more important than, or caused by the other. Professionals may define the illness they are currently treating as primary in order to meet the requirements of funding agencies. With the increase in the number of very young people abusing alcohol and drugs at an age before severe mental illnesses are usually expressed, such temporal distinctions can be arbitrary and misleading. Minkoff believes

that when two disorders are of major concern, it may be more appropriate to classify both as primary.[32] There is a growing consensus in the field that when clients have two primary disorders, these problems should be treated in an integrated or simultaneous manner (see Chapter 13).

ASSESSMENT

The work of the WHO, the APA, and the NCADD has all been important in establishing better ways to diagnose alcohol and drug disorders, but these diagnostic tools do not provide all the information needed to plan for the client's treatment. Various assessment tools such as the Addiction Severity Index (ASI),[33] have been used to gain a better understanding of clients' overall functioning. The ASI is a structured interview accompanied by a numerical scoring system to indicate the severity of the patient's or client's problems in seven life areas: alcohol, drugs, vocational, family and social supports, medical, psychological-psychiatric, and legal. It can be administered by chemical dependency professionals and other human service professionals who have been trained in its use. The ASI has a follow-up version which has also contributed to its use in treatment and research to measure client progress and to assess the effectiveness of treatment programs. Training materials and workshops are available to initiate staff in its use. Similar instruments for use with adolescents have also been developed.[34]

The information obtained from screening, diagnosis, and assessment is used to determine the type of substance abuse treatment needed by the client. In Chapter 6 we describe the components of the chemical dependency treatment system, indicating the types of clients that are likely to benefit from each service. Since many alcoholics and addicts initially seek help for marital, family, job, legal, or health problems rather than for alcohol or drug problems, it is incumbent on helping professionals from all disciplines and in various treatment settings to be knowledge-able about screening, diagnosis, and assessment for chemical dependency problems. Similarly, tools such as the ASI are important to professionals in the chemical dependency field, because they are concerned with the client's overall quality of life. Babor and coworkers believe that the jury is still out on whether the unidimensional approach (in which the treatment goal of abstinence is expected to result in improvement in other areas of the client's life) is as useful as the multidimensional approach (which suggests the client's problems in all areas be targeted for treatment since abstinence alone may not resolve them).[35] But the multidimensional or systems view of assessment and treatment seems to have taken precedence over the view that chemical dependency is a unitary phenomenon[36] and that treating alcohol or drug abuse is the only concern of chemical dependency professionals.

We are especially concerned with taking the client's social history, because it is the type of assessment that exemplifies the systems or ecological perspective of this book.* Our discussion is intended to alert the new professional to some of the issues involved in doing a thorough assessment, focusing on the strengths as well as the problems of the client.[37] There are many formats for doing social histories from checklists to structured interviews to more open-ended formats. The social history outline found in Table 5.6 can be used to structure an assessment or intake interview with an adult who admits a substance abuse or dependency problem. A skillful interviewer may also be able to use this tool to reduce defensiveness in clients who are less willing to discuss their alcohol or drug use and to begin to engage the client in the treatment process and increase motivation for change.[38] While not exhaustive of all the avenues that can be explored with a client, the topics and questions suggested in the outline can help the interviewer capture

---

* I wish to thank William J. McCabe who taught me about many of the elements in this social history.

information both about problems in the client's life and about the assets the client brings to the recovery process. The format of the social history is flexible and can be adjusted depending on the client and treatment setting. Sometimes a comprehensive intake interview or social history is done at an initial session. In other cases, the material is obtained over several sessions. Clients may initially give limited answers to questions but reveal more information over time as comfort and trust with the treatment professional increases. Assessment is not a single event; it takes place throughout the treatment process as clients' needs and circumstances change.

In conducting a social history, the interviewer determines which questions to ask at a given time and the order of the questions. In discussing each section of this social history, we comment not only on the type of information that might be gathered, but also on the reasons for gathering it. Often the social history starts with information considered to be least threatening to the client. The sections on education and employment may be good starting points. Basic questions about how much education the client has had and whether the client has professional or vocational education are generally considered routine and are usually easily answered by clients without resistance.

Education

School adjustment may be a useful avenue to explore, especially for younger clients, as it may be particularly relevant to their current situation. For older clients, the interviewer may ask whether he or she liked school, did well, and fit in at school or if school was a frustrating or unsatisfactory experience? Did the client initiate alcohol and/or other drug use or abuse in primary or secondary school or in college? Were his or her friends involved in alcohol and drug use in the same way? These questions may help establish the time frame and circumstances during which alcohol or drug use first became a problem. If the client has no high school diploma or no

TABLE 5.6 The Social History As It Relates to Drinking and Drug Use

I. EDUCATION
   A. How long did the client stay in school?
   B. How did the client like or feel about school?
   C. Did the client do well in school?
   D. What work is the client educated to do?
   E. Did the client have a history of alcohol and/or other drug use or abuse during the school years?
   F. Did the client have friends and close relationships during the school years? If so, were these individuals alcohol or drug users/abusers?

II. EMPLOYMENT
   A. What is the client's current job or when did the client last work?
   B. What other jobs has the client held?
   C. How often has the client changed jobs?
   D. What is the client's favorite type of work?
   E. Has the client experienced job difficulties and what seems to be the causes of these problems?
   F. If the client is not working, is financial support being obtained from other sources?

III. MILITARY HISTORY (IF APPLICABLE)
   A. If not currently in the military, what type of discharge did the client receive?
   B. What was the client's last rank in the military?
   C. What were the client's patterns of socialization in the military?
   D. How long did the client remain in the military?
   E. If the client experienced problems in the military, were they related to alcohol, other drug use, or other factors?

IV. MEDICAL HISTORY
   A. Does the client have current or past medical problems?
   B. Has the client ever been hospitalized for medical problems?
   C. Are past medical records available?
   D. Is the client currently taking medications or has the client taken medications in the past?
   E. Has the client abused prescription or non-prescription drugs?
   F. Are any of the client's medical problems directly related to or exacerbated by the use of alcohol or other drugs?

V. DRINKING AND DRUG USE HISTORY
   A. What drugs does the client use and what does the client drink (including any technical products)?
   B. How often does the client consume alcohol or other drugs?
   C. How much alcohol and/or drugs does the client use?
   D. What is the client's drinking or drug use pattern (daily, weekend, periodic, etc.)?
   E. When did the client's drinking or drug use begin?
   F. Does the client give a "reason" for his/her drinking or drug use?
   G. Has the client experienced periods of abstinence?
   H. Has the client experienced blackouts or other indications of chemical abuse problems?
   I. Has the client experienced withdrawal symptoms from alcohol or other drugs?
   J. Has the client ever received treatment for a drinking or other drug problem?
   K. Are records of past treatment available?

VI. PSYCHOLOGICAL-PSYCHIATRIC HISTORY
   A. Does the client express feelings of being tense, lonely, anxious, depressed, etc.?
   B. Has the client ever contemplated, threatened, or attempted suicide?
   C. Has the client received any counseling or psychiatric treatment on an outpatient basis?
   D. Has the client ever had a psychiatric hospitalization?
   E. Are records of past treatment available to determine the exact nature of the problem?

VII. LEGAL INVOLVEMENT (IF APPLICABLE)
   A. Is the client currently on probation or parole or incarcerated?
   B. What types of charges or other legal problems has the client had?
   C. Are legal charges related to alcohol or other drug use?
   D. Does the client have any charges pending? If so, does the client believe that chemical dependency treatment will result in reduced legal penalties?
   E. If client was arrested for DWI, what was his/her blood alcohol level?

VIII. FAMILY HISTORY
   A. What are the drinking and drug use habits of members of the client's family of origin (mother, father, grandparents, siblings, aunts, uncles, etc.)?
   B. Are there persons in the client's family of origin who have alcohol or other drug abuse problems?
   C. What were the attitudes towards drinking alcohol and the use of other drugs in the client's family of origin?
   D. How does the client describe his/her relationship with other family of origin members?
   E. Was there a history of psychological or physical (including sexual) abuse in the family?
   F. What is the client's current relationship with family members?

IX. RELATIONSHIP WITH SPOUSE, CHILDREN, AND OTHER SIGNIFICANT INDIVIDUALS
   A. What is the client's current marital status and marital history?
   B. If the client has a spouse or other partner, what is the quality of the relationship?
   C. What are the drinking and drug taking habits of the partner?
   D. If the client has children, what is his/her relationship with them?
   E. What are the drinking and drug taking habits of the children?
   F. Are the spouse or children experiencing significant problems (psychological or physical abuse, financial problems, etc.)?
   G. What are the client's living arrangements?
   H. What is the extent of the client's other social relationships?

X. WHY IS THE CLIENT COMING TO SEE YOU AT THIS POINT IN TIME (for example are there legal, medical, family, work, or other pressures to do so)?

college or vocational education, and wishes to pursue further education, the chemical dependency professional may note the client's need for a referral to a GED program or other educational or vocational program. If the client did well in school and has substantial education, these may be noted as assets to recovery.

Employment

Questions about employment often follow logically after questions about education. Is the client currently employed and is the client's job secure, or has it been threatened by substance abuse? During assessment interviews, individuals (such as those referred by an employee assistance program or by the correctional system) may deny employment problems related to alcohol or drug use. The pattern of employment—whether it is stable or erratic—is important to note. An erratic employment history is not necessarily the result of a substance abuse problem, but it may be an indication of it or other problems in the client's life. Discussion of employment may provide an opportunity for the assessment specialist to help clients identify how alcohol or drug abuse has negatively affected their work. Another clue to problems may be the client's employment in a job that is well below his or her educational level. For example, an individual with a graduate degree may be working in a convenience store. Perhaps this work is what the individual prefers, perhaps this is the only work available, or perhaps personal problems like chemical dependency have interfered with other employment. Seeming incongruities in the individual's life such as this can be explored to help determine if substance abuse is a problem.

The client may have a job that is an obstacle to recovery. An obvious example is working as a bartender where constant exposure to alcohol presents a problem for the client. Or perhaps the individual spends long periods on the road alone and is used to going to bars at night to relieve loneliness or boredom. Some clients frequently entertain business associates in settings where the use of alcohol or other drugs is common or expected. For some of these individuals, referrals to outpatient counseling to learn how to engage in alternative activities or to assertiveness training to learn how to refuse drinks or drugs may prove useful; for others, a key to attaining sobriety may include employment changes. A referral to a vocational rehabilitation agency, an employment counselor, or an employment agency, may be appropriate. These referrals may be made at the time of the intake or assessment interview or at a later date, depending upon the client's circumstances. Some clients are immediately in need of a job. Professionals who work with "skid row" or homeless clients generally know the street corners in town where a client can try to get a day labor job or they know employers who hire and pay individuals by the day. The professional's interest in the whole client, not just the client's substance abuse problem, is reflected in addressing employment concerns. Productive employment can be a useful tool in maintaining sobriety. For some clients, current employment may be identified as an asset. For example, an individual referred by an employee assistance program may have a job that he or she is anxious to keep. The interviewer may also ask questions about work hours or work habits that may be appropriate in determining whether the client is currently working to the detriment of other aspects of his or her life.

When clients are not working, it may be appropriate to inquire about their current means of support. They may be receiving public assistance or Social Security payments, or they may need a referral to apply for these benefits. Some clients may be getting help from family or friends, or they may be dealing drugs or engaging in other criminal activity to support themselves.

Military History

Questions about military service are often not asked unless the client is currently in the service or is in a Veterans Administration facility. However, these questions may be important, because many young people are introduced to alcohol and other drugs while in the military. A problematic military history may have been the result of alcohol or drug abuse. Questions that might be asked to probe into this area involve the rank or ranks the client held in the military and the type of discharge the individual received. For example, being demoted ("busted") in rank or receiving a medical, general, administrative, or dishonorable discharge may have been a consequence of alcohol or drug problems.

Medical History

An obvious reason that questions about medical problems are asked is to determine if they may be related to substance abuse. The client may not have made a connection between his or her medical problems (for example, sores, gastritis, or neuropathy) and the use of alcohol or other drugs. Some medical problems are not caused by substance use or abuse but alcohol and drug use may be contraindicated if the client has a particular condition (such as diabetes or epilepsy). Another reason to ask these questions is to determine if the client is receiving appropriate care for any current medical problems. If the client does not have personal resources to obtain medical attention, the interviewer may act as a referral source to community clinics, the local health department, or other services, although may communities lack the resources to provide anything but emergency medical care to these individuals.

Also important are any medications the client is taking, both physician prescribed and over the counter. Some clients are taking medication but do not understand what it is, only that the doctor told them to take it. Many are unaware of the adverse consequences that alcohol can have when combined with medications, such as the synergistic effect of alcohol and minor tranquilizers or of the contraindications of combining illicit drugs with prescribed medications. An important reason that health questions are asked in residential programs is for staff to be prepared if the client experiences medical problems. For example, a history of epilepsy would be of concern in order for staff to be prepared for seizures, and it is important to know if a history of seizures is related to epilepsy or to alcohol or drug withdrawal. There is a growing body of literature on those who are dually diagnosed with chemical dependency problems and major physical disabilities (see Chapter 13). A release signed by the client is generally needed to obtain information about prior health history and medical treatment. It is typical to request a release if this information would be useful in assisting the client in the chemical dependency treatment setting.

Legal History

Questions about the client's legal problems are also important. Many referrals to chemical dependency treatment programs are motivated by the legal system. A brush with the law may help the client confront a chemical dependency problem, or a client may seek treatment in the hope of obtaining a lighter or deferred sentence. Probation and parole officers and attorneys frequently make referrals to chemical dependency programs. Those convicted of a driving while intoxicated (DWI) or driving under the influence (DUI) offense may routinely be required by the court to submit to a screening or assessment to determine whether they have an alcohol or drug problem.

Often a client admits to having gotten into legal difficulties as a result of using alcohol or drugs but denies an inability to control alcohol or other drug use. An important clue to a drinking problem in these cases may be blood-alcohol level (BAL) or blood-alcohol content (BAC). BAL or BAC are frequently measured by a breathalyzer or intoxilizer, typically following arrest on suspicion of DWI or DUI. A high level may be an indication of tolerance to alcohol or alcohol dependency. For example, a person with a 0.20 percent BAL may deny a problem, but 0.20 is twice what is commonly referred to as the "legal limit" of 0.10 percent in most states (in a few states it is 0.08 percent). Most people would be unable to drive at a 0.20 level, yet those with a high tolerance may be able to do so. Asking how much alcohol was consumed before the arrest may be another clue to the client's candidness in responding to questions. When an individual says she had two cocktails, but her BAL was 0.20, something is amiss. Two cocktails (the type typically served in a bar) would not produce such a high BAL. Sometimes a blood test is used to determine BAL or the presence of other drugs. In accidents where a person is seriously injured and is taken to the hospital, the use of a blood test is common. Previous DWI or DUI arrests or other history of alcohol- or drug-related arrests are also strong clues to consider. Most nonproblem drinkers do not make the mistake of getting a second DWI or DUI, because the consequences are just not worth it. The person with an unrecognized problem is far more likely to make this costly misjudgment.

Other common types of alcohol- and drug-related arrests are public intoxication (in locations where this offense is still a crime), disorderly conduct, and offenses related to the possession and sale of controlled substances. Transient substance abusers are frequently arrested for vagrancy. Arrests for family violence may also be indicative of chemical abuse. Of course, white-collar crime, such as embezzlement and forgery, may also be the result of a drug habit. With the advent of drug screening in the workplace, urinalysis, previously used most by the criminal justice system and in therapeutic communities, has become an increasingly common detection tool.

Clients may bring other legal problems to the attention of the interviewer such as fears that past behavior may result in prosecution if discovered. Other legal matters worrying clients may be how to deal with an abusive partner or civil matters such as eviction notices and child custody or child support. Referrals to legal services may help clients put these problems in perspective so that they can avail themselves of treatment.

Drinking and Drug History

Naturally, the individual's drinking and drug history are paramount in conducting an assessment for chemical abuse or dependency. What psychoactive drugs has the client used in his or her life, and what are the current drugs used including frequency and amount of use? In some cases this will also involve asking if the individual has ingested "technical" products which contain alcohol not meant for human consumption, such as rubbing alcohol, after-shave lotion, Sterno, and so on. What problems have been experienced as a direct result of the drug use or abuse such as blackouts or violent behavior or withdrawal symptoms like tremors, seizures, hallucinations, or delirium tremens? In obtaining information from or about clients who are not detoxified, it is especially helpful to know about previous withdrawal symptoms that the client has experienced. Such information may indicate the need for immediate referral to a detoxification program and can be very helpful to the medical staff assisting the client through withdrawal. Unfortunately, the client may not be in a position to provide this information, and others who know the information may not be available. This is frequently the case when a transient substance abuser is brought to a hospital emergency department or to a community detoxification center (see Chapter 6).

It is also important to know if the individual has made attempts to stop using alcohol or other drugs in the past and if there have been periods of abstinence (no alcohol or drug use often referred to as "sober time" or being "clean"). These periods may also indicate that the individual is an alcohol or drug abuser, since others usually do not need to make special efforts at abstinence. Periods of abstinence should be considered an asset, and the chemical dependency counselor can discuss with the individual behaviors which may have contributed to the ability to remain alcohol or drug free (also see Chapter 6). Another question is whether the client has had previous treatment for alcohol or other drug problems. A release is generally obtained from the individual to obtain treatment records or to talk with previous treatment providers in order to gain a better understanding of the client's progress and setbacks in treatment. Information of this nature may also be helpful in determining whether the client is best served in an inpatient or outpatient chemical dependency treatment program.

A possible avenue to explore is whether the individual perceives that his or her alcohol or drug problems were precipitated by particular events or circumstances. This may seem like an unusual question since no one really knows the causes of chemical dependency. Asking the question is not done to give the client an opportunity to place blame on some internal or external factor. It is done to understand better the client's own perception of the roots of his or her chemical dependency. This is a reflection of the principle of "starting where the client is." Many clients need help in understanding the dynamics of chemical dependency and its development. Remember the client mentioned earlier who blamed his drinking on a divorce that occurred ten years ago. He may be correct in identifying that drinking or other drug use escalated at that point, but he is probably incorrect if he thinks that reuniting with his spouse will solve the problem. The professional taking the social history may make note, however, that this will be an important point to which to return with the client. Additionally, knowing events that precede drinking or drug use may help to establish plans that can avert relapse (see Chapter 6 regarding relapse).

Psychological and Psychiatric History

Psychological or psychiatric history is yet another aspect of the diagnosis and assessment process. Has the client had past mental problems? Of particular concern are current psychological or psychiatric problems the client is experiencing, especially thoughts or plans related to suicide. Substance abusers, particularly those who use depressants like alcohol, are at high risk for suicide. A referral for psychiatric evaluation or to an inpatient psychiatric unit may be an immediate necessity. Some clients with chemical dependency problems have serious mental disorders such as schizophrenia or they may have personality disorders or other mental problems (also see Chapter 13). If adequate information on mental history is not available and mental health problems are suspected, a psychological or psychiatric evaluation should be obtained. This information will help to establish an accurate diagnosis and determine the range of services the client needs and who may best treat the client. A referral to a mental health program or, where available, a program specifically for those with dual diagnoses of chemical dependency and mental disorders may be the best alternative. Dually diagnosed individuals may also be directed to self-help groups designed specifically for them.

Family History

The family history section of the assessment refers to the client's family of origin. These questions should probably be asked after some rapport has been established, because this subject can be particularly emotionally charged for the client. Since many alcoholics have alcoholic parents, it is useful to note whether the parents had entered recovery, and if so, at what point in the client's life. Did other family members such as siblings, aunts, uncles, or grandparents have drinking or drug problems? Other useful information concerns family attitudes about alcohol and drug use. Was there an intolerant attitude toward any use of alcohol? Was drinking or drug use seen as acceptable, and how was abuse of these substances viewed? To what extent were family attitudes related to particular cultural, ethnic, or religious beliefs (also see Chapter 11)? Checking for a history of psychiatric problems and other problems of family members may also be helpful to understanding the client's situation.

Questions about the client's current relationship with members of his or her family of origin are also important. Is the client in contact with other family members or estranged from them? Are family members seen as potentially supportive of the client's recovery or might they present obstacles by reinforcing or encouraging the client's drug use? It may be appropriate to consider involving family members in the client's treatment. How much the client is asked to reveal about his or her family of origin will depend on the treatment setting and its purpose. In a brief detoxification program, medical history is more important than family history. In an intensive inpatient or extended outpatient treatment setting, the social history may delve further into family matters.

Not so many years ago, chemical dependency professionals were unlikely to ask clients questions about previous physical, sexual, or emotional abuse inflicted on them by family members or others. However, as professionals began hearing about this from clients, particularly women, it could not continue to be overlooked. These problems may surface during treatment and can present serious obstacles to recovery if not addressed appropriately. Physical, sexual, and psychological abuse may or may not be addressed in the initial assessment interview, depending on professional judgment. Unless the client offers this information, it may be premature to broach these problems because they are too distressing to confront so early in the treatment process, and they may be better handled once a relationship between client and professional has developed.

Current Family and Social Relationships

Other vital questions concern the client's relationship to any current or former spouse, other partners, or children. If the client's sexual orientation is not clear, the professional should take care not to make an erroneous assumption (also see Chapter 13 on gay men and lesbians). How do the client's "significant others" perceive his or her drinking or drug use? Are they aware that the client has come for help? Are they similarly engaged in alcohol or drug use, or have they pushed the client to contact the treatment program? Including significant others in the treatment process can be helpful for all parties involved. The interviewer should explore whether significant others are likely to be supportive or not and inquire as to whether the client

wishes to involve them in the treatment process. Clients are usually encouraged to do so. However, they may be reluctant, especially if there are concerns about retaliation from an abusive partner. Or the client may be threatened with an unwanted separation or divorce, and his or her partner may wish to sever all ties rather than participate in treatment. Occasionally, child abuse or neglect becomes apparent or is suspected, or threats on a partner's life are made and may have to be reported to authorities in keeping with state statute or the "duty to warn."

Stable living arrangements make the process of becoming alcohol and drug free easier, but some clients are living with other alcoholics or addicts or have no suitable home. Professionals working in the alcohol and drug rehabilitation fields have always worked with clients who are drifters or who have found themselves with no roof over their heads. Deinstitutionalization of persons with mental illness, unemployment, and lack of affordable housing in addition to alcohol and drug abuse have added to the ranks of persons who need housing referrals or referrals to residential treatment programs in order to make rehabilitation a viable option.

Questions about close friends, other social relationships, and involvement with organizations and associations also help to determine the extent of social supports the client has in the community. Religious affiliation or involvement is addressed to determine if it may be an avenue of support and spiritual strength, or if the client's church or religious group holds punitive attitudes toward alcohol and drug abusers that have contributed to the client's guilt or denial. Many clients need assistance in establishing friendships with sober individuals and pursuing activities not centered on alcohol and drug use.

Why the Individual Is Seeking Services

Finally, if it is not clear why the individual is seeking services at this particular time, the interviewer may want to inquire about this. Many clients have abused psychoactive drugs for a long time, but have not previously sought help. Is there some particular concern—threat of job loss, of divorce, of legal consequences, and so on—that has motivated the individual to seek help at this time? Or perhaps as the saying goes, the individual is just, "sick and tired of being sick and tired."

Initial appointment or assessment interviews may be done free of charge even by private-for-profit programs as a way of encouraging people to consider some type of treatment or to encourage use of a particular program. For clients who want further services, the initial appointment may also involve obtaining information about insurance or other health care coverage to determine if the individual has a viable method of paying for treatment. If the client does not have the financial resources required by the program or needs services not offered by the program, professionalism generally requires that a referral to another resource be offered.

DENIAL, RESISTANCE, AND MOTIVATION TO RECOVERY

It is probably not possible to work in a substance abuse treatment program without hearing the terms *denial* and *resistance* during the course of the workday. Tarter and his associates describe the ways in which the term "denial" has been used in the field of chemical dependency.

Denial . . . has frequently been used to explain an alcoholic's failure to recognize the role of his feelings in instigating and sustaining drinking. Denial has also long been believed to reflect a conscious refusal by an alcoholic to recognize the effects of continued and excessive drinking on himself and his environment, thereby contributing to the alcoholic's resistance to initiating treatment, as well as ensuring poor treatment prognosis. Within the rubric of psychodynamic theory, denial has been conceptualized as an ego defense, and as such is considered to be indicative of an unconscious attempt by an alcoholic to protect himself from the threatening or aversive aspects of drinking behavior.[39]

As a largely unconscious process, denial differs from lying or an outright attempt at deceit.[40] Tarter and coworkers propose a biopsychological interpretation of denial suggesting that some alcoholics have a "disturbed arousal regulation process" in which they fail "to perceive or label internal cues accurately."[41] This causes them to underestimate the severity of stress in their lives, thereby promoting denial.

Everyone employs defense mechanisms to cope with life's stresses and strains. For example, news of the death of a family member or that one has a serious illness may be initially met with denial.[42] In these cases, denial initially serves a protective function until the individual can begin to integrate the event and move along to the next stages of the grief process. Clearly, it is necessary to utilize some level of defenses in order to maintain healthy psychological functioning, but when one is unable to move past denial, well-being can become impaired. This is frequently the case with the individual who has a substance abuse or dependency problem. As Weinberg puts it:

Denial is a way the human mind often deals with a situation involving incompatible perceptions, thoughts, or behaviors. In the case of drinking problems, the two elements are the powerful reinforcement derived from the drug and the unwanted side effects produced at the same time. The former is comprised of positive reinforcement (euphoria and energy) and/or negative reinforcement (temporary reduction of such unwanted feelings as tension, depression, self-hate, boredom, and sexual inadequacy).[43]

Another function of denial is to shield substance abusers from feelings of hopelessness.[44] Kinney notes that many patients are actually unaware that their problems are a result of substance abuse.[45]

Both Weinberg and Kinney and Leaton recommend helping clients reduce their denial gradually since it is serving an important, protective function.[46] An important task of the treatment professional is to help the client recognize the relationship between his or her drug abuse and its negative consequences. To facilitate this process with cocaine abusers, Washton has developed the Cocaine Abuse Assessment Profile (CAAP) which is described as being useful in assessment and in addressing denial.[47] The many questions about drug use and its consequences contained in the profile can help patients understand the magnitude of their substance abuse and the need for treatment.

Family members and other loved ones are also likely to engage in denial. It is equally painful for them to recognize that one of their members is chemically dependent. They may blame themselves for the client's problem, or they may just be plain embarrassed that this could be happening to them. Consequently, substance abusers and their loved ones reinforce each other's denial. In a well-known pamphlet published by Al-Anon, Reverend Joseph L. Kellerman likened the process of denial to being on a merry-go-round, but he noted that "the alcoholic cannot keep the merry-go-round going unless the others [family, friends, employers, etc.] ride it with him and help him keep it going."[48] When a couple or more than one member of the family is chemically dependent, denial can be especially strong.

In addition to denial, clients and their significant others may use a variety of other defenses. These include rationalization (attempts to find reasons to explain or excuse the chemical use), projection (blaming or attacking others for problems), avoidance or evasion of discussions of chemical use, recollection of the positive effects and experiences associated with chemical use, minimization of chemical use and its effects, and repression of painful events and feelings.[49] But George says that "denial is a more prominent approach, because it blocks the need for the use of the other defense mechanisms entirely."[50] It is also important to remember that the individual's defensiveness may result in behaving in grandiose, aggressive, and belligerent ways when often their feelings, especially during periods of sobriety, are actually those of remorse, guilt, inferiority, and helplessness.

Just as clients vary in their expression of denial and other defenses, they also vary in the extent to which they enter treatment voluntarily. Individuals who call a twenty-four-hour crisis line asking for help with a drug problem or those who walk into an outpatient alcoholism treatment program are generally considered voluntary referrals. Of course, external factors may have motivated them to request help—fear that their marriage or their work is suffering. Less voluntary clients may be those who have been committed or ordered to treatment through civil procedures. In these cases family members or others have appealed to the court because the individual has refused to seek help and is in serious danger due to alcohol or drug abuse. (These laws and procedures vary by state.) Other clients have been referred by their employer because their job is at stake or they may have been told by their probation officer that it is treatment or jail. These clients may recognize the problem and may participate willingly in treatment, or they may attend simply to remain employed or to fulfill the terms of their court order. Resistance to treatment varies with the individual's willingness or ability to terminate substance abuse and desire to engage in the treatment process. It may take some time for treatment providers to develop rapport with clients and to help them work through their defenses, but clients who come to counseling sessions or stay in halfway houses or therapeutic communities and never engage in the treatment process may be told that there is nothing more the treatment program can do for them at this time.

When individuals come to a treatment program to satisfy others but are not seeking long-term services (at least not at this time), they may be hoping for the "one-session cure." While this may sound flip, the one-session cure happens every day in chemical dependency treatment. It works like this:

Following the assessment interview, the individual thanks the interviewer, saying he now understands the problem, and is sure he can quit or control his drug use. Unless the individual is in an immediate life-threatening situation, it is usually not possible for treatment providers to force or coerce someone into receiving services, even if the situation is severe. Some professionals object to the idea that a client would be forced or coerced at all. Treatment providers generally consider their services voluntary. They cannot force someone to participate in treatment, even if he or she is under a civil court order or is required to attend by a parole or probation officer. However, the life-threatening nature of alcohol or drug dependency and the problems they pose for other individuals or the community may make some degree of coercion necessary, and there is ample evidence that this can be helpful.[51]

If the individual appears to have an alcohol or drug problem but resists treatment, the assessment specialist may encourage him or her to attend an educational program, a few individual or group counseling sessions, or some meetings of a self-help group before rejecting the notion of treatment entirely. If none of these alternatives is accepted, the professional may be supportive of the individual for his or her willingness to come in at all, being sure to leave the door open should he or she want to return later. Sometimes individuals are willing to make an agreement with the assessment specialist—if they use more than specified amounts of alcohol or drugs during a given time period or encounter negative consequences of alcohol or drug use, they will concede that they cannot control their use, and they agree to recontact the assessment specialist for treatment. This approach sometimes works in helping individuals identify alcohol and drug problems, especially those who are certain that they are in control of the situation. Some chemical dependency specialists may use more confrontive or direct approaches, depending on the client and the situation.

Finally, it may be useful to remember that calling a client unmotivated or resistant to treatment may be unfair or unwarranted. There is a great deal we do not know about substance abuse and dependency. For example, why is it that alcoholics or addicts with dozens of admissions to detox are able to maintain sobriety or stay "clean" after many unsuccessful attempts? The approaches available to treat substance abuse are relatively limited. We rely heavily on psychologically or cognitively based approaches, despite increasing evidence of a genetic component to these problems. Given that there are probably many types of alcoholism and drug addiction with complex etiologies, we do not yet have the tools to treat all individuals successfully and this, rather than lack of motivation, may be at the heart of why so many do not maintain recovery.

CONFIDENTIALITY

Respect for client confidences is an important aspect of the codes of ethics of most human service professionals. In addition, professionals working with chemically dependent clients should be aware of the portion of the *Federal Register* called "Confidentiality of Alcohol and Drug Abuse Patient Records" (42 CFR, Part 2). It details information that chemical dependency professionals need to know to protect their clients and themselves. We describe some of its major points and discuss other issues relevant to confidentiality. These comments are no substitute for good legal counsel and are meant only to suggest some of the issues in the field.

Without an individual's permission, treatment providers usually may not reveal whether or not he or she is a patient or client in a chemical dependency treatment facility or any other information about the individual or his or her treatment. Providing information to those outside the treatment program or requesting information from other sources generally requires the client's written permission. A client's written authorization to release information must state the name of the agency, program, or individual that is requesting the information; the type of information that the client wishes to be provided; the purpose for which the information will be used; the agency, program, or individual from which the information is requested; the date the release is signed and the date on which the release expires; and the client's signature and a witness's signature as written proof of permission.

As noted earlier, staff may wish to obtain certain types of information, such as medical or psychological information, that may help them better serve the client. A release of information form may also be required for the staff to communicate with the client's spouse or other loved ones, since it should not be assumed that these individuals know that the client is receiving treatment or that the client wants the staff to communicate with them. Professional conduct also suggests that information about the client not be shared or discussed with other staff in the facility unless they have a need to know this information to serve the client or in cases where a consultation is needed. Clients should also be informed of the extent to which staff may need to share information with each other.

Sometimes the client requests that the treatment program give information to others. For example, a client may want his employer to know that he is attending treatment, but he may not want any other details of his treatment revealed. In other cases, a client may be anxious for the treatment provider to explain at greater length to her probation officer how well she has progressed in treatment.

Exceptions to the right to confidentiality should be explained to the client. For example, under certain circumstances, treatment records of alcohol and drug abuse patients may be subject to subpoena or court order. Attempts may be made to subpoena records in cases where there are criminal charges against the client, in child custody cases, or under other circumstances. The issue of what to record in clients charts or files is an important one. Additionally, many helping professionals do not enjoy privileged communication with their clients; that is, they can be ordered by the courts to provide information even about matters not contained in the client's case record. In situations where the information may be damaging, professionals may be given an opportunity to explain to the court why they think releasing information would not be appropriate, and the court makes a decision on the matter.

In a medical emergency, information necessary to save the client's life may be released. In cases where the client may be harmful to himself or herself, such as in the case of threatened suicide, the professional has a responsibility to seek protection for the client through an appropriate mental health referral. Sometimes this involves asking the local mental health crisis team or law enforcement agency which handles these problems to intervene. If a client threatens serious harm to another, there may be a duty to warn this person, and the professional may be liable for injury sustained if no warning was issued. Child abuse and neglect must be reported according to state statute. There may also be state laws regarding reporting of elder abuse and other crimes.

Legal issues arise more frequently than ever in the chemical dependency field as they do in most fields, yet the appropriate responses are not always clear. Questions about what procedures to follow if law enforcement officers call about a client or arrive at the door with an arrest warrant for a client or a subpoena for a file are not unusual. Good legal counsel is important; so is education about legal matters, since staff may have to respond quickly.

Chemical dependency researchers may be afforded special confidentiality protections by obtaining a "certificate of confidentiality" from a federal agency such as the National Institute on Alcohol Abuse and Alcoholism or the National Institute on Drug Abuse. The certificate covers information obtained for research (not treatment) purposes only. It is particularly useful to obtain this protection when subjects are asked about alcohol and drug use or illegal activity (for example, illicit drug use or crimes committed) since it is designed to prevent researchers from having to release information in any type of court (administrative, civil, criminal, etc.). The research must be legitimate, but it need not be funded by the federal government or other external source to qualify for this certificate.

REFERRALS

Human service professionals of all types and in virtually all settings encounter chemically dependent individuals and their loved ones. From the elementary school to the child welfare agency to the workplace to the nursing home, chemical dependency problems appear. While all social workers, psychologists, and other human service professionals should be adept at recognizing these problems, many are not qualified to officially diagnose and treat them. When this is the case, a referral for further assessment or services is indicated. Some agencies, for example, family service agencies, may be able to provide these services in house; in other cases knowing the local alcohol and drug abuse treatment agencies, their purposes, and their staff members can facilitate a referral. For example, a child protective services (CPS) worker suspects that a child neglect case is due to alcohol abuse, but he needs a confirmatory diagnosis to require that the mother seek treatment. Knowing the woman's limited financial resources, he refers her to a community mental health center with a substance abuse treatment component. An adult protective services worker contacts an inpatient chemical dependency treatment to assist with a client whose addiction to minor tranquilizers is preventing her from functioning independently. Or a parole officer makes sure a bed in a therapeutic community for offenders with chemical dependency problems will be available before the release date of a heroin addict on her caseload.

Chemical dependency professionals not only accept referrals, they frequently make referrals to other agencies. As indicated in our discussion of assessment, chemically dependent clients often need additional services; vocational guidance, parent education, medical care, public assistance, and legal assistance are just a few. Keeping abreast of the services available in the community and developing cooperative working relationships with those who provide them are important professional responsibilities. Some agencies, such as the local offices of the state vocational rehabilitation agency, may have a particular counselor or counselors who work with substance abusers, or counselors may have general caseloads that include substance abusers as well as those with other disabilities. Informal knowledge of staff of other agencies that are most favorably disposed to working with chemically dependent clients can be a big help, and it does not take long to learn who these individuals are.

Making a referral on which the client follows through can involve more than writing a name and a phone number on a piece of paper. No one wants to act as an enabler (in the negative sense of the word) or increase a client's dependency, but calling ahead for a client, letting the client know specifically for whom to ask, and informing the client of the referral's purpose and what the referral source may or may not be able to do can be helpful. Clients with severe mental or physical disabilities may need extra support or assistance. This may mean providing transportation, accompanying them to the referral agency, or helping them complete application forms and compile necessary information. Clients who are desocialized or are particularly unassertive may also benefit from someone to accompany them until they can learn to negotiate these situations themselves. Additional obstacles such as lack of child care or language barriers may also need to be addressed before a client can take advantage of referrals. In making referrals for health care, it is particularly helpful to know if the client has private health insurance, belongs to a health maintenance organization (HMO), receives Medicaid or Medicare, or has another type of coverage.

Many agencies have intake workers whose job it is to interview new referrals and see that they are directed to the appropriate staff and services. Appointments may be set in advance or walk-in appointments may be accepted; some agencies allot specific times each day or week for new referrals. Many professionals also refer clients to self-help groups like Alcoholics Anonymous and Narcotics Anonymous (see Chapter 6), but making these referrals is different. These groups are not staffed by professionals, and arrangements for clients generally cannot be made in advance. Anonymity of self-help group members is often stressed, so the client cannot be given the name of an individual to call. The professional can give the client a list of meeting times or encourage the client to call the group for information.

Many self-help groups have telephone lines that are staffed twenty-four hours a day; others have twenty-four-hour answering services. Some have limited hours when telephones are staffed, and they may use a recording to give callers information or allow them to leave messages at other times.

Giving clients a list of meetings is not necessarily the most effective way of making referrals to self-help groups. Many members did get to their first meetings solely on their own, but clients are frequently hesitant to go to a group about which they know very little. Professionals can make the process considerably easier. One way is to educate clients about what to expect in advance.

Facilitating a referral to a self-help group may be easiest for those who "wear two hats." This phrase refers to individuals who are both human service professionals and members of self-help groups. Initially, they might accompany clients to a meeting or two, introduce them to other members, and explain what "working" a self-help program is about. Professionals who are not members of these self-help groups may assist by accompanying the client to an "open" meeting where those who are not alcoholics or addicts are welcome. Perhaps a more use-ful method is for professionals to become acquainted with self-help group members who do "twelve-step work." Twelve-step work refers to the desire of AA or NA members to take the message of the self-help group to others. Many communities have a number of self-help groups. Even professionals who are also recovered or recovering alcoholics or drug abusers do not attend all the groups in their community. Some groups are only for men, some are only for women, some are for Spanish speakers, and some are for gay men or lesbians. It is not possible for someone who wears two hats to fit in all the groups that their clients might need. Neither is it healthy for counselors to fill all these roles for clients. Clients need to widen their circle of recovering individuals, and professionals do not have time to fill this function for all their clients. It may be more effective for professionals to know a number of recovering individuals in the community who are available to assist newcomers to the many self-help groups that have emerged for chemically dependent individuals. There are also self-help groups for loved ones (spouses, partners, children, and other family members and friends) such as Al-Anon and Naranon. Similar procedures can be used to make referrals to these groups. It is also more difficult for clients to fail to follow through on a referral when arrangements have been made for someone to pick them up at their home or to greet them at the door of the meeting place. The client is also more likely to stay for the entire meeting and to return when members have made them feel welcome.

Some individuals are not only referred to self-help groups by the courts, they are required by the courts to attend. Self-help groups regard themselves as strictly voluntary programs, but many do allow the secretary of the group to sign slips of paper so that attendees can verify their presence at the meeting.

SUMMARY

This chapter discussed screening, diagnosis, assessment, and referral which are the first steps in treating individuals with alcohol or drug abuse problems. Many tools are available to assist professionals in determining whether an individual has an alcohol or drug abuse problem. Clients and their loved ones may, however, be resistant to these processes, and helping them overcome denial is often a prerequisite to their accepting help. Engagement of clients during these early stages of treatment requires not only knowledge of chemical dependency but also the skills and talents required to develop rapport and build relationships with clients.

There is much to be learned about an individual before a treatment plan can be developed. A thorough assessment includes knowledge about medical, psychiatric, family, legal, educational, and employment history, as well as other aspects of social functioning. The information obtained will help medical personnel make an immediate determination about whether the client needs medical detoxification and whether this should be done in a hospital, community detoxification center, or on an outpatient basis. It will also help other treatment staff determine whether intensive inpatient treatment, outpatient care, or other chemical dependency services are most appropriate for this individual. The assessment process is also used to identify other needs of the client so that appropriate referrals can be made. The inclusion of family or other individuals in the client's treatment is still another decision to be addressed following assessment. Professionals continue to use their assessment skills throughout the treatment process as the client's needs and circumstances change. In the next chapter we look more closely at the components of the treatment system that can benefit clients and their loved ones during recovery.

ENDNOTES

1. Also see National Institute on Alcohol Abuse and Alcoholism (NIAAA), *Seventh Special Report to the U.S. Congress on Alcohol and Health* (Rockville, MD: U.S. Department of Health and Human Services, 1990), Chapter VIII.

2. See ibid. for a discussion.

3. J. A. Ewing and B. A. Rouse, "Identifying the Hidden Alcoholic," paper presented at the 29th International Congress on Alcohol and Drug Dependence, Sydney, Australia, February 3, 1970, cited in John A. Ewing, "Detecting Alcoholism, The CAGE Questionnaire," Journal of the American Medical Association, Vol. 252 (1984), pp. 1905–1907, Copyright 1984, American Medical Association; and Demmie Mayfield, Gail McLeod, and Patricia Hall, "The CAGE Questionnaire: Validation of a New Alcoholism Screening Instrument," *American Journal of Psychiatry,* Vol. 131 (1974), pp. 1121–1123.

4. Ewing, "Detecting Alcoholism," and Booker Bush, Sheila Shaw, Paul Cleary, Thomas L. Delbanco, and Mark D. Aronson, "Screening for Alcohol Abuse Using the CAGE Questionnaire," *American Journal of Medicine,* Vol. 82 (1987), pp. 231–235.

5. Kathleen Sciacca, Dual diagnosis workshop, Austin, TX: Texas Department of Mental Health and Mental Retardation, May 1990.

6. Melvin L. Selzer, "The Michigan Alcoholism Screening Test: The Quest for a New Diagnostic Instru-

ment," *American Journal of Psychiatry,* Vol. 127 (1971), pp. 1653–1658.

7. See Dan J. Lettieri, Jack E. Nelson, and Mollie A. Sayers (eds.), *Alcoholism Treatment Assessment Research Instruments,* Treatment Handbook Series 2 (Rockville, MD: National Institute on Alcohol Abuse and Alcoholism, 1985), and Harvey A. Skinner, "A Multivariate Evaluation of the MAST," *Journal of Studies on Alcohol,* Vol. 40 (1979), pp. 831–844.

8. Melvin L. Selzer, Amiram Vinokur, and Louis van Rooijen, "A Self-administered Short Version of the Michigan Alcoholism Screening Test (MAST)," *Journal of Studies on Alcohol,* Vol. 36 (1975), pp. 117–126.

9. Alex D. Pokorny, Byron A. Miller, and Howard B. Kaplan, "The Brief MAST: A Shortened Version of the Michigan Alcoholism Screening Test (MAST)," *American Journal of Psychiatry,* Vol. 129, No. 3 (1972), pp. 342–345.

10. Thomas F. Babor, Juan Ramon de la Fuente, John Saunders, and Marcus Grant, *AUDIT, The Alcohol Use Disorders Identification Test, Guidelines for Use in Primary Health Care* (Geneva: World Health Organization, 1992).

11. Harvey A. Skinner, "The Drug Abuse-Screening Test," *Addictive Behaviors,* Vol. 7 (1982), pp. 363–371.

12. Glenn A. Miller, *The Substance Abuse Subtle Screening Inventory Manual* (Bloomington, IN: The SASSI Institute, 1985).

13. Linda A. Morton, *The Risk Prediction Scales* (Indianapolis, IN: Department of Mental Health, Division of Addiction Services, 1978).

14. Craig MacAndrew, "The Differentiation of Male Alcoholic Outpatients from Nonalcoholic Psychiatric Outpatients by Means of the MMPI," *Quarterly Journal of Studies on Alcohol,* Vol. 26 (1965), pp. 238–246.

15. Lettieri et al., *Alcoholism Treatment Assessment Research.*

16. NIAAA, *Seventh Special Report,* Chapter VIII; National Institute on Alcohol Abuse and Alcoholism, "Alcohol Alert," No. 12, PH294, April 1991, and John P. Allen, "The Interrelationship of Alcoholism Assessment and Treatment," *Alcohol Health and Research World,* Vol. 15, No. 3 (1991), pp. 178–185.

17. Also see Deborah S. Hasin, "Diagnostic Interviews for Assessment: Background, Reliability, Validity," *Alcohol Health & Research World,* Vol. 15, No. 4 (1991), pp. 293–302.

18. *BSW/MSW Curriculum Enhancement Project on Alcohol and Other Drugs,* funded by Center for Substance Abuse Prevention, contract #277-91-2006, July 1991– June 1994.

19. Richard K. Fuller, "Can Treatment Outcome Research Rely on Alcoholics' Self-reports?" *Alcohol Health & Research World,* Vol. 12, No. 3 (1988), pp.

180–186; NIAAA, *Seventh Special Report,* Chapter VIII; and Michie Hesselbrock, Thomas F. Babor, Victor Hesselbrock, Roger E. Meyer, and Kathy Workman, "'Never Believe an Alcoholic?' On the Validity of Self-Report Measures of Alcohol Dependence and Related Constructs," *The International Journal of the Addictions,* Vol. 18, No. 5 (1983), pp. 593–609.

20. Fuller, "Can Treatment Outcome Research Rely on Alcoholics' Self-Reports?"

21. Harvey A. Skinner, "Assessing Alcohol Use by Patients in Treatment," in Reginald G. Smart, Howard D. Cappell, Frederick B. Glaser et al. (eds.), *Research Advances in Alcohol and Drug Problems,* Volume 8 (New York: Plenum Press, 1984), pp. 183–207.

22. Hesselbrock et al., "'Never Believe an Alcoholic?'" also see Babor et al., *AUDIT,* p. 8.

23. *Alcohol Health & Research World,* Vol. 15, No. 4 (1991), is devoted to definitions and diagnostic criteria of alcoholism including the history of work in this area.

24. Criteria Committee, National Council on Alcoholism (now National Council on Alcoholism and Drug Dependence), New York, "Criteria for the Diagnosis and Treatment of Alcoholism," *Annals of International Medicine,* Vol. 77 (1972), pp. 249–258, and *American Journal of Psychiatry,* Vol. 129 (1972), pp. 127–135. Copyright 1972, The American Psychiatric Association.

25. Frank A. Seixas, "Criteria for the Diagnosis of Alcoholism," in Nada J. Estes and M. Edith Heinemann, *Alcoholism: Development, Consequences, and Interventions,* 2nd ed. (St. Louis, MO: C. V. Mosby, 1982), pp. 49–67.

26. NIAAA, *Seventh Special Report.*

27. American Psychiatric Association, *Diagnostic and Statistical Manual of Mental Disorders,* 3rd ed., rev. (Washington, DC: The Association, 1987).

28. See Hasin, "Diagnostic Interviews for Assessment," for a review of these and other procedures.

29. NIAAA, *Seventh Special Report,* Chapter VIII.

30. NIAAA, *Seventh Special Report,* p. 186.

31. Criteria Committee, "Criteria for the Diagnosis and Treatment of Alcoholism." Copyright 1972, The American Psychiatric Association.

32. Kenneth Minkoff, "Dual Diagnosis Workshop" (Austin: Texas Department of Mental Health and Mental Retardation, May 1990).

33. A. Thomas McLellan, Lester Luborsky, George E. Woody, and Charles P. O'Brien, "An Improved Diagnostic Evaluation Instrument for Substance Abuse Patients: The Addiction Severity Index," *The Journal of Nervous and Mental Disease,* Vol. 168 (1980), pp. 26–33; and A. Thomas McLellan, Lester Luborsky, John Cacciola, Jeffrey Griffith, Frederick Evans, Harriet L. Barr, and Charles P. O'Brien, "New Data from the Addiction Severity Index: Reliability and Validity in Three Centers," *The Journal of Nervous and Mental Disease,* Vol. 173, No. 7 (1985), pp. 412–423.

34. See, for example, Alfred S. Friedman and Arlene Utada, "A Method for Diagnosing and Planning the Treatment of Adolescent Drug Abusers (The Adolescent Drug Abuse Diagnosis [ADAD] Instrument)," *Journal of Drug Education,* Vol. 19, No. 4 (1989), pp. 285–312.

35. Thomas F. Babor, Zelig Dolinsky, Bruce Rounsaville, and Jerome Jaffe, "Unitary versus Multidimensional Models of Alcoholism Treatment Outcome: An Emperical Study," *Journal of Studies on Alcohol,* Vol. 49, No. 2 (1988), pp. 167–177; also see A. Thomas McLellan, Lester Luborsky, George E. Woody, Charles P. O'Brien, and Ruben Kron, "Are the Addiction-Related Problems of Substance Abusers Really Related?" *The Journal of Nervous and Mental Disease,* Vol. 169 (1981), pp. 232–239.

36. E. Mansell Pattison, Mark B. Sobell, and Linda C. Sobel, *Emerging Concepts of Alcohol Dependence* (New York: Springer, 1977), especially Chapter 1; Babor et al., "Unitary Versus Multidimensional Models of Alcoholism Treatment Outcome"; and Edward J. Callahan and Ella H. Pecsok, "Heroin Addiction," in Dennis M. Donovan and G. Alan Marlatt, *Assessment of Addictive Behavior,* (New York: Guilford Press, 1988), pp. 390–418.

37. NIAAA, *Seventh Special Report,* p. 186.

38. See William R. Miller, "Motivation for Treatment: A Review with Special Emphasis on Alcoholism," *Psychological Bulletin,* Vol. 98, No. 1 (1985), pp. 84–107; also see Dennis M. Donovan, "Assessment of Addictive Behaviors, Implications of an Emerging Biopsychosocial Model," in Donovan and Marlatt, *Assessment of Addictive Behaviors,* especially pp. 26–29.

39. Ralph E. Tarter, Arthur I. Alterman, and Kathleen L. Edwards, "Alcoholic Denial: A Biopsychological Interpretation," *Journal of Studies on Alcohol,* Vol. 45, No. 3 (1984), pp. 214–218.

40. Rickey L. George, *Counseling the Chemically Dependent, Theory and Practice* (Englewood Cliffs, NJ: Prentice Hall, 1990), pp. 36–37.

41. Tarter et al., "Alcoholic Denial," pp. 214–215.

42. Jean Kinney, *Clinical Manual of Substance Abuse* (St. Louis, MO: Mosby Year Book, 1991).

43. Jon R. Weinberg, "Counseling the Person with Alcohol Problems," in Nada J. Estes and M. Edith Heinemann, *Alcoholism: Development, Consequences, and Interventions,* 3rd ed. (St. Louis, MO: C. V. Mosby), p. 367.

44. George, *Counseling the Chemically Dependent.*

45. Kinney, *Clinical Manual of Substance Abuse,* p. 2.

46. Weinberg, "Counseling the Person with Alcohol Problems," and Jean Kinney and Gwen Leaton, *Loosening the Grip: A Handbook of Alcohol Information,* 4th ed. (St. Louis, MO: Mosby Year Book, 1991).

47. Arnold M. Washton, Nannette S. Stone, and Edward C. Hendrickson, "Cocaine Abuse," in Donovan and Marlatt, *Assessment of Addictive Behaviors,* p. 372.

48. Joseph L. Kellerman, "Alcoholism, A Merry-Go-Round Named Denial" (New York: Al-Anon Family Group Headquarters, 1969), copyright © 1969 by Al-Anon Family Group Headquarters, Inc. Reprinted by permission of Al-Anon Family Group Headquarters, Inc.

49. See George, *Counseling the Chemically Dependent,* and Vernon E. Johnson, *I'll Quit Tomorrow* (New York: Harper and Row, 1973).

50. George, *Counseling the Chemically Dependent,* p. 36.

51. See, for example, Carl G. Leukefeld and Frank M. Tims (eds.), *Drug Abuse Treatment in Prisons and Jails,* NIDA Research Monograph 118, DHHS Publication No. (ADM) 92–1884 (Rockville, MD: U.S. Department of Health and Human Services, 1992); Carl G. Leukefeld and Frank M. Tims (eds.), *Compulsory Treatment of Drug Abuse: Research and Clinical Practice,* NIDA Monograph 86, DHHS Publication No. (ADM) 89–1578 (Rockville, MD: U.S. Department of Health and Human Services, 1988); Harrison M. Trice and Janice M. Beyer, "Job Based Alcoholism Programs: Motivating Problem Drinkers to Rehabilitation," in E. Mansell Pattison and Edward Kaufman, *Encyclopedic*

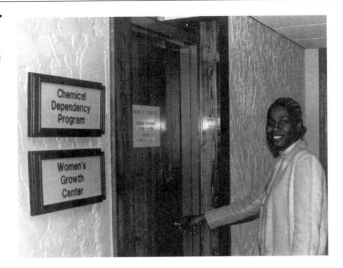

6

Treatment— the system of care

This chapter describes the system of care available to those with substance abuse or dependency problems. Once diagnosis and assessment are complete, the next step in assisting clients is to select the type or types of treatment that will meet their needs as closely as possible. The phrase "matching clients to treatment" has been used to describe this part of the helping process. To do this, it is necessary to be knowledgeable about all the components of the system of care available to those with substance abuse or dependency, as well as self-help groups. While we want to provide clients with the most optimal treatments and services, there are many limitations that can prevent this from happening. Particular services may not be available in a given locale. Clients may not have the financial resources to obtain services. Clients and the professionals they encounter may not be aware of resources. In many cases, clients get whatever is available without much regard for their particular needs and circumstances. This chapter covers each of these topics and discusses the treatment outcome assessment or evaluation literature—just how successful is chemical dependency treatment?

COMPONENTS OF THE TREATMENT SYSTEM

We have conceptualized the treatment system for chemical abuse and dependency clients using a continuum of care[1] comprised of nine major components that are most commonly offered to clients: (1) detoxification, (2) intensive treatment (provided on an inpatient or outpatient basis), (3) residential services, (4) other outpatient services, (5) pharmacotherapy, (6) aftercare, (7) maintenance, (8) education and psychoeducation, and (9) adjunctive services. While some individuals may require all these services, others need particular components. The continuum represents a comprehensive service delivery system designed to meet the biopsychosocial needs of clients. We also briefly consider some nontraditional methods of treatment which have recently been used with substance abusers.

Detoxification Programs

Many chemically dependent individuals begin their treatment with detoxification services. These services are needed when an individual has a physical dependence on alcohol or other drugs that results in withdrawal symptoms when drug use is terminated. While very mild symptoms may not require medical attention, and many individuals withdraw on their own, those with more severe symptoms may require professional care. The individual's medical, psychological, and social situation will help to determine whether detoxification is done on an inpatient basis in a hospital, in another inpatient setting, or on an outpatient basis.

Medical, Hospital Detoxification. Medical, hospital detoxification takes place in a general hospital or in a hospital or hospital unit specifically designed for chemical dependency treatment. Hospitals require that a physician admit the patient before services, including detoxification, can be rendered. Some individuals have a private physician who can admit them to a general hospital for detoxification. If the physician is sensitive to chemical abuse and dependency, the patient may be encouraged to engage in further treatment for addiction.

In many cases, those dependent on alcohol and drugs have medical emergencies (such as acute withdrawal symptoms, overdoses, or accidents) that cause them to use emergency rooms at local hospitals. These are generally public hospitals which must treat individuals whether or not they have a private physician or the means to pay for their treatment. Too often the individual is treated and released without referral to other services. Some general hospitals have medical and counseling staff knowledgeable about the social as well as the medical aspects of chemical dependency. These staff increase the likelihood that patients will be referred to chemical dependency treatment programs following detoxification or emergency treatment.

Hospitals which have chemical dependency treatment units and specialty hospitals devoted to the treatment of chemical dependency often have detoxification programs that also provide assessment for longer-term chemical dependency services as well as referral to other social services. Immediately following detoxification, clients can be transferred to intensive inpatient or outpatient chemical dependency treatment units at these or other appropriate facilities.

State mental hospitals may also have wards for addiction treatment, and some include detoxification services. While the preference today is to treat alcoholics and drug addicts in community facilities, involuntary patients with dual diagnoses of substance abuse and mental disorders are still likely to receive treatment in state hospitals.

Medical, Nonhospital Detoxification. Other types of facilities in which withdrawal is done on an inpatient basis are community-based detoxification centers, sometimes referred to as medical, nonhospital or "social setting" detoxification.[2] Staff include physicians and nurses, as well as other professionals who provide psychosocial services to patients. The bulk of the funding for community detoxification centers comes from the public sector. These detoxification facilities sprang up around the country following passage of the federal Comprehensive Alcohol Abuse and Alcoholism Prevention, Treatment and Rehabilitation Act of 1970 (also known as the

Hughes Act after its primary sponsor, Senator Harold Hughes). The act emphasized improved services for alcoholics and decriminalization of public intoxication by states and communities. In the 1970s these detoxification centers were called "sobering-up stations"[3] for alcoholics and are now formally referred to as "primary care centers." Most patients and staff simply call them "detox." Many centers still focus on treating alcohol withdrawal, but some may assist those withdrawing from other types of drugs.

Prior to the establishment of these community detoxification programs, jailers were the detox agents for many public inebriates sent to the local "drunk tank."[4] Jailers often gave these individuals alcohol to ward off withdrawal symptoms and to help them detoxify. The term "revolving door" described public inebriates whose life was a cycle of drinking, public intoxication arrests, and short jail terms (often thirty, sixty, or ninety days). Community detoxification centers were intended to help alcoholics break this cycle. Community "detox" centers are not always the finest-looking facilities in town, but they are a vast improvement over the treatment alcoholics generally received while incarcerated.

Patients in community detoxification centers may be self-referred; brought by a relative or friend; or referred by community gatekeepers such as the police, probation or parole officers, health department staff, the clergy, or social agency personnel. Admission procedures vary. Some require screening by a physician before the patient is sent to the center. This is done to prevent inappropriate admissions to the detoxification program. For example, an individual may have ingested some alcohol or another drug, but may actually be experiencing a psychiatric emergency requiring care in a mental hospital, or the individual may be having a medical crisis requiring treatment in a general hospital. Some community detox centers permit nurses to admit patients and rely on nurses to provide most of the medical care. There are "standing orders" which provide instructions for how to care for patients with varying degrees of withdrawal symptoms. One or more physicians come daily to examine patients and provide special instructions and are on call for emergencies. Community detoxification centers have been highly successful in helping patients detoxify safely and their costs are substantially less than hospital care.

There are some limitations to the assistance that can be provided in community centers. For instance, patients needing detoxification who also have another medical emergency, such as a laceration or a broken bone, must generally be attended to in a hospital or emergency medical center before admission to the nonhospital detoxification program. Sometimes patients do not arrive at the detoxification center early enough to receive medical attention that will prevent the most serious withdrawal symptoms like repeated seizures or delirium tremens (DTs). Medical management of these problems may be beyond the scope of the community center, and the patient may have to be transferred to a hospital.

Since the primary concern of community detoxification programs is chemical dependency treatment, more is usually done to link the client to additional services needed for recovery than in general hospitals where the staff may be overwhelmed with medical emergencies. While at the detoxification program, patients are often provided alcohol and drug education and receive initial counseling and referral services. They are usually expected to participate in educational group sessions just as soon as they are physically able. Loved ones may also be briefly counseled about the need for additional treatment for themselves as well as the patient. Alcoholics Anonymous or other self-help groups may hold meetings at these "detox" centers in order to introduce patients to these programs and to encourage them to pursue recovery. Members act as role models and give patients hope that recovery is possible.

Patients in community detoxification programs are often of lower socioeconomic status. Many are transients who do not have private health insurance or other coverage.

Services are generally charged on a sliding scale based on the patient's ability to pay, but many bills are never collected. Those with very limited resources may not be charged at all. The number of beds in a center usually varies with the size of the city or community served. Rural areas may have no community detox center, and those needing services may have to travel long distances to obtain care.

The day-to-day operation of community detoxification programs differ. In some centers, patients are required to wear hospital gowns which can deter elopements (patients leaving without the staff's knowledge). In other centers, patients wear their own clothes to help preserve their dignity and to minimize the medical atmosphere which is thought to prolong physical symptoms of withdrawal. Many indigent patients living on the streets own only the clothes on their backs. Detoxification staff provide services as basic as washing their clothing or offering clean, donated clothing.

Admissions procedures generally involve a search or check of the individual's possessions. Occasionally a patient checks in with a weapon (a knife or gun) that must be properly secured or disposed of. More often, the individual arrives with alcohol or other drugs that must be confiscated. Patients are generally allowed visitors, but some friends have been known to smuggle alcohol or drugs to the patient. Like other treatment settings, detoxification centers have developed a culture of their own.

Whether patients are treated in a hospital or in a community detoxification program, medical personnel observe the patient and assess the severity of withdrawal symptoms to determine the medical regimen needed. Often the medical personnel do not know what drugs the patient has ingested, how much has been ingested, and over what period of time. They may be unaware of the withdrawal symptoms the patient has experienced in the past. Therefore, they must proceed cautiously before administering any medications for withdrawal (such as Librium for alcohol withdrawal, phenobarbital for barbituate withdrawal, or methadone for heroin

withdrawal).[5] Treatment, including the type and amount of medication, if any, to be administered, will depend on whether the patient's withdrawal symptoms are mild, moderate, or severe. Patients often ask for or demand additional medication to further mitigate physical and psychological discomfort. This is not surprising given that this is how patients have medicated themselves before entering the detoxification program. When medical staff feel that additional medication is not warranted, they generally respond with verbal encouragement and support that the symptoms will pass.

The stay in detoxification programs is generally brief but depends on the drugs on which the patient is dependent.[6] For example, the acute problems associated with alcohol withdrawal are likely to pass in a few days, while the period for barbituate withdrawal is longer. Sedative-hypnotic withdrawal presents particular dangers due to the possibility of seizures or DTs. Withdrawal from more than one drug further complicates matters. Patients are detoxified from each drug sequentially, beginning with the drug that produces the most serious withdrawal symptoms. The type of drugs to which the patient is addicted and the severity of symptoms and other complicating medical conditions will also determine the setting in which withdrawal is accomplished.

Since there is usually a high demand for the beds in community detoxification programs, patients are typically not encouraged to stay longer than necessary. As soon as the danger of medical problems has passed, staff may be pressed to refer the patient elsewhere, such as to an inpatient or outpatient treatment center, a halfway house, or the Salvation Army or a mission. Some alcoholics and addicts are reluctant to leave. For them the detox center is a shelter or temporary home because they have no other residence.

Other individuals do not wish to be treated in the detoxification center at all and may leave or try to leave before the dangers of withdrawal have passed. While some are referred by the courts or are under pressure from authorities (such as the probation department or child welfare agency) to enter the center, patients are generally considered voluntary admissions. Voluntary patients cannot be required to stay, although local law enforcement may be called if a patient considered dangerous to himself or herself or to others attempts to leave. Some patients are committed involuntarily under civil procedures. Should these patients elope or otherwise leave against medical advice or without permission, staff may be required to notify the appropriate authorities.

Outpatient Detoxification. When withdrawal problems can be medically managed without the need for inpatient treatment, outpatient (ambulatory) care may be an economical alternative.[7] The use of outpatient detoxification is contingent on the patient's social and psychological state. Suicidal or severely depressed patients are obviously not good risks for outpatient detoxification, and outpatient detoxification is not a viable option if the patient lacks the ability or supervision to comply with the treatment protocol. Available emotional supports should also be considered. While there are advantages of inpatient detoxification, such as continual medical su-

pervision, a study by Hayashida and his colleagues indicates that patients requesting detoxification for mild-to-moderate alcohol withdrawal syndrome can be successfully detoxified on an outpatient basis if they are screened to ensure that they do not have complicating medical and psychiatric problems.[8] These findings are particularly interesting given the low socioeconomic status of the alcoholic patients who participated in the study and their lack of social supports, including some with unstable living arrangements. Gerstein and Harwood also recommend consideration of alternatives to inpatient hospital detoxification for clients addicted to other types of drugs, and they provide guidelines for making referrals to these settings.[9]

Finally, medical treatment is not always needed to terminate drug use. Some users experience physical discomfort mild enough that medical attention is not required. Others use drugs such as some hallucinogens with no reported physical dependence.[10] These individuals may, however, need emotional support in their efforts to become drug free. Chemical dependency programs offer a number of services to assist in this process such as outpatient services (described shortly), drop

A Community Detoxification Center Patient*

Ed Welch, a white male in his late forties, was well known at the community detox center. He had been admitted about six times in the last year as a result of his dependence on alcohol. Ed's most prominent withdrawal symptom was severe tremors. His medical history also included several bouts of severe gastritis. The medical staff was always able to manage his care without referral to the hospital, and it was amazing how much better he looked after a five-day stay. Ed was a cooperative and quiet patient. He worked as a welder and his boss would bring him in when he got drunk. As soon as he was sober, Ed's boss would put him back to work. Ed was divorced, never saw his grown children,

and didn't seem to have any friends. He had no trouble downing two fifths of whiskey when he went on a binge. The detox staff was never able to get Ed to enter the halfway house or to attend outpatient groups. It seemed that the thing Ed liked least was talking. He came to AA sometimes but never said much. Ed did get an AA sponsor, a member with a history a lot like Ed's. Ed often managed to put a few months of sobriety together, but his binges, although less frequent, continued, and he returned to the detox center intermittently.

*All clients described in this chapter are fictitious or represent composite cases.

in centers, and twenty-four-hour crisis lines, which increase the availability of emotional support. Termination of drug use is the first and usually the briefest step in the recovery process.[11] While some individuals recover spontaneously on their own, many require professional assistance. Following detoxification services, they are likely to need additional components on the continuum of care.

Intensive Treatment

The next component on the continuum of care, intensive treatment, has burgeoned since the 1970s. Intensive treatment used to be thought of synonymously with inpatient care, but it is now also offered on an outpatient basis.

Intensive Inpatient Care. Intensive inpatient treatment programs originated primarily to assist alcoholics but now also include those with other drug problems. They often last for twenty-eight or thirty days, which coincidentally is the maximum period that many health insurers will pay for this care. Some programs are longer, such as six weeks, or individual patients' stays may be longer depending on their treatment needs and the type and severity of their addiction (but major insurers have recently considered reducing coverage to fewer days). Intensive inpatient treatment may be the logical choice when an individual is unlikely to remain alcohol or drug free in his or her current situation due to psychological, family, or environmental stressors. For example, the individual may have suicidal ideation or may be living on the streets or with a nonsupportive partner.

Intensive inpatient treatment programs may be located in a special unit of a general hospital, or they may be offered by a specialty hospital or other inpatient facility devoted to mental health or chemical dependency treatment. As noted earlier, these programs often have their own detoxification component, and patients can be easily transferred to intensive treatment once the danger of severe withdrawal symptoms has passed.

Many intensive inpatient treatment facilities are privately owned and intended to earn profit; others are private, not-for-profit or public facilities. The number of these programs, especially among the private sector, has increased tremendously in the last two decades. Several factors are responsible for this growth. First is public recognition that chemical dependency can be treated successfully. Second, health insurers have succumbed to pressure to cover substance abuse treatment, and third, almost everyone now recognizes the importance of this treatment in reducing overall health care costs. Inpatient care is, however, quite expensive. A fee of $10,000 or more is common for a four-week inpatient stay in a private treatment program. Occasionally, private facilities offer "scholarships" or fee waivers as a community service to clients who do not have health care coverage and cannot afford to pay themselves. Private, not-for-profit or public programs often use a sliding scale to assess patient fees. Clients without financial resources may not be charged, but there is often more demand than there are treatment slots available. While it is usually possible to get immediate admission to a for-profit program, not-for-profit and public programs are likely to have a waiting list. Maintaining sobriety while awaiting admission to a public or not-for-profit program can be a challenge for clients. As the HIV epidemic has made Americans ever more aware of the consequences of drug abuse, more individuals and organizations are calling for chemical dependency treatment on demand.[12]

Although there is some variation in the treatment services offered in these inpatient programs, many are similar to what is called the "Minnesota model." This model, developed by alcoholism treatment centers in Minnesota during the 1940s and 1950s, "is an abstinence oriented, comprehensive, multiprofessional approach to the treatment of the addictions, based upon the principles of Alcoholics Anonymous."[13] The services most commonly offered by these programs are education about chemical dependency, group and individual counseling or therapy, and an introduction to self-help programs. Other services promote general health and well-being. Examples are lectures on adopting good nutritional habits and individual consultation on developing daily menus, exercise periods, plans for incorporating a fitness program into one's daily routine, and social and recreational alternatives to drug use. Improving communication skills, practicing assertiveness, and learning to reduce stress may also be introduced. There are, of course, limits on what can be accomplished in a four- to six-week period. Many clients are only beginning to come to grips with their substance abuse or dependency problem in this early stage of recovery. Only so much information can be processed and retained in a short period of time, especially by those with long-term dependency who are newly detoxified.

Programs vary in the methods used to involve loved ones and the extent of these services. Education is one means, beginning with basic information on alcohol and drugs and definitions of addiction. Chemical dependency as a "family disease" and "codependency" generally receive attention (see Chapter 10). Loved ones may also be introduced to self-help groups such as Al-Anon and Naranon. Therapy sessions may be scheduled for individual families or families may meet in groups. Some family groups are just for spouses or other adult partners; others include children, parents, and others important in the client's life. In some programs, family members, particularly spouses or other adult partners, spend a week or so in residence at the program.

Intensive Outpatient Care. During the last decade, reliance on intensive inpatient treatment for so many chemically dependent individuals has been questioned. Most of the alcoholism research literature indicates no difference in the effectiveness of inpatient versus outpatient treatment,[14] and inpatient treatment is considerably more expensive than outpatient treatment. Professionals directed chemically dependent individuals to

inpatient treatment because they assumed it was the best alternative or due to the lack of other treatment alternatives. In addition, insurance policies often limited coverage to inpatient care. Patients were told that inpatient treatment came first, regardless of their personal circumstances. But insistence on inpatient treatment may have alienated potential clients concerned about disruption to their work and family life. Single parents, those with limited financial resources, and those concerned about explaining a long job absence may see outpatient care as their only viable treatment option. Intensive outpatient treatment is becoming the preferred service for those who can continue to function at home and in the community. While some clients need relief from the stresses of their current environment to benefit from treatment, and others may have psychiatric disorders that contraindicate outpatient treatment, matching clients to the least restrictive treatment suitable to their needs is an appropriate goal of treatment planning.

The services provided in intensive outpatient treatment are the same as those provided during inpatient treatment, but clients work at their regular jobs or care for their families during the day and usually attend treatment in the evenings or on weekends. A typical program involves participation four nights a week over a ten- to twelve-week period. A variation on this form of outpatient treatment is known as day treatment or partial hospitalization. Participation in a day treatment program often lasts longer than other forms of intensive treatment and is used by clients who are not yet able to function in the community by holding regular jobs or caring for their families. Some of these clients have a combination of psychiatric disorders and substance abuse disorders. Others have substantial physical impairment that may require a longer period of rehabilitation, or they may have substantial cognitive impairments from substance abuse and need additional time in learning communication, vocational, or other skills before a complete return to the community can be made. Some clients attend day treatment following intensive inpatient chemical dependency treatment or inpatient psychiatric treatment.

Residential Programs

Also on the continuum are a number of residential services including halfway houses, therapeutic communities, domiciliaries, and missions. Each serves a different purpose.

Halfway Houses. Halfway houses (sometimes called rehabilitation facilities) are another important part of the continuum of care for many alcoholics and addicts. According to Rubington, "The halfway house may be defined as a transitional place of indefinite residence of a community of persons who live together under the rule and discipline of abstinence from alcohol and other drugs."[15] Halfway houses may be publicly subsidized, privately owned, or church sponsored.[16]

Many halfway house residents have lost their jobs and financial assets, are estranged from family and friends, or lack social and independent living skills. Most halfway houses serve clients who enter more or less voluntarily, but some are solely for those who are mandated to become residents by the criminal justice system.

The term halfway house refers to half way back into the community. Residents sometimes used to progress from a quarterway house to a halfway house and later to a three-quarter-way house where they were considered to be close to a complete return to the community. The term halfway house is primarily used today. As residents move through recovery, they usually earn greater amounts of responsibility and more privileges in the halfway house, similar to the progression from quarterway to three-quarter-way houses.

The structure of halfway houses and the services they offer vary considerably.[17] Some are highly structured with a specific treatment regimen that consumes almost all the residents' time. Others are loosely structured and are more like boarding homes with some supervision or requirements to get a job and attend self-help meetings. The structure of

many halfway houses falls in between these two extremes and incorporates treatment and self-help groups along with expectations that residents seek and maintain employment.

The size of the staff and their credentials vary. Many halfway houses are supervised twenty-four hours a day by managers who are themselves "recovered" or "recovering" alcoholics or addicts.[18] Some managers have formal education in the helping professions or in chemical dependency treatment, but this may not be a job requirement. Other halfway house staff (therapists, vocational counselors, etc.) come from a variety of educational backgrounds. Halfway house residents may have a case manager or primary therapist who coordinates the various services they need. Other staff may specialize in group treatment or in vocational services.

Some programs require clients to have at least weekly individual counseling or therapy sessions and to participate in group treatment. Seeing that clients get a job is often a priority in halfway house programs. Other services may include education about independent living skills and communication as well as nutritional counseling, exercise, and instruction on maintaining good health and mental health. Participation in recreational activities and developing social skills is also encouraged because of the desocialization of clients whose problems are severe enough to warrant referral to a halfway house. Attendance at self-help meetings, often several times a week, is a frequent requirement. One of the local AA or NA groups may meet at the halfway house, and residents also attend meetings in the community. Halfway house staff may work closely with staff of other community agencies to ensure that their clients receive other services such as vocational rehabilitation and health care. Clients may also be assisted in applying for food stamps which can help the halfway house defray food costs. Residence in a halfway house provides an opportunity to address many of the client's needs.

Residents may be admitted to the halfway house on the recommendation of an individual staff member, or there may be a client "staffing." A staffing generally involves the client meeting with a small group of staff members who ask the client questions about his or her motivation to enter the halfway house.[19] The staff members may then vote or come to a consensus on whether or not to admit the individual. To gain entrance, clients must usually agree to participate in all halfway house activities and to abide by other rules, which include no drinking of alcohol and no use of drugs except as approved by medical staff. Residents are generally not allowed to keep their own medications but are given access to them by staff. Other rules are no violence and no sex in the house. Residents are usually obligated to report violations of the rules by other residents.[20] They are also expected to keep their personal living area clean, and general household chores such as cooking and cleaning are shared or rotated. Visitors and personal telephone calls may be restricted to specified times. Passes or leaves of absence are generally limited at first but increase as the client makes progress. Policies regarding readmission after rule violations, especially drinking or drug use, differ among programs with some more lenient than others.

Some programs have resident or community governments. Residents take turns acting as the chairperson and weekly meetings are held to discuss and solve problems in the house such as individuals not doing their chores, knowledge or suspicion of individuals drinking or using drugs, interpersonal conflicts between residents, and so forth. Resident governments are established to help clients learn rational means of problem solving. Staff may participate in all or a portion of these meetings to work out problems, especially conflicts between residents and staff. This gives staff an opportunity to model problem-solving and discussion skills for residents.

The length of time clients may remain in halfway house programs varies. Some have limits of thirty, sixty, or ninety days or more. Houses with shorter lengths of stay help clients get back on their feet but are concerned that they not foster dependency, or the demand for their services is so high that they cannot accommodate clients longer. In other houses the stay is open ended and is determined by client needs. The philosophy of open-ended programs is that residents need a period of treatment commensurate with the length and severity of their chemical dependency before they can achieve sufficient stability to live independently.

Clients are generally charged something for their room, board, and treatment while at the halfway house. Fees are usually quite modest compared to what it would cost to receive treatment and live elsewhere. In addition to the need to defray program costs, reasons commonly used to support charging halfway house residents are (1) it helps them learn or relearn to accept responsibility, (2) services that involve a fee are more highly valued than those that are free, and (3) those that are not serious about treatment will be deterred from entering the program. Some clients are employed and pay the fees themselves. Others may be sponsored for a period by treatment or rehabilitation agencies such as a state's vocational rehabilitation program. Occasionally, a client receives some type of public assistance or disability payment.[21]

Some halfway houses serve men only or women only, but others serve both. While still very few in number, some innovative programs allow women to bring their children; these programs generally offer the services found in most halfway house programs while also helping mothers improve their parenting skills. Services are also offered to the children to foster their development and to help them understand chemical dependency.

Therapeutic Communities. While halfway houses were originally designed to serve alcoholics, therapeutic communities (TCs) originated to treat addicts who abused heroin or other illegal drugs. TC staff are often recovered or recovering addicts. The first therapeutic community for drug addicts, Synanon, began in 1958. It was based on a combination of ideas from Alcoholics Anonymous and therapeutic communities for those with psychiatric problems.[22] Daytop Village and Odyssey House are also well known TCs. TC

A Halfway House Resident

Maxine Jones, known as Maxey by the residents at the halfway house, was 35 when some friends first brought her to the detox center. She was known for being loud and violent when drinking and using drugs, but outgoing and friendly when sober. A counselor encouraged her to get into the halfway house and to join a treatment group for women with alcohol and drug problems. Maxey stayed at the house for 14 months, celebrating her first AA birthday there. During her stay in the halfway house, Maxey got a job in a factory with the help of the vocational rehabilitation counselor. She worked on a regular basis and did her share around the halfway house. She faithfully attended all treatment sessions and more than the required number of AA and NA meetings. Maxey was one of the few women residents at the

halfway house, but she got along well with the men and often planned picnics and social events for the residents. Maxey seemed to have gotten what she could from the halfway house program, and she and her counselor decided it was time to live on her own. Maxey took a small apartment and kept going to AA and NA meetings, but after two or three months, no one saw Maxey. Her counselor found her drunk, but Maxey said she was too embarrassed to go back to detox. Two weeks later, after an altercation with the manager at her apartment complex, Maxey was back in detox. She decided to try living on her own again and attend outpatient treatment rather than return to the halfway house, but occasionally she stopped by to visit her friends there.

residents often began drug involvement at a young age and have not mastered the developmental tasks of adulthood.[23] As a result, TCs are likely to focus on habilitation as well as rehabilitation of residents.[24] These residential programs may be thought of as a combination of intensive treatment and residential care. The recommended stay in these programs is often longer than in halfway houses, and a year or even two is not considered atypical if the resident "works" the entire program.

Therapeutic communities rely on group process and peer pressure to get residents to address their problematic behaviors. Reality therapy[25] is often the underlying treatment philosophy. Confrontation is used to break the denial that is generally a part of chemical dependency. Many professionals are initially quite surprised at the intensity of the confrontation in individual and group counseling sessions, but both TCs and other chemical dependency treatment programs seem to have toned this down in recent years. The dropout rate from TCs is high, due perhaps to the rigors of these programs.

While many halfway houses expect clients to obtain jobs quickly, therapeutic communities tend to believe a longer period of treatment is needed before the resident is capable of holding an outside job and has earned the privilege of working outside the facility. To teach employment behaviors and skills, some TCs operate cottage industries where residents work in enterprises such as a greenhouse, duplication service, or other small business.

Clients start with few privileges and earn additional privileges as they progress in the TC program. New residents are often assigned the most menial house chores. Progress is measured by abstinence from drugs, active participation in treatment, and adherence to program rules. Urine "drops" may be used to monitor abstinence. Moving up to the next level in the program may be based on a vote of residents and staff. Residents may graduate to become staff of therapeutic communities. Gerstein and Harwood describe today's therapeutic communities as "a remarkable merger of the therapeutic optimism of psychiatric

A Therapeutic Community Resident

Susan Murphy was 18 when she entered a therapeutic community. She was skinny with long, scraggly black hair and a tatoo of a former boyfriend's name on her left hand. She had run away from home at least a dozen times during her teen years, because she and her mother and stepfather never got along. Susan spent many nights on the streets or in runaway shelters. She was a high school dropout and had never had a job for more than a few weeks. Susan was convinced by staff of a criminal justice diversion program to enter the TC after she was picked up on a vagrancy charge and her rap sheet indicated several other infrac-

tions. Susan had used many types of drugs. She was particularly fond of amphetamines but did not want to start mainlining drugs like her current boyfriend. Susan hated the TC at first and found it difficult to take the strong feedback from staff and other residents about her attitude of blaming others for her problems. She almost left several times but she did manage to remain for a year and earned a GED along with twelve months of "clean" time. Susan is now a graduate of the TC and is in vocational school learning computer technology, attends Narcotics Anonymous regularly, and likes to sponsor new members.

medicine and the disciplinary moralism of the criminal perspective."[26]

Domiciliaries. Domiciliaries, another type of residential facility, assist those with severe physical or mental debilitation from alcohol or other drug dependency. Some of these individuals need an extensive period of recovery before they move to a halfway house. For others, the domiciliary will become their long-term home, because their impairments make a successful return to independent living unlikely. Some domiciliaries are referred to as "farms," because they are on the outskirts of town on large pieces of property with gardening sometimes a primary activity of residents.

Domiciliaries usually have twenty-four-hour staff supervision. Residents are given responsibilities or participate in activities commensurate with their abilities. The care provided may be largely custodial but there may be some group treatment, especially to promote socialization. Domiciliaries are generally more lenient in reaccepting a client following alcohol or drug use than halfway houses or therapeutic communities. The Veterans Administration operates a number of domiciliaries that serve those severely debilitated by alcoholism, drug dependency, or other physical and mental disorders. There

are also other publicly supported domiciliary-type facilities in a number of communities. Residents whose condition deteriorates to the point that they are nonambulatory or in need of psychiatric or nursing home care are referred to appropriate facilities.

Missions. For years, facilities like the Salvation Army[27] and rescue missions have assisted those who are homeless, transient, or living on the streets due to a variety of problems such as substance abuse, mental illness, or the inability to secure a job. Some of these facilities are better classified as halfway houses, because residents spend several months at them receiving treatment and working (perhaps in one of their thrift shops). A religious program is generally a component of services.[28] In most cases, the stay at these facilities is brief (a night or two). In street lingo, brief stays are often referred to as "three hots and a cot" (three meals and a bed in which to sleep). Those staying overnight receive an evening meal and may be expected to attend a prayer or spiritual service designed to motivate them to find a new way of life. Following an early breakfast (sometimes toast, coffee, and grits), they are generally expected to leave the premises, and those planning to spend another night usually are not permitted to return until evening check in time.

They may be assisted in finding a few hours or a day's work. The cost of staying overnight might be a few dollars. Some facilities do not charge, or they may give a free night once every month or two.

The staff of public and not-for-profit substance abuse programs frequently refer individuals with alcohol and drug abuse problems who have no where else to go or who are not interested in treatment to these facilities. Some substance abuse programs have funds that can be used to pay for a night or two at a mission or shelter for alcoholics and addicts while they try to find a job, make arrangements to get a bus ticket home, or await admission to an inpatient chemical dependency treatment center or a halfway house.

Chemically dependent individuals are also making use of community shelters for homeless persons which have increased in number in recent years. Missions and shelters generally do not admit those who are intoxicated or who are experiencing serious withdrawal symptoms. Some missions have been criticized for their moralistic approach to substance abuse and for their exploitation of clients' labor; however, they have historically provided a safe haven for those who would otherwise be sleeping on the streets or in the woods.[29]

Outpatient Services

Outpatient services also occupy a place in the system of care. Some clients use outpatient services following detoxification, intensive treatment, or halfway house services. Those with early stage or less severe problems may begin treatment with this component. For example, a substance abuser experiencing early signs of family or other social problems, who is not physically addicted, and who is employed, may be well served by an outpatient program.

Outpatient services are usually some type of counseling—individual, couple, family, or group. The theoretical orientations and treatment philosophies of those who provide these services vary considerably. The frequency with which clients receive outpatient services also varies. Sessions are often weekly but may be more or less frequent.

The content of outpatient treatment sessions is quite similar to topics initiated in intensive and residential treatment. Examples are how to remain alcohol and drug free, dealing with depression or loneliness, fostering positive social relationships, and increasing self-esteem. Other services may involve teaching relaxation or stress reduction techniques. Obstacles to recovery, such as a previous history of physical or sexual abuse, may also be addressed. Since no single human service professional is equipped to treat all the problems clients may present, referral to other professionals may be needed. For example, clients with sexual dysfunctions may need the assistance of a certified sex therapist.

Today, outpatient chemical dependency services are offered by many types of providers under various auspices. Service providers include psychiatrists, psychologists, nurses, social workers, marriage and family therapists, and various types of counselors (such as rehabilitation and pastoral), as well as chemical dependency counselors (some who have degrees in the helping professions and others who do not). State laws governing these groups vary, but increasingly human service professionals, including those who treat alcoholics and addicts, are required by state law or by community norms to be licensed or certified. State laws and insurance companies determine which professionals can collect third-party payments for their services.

Outpatient services are provided under public; private, not-for-profit; private, for-profit; and church auspices. Some outpatient programs are attached to hospitals; others are part of community mental health centers or community alcohol and drug treatment centers. Practitioners in the chemical dependency field may also offer their services in private, individual or group practices. Health maintenance organizations (HMOs) and employee assistance programs (EAPs) may offer outpatient chemical dependency services directly using their own personnel or through arrangements with other agencies and individuals who provide chemical dependency services.

Like other services, outpatient chemical dependency treatment may be covered under the individual's health care plan, or the client may pay for it directly. In public or not-for-profit programs, a sliding scale may be used. Private practitioners usually charge fees based on local market rates; some use sliding scales or provide some treatment on a pro bono basis as a service to the community.

Individual Counseling. Individual outpatient counseling involves only the client and the human service professional. The preference in chemical dependence treatment has been for group therapy with individual treatment used as an adjunct[30] or to treat specific problems such as sexual dysfunction or other problems not necessarily appropriate for the chemical dependency treatment group. Chemical dependency treatment providers may see clients on an individual basis initially while encouraging them to consider group treatment and self-help groups. While group treatment may be recommended, clients may opt for individual treatment, because they feel individual treatment will be more effective or because group participation seems too threatening or will not protect their anonymity.

Group Treatment. Group treatment is frequently offered as the "treatment of choice" to those with alcohol and drug problems on the grounds that they can benefit from the experiences of and interactions with others who are facing the challenges of maintaining sobriety.[31] Levine and Gallogly write that:

Groups for alcoholics can serve many purposes:

1. help reduce the denial and facilitate the acceptance of alcoholism
2. increase the motivation for sobriety and other changes
3. treat the emotional conditions that often accompany drinking (i.e., anxiety, depression, hostility)
4. increase the capacity to recognize, anticipate, and cope with situations that may precipitate drinking behavior
5. meet the intense needs of alcoholics for social acceptance and support.[32]

Groups are almost always a component of intensive chemical dependency treatment programs and are also offered by other outpatient programs.

The composition of outpatient chemical dependency treatment groups varies. Groups usually have several members, but more than twelve is generally considered too large to allow everyone to participate actively. Participation may be limited to clients who share certain characteristics. For example, the groups may be composed of only male or only female members, gay men or lesbians, those in particular age groups, or white-collar or blue-collar workers. Larger communities or programs which serve many clients tend to offer more groups. There are usually one or two group leaders. Co-ed groups may have male and female leaders, while groups for men or women generally have a leader or leaders of the same gender.

Groups may be closed or open ended. In a closed-ended group, members usually start together and contract for a certain number of sessions. At the end of the sessions, members may be asked if they wish to contract for additional group sessions. An advantage of the closed-ended group is continuity of membership, but if there are many dropouts, those remaining may become discouraged, and the number may dwindle below what is necessary to carry on effective group sessions. In an open-ended group, members may join at different times, and there may be no commitment to attend a specific number of sessions. An advantage of the open-ended group is that more experienced members, especially those who are making progress or who have learned from mistakes, share their experiences with other members; however, disruptions may occur as members leave and new members are introduced to the group and the group process.

The amount of structure imposed by group leaders varies. In more structured groups, the leader may present topics for discussion and use preplanned exercises, while in less structured groups, the leader may ask clients to present topics for discussion that are of current concern to them. A great deal has been written on group treatment, some of it specific to substance abusers.[33]

Group treatment is also provided to the loved ones of chemically dependent individuals. Some groups include all types of family members—spouses or other partners, children, parents, and siblings. Membership in other groups may be limited to spouses or other partners, to young children, or to adult children (see Chapters 10 and 12). The goals of these groups are usually to help family members understand the dynamics of chemical dependency, relieve guilt, build self-esteem, avoid enabling, and focus on becoming healthier and happier individuals.

Conjoint Therapy. Conjoint therapy, often called marital therapy, is another outpatient service. (The term "marital" is outmoded for many clients given the range of relationships that people may experience.) While couples may participate in conjoint treatment at any time, it is often offered after the client receives initial inpatient or outpatient services for chemical abuse or dependency and has maintained some sobriety. Before participating in conjoint treatment, the nonchemi-

cally dependent partner may also have attended educational sessions or group therapy. Initially, conjoint therapy may help the couple explore how chemical dependency or other problems have affected their relationship. Ventilation of hurt and anger may be important at this stage. The topics may then progress to improving communications, working out problems, and reacting to lapses or relapses should they occur. Conjoint treatment may lead to a strengthening of the relationship, but it may become a forum for determining that the relationship was never satisfactory or that it is not repairable. Some practitioners treating chemically dependent clients and their partners are marriage and family therapists or are otherwise qualified to treat couples and families. Others are not equipped to do extensive work in these areas and refer clients when these services are needed.

Family Therapy. Still another type of outpatient service is family therapy (discussed more fully in Chapter 10). Similar to conjoint therapy, family therapy focuses on the effects of chemical dependency on the particular

An Outpatient Client

Mitch Wheeler, 26, was friendly and cheerful when sober, someone who was always described as a nice guy, but his wife would not put up with his drug use and left him. To make matters worse, he flunked out of college after changing majors three times and got a DWI. He was out of work and had little choice but to move in with his mother and to try to stay away from alcohol, marijuana (his favorite drug), and whatever else came his way. Mitch got a part-time job with a moving company and also enrolled part-time at the junior college. He joined an outpatient group for young people at the community alcohol and drug treatment program after deciding it was time to "grow up." Mitch enjoyed attending the group. The discussions of topics among his peers always seemed rel-

evant to him, and the socialization before and after group helped assuage his loneliness. Mitch felt he really fit in with the group members, unlike those at school and at work who had no idea what it was like to have a drug problem. He also attended AA and NA a few times a week. Mitch would stay off alcohol and drugs for a few months and then get high. After his mother became tired of his behavior and threw him out, Mitch got a girlfriend he met at NA to let him move in with her. With her urging, he went back to his therapy group and to AA and NA. Mitch eventually celebrated a year of sobriety. Friends have told him he would make a good counselor. After giving it serious consideration, he is now working on his certification in chemical dependency treatment.

family, reducing family dysfunction and improving family communications and relationships. Family members may have participated in educational sessions or in family groups before beginning family therapy. All members of the current nuclear family are usually invited to participate, although some may not agree to do so. Members of the extended family such as the parents of an adult chemical abuser may be included, especially if they are directly enabling the client. The client and extended family members may also be seen together if the client is working to resolve family-of-origin issues.

Pharmacotherapy

Several types of drugs are used to assist alcoholics and addicts in recovery following detoxification. Each type serves a different purpose. While no drug is a magic elixir, several can apparently be helpful in maintaining abstinence under appropriate conditions.

Antabuse. Disulfiram, best known by the trade name Antabuse, is used in the treatment of alcoholics; it is referred to as a deterrent drug.[34] Antabuse does not reduce the desire to drink. Instead, it is described as "buying time" or as an "insurance policy," because those taking it know they will become violently ill if they drink. The value of Antabuse is thought to be its ability to deter impulsive drinking. It is recommended as an adjunct to other treatment services, not as a sole treatment.

Antabuse interferes with the normal metabolism of alcohol, resulting in a serious physical reaction if even a small amount of alcohol is ingested. Those taking it must avoid all alcohol, including that found in prescription and over-the-counter drugs and other products that may contain alcohol such as mouth wash and skin lotions. Paraldehyde, which is sometimes used to prevent DTs in alcoholics, will also cause a severe reaction. Inhaling alcohol fumes in closed quarters might also result in some reaction. Antabuse-ethanol reactions may involve a variety of symptoms, including flushing, increased

pulse and respiration, sweating, weakness, decreased blood pressure, a severe headache, vomiting, and confusion. Reactions may also result in heart failure and other life-threatening problems, and some deaths have been reported. A patient should be completely detoxified from alcohol before beginning Antabuse treatment.

Antabuse is contraindicated for those with certain conditions such as serious mental illness, heart disease, diabetes, epilepsy, or pregnancy. Patients must fully understand the consequences of using alcohol while taking Antabuse before beginning this treatment. Antabuse should not be given to those who are intellectually unable to appreciate these consequences. Patients should also be aware that if they do decide to return to drinking, several days must elapse following the last dose of Antabuse to avoid a reaction. Since serious Antabuse-ethanol reactions can occur, it also seems that patients should be screened for their desire to take this drug.

Side effects of Antabuse (not related to the ingestion of alcohol) may include skin eruptions or rashes, drowsiness, headaches, and reduced sexual performance. These symptoms often abate following an initial period of adjustment to the drug, or the dosage may be reduced to prevent these symptoms. More severe effects such as neuritis and psychoses may require discontinuing the drug. Patients usually take Antabuse once a day. Antabuse was originally given in larger doses than are prescribed today (disulfiram skin implants were used in some countries). Side effects and complications from reactions were more severe. It was determined that lower doses were safer and effective.

Although this description of Antabuse may sound rather frightening, many clients have used it, apparently with success.[35] Patients generally carry a card with them indicating that they are taking Antabuse. Like a medical alert bracelet, this card helps medical personnel respond if a reaction or other emergency occurs. Some patients do attempt drinking while on Antabuse and usually end up in a hospital emergency room. Ewing recommends the use of contracts with patients

A Client Taking Antabuse

James Burrey was told by his probation officer to see an alcoholism counselor after he appeared in court one day on a DWI probation violation. His probation officer also required that he take Antabuse and get treatment. James was a 45-year-old chronic alcoholic. He had a fifth grade education and limited social skills and worked as a laborer. The day of their first meeting, James was quite rude to the alcoholism counselor, but he had little choice except to do what his probation officer said, and the counselor had little choice but to try to help him. James began taking Antabuse, stayed in the halfway house for a short time, came to group treatment, and gained his first sober time. He did quite well. James remarked that he never knew he could feel so good until he started taking Antabuse. Without Antabuse, he might never have gotten enough sober time together to know this feeling, and his counselor may never have realized James's many positive qualities.

taking Antabuse, including having a family member or friend supervise the daily dose.[36]

Originally, it was hoped that Antabuse would provide an answer for many alcoholics. The criminal justice was enthusiastic about its use and ordered many of its alcoholic charges to take the drug if it was not contraindicated by other medical conditions. Patients reported to the probation and parole office or an alcoholism treatment program to take their Antabuse each day or every other day under supervision. Those who did not wish to comply learned that the drug (which looks like a large aspirin) could be slipped under the tongue and disposed of upon leaving. Those administering Antabuse quickly became aware of this practice and began crushing the pill and mixing it with juice. The patient drank the mixture and then talked with the individual administering it to ensure compliance. Reports of patients ingesting large amounts of ascorbic acid before taking Antabuse to limit reactions[37] or resorting to self-induced vomiting soon followed. Drugs similar to Antabuse have been used in countries other than the United States. Like other forms of treatment, Antabuse may work best for those who wish to use it.

Methadone. Methadone is a synthetic narcotic drug. In addition to its use in narcotic detoxification, it is also used in longer-term chemical dependency treatment as a substitute for the narcotic analgesic drugs. It is best known for its use with heroin addicts beginning in the 1960s. Methadone appears to deter addicts from pursuing illegal activities to support their drug habit, but its use remains controversial. Detractors argue that it replaces one drug with another rather than promoting a treatment goal of abstinence. Witters and Venturelli summarize the advantages and disadvantages of methadone maintenance:

The advantages of methadone over other forms of maintenance therapy are (1) the drug can be administered orally; (2) it has a duration of action in the body of 24 to 36 hours, compared to heroin's action of four to eight hours; (3) no serious side effects are seen at maintenance doses; (4) at sufficient dose levels methadone will almost completely block the effects of heroin; and (5) when taken orally, it does not produce euphoric effects of its own. Disadvantages of methadone maintenance include (1) the person taking it will have a drug dependence on methadone; and (2) it will not prevent the addict from taking other drugs that may interfere with treatment and rehabilitation.[38]

Controversies persist about the safety and health problems of methadone maintenance and how frequently users sell it to obtain illicit drugs. Gerstein and Harwood provide an extensive discussion of these controversies, including the issue of methadone's use as a social control mechanism versus its therapeutic value to the individual client.[39] Some communities do not have methadone maintenance clinics because they do not wish to attract heroin users to their area.

Methadone maintenance is intended only for those with a severe narcotic dependence. While some use methadone for a short period before completely withdrawing, others use it indefinitely. Methadone maintenance treatment can only be provided by approved programs. Methadone provides the addict an opportunity for life stabilization and allows the individual to participate in a wide range of habilitative or rehabilitative services. Like Antabuse, methadone maintenance is not recommended as a sole treatment but as an adjunct to other therapeutic services; however, the extent to which methadone clients participate in other services varies.

Patients take methadone orally once a day, typically combined with a sweet drink, at outpatient clinics which also offer other services to clients. Addicts taking methadone may complain about weight gain and insomnia, but these problems have been attributed to factors such as increased alcohol consumption and to personal characteristics of users rather than to the methadone itself.[40] Alcoholism can emerge as a significant problem for narcotics addicts in methadone maintenance programs and must also be addressed.[41] The drug use of clients on methadone maintenance is usually monitored through urinalyses. As clients make progress in treatment they may be allowed to take a Sunday dose of methadone home or may be allowed to come to the clinic every other day and take a dose home for the intervening day. A team approach to treatment is used in many methadone maintenance programs. Team members may jointly decide on the course of treatment for the client, including decisions to adjust the client's dose of methadone, add or revoke privileges, or conclude the client's treatment.[42]

Another drug that shows promise in maintaining narcotic addicts is levo-alpha-acetyl-methadol (LAAM), a methadone analog with longer-lasting effects.[43] Patients can take it every two or three days rather than daily. It has been tried experimentally but has not yet been approved for regular use.

Naltrexone. Naltrexone is an improved version of the drug naloxone.[44] Both are synthetic drugs called narcotic antagonists. Naltrexone is useful in treating narcotic overdose because it can reverse respiratory depression produced by these drugs. It is also used in the longer-term treatment of narcotic addicts. In long-term treatment, both methadone and naltrexone work to block the effects of narcotics, preventing addicts from experiencing the euphoria these drugs produce. Without this effect, "the recovering opiate addict learns to *not* associate drug use with reward."[45] However, methadone is a substitute for narcotic drugs, while naltrexone reverses their effects. Naltrexone is also reportedly nonaddicting.[46] The effects of naltrexone last for a few days. Like Antabuse and methadone, narcotic antagonists are recommended as an adjunct to inpatient or outpatient treatment. In their assessment of the use of narcotic antagonists in treatment, Witters and Venturelli state: "Naltrexone is best suited for adolescent heroin users with relatively short experience with heroin, for recently paroled prisoners who have been abstinent while incarcerated, and for persons who have been on methadone maintenance who wish to go off, but who are afraid of relapsing to heroin."[47] The effective use of narcotic antagonists is dependent on the individual's motivation to remain "clean," since the drug itself does not provide positive effects; monitoring may therefore be necessary to ensure compliance.[48]

Naltrexone has also recently been reported to improve treatment outcomes of alcoholics and cocaine addicts.[49] While naltrexone blocks only the effects of opiates, it does so by inhibiting the production of endorphins (the brain's natural morphinelike or "endogenous opiate" substances). This may also make other psychoactive drug use less pleasurable, thereby reducing the amount consumed should a client decide to drink or use drugs and reducing the likelihood of a full relapse should some alcohol or other drug be consumed.

Clonidine. Clonidine is an antihypertensive drug that seems promising in treating opiate withdrawal. We include it in our discussion of longer-term drug treatment, because it can substantially reduce the rather long period it takes to withdraw from opiates. This may encourage addicts to complete a withdrawal regimen and hopefully to enter inpatient or outpatient treatment. Clonidine is described by Witters and Venturelli as "the first non-addictive, noneuphoriagenic prescription medication with demonstrated efficacy in relieving the effects of opiate withdrawal" such as depression, craving, irritability, and anxiety.[50] However, not everyone can tolerate this drug since one side effect is lowered blood pressure.

Aftercare

Aftercare, the sixth of the treatment system components on the continuum of care, is an extension of intensive treatment, residential, and outpatient programs. Aftercare provides an opportunity for program staff to assist clients in monitoring their progress and to address problems or obstacles to maintaining recovery before they result in serious consequences. Clients participating in aftercare are usually encouraged to continue participation in self-help groups.

Perhaps the most important part of aftercare is learning and practicing the skills needed to prevent lapses and relapses. An important key to teaching relapse prevention seems to be in increasing clients' perceptions that they can successfully cope with situations that pose risks of drinking or drug use.[51] Marlatt and Gordon,[52] Gorski and Miller,[53] and others[54] have written extensively on relapse prevention and management and recommend the use of a number of behavioral and cognitive techniques. Clients generally identify their behaviors and other factors, referred to as "warning signs" or "triggers," that usually precede their desire to drink or use drugs or their actual use of alcohol or drugs.[55] Clients then learn techniques to avoid or defuse the particular situations that threaten their sobriety. For example, a trigger may be a fight with a spouse. This trigger may be defused by teaching clients anger control techniques such as absenting themselves from the situation until they have cooled off and can discuss the problem rationally. Practicing relaxation and stress reduction techniques or other healthy life-style habits can also be use-

ful in preventing relapses and as essential components of one's aftercare program.[56]

Marlatt and Gordon suggest that clients also develop plans to follow if drinking or drug use does occur.[57] One strategy in this regard is to teach clients that consuming a small amount of alcohol or drugs, which some refer to as a "lapse" or "slip," need not necessarily result in a full-blown relapse and that it is possible to take measures to avert a relapse. Contracting may be used to accomplish this purpose. For example, a client may develop a written or verbal agreement with a professional or another individual to call for assistance should they begin to drink or use drugs. Since clients are often embarrassed or ashamed or feel they have let others down once alcohol or drug use commences, they may fail to stop and seek help. The contract can help them acknowledge that there is a way to conclude the episode successfully.

Aftercare services are provided in many ways. Individual sessions may be used but group meetings are more common. Telephone contacts may also be used. Clients may participate weekly, biweekly, monthly, or bimonthly, depending on the program and the client's needs. Some treatment centers charge a flat fee for services, which includes participation in an aftercare program. The duration of aftercare for alcoholics and addicts may be from a few months to a few years.[58]

Maintenance

Maintenance is a particularly important part of the treatment continuum, because it lasts throughout the individual's life. However, it generally receives the least attention. Approaches to maintenance vary depending on the individual's need and preferences. Perhaps the most popular method of maintenance is the use of self-help groups discussed at the end of this chapter. Some people drop into aftercare services or contact a professional as they feel the need. Practicing the relapse prevention techniques learned in intensive treatment, outpatient services, or aftercare components is also an important part of a long-term maintenance program.

Education and Psychoeducation

Didactic education about chemical abuse and dependency is also part of the continuum. It is an essential element of almost all the components of the service system we have discussed. Whether it is education about the physiological effects of alcohol and other drugs presented to patients during their brief stay in detoxification programs, or education about the effects of chemical dependency on the family presented to clients and their loved ones during intensive treatment, accurate information can address misconceptions, present the controversies in the field, and provide a foundation for rehabilitation and recovery.

Psychoeducation is become increasingly popular in the human service professions. It combines the presentation of didactic information to increase knowledge with a variety of other techniques to help clients make desired changes and to provide support. Among the methods employed as part of psychoeducation are role plays (for example, to practice communication or assertiveness skills), structured exercises (such as genograms or other family exploration exercises), homework assignments (reading, charting behaviors, or keeping journals), and group discussion.

While education or psychoeducation are part of all the components of treatment, they can also be primary services occupying their own place on the continuum of care. For example, in addition to license suspension and any jail term, those convicted of driving while intoxicated (DWI) or driving under the influence (DUI) are usually required to attend an educational program. These programs describe the effects of alcohol and other drugs on behavior, allow participants to review the circumstances that led to their arrest and how to avoid such problems in the future, present the signs and symptoms of chemical abuse and dependency, and help participants consider whether they are comfortable with their current use of alcohol or

other drugs. Students in DWI or DUI courses may be screened for chemical abuse or dependency and referred to treatment if indicated, but many do not meet the criteria for these problems.

Education and psychoeducation may also be the primary services offered to youth apprehended by law enforcement on minor-in-possession charges or other infractions. The juvenile courts may also require parents to attend educational sessions when their child has been involved in an alcohol- or drug-related incident. High schools, colleges, and universities have established alcohol and drug education courses for those referred for disciplinary action after causing disturbances or damaging property while drunk. These institutions are also using education and psychoeducation to help students explore the relationship between alcohol, other drugs, and sexual behavior, including contracting sexually transmitted diseases, and the role of alcohol and drugs in sexual assault. Education as a tool in preventing chemical abuse and dependency is discussed at length in Chapter 7.

Adjunctive Services

The final component comprising our continuum is adjunctive services, introduced in the previous chapter on screening, diagnosis, and referral. In addition to chemical abuse or dependence, the systems or multidimensional approach requires the remediation of employment, legal, family, health, and other problems the client is experiencing. A referral is sufficient for many clients to avail themselves of these adjunctive services. Others need additional assistance. For some this may involve coordinating and monitoring adjunctive services for the client. The terms "case management" or "care management" are used to describe these coordination and monitoring functions. Some state, county, and local agencies have special case management units to assist clients with multiple problems. Clients served by these units generally (1) have problems which are severe and

The Two-Tier System of Alcohol and Drug Treatment*

One of the *most* important policy issues regarding drug and alcohol abuse is how treatment services are organized and delivered. According to a recent national evaluation of treatment systems, *"there are two highly contrasting tiers of drug treatment— one for the poor under public sponsorship and one for those who can pay with private insurance or out-of-pocket funds."** These two tiers parallel the general medical delivery systems that serve the affluent and well insured (private medical centers) and the poor and underinsured (public hospitals and clinics), but the differences in the drug treatment systems are even more pronounced.

Public-tier providers consist primarily of publicly owned programs or private, not-for-profit programs. The bulk of their operating funds come from governmental sources. This system of care includes small outpatient clinics in about two thousand communities throughout the nation, as well as a number of large residential facilities and methadone maintenance programs. Its origins are found in government's "wars" on crime and poverty beginning in the late 1960s. In many ways it still is an adjunct to the criminal justice system.

The private tier is made up of about 1,275 providers serving clients who have private health insurance or adequate financial resources to pay for their own treatment. This tier developed primarily from private hospital units that originally focused almost exclusively on the medical treatment of alcoholism. It was an almost invisible component of the treatment system until 1980, but its growth in recent years has been tremendous. Its financial base has begun to match that of the public tier. The most rapid growth is occurring within the ranks of the *for-profit* providers, which charge clients far more for their care than the public sector.

There is less overlap between these two tiers of drug treatment providers than is found within the general medical delivery system. Those with financial resources or private insurance rarely seek treatment from programs that serve indigent clients, and public subsidies for the less affluent drug abuser are rarely adequate to cover the cost of private treatment. Public clients are generally these with longer histories of drug abuse, are more likely to be polydrug abusers, to be unemployed, to be unskilled, and to have a criminal record.[†] They also have greater deficits in health, education, and family functioning, characteristics which mitigate against successful rehabilitation.

One group of clients that is particularly difficult to serve is those that are homeless. These clients will obviously not be served by the private tier, and they frequently find it difficult to get services from the public tier. Without a permanent address it is often difficult to qualify for publicly subsidized services. Recent studies of homeless individuals generally indicate that between one-fourth and one-third of this population are chronic alcoholics,[‡] and many others regularly abuse illicit drugs.[§] It is common for homeless alcoholics and drug abusers to get caught in the "revolving door"—to be "recycled" from detoxification centers to homeless shelters back to the streets, and once again to detoxification programs. Very few treatment programs are designed specifically for these individuals.

Federal funding has played a major role in shaping the public-tier alcohol and drug treatment system, primarily through the (former) Alcohol, Drug Abuse, and Mental Health Administration's (ADAMHA) categorical and block grant funds. Federal funding peaked in 1980, slowly decreased, and then stabilized until 1989 when it began to grow again (Table 6.1). Perhaps even more interesting is the fact that the portion of this federal funding for *drug* (rather than alcohol) treatment declined precipitously between 1980 and 1986, at the very time when the problem of drug abuse was gaining national attention.

TABLE 6.1 Federal Appropriations for Drug, Alcohol, and Mental Health Treatment Provided Through ADAMHA Categorical and Block Grants, 1980–1989 (in millions of dollars)

Year	ADMS[1] Block Grant	ADTR[2] Supplement	Estimated Portion for Drug Treatment
1980	625	—	256
1981	543	—	136
1982	428	—	107
1983	468	—	117
1984	462	—	92
1985	490	—	98
1986	468	—	93
1987	508	163	167
1988	487	156	160
1989 (est.)	765	—	260
1990 (est.)	1,133	—	448

[1] Alcohol, Drug, and Mental Health Services (ADMS).

[2] Alcohol and Drug Treatment (ADTR) supplemental appropriation, 1987–1988.

Source: Adapted from Dean R. Gerstein and Henrick R. Harwood, *Treating Drug Problems,* Vol. 1 (Washington, DC: National Academy Press, 1990), p. 215. Reprinted with permission from *Treating Drug Problems, Volume 1.* Copyright 1990 by the National Academy of Sciences. Courtesy of the National Academy Press, Washington, DC.

Between 1969 and 1975, the federal government put the major portion of its drug abuse funding into treatment programs, but by 1989 law enforcement programs received $680 million, and treatment programs received $520 million. Adjusting for inflation, the real value of funding decreased by 21 percent from 1976–1987.

State and local government expenditures for drug treatment programs from all sources accounted for about 37 percent of all expenditures in 1987. Both the federal and state and local proportions of total (public and private) drug treatment funding decreased between 1976 and 1987, while private funding increased from 5 percent to 38.5 percent of the total (Figure 6.1). Private funding is now the major source of support for drug treatment.

FIGURE 6.1

Funding Sources for Drug Treatment in 1976 (Total Expenditures: $603 Million). *Source:* National Institute on Drug Abuse, 1976–1980

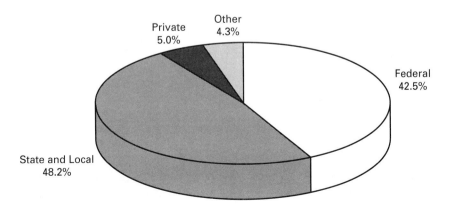

Funding Sources for Drug Treatment in 1987 (Total Expenditures: $1.311 Billion) *Source:* Institute of Medicine Analysis of the 1987 National Drug and Alcoholism Treatment Utilization Survey.

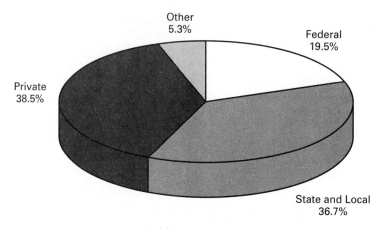

Other
5.3%

Federal
19.5%

Private
38.5%

State and Local
36.7%

Source: Dean R. Gerstein and Henrick R. Harwood, *Treating Drug Problems,* Vol. 1 (Washington, DC: National Academy Press, 1990), p. 213. Reprinted with permission from *Treating Drug Problems, Volume 1.* Copyright 1990 by the National Academy of Sciences. Courtesy of the National Academy Press, Washington, DC.

The public tier of treatment provides detoxification for chronic alcoholics who cannot afford treatment elsewhere, methadone maintenance for heroin addicts, and both inpatient and outpatient services for less affluent drug users of all kinds. Public tier clients are likely to experience longer waiting lists in gaining access to treatment, and they spend less time with treatment personnel; the public tier spent $1,240 per client in 1987 compared to $2,450 spent by the private tier for each client served. Perhaps it is time we added a proposal to equalize the quality of drug and alcohol treatment to a plan for national health insurance.

---

*Most of this section relies on Dean R. Gerstein and Henrick R. Harwood (eds.), *Treating Drug Problems,* Volume 1, Chapter 6 (Washington, DC: National Academy Press, 1990), quote is from pp. 200–201.

†Robert L. Hubbard, Mary Ellen Marsden, J. Valley Rachal, Henrick J. Harwood, Elizabeth R. Cavanaugh, and Harold M. Ginzburg, *Drug Abuse Treatment: A National Study of Effectiveness* (Chapel Hill: University of North Carolina Press, 1989).

‡Ellen L. Bassuk, "The Homeless Problem," *Scientific American,* Vol. 251, No. 1 (July 1984), pp. 28–33.

§Leanne G. Raivlin, "A New Look at the Homeless," *Social Policy* (Spring 1986), pp. 3–10.

---

persistent, (2) have a history of involvement with the chemical dependency or mental health service delivery systems or both, and (3) have had difficulty in utilizing available services. Monitoring is done through contacts with the client, available family members or friends, and with the service providers. This function can prevent crises through the early identification of new problems and the recognition of recurring problems.[59]

TREATMENT EFFECTIVENESS AND CLIENT MATCHING

The previous pages of this chapter addressed the components of the continuum of care and discussed the types of clients that might logically be referred to them. For example, those with a strong physical dependence on drugs generally need detoxification services. The withdrawal symptoms they may face, their psychiatric status, and the types of social supports available to them are factors that might be used to determine whether inpatient or outpatient detoxification would be recommended for the client.

Some tools are available to help clinicians identify an appropriate level of care for a patient or client. For example, the American Society of Addiction Medicine (ASAM) has published *Patient Placement Criteria for the Treatment of Psychoactive Substance Use Disorders.* An overview of the organization's Adult Admission Criteria is found in Table 6.2. Level I is outpatient treatment, Level II is intensive outpatient treatment, Level III is medically monitored intensive inpatient treatment (generally corresponding to what we have called intensive inpatient treatment, and Level IV is medically managed intensive inpatient treatment (corresponding to the settings we have described as medical, hospital detoxification). The level of treatment recommended is suggested by the six dimensions in the left-hand column of the figure such as withdrawal potential and other medical complications, emotional and behavioral condition, treatment acceptance, relapse potential, and the individual's environment. Rather than conceptualizing treatment as fixed interval or fixed length of stay programs, there is also a growing recognition in the field that the system of care be flexible, allowing patients or clients to move to more or less intensive levels as changes in their situations arise.[60] This requires that tools such as the ASAM criteria be used not only to assess but also to reassess the client during the course of treatment.

Clinical judgments are often not the only criteria for selecting treatment. These decisions can be influenced by clients' preferences. For example, a client and his or her family may not see inpatient treatment as a viable alternative, but they may be willing to use outpatient treatment. Other times the method of care is determined by available resources,[61] as our discussion of the two-tier system of chemical dependency services indicated. These are some of the factors that impinge on the treatment of those with substance abuse and dependency problems in the real world.

But what if our only concern was to select the most effective treatment for the client? Do we have empirical evidence that treatment really makes a difference? Do those who receive treatment fare better after treatment than they did before, and do they fare better than those who do not receive treatment? In general, research indicates that the answer to these questions is yes,[62] but our questions about effectiveness are more complex than this. For example, are some forms of treatment (modality, duration, and theoretical perspective) more effective than others? Differential matching of clients to treatment is also of interest, that is, are the particular characteristics of clients (socioeconomic status, marital status, motivation, and so forth) associated with better outcomes in some forms of treatment than others? Do factors such as the personality, gender, or other characteristics of chemical dependency treatment providers make a difference? Finally, if we are concerned about the client's biopsychosocial functioning, what outcome measures should be used to assess family, social, employment, legal, and health status in addition to abstinence or reduced alcohol and other drug use.[63] This section offers an overview of what is known about the effectiveness of treatment and where research still needs to take us. Useful syntheses of information on the effectiveness of alcoholism treatment are provided by NIAAA.[64] Large national studies including the Drug Abuse Reporting Program (DARP) and the Treatment Outcome Perspective Study (TOPS) provide data on drug treatment, and a comprehensive analysis by Gerstein and Harwood is valuable in digesting the information on the effectiveness of treatment for illicit drug use.[65]

Detoxification Services

From a purely medical standpoint, detoxification can be successfully accomplished on an inpatient basis in a hospital, and often in inpatient nonhospital settings as well as on an outpatient basis in appropriate

TABLE 6.2 Adult Patient Placement Criteria for the Treatment of Psychoactive Substance Use Disorders.

THE AMERICAN SOCIETY OF ADDICTION MEDICINE

ADULT PATIENT PLACEMENT CRITERIA FOR THE TREATMENT OF
PSYCHOACTIVE SUBSTANCE USE DISORDERS

LEVELS OF CARE	LEVEL I OUTPATIENT TREATMENT	LEVEL II INTENSIVE OUTPATIENT TREATMENT	LEVEL III MEDICALLY MONITORED INTENSIVE INPATIENT TREATMENT	LEVEL IV MEDICALLY MANAGED INTENSIVE INPATIENT TREATMENT
CRITERIA DIMENSIONS				
1 ACUTE INTOXICATION AND/OR WITHDRAWAL POTENTIAL	No withdrawal risk.	Minimal withdrawal risk.	Severe withdrawal risk but manageable in Level III.	Severe withdrawal risk.
2 BIOMEDICAL CONDITIONS AND COMPLICATIONS	None or very stable.	None or non-distracting from addiction treatment and manageable in Level II.	Require medical monitoring but not intensive treatment.	Require 24-hour medical, nursing care.
3 EMOTIONAL/BEHAVIORAL CONDITIONS AND COMPLICATIONS	None or very stable.	Mild severity with potential to distract from recovery.	Moderate severity needing a 24-hour structured setting.	Severe problems requiring 24-hour psychiatric care with concomitant addiction treatment.
4 TREATMENT ACCEPTANCE/RESISTANCE	Willing to cooperate but needs motivating and monitoring strategies.	Resistance high enough to require structured program, but not so high as to render outpatient treatment ineffective.	Resistance high enough despite negative consequences and needs intensive motivating strategies in 24-hour structure.	Problems in this dimension do not qualify patient for Level IV treatment.
5 RELAPSE POTENTIAL	Able to maintain abstinence and recovery goals with minimal support.	Intensification of addiction symptoms and high likelihood of relapse without close monitoring and support.	Unable to control use despite active participation in less intensive care and needs 24-hour structure.	Problems in this dimension do not qualify patient for Level IV treatment.
6 RECOVERY ENVIRONMENT	Supportive recovery environment and/or patient has skills to cope.	Environment unsupportive but with structure or support, the patient can cope.	Environment dangerous for recovery necessitating removal from the environment; logistical impediments to outpatient treatment.	Problems in this dimension do not qualify patient for Level IV treatment.

Note: This overview of the Adult Admission Criteria is an approximate summary to illustrate the principal concepts and structure of the criteria.

Source: American Association of Addiction Medicine and National Association of Addiction Treatment Providers, *Patient Placement Criteria for the Treatment of Psychoactive Substance Abuse Disorders* (Washington, DC: American Society of Addiction Medicine, March 1991), p. 109.

circumstances.[66] While Hayashida and colleagues present initial evidence that alcoholics of low socioeconomic status can comply with outpatient detoxification regimens,[67] Gerstein and Harwood believe that the jury is still out on which type of detoxification setting may be most effective in ensuring that drug addicts complete detoxification.[68]

Gordis and Sereny[69] and Gerstein and Harwood[70] also note that medically safe withdrawal is only one goal of detoxification programs; more important in the long run is whether participation in a detoxification program promotes further use of treatment and rehabilitation services by clients. In their review of the effectiveness of detoxification programs for illicit drug users, Gerstein and Harwood conclude that "consistently, without subsequent treatment, researchers have found no effects from detoxification that are discernibly superior to those achieved by untreated withdrawal in terms of reducing subsequent drug-taking behavior and especially relapse to dependence."[71] A review by Snair indicates "only small positive effects" from detoxification programs in reducing drug use.[72] Although the literature is scant and reports of success rates vary, reviews often reflect that disappointingly small number of alcoholics and addicts continue in treatment following detoxification services.[73] Tests of methods that will improve client compliance following detoxification are needed.[74]

Intensive Treatment and Outpatient Services

The first studies of Minnesota model intensive treatment programs were conducted in the 1950s.[75] In a review of the effectiveness of these programs, Cook found few "serious" studies; like criticisms of much chemical dependency research, he noted that "the need [is] for further research incorporating control or comparison treatment groups, longer follow-up, more rigorous assessment procedures, and clearly defined diagnostic/outcome criteria."[76] On a positive note, however, he concluded that "despite exaggerated claims of success, [the Minnesota model]

appears to have a genuinely impressive 'track record' with as many as two-thirds of its patients achieving a 'good' outcome at 1 year after discharge."[77] Gerstein and Harwood indicate that those who primarily abuse alcohol appear to have better outcomes in these inpatient programs than do clients who primarily abuse illicit drugs.[78]

Many follow-up studies are based on clients' self-reports of their drinking or other drug use following inpatient or outpatient care. Sometimes clients are also asked to report on their employment, family functioning, illegal activity, and compliance with additional treatment and self groups following discharge. The accuracy of self-reports has been debated, but evidence tends to support their usefulness (see Chapter 5).[79] In some cases, collaterals, records, or laboratory tests (for example, urine toxicologies) are used to validate clients' self-reports at follow-up. These additional sources increase confidence in the information provided about treatment outcomes.

Many questions about intensive inpatient treatment remain unanswered. For example, are particular components or combinations of components of these inpatient programs the keys to client's success, or is the total package of services necessary to promote recovery?[80] One question that has been addressed is whether inpatient or outpatient services produce better results. In a review of treatment modalities, the NIAAA concluded that almost all studies have found no reported differences in the outcomes associated with inpatient and outpatient care (including partial hospitalization and day treatment) of alcoholics.[81] Even one group of researchers who found that hospital treatment produced better overall results than community treatment wrote that "Noteworthy . . . were the findings that the IC [community] treatment was effective for some patients and that both IH [hospital] and IC treatment were relatively ineffective for other patients."[82] A 1991 study of alcoholics treated through an employee assistance program did find that inpatient treatment followed by AA attendance produced better outcomes with regard to drinking and drug use than did AA alone or allowing employees to select their treatment; however, no differences were found on job outcomes.[83] Goodwin cautions that inpatient programs not be abruptly abandoned since the studies to date vary greatly in the treatment used, the populations studied, and evaluation methodologies used,[84] and an article in *Psychiatric News* cautioned against abandoning intensive inpatient treatment in an effort to cut costs in this era of "managed care."[85]

But given that most researchers accept that outpatient treatment for alcoholism generally appears to be as effective as inpatient, it is interesting that the number of intensive outpatient programs has not grown faster. This may be due to the heavy investment of private companies in inpatient facilities, the large amounts charged to clients receiving inpatient care, and resistance to the changes involved in converting to outpatient services. The rising costs of health care and efforts at health care reform may serve to change this.

Snair found outpatient drug-free programs "to be moderately to highly effective in reducing drug use" and also helpful in reducing criminal behavior,[86] but Gerstein and Harwood report that illicit drug abusers have better compliance rates with therapeutic communities and methadone maintenance than with outpatient treatment.[87] One study of military veterans who were cocaine abusers (90 percent were black), found that inpatients were significantly more likely to complete treatment than were those who participated in a day hospital program.[88]

Although group therapy has been recommended as the treatment of choice for chemical dependency, there are many forms of this type of treatment. Brandsma and Pattison's review of about thirty studies generally indicates positive effects of group therapy as part of a treatment program but also a critical need to more clearly define these treatments, especially in efforts to empirically validate their effectiveness.[89] Solomon adds that the lack of studies comparing group with individual treatment for alcoholics makes it difficult to determine whether one modality is better

than the other and that we do not know which types of groups work best with which types of clients.[90]

Marital or conjoint treatment has also shown some promising results for alcoholic clients, but the benefits may be more pronounced in the short run.[91] McCrady and her colleagues randomly assigned alcoholic patients to three treatment conditions: (1) joint hospital admission for the alcoholic and spouse, (2) hospital admission for the alcoholic with the spouse participating in treatment, and (3) hospital admission for the alcoholic and no treatment for the spouse.[92] Initial results indicated that the alcoholics in the first two groups drank less than did those who received treatment by themselves. Four years later, however, there were no statistically significant differences in drinking or other treatment outcomes among the three groups. McCrady then decided to test outpatient treatment for couples. She and her colleagues randomly assigned couples to three behavioral types of outpatient treatment: minimal spouse involvement, alcohol-focused spouse involvement, or alcohol-focused plus behavioral marital therapy.[93] A six-month follow-up indicated positive benefits for all groups with the alcohol-focused plus behavioral marital therapy group generally having better outcomes such as a more rapid decline in drinking and greater maintenance of reduced drinking.

Residential Services

Attempts have been made to study halfway houses services, but most have used small samples or have other serious methodological flaws.[94] Rubington's review indicates that long-term sobriety remains an illusive goal for most halfway house residents, that "studies do not give the halfway house high marks when grading their efforts as rehabilitative agencies," and that the construction of most studies makes it "rather hard to arrive at any important theoretical conclusions based on these negative results."[95]

Annis and Liban conducted a study of thirty-five males who entered halfway houses following detoxification.[96] They matched them with controls who did not enter halfway houses following detoxification (on characteristics such as criminality and employment as well as demographics). There were no posttreatment differences in the drinking behaviors of the client groups, but clients who had participated in the halfway house programs were more likely to refer themselves to a detoxification program after drinking. These researchers suggest that clients may need longer-term services, since most did not remain in the halfway house for more than three months. The findings of Van Ryswyk and colleagues using a larger sample of 641 former residents from eight halfway houses were much more positive. They conducted a secondary data analysis rather than an experimental study, but compared with preadmission functioning, these individuals had fewer detox admissions, used public assistance less, had fewer encounters with the criminal justice system, had greater abstinence, and had better employment outcomes.[97]

Orford and Velleman reviewed the evaluation literature on halfway house programs in the United States, Canada, and the United Kingdom.[98] (In the United Kingdom, these programs go by the more generic name of hostels.) Like Annis and Liban, their review indicates that most clients do not achieve the optimal length of stay in a halfway house which some think is three to nine months. While there is apparently no empirical evidence validating the most beneficial length of stay in a halfway house, the treatment literature generally associates better outcomes with longer lengths of stay. Reports indicate that most clients leave without staff approval, often after drinking or after a dispute.[99] In a study of twenty-nine residents and staff of a halfway house in England, Velleman found that residents who left prematurely were less liked by staff and that staff spent less time with them; residents who left prematurely felt more negatively about lack of privacy, felt life could be better outside the halfway house, had more negative attitudes about staff, and thought that their expectations about the halfway house were not met.[100] Velleman recommends attention to these factors to prevent clients from leaving prematurely. There are conflicting results on whether clients' length of stay in halfway houses is affected by the degree of structure or institutional atmosphere of these facilities.[101]

Given that many residents stay sober while in halfway houses but have high relapse rates after leaving, we have often wondered whether independent living is a viable goal for some residents.[102] Many clients seen in halfway houses are severely debilitated. For some, this type of communal living may promote sobriety, and regardless of independent living skills that are learned, living alone after discharge can be isolating and may promote drinking or drug use.

Gerstein and Harwood draw these primary conclusions from the treatment effectiveness literature on therapeutic communities serving drug abusers: (1) drug use and criminal activity are reduced and social productivity is increased both during and after treatment, (2) length of stay in treatment is the best predictor of outcome with at least three months of treatment needed and better results indicated for those who spend longer periods (up to eighteen months) in treatment, and (3) those who participate in and those who graduate from treatment do better than do those who fail to enter or dropout of treatment, respectively.[103] Snair's review also confirms the effectiveness of therapeutic communities in reducing drug use and criminal behavior.[104]

Shelters and Missions

Evaluating the effectiveness of shelters and missions is particularly difficult because of the transient nature of the clientele served by these programs. Jacobson reviewed the findings from the few evaluative studies available and concluded that among former clients who could be located, there did seem to be some reduction in drinking.[105] Katz's follow-up study of about 100 residents of two Salvation Army Men's Social Service Centers indicated "that men going through the program were, as a group, 'better off' afterward than before. They showed greater residential stability and reported better health" and "a greater portion . . . showed an improved drinking pattern than showed vocational improvement."[106] Since the bulk of the residents stayed from one to four months and received multiple services, the program functioned more like a halfway house than a transient shelter. Another follow-up study of Salvation Army alcoholism treatment programs showed client improvement in seven of nine areas of client functioning including abstinence, psychological well-being, and occupational functioning, but not in hospitalization for alcoholism or social functioning.[107] Clients were encouraged to stay six months but the median stay was sixty-three days. An important note about this study was that a high proportion (82 percent) of the original 121 participants were located at follow-up.

Jacobson concludes that although the long-term effects of shelter residence are not clear, experience tells us that the short-term effects are generally positive—there is interruption of the individual's drinking, meals and safety are provided, and the individual may be referred to other helping resources such as employment services, medical services, halfway houses, self-help and spiritual programs, or other services.[108] Like halfway houses, shelters and missions have not attracted much empirical study as of late.

Pharmacotherapy

More is known about the effectiveness of methadone maintenance than about other types of treatment for illicit drug users.[109] Snair's review found these programs "to be moderately to highly effective in reducing drug use and criminality."[110] Gerstein and Harwood caution that methadone maintenance is not the answer for all heroin addicts, but in spite of controversies about this treatment, it generally produces favorable results:

There is strong evidence from clinical trials and similar study designs that heroin-dependent individuals have better outcomes on average (in terms of illicit drug consumption and other criminal behavior) when they are maintained on methadone than when they are not treated at all or are simply detoxified and released, or when methadone is tapered down and terminated as a result of unilateral client request, expulsion from treatment, or program closure.[111]

Given individual client differences, higher rather than lower doses of methadone seem to produce more positive results.[112] The benefit-to-cost ratio associated with methadone maintenance is substantial.

There is some initial evidence on the use of naltrexone with federal probationers who are dependent on opiate drugs. In a project involving a small group of federal probationers taking this drug, half were still participating at six months. Participants reported few negative side effects of the drug, but the researchers believe that, "the greatest challenge facing the project is the current low rate of identifiable opiate abuse and the epidemic use of cocaine."[113] Despite the drug's utility, they also report that it lacks acceptability among patients.

Effects of Antabuse with alcoholics have been modest, and among those who use it successfully, questions arise as to whether it is their desire and motivation to remain sober,[114] fear of becoming sick,[115] or some other corollary that actually promotes positive outcomes. A recent controlled study by Fuller and his colleagues has cast some doubt on Antabuse's usefulness. In the authors' words, "We concluded that disulfiram may help reduce drinking frequency after relapse, but does not enhance counseling in aiding patients to sustain continuous abstinence or delay the resumption of drinking."[116] McNichol and Logsdon seem more optimistic in their review of the research to date; they state that "results have been encouraging but far from definitive" with success rates from 19 to 89 percent.[117] In their view, the benefits of Antabuse far outweigh the few risks associated with its use, particularly in light of the devastating impact of alcoholism. McNichol and Logsdon also make suggestions for improving the research on the effectiveness of this adjunct to treatment by studying supervised rather than unsupervised administration of the drug and by eliminating sampling bias.

Aftercare

NIAAA's review of the research literature indicates that "available data do support the traditional view of the importance of aftercare services in alcoholism treatment."[118] Alcoholics who participate in aftercare and who participate longer seem to have better outcomes than do those who do not participate or who participate for shorter periods.[119] With respect to treatment of illicit drug users, Gerstein and Harwood note that "the extended follow-up or aftercare phase is seldom if ever a strong and integrated program element."[120] As a result, the effectiveness of this program component following intensive treatment for drug use has not been well studied.

Maintenance

Perhaps the most striking statement that can be made about those treated for chemical dependency is that their relapse rates are very high, regardless of the type of treatment they received. In fact, these high rates (perhaps two-thirds or more of alcoholic clients relapse) make the literature on effectiveness of each of the components of treatment difficult to evaluate.[121] Rather than total prevention of relapse, chemical dependency specialists have come to realize that the goals of reduced drug use and longer periods of abstinence are also indicators of success. Studies on the efficacy of teaching relapse prevention to alcoholics as a maintenance strategy have yielded some positive results, but a return to drinking at some level still occurs for many clients.[122]

Alcoholics and addicts frequently use self-help groups (discussed shortly) as aftercare and maintenance programs. Studies of AA used in this manner generally show positive results in helping alcoholics maintain sobriety.[123]

Adjunctive Services

If human service professionals are to continue to support a systems, multidimensional, or biopsychosocial view of substance abuse treatment, it is necessary to demonstrate that treatment of problems in addition to the substance abuse or dependency promotes better outcomes for clients. We can point to some evidence that attention to the client's other problems is also important. For example, a study of supported work demonstration programs indicated that compared to controls, substance abusers participating in these programs had greater employment and less criminal activity, even though drug use did not differ between the two groups.[124] Additional indications that treatment of clients' problems in addition to chemical dependency may be needed comes from McLellan and his colleagues.[125] They followed 742 male veterans after treatment for substance abuse and found "little relation" between the severity of the client's substance use and functioning in most other life areas, including employment. These findings indicate that substance abuse treatment alone may not be sufficient to improve the clients' functioning in other areas. Employment problems and other problems may require specific interventions.

Other Treatment Effectiveness Issues

In addition to issues about the effectiveness of each component of the system of care, some concerns cut across components. They include length of treatment, client and therapist characteristics, and theoretical approaches to treatment.

Length of Stay. In general, Gerstein and Harwood report that improvement among illicit drug users is positively related to length of stay in treatment whether clients participated in inpatient therapeutic communities, outpatient methadone maintenance programs, or other outpatient services.[126] Alcoholism service providers and researchers are also concerned with this issue. The evidence on length of stay for alcoholic clients is somewhat equivocal with studies tending to show one of two findings: either there is no difference or longer stays are associated with more positive outcomes.[127]

Client Characteristics. Some of the clearest evidence from alcoholism treatment outcome studies is that the strongest predictors of outcome are client characteristics rather than the type, length, or intensity of the treatment received.[128] Clients who are "married, stably employed, free of severe psychological impairments, and of higher socioeconomic status" are more likely to have positive outcomes.[129]

Two frequently cited studies by McLellan and his colleagues, conducted on all-male samples of veterans with alcohol, drug problems, or both, indicate that treatment is generally effective and that when patients are matched to the appropriate type of treatment based on their personal characteristics, effectiveness can be improved.[130] For example, patients who had low psychiatric severity scores did well in outpatient treatment, while those with high scores needed inpatient treatment. Another important finding of this research is that patients with less severe psychiatric symptoms did better than did those with more severe symptoms, regardless of the type of treatment they received. This also indicates the need for special interventions for those with severe mental disorders (also see Chapter 13).

These findings support the need to match clients with appropriate treatment, but they also point to the need to develop programs which compensate for factors that appear to inhibit positive outcomes for clients, specifically, marital instability, unstable employment, low incomes, and severe psychiatric symptoms. Progress is being made in addressing some of these issues. For example, some communities now have programs designed specifically for those with dual diagnoses (comorbidity) of substance abuse and mental disorders. While vocational rehabilitation has long been an adjunct to substance abuse treatment, some studies indicate that relatively few substance abusers actually get this service, despite its reported effectiveness in helping clients obtain and maintain employment.[131] Services that would improve clients' abilities to develop long-term, stable, personal relationships would also logically be expected to help and should be tested for their usefulness.

Therapist Characteristics. An area particularly lacking study is the characteristics of treatment providers that might influence client outcomes. McLachlan studied 94 alcoholics (20 were women) and found that those who were similar to their group therapist in terms of conceptual level (defined as interpersonal development) did better in maintaining abstinence than did patients whose therapist did not match their conceptual level.[132] Valle's work indicates that clients who had counselors with higher levels of interpersonal functioning (based on an assessment of their empathy, genuineness, concreteness, and respect) showed fewer relapse-related outcomes.[133] While Valle's findings seem reasonable, their generalizability is limited since the six counselors studied were recovering alcoholic men (although they had different educational backgrounds), and the clients were mostly males and all were white. Costello reviewed fifty-eight studies of the effectiveness of alcoholism treatment programs and found more effective programs to have staff who made home visits and reached out to collaterals.[134] Researchers have been more likely to study client characteristics than the characteristics of treatment providers.

Theoretical Perspectives. A cornucopia of theoretical perspectives have been used to treat substance abusers—reality therapy, rational emotive therapy, rational behavior therapy, transactional analysis, gestalt, several aversion treatments, and a variety of other behavioral, cognitive, and psychodynamic approaches. According to NIAAA, "in contrast to classical, dynamic, insight-oriented psychotherapy, alcoholism counseling is directive, supportive, reality centered, focused on the present, short term, and oriented toward real world behavioral changes."[135] This is also true of the treatment of illicit drug abusers. In general, we have noted that positive effects can accrue from alcohol and drug abuse treatment. On the other hand, traditional, insight-oriented treatment has historically been viewed as ineffective in helping clients terminate drug use. Explanations for this perceived ineffectiveness are that the causes or etiology of substance abuse problems are not known, and that even knowing the causes of one's chemical dependency may still not result in abstinence. But in one study using random assignment of 260 male court referrals, Brandsma and his colleagues found that those given rational behavior therapy or insight-oriented treatment did better in reducing drinking than those referred to an AA-focused discussion group.[136] The insight group had the fewest legal problems, and those in all groups did better than controls who pursued their own treatment arrangements.

Interpretation of research studies on the effects of interventions from various theoretical perspectives has been hampered by a lack of specification of what constituted the psychotherapeutic intervention.[137] There also has been little controlled investigation to determine what theoretical perspectives might be most useful. Perhaps insight-oriented psychotherapy or other theoretical perspectives should not be summarily dismissed. At a minimum, substance abusers who wish to address additional concerns following sobriety may benefit from a variety of treatment perspectives.

There is a substantial body of literature on aversion therapies in the treatment of alcoholism. Studies have shown varying effects with samples of patients exposed to chemical aversion using emetic (nausea-producing) drugs.[138] As with other types of treatment, clients with greater social stability and greater motivation for treatment seem to fare better.[139] Electrical aversion therapy has been less effective, and less is known about the effectiveness of covert sensitization.[140] "Covert sensitization employs imagery of unpleasant stimuli to elicit the aversive responses needed to accomplish . . . counter conditioning," and Shorkey calls it the only aversive conditioning technique that can practically be employed by most human service professionals.[141] Nathan and Briddell add that used alone, none of these aversive conditioning methods has proven effective.[142] Most chemical dependency practitioners do not use these approaches. A recent report indicated that one corporation "has discontinued the use of aversion therapy in all 21 of its hospitals to improve its ability to recruit patients."[143]

It is probably accurate to say that chemical dependency treatment providers bring diverse theoretical perspectives to their work, and that many have developed theoretical perspectives of their own that are a combination of approaches. In many cases, treatment is done using a "seat-of-the-pants" approach in an attempt to find everything or anything that might work with a particular client. The results of many studies conducted to date provide positive findings about what can be accomplished with chemical dependency treatment, but like most research it often raises more questions than it answers. While every chemical dependency treatment program provides a natural laboratory for research, treatment providers and programs rarely conduct any studies besides client follow-up. Most of the research is done by a small core of academic and clinical researchers in a small number of treatment settings. Client demands for services, lack of knowledge of research methods, and lack of funding prevent the conduct of more research, but there is a growing awareness among human service professionals about the need for systematic evaluation of their work. Although the use of these methods is beyond the scope of this volume, we hope that more treatment providers will seriously pursue preparation in the use of research techniques.

Nontraditional Treatments

Controlled Drinking. Our section on nontraditional treatments begins with a discussion of "controlled drinking." This term has been used to describe both the desire of some alcoholics to drink in a socially acceptable manner and the treatment goal of teaching alcoholics to drink in a socially acceptable manner. The idea of teaching alcoholics to drink in a controlled manner has been met with more than spirited debate. Although it is not a new subject, we include it in this section since it is not a routine treatment offered in chemical dependency programs where the goal for clients is usually abstinence. Yet we know that many clients or potential clients reject total abstinence, and apparently some people who have drunk in an alcoholic manner may go on to adopt more moderate drinking practices.[144] Our discussion is limited to alcohol, since the controlled use controversy has centered on this substance. However, some people apparently use drugs like marijuana and even heroin or other narcotics (called "chipping") in a controlled manner throughout their lives.[145]

The controversy over controlled drinking gained momentum in the 1970s when researchers from the Rand Corporation published an NIAAA-funded study entitled *Alcoholism and Treatment*.[146] Similar to reports by Pattison and colleagues,[147] they found that 18 months following contact with an alcoholism treatment program, a number of the male patients that comprised the study sample reported that they were drinking in a so-called controlled (nonproblematic) fashion or were alternating between drinking and abstention even though they had been treated in traditional, abstinence-oriented programs. A second follow-up conducted four years after treatment found that 46 percent were in remission (that is, 28 percent were currently abstinent and 18 percent were "drinking without problems"; the remaining 54 percent were drinking "with problems."[148] There have, of course, been methodological criticisms of the studies, but the studies generated a great deal of controversy among those interested in alcoholism because of the implications that some alcoholics may be able to drink in a controlled manner.

For those who were upset, the work of Mark and Linda Sobell added to their consternation. The Sobells used "individualized behavior therapy" in an effort to teach some gamma alcoholics to drink in a controlled manner while comparing them with gamma alcoholics who were treated with a goal of abstinence.[149] Patients were selectively assigned to a treatment goal of controlled

drinking or abstinence based on factors such as their desire to become abstinent and whether they had social supports available to assist in accomplishing a goal of controlled drinking. The individualized behavior therapy used to teach patients controlled drinking included identification and practice of alternative responses to excessive drinking, electric shocks, education, comparison of videotapes of themselves when drunk and sober, and other procedures. (Other techniques that have been used include teaching clients to discriminate their blood-alcohol level.) Following a two-year evaluation, the Sobells concluded from treatment outcomes that *some* alcoholics could successfully pursue controlled drinking as a goal given treatment by a professional skilled in using this approach; they cautioned that this did not mean that all or a majority of alcoholics would be appropriate for this treatment.[150] Several attacks of this work followed. In an effort to discern what later happened to the original twenty subjects taught controlled drinking, Pendery and her colleagues conducted a ten-year follow-up.[151] They found that only one had continued to engage successfully in controlled drinking, eight continued to drink problematically, six had become abstinent, four had died from alcoholism, and one was missing. How these twenty alcoholics would have fared if treated in an abstinence-oriented program from the outset cannot be determined.

Pomerleau and colleagues also conducted a related study in the 1970s and found mixed results when they randomly assigned 32 middle-class volunteers who were problem drinkers to two treatment conditions.[152] One they described as traditional, insight-oriented psychotherapy using confrontation and emphasizing abstinence. The other was behavioral self-control training using positive reinforcement and emphasizing moderation. Substantially more traditional treatment subjects dropped out, but among those remaining in treatment, both groups significantly reduced their drinking.

Have professionals rejected the goal of controlled use for those with alcohol and drug problems? Many think we should, and few ever attempted to use this treatment approach, yet some people seem to moderate or reduce their use and remain functioning members of society or show improvement in other areas of their lives.[153] Maintaining high ethical standards in substance abuse treatment and research is a necessity, but it is also true that emotion can inhibit the pursuit of knowledge in the field. Given high relapse among treated alcoholics and addicts, it is critical that we remain open to scientific investigation that might lead to improved methods of helping individuals eliminate or moderate their use of chemicals. We want to be neither too restrictive in our approaches nor too free in our willingness to grasp at new straws.

Acupuncture. Recent reports of new treatments for chemical dependency include the use of acupuncture and alpha-theta brainwave training (a biofeedback technique). The small number of studies on these methods makes it difficult to draw conclusions about their effectiveness, either as adjuncts to treatment or as alternatives to traditional treatment, but fresh approaches are needed.

In theory, acupuncture, an ancient Chinese approach to treating medical and psychological problems with the use of needles, is said to work in the following way:

Energy (Chi) from oxygen and food flows through the organs and body where it is transformed and distributed. The acupuncturist assesses (through symptoms, physical examination and pulse diagnosis) the homeostasis of this energy and intervenes with treatment if it is out of balance.[154]

Acupuncture may promote the production of beta-endorphins or other naturally occurring substances in the body, but the precise mechanisms through which it might work are not known.[155]

Brumbaugh enthusiastically discusses the use of auricular (ear) acupuncture with detoxification patients and in treatment following detoxification.[156] He reports that there are over 175 such detoxification programs in the United States. Acupuncture in longer-term chemical dependency treatment has apparently been used most extensively with volunteers from the criminal justice system. Individuals are being treated with the procedure in groups, minimizing the time and the costs of the treatment. Acupuncture has been used with various drug addictions, including alcohol, heroin, and crack cocaine. The procedure has been used for about twenty years at Lincoln Hospital's Substance Abuse Division in New York. A group called the National Acupuncture Detoxification Association has emerged with a suggested protocol for the use of acupuncture in detoxification.

The literature on the use of acupuncture with alcoholics and drug abusers is interesting, but few controlled trials of acupuncture have been published. Bullock and his colleagues found positive results in two controlled, single-blind studies with severe, chronic alcoholics.[157] Control subjects were less likely to complete treatment, reported a greater desire to drink, and had significantly more episodes of drinking and detoxification admissions than experimental subjects. The experimental groups received acupuncture at points thought to be specific for substance abuse treatment while the controls received it at nonspecific points. The subjects in these studies were given a place to live during the treatment, but other than Alcoholics Anonymous, no traditional chemical dependency treatment was provided. These researchers suggest that acupuncture may not only be an effective adjunct to treatment but may be useful for clients who have not fared well with other treatment approaches. Worner and associates, on the other hand, found no difference in treatment or control subjects, all of whom were lower socioeconomic status alcoholics, with respect to attendance at AA or treatment, treatment completion, detox admissions, or relapses.[158] Subjects were randomly assigned to one of three groups: point-specific acupuncture along with standard, outpatient alcoholism treatment, needleless or sham acupuncture with standard treatment, or standard treatment only. They found that many individuals were unwilling to receive acupuncture treatment. Worner reported a much higher dropout rate from the point-specific acupuncture treatment group than did Bullock. Given their lack of success with acupuncture and potential medical problems that can arise from the use of acupuncture, Worner and associates "caution against the routine use of this treatment until more randomized control trials demonstrate a beneficial effect."[159]

Biofeedback. Various stress reduction or relaxation techniques such as progressive muscle relaxation and relaxation imagery have been used as adjuncts in the treatment of chemical abusers.[160] Other approaches such as hypnosis and meditation have also been tried. The hope is that reducing stress and promoting relaxation will lead to better treatment outcomes for clients. Alpha-theta brainwave training is a newer relaxation approach being used with alcohol and drug abusers. Like acupuncture, it is administered by those with specialized training. Peniston and Kulkosky have been studying the use of alpha-theta brainwave training with alcoholics and with veterans with posttraumatic stress disorder.[161] The purpose of this training is to increase alpha and theta brain rhythms since it is suspected that alcoholics are deficient in these brain activities and that increases in these activities may promote better treatment outcomes. Peniston and Kulkosky explain the procedures they use such as placement of electrodes, audio feedback, and temperature biofeedback. Their controlled study of thirty individuals indicated that the experimental group showed improvements (increases) in alpha and theta activity and had less depression and fewer relapses at thirteen months following treatment compared to controls. Additional studies will be helpful, since Witters and Venturelli report that while those who have learned biofeedback feel it is helpful, their treatment outcomes have not been better than those of other patients.[162]

SELF-HELP GROUPS

Self-help groups have been part of the recovery of alcoholics and addicts since the 1930s.

They are an important component of the system of care but are not part of the continuum of services provided by professionals. Instead, they are composed of volunteers who both "work the program" and maintain these loosely structured organizations. In most cases, members take turns chairing the meetings or acting as secretary.

Alcoholics Anonymous

The best-known self-help group is Alcoholics Anonymous (AA). AA has been described as everything from a form of psychotherapy[163] to having an "antipsychotherapy attitude."[164] It has also been described in systems terms as "a model for synthesizing biomedical, psychosocial, and environmental approaches to arresting alcoholism and achieving what AA members term 'contented sobriety.'"[165] Regardless of how one views AA, it began in 1935, well before most professionals took a serious interest in assisting alcoholics. The founders of AA were two men, a physician and a stockbroker, who shared with each other their problems with alcohol and supported each other in maintaining sobriety. Alcoholics Anonymous estimates that it now has more than 87,000 groups[166] and more than 1.5 million members.[167] Groups meet throughout the United States and many other countries. A directory is available to help members locate meetings, and almost every phone book in the United States lists a local number for the organization. Local groups operate rather independently, although the General Service Office, located in New York City, provides kits to assist in starting groups and offers a great deal of literature addressed to recovering persons, their friends and family members, and the various professionals who help alcoholics.

AA is referred to as a fellowship. More than meetings, it is a program for the recovering alcoholic to "work" on a daily basis. The program is based on twelve steps (reproduced in Table 6.3) that refer to the individual's powerlessness over alcohol, the need to recognize one's shortcomings and to make amends, and reliance on a higher power.

TABLE 6.3

The Twelve Steps of Alcoholics Anonymous	The Twelve Traditions of Alcoholics Anonymous
1. We admitted we were powerless over alcohol—that our lives had become unmanageable.	1. Our common welfare should come first; personal recovery depends upon A.A. unity.
2. Came to believe that a Power greater than ourselves could restore us to sanity.	2. For our group purpose, there is but one ultimate authority—a loving God as He may express Himself in our group conscience. Our leaders are but trusted servants; they do not govern.
3. Made a decision to turn our will and our lives over to the care of God *as we understood Him.*	3. The only requirement for A.A. membership is a desire to stop drinking.
4. Made a searching and fearless moral inventory of ourselves.	4. Each group should be autonomous except in matters affecting other groups or A.A. as a whole.
5. Admitted to God, to ourselves and to another human being the exact nature of our wrongs.	5. Each group has but one primary purpose—to carry its message to the alcoholic who still suffers.
6. Were entirely ready to have God remove all these defects of character.	6. An A.A. group ought never endorse, finance, or lend the A.A. name to any related facility or outside enterprise, lest problems of money, property, and prestige divert us from our primary purpose.
7. Humbly asked Him to remove our shortcomings.	7. Every A.A. group ought to be fully self-supporting, declining outside contributions.
8. Made a list of all persons we had harmed, and became willing to make amends to them all.	8. Alcoholics Anonymous should remain forever nonprofessional, but our service centers may employ special workers.
9. Made direct amends to such people wherever possible, except when to do so would injure them or others.	9. A.A., as such, ought never be organized; but we may create service boards or committees directly responsible to those they serve.
10. Continued to take personal inventory and when we were wrong promptly admitted it.	10. Alcoholics Anonymous has no opinion on outside issues; hence the A.A. name ought never be drawn into public controversy.
11. Sought through prayer and meditation to improve our conscious contact with God, *as we understood Him,* praying only for knowledge of His will for us and the power to carry that out.	11. Our public relations policy is based on attraction rather than promotion; we need always maintain personal anonymity at the level of press, radio, and films.
12. Having had a spiritual awakening as the result of these steps, we tried to carry this message to alcoholics, and to practice these principles in all our affairs.	12. Anonymity is the spiritual foundation of all our traditions, ever reminding us to place principles before personalities.

These steps have been adapted by many other self-help groups for chemically dependent individuals, such as Narcotics Anonymous, and a wide variety of other groups concerned about problems ranging from overeating and gambling to sexual behavior. Another important aspect of AA is its twelve traditions (see Table 6.3) recognizing the group's concerns about anonymity, not taking stands on outside issues, and so forth. Some alcoholics never seek professional assistance and, instead, have relied on Alcoholics Anonymous to help guide them toward recovery. Others use a combination of professional assistance and self-help groups. The self-help movement does not appeal to all recovering individuals. Some professionals question its utility, believing that it is best reserved for certain types of individuals. However, it is probably accurate to say that most human service professionals concerned about chemical dependency not only refer their clients to self-help groups but strongly encourage them to participate.

The only requirement for membership in AA is a desire to stop drinking. There are no application forms or other requirements for participation. Individuals who come to meetings intoxicated or not completely detoxified are usually allowed to remain unless they cause disruption or appear to need immediate medical attention. There are no dues or fees for membership. The groups are supported by contributions of members and outside donations are not accepted. Since anonymity is stressed, only first names are used at meetings, and members are reminded to "leave what they hear at the meeting" so as not to violate the confidences of others.

A mainstay of the group is its meetings which are usually about one hour long. In large cities, it is not surprising to find meetings being conducted around the clock every day of the week. Smaller communities generally having fewer meetings. Some cities have AA clubs where members can drop in whenever they wish.

When AA began, its membership was largely men. Only a few brave women ventured into the meetings, but today women are a sizable portion (35 percent) of members.[168] Some AA groups are designated for women only (see Chapter 15) or men only. Other groups are for young people (although anyone young at heart is usually permitted to attend) or for members of particular ethnic groups with meetings conducted in their native languages (see Chapter 11). Gay men and lesbians (see Chapter 12), members of particular professions, and nonsmokers have also organized groups. Again, community size is usually a predictor of the variety of meetings. Sometimes the composition of the group is defined by the location in which the meeting is held—an affluent residential neighborhood, the deteriorating downtown section of a city, or a prison.

Many outsiders think AA is a religious program. The twelve steps do include references to God, but AA is probably better described as a spiritual program.[169] God is considered a "higher power" defined according to individual preference. For some, it is God in the traditional sense of organized religion; for others it may be the AA group, or virtually any other spiritual or physical entity. Religious aspects of meetings seem stronger in some groups than in others, but some atheists and agnostics have successfully recovered through the program.[170] Various ethnic groups have adapted the principles and format of AA according to their beliefs and customs (see Chapter 11). Groups seem to develop their own personalities depending on their membership. Newcomers may be encouraged to attend the meetings of several different groups and to select those in which they feel most comfortable. They are also encouraged to attend "ninety meetings in ninety days" in order to break old patterns, to become fully immersed in the program, and to not give up too quickly.

The overall structure of AA meetings is generally consistent in that they begin and end in the same manner, with readings from the *Big Book* of Alcoholics Anonymous and prayers, but there are different meeting formats. A speaker's meeting is devoted to one or more testimonials by members who are from the local community or invited from out of town. Members sometimes call these talks "drunkalogues." Speakers tell their "story," usually beginning with the circumstances surrounding their use and abuse of alcohol and their development of alcoholism. Stories generally contain a number of the negative consequences that the alcoholic experienced while drinking and the way in which the alcoholic was able to recover, including their introduction to and use of AA. The stories assist members, especially "newcomers," in realizing that it is possible to recover, no matter how bad one's problems. They are also cathartic for the storyteller. Birthday meetings at which members celebrate each year of their sobriety are often combined with speakers' meetings.

Another format is discussion meetings. At these meetings, the chairperson may offer a topic for discussion (such as guilt, resentments, loneliness, friendships, intimacy) or ask members to suggest a topic. Members may volunteer comments on their personal experiences, or the chairperson may proceed in round-robin fashion. Members who do not wish to speak are usually not pressured to do so and may simply say "I pass" when their turn comes. In this sense, AA differs from group therapy or other forms of group treatment in which members are expected to verbalize their thoughts and interact with other members during sessions.

At step meetings, the chairperson leads a discussion of one of the twelve steps of AA. Members comment on points that helped them work the step or the problems they are encountering in working that step. There is no one way, or even recommended ways, to work each step. Members offer their thoughts, but each is free to work the step in a manner suitable to him or her. Big Book meetings are another type of meeting. The book *Alcoholics Anonymous,* usually referred to as the *Big Book,* recounts the story of the birth and development of AA and contains the stories of various members. These meetings focus on discussion of passages from the book.

Tokens are among the symbols used in meetings. For example, poker chips of different colors may be given after one, two, three, and six months of continuous sobriety to recognize the progress the individual has made. At birthday meetings, members with one or more years of continuous sobriety are presented with a special memento, such as a silver dollar with a hole drilled in it to commemorate each year of sobriety.

Slogans for living such as "one day at a time" and "live and let live" are frequently heard at AA and are often displayed on the walls of the meeting room. Meetings generally close with "Keep coming back; it works."

AA conventions are held around the country, and local groups often sponsor social and recreational activities such as dances and family picnics to provide an atmosphere where members can enjoy themselves without exposure to alcohol. For some recovering alcoholics, AA is the focus of their lives. Some

have criticized this as an inability to lead a normal life; others call it an individual choice. There are no rules telling a member how often to attend meetings. Many individuals go frequently in the early stages of their sobriety and then less frequently as their length of sobriety increases. In the early stages of sobriety, failing to attend meetings is often considered a "red flag" or a precursor to a "slip" (a lapse or relapse).

Sponsorship is another aspect of AA and many other self-help programs. Newcomers who wish may ask a member to serve as their sponsor. A sponsor has usually been an AA member for some time and has achieved a substantial period of sobriety, but there are no requirements to serve in this capacity. Newcomers are encouraged to select sponsors whom they feel have "solid sobriety" and with whom they feel comfortable discussing their recovery. They may also be encouraged to select a sponsor of the same gender to avoid confusing issues of recovery and sexual intimacy (issues in AA for gay men and lesbians are discussed in Chapter 12). The individual who is asked to be a sponsor is free to accept or decline. Sponsors can be a valuable resource, especially when they are readily available to provide support and encouragement. This is particularly important to members when they experience a crisis such as a strong desire to drink or when they want help with understanding various aspects of the AA program.

Why are so many people attracted to AA? It may well be due to the camaraderie—the idea that there are others who have been there, who have recovered, and who understand. The fellowship of AA and other self-help groups is a strong one. Visitors and newcomers are often struck by the way members introduce themselves and are acknowledged by fellow members. When members speak at the meetings they usually begin by saying, "I'm so-and-so, and I'm an alcoholic," to which the group responds in chorus, "Hi, so-and-so!" Members and visitors are impressed with the unconditional acceptance of the alcoholic. Visitors sometimes remark that the interaction between members was so positive, they wished they were alcoholics! On the other hand, visitors and newcomers may be concerned about some of the behavior at meetings. For example, members may come and go as they wish during meetings which can seem disruptive, or they may offer comments but do not always receive responses to their remarks which can seem disrespectful.

AA and similar self-help groups for alcoholics and addicts have closed and open meetings. Closed meetings are only for those who consider themselves alcoholics or addicts. These meetings provide greater assurance to the alcoholic or addict that they are among those who share the same problem and that their anonymity will be respected. Open meetings also serve an important purpose. They allow professionals, family members and friends, those who think they might have a problem, and others to learn more about self-help groups, the problems they address, and the people they help. They are an important resource for every community. Anyone considering a career working with chemically dependent clients should attend these meetings.

Research and Self-help Groups

AA has been touted as having helped more people recover from alcoholism than any other program.[171] Some have called this aggrandizement "an ill-considered hyperbole,"[172] and others warn that even questioning the effectiveness of AA might cause "surprise, annoyance, anger, exasperation, shock, or perhaps even rage" among some individuals.[173] The informal structure of the organization and its groups[174] and the concern for members' anonymity have deterred researchers from conducting studies on AA in spite of its unique approach and its large following. In 1976, Bebbington wrote that given the nature of AA, "it seems unlikely to be possible to assess its effectiveness in a scientific manner."[175] He noted the bias in studies of AA because members self-select into the program and because samples have been of the convenience types. Using the principles of scientific inquiry, suggestions have been

made about how researchers should go about studying AA.[176] While most studies do not meet these criteria, we consider the efforts that have been made to study AA.

Two types of studies of interest are (1) descriptive studies of members and (2) studies of AA's effectiveness. Descriptive studies include periodic membership surveys of the organization as well as the efforts of other researchers to investigate those most likely to affiliate with AA. In 1981 Ogborne and Glaser summarized the affiliation literature:

Researchers have found that affiliates of AA are more likely to be men, over 40 years of age, white, middle- or upper-class and socially stable. AA affiliation has been associated with binge drinking, physical dependence on alcohol, loss-of-control drinking, and the loss or threatened loss of a valued life-style because of drinking. It has also been associated with an authoritarian personality, strong affiliative needs, proneness to guilt, and external locus of control, field dependence, cognitive simplicity, formistic thinking, a low conceptual level, high autokinesis scores, a religious orientation, existential anxiety and a tendency to conform.[177]

They warned that given the state of the research, these "characteristics should be viewed only as a set of working hypotheses."[178] However, Baekeland suggested that physicians "not blindly recommend AA to patients who are unlikely to accept it (. . . non- or antireligious, uncomfortable in groups) but rather to those likely to profit from it."[179]

Later reviews of the affiliation literature have found considerable variation among AA members.[180] Emrick's conclusion was that "until specific affiliation characteristics are identified, prudence suggests viewing all alcoholic patients in conventional alcoholism treatment as possible members of AA, while at the same time recognizing that many alcohol-dependent patients recover from their alcohol problems without ever joining the organization."[181]

Keeping the methodological problems of studies in mind, the bulk of literature on the effectiveness of AA generally indicates the positive results of affiliation. Baekeland reported that as a primary treatment, "AA seems to do about as well as alcohol clinics."[182] Vaillant's study of over 600 men found that among some of the study's subgroups, more recovered individuals had begun stable abstinence while participating in AA than other treatment, but those who sought clinic treatment seemed equally as likely to achieve stable abstinence through this form of treatment as they were through AA.[183] In a 1980 review of the literature, Miller and Hester found abstinence rates of AA members of 26 to 50 percent after one year; while the studies did not use controls, these rates were reportedly similar to other types of treatment.[184] Emrick found abstinence rates of 40 to 50 percent among "long-term, active AA members," which he reported as being higher than rates among "professionally treated alcoholics."[185] When Brandsma and colleagues randomly assigned court referrals to AA-type discussion groups and several other treatments, AA had the highest dropout rate.[186] Since subjects were under coercion to receive help, findings may not generalize to individuals in other circumstances.

Baekeland suggested that AA might appeal to more individuals when used as an adjunct to other treatment,[187] but he acknowledged that this had not been verified in the scientific literature. Recent studies give credence to this hypothesis. In a four-year follow-up of 225 patients discharged from an addiction treatment program, Pettinati and colleagues found that AA attendance was more likely to be associated with maintaining abstinence than were other posttreatment interventions such as additional inpatient or outpatient treatment.[188] Similarly, in a study of women alcoholics, Corrigan found that prior AA attendance, prior inpatient treatment, and prior outpatient treatment all contributed equally to explaining abstinence as did current AA attendance; however, additional outpatient or inpatient treatment was negatively related to abstinence.[189] In a 1987 review of the literature, Emrick found that those who combined AA and other treatment did as well or better than those whose only involvement was with AA.[190] A ten-year follow-up study of

male and female patients who had received intensive inpatient treatment revealed that "involvement in Alcoholics Anonymous (AA) predicted abstinence, suggesting successful outcome for patients who undergo a treatment regimen, which bridges patients into AA involvement."[191]

Like the literature on treatment effectiveness, research is needed on many aspects of self-help groups. Research might help to determine the process through which affiliation with these groups occur, who tends to benefit from this involvement, and the mechanisms of these groups that actually help to produce change.

Narcotics Anonymous and Other Self-help Groups

Next to AA, Narcotics Anonymous (NA) probably has the greatest name recognition of all the self-help groups for chemically dependent individuals. NA began in the 1950s. Groups were often started by AA members who were also drug addicts; like AA, NA emphasizes taking individual responsibility for problems.[192] The twelve steps and twelve traditions of NA are almost identical to AA's with drug terminology substituted for alcohol terminology. Why did NA emerge separately from AA? Before the advent of increased polydrug abuse, there were many more "pure alcoholics." Some alcoholics were uncomfortable with narcotics addicts whom they associated with the criminal element. Alcoholics also abuse a drug, but it can be obtained within the law. Today, however, it is common to hear attendees at AA or NA meetings introduce themselves as alcoholics and addicts.

Cocaine Anonymous is another group that has emerged with the increased use of this drug. While cocaine abusers would likely be welcome at NA or AA meetings, the unique aspects of preference for a particular drug, such as life-style differences, may have encouraged the emergence of yet another self-help group.

There are a variety of other self-help groups for alcoholics and addicts. Women for Sobriety (WFS) was developed by Jean

Kirkpatrick who feels that AA has a male orientation and that women need alternatives to help them in their sobriety. WFS is discussed further in Chapter 15. Gay Alcoholics Anonymous and Alcoholics Together, for gay men and lesbians, are discussed in Chapter 12. More recently, the Secular Organization for Sobriety (S.O.S.), also called Save Our Selves, has emerged as a "cognitively-based" group to assist those "uncomfortable with a perceived religious emphasis" in many self-help groups.[193]

Other variations of self-help groups have also emerged. Some are run by a combination of volunteers and staff members from chemical dependency, mental health, or other treatment programs. Nurco and his colleagues discuss a project using this approach to assist narcotic addicts.[194] Groups now emerging for those with dual diagnoses of substance abuse and mental illness or substance abuse and mental retardation are often organized and led by a professional or they may be co-led by a professional and a dually diagnosed, recovering individual (see Chapter 13).

There are also groups for the loved ones of alcoholics and addicts. The first to emerge was Alanon, founded by the wife of one of AA's founders (see Chapter 10). Naranon is for the loved ones of narcotic addicts. Alatot and Alateen are especially for the children of alcoholics.

SUMMARY

This chapter reviewed the components of the treatment system commonly used by those with alcohol or drug problems. A wide range of treatments are available to these individuals and their loved ones. Many of these methods show promising results in helping those who seek professional assistance in their recovery, and chemical dependency professionals must be able to match clients with the treatments that are most likely to meet their needs. Self-help groups were among the first approaches to aid individuals with chemical dependency problems. They remain an important component of the helping system

and have grown in number and in their application to other types of problems. Research has begun to address many of the questions that have been raised about the effectiveness of treatment and self-help approaches. There is still much knowledge to be gained, especially in light of the fact that much of the etiology of chemical abuse and dependency remains a mystery and relapse rates remain high.

ENDNOTES

1. For other descriptions of the continuum of care, see Benjamin Kissin and Henri Begleiter (eds.), *The Biology of Alcoholism, Treatment and Rehabilitation of the Chronic Alcoholic* (New York: Plenum Press, 1977), and Daniel John Anderson, "Delivery of Essential Services to Alcoholics Through the 'Continuum of Care,'" *Cancer Research,* Vol. 39 (July 1979), pp. 2855–2858.

2. Also see Kissin and Begleiter, *The Biology of Alcoholism.*

3. Enoch Gordis and George Sereny, "Controversy in Approaches to Alcoholism," in Victor M. Rosenoer and Marcus Rothschild (eds.), *Controversies in Clinical Care* (New York: Spectrum Publications, 1981), pp. 37–55.

4. Earl Rubington, "Staff Problems in Halfway Houses," *Alcoholism Treatment Quarterly,* Vol. 2, No. 2 (Summer 1985) pp. 29–47.

5. For information on the treatment of withdrawal, see Dennis F. Moore, "Detoxification," in Gerald Bennett, Christine Vourakis, and Donnas S. Woolf (eds.), *Substance Abuse, Pharmacologic, Developmental, and Clinical Perspectives* (New York: John Wiley and Sons, 1983), pp. 328–340.

6. See Chapter 1 for a description of the various types of drugs and associated withdrawal problems. Also see Bennett et al., *Substance Abuse.*

7. Motoi Hayashida, Arthur I. Alterman, Thomas McLellan, Charles P. O'Brien, James J. Purtill, Joseph R. Volpicelli, Arnold H. Raphaelson, and Charles P. Hall, "Comparative Effectiveness and Costs of Inpatient and Outpatient Detoxification of Patients with Mild-to-Moderate Alcohol Withdrawal Syndrome," *The New England Journal of Medicine* (February 9, 1989), pp. 358–365, and Dean R. Gerstein and Henrick J. Harwood (eds.), *Treating Drug Problems,* Vol. 1 (Washington, DC: National Academy Press, 1990), pp. 125–126, reprinted with permission from *Treating Drug Problems,* Volume 1, copyright 1990 by the

National Academy of Sciences, courtesy of the National Academy Press, Washington, DC.

8. Hayashida et al., "Comparative Effectiveness and Costs."

9. Gerstein and Harwood, *Treating Drug Problems;* also see National Institute on Alcohol Abuse and Alcoholism (NIAAA), *Sixth Special Report to the U.S. Congress on Alcohol and Health* (Rockville, MD: U.S. Department of Health and Human Services, 1987); and National Institute on Alcohol Abuse and Alcoholism (NIAAA), *Seventh Special Report to the U.S. Congress on Alcohol and Health* (Rockville, MD: U.S. Department of Health and Human Services, January 1990).

10. Drug Enforcement Administration, *Drugs of Abuse,* 1989 ed. (Washington, DC: U.S. Department of Justice, 1989).

11. Gordis and Sereny, "Controversy in Approaches to Alcoholism."

12. *Report of the Presidential Commission on the Human Immunodeficiency Virus* (Washington, DC: U.S. Government Printing Office, 1988).

13. Christopher C. H. Cook, "The Minnesota Model in the Management of Drug and Alcohol Dependency: Miracle, Method or Myth? Part I. The Philosophy and the Programme," *British Journal of Addiction,* Vol. 83 (1988), p. 625; also see NIAAA, *Seventh Special Report to the U.S. Congress on Alcohol and Health,* p. 262.

14. NIAAA, *Sixth Special Report to the U.S. Congress on Alcohol and Health.*

15. Earl Rubington, "The Role of the Halfway House in the Rehabilitation of Alcoholics," in Kissin and Begleiter, *The Biology of Alcoholism,* p. 352; also see Anderson, "Delivery of Essential Services to Alcoholics Through the 'Continuum of Care.'"

16. Rubington, "The Role of the Halfway House in the Rehabilitation of Alcoholics."

17. Allan C. Ogborne, T. R. Ian Wiggins, and Martin Shain, "Variations in Staff Characteristics, Programmes and Recruitment Practices Among Halfway Houses for Problem Drinkers," *British Journal of Addiction,* Vol. 75 (1980), pp. 393–403, and Rubington, "Staff Problems in Halfway Houses."

18. Rubington, "Staff Problems in Halfway Houses."

19. Ibid.

20. Ibid.

21. For additional information on halfway houses, see Jim Orford and Richard Velleman, "Alcoholism Halfway Houses," in E. Mansell Pattison and Edward Kaufman (eds.), *Encyclopedic Handbook of Alcoholism* (New York: Gardner Press, 1982), pp. 907–922; Rubington, "The Role of the Halfway House in the Rehabilitation of Alcoholics"; and Rubington, "Staff Problems in Halfway Houses."

22. Some of this section relies on Weldon Witters and Peter Venturelli, *Drugs and Society;* 2nd ed., (Boston: Jones and Bartlett, 1988), pp. 332–333, ©1988 Boston: Jones and Bartlett Publishers. Reprinted by permission, and Oakley Ray and Charles Ksir, *Drugs, Society, & Human Behavior,* 5th ed. (St. Louis, MO: C. V. Mosby, 1987), pp. 371–372.

23. Witters and Venturelli, *Drugs and Society.*

24. Gerstein and Harwood, *Treating Drug Problems;* also see this reference for information on therapeutic communities.

25. William Glasser, *Reality Therapy* (New York: Harper Colophon Books, 1965).

26. Gerstein and Harwood, *Treating Drug Problems,* p. 352; for additional information on therapeutic communities, see Cook, "The Minnesota Model in the Management of Drug and Alcohol Dependency."

27. Lawrence Katz, "The Salvation Army Men's Social Service Center: II. Results," *Quarterly Journal of Studies on Alcohol,* Vol. 27 (1966), pp. 636–647.

28. Ibid.

29. George R. Jacobson, "The Role of Shelter Facilities in the Treatment of Alcoholics," in Pattison and Kaufman, *Encyclopedic Handbook of Alcoholism,* pp. 894–906.

30. NIAAA, *Seventh Special Report to the U.S. Congress on Alcohol and Health.*

31. Sandra C. Anderson, "Group Therapy with Alcoholic Clients: A Review," *Advances in Alcohol and Substance Abuse,* Vol. 2, No. 2 (1982), pp. 23–40.

32. Baruch Levine and Virginia Gallogly, *Group Therapy with Alcoholics, Outpatient and Inpatient Approaches* (Beverly Hills, CA: Sage, 1985), p. 15.

33. Also see Irving D. Yalom, "Group Therapy and Alcoholism," *Annals of the New York Academy of Sciences,* Vol. 233 (1974), pp. 85–103; David R. Doroff, "Group Psychotherapy in Alcoholism," in Kissin and Begleiter, *The Biology of Alcoholism,* pp. 235–258; and Philip J. Flores, "Modifications of Yalom's Interactional Group Therapy Model as a Mode of Treatment for Alcoholism," *Group,* Vol. 6, No. 1 (1982), pp. 3–16.

34. Much of this section is based on John A. Ewing, "Disulfiram and Other Deterrent Drugs," in Pattison and Kaufman, *Encyclopedic Handbook of Alcoholism,* pp. 1033–1042; also see *Antabuse* (Tallahassee, FL: Department of Health and Rehabilitative Services, July 1973); and *Physicians' Desk Reference, 47th ed.* (Medical Economics Data, 1993), pp. 2540–2541.

35. Ronald W. McNichol and Steven A. Logsdon, "Disulfiram: An Evaluation Research Model," *Alcohol Health & Research World,* Vol. 12, No. 3 (1988), pp. 202–209.

36. Ewing, "Disulfiram and Other Deterent Drugs."

37. Ibid.

38. Witters and Venturelli, *Drugs and Society,* pp. 329–330; also see their book for a discussion of methadone maintenance.

39. Much of the remainder of this section relies on Gerstein and Harwood, *Treating Drug Problems;* also see Ray and Ksir, *Drugs, Society, & Human Behavior,* pp. 367–369.

40. Gerstein and Harwood, *Treating Drug Problems.*

41. Warren K. Bickel, Ira Marion, and Joyce H. Lowinson, "The Treatment of Alcoholic Methadone Patients: A Review," *Journal of Substance Abuse Treatment,* Vol. 4 (1987), pp. 15–19.

42. Gerstein and Harwood, *Treating Drug Problems.*

43. See Gerstein and Harwood, *Treating Drug Problems,* and Witters and Venturelli, *Drugs and Society.*

44. Some of this paragraph relies on Witters and Venturelli, *Drugs and Society.*

45. "Naltrexone: Breakthrough Treatment for Many Addictions?," *The Facts About Drugs and Alcohol,* Vol. 1, No. 4 (A Publication of the University of Florida College of Medicine) (1992), p. 1.

46. Ibid.

47. Witters and Venturelli, *Drugs and Society,* p. 331.

48. Ibid.

49. This paragraph relies on "Naltrexone: Breakthrough Treatment for Many Addictions"; also see "New Drug Update," *News & Views* (Newsletter of the Texas Research Society on Alcoholism), Vol. 3, No. 1 (1993).

50. This paragraph relies on Witters and Venturelli, *Drugs and Society,* especially p. 240. Also see National Institute on Drug Abuse, *Drug Abuse and Drug Abuse Research, The Third Triennial Report to Congress from the Secretary, Department of Health and Human Services* (Rockville, MD: Alcohol, Drug Abuse, and Mental Health Administration, 1991), pp. 56–57 for a discussion of the research on Clonidine.

51. Helen M. Annis and Christine S. Davis, "Self-Efficacy and the Prevention of Alcoholic Relapse: Initial Findings from a Treatment Trial," in Timothy B. Baker and Dale S. Cannon (eds.), *Assessment and Treatment of Addictive Disorders* (New York: Praeger, 1988), pp. 88–112, and NIAAA, *Seventh Special Report to the U.S. Congress on Alcohol and Health.*

52. G. Alan Marlatt and Judith R. Gordon, *Relapse Prevention: Maintenance Strategies in the Treatment of Addictive Behaviors* (New York: Guilford Press, 1985).

53. Terrence T. Gorski and Merlene Miller, *Staying Sober: A Guide for Relapse Prevention* (Independence, MO: Independence Press, 1986).

54. Also see Annis and Davis, "Self-Efficacy and the Prevention of Alcoholic Relapse," and Dennis C. Daley, *Relapse Prevention Workbook for Recovering Alcoholics and Drug Dependent Persons* (Holmes Beach, FL: Learning Publications, 1986); and Dennis C. Daley, *Relapse Prevention: Treatment Alternatives and Counseling Aids* (Blue Ridge Summit, PA: Tab Books, 1989).

55. Gorski and Miller, *Staying Sober,* and CENAPS Corporation, "The Relapse Dynamic" (Hazel Crest, IL: The CENAPS Corporation, no date).

56. Marlatt and Gordon, *Relapse Prevention.*

57. This paragraph relies on ibid.

58. Gerstein and Harwood, *Treating Drug Problems.*

59. Marie Weil, James M. Karls, and assoc., eds., *Case Management in Human Service Practice* (San Francisco: Jossey-Bass, 1985); also see Texas Department of Mental Health and Mental Retardation, *Case Management System Components by Mental Health and Mental Retardation Authorities,* June 1984.

60. Frances B. Hamm, "Organizational Change Required for Paradigmatic Shift in Addiction Treatment," *Journal of Substance Abuse Treatment,* Vol. 9 (1992), pp. 257–260.

61. Also see Peter E. Nathan, "Outcomes of Treatment for Alcoholism: Current Data," *Annals of Behavioral Medicine,* Vol. 8, Nos. 2–3 (1986), pp. 40–46.

62. NIAAA, *Sixth Special Report to the U.S. Congress on Alcohol and Health;* NIAAA, *Seventh Special Report to the U.S. Congress on Alcohol and Health;* and Gerstein and Harwood, *Treating Drug Problems.* For additional articles on alcoholism and drug treatment evaluation, see Louis S. Harris (ed.), *Problems of Drug Dependence 1989, Proceedings of the 51st Annual Scientific Meeting, The Committee on Problems of Drug Dependence,* National Institute on Drug Abuse, Research Monograph 95 (Rockville, MD: NIDA, 1990).

63. Kenneth W. Wanberg, John L. Horn, and Donald Fairchild, "Hospital Versus Community Treatment of Alcoholism Problems," *International Journal of Mental Health,* Vol. 3, Nos. 2–3, pp. 160–176; E. Mansell Pattison, Mark B. Sobell, and Linda C. Sobell, *Emerging Concepts of Alcohol Dependence* (New York: Springer, 1977); A. Thomas McLellan, Lester Luborsky, George E. Woody, Charles P. O'Brien and Ruben Kron, "Are the 'Addiction-Related' Problems of Substance Abusers Really Related?" *The Journal of Nervous and Mental Disease,* Vol. 169, No. 4 (1981), pp. 232–239; Chad D. Emrick and Joel Hansen, "Assertions Regarding Effectiveness of Treatment for Alcoholism: Fact or Fantasy?," *American Psychologist* (October

1983), pp. 1078–1088; P. Joseph Frawley, "Defining Desirable Treatment Outcomes," *Alcohol Health and Research World*, Vol. 12, No. 3 (1988), pp. 210–213; Thomas F. Babor, Zelig Dolinsky, Bruce Rounsaville, and Jerome Jaffe, "Unitary Versus Multidimensional Models of Alcoholism Treatment Outcome: An Empirical Study," *Journal of Studies on Alcohol*, Vol. 49, No. 2 (1988), pp. 167–177; and Edward J. Callahan and Ella H. Pecsok, "Heroin Addiction," in Dennis M. Donovan and G. Alan Marlatt, (eds.), *Assessment of Addictive Behaviors* (New York: The Guilford Press, 1988), pp. 390–418 and Stephen A. Maisto and Gerard J. Connors, "Assessment of Treatment Outcome," pp. 421–453 in same book.

64. NIAAA, *Sixth Special Report to the U.S. Congress on Alcohol and Health;* NIAAA, *Seventh Special Report to the U.S. Congress on Alcohol and Health.*

65. Gerstein and Harwood, *Treating Drug Problems.*

66. See NIAAA, *Sixth Special Report to the U.S. Congress on Alcohol and Health;* Gerstein and Harwood, *Treating Drug Problems.*

67. Hayashida et al., "Comparative Effectiveness and Costs of Inpatient and Outpatient Detoxification of Patients with Mild-to-Moderate Alcohol Withdrawal Syndrome."

68. Gerstein and Harwood, *Treating Drug Problems.*

69. Gordis and Sereny, "Controversy in Approaches to Alcoholism."

70. Gerstein and Harwood, *Treating Drug Problems.*

71. Ibid., p. 176.

72. Joanne R. Snair, *Report on Evaluation Research Review Conducted for the Governor's Study Commission on Crime Prevention and Law Enforcement* (Tallahassee, FL: Florida State University, October 1989, rev.), p. 6.

73. NIAAA, *Sixth Special Report to the U.S. Congress on Alcohol and Health;* Gerstein and Harwood, *Treating Drug Problems.*

74. Gordis and Sereny, "Controversy in Approaches to Alcoholism."

75. Cook, "The Minnesota Model in the Management of Drug and Alcohol Dependency: Miracle, Method or Myth? Part I. The Philosophy and the Programme," and Christopher C. H. Cook, "The Minnesota Model in the Management of Drug and Alcohol Dependency: Miracle, Method or Myth? Part II. Evidence and Conclusions," *British Journal of Addiction*, Vol. 83 (1988), pp. 735–748.

76. Cook, "The Minnesota Model, Part II," p. 735.

77. Ibid., p. 746.

78. Gerstein and Harwood, *Treating Drug Problems*, p. 190.

79. Richard K. Fuller, "Can Treatment Outcome Research Rely on Alcoholics' Self-Reports?" *Alcohol Health and Research World*, Vol. 12, No. 3 (1988), pp. 180–186.

80. John D. Swisher, "Evaluating Professional Counseling in Alcoholism Treatment," *Alcohol Health and Research World*, Vol. 12, No. 3 (1988), pp. 176–179.

81. NIAAA, *Sixth Special Report to the U.S. Congress on Alcohol and Health.*

82. Wanberg et al., "Hospital Versus Community Treatment of Alcoholism Problems," p. 174.

83. Diana Chapman Walsh et al., "A Randomized Trial of Treatment Options for Alcohol-abusing Workers," *The New England Journal of Medicine*, September 12, 1991, pp. 775–782, and Ron Winslow, "New Study Shows Inpatient Treatment May Be Best Course for Problem Drinkers," *The Wall Street Journal*, September 12, 1991, pp. B–1 and B–4.

84. Donald W. Goodwin, *Alcoholism*, (Kalamazoo, MI: The Upjohn Co., 1990).

85. "Efforts to Shift Substance Abuse Treatment to Outpatient Settings Has Patients 'Reeling,'" *Psychiatric News*, March 15, 1991, pp. 2 & 25.

86. Snair, *Report on Evaluation Research Review*, p. 6.

87. Gerstein and Harwood, *Treating Drug Problems.*

88. Charles P. O'Brien, Arthur Alterman, Dan Walter, Anna Rose Childress, and A. T. McLellan, "Evaluations of Treatment for Cocaine Dependence," in Louis S. Harris (ed.), *Problems of Drug Dependence 1989: Proceedings of the 51st Annual Scientific Meeting* (Rockville, MD: U.S. Department of Health and Human Services, 1990), pp. 78–84.

89. Jeffrey M. Brandsma and E. Mansell Pattison, "The Outcome of Group Psychotherapy Alcoholics: An Empirical Review," *American Journal of Drug and Alcohol Abuse*, Vol. 11, Nos. 1 & 2 (1985), pp. 151–162; also see Doroff, "Group Psychotherapy in Alcoholism."

90. Susan D. Solomon, "Individual Versus Group Therapy: Current Status in the Treatment of Alcoholism," *Advances in Alcohol and Substance Abuse*, Vol. 2, No. 1 (1982), pp. 69–86.

91. NIAAA, *Seventh Special Report to the U.S. Congress on Alcohol and Health.*

92. Barbara S. McCrady, Judith Moreau, Thomas J. Paolino, Jr., and Richard Longabaugh, "Joint Hospitalization and Couples Therapy for Alcoholism; A Four-Year Follow-up," *Journal of Studies on Alcohol*, Vol. 43, No. 11 (1982), pp. 1244–1250.

93. Barbara S. McCrady, Nora E. Noel, David B. Abrams, Robert L. Stout, Hilary Fisher Nelson, and William M. Hay, "Comparative Effectiveness of Three Types of

Spouse Involvement in Outpatient Behavioral Alcoholism Treatment," *Journal of Studies on Alcohol,* Vol. 47, No. 6 (1986), pp. 459–467.

94. H. M. Annis and C. B. Liban, "A Follow-up Study of Male Halfway-House Residents and Matched Nonresident Controls," *Journal of Studies on Alcohol,* Vol. 40, No. 1 (1979), pp. 63–69.

95. Rubington, "The Role of the Halfway House in the Rehabilitation of Alcoholics," p. 363.

96. Annis and Liban, "A Follow-up Study of Male Halfway-House Residents and Matched Nonresident Controls."

97. Carol Van Ryswyk, Margaret Churchill, Joan Velasquez, and Richard McGuire, "Effectiveness of Halfway House Placement for Alcohol and Drug Abusers," *American Journal of Drug and Alcohol Abuse,"* Vol. 8, No. 4 (1981–82), pp. 499–512.

98. Some of this section relies on Orford and Velleman, "Alcoholism Halfway Houses."

99. Shirley Otto and Jim Orford, *Not Quite Like Home: Small Hostels for Alcoholics and Others* (New York: John Wiley and Sons, 1978), and Alan C. Ogborne, H. M. Annis, and M. Sanchez-Craig, *Report of the Task Force on Halfway Houses* (Toronto: Addiction Research Foundation, 1978) cited in Orford and Velleman, "Alcoholism Halfway Houses."

100. Richard Velleman, "The Engagement of New Residents: A Missing Dimension in the Evaluation of Halfway Houses for Problem Drinkers," *Journal of Studies on Alcohol,* Vol. 45 (1984), pp. 251–259.

101. See Orford and Velleman, "Alcoholism Halfway Houses," and Rubington, "Staff Problems in Halfway Houses."

102. Also see Orford and Velleman, "Alcoholism Halfway Houses."

103. Gerstein and Harwood, *Treating Drug Problems.*

104. Snair, *Report on Evaluation Research Review.*

105. Jacobson, "The Role of Shelter Facilities in the Treatment of Alcoholics."

106. Katz, "The Salvation Army Men's Social Service Center," p. 642.

107. Rudolf H. Moos, Barbara Mehren, and Bernice S. Moos, "Evaluation of a Salvation Army Alcoholism Treatment Program," *Journal of Studies on Alcohol,* Vol. 38, No. 7 (1978), pp. 1267–1275.

108. Jacobson, "The Role of Shelter Facilities in the Treatment of Alcoholics."

109. Gerstein and Harwood, *Treating Drug Problems.*

110. Snair, *Report on Evaluation Research Review,* p. 6.

111. Gerstein and Harwood, *Treating Drug Problems,* p. 153.

112. Ibid.

113. David S. Metzger, James Cornish, George E. Woody, A. Thomas McLellan, Patrick Druley and Charles P. O'Brien, "Naltrexone in Federal Probationers," in Louis S. Harris (ed.), *Problems of Drug Dependence 1989: Proceedings of the 51st Annual Scientific Meeting* (Rockville, MD: U.S. Department of Health and Human Services, 1990), p. 466.

114. NIAAA, *Sixth Special Report to the U.S. Congress on Alcohol and Health.*

115. Richard K. Fuller, Laure Branchey, Dennis R. Brightwell, Robert M. Derman, Chad D. Emrick, Frank L. Iber, Kenneth E. James, Roy B. Lacoursiere, Kelvin K. Lee, Ilse Lowenstam, Iradj Maany, Dewey Neiderhiser, James J. Nocks, and Spencer Shaw, "Disulfiram Treatment of Alcoholism: A Veterans Administration Cooperative Study," *Journal of the American Medical Association,* Vol. 256, No. 11 (September 19, 1986), pp. 1449–1455.

116. Ibid., p. 1449.

117. McNichol and Logsdon, "Disulfiram: An Evaluation Research Model."

118. NIAAA, *Sixth Special Report to the U.S. Congress on Alcohol and Health,* p. 130.

119. See, for example, R. Dale Walker, Dennis M. Donovan, Daniel R. Kivlahan, and Michael R. O'Leary, "Length of Stay, Neuropsychological Performance, and Aftercare: Influences on Alcohol Treatment Outcome," *Journal of Consulting and Clinical Psychology,* Vol. 51, No. 6, pp. 900–911.

120. Gerstein and Harwood, *Treating Drug Problems,* p. 172.

121. NIAAA, *Sixth Special Report to the U.S. Congress on Alcohol and Health.*

122. Annis and Davis, "Self-Efficacy and the Prevention of Alcoholic Relapse: Initial Findings from a Treatment Trial," and NIAAA, *Seventh Special Report to the U.S. Congress on Alcohol and Health.*

123. Chad D. Emrick, "Alcoholics Anonymous: Affiliation Processes and Effectiveness as Treatment," *Alcoholism: Clinical and Experimental Research,* Vol. 11, No. 5 (1987), pp. 416–423, and Ann M. Bradley, "Keep Coming Back: The Case for a Valuation of Alcoholics Anonymous," *Alcohol Health & Research World,* Vol. 12, No. 3 (1988), p. 198.

124. Manpower Demonstration Research Corporation, *Summary and Findings of the National Supported Work Demonstration* (Cambridge, MA: Ballinger, 1980).

125. McLellan et al., "Are the 'Addiction-Related' Problems of Substance Abusers Really Related?"

126. Gerstein and Harwood, *Treating Drug Problems.*

127. NIAAA, *Sixth Special Report to the U.S. Congress on Alcohol and Health.*

128. Nathan, "Outcomes of Treatment for Alcoholism: Current Data."

129. NIAAA, *Seventh Special Report to the U.S. Congress on Alcohol and Health,* p. 130; also see Chad D. Emrick and Joel Hansen, "Assertions Regarding Effectiveness of Treatment for Alcoholism: Fact or Fantasy?," *American Psychologist* (October 1983), pp. 1078–1088.

130. A. Thomas McLellan, George E. Woody, Lester Luborsky, Charles P. O'Brien, and Keith A. Druley, "Increased Effectiveness of Substance Abuse Treatment: A Prospective Study of Patient-Treatment 'Matching,'" *The Journal of Nervous and Mental Disease,* Vol. 171, No. 10 (1983), pp. 597–605, and A. Thomas McLellan, Lester Luborsky, George E. Woody, Charles P. O'Brien, and Keith A. Druley, "Predicting Response to Alcohol and Drug Abuse Treatments," *Archives of General Psychiatry,* Vol. 40 (1983), pp. 620–625.

131. Sherry Deren and Joan Randell, "The Vocational Rehabilitation of Substance Abusers," *Journal of Applied Rehabilitation Counseling,* Vol. 21, No. 2 (1990), pp. 4–6.

132. John F. C. McLachlan, "Therapy Strategies, Personality Orientation and Recovery from Alcoholism," *Canadian Psychiatric Association Journal,* Vol. 19, No. 1 (February 1974), pp. 25–30.

133. Stephen K. Valle, "Interpersonal Functioning of Alcoholism Counselors and Treatment Outcome," *Journal of Studies on Alcohol,* Vol. 42, No. 9 (1981), pp. 783–790.

134. Raymond M. Costello, "Alcoholism Treatment and Evaluation: In Search of Methods. II. Collation of Two-Year Follow-up Studies," *The International Journal of the Addictions,* Vol. 10, No. 5 (1975), pp. 857–867.

135. NIAAA, *Sixth Special Report to the U.S. Congress on Alcohol and Health,* p. 127.

136. Jeffrey M. Brandsma, Maxie C. Maultsby, Jr., Richard J. Welsh, *Outpatient Treatment of Alcoholism: A Review and Comparative Study* (Baltimore, MD: University Park Press, 1980).

137. NIAAA, *Sixth Special Report to the U.S. Congress on Alcohol and Health.*

138. Ibid.

139. Ibid.

140. Ibid.

141. Clayton T. Shorkey, "Use of Behavioral Methods with Individuals Recovering from Psychoactive Substance Dependence," in Donald K. Granvold (ed.), *Cognitive and Behavioral Treatment: Methods and Applications* (Belmont, CA: Brooks/Cole Publishing, forthcoming, 1993).

142. Peter E. Nathan and D. W. Briddell, "Behavioral Assessment and Treatment of Alcoholism," in Kissin and Begleiter, *The Biology of Alcoholism,* pp. 301–349.

143. Dale S. Cannon, Timothy B. Baker, Antonio Gino, and Peter E. Nathan, "Alcohol Aversion Therapy: Relationship Between Strength of Aversion and Abstinence," in Timothy B. Baker and Dale S. Cannon (eds.), *Assessment and Treatment of Addictive Disorders* (New York: Praeger, 1988), p. 205.

144. Pattison, Sobell, and Sobell, *Emerging Concepts of Alcohol Dependence,* see Chapter 6, and David J. Armor, J. Michael Polich, and Harriet B. Stambul, *Alcoholism and Treatment* (Publication R-1739-NIAAA) (Santa Monica, CA: Rand Corporation, 1976, also published by John Wiley and Sons, New York, 1978).

145. Callahan and Pecsok, "Heroin Addiction," p. 392.

146. Armor et al., *Alcoholism and Treatment.* Some of this section relies on Ray and Ksir, *Drugs, Society, & Human Behavior,* see pages 363–364.

147. Pattison et al., *Emerging Concepts of Alcohol Dependence.*

148. J. Michael Polich, David J. Armor, and Harriet B. Braiker, *The Course of Alcoholism: Four Years After Treatment* (R-2433-NIAAA) (Santa Monica, CA: Rand Corporation, 1980, also published by John S. Wiley and Sons, 1981).

149. Mark B. Sobell and Linda C. Sobell, "Individualized Behavior Therapy for Alcoholics," *Behavior Therapy,* Vol. 4 (1973), pp. 49–72; and Mark B. Sobell and Linda C. Sobell, "Alcoholics Treated by Individualized Behavior Therapy: One Year Treatment Outcome," *Behaviour Research and Therapy,* Vol. 11 (1973), pp. 599–618.

150. Mark B. Sobell and Linda C. Sobell, "Second-Year Treatment Outcome of Alcoholics Treated by Individualized Behavior Therapy: Results," *Behaviour Research and Therapy,* Vol. 14 (1976), pp. 195–215, reprinted in Pattison et al., *Emerging Concepts of Alcohol Dependence,* pp. 300–335.

151. Mary L. Pendery, Irving M. Maltzman, and L. Jolyon West, "Controlled Drinking by Alcoholics? New Findings and a Reevaluation of a Major Affirmative Study," *Science,* Vol. 217 (July 9, 1982), pp. 169–175.

152. Ovide Pomerleau, Michael Pertschuk, David Adkins, and John Paul Brady, "A Comparison of Behavioral and Traditional Treatment for Middle-Income Problem Drinkers," *Journal of Behavioral Medicine,* Vol. 1, No. 2 (1978), pp. 187–200.

153. Ray and Ksir, *Drugs, Society, & Human Behavior,* p. 364.

154. T. M. Worner, B. Zeller, H. Schwarz, F. Zwas, and D. Lyon, "Acupuncture Fails to Improve Treatment Out-

come in Alcoholics," *Drug and Alcohol Dependence,* Vol. 30, (1992), pp. 169–173.

155. Alex G. Brumbaugh, "Acupuncture: New Perspectives in Chemical Dependency Treatment," *Journal of Substance Abuse Treatment,* Vol. 10 (1993), pp. 35–43.

156. This paragraph relies on ibid.

157. Milton L. Bullock, Andrew J. Umen, Patricia D. Culliton, and Robert T. Olander, "Acupuncture Treatment of Alcoholic Recidivism: A Pilot Study," *Alcoholism: Clinical and Experimental Research,* Vol. 11, No. 3 (1987), pp. 292–295; and Milton L. Bullock, Patricia D. Culliton, and Robert T. Olander, "Controlled Trial of Acupuncture for Severe Recidivist Alcoholism," *The Lancet,* June 24, 1989, pp. 1435–1439.

158. Worner et al., "Acupuncture Fails to Improve Treatment Outcome in Alcoholics."

159. Ibid., p. 173.

160. Shorkey, "Use of Behavioral Methods with Individuals Recovering from Psychoactive Substance Dependence."

161. Eugene G. Peniston and Paul J. Kulkosky, " $\alpha - \theta$ Brainwave Training and β-Endorphin Levels in Alcoholics," *Alcoholism: Clinical and Experimental Research,* Vol. 13, No. 2 (March/April 1989), pp. 271–279, and Eugene G. Peniston and Paul J. Kulkosky, "Alpha-Theta EEG Biofeedback Training in Alcoholism & Post-Traumatic Stress Disorder," *International Society for the Study of Subtle Energies and Energy Medicine,* Vol. 2, No. 4 (1992), pp. 5–7.

162. Witters and Venturelli, *Drugs and Society.*

163. Brandsma et al., *Outpatient Treatment of Alcoholism: A Review and Comparative Study;* Nick Kanas, "Alcoholism and Group Psychotherapy," in Pattison and Kaufman, *Encyclopedic Handbook of Alcoholism,* pp. 1011–1021, and Sheldon Zimberg, "Psychotherapy in the Treatment of Alcoholism," also in Pattison and Kaufman, *Encyclopedic Handbook of Alcoholism,* pp. 999–1010.

164. Doroff, "Group Psychotherapy in Alcoholism."

165. Bradley, "Keep Coming Back: The Case for a Valuation of Alcoholics Anonymous," p. 198.

166. Alcoholics Anonymous World Services (AAWS), "Alcoholics Anonymous 1989 Membership Survey" (New York: AA, 1990).

167. "A.A. at a Glance" (New York: A.A. General Service Office, no date).

168. AAWS, "Alcoholics Anonymous 1989 Membership Survey."

169. Alcoholics Anonymous World Services, *Forty-four Questions and Answers About the A.A. Program of Recovery from Alcoholism* (New York: AA, 1952).

170. Ibid.

171. Mary Sheeren, "The Relationship Between Relapse and Involvement in Alcoholics Anonymous," *Journal of Studies on Alcohol,* Vol. 49, No. 1 (1988), pp. 104–106, and Frederick Baekeland, "Evaluation of Treatment Methods in Chronic Alcoholism," in Kissin and Begleiter, *The Biology of Alcoholism,* p. 406.

172. Paul E. Bebbington, "The Efficacy of Alcoholics Anonymous: The Elusiveness of Hard Data," *British Journal of Psychiatry,* Vol. 128 (1976), pp. 572–580.

173. Frederick B. Glaser and Alan C. Ogborne, "Does A.A. Really Work?" *British Journal of Addiction,* Vol. 77 (1982), pp. 123–129.

174. Ibid.

175. Bebbington, "The Efficacy of Alcoholics Anonymous: The Elusiveness of Hard Data," p. 572; also see Baekeland, "Evaluation of Treatment Methods."

176. Bebbington, "The Efficacy of Alcoholics Anonymous: The Elusiveness of Hard Data"; also see Glaser and Ogborne, "Does A.A. Really Work?"

177. Alan C. Ogborne and Frederick B. Glaser, "Characteristics of Affiliates of Alcoholics Anonymous," *Journal of Studies on Alcohol,* Vol. 42, No. 7 (1981), p. 670.

178. Ibid., p. 670.

179. Baekeland "Evaluation of Treatment Methods," p. 408.

180. Emrick, "Alcoholics Anonymous," and Bradley, "Keep Coming Back: The Case for a Valuation of Alcoholics Anonymous."

181. Emrick, "Alcoholics Anonymous," p. 418.

182. Baekeland "Evaluation of Treatment Methods," p. 407.

183. George E. Vaillant, *The Natural History of Alcoholism* (Cambridge, MA: Harvard University Press, 1983).

184. William R. Miller and Reid K. Hester, "Treating the Problem Drinker: Modern Approaches," in William R. Miller (ed.), *The Addictive Behaviors: Treatment of Alcoholism, Drug Abuse, Smoking, and Obesity* (Oxford: Pergamon Press, 1980), pp. 11–141.

185. Emrick, "Alcoholics Anonymous," p. 416.

186. Brandsma et al., *Outpatient Treatment of Alcoholism: A Review and Comparative Study.*

187. Baekeland "Evaluation of Treatment Methods," p. 407.

188. Helen M. Pettinati, A. Arthur Sugerman, Nicholas DiDonato, and Helen S. Maurer, "The Natural History of Alcoholism over Four Years After Treatment," *Journal of Studies on Alcohol,* Vol. 43, No. 3 (1982), pp. 201–215.

189. Eileen M. Corrigan, *Alcoholic Women in Treatment* (New York: Oxford University Press, 1980).

190. Emrick, "Alcoholics Anonymous."

191. Gerald M. Cross, Charles W. Morgan, Al J. Mooney, Carolyn A. Martin, and John A. Rafter, "Alcoholism Treatment: A Ten-Year Follow-up Study," *Alcoholism: Clinical and Experimental Research,* Vol. 14, No. 2 (1990), p. 169.

192. Some of this paragraph relies on David N. Nurco, Norma Wegner, Philip Stephenson, Abraham Makofsy, and John W. Shaffer, *Ex-Addicts' Self-Help Groups, Potential and Pitfalls* (New York: Praeger, 1983).

193. G. J. Connors, K. H. Dermen, and M.R. Duerr, "Characteristics of Participants in a secular Self-Help Organization: Findings from a Survey of S.O.S. Members, " presented at the Research Society on Alcoholism, Annual Scientific Meeting, San Antonio, TX, June, 1993.

194. Nurco et al., *Ex-Addicts' Self-Help Groups.*

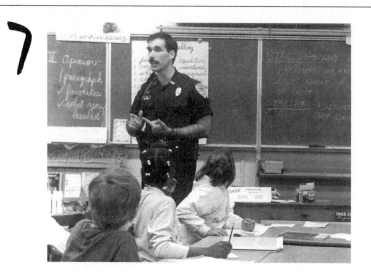

7

Preventing alcohol and drug problems

INTRODUCTION

The concept of "prevention" can be operationalized in a number of different ways. Most people seem to equate the term with the prevention of alcohol and other drug abuse, especially among children and adolescents. It is also frequently associated with a specific preventive method used with young people, that is, education. This is a relatively narrow view of prevention. During the last decade our outlook on prevention has broadened considerably to include new goals, other populations, and additional strategies.

Several factors have contributed to this broader view of prevention. For example,

there has been increasing involvement of volunteers and local action-oriented groups such as Mothers Against Drunk Driving (MADD), Students Against Driving Drunk (SADD), the Group Against Smoking Pollution (GASP), and hundreds of parent and community-based antidrug organizations. These groups have succeeded in developing specific *constituencies* for prevention programs, something that has been lacking in earlier efforts focused primarily on school children. It is difficult to disagree with their very specific objectives such as protecting the public from drunk drivers or making the air in office buildings safe to breathe. They are also free of the prior disciplinary and professional constraints that have handicapped many of the professionals working in prevention programs. MADD and SADD have not hesitated to take their concerns directly to the legislative arena to get their point of view across. Neighborhood

groups have organized public demonstrations outside the homes of suspected drug dealers. They have also provided surveillance of suspected drug dealers and supplied the police with information on drug transactions.

Saying "No" to Crack Gangs: Angry citizens fight back against the drug trade

The section of Brooklyn, N.Y., that surrounds the Muslim mosque At-Taqwq smells pleasantly of West Indian food. People walk unhurried down the street, pausing to chat with friends. From the mosque comes a musical wailing, calling worshippers to prayer. In the late afternoon sunlight, the neighborhood—though it lies deep in a crime-ridden ghetto—seems calm.

It was not always so. Just two months ago these same streets formed a battle zone crossed only at great risk. Drug dealers operated out of 12 crack houses and openly hustled their goods on the street. Addicts robbed passers-by at gunpoint. There were sidewalk killings. Shops closed down, their customers scared away. Residents lived in terror, some afraid to go near their windows. Then a group of Muslims decided to take back the neighborhood. Arming themselves with walkie-talkies and a we're-not-going-to-take-it-anymore attitude, they began to patrol the area around the mosque 24 hours a day. The Muslims got the police to flush out the crack houses, then parked themselves cross-armed in the doorways. When would-be drug buyers came by the Muslims told them they were gone. If patrol members spotted a crack transaction on the street, they boldly placed themselves between the dealer and the buyer and contacted the police through the radios. The effectiveness of the vigil has surpassed everyone's expectations. "We closed down the crack houses last October, but within weeks they were back operating at full scale," recalls Capt. Thomas Baumann of the 79th Precinct. "This time they stayed shut."

In cities across the country, citizens are began fighting back against crack. The battle is taking many forms, from gutsy street

confrontations to anti-drug programs in schools, but there is one common thread: a sense that the crack epidemic and the gang violence that attends it spiraling out of control. Ghetto residents once wary of the police now cooperate with the law. Parents who once saw no evil now seek out trouble in city parks. Ex-addicts and gang members lecture children on the evils of drug gangs. Groups with names like Mothers Against Gangs, Teenagers in Action and Southside Concerned Black Men are establishing telephone hot lines, camping out in known drug zones and forming hall patrols in schools. Whether in Chicago, Los Angeles, New York or Atlanta, the message is the same: it's time for everyone to get involved.

In Brooklyn the Muslims' confrontational approach is an extreme example, inspired in part by an anti-drug religious creed. More typical are harassment tactics like those adopted by residents around East 14th Street in Manhattan. Linking up with local block associations, a group called East Villagers Against Crack advertised its presence in six inch letters on an abandoned theater marquee: "You Buy We Spy" and "Drug Dealers Out." EVAC formed street patrols and sent letters to all neighborhood residents urging that they join the fight against drugs in the area. "The community has to come forward," says Bill Hopkins of the New York State Substance Abuse Services. "If people keep running into their houses too afraid to say anything to police, the drug gangs are going to take over the streets.

Continued presence

Unfortunately, community pressures often succeed only temporarily, or simply push drug gangs down the road a piece.

When a shopping plaza in southwest Atlanta became overrun with crack dealers last year, a neighborhood resident named Michael Langford decided to take action. Langford convinced 10 other men to camp out on a drug corner one night and organized an anti-drug rally the next day. The dealers vacated the corner—but not before one of them came up to Langford and said, "I could blow you away right here." Several days after the stakeout, the dealers were back. "It's not as bad as it was, but it's not what it should be either," says Langford. "That's why it has to be a constant, continual presence."

Maintaining that presence can be dangerous. Armed with money, guns and brazen indifference to violence, crack gangs seldom give up their turf without a fight. Last year a minister in Compton, Calif., just south of Los Angeles, organized several anti-drug marches that gained considerable media attention. Several weeks ago the minister (who did not want his name used in this article) walked into his office to find the bloody head of a dog on his desk and a note warning him to stop his crusade or expect the same fate.

The Community Youth Gang Services in Los Angeles has developed a multifaceted approach. A city and county organization with a $2 million annual budget, the CYGS is made up of both former gang members and professional social workers. Last year CYGS persuaded more than 120 gang members to give up the life. They also helped 350 ghetto families with everything from counseling to funeral arrangements and secured 47 truces between rival gangs. In the process, CYGS night supervisor Kenneth Wheeler 29, took a stray bullet in the chin. But he has no intention of quitting. "I feel I'm doing something." He says "I'm tired of seeing all these youngsters get killed. Someone has to tell them there's a better way."

Source: *Newsweek* March 28, 1989, p. 29.

Community groups have been pushing for broad changes in policies and practices at all levels, from the grass-roots to Washington, and they have evolved a national leadership to advocate for reform. There is evidence of the impact of this new movement in such issues as Proposition 99 in California. Despite a $20 million campaign by the tobacco industry to defeat it, voters passed an initiative raising taxes on tobacco products by 25 cents and designating the money for youth-oriented preventive education, research, and health care for people with tobacco-related medical problems.[1]

The new approach is more consistent with a "harm reduction" model of prevention rather than the "zero tolerance" philosophy that is apparently still favored by the law enforcement agencies of our federal government (see Chapter 8). The objectives of a harm reduction approach are to reduce the mortality and morbidity associated with alcohol and drug-related *problems* as well as to reduce the rates of abuse for alcohol and drugs. The new, more comprehensive view includes social, cultural, and legislative aspects of prevention rather than emphasizing individual responsibility.[2] Environmentally and culturally targeted approaches focus on the social and economic aspects of alcohol availability and stress objectives designed to reduce the severity of alcohol-related injuries.[3] Some environmentally oriented programs have specifically targeted young people. Perhaps the best example of the approach was the change in "minimum age of consumption" laws during the early 1980s.[4] The social aspects of prevention are stressed in ad campaigns that repeatedly tell us that "Friends don't let friends drive drunk." At the cultural level, when new legal drugs (cigarettes and alcohol) were recently introduced specifically for young urban Afro-Americans, organized opposition quickly let the manufacturers and retailers know that this was not an acceptable practice.

This is a utilitarian approach, one that argues for the greatest good for the greatest number of people, and one that recognizes that the indirect consequences of abuse and dependency may be far more serious and widespread than is generally believed.[5] Perhaps the best example is the high fatality rate associated with alcohol-related automobile accidents. Another is the high rate of infection (hepatitis, AIDS, etc.) associated with needle-sharing among intravenous drug users. Still another is the high crime rates associated with using certain illicit drugs such as heroin. Advocates of harm reduction approaches assume that certain drugs will always be abused. If we recognize that college fraternities probably will always abuse alcohol, we might turn our efforts toward preventing "frat boys" from driving while intoxicated. A more realistic approach to intravenous drug use might be able to halt the spread of certain diseases by providing clean needles and syringes to heroin addicts.

Using a traditional public health model, prevention efforts may be classified as *primary,* *secondary,* or *tertiary.* Preventing new cases from occurring, such as in convincing a classroom of youngsters to not smoke, is primary prevention. Reducing the number of existing cases, generally by identifying and treating those who have a drug or alcohol problem, is secondary prevention. The effort to avoid relapse and maintain the health of those who have been treated is tertiary prevention.[6]

Preventive strategies also may be grouped into five major categories: public information and education, service measures, technologic measures, legislative and regulatory measures, and economic measures. Some of these strategies may be directed at preventing or decreasing the use or abuse of alcohol or drugs; others focus on reducing or eliminating the harmful consequences of alcohol and drug use, both to the user and the larger society. All of these will be discussed in the following pages, but first we will turn our attention to a brief overview of prevention efforts.

OVERVIEW OF PREVENTION

Drug problems among American youth became a public concern in the middle to late 1960s. Obviously, young people had been abusing alcohol as long as anyone could remember, but prevention efforts were relatively puny until large numbers of children began experimenting with *illicit* drugs. The majority of prevention programs focused on ways to reduce demand for drugs and alcohol, most often by trying to change individual behavior. Few of these programs have had successful results beyond superficial and transient changes in knowledge and attitudes.[7] One can change both knowledge and attitudes concerning drugs only to discover that it has little effect on behavior.[8] The research and evaluation methodologies used in most of these programs are also quite weak, and few of them have addressed any significant theoretical issues that cut across common areas of concern regarding alcohol, tobacco, and illicit drugs. Do peer influences operate in the same manner regarding both legal and illegal drugs? Is gender a factor in the success of prevention programs? If a prevention program is assessed a "failure," do we know *why* it failed? Despite the seriousness of polydrug use, programs focusing on alcohol, tobacco, and other drugs have maintained their conceptual distinctness, and professionals working in the prevention field also have tended to focus on differences in their areas of specialization rather than to seek common ground.[9]

PUBLIC INFORMATION AND EDUCATION

Information and education are explicit elements in most drug and alcohol prevention programs. Tremendous emphasis has been placed on public information and school-based education as a primary means of prevention throughout the United States. However, these approaches to changing behaviors rooted in deeply held social values have been marginally effective, at best.[10] Nevertheless, it is still widely accepted that informational approaches should be included in programs designed to prevent drug use.[11]

Under highly specific conditions public information campaigns can sometimes achieve certain limited goals. There is evidence that programs directed at increasing the number of people inoculated for infectious diseases, increasing the response rates for census reports, and getting taxpayers to file by the deadline all have met with a measure of success.[12] Health education in the public schools is another matter, however.[13] This should come as no surprise, since health education has never been accorded a high priority in the public schools. Teachers often view it as an intrusion and a drain on the "legitimate" goals of the educational process. Programs are ill conceived, lack clear-cut objectives, and are not designed to engage student interest and involvement. Teachers generally receive little training in how to present the material. Students, perhaps reflecting school and teacher attitudes, typically regard health education as a required bore. It is no wonder that programs are, at best, marginally effective.[14]

Public information and education efforts directed at adults have been much more limited. The primary adult educational programs are "DUI schools." These are designed for persons who generally have long histories of DUI violations and even longer histories of alcohol abuse, but many of their clients are probably not alcoholics. With such a varied group of clients, it is not surprising that their effectiveness is also marginal. Paradoxically, they are probably more successful with the substantial number of students who are not really alcoholic or drug dependent.

We have witnessed a dramatic increase in mass media campaigns dealing with alcohol, drugs, and smoking in recent years. Strategies are aimed at getting children to "just say no" to drugs, at convincing adults to drink in moderation, at convincing drivers to not get behind the wheel after drinking, and at convincing everyone to quit smoking. These strategies appear to have had limited success

regarding smoking (not among teenage girls), but the jury is still out on alcohol and drug abuse prevention. Even the modest decrease in alcohol consumption among certain subgroups is very difficult to tie directly to prevention efforts. With few exceptions, the evidence that we do have is no cause for optimism.[15]

Programs Directed at Children and Adolescents

Throughout the 1970s most drug abuse prevention programs were educational in nature, were directed at adolescents, and were implemented through the schools. Early programs relied on providing information and using "scare" tactics. These programs were generally so ineffective that they were denounced by the federal government's Special Office for Drug Abuse Prevention (SODAP). In fact SODAP was so disillusioned that it imposed a temporary ban on the funding of drug information programs.[16]

Growing evidence of the ineffectiveness of these strategies led to a trend toward use of "affective education" and other alternative approaches.[17] Affective programs assumed that adolescents would be deterred from using drugs if their self-esteem, interpersonal skills, and techniques for decision making and problem solving could be improved. Recreational activities, community service projects, and involvement in the arts were stressed as a way of providing meaningful, fulfilling experiences that would counteract the attractions of drugs. Unfortunately, there is little evidence that this approach has been any more effective than simply providing information.[18] This model was developed as a result of research on the correlates of drug-using behavior primarily among delinquents and addicts.[19] These studies identified drug-abusing youth as less likely to participate in clubs, youth organizations, and religious activities. Generalizing from that population to "normal" adolescents may have led to a faulty model for our prevention efforts.

Early smoking prevention programs were also information oriented and frequently resorted to "scare" tactics, such as showing students photographs of cancerous and healthy lungs. Like the early alcohol and drug prevention programs, they had little impact on long-term behavior. Confronted with this lack of success, some researchers began to consider ways of addressing the social milieu in which young people begin smoking. This eventually resulted in a new generation of smoking programs that have been somewhat more successful.

Drawing on Evan's "social inoculation" theory[20] and McGuire's concept of "cognitive inoculation,"[21] this approach argues that if adolescents are provided with counterarguments and techniques with which to resist peer pressures to smoke, as well as factual information about smoking, they are more likely to abstain. Most of the new generation of smoking prevention programs focus on the short-term effects of smoking rather than long-term health consequences. ("When he kisses you, do you really want your breath to smell like an ashtray?") The impact of this new approach is well documented in delaying young people's use of tobacco for up to two years.[22] However, longer-term effects have not been demonstrated, and even the short-term effects appear to decay with time.[23]

Many elements from the social inoculation and affective education models were used in developing Project DARE (Drug Abuse Resistance Education). This program was originally developed as a joint project of the Los Angeles Police Department and the Los Angeles Unified School District, and it is now operated in several hundred communities across the nation. Project DARE is designed to help fifth and sixth grade students recognize and resist peer pressure that frequently leads to experimentation with alcohol and drugs. Several lessons focus on building self-esteem, while others emphasize the consequences of using alcohol or drugs and identify alternative ways of coping with stress, gaining peer acceptance, or having fun. Most important, students learn and practice specific strategies for responding to peers who offer them drugs. Ways to say "no" include changing the subject, walking away or ignor-ing the person, or simply saying "no" and repeating it as often as necessary. The curriculum is organized into seventeen classroom sessions (see Table 7.1) conducted by a police officer, coupled with other activities to be taught by the regular classroom teacher.[24]

One of the earliest evaluations of the DARE program found that students who received the full-semester DARE curriculum during the sixth grade had significantly lower use of alcohol, cigarettes, and other drugs. The impact was much greater for boys (who used more drugs to begin with) than for girls, however.[25] A later longitudinal (three-year) study found significantly lower use rates by DARE graduates for all drugs except tobacco.[26] One of the more recent evaluations of a DARE program in Lexington, Kentucky, found significant differences in student attitudes concerning drug use, but no differences in self-reported drug use.[27]

The most important conclusion to be reached after twenty years of organized prevention programming is that no single strategy has demonstrated a long-term impact, and many of the experts now believe that it may be a mistake to think in terms of a single-strategy solution. In many respects life has become more complicated for the current generation. Experimentation may be a normal rite of passage for many youth—a phase that most will outgrow. Previous generations of youth experimented mostly with alcohol. The greater availability of illicit drugs provides today's youth with a greater variety of choices. Prevention efforts, therefore, must become more comprehensive. A mixture of public information and education programs with the other measures described shortly may result in a more effective approach to prevention.

SERVICE MEASURES

Service measures (detoxification, therapeutic communities, twenty-eight-day treatment programs, Alcoholics Anonymous, etc.) are aimed at ameliorating or reversing a condition resulting from alcohol or drug use or reducing

TABLE 7.1 DARE Lessons

The DARE curriculum is organized into seventeen classroom sessions conducted by the police officer, coupled with suggested activities taught by the regular classroom teacher. A wide range of teaching activities are used: question-and-answer, group-discussion, and role-play and workbook exercises, all designed to encourage student participation and response.

Each lesson is briefly summarized below, giving a sense of the scope of the DARE curriculum and the care taken in its preparation. All of these lessons were pilot tested and revised before widespread use began.

1. **Practices for Personal Safety.** The DARE officer reviews common safety practices to protect students from harm at home, on the way to and from school, and in the neighborhood.

2. **Drug Use and Misuse.** Students learn the harmful effects of drugs if they are misused as depicted in the film "Drugs and Your Amazing Mind."

3. **Consequences.** Focus is on the consequences of using and not using alcohol and marijuana. If students are aware of those consequences, they can make better informed decisions regarding their own behavior.

4. **Resisting Pressure to Use Drugs.** The DARE officer explains different types of pressure—ranging from friendly persuasion and teasing to threats—that friends and others exert on students to try tobacco, alcohol, or drugs.

5. **Resistance Techniques: Ways to Say No.** Students rehearse the many ways of refusing offers to try tobacco, alcohol, or drugs—simply saying no and repeating it as often as necessary, changing the subject, walking away, or ignoring the person. They learn that they can avoid situations in which they might be subjected to such pressures and can "hang around" with nonusers.

6. **Building Self-esteem.** Poor self-esteem is one of the factors associated with drug misuse. How students feel about themselves results from positive and negative feelings and experiences. In this session students learn about their own positive qualities and how to compliment other students.

7. **Assertiveness: A Response Style.** Students have certain rights—to be themselves, to say what they think, to

say no to offers of drugs. The session teaches them to assert those rights confidently and without interfering with others' rights.

8. **Managing Stress Without Taking Drugs.** Students learn to recognize sources of stress in their lives and techniques for avoiding or relieving stress, including exercise, deep breathing, and talking to others. They learn that using drugs or alcohol to relieve stress causes new problems.

9. **Media Influences on Drug Use.** The DARE officer reviews strategies used in the media to encourage tobacco and alcohol use, including testimonials from celebrities and social pressure.

10. **Decision Making and Risk Taking.** Students learn the difference between bad risks and responsible risks, how to recognize their choices, and how to make a decision that promotes their self-interests.

11. **Alternatives to Drug Abuse.** Students learn that to have fun, to be accepted by peers, or to deal with feelings of anger or hurt, there are a number of alternatives to using drugs and alcohol.

12. **Role Modeling.** A high school student selected by the DARE officer with the assistance of the high school staff visits the class, providing students with a positive role model. Students learn that drug users are in the minority.

13. **Forming a Support System.** Students learn that they need to develop positive relationships with many different people to form a support system.

14. **Ways to Deal with Pressures from Gangs.** Students discuss the kinds of pressures they may encounter from gang members and evaluate the consequences of the choices available to them.

15. **DARE Summary.** Students summarize and assess what they have learned.

16. **Taking a Stand.** Students compose and read aloud essays on how they can respond when they are pressured to use drugs and alcohol. The essay represents each student's "DARE Pledge."

17. **Culmination.** In a schoolwide assembly planned in concert with school administrators, all students who have participated in DARE receive certificates of achievement.

Source: U.S. Department of Justice, Office of Justice Programs, Bureau of Justice Assistance, *An Introduction to DARE: Drug Abuse Resistance Education,* 2nd ed. NCJ 129862 (Washington, DC: U.S. Government Printing Office, October 1991), pp. 12–13. Reprinted with the permission of the Los Angeles Unified School District.

the chances of its onset among members of a high-risk population. In traditional community health terms, such measures usually fall into the secondary or tertiary prevention category. Service measures are not generally emphasized in prevention because of their ameliorative or restorative nature. Their lack

of popularity among prevention experts is due to the fact that, by definition, they are directed toward the remediation of a problem rather than preventing new cases from occuring.

Service measures are also labor intensive and, therefore, comparatively expensive. They may often require large capital outlays for facilities and personnel, making them not particularly cost effective. In all other fields of public health, a compelling reason for providing prevention services is that it is less expensive to prevent an illness from occuring than it is to "cure" a patient. Service measures also are usually focused on the individual, while prevention specialists are more comfortable with strategies that apply to large populations. Finally, when mandated to "do prevention," service providers are inclined to allocate resources to services while neglecting other preventive measures.[28] Faced with dealing with the serious nature of a client's alcohol or drug problem, most counselors or therapists find little time for "prevention work."

Early intervention services, such as those provided in occupational alcoholism programs, "troubled worker" programs, or employee assistance programs, are a common type of secondary prevention. These programs are oriented toward employees whose work performance is impaired by the use of drugs or alcohol. The reported "success" rates of these programs are impressively high, even though few evaluations actually rely on hard data.[29] (A relatively recent article states unequivocally that, "Treatment offered with job retention as leverage generally proves highly effective."[30] No supporting data are provided.) Most referred employees are alcoholics or addicts with long-standing problems, rather than individuals who are "at risk" for chemical dependency.*

According to a recent study by Roman and Blum, however, only about 4 percent of the employees in a firm with such a program consult the employee assistance program (EAP) in a given year, and only 1.5 percent specifically present a substance abuse problem.[31] Another recent report indicates that the employer is mentioned as a primary motivator for treatment admission by only one-sixteenth of inpatients and one-tenth of outpatients.[32]

Chemical dependency manifests itself in the workplace in four ways. First, the employee may be chemically dependent. Second, the employee may be affected by a spouse, child, or other loved one who is chemically dependent. Third, an employee may be an adult child of a chemically dependent parent. Finally, employees may be selling or using drugs in the workplace.[33] To intervene at the earliest possible stage of dependency, supervisors are taught to be alert for the following common symptoms of alcohol or drug abuse:

Chronic absenteeism

Change in behavior

Physical signs

Spasmodic work pace

Lower quantity and quality of work

Partial absences

Lying

Avoiding supervisors and coworkers

On-the-job drinking or drug use

On-the-job accidents and lost time from off-the-job accidents[34]

Assuming that early identification and treatment are achieved in a workplace program, the chances of recovery should be increased because:

The threat of job loss is a significant motivator.

The family may still be present to provide emotional support.

Physical health has not deteriorated seriously.

The client's financial resources are not depleted.

Workplace programs use early intervention (service) measures as one component of more comprehensive prevention efforts. Other components include information sessions, substance abuse issue discussion (often at lunch time), posters and pamphlets, use of peer pressure, and financial incentives. Such incentives may take the form of cash awards to employees who quit smoking or reduced insurance rates for healthy life-styles.

---

*For a comprehensive treatment of workplace programs, see Gary M. Gould and Michael Lane Smith (eds.), *Social Work in the Workplace: Practice and Principles* (New York: Springer, 1988).

Employers are convinced that a healthier work force results in greater organizational efficiency and higher profits.

Although we considered DUI programs earlier as educational prevention, they also could be considered as early intervention. In addition to the educational component, offenders are offered treatment and probation instead of fines, jail, or other punishment. The effectiveness of "treatment" offered under such compulsion is questionable, however.[35] Just as in workplace programs, the clients are also likely to be those with long-standing problems of chemical dependency, so the appropriateness of the "early intervention" label is equally questionable.

A number of pilot early detection, screening, and treatment programs have been funded by the U.S. Department of Justice. In Miami, for example, juvenile offenders are routinely screened at detention through urine analysis. Those who test positive for any of five major drugs (about 85 percent) are referred for treatment at local agencies. Because of a lack of follow-up, however, fewer than half the youths referred actually go to treatment, and only about one-third of them complete a treatment program.[36]

TECHNOLOGIC MEASURES

In the traditional public health prevention model, technologic measures refer to "modifications in the noxious agent or the environment in which it operates that will affect the relationships among the agent, the environment, and members of a population to reduce the rate of occurrence of a disorder."[37] Although relatively new in chemical dependency, technologic measures are commonplace in occupational health and safety, transportation, and water sanitation.

Efforts to alter the noxious agent itself generally have been limited to modifications of alcohol and tobacco products. Cigarette makers produce a variety of "light" brands that are lower in nicotine. Manufacturers of distilled spirits have actually decreased the average amount of absolute alcohol in their products over the past decade, and more brands of low-alcohol beer become available each year. At first these low-alcohol brands seemed to be socially acceptable only in Europe, but they have now become quite popular in the United States. Biomedical researchers are still searching for a breakthrough that will eliminate the negative physiologic and psychologic effects of alcohol. Some even have hope of developing a practical "sobering-up" pill.

As we mentioned in Chapter 6, antagonist therapies have been developed for drugs such as heroin addiction. Drugs such as naloxone, naltrexone, and cyclazocine block the effects of opiate drugs but do not prevent withdrawal symptoms. Patients are withdrawn from heroin before being given these drugs. The addict who then returns to using heroin while taking a narcotic antagonist will find it impossible to get high.[38] While not technically an antagonist, methadone is a drug used to prevent symptoms of heroin withdrawal, and it also diminishes the effects of heroin. The heroin addict who is taking methadone will not be able to get the same "high" from using heroin.

Antabuse (disulfiram) is a drug that prevents the normal metabolization of alcohol. A person who ingests alcohol while taking antabuse will experience an accumulation of acetaldehyde, resulting in severe physical consequences such as difficulty in breathing, nausea, dizziness, vomiting, and blurred vision. In some cases people are able to continue drinking despite the symptoms, however.[39]

Other technologic measures are designed to make the environment safer for the person who uses alcohol or drugs. These measures do not prevent the use of alcohol or drugs, but protect both the user and innocent people from the effects of use. Passive restraints and air bags in automobiles are perhaps the best examples. Various devices have also been developed to prevent an intoxicated person from turning on the ignition of an automobile, but none are practical for widespread use at this point. Fire-retardant or fireproof clothing, bedding, and furniture also protect users who pass out or "nod off" while smoking.

Many cities have established a "tipsy taxi" service for drivers who have had too much to drink. In Tallahassee, Florida, for example, the city operates a free taxi service available to anyone on major holidays when overdrinking is traditionally a problem. In the same city, Florida State University offers a free chauffeur service to all its students on a year-round basis. Alcohol-related traffic fatalities have fallen since these services were introduced.

Many communities are providing free needles and syringes to intravenous drug users in an attempt to slow the spread of infectious diseases such as AIDS. These programs have spread much faster in European nations, partly because of a more liberal attitude toward such prevention efforts and partly because the laws are more conducive to these approaches. In many communities in the United States, there is a feeling that providing free needles and syringes *encourages* drug use. In many states, needles and syringes are available only through a physician's prescription.

Some communities have attempted to get around this problem by educating intravenous drug users in methods of cleaning their equipment before using it again or sharing it with another user. Both San Francisco and New York City launched efforts in the late 1980s to educate these drug users to "bleach their works" before state courts eventually allowed the distribution of needles and syringes.

LEGISLATIVE AND REGULATORY MEASURES

Legislative and regulatory measures regarding drug use can be employed to raise revenue, safeguard public health or morals, provide both political and economic rewards, or *prevent* drug use or abuse. In this chapter we will discuss only the latter purposes. The others will be deferred until the next chapter, where we deal with the concept of regulation in considerably greater depth.

Throughout the eighteenth and nineteenth centuries, there were many local and state laws restricting the sale of alcohol, culminating in 1917 in national prohibition. Whatever the failings of this "noble experiment," we know that one of its primary purposes was achieved—a substantial decrease in the consumption of beverage alcohol.[40] Other legislation has controlled the hours and location of sale for alcoholic beverages, and there have been long-standing laws against serving alcohol to minors. These laws are also intended to reduce consumption, frequently among specific populations. Still other laws have placed restrictions on certain activities associated with drinking (gambling, nude dancing, driving a car, boat, or airplane, etc.) as a way of protecting the public from some of the "side effects" of drinking alcohol. So-called "dramshop" laws have been revived to make it illegal for bartenders or other servers to serve alcohol to obviously intoxicated persons. Several lawsuits and court decisions upholding server liability laws have impressed on tavernkeepers the need for better training of their personnel. Perhaps this desire to reduce liability will lead to a reduction of some alcohol problems.[41]

Regulation of other psychoactive drugs is much less complicated. In most cases we either have no law restricting the use of a drug (such as gasoline, glue, and other inhalants), or it is simply illegal to use or possess it (heroin). In relatively few cases (marijuana) a drug may be illegal except for certain limited medical purposes. Regulation of most of these drugs came much later than for alcohol, however. Opiates were not made illegal until the Harrison Act of 1914. Although many states had prohibitions against its use, marijuana was not outlawed nationally until the Marijuana Tax Act of 1937. Recently there have been many more drugs added to the list of controlled substances, but there is little evidence that these prohibitions have significantly impacted the drug trade or drug use.[42] The general failure of law enforcement efforts regarding illicit drug use is discussed at some length in the next chapter.

Advertising and the Media

Both legislation and self-regulation have resulted in restrictions on the advertising of alcohol and tobacco products, although the

The Malt Liquor Wars: News from the Front

" . . . grab a six-pack and get your girl in the mood quicker

Get your jimmy thicker, with St. Ides Malt Liquor."

From a radio ad for St. Ides

Malt Liquor, Summer 1991

"Behind every empty bottle (of malt liquor) is an argument, or a murder or some s—t," says the flamboyant Chuck D., principal spokesperson for the politically-oriented rap group Public Enemy. Chuck D. has been traveling the country for months, willingly forgoing the lucrative summer touring season to spread his band's strong and unequivocal anti-malt liquor message.

That campaign has now moved to a whole new level with his initiation of a $5,000,000 lawsuit against St. Ides for illegally using a "sample" from a Public Enemy recording featuring his voice in a radio ad.

"In our conversations with the head of the company, Minott Wessinger, the impression that he tried to leave with us was that [the ad] had not aired for that long and that it was not widely disseminated", says Public Enemy's legal counsel Lisa E. Davis. "We were being told [that it aired] during a three-week period. We didn't know what the markets were, then found out, in terms of the damage to reputation, that it's been aired in major communities on rap shows. So it's hitting the core audi-

ence for Public Enemy, and giving these youths the impression that PE is 'down' with this malt liquor."

Chuck D. and other opponents of malt liquor marketing are angry about more than just the intensive marketing of higher octane beers to African American and Latino youth (St. Ides has the highest alcohol content of any malt liquor available for mass consumption—a full 8%, which is 80% more than regular beer)—it's the irresponsible and stereotype-reinforcing way the marketing is done.

This sampling of commercials aimed squarely at black youth speaks for itself:

#1 RAPPER: Step right up, step right up, step right up, son, And try this new beer, but are you over 21?

ICE CUBE: Yes I am mister, so please pass the bottle

(AN L.A. RAPPER): 'Cause I've been drinking ever since I could swallow.

RAPPER: O.K. One of these is St. Ides, we took off this sticker s'if you were blindfolded do you think you could pick it?

ICE CUBE: The other ones are alright, That may be true, g. (slang for gangster) But y'all can't fool me 'Cause I know the the S-T-I-D-E-S has gotta be the best

Source: I.B.C.A. Scope, Summer 1991, pp. 1–2.

---

accompanying box causes one to wonder if these restrictions are adequate. Industry standards prohibit the advertising of hard liquor on television, and although beer, malt liquor, and wine can be advertised, no one may be shown actually drinking it. There are strong arguments for restricting the advertising of these products in all media, because they frequently appeal to young people who are particularly susceptible to suggestions that wealth, success, or peer approval may be related to using the "right" kind of alcohol or

tobacco products. It must be said, however, that the long-term effects of current restrictions on advertising appear to be minimal.[43]

Ads for alcoholic beverages are well researched, slickly produced, and reinforced by well-organized promotions at the local retail level. After the Coca-Cola Company bought Taylor Wines in the late 1970s, it set out to promote the image of wine as a drink to be consumed regularly rather than just on special occasions. Within a short time the amount of advertising in the wine industry nearly doubled, partly because of Coca-Cola's aggressive marketing techniques.[44]

While there are restrictions on advertising alcoholic beverages, there are no restrictions on the use of alcohol by actors in television programs. Consumption of alcoholic beverages is frequent in TV programs (although the incidence of actors smoking has decreased). Attempts to curtail youth from buying alcohol by restricting advertising may be undone by the frequent images of alcohol use in television programs.

The effect of advertising on consumption and the portrayal of alcohol drinking by the mass media are controversial issues on which there is no definitive evidence. A recent review of the literature on advertising concludes that (1) marginal changes in expenditures for alcohol advertising have little or no effect on total alcohol consumption and (2) existing studies shed "virtually no light" on the relationship between advertising and alcohol abuse.[45] One national survey of 1,200 respondents aged 12 to 22 did find a moderately strong positive correlation between the amount of day-to-day exposure to ads for alcoholic beverages, on the one hand, and alcohol consumption and drinking in dangerous situations, on the other.[46] Both the advertising and the brewing industry recently have come under heavy criticism for directing advertising campaigns at minority groups. A case in point is the advertising of "PowerMaster," a high-alcohol malt liquor, in media targeted toward low-income minorities.[47] (The tobacco industry also had developed a new cigarette with plans to market it primarily to Afro-Americans. Fortunately, public opinion and political pressure resulted in the cancellation of both campaigns.)

According to Wallack, however, any findings that indicate an association between advertising and increased consumption contradict a larger body of previous research that has failed to substantiate such a relationship.[48] (One *must* wonder—if advertising doesn't increase consumption, why advertise? The alcoholic beverage industry spends over *$1 billion* yearly advertising its products.[49])

Advertising is not the only way images of alcohol use are disseminated. In his study of Hollywood's treatment of the alcoholic, Denzin found 664 movies that used alcoholism as a major theme between 1909 and 1991.[50] Many of those, such as *Harvey* and *Arthur* depict the main characters as "happy alcoholics" with no particular need to deal with their alcohol problems. More recent movies (*Clean and Sober, Barfly, The Boost*) have presented a much more realistic appraisal of both alcoholism and drug abuse. A series of articles in the *Christian Science Monitor* described television's portrayal of alcohol use beginning in 1975. Among prime-time shows in the spring of 1975, scenes involving alcohol use were found in 201 of 249 shows.[51] A study of drinking on daytime soap operas viewed 79 half-hour segments over a five-day period and found 236 events involving alcoholic beverages and only 205 involving soft drinks.[52] In 1980, the top ten prime-time series and the top soap operas were studied at Michigan State University. The rate of alcohol consumption averaged 8.13 incidents per hour on the top ten series and 2.25 per hour on the soap operas. Alcohol use was shown in an almost entirely positive context, with no indication of potential risk.[53] This seems strange, indeed, for a medium whose code does not allow the commercial advertising of any "hard" liquor nor the actual drinking of wine or beer during a commercial!

In 1982, one team of researchers developed a strategy for "cooperative consultation" to work with media personnel toward the realistic portrayal of alcohol use on television and in other media.[54] Later that same year, three alcohol-related tragedies rocked Hollywood. Two celebrities, Mary Martin and Janet Gaynor, were critically injured when a drunk driver crashed into their taxi. Next, William Holden died alone in his room because he was too drunk to know that he was bleeding to death. Finally, Natalie Wood, after drinking "a few" glasses of wine, slipped off the side of a boat and drowned. Not long after these events, one of the major networks televised a news series called "The Hollywood Alcoholic." The result of this new realization of the dangers of alcoholism was an effort by a caucus of producers, writers, and directors to produce guidelines for dealing with alcohol use on television and in the movies.[55]

1. Try not to glamorize the drinking or serving of alcohol as a sophisticated or an adult pursuit.
2. Avoid showing the use of alcohol gratuitously in those cases in which another beverage might be easily and fittingly substituted.
3. Try not to show excessive drinking without consequences or with only pleasant consequences.
4. Try not to show drinking alcohol as an activity that is so "normal" that everyone must indulge. Allow characters a chance to refuse an alcoholic drink by including nonalcoholic alternatives.
5. Demonstrate that there are no miraculous recoveries from alcoholism; normally it is a most difficult task.
6. Don't associate drinking alcohol with macho pursuits in such a way that heavy drinking is a requirement for proving one's self as a man.
7. Portray the reaction of others to heavy alcohol drinking, especially when it may be a criticism.

There have been some notable efforts by the media since then to incorporate these guidelines into their programming. Captain Ferillo on "Hill Street Blues" and at least one of his officers were depicted in several episodes in a difficult struggle against alcoholism. A made-for-TV movie, "Shattered Spirits," honestly portrayed the struggle of a family against alcoholism in a realistic manner. The movie *Clean and Sober* not only dealt honestly with the alcoholism and drug addiction of its major characters, but also won rave reviews from the critics. Public service announcements regularly warn young people about the dangers of alcohol and drug abuse and urge them to "just say no."

At the same time, however, it is still easy to find the gratuitous portrayal of alcohol use in the media. While there is little or no evidence that television programming has increased consumption, it is the National Association of Broadcaster's position that alcohol use should be *deemphasized* on television. The truth is that the rate of drinking on television still seems to be much greater than in real life. According to one estimate, a person

under the legal drinking age will be exposed to approximately three thousand acts of drinking during a year of television viewing.[56] Is it any wonder that young peoples' T-shirts sport such popular themes as "Party Till you Puke" and "Avoid Hangovers, Stay Drunk"? Obviously, television and the other mass media are not entirely to blame, and they have taken certain steps to improve programming. They generally do not, however, provide the proper messages to young people about the use of alcohol.

All states have legislation prohibiting the sale of both alcohol or tobacco products to underaged youth. While the enforcement of alcohol laws have been a great concern to local and state law enforcement authorities, only recently have they put much efforts into enforcing the tobacco laws. In a recent study in California, minors aged 14 to 16 years attempted to purchase cigarettes in 412 stores and from thirty vending machines. They were successful in 74 percent of the stores and 100 percent of the vending machines.[57] The situation may be changing, however. A large Maryland convenience store chain was convicted in 1991 of routinely selling cigarettes to underaged youth and fined several million dollars.[58]

Health warnings also have been mandated for alcohol and tobacco products. Everything from "lite" beer to 100-proof vodka must carry a government warning concerning the risk to pregnant women of birth defects and the risk to everyone of impaired driving ability.

Government Warning: (1) According to the Surgeon General, women should not drink alcoholic beverages during pregnancy because of the risk of birth defects. (2) Consumption of alcoholic beverages impairs your ability to drive a car or operate machinery, and may cause health problems.

Tobacco products warn the user of a plethora of possible diseases. (Most of these warnings give new meaning to the term "fine print." Look closely at the container the next time you purchase an alcoholic beverage.) The impact of the warnings is unknown, but some argue that they may actually serve to protect the manufacturers from liability by providing the consumer with an adequate warning of potential risks involved in using the product.

In addition to restrictions on advertising, we have placed some restrictions on the use of tobacco products. By 1987 there had been restrictions placed on tobacco use in the workplace by thirty-two states and in other public places such as restaurants in twenty-three states. In addition national restrictions were placed on smoking on airlines, and smoking is almost universally prohibited in public hospitals and other health facilities. Tobacco companies have hotly contested these prohibitions, of course.[59]

Drinking-and-driving prevention has been the subject of much legislation since the advent of the automobile. Research in the United States, England, and Scandinavia indicates that no one single approach to preventing driving under the influence (DUI) is preferable, but there is a constellation of measures that seems to be effective under various circumstances. These include vigorous enforcement of DUI laws, rapid application of sanctions, and clear-cut regulations that are widely publicized. Heavy fines appear to be about as effective as the revocation of driving privileges or mandatory "DUI schools" or other treatment. Some of the more controversial methods, such as roadblocks used to ferret out impaired drivers, have proven less effective.[60] They also have been criticized as infringement on civil liberties, but so far the courts have generally allowed the practice to continue.

ECONOMIC MEASURES

The difference between legislative-regulatory measures and economic measures is primarily one of emphasis. The price of alcohol or tobacco, for example, may be a matter of a producer's competitive strategy to capture a share of the market for its product. On the other hand, price also reflects federal and state legislation governing the rate of taxation for that product. Whether it happens because of company policy or government decree, the impact of a price increase or decrease on the consumer is likely to be much the same. Several recent studies have indicated that the consumption of alcohol is relatively sensitive to price and that everything from cirrhosis to traffic fatalities could be reduced by increasing prices.[61] The increase in prices in the underground market after the passage of Prohibition in 1917 was undoubtedly one of the major factors in the dramatic decrease in consumption. The demand for tobacco products seems to be even more sensitive to price, especially among younger users. Increasing taxes on cigarettes may be the most effective way of convincing novice users, such as adolescents, to not smoke.[62] When it comes to illicit drugs such as marijuana, there is little doubt that consumption increases as prices fall.[63] One of the few successes of the "war on drugs" may be in maintaining prices at a relatively high level, thereby deterring some potential users.

In addition to pricing policies, other economic measures include such items as allocating tax revenues from the sale of drugs to prevention programs (such as Proposition 99, described earlier), reducing insurance premiums for those who abstain from alcohol and tobacco, and tax incentives that discourage drug use. (Recent income tax reforms have disallowed the "three martini" lunch.) It is not uncommon for government to use an economic measure as a subterfuge for prohibiting drugs. For example, the Marijuana Tax Act of 1934 placed a $100 per ounce tax on marijuana. Texas has a drug tax law that requires those who buy or possess illegal drugs to purchase tax stamps for them. Failure to do so results in a tax law violation. These laws are often called "Al Capone" laws because of the prosecution of that notorious gangster, who sold bootleg liquor, under the tax evasion statutes.

SUMMARY

Prevention sounds like a good idea, but how does one measure its effect? To know whether a prevention program *really* works, we would have to hold a number of important factors constant while a prevention intervention is implemented. We would probably need to randomize the target population between the program and a control group, and we would need to study this cohort over a relatively long period of time. Our current state of knowledge regarding prevention programs is largely anecdotal and incomplete. Our best information generally comes from correlational studies.

From a logical perspective, we know that if we can prevent a population from using a drug, morbidity and mortality rates will be reduced. We have a pretty good idea that education and public information approaches do not seem to be effective, especially for those persons with the most serious problems. Those techniques that do work are relatively limited in their scope. Swift and certain law enforcement for DUI offenses seem to work. Heavy fines are also effective. Price has a strong deterrent effect on the use of certain drugs. Minimum age of purchase legislation keeps many younger drivers alive. In the next chapter we will see that many other law enforcement strategies, such as long prison terms, do not seem to be very effective prevention tools.

The focus of prevention efforts seems to have shifted away from reliance on the traditional educational and public information approaches to a "harm reduction" philosophy. We must try not only to reduce the use and abuse of harmful drugs, but work to ameliorate the consequences of those drugs. Preventing the spread of AIDS and decreasing traffic fatalities are just as legitimate prevention goals as reducing intravenous heroin use or the consumption of alcoholic beverages. Guided by this philosophy, there are many other approaches still to be tried. For example, it has been suggested that makers of fortified wines be required to supplement them with vitamins and minerals. The alcoholics who buy these products are especially prone to malnutrition, which is at least partly a result of their alcoholism. Or what about levying special taxes on products we know to be detrimental to our health (primarily tobacco

and alcohol) and dedicating them to the provision of additional health care services?

ENDNOTES

1. Lawrence Wallack and Kitty Corbett, "Illicit Drug, Tobacco, and Alcohol Use Among Youth: Trends and Promising Approaches in Prevention," in Hank Resnik, S. E. Gardner, R. P. Lorian, and C. E. Marcus, "Youth and Drugs: Society's Mixed Messages," *OSAP Prevention Monograph No.6*, Alcohol, Drug Abuse, and Mental Health Administration, Office for Substance Abuse Prevention (Rockville, MD: U.S. Department of Health and Human Services, Public Health Service, 1990), p. 16.

2. Ibid., pp. 5–29.

3. Joel M. Moskowitz, "The Primary Prevention of Alcohol Problems: A Critical Review of the Research Literature," *Journal of Studies on Alcohol*, Vol. 50, No. 1 (1989), pp. 54–88.

4. A. C. Wagenaar, "Youth, Alcohol, and Traffic Crashes," paper presented at Prevention Research Center Workshop, Berkeley, CA, 1986.

5. Howard T. Blane, "Preventing Alcohol Problems," in Nada J. Estes and M. Edith Heinemann (eds.), *Alcoholism: Development, Consequences, and Interventions*, 3rd ed. (St. Louis: C. V. Mosby, 1986), pp. 78–90.

6. Jean Kinney and Gwen Leaton, *Loosening the Grip: A Handbook of Alcohol Information* (St. Louis, MO: Times Mirror/Mosby College Publishing, 1987).

7. M. Klitzner. *Report to Congress on the Nature and Effectiveness of Federal, State, and Local Drug Prevention/Education Programs—Part 2: An Assessment of the Research on School-Based Prevention Programs*, prepared for the U.S. Department of Education, Office of Planning, Budget and Evaluation (Vienna, VA: Pacific Institute for Research and Evaluation, 1988). Also see Nancy S. Tobler, "Meta-Analysis of 143 Adolescent Drug Prevention Programs: Qualitative Outcome Results of Program Participants Compared to a Control or Comparison Group," *Journal of Drug Issues*, Vol. 16, No. 4 (1986), pp. 537–567.

8. Kinney and Leaton, *Loosening the Grip*.

9. Wallack and Corbett, "Illicit Drug, Tobacco, and Alcohol Use Among Youth," 1990.

10. Howard T. Blane, "Education and Prevention of Alcoholism," in Benjamin Kissin and Henri Begleiter (eds.), *The Biology of Alcoholism*, Volume 4 (New York: Plenum Press, 1976). Also see Robert L. Bangert-Downs, "The Effects of School-Based Substance

Abuse Education—A Meta-Analysis," *Journal of Drug Education,* Vol. 18, No. 3 (1988), pp. 243–265.

11. Wallack and Corbett, "Illicit Drug, Tobacco, and Alcohol Use Among Youth," 1990.

12. Blane, "Preventing Alcohol Problems."

13. Howard T. Blane, *Health Education as a Preventive Strategy,* in Tripartite Conference on Prevention (Washington, DC: Alcohol, Drug Abuse, and Mental Health Administration, 1977).

14. Blane, "Preventing Alcohol Problems."

15. Steve Olson and Dean R. Gerstein, *Alcohol in America: Taking Action to Prevent Abuse* (Washington, DC: National Academy Press, 1985), pp. 82–94.

16. Wallack and Corbett, "Illicit Drug, Tobacco, and Alcohol Use Among Youth," 1990.

17. Ibid.

18. G. Nicholas Braucht and Barbara Braucht, "Prevention of Problem Drinking Among Youth: Evaluation of Educational Strategies," in P. M. Miller and T. D. Nirenberg (eds.), *Prevention of Alcohol Abuse* (New York: Plenum Press, 1984).

19. Richard Dembo, "Key Issues and Paradigms in Drug Use Research: Focus on Etiology," *Journal of Drug Issues,* Vol. 16, No. 1 (1986), pp. 1–4.

20. Richard I. Evans, R. M. Rozelle, Maurice B. Mittelmark, William B. Hansen, A. L. Bane, and J. Havis, "Deterring the Onset of Smoking in Children: Knowledge of Immediate Physiological Effects and Coping with Peer Pressure, Media Pressure, and Parent Modeling," *Journal of Applied Social Psychology,* Vol. 8, No. 2 (1978), pp. 126–135.

21. William J. McGuire, "The Nature of Attitude and Attitude Change," in G. Lindzay and E. Aronson (eds.), *Handbook of Social Psychology,* 2nd ed., Volume 3 (Reading, MA: Addison-Wesley, 1969).

22. William J. McCarthy, "The Cognitive Developmental Model and Other Alternatives to the Social Deficit Model of Smoking Onset," in C. S. Bell and R. Battjes (eds.), *Prevention Research: Deterring Drug Abuse among Children and Adolescents.* (Rockville, MD: U.S. Department of Health and Human Services, 1985), pp. 153–169.

23. Wallack and Corbett, "Illicit Drug Use," 1990.

24. William DeJong, "A Short-Term Evaluation of Project DARE (Drug Abuse Resistance Education): Preliminary Indications of Effectiveness," *Journal of Drug Education,* Vol. 17, No. 4 (1987), pp. 279–294.

25. Ibid.

26. The Evaluation and Training Institute, "DARE Longitudinal Evaluation Annual Report: 1987–88," unpublished.

27. Richard R. Clayton, Anne Cattarello, L. Edward Day, and Katherine P. Walden, Persuasive Communication and Drug Prevention: An Evaluation of the D.A.R.E. Program," in Lewis Donohew, Howard Sypher, and William Bukoski (eds.), *Persuasive Communication and Drug Abuse Prevention* (Hillsdale, NJ: Lawrence Erlbaum Associates, 1991).

28. Blane, "Health Education."

29. Norman R. Kurtz, Bradley Googins, and William C. Howard, "Measuring the Success of Occupational Alcoholism Programs," *Journal of Studies on Alcohol,* Vol. 45, No. 1 (January 1984), pp. 33–45.

30. Meryl Nadel, Alice W. Petropoulos, and Nelson Feroe, "Alcoholism Treatment Resources: Which One When?" in David Cook, Christine Fewell, and John Riolo (eds.), *Social Work Treatment of Alcohol Problems* (New Brunswick, NJ: Rutgers Center of Alcohol Studies, 1983), p. 14.

31. Paul M. Roman and T. C. Blum, "Employee Assistance and Drug Screening Programs," in Dean R. Gerstein and Henrick J. Harwood, *Treating Drug Abuse,* Volume 2 (Washington, DC: National Academy Press, 1990).

32. P. A. Harrison and N. G. Hoffman, *Adult Outpatient Treatment: Perspectives on Admission and Outcome* (St. Paul, MN: Chemical Abuse/Addiction Treatment Outcome Registry, Ramsey Clinic, 1988).

33. Diana M. DiNitto, "Drunk, Drugged, and on the Job," in Gary Gould and Michael Lane Smith, *Social Work in the Workplace* (New York: Springer, 1988), p. 77.

34. Kinney and Leaton, *Loosening the Grip,* p. 222.

35. Ross Homel, *Policing and Punishing the Drinking Driver: A Study of General and Specific Deterrence* (New York: Springer, 1988).

36. Interview with Miami/Dade County Juvenile Screening, Detection, and Treatment program officials, Miami, FL, June 7, 1991.

37. Blane, "Preventing Alcohol Problems," p. 84.

38. Ibid., p. 246–247.

39. Jason M. White, *Drug Dependence* (Englewood Cliffs, NJ: Prentice Hall, 1991), p. 243–244.

40. William A. McKim, *Drugs and Behavior,* 2nd ed. (Englewood Cliffs, NJ: Prentice Hall, 1991), p. 90.

41. Olson and Gerstein, *Alcohol in America,* pp. 62–68.

42. James A. Inciardi, *The War on Drugs* (Palo Alto, CA: Mayfield, 1986).

43. Kenneth E. Warner, "Clearing the Airwaves: The Cigarette Ad Ban Revisited," *Policy Analysis,* Vol. 4 (1979), pp. 435–450.

44. Olson and Gerstein, *Alcohol in America,* p. 85.

45. Federal Trade Commission, Bureau of Consumer Protection and Economics, "Omnibus Petition for Regulation of Unfair and Deceptive Alcoholic Beverage Advertising and Marketing Practices," Docket No. 209–46. March 1985.

46. Charles Atkin, Kimberly Neuendorf, and Steven McDermott, "The Role of Alcohol Advertising in Excessive and Hazardous Drinking," *Journal of Drug Education*, Vol. 13 (1983), pp. 313–326.

47. "A Real Brew-Haha," *Time,* July 1, 1991, p. 56.

48. Lawrence Wallack, "Practical Issues, Ethical Concerns and Future Directions in the Prevention of Alcohol-Related Problems," *Journal of Primary Prevention,* Vol. 4 (1984), pp. 199–224.

49. Steve Olson and Dean R. Gerstein, *Alcohol in America: Taking Action to Prevent Abuse* (Washington, DC: National Academy Press, 1985), p. 94.

50. Norman K. Denzin, *Hollywood Shot by Shot: Alcoholism in American Cinema* (Hawthorne, NY: Aldine De Gruyter, 1991), p. 6.

51. John Dillin, "TV Drinking: How Networks Pour Liquor Into Your Living Room," *Christian Science Monitor,* Vol. 67, No. 151, pp. 1ff.

52. W. Garlington, "Drinking on Television: A Preliminary Study with Emphasis on Method," *Journal of Studies on Alcohol,* Vol. 38 (1977), pp. 2199–2205.

53. B. Greenberg, C. Fernandez-Collado, D. Graef, F. Dorzenny, and C. Atkin, *Trends in Use of Alcohol and Other Substances on Television* (East Lansing, MI: Department of Communication, Michigan State University, 1981).

54. Warren K. Breed and James R. DeFoe, "Effecting Media Change: The Role of Cooperative Consultation on Alcohol Topics," *Journal of Communication,* Vol. 32 (1982), pp. 100–111.

55. Gerstein, *Toward the Prevention,* p. 97.

56. Greenberg, *Trends in Use of Alcohol.*

57. David Altman, Valodi Foster, Lolly Rasenick-Douss, and Joe Tye, "Reducing the Illegal Sale of Cigarettes to Minors," *Journal of the American Medical Association,* Vol. 261 (1989), pp. 80–83.

58. *Tallahassee Democrat,* "Chain Fined for Sales to Minors" Sec. C, p. 2, August 18, 1991.

59. Mosher, "Drug Availability," p. 137.

60. American Bar Association, Criminal Justice Section, *Drunk Driving Laws & Enforcement: An Assessment of Effectiveness.* (Washington, DC, American Bar Association, 1986).

61. Olson and Gerstein, *Alcohol in America,* p. 51.

62. James F. Mosher, "Drug Availability in a Public Health Perspective," in Hank Resnik et al., *Youth and Drugs: Society's Mixed Messages,* 1990, p. 152.

63. Ibid., pp. 129–168.

8

Regulating drugs and their consequences

One of the major obstacles to the successful prevention and treatment of chemical dependency problems is that we have no clear understanding of the etiology of drug abuse or dependence *at the level of individual pathology* (Chapter 2). From a clinical perspective, therefore, it is difficult (some would say impossible) to match an individual's treatment needs with a particular treatment modality that is best suited for those needs. We do know, however, that there are a number of social, cultural, and environmental factors that influence an individual's probability of using drugs. Unfortunately, we tend to plan treatment for chemical dependency as if it were only an *individual* phenomenon,

ignoring important *systemic* causes and consequences. While most of the previous chapters have focused more directly on clinical issues, we now turn to some important public policy issues related to drug availability, use, and treatment. We will continue and expand our discussion, begun in Chapter 7, regarding the types of collective action that society may employ in controlling the use of drugs. We also will continue the debate concerning the legalization of certain drugs within the context of broad public policy issues. Public policies regarding drug use and addiction include much more than the *legality* of manufacturing, selling, and using drugs, however. Public policy is concerned with controlling or limiting the use of specific drugs, restricting use to specific segments of the population (such as adults, cancer patients, etc.), avoiding the *misuse* of drugs, enhancing governmental revenues through the collection of taxes on drugs (especially alcohol), and protecting domestic drug producers from foreign competition. Finally, we will turn to one of the most troubling policy issues regarding drug use: what to do about the relationship between drugs and crime. It is clear that we are losing the "war on drugs," and we are desperate for an alternative course of action.

SOCIOCULTURAL INFLUENCES ON PUBLIC DRUG POLICY

Public policies regarding drugs vary widely throughout the world. They have also varied widely within nations during the last few centuries. Until the early part of this century, very few drugs were strictly regulated by any government.[1] Public policies that are now common in modern Western societies cannot be considered historical norms.[2]

Variations between cultures depend partly on historical accident: peyote grew in the American Southwest, heroin in Asia, and cannabis from the Middle East to India. Beverage alcohol is the most nearly universal psychoactive drug. As locally produced-drugs were spread by international trade, the culture of the importing nation had a profound impact on public policy toward these new drugs. When it was first introduced to Europe, tobacco was used primarily as a medicine in some countries and as a mild stimulant in others. In Russia it was used as an intoxicant by means of deep and rapid inhalation.[3]

Drugs associated with ceremonial and religious use are generally treated differently from other drugs. Alcohol commonly was used by a great many people in ceremonies and rituals, often to the point of intoxication. But these same people rarely used alcohol outside of these rituals and ceremonies until very recently. The same can be said of marijuana use in some areas of India.[4] Where use

of a drug is a very old, traditional practice, such as opium use in Arab countries, it is usually restricted to the adult male population.[5]

Religious beliefs and practices may either inhibit or reinforce the use of particular drugs. Psychoactive drugs were frequently viewed in traditional societies either as a gift from God or as "the devil's brew." The Indians of both North and South America used hallucinogenic drugs as a part of religious rituals. Indeed, American Indians are still fighting for the right to use peyote legally in ceremonies sanctioned by the Native American Church. The cactus plant from which the drug is obtained is believed to be a gift from God to man. On the other hand, the strong religious injunctions against the use of alcohol in many Muslim countries severely restricts its use. This ban was decreed by the prophet Mohammed and still carries the force of law in countries such as Saudia Arabia.[6]

Sociocultural differences are also found in conceptions of the role of government regarding the health and welfare of its citizens, and these different conceptions influence public policy responses to the use of drugs.[7] Thus Sweden, Norway, and Finland have introduced retail liquor monopolies as a way of limiting consumption. The former Soviet Union has a complete state monopoly on the production, distribution, and sale of alcohol. In America, several states have adopted a monopoly distribution system for distilled spirits but not for wine and beer. Other states allow competitive retailing but control the hours and location of sales. Some states allow beer and wine sales in supermarkets, convenience stores, and gas stations, while other states restrict such sales to "liquor" stores. Communities in states with "local option" laws may simply prohibit the sale of alcoholic beverages.

ECONOMIC AND POLITICAL FACTORS

In Ireland, where the giant Guiness brewery is the largest single private employer, the largest exporter of beer in the world, and operates one of the largest charitable foundations in the nation, legislation controlling or regulating alcohol production or sales is difficult to pass. Private physicians and college professors still relay the message to their patients and students that moderate alcohol use is a healthy practice. Only recently has the prevention of alcohol abuse been placed on the public agenda.[8] Efforts to control the use of other drugs is quite commonplace, however.

Why do societies decide to regulate some drugs, prohibit other drugs, and ignore some drugs altogether? In many cases the production and supply of the entrenched drugs such as alcohol, nicotine, and caffeine are sources of wealth and power in society.[9] Permissive policies toward other drugs may simply have represented a threat to business. Since coffee could not be grown in Europe, it was necessary to import it. The Germans saw this as a threat to their beer industry, and the English imposed heavy taxes on coffee as a way of protecting tea produced in British colonies.

It is easy to understand why American distillers and brewers may oppose the legalization of other drugs. Depending on the degree to which newly legalized drugs could be substituted for alcohol, they stand to lose a great deal of money. On the other hand, some say that the American tobacco industry has already "geared up" to produce marijuana cigarettes in the event that cannabis is legalized.[10] This new market could take up some of the slack resulting from declining cigarette sales.

Economic factors also have an impact on the enforcement of existing drug laws. It would be counterproductive for the tobacco industry to favor strict enforcement of the age limitation for the purchase of cigarettes when *all* their future customers, not to mention the fastest-growing segment of their current market, are under 18 years of age.

The socioeconomic status, political position, and race of drug *users* also must be considered. Heroin and crack cocaine are still regarded as being most common in black ghettoes. Most experts agree that these are the drugs least likely to be legalized. When marijuana was perceived to be a drug used mostly by Afro-Americans, Hispanics, and a few eccentric literary figures and musicians, there was not much support for its legalization. Now that hundreds of thousands of middle-class college students have used the drug, there is much more support for its "decriminalization"—even in otherwise conservative states such as Nebraska.[11]

CHANGES IN DRUG USE PATTERNS

The types of drugs and manner of their use within a society vary over time. A society with few or no restrictions in one historical period may have comprehensive regulations of most drugs during another time.[12] Traditional societies tended to have available a rather narrow range of drugs, and they were frequently used in religious rituals or ceremonies. This type of limited use was not viewed as a cause for alarm. Eventually international trade brought new types of drugs to practically every nation. New drugs presented a threat because they were used recreationally, their effects were not known, and their users were regarded as deviant. This called for regulation.

Changes in the manner of use of a single drug also have resulted in pressures for regulation and control. Oral administration or smoking of drugs such as opium and heroin presented fewer threats to the users' health and safety than did intravenous injection. Little thought was given to the drinking of small amounts of cocaine in soft drinks such as Coca-Cola, since the consequences of this type of use represented no more of a threat to the user than the chewing of coca leaves by South American aborigines. "Snorting" coke brought more immediate results, but it was not regarded as truly dangerous until users began to inject a soluble form with a hypodermic needle. Intravenous use not only makes possible an instantaneous high, but also brings the risk of addiction and the additional hazards of hepatitis, AIDS, and other diseases. Finally, the discovery of a new form of smokable "crack" cocaine brought even greater risks of addiction. The use of cocaine itself does not seem to be as much an issue as the form of administration.

THE NATURE OF DRUG CONTROL

The most obvious function of drug control, and the primary reason cited by our lawmakers, is to decrease the amount of a particular drug that is used. In some cases, such as heroin, the goal is complete prohibition. In other cases, such as cocaine, the goal may be to limit use of the drug to medical practice. In still other cases, such as alcohol, government may allow general use by adults, but seek to control the amount used by price controls, taxes, number of outlets, and the hours of sale. Because of the particular importance of alcohol regulation in the United States, we have a special section on this issue in the following pages.

The Harrison Narcotics Act of 1914 was primarily a labeling and registration act, and its purpose was to restrict the distribution of narcotic drugs to physicians and pharmacists. Prior to this act, access to opium derivatives was not officially restricted. After 1914, distributors had to register with the Treasury Department.

Most legal drugs are taxed. Since they are widely used commodities in any modern economy, governments have discovered that they can be a significant source of tax revenue. In most cases the tax is imposed primarily for the purpose of raising revenue, but taxes on drugs are also used to regulate trade in one way or another. Such was the case of Britain's tax on Jamaican rum or Indian tea that was destined for other colonies. Alcoholic beverages were first subjected to federal taxation in the United States in 1791, and a liquor excise was the first internal revenue law enacted by Congress under the Constitution. As late as 1907, these revenues constituted 80 percent of all federal internal tax collections![13]

Drug taxes almost always have a dual purpose of decreasing consumption and raising revenue. Sometimes the revenues from taxes on a drug are only incidental to the primary purpose of the tax, restricting *use* of the drug. (The Marihuana Tax Act of 1937 used a tax to outlaw marijuana. Marijuana approved for medical use was taxed at $1.00 per ounce. Marijuana used for other purposes was taxed at $100.00 per ounce.[14]) Both the amount of revenue raised and the success of the tax in curbing consumption depends on the degree of *price elasticity* of the product being taxed. The elasticity of any particular drug depends on a number of factors, such as (1) the degree to which another drug may be substituted for it, (2) the availability of the drug, (3) the addictive power of the drug, and (4) the cost of the drug, including taxes. It is generally agreed that taxes on alcoholic beverages diminish their consumption[15] but that distilled spirits are less price elastic than beer.[16] In other words, a tax on distilled spirits would result in a smaller decrease in consumption than the same tax on beer. The relative elasticity of illicit drugs is less well known.

ASSUMPTIONS UNDERLYING REGULATION

There are a number of important assumptions underlying any government's efforts to control drug use. One is that, whenever drugs are used, there are victims. Victims may be the actual users of drugs, or they may be innocent bystanders—those who passively inhale cigarette smoke or who are maimed or killed by drunken drivers. There are those who argue that use of drugs is a "victimless" crime which has no major adverse consequences for the rest of society, but this view is not consistent with governmental regulation.[17]

Closely related to this is a second assumption that governments have the responsibility for enhancing the general welfare. A nation with a large proportion of drug users would be at an economic disadvantage in the world market because of reduced work output by drug users and the need to divert resources to handle the health and welfare needs of users. In regulating drugs as a way of promoting the general welfare, government walks a fine line between benefiting the majority of its citizens and encroaching on the individual liberties of a few. This potential conflict frequently appears when governments declare "smoke-free" workplaces or prohibit the possession of alcoholic beverages in a public park.

Governments find it just as difficult to distinguish *nonproblem* from *problem* drug use as distinguishing *use* and *misuse* (Chapter 1), but they do it anyway. Those drugs that are perceived not to cause problems (such as caffeine) are subjected to few controls. Those that are deemed to be troublesome but are impossible to prohibit because of widespread public use and acceptance, and because they are easily produced (such as alcohol), are tightly regulated. Those perceived to be the most problematic (heroin, cocaine) are generally banned.

These divisions between problem and nonproblem use are somewhat arbitrary, and the reasons for regarding drugs as acceptable or not are largely historical rather than pharmacological. For example, alcohol produces marked changes in behavior, has dangerous physical effects, and is powerfully addicting. Many experts believe that it is highly unlikely that we would ever completely legalize any other drug with such undesirable consequences.[18]

REGULATION OF ALCOHOL

Alcohol is tightly regulated in most countries and banned in a few. It remains an extremely popular drug despite its adverse consequences and the problems of addiction associated with its use. Because of its special position in most societies as an historically controlled, but legal, psychoactive drug, it deserves special attention in this chapter.

The Lessons of Prohibition

Although it is widely believed that the Eighteenth Amendment to the U.S. Constitution was a failure and that it demonstrated once and for all the futility of governmental

attempts to legislate morality, this is not a completely accurate account of the effects of Prohibition.[19] This "noble experiment" was a failure in the sense that it bred contempt and open defiance of law and order, and it also fostered the growth of organized crime. No one denies that the Volstead Act was widely violated and that smuggling, moonshining, and speakeasies all thrived during the Prohibition era. On the other hand, there is considerable evidence that the consumption of alcoholic beverages declined considerably, especially among the working class. The most reliable indicators of heavy consumption, including acute alcohol overdose mortalities, liver cirrhosis, and hospital admissions for alcoholic psychosis, dropped well below their pre-Prohibition levels.[20] These declines were related to the price of alcohol, which tripled or quadrupled in parts of the nation after the Eighteenth Amendment took effect.[21] It can be expensive to deal in the underground economy!

According to Moore and Gerstein, there are three principal lessons of Prohibition that should be remembered in any future attempts to regulate the supply of beverage alcohol:[22]

1. Drinking customs in the United States are strongly held and resistant to frontal assault. It is well beyond the will or capacity of government ever to eradicate the customary demand for alcoholic beverages.

2. A criminal supply network emerges—if not instantly, then within a few years—if production and sale of alcoholic beverages are outlawed. The prices and extent of this criminal supply depend on the degree of public support for the law and the resources devoted to law enforcement.

3. The quantity of alcohol consumption and the rates of problems varying with consumption can, however, be markedly reduced by substantial increases in real prices and reductions in the ease of availability.

One lesson of Prohibition is that an abrupt legislative decree banning beverage alcohol will not work in our society. This seems to be the most well-remembered lesson. In fact, it may be responsible for tendency of many of those interested in alcohol problems to "disassociate themselves from the taint of temperance."[23] An equally important lesson, but one that we seem to have forgotten, is that regulation *can* reduce consumption and alcohol-related problems.

Current U.S. Policies

Today all states in the United States set a minimum age for the legal consumption of alcohol and prescribe penalties for retailers who knowingly sell to underage customers. Some states assess penalties even when a retailer mistakenly sells alcohol in good faith to a minor with a fake ID. Under pressure from the federal government, including the threat of withholding highway trust funds, the minimum age has shifted back to 21 years. All states also impose special excise taxes on alcoholic beverages, and most have restricted advertising, hours of sale, and credit sales (charge accounts, credit cards, etc.).

Beginning in the 1930s, eighteen states chose to create state or county monopolies to control both wholesale distribution and retail sales of distilled spirits. The remaining states adopted licensing systems in which state regulatory agencies are empowered to license wholesalers and retailers and to promulgate and implement other rules and regulations regarding beverage alcohol sales.

While the Twenty-first Amendment left the "dry" option open to individual states, all of them now permit alcoholic beverage sales in at least part of the state. Only about 3.5 percent of the population still resides in dry counties.[24] In most cases the dry counties are predominately rural areas, and they tend to be concentrated in the South. Even there, however, drinking usually is allowed in certain lodges, fraternal organizations, and "private" clubs.

Taxes and Price Controls. A fundamental law of economics is that as the price of something goes up, *ceteris paribus,* people will generally buy less of it. Thus, as prices for alcoholic beverages rapidly rose during Pro-

hibition, demand decreased.[25] The same effect, in reverse, may also be partly responsible for the increase in per capita consumption that has occurred since the last major increase in federal taxes in 1951. Between 1967 and 1984, the real price of liquor dropped by almost one-half! One reason for this dramatic decrease in price was the fact that the federal excise taxes were not based on the price of the beverage, but instead were tied directly to the volume. Some critics have argued that the most important feature of federal policy in alcohol abuse prevention during the past several decades is the failure to index excise taxes on liquor to the consumer price index.[26]

In addition to taxes, many state governments had also influenced alcohol prices through "fair trade laws" and, in monopoly states, by administrative fiat. States with liquor monopolies may still set prices by decree in state-owned liquor stores, but the courts have eliminated price fixing by the liquor industry through fair trade laws. The method used to set prices may make a great difference to the state treasury, but it matters very little to the consumer. A price increase that arrives through taxation, price fixing, or administrative decree is all the same to the customer at the checkout stand. All three methods equally affect demand for the product.

Perhaps the most comprehensive analysis of the connection between alcohol prices, consumption, and alcohol-related problems was accomplished by Philip J. Cook. His examination of changes in liquor tax increases over a fifteen-year period demonstrated that even relatively small changes in prices influence not only the consumption of alcohol but the most serious health effects as well.[27] Similar decreases in consumption, heavy drinking, and alcohol-related problems due to price increases also have been noted in other countries.[28]

Does a decrease in overall consumption within a population also affect the drinking patterns of "heavy" drinkers? The pioneering work of Ledermann[29] and subsequent studies by several others confirm that even a significant proportion of problem drinkers in any population will reduce their consumption as overall consumption is reduced.[30] Some have suggested that regulation aimed at prevention of problem drinking might be more effective if specific taxes were levied on particular beverages favored by heavy drinkers, such as cheap brands of fortified wine.[31] However, this may just encourage switching to other alcoholic beverages. This argument also favors keeping the tax tied to the volume of alcohol sold, rather than the purchase price, since the former approach would have a greater impact on alcoholics, especially poor alcoholics who customarily purchase the cheaper types and greater quantities of alcoholic beverages.

Even though taxes on alcohol constitute a relatively small proportion of governmental budgets, governments closely consider the implications of these tax levels on their revenues. This is especially true during the recent past years of serious budget crises. President Bush's promise of "no new taxes" was quickly amended in 1990 to allow consideration of both alcohol and tobacco "sin" tax increases. Governments are most certainly aware of the danger of raising taxes to such a high level that revenues may actually decrease from a reduction in sales. As long as the alcoholic beverage lobby still exerts any influence in legislative circles, taxes are unlikely to rise to such levels. Consider the comments of an Ohio legislator:

"If the main, publicly stated objective from a policy standpoint is to reduce consumption through taxation, I believe it will create substantial problems in building coalitions in the legislature. A lot of folks make a good living selling alcoholic beverages, and they have for years contended that tax policy affects consumption. If a bill goes to a . . . committee, . . . it will have a hard time getting out of that committee because such committees are dominated by people who are generally friendly to the (alcoholic beverage) industry."[32] Still, if governments have no choice but to raise income taxes or "sin" taxes, and the amount of additional revenue needed is moderate, the latter are politically less volatile.

There are a number of other mechanisms by which government may influence the price and thereby control demand for alcohol. Until recently, our tax laws heavily subsidized alcohol consumption by allowing tax deductions for beverages purchased with business-related meals. Another example is the long-standing practice of selling alcoholic beverages at greatly discounted prices on U.S. military bases, a practice that strongly encouraged drinking by both uniformed and civilian employees and their families. Fortunately, the military establishment has realized that many problems were caused by selling cheap alcohol, and current policies are changing this practice.

Control of Distribution. In addition to taxation and monopolistic price controls, government can do much to regulate the consumption of alcohol by controlling its distribution. It can do this by adopting and implementing policies regarding the number, size, and location of outlets, hours of business for package stores and bars, advertising practices, and the minimum legal drinking age.

The matter of licensing retail sales is generally a function of state and local governments. A number of earlier studies have attempted to determine the effect of outlet density on alcohol consumption, but there appears to be no relationship.[33] A quasi-experimental study in Ontario compared sales to residents of two cities located some miles apart, both of which were served by a package store located in one of them. Per capita sales were roughly equal for these two cities, despite the considerable differences in accessibility.[34] Outlet density may be more a result than a cause of demand in communities that treat alcohol sales as a proper function of the free market.[35]

Monopoly distribution systems also do not seem to have any appreciable effect on alcohol sales. In the Commonwealth of Independent States (CIS, formerly the Soviet Union), for example, consumption is high and alcoholism is a major social problem.[36] A comparison of states in the United States that have monopoly distribution systems with those that allow private competition showed no difference in levels of consumption or indicators of alcohol-related health problems.[37]

There is little evidence that restricting the hours of sale reduces consumption. In fact, a study of changes in the hours of sale over a twenty-five year period concluded that "Sunday closing" laws (sometimes called "blue" laws) and earlier closing hours had the opposite effect: more sales![38] However, other changes in availability have been related to increased consumption. These include a gradual easing of restrictions on alcohol sales since World War II. Liquor-by-the-drink is now available in almost every large city, wine and beer are routinely sold in grocery stores and gas stations, mixed drinks are available in restaurants, and sporting events often realize as much profit from the sale of alcohol as from the sale of tickets.

Blose and Holder found a significant increase in alcohol sales and alcohol-related automobile accidents immediately after North Carolina adopted liquor-by-the-drink.[39] When Idaho, Maine, Virginia, and Washington made wine available for sale in grocery stores, wine consumption rose significantly.[40] Anyone who has ever attended a professional baseball or football game where alcoholic beverages are sold can attest to their popularity. Consumption at sporting events has become such a problem in some communities that local officials have imposed "beer-free" games on the fans. Several major stadiums no longer sell any beer after the seventh inning of major league baseball games—with no significant effect on attendance.

The effect of increased availability on consumption is not peculiar to the American culture. One recent study of the liberalization of alcohol laws in Finland showed a remarkable *doubling* of consumption in just seven years. The Alcohol Act of 1969 had abolished restrictions on sales in rural areas, lowered the drinking age, and permitted retail shops to sell beer with a higher alcohol content. By 1975 the Finns were drinking 156 percent more beer, 96 percent more spirits, and 87 percent more wine. (Another curious fact is that Finnish drivers already had a higher rate of DUI than other Europeans *before* the liberalized liquor laws.[41] This happened despite a lower rate of drinking—indicating, perhaps, that enforcement was more strict in Finland.)

Drinking Age. Perhaps no other area of alcohol policy has been so emotionally charged as the minimum legal age for purchasing and consuming alcoholic beverages. Minimum age restrictions are based on the assumption that alcohol use is more harmful for young persons than it is for adults. There always has been some variation in this age among the states, but historically most have used the age of 21 as the minimum age for unrestricted purchases. This continues to be a point of contention among the young, since they can now vote and be drafted into military service at age 18. Between 1970 and 1973, twenty-four states reduced their minimum drinking ages, reasoning that 18- to 21-year-olds should have all the rights and responsibilities of adulthood.[42]

During that period an enormous amount of research was conducted on the impact of lowering the minimum age of purchase. One conclusion stood out quite clearly: lower drinking ages were associated with significant increases in the rate of automobile crashes among young people.[43] Estimates of the increase in fatality rates were found to be 7 percent among those states that had dropped their minimum ages from 21 to 18 years of age.[44]

Partly because of this evidence, fifteen states raised their minimum drinking ages back to 21 between 1975 and 1982. Among thirteen of these states that were studied, automobile crashes were reduced from a minimum of 14 percent to a maximum of 29 percent.[45] Another study of nine states that raised their minimum drinking age between 1975 and 1979 found a *41 percent* decrease in nighttime single-vehicle fatalities.[46] With such convincing evidence in hand on the effect of minimum age legislation, Congress passed a law in 1984 that would have reduced federal highway funds for any state that had not raised its minimum drinking age to 21 years by 1986. Despite the outcry on college campuses and frantic lobbying by the alcohol lobby, most states complied by the deadline. Louisiana held out until its highway system could no longer survive without federal funds.

One of the other arguments against a lower minimum age is that it makes it just that much easier for 16- and 17-year-old students who have 18-year-old friends to obtain alcohol. (Remember, a majority of high school seniors will be 18 years old before their graduation.) There is some limited support for this argument, but it appears that beer is the only type of alcoholic beverage to have been affected appreciably by changes in the minimum age laws.[47]

Driving Under the Influence. In most situations, the possession and use of alcohol by adults is completely legal. However, when a legally intoxicated individual (someone with a blood-alcohol concentration of 0.10 percent in most states) attempts to drive an automobile, a *crime* has been committed. Driving under the influence (DUI) or driving while intoxicated (DWI) is a criminal offense in all fifty states and the District of Columbia. (Most states also have laws against having any kind of open container of alcohol in a moving motor vehicle.)

At least half of all traffic fatalities involve alcohol. An estimated 40 percent of the traffic related deaths that occur each year result from accidents in which one or more drivers exceeded the legal limit for intoxication. Another 10 percent of these fatalities involved drivers with lower levels of alcohol.[48] There are indications that the incidence of alcohol-related fatalities resulting from other accidents (light aircraft and boating accidents, falls, etc.) is even higher.[49]

All states have laws against driving under the influence of alcohol or driving while intoxicated, with the most common standard for either set at a blood-alcohol concentration (BAC) of 0.10 percent.[50] A few states and a number of other countries have lower levels. Sometimes called the blood-alcohol level (BAL), this figure is determined by the ratio of the weight of alcohol to the volume of blood, grams per 100 milliliters (G/100ml). In states with "per se" laws, it is an offense to

drive with a BAC at or above the specified-value. A defendant may be convicted on the basis of chemical test evidence alone. Other states use a particular BAC as a "presumptive standard," allowing the defendant to introduce evidence that he or she was not, in fact, impaired at the prescribed limit.[51] The question of how effective these laws are in influencing the rate of drunken driving is still unsettled. Some moderately persuasive evidence does suggest that effectively enforced drunk driving laws deter drunken driving and reduce the accidents and fatalities associated with them.

The most thorough study of drunk driving laws is possibly that of the British Road Safety Act (RSA) of 1967. This act provided a "per se" BAC limit of 0.08 percent, and the first offense was a mandatory one-year suspension of the license. The new law was also preceded by a great deal of publicity. Ross's evaluation of the RSA found a 23 percent decline in auto fatalities, a decline in other auto injuries, and a decline in BAC levels of injured drivers—all within the first few months after implementation. Unfortunately, these improvements gradually flattened out and then began to rise by the end of 1970. The explanation for these events was that the well-publicized passage of the RSA convinced many drivers that the risk of arrest and punishment would be much higher than it had been. Although they were deterred from drinking before driving and from driving after drinking, law enforcement did not markedly increase the certainty of either detection or punishment, and drivers gradually returned to their old habits as this became known to the public.[52]

In the United States an evaluation of thirty-five alcohol safety action programs between 1970 and 1977 concluded that twelve of the programs had produced a decrease in nighttime auto fatalities, an accepted indicator of drunken driving.[53] Nevertheless, there continues to be a great deal of controversy over DUI laws. In most states a common result of a DUI conviction is the administrative suspension of the driver's license. No one could deny the logic (and perhaps the justice) of this method. However, police report that a very large proportion of DUIs involve drivers whose licenses already have been suspended for previous DUI convictions. Even in states like Florida, with *mandatory* jail sentences for second offenses, it is not at all uncommon for persons arrested on DUI charges for the second, third, or later offenses to serve no time in jail at all.[54] One reason the courts cite for not strictly enforcing DUI laws is that they impose "new and heavy demands on courts, incarceration facilities, and probation services" at a time when the criminal justice system is already overloaded (no pun intended) with more "serious" crimes.[55] Prosecuting attorneys frequently feel that tough mandatory sentences for drunk drivers are ineffective and may actually raise public expectations to unrealistic levels.[56] Organizations such as Mothers Against Drunk Driving (MADD) and Students Against Driving Drunk (SADD) have reacted by bringing even greater pressure for tougher sentences, especially for drunk drivers who kill or injure another person. Such pressure has resulted in much political posturing by state and local politicians, but few effective solutions. Some judges have resorted to bizarre sentences such as mandating a convicted drunken driver to place a "Drunken Driver" plate or tag on the family automobile. Needless to say, other family members who drive this automobile suffer needless embarrassment.

Another popular approach in dealing with drunken drivers is the "sobriety checkpoint." The typical procedure is for local police to set up unannounced roadblocks along certain routes and stop vehicles, sometimes at random, to check for indications of alcohol impairment. This strategy provides a highly visible method of approaching the problem that is generally supported by the public, but there is little evidence of its effectiveness.[57] Its chief virtue lies in its symbolic reassurance to the public that something is indeed being done! Sobriety checkpoints are regarded by some motorists as a nuisance, especially in heavy traffic, and have been challenged by others as an unconstitutional invasion of privacy. So far,

however, the courts have upheld the legality of this approach in most instances.[58]

Like drug use and possession, drunk driving lacks the usual criminal motives of gaining property or harming another person. DUI offenses are also unique in that a physical test (breathalyzer, blood analysis, etc.) is used and compared against a state standard to determine whether or not a crime has been committed. Drunk driving offenses are also frequently handled administratively rather than judicially through driver's licensing regulation. This means that one could have a driver's license suspended without any judicial safeguards. In most states when drivers receive their licenses, they agree to take a breath or blood test if they are stopped on suspicion of driving while intoxicated. Refusal to take a test upon request is a violation of the licensing agreement and can result in automatic suspension or revocation of the license through an administrative process. Forty-two states have such sanctions.[59]

Between 1970 and 1986 arrests for drunk driving increased by 223 percent, while the number of licensed drivers increased by only 42 percent.[60] Although much of this increase can be attributed to concentrated law enforcement efforts, some increase was almost certainly due to the trend in the early to mid-1970s for the states to lower the minimum age for the purchase of alcoholic beverages, largely in response to the ratification of the Twenty-sixth Amendment (1971), which extended the right to vote to 18-year-olds. By 1983 19-year-olds could legally drink in twenty-seven states, and 18-year-olds could legally drink in thirteen states.

DUI arrest rates for youth age 18–19 peaked in 1982; for 20-year-olds they peaked the next year. The number of DUI arrests for those age 18–20 decreased by 24 percent by 1986. This abrupt reversal of DUI trends among our youth may be the result of the states once more raising their minimum legal drinking ages.[61] By 1987 only five states still allowed anyone under the age of 21 to purchase alcohol.[62]

A special survey in 1983 revealed that about three-fourths of all DUI offenders previously had been convicted of a crime. About half had previous DUI convictions. The median age of a DUI offender was 32, and about one-third worked as a laborer or in a construction trade. Another one-third were unemployed at the time of their arrest. The typical DUI offender was white (85.6 percent) and male (94.7 percent) and had consumed the equivalent of twelve bottles of beer just prior to arrest.[63]

Insurance/Liability Laws. Public policy is sometimes intended to indirectly affect the consumption of alcohol through such measures as the regulation of insurance rates. Drivers with DUI convictions may face higher insurance premiums or, in some cases, they may be unable to purchase automobile insurance. Since many of these drivers will continue to drive without insurance, these laws may actually be harmful to the larger population. There is no evidence indicating that higher insurance premiums have actually reduced consumption.

Another indirect measure involves server liability or "dram shop" laws. In a majority of states, commercial establishments that serve alcoholic beverages are civilly liable to those who suffer harm or injury as the result of an intoxicated or underage person's irresponsible use of alcohol. The typical dram shop law imposes civil liability for damages caused by an establishment's serving alcohol to "visibly intoxicated or underage customers."[64] (Criminal liability may also be attached when a minor is involved.) The courts also have held that even without a dram shop law, civil liability can be imposed on a tavern under common law.[65] One result of these laws has been the provision of better training to servers to help them learn how to recognize and "cut off" a customer who is intoxicated and to see that they get home safely. Some communities have established training programs for servers on methods of referring problem drinkers to appropriate treatment services.

More recently, decisions in a number of states have extended common law liability from commercial establishments to social hosts who provide alcohol to their intoxicated or underage guests.[66] Even though there are many good reasons to retain these policies, there is no published research indicating that dram shop or server liability laws have affected the use of alcohol.[67] Many feel that the laws have been too vague to persuade servers to change their policies. Also many establishments buy insurance to cover their liability, and insurance companies have often shortcut the intent of the laws by settling out of court on unjustified claims.[68]

CONTROL OF ILLICIT DRUGS

Public policies regarding illicit drugs have not reached the degree of specificity that is found in policies regarding alcohol use. The primary debate surrounding illicit drugs is whether it is possible to control their use through law enforcement. The current failure of public policy to deal with the drug problem is the logical outgrowth of policies pursued by the federal government over the past decade. Since the election of Ronald Reagan in 1981, federal policy has been much more concerned with preventing recreational drug use than with helping habitual users. During Reagan's first term, funding for drug treatment fell by almost 40 percent, adjusting for inflation.[69] A staff member of the Democratic Study Group in the House of Representatives estimates that Washington, DC, has twenty thousand crack addicts and seventeen thousand IV drug users, but treatment facilities are available to help no more than four thousand of them.[70]

During the 1988 presidential campaign, the drug issue was never far from the political spotlight, and according to most opinion polls, drug problems were the nation's leading concern. At his inauguration, President Bush promised, "This scourge will end," and in September 1989, he devoted an entire speech to the subject.[71] Today the "war on drugs" commands relatively little attention. The candidates in the 1992 presidential race seldom mentioned the drug issue, and the extent of media interest in the subject seems to be Bill Clinton's denial that he inhaled marijuana while attending Oxford.

The approach chosen by the Bush administration was one of "zero tolerance." This approach emphasizes law enforcement toward the end of completely eradicating illegal drugs, and it appears to be based on the following assumptions: (1) that if there were no drug abusers, there would be no drug problem, (2) that the market for drugs is created not only by availability, but also by demand, (3) that drug abuse starts with a willful act, (4) that the perception that drug users are powerless to act against the influences of drug availability and peer pressure is an erroneous one, (5) that most illegal drug users can choose to stop their drug-taking behaviors and must be held accountable if they do not, (6) that individual freedom does not include the right to self and societal destruction, and (7) that public tolerance for drug abuse must be reduced to *zero*.[72] This policy means that possession of even the smallest amounts of illicit drugs may result in the seizure and confiscation of an individual's automobile, home, or other property. Some see this as a serious threat to our civil liberties.

Although still woefully inadequate, the Bush administration did increase treatment funding by 50 percent, to $1.6 billion. At the same time, the administration continued its preoccupation with casual middle-class drug use, not with addiction or habitual use.

The nation's first "drug czar," William Bennett, had developed a strategy of seeking out and punishing casual, nonaddicted users. He also insisted that all drugs were equally pernicious,[73] a somewhat incongruous philosophy

Needle Exchange Urged to Break AIDS-Drug Link

WASHINGTON—The National Commission on AIDS Tuesday sharply criticized the federal government for what it said was a "bewildering and tragic" failure to address the close link between HIV infection and drug abuse, which produces one-third of all new AIDS cases.

In a report titled "The Twin Epidemics of Substance Use and HIV," the commission endorsed needle exchange programs to reduce the spread of AIDS among drug users.

The commission called for full federal support of "outreach" programs that provide addicts with sterile needles while counseling them to enter treatment. And it said 11 states and the District of Columbia should lift laws prohibiting the sale or possession of syringes without a prescription.

The prescription requirement, it said, encourages the sharing of contaminated needles, thus increasing the risk of transmission of the human immunodeficiency virus, which causes AIDS.

The report was particularly critical of the federal Office of Drug Control Policy, which it said virtually ignores the link between AIDS and drug abuse and neglects treatment measures to fight the problems in tandem.

The director of National Drug Control Policy, Bob Martinez, said the report offered "no clear scientific evidence" that needle-exchange programs reduce what he called "risk-taking" behavior related to the transmission of the AIDS virus.

Dr. Don Des Jarlais, a member of the AIDS commission and director of research on chemical dependency at Beth Israel Medical Center in New York, said there were "tens of studies that give evidence that needle-exchange programs work."

Researchers reported last month that the New Haven program, authorized by the Connecticut Legislature and carried out in a partnership between the state drug program and the Yale University medical school, reduced the rate of infections among drug users in the city by 33 percent.

Source: *Austin American-Statesman*, August 7, 1991.

for a two-pack-a-day smoker! The next drug czar, former Florida governor Bob Martinez, shied away from the public spotlight and made few changes in Bennett's approach. Four months into the Clinton presidency, a new drug czar has yet to be confirmed.

Other nations have chosen other strategies. The Netherlands has legalized the use of certain drugs such as marijuana. While Britain has a reputation for legalization, its approach to controlling illicit drugs really is one of "harm reduction" through methadone maintenance or needle/syringe exchange programs. Many experts feel that the United States is rather myopic in considering other options. Several states still prohibit the distribution of hypodermic needles or syringes without a prescription, making it impossible to operate a "legal" needle/syringe exchange program.

In the United States, efforts to control illicit drugs have been hampered by the great degree of fragmentation of federal, state, and local drug enforcement programs. A recent report from the Comptroller General indicates that the supply and demand of illicit drugs have remained relatively constant despite the massive increase in federal drug control efforts. In fact, he seriously questioned the ability of governmental efforts to regulate illegal drugs in the absence of "factual information about which anti-drug programs work best."[74] It is the recognized failure of antidrug enforcement policies that gave rise to the current debate on legalization of illicit drugs.

According to Dale Masi, an expert on employee assistance programs, the legalization of illicit drugs signals "the inevitability that use will increase." She testified before Congress that this approach "cannot be reconciled with ethical principles because it would be implemented with recognition of the increased personal and social destruction connected with drug abuse that would result. We, as a civilized society, are responsible for preventing disease and destruction, not spreading them."[75] This view is not accepted by all the experts, however. A New York State Senator, Joseph Galiber, proposed the legalization of *all* drugs. His plan is intended to eliminate criminal drug trafficking by allowing the sales of currently prohibited drugs in the same place and manner as alcohol. Similar restrictions on minimum age for purchase, hours of sale, location of stores, and so on would apply to drugs sales just as to current alcohol sales.[76]

Other testimony favored various compromise proposals, such as the legalization of the "less harmful forms" of illicit drugs. These advocates all favored the legalization of marijuana, and some favored legalizing certain forms of cocaine (coca leaves) and opiates (smokable opium).[77] Compromise proposals frequently advocate some degree of "decriminalization" for particular drugs rather than complete legalization. This approach sometimes suggests a civil rather than a criminal penalty for the use or possession of a controlled substance. On other occasions it suggests that no penalty be attached to use but that sales be subjected to criminal penalties. This leaves users in the awkward position of being legally entitled to use a drug, but having no legal means to obtain it.[78] We could also use the tax laws as a way of imposing civil penalties on the use or possession of a drug, as we did with marijuana in 1937.

The War on Drugs

Richard Nixon was the first president to declare "war" on drugs. He did this in 1971 as he also introduced stronger criminal penalties for drug dealers and proposed a rapid expansion of drug treatment facilities, especially those specializing in heroin addiction.[79] All subsequent presidents have continued this effort, with each promising to increase the war effort against drugs.

The "war on drugs" was simply a continuation of the policies espoused in the Harrison Act in 1914, in which the federal government relied on a variety of approaches to reduce both the demand for and the supply of illicit drugs. The major changes are seen in the massive amount of funding for law enforcement, the perceived seriousness of the problem of drug abuse, and the advanced technological strategies for controlling drugs. We now use Bell 209 assault helicopters, Navy EC-2 and Air Force AWACS "eye-in-the-sky" aircraft, "Fat Albert" surveillance balloons, "Blue Thunder" high-performance Coast Guard vessels, and NASA satellites.[80] The war analogy may seem appropriate in halting the operation of large drug cartels, but it seems inappropriate when it comes to dealing with other aspects of drug abuse. The war analogy seems especially inappropriate regarding efforts to prevent or treat drug abuse by our children.[81]

Critics of the war on drugs have declared it "a losing battle," "almost an afterthought," and "hype from an Administration and Congress eager to justify the expenditure of billions of dollars for law enforcement."[82] These "get-tough" efforts may sound good to the public, but no serious student of drug policy is encouraged by our efforts at law enforcement in the attempt to reduce illegal drug use.

The Economics of Drug War/Peace

One of the principal criticisms of the war on drugs is that it simply hasn't worked. Our best estimates indicate that only 10 percent of the major illicit drugs smuggled into the United States are interdicted.[83] Drug-related emergency room admissions, drug-related arrests, and casual drug use continue to rise.[84] Prison populations are exploding because of drug-related crime. This problem is so severe that even though many penalties for drug-related crimes have been increased, actual sentences served have decreased. Corrections officials are highly critical of this "revolving-door" approach. As new drug offenders are incarcerated, some other prisoners have to be released simply to make room for them. Minority offenders are particularly affected by drug law enforcement. In Florida, the majority of all black adults sentenced to prison are there because of illicit drugs.[85]

Another major criticism is that we cannot afford the cost of the war on drugs. From 1981 through 1988 the federal costs alone totaled $16.5 billion.[86] The current cost of the war on drugs for all levels of government is $30 billion per year, and former head of the National Drug Control Policy Office, William Bennett, implied that at least $10 billion more per year will be needed just to incarcerate additional drug users.[87]

Our present policies on illicit drugs have also amounted to a type of regressive tax: it has dramatically increased the profits of drug dealers while placing additional economic burdens on the residents of inner cities to provide more law enforcement and to ameliorate the effects of crime. In 1989 federal agents discovered and confiscated 20 tons of cocaine in a California warehouse. This was reported to be the largest seizure of illegal narcotics ever (although drug seizure records continue to be broken). Both politicians and police officials heralded it as proof not only of the severity of the drug problem but also of the success of our interdiction efforts. However, it is questionable whether the raid prevented a single person from using cocaine. No drug lord or street dealer was put out of business, and no additional addicts were driven to seek treatment. This event had no perceptible impact on the public's attitude toward drug use. People who wanted cocaine were still able to find it.[88]

A recent article on the costs of the drug war estimated that the legalization and taxation of marijuana and cocaine (powder, not crack) would result in a net savings of about $25.25 billion per year. Legalization of these drugs would save $10 billion a year in federal law enforcement, $10 billion a year in state and local prosecution, $8 billion a year in other law enforcement costs, $6 billion a year in the value of stolen property associated with drug use, and $3.75 billion a year by eliminating the "match" for Colombians' drug profits. We would also receive additional tax revenues of about $12.5 billion. These gains amount to $50.25 billion.

If drug use were to rise by 25 percent because of legalization, it would result in an additional social cost (health costs, stolen property, loss of income, etc.) of about $25 billion. This would leave the net gain of "drug peace" at $25.25 billion per year! Drug peace would be a less costly alternative to the drug war, according to these estimates, unless legalization led to a *doubling* of the number of marijuana and cocaine users. At this point the net economic benefits of drug peace would be zero.[89] Of course, all these estimates rely on assumptions which are highly speculative, at best. We have no reliable way of predicting how much drug use would increase under a policy of legalization or decriminalization. We know that in Britain the number of addicts seeking treatment increased after passage of the Dangerous Drugs Act (which decriminalized the use of heroin and other illicit drugs), but we do not know to what extent drug *use* increased or decreased. There is some evidence that marijuana use decreased immediately after the Dutch government decriminalized its use in 1976, however.[90] Both England and the Netherlands are far different from the United States in culture and economic demographics. We cannot assume that Washington, DC, would react to legalization in the same manner as London or Amsterdam. The Netherlands has a homicide rate only one-eighth that of the United States. Important aspects of their overall drug policy are also very different.

Mandatory treatment of drug abuse is simply not an acceptable approach in the Netherlands. The Dutch also regard "successful" treatment as that which improves the life of the drug user. Abstinence is not a primary treatment objective.[91]

Issues Regarding Legalization

We must remember that in the absence of any convincing empirical data regarding the effectiveness of alternative policies toward illicit drugs, our political system encourages the use of symbolic values (such as increased law enforcement) that become just as important, if not more important, than any tangible outcomes. Thus the debate over the legalization of illicit drugs has developed very strong moral overtones.

Have Drug Laws Created Problems Worse than the Drugs Themselves? Is it reasonable to say that our present drug policies are responsible for increased corruption, violence,

street crime, and disrespect for the law? There is obviously much truth in these assertions. One could easily argue that our present policies have made the sale of illicit drugs a highly profitable enterprise—so profitable that "turf" wars among cartels and neighborhood dealers alike have led to remarkable increases in the homicide rate. One only has to read the headlines in any Washington, DC, newspaper to learn that the great majority of homicides in the nation's capital (also the nation's *murder* capital) is drug related. On the other hand, the evidence suggests that among the majority of street drug users who are involved in crime, their criminal careers were well established prior to the onset of their drug use.[92] As we mentioned in the previous chapter, their drug involvement may be due primarily to their involvement in a criminal subculture.

Perhaps more important is that our present laws, coupled with the propaganda we fed to our children for two generations about the consequences of drugs such as marijuana, have resulted in disbelief and widespread criminal violations. There is a direct parallel between this situation and the consequences of Prohibition, during which the law made criminals of millions of otherwise honest citizens.

Has Law Enforcement Failed in Reducing the Supply and the Demand for Drugs? A closely related argument often made by advocates of legalization is that the $30 billion a year currently spent for law enforcement could be better used for the treatment and prevention of drug abuse. *Casual* drug use, especially among young people, has steadily declined since 1980.[93] Whether this decline is related to present drug enforcement efforts is highly questionable, however. It is just as likely that increased public awareness of drug problems has contributed to this decline. Unfortunately, the latest data on regular users could hardly be more discouraging. According to National Institute on Drug Abuse (NIDA), the number of people who use cocaine at least once per month had increased by 18 percent since 1988, and the number of weekly users increased by 29 percent—to 855,000.[94]

Can We Stop the Use of Drugs That a Significant Segment of the Population Are Committed to Using? We simply cannot arrest, prosecute, and punish such large numbers of people, especially in a liberal democracy in which the government must not unduly interfere with personal behavior. Attempting to enforce draconian measures against drug users will not only bankrupt us, but it is also an imminent threat to our civil liberties.

Is Illicit Drug Use as Great a Threat to Our Society as the Legally Sanctioned Use of Alcohol and Tobacco? The surgeon general of the United States estimated that cigarette smoking (the number *one* preventable cause of death) alone killed more than 390,000 persons in 1989.[95] Cigarette smoking kills more people each year than all other drugs combined and is virtually always addicting. Sales of tobacco are not just legal; they are actually *subsidized* by government programs providing price supports for tobacco growers! The number of deaths directly caused by beverage alcohol each year is approximately 100,000, and another 100,000 deaths are described as having alcohol consumption as a "contributing factor."[96] These figures are almost certainly conservative estimates of alcohol-related deaths. Compare these figures with the estimated mortality rate of six thousand deaths from illicit drug use, and one must wonder why cocaine, marijuana, and heroin are regarded as being so dangerous.[97] If we want to focus on a strong drugs-crime connection, we should remember that more than half of all persons convicted of a violent crime were "under the influence" of alcohol at the time the crime was committed.[98]

Mark Kleiman, a former Reagan administration Department of Justice staff, has suggested raising the tax on cigarettes to a dollar per pack. He estimates that this would reduce the number of smokers by 10 percent, thereby saving 40,000 lives a year.[99]

What Are the Possible Benefits of Legalization? Among the expected benefits are cheaper drug prices, a decrease in drug-related crime, less corruption of governmental officials, and a destruction of the power base of drug lords and criminal syndicates. In addition, our legal system would be free to use its resources to provide treatment to those who are addicted, to prosecute and punish "real" criminals, and to eliminate the threat to civil liberties contained in our present policies. Finally, government-sanctioned sales outlets could provide "quality control" for drug users and could collect badly needed tax revenues.

Would Legalization Result in Increased Drug Use, Loss of Productivity, and Higher Health Care Costs? On the other hand, legalization could imply approval and lead to increased use. (If arguing that drug legalization would persuade people that drugs are safe, then the obvious implication is that we need to reconsider our policies on alcohol and tobacco!)

As we mentioned earlier, marijuana use actually fell in the Netherlands after it was decriminalized. Even if drug use were to increase with legalization, however, the economic benefits of "drug peace" would in all likelihood pay for the additional costs of increased usage, both socially and economically. As the earlier analysis indicated, the break-even point would be close to a 100 percent increase, and not even the most severe critics of legalization are predicting such dire consequences.

Will Drug Users Seek Greater Quantities and Higher Potencies of Drugs on the Black Market? This is probably true if government legalizes drugs but restricts the amount that a person can legally purchase. In order to work, legalization must make drugs available at all levels of quantity and potency. Otherwise, a black market in drugs will continue.

Will Legalizing "Soft" Drugs Like Marijuana Lead Its Users to More Harmful and Addictive Drugs? If we want to restrict "gateway" drugs (drugs that young people use that appear to be precursors of later drug use), then we should place restrictions on alcohol and tobacco, *especially* tobacco. Moreover, keeping marijuana illegal forces buyers into a black market where they are likely to be offered other illegal drugs. Finally, some sixty million Americans have tried marijuana, and the number of cocaine addicts is estimated at only one million. Most of these people do not graduate to stronger drugs. The gateway effect is apparently not very strong.

Proposals for the legalization or decriminalization of drugs are incomplete and imperfect. There are still too many unanswered questions for us to change course abruptly on these policy issues. Before we can seriously consider radical alternatives to the war on drugs, we need to answer such questions as:

What drugs should be legalized? Marijuana? Heroin? Cocaine? If cocaine is to become legal, should we legalize *all* forms such as cocaine powder and crack?

What potency levels should be permitted? Or should there be any controls on potency?

Should there be age limits as to who *can* and *cannot* purchase drugs? Should we have a 16- or 18-year-old minimum age for purchasing marijuana or Quaaludes and a 21-year-old limit for cocaine or heroin?

Should we limit drug use to those persons who are already addicted to them? If so, what do we say to the heroin user who wishes to purchase cocaine?

Where should drugs be sold? Over-the-counter in drugstores and supermarkets? In liquor stores? Vending machines?

Will advertising of drugs be allowed? In which media? How will we prevent drug advertising from encouraging children to try the product?

If drugs are legal, will we still place restrictions on drug use by transportation workers, police officers, military personnel? Will we treat drugs like alcohol and only forbid on-duty use? Will it

---

Alaskans Practice Benign Neglect of New Anti-Pot Law

ANCHORAGE—Tom Walls liked his marijuana best in the morning—two or three puffs, he says, to clear his bronchial passages, calm his nerves and get a jump-start on a happy day.

For nearly 16 years, there was no problem with that. Alaska's marijuana law, the most liberal in the country, allowed residents to have up to four ounces in the home. As the war on drugs raged across the rest of the United States, Alaska, to the embarrassment of some and the glee of others, remained something of a sanctuary.

Until November. Then voters passed an initiative to recriminalize marijuana. Though the margin was narrow—legal marijuana received more votes than the winning candidate for governor—the party, it appeared, was over.

But today, Tom Walls still enjoys his marijuana in the morning. The law, which went into effect in March, is being contested in court. And police agencies, saying they have better things to do, acknowledge that they aren't enforcing it, at least not vigilantly.

"People didn't start smoking it when it became legal, and they're not stopping because it has become illegal," said Anchorage lawyer Bob Wagstaff, who has filed a lawsuit challenging the new law. "In fact, there's some thought that some people who quit have taken it up again as a form of rebellion."

"People moved here because Alaska has less oppressive laws, and some moved here particularly because of the marijuana law. But then they became complacent and didn't guard against this sort of erosion of rights," said Walls, who belongs to a pro-marijuana group called Alaskans for Hemp Awareness, which was established after the referendum passed.

In mid-March, members protested the new law by staging a pot party—the "Idita-toke," named in honor of the Iditarod sled dog race—in an Anchorage hotel room. They called police to come arrest them. Police, saying they had higher priorities, never came.

Source: *Miami Herald,* June 8, 1991.

be permitted to require drug-testing of employees for a *legal* drug?

Merely asking these questions will anger many people, but we must begin to fashion a comprehensive, consistent, and enforceable policy regarding the use of drugs. These questions, and many others, must be answered before the political system is ready to consider an abrupt change in policy. Without a minimum degree of consensus on a number of these issues, we are not likely to deviate much from our present course. An interesting illustration depicting the ambivalence of state policymakers on the legalization of marijuana is found in Alaska.

DRUGS, ALCOHOL, AND CRIME

That there is a relationship among alcohol, drugs, and crime is certain. The exact nature of that relationship is quite complex, however, and scholars are still putting the pieces together. David Rasmussen and his colleagues argue that the great majority of persons who are arrested for drug offenses are *not* participating in other types of more violent criminal activity.[100] On the other hand, we know from current research that the great majority of persons arrested in urban areas for all crimes test positive for illicit drug use.[101] The effects of substance abuse on crime depends on (1) *what* drug is being used, (2) *who* is using the drug, (3) the relationship of the user to subcultures tolerant of other forms of social deviance, (4) law enforcement policies regarding drug use, and perhaps most important of all, (5) *who* is conducting the research.

It is almost tautological that people who use drugs (except for alcohol and certain legal prescription drugs) are, *ipso facto*, violating criminal laws. One simply cannot use heroin, hashish, or cocaine without committing a criminal act. There are some very persuasive arguments that society forces drug users to become criminals because of our unreasonable definitions of drug use per se as a criminal act. Labeling theorists such as

Lemert argue that the secondary deviance that attaches to a person who is arrested or incarcerated for drug offenses can be far more destructive than the consequences of the drug use itself.[102] For the most part, however, society seems to be more concerned with whether other nondrug crime, particularly "street crime," is a direct result of drug-taking behavior. Labeling, stigmatization, and secondary deviance are rather remote issues for citizens facing a crime wave.

Two hypotheses currently dominate the drugs-crime controversy. The first maintains that the "addict of lower socio-economic class is a criminal primarily because illicit narcotics are costly and because he can secure his daily requirements only by committing crimes that will pay for them."[103] This hypothesis maintains that criminality is a more or less direct consequence of physical dependence and tolerance that requires ever-increasing doses of a drug that is economically unavailable to the addict with limited financial means. The other hypothesis maintains that the "principal explanation for the association between drug abuse and crime . . . is likely to be found in the subcultural attachment" of the drug abuser to criminal associations, identifications, and activities of other persons who are addicted.[104] This hypothesis has more currency with the "hard" drugs such as heroin, a drug that is closely associated with a criminal subculture. It is less fruitful when applied to the "soft" drugs such as marijuana, as most middle-class college students could eagerly testify. Even cocaine seems to be a favorite drug of businessmen, "yuppies," and other middle-class citizens.

There is another category of crime, frequently identified as "domestic violence" (wifebeating, child abuse, etc.) that has been linked to alcohol or drug abuse so frequently and so consistently that one might also hypothesize a direct, causal relationship between drug use and certain crimes of violence.[105] Alcohol especially is said to have a "disinhibiting" effect that unleashes emotions such as rage, or at least lessens the ability to control rage.[106] In a study of 234 "women abusers" appearing before the court in Indianapolis,

60 percent had been under the influence of alcohol, and 21.8 percent had been under the influence of other drugs when they physically assaulted their spouses or partners. The men who were using alcohol or drugs generally displayed greater violence toward the women.[107]

On the other hand, with few exceptions there is no evidence of a clear cause and effect relationship between alcohol or drug use and violent behavior. Drugs such as PCP and amphetamines are known to affect the brain in some way that triggers violent behavior.[108] However, CNS depressants and marijuana generally alter behavior in the *opposite* direction.[109] There are reasons to suspect that much of the domestic violence that occurs under the influence of alcohol or drugs is preplanned. According to the "disavowal" theory, the abuser simply gets drunk or gets "high" so that he will have an excuse for beating his wife or children. By doing so, both his family and society may treat him less severely.[110]

There is considerable evidence that most of the current problems of the criminal justice system can be attributed, either directly or indirectly, to drugs—jail overcrowding, court backlogs, increased crime, prison overcrowding, inmate violence, and the increased costs of incarceration. Strains on the system caused by the increased use of drugs have resulted in frequent crisis management and a "continuing search for more effective ways for the system to absorb the increase in drug arrests and to reduce the cycle of drug use and arrest for these defendants."[111]

The data that we will discuss on the following pages show an undeniable relationship among alcohol, drugs, and crime. One task will be to understand whether the socioeconomic class approach, the subcultural attachment approach, or some other hypothesis best explains the nature of that relationship. First, we will look at drug law violations (manufacture, use, and sales) as crime. Next, we will examine the substance abuse and criminal histories of persons arrested or incarcerated for nondrug crime. Third, we will review the research on substance abuse and domestic violence. Finally, we will examine current trends in the drugs-crime relationship, and we will review current policies regarding drugs and crime.

ALCOHOL AND DRUG LAW VIOLATIONS

It is no secret that crime statistics are regarded by "the experts" as seriously flawed. Despite such impressive titles as *Uniform Crime Reports* that fill the basements of university libraries, there is actually very little *uniformity* in reporting practices. Crime statistics are based on reports taken by thousands of local police officers and county sheriffs. Crime statistics in a community may change dramatically overnight with a change in reporting procedures. Police commissioners arguing for larger budgets have been known to create their own crime waves by simply altering departmental rules for reporting crime.

Anyone doing research on juvenile delinquency certainly has been frustrated by the tremendous variability in state and local reporting procedures. Only about two-thirds of the states regularly report juvenile crime data to a central national registry, and many local jurisdictions are not required to report to a central state agency. There is no way to determine how many juveniles were arrested in Texas or Illinois (or several other states) for drug law violations, except by reviewing records of local police. (Imagine examining the records of 254 county sheriffs and hundreds of city police departments in a state like Texas!)

Crime data, although seriously flawed, can be of some help in understanding the drugs-crime relationship, however. Some categories of drug-related offenses, such as adult arrests for drug law violations, are reported with much greater regularity and consistency. Also, we can assume that the direction of error in crime data is toward *underreporting*. On a nationwide basis, we can assume that the degree of underreporting is fairly consistent from one year to the next. Therefore, if we see dramatic changes occurring over a period of years, we may still be able to identify specific trends.

It is obvious from Table 8.1 that there has been a dramatic increase in adult arrests for drug violations during the past decade. In fact, between 1981 and 1990 there was a 110 percent increase in these arrests. Does this mean that there was a comparable increase in illegal drug manufacture, sale, or possession during that period? We can't say. In some communities there may actually be much smaller increases or possibly even a decrease. Other data indicate that the overall crime rate peaked and began to decrease during this period.[112] Despite this trend, vigorous enforcement of drug laws could still produce an increasing number of arrests in this category each year. This is shown quite clearly by the fact that *federal* arrests for drug law violations increased by 134 percent between 1980 and 1986.[113] In other communities the increase in drug law violations may be a thousandfold, but it appears from the statistics to be much smaller, because the police are understaffed and simply cannot keep up with the increased crime. All we know for certain from these data are that *arrests* have increased by 110 percent.

Juvenile arrest data indicate that a somewhat smaller proportion of youth under age 18 are arrested for drug-related offenses— about 9 percent in 1985.[114] However, this figure masks some alarming increases in drug law violations for certain subgroups. Among male juveniles arrested, over 12 percent were charged with a drug offense. For *black* males under 18, the rate was almost 25 percent.

DRUG USE BY CRIMINALS

In a special survey of state prison inmates in 1979, 42.7 percent of the 288,086 offenders either had been convicted of a drug crime or had been daily users of illegal drugs in the month preceding the offense for which they were incarcerated. In 1986, 46.8 percent of more than the half million prisoners in state institutions were found to be similarly involved in drugs.[115]

TABLE 8.1 Estimated Number of Court Commitments and Adult Arrests for Selected Serious Offenses and Drug Offenses, 1960–1990

Year	*Estimated Number of Adult Arrests*		
	Selected Serious Offenses	All Drug Offenses	Drug Trafficking
1960	250,465	—	—
1964	291,146	—	—
1970	395,679	322,314	—
1974	574,730	474,897	—
1978	616,656	479,950	86,391
1981	697,847	468,056	93,143
1982	754,742	584,850	119,309
1983	709,525	583,474	128,948
1984	679,032	623,719	137,218
1985	688,795	718,597	170,307
1986	757,587	742,687	186,414
1987	749,651	849,521	219,176
1988	840,633	1,050,576	287,858
1989	897,252	1,247,763	404,275
1990	881,466	1,008,332	318,633

Source: U.S. Department of Justice, Office of Justice Programs, Bureau of Justice Statistics, *Prisoners in 1991* (Washington, DC: U.S. Government Printing Office, May 1992), p. 8.

In the 1979 study, about 35 percent of the property offenders and 38 percent of the robbers had been under the influence of drugs at the time of the crime. Somewhat fewer rapists (22 percent) and murderers (21 percent) had been under the influence of a drug. In a 1983 study of jail inmates about one-third of all property offenders and one-fourth of all violent offenders reported that they were under the influence of a drug at the time of their offense. Nearly half of the offenders had been drinking alcohol just prior to committing the crime.[116] (Since these figures are from self-reports, there is always the possibility that inmates may have overreported drug use as an excuse for their behavior. With the exception of cocaine users, however, self-reports have proven to be a reasonably reliable indicator of drug use.[117])

In the 1986 study, 28 percent of prison inmates reported a past drug dependency. The drugs most frequently mentioned were heroin (14 percent), cocaine (10 percent), and marijuana or hashish (9 percent). At the time of the offense, 17 percent were under the influence of drugs only, 19 percent were under the influence of alcohol only, and 18 percent were under the influence of both drugs and alcohol. More than half said they had taken illegal drugs during the month before committing the crime, and 43 percent said that they had used drugs on a daily basis just prior to committing the crime.[118]

A very high level of drug use was found in a recent study of persons arrested in major metropolitan areas (Table 8.2). In New York City, 80 percent of all females arrested tested positive for drug use. It is interesting that a higher percentage of female arrestees tested positive in several of these cities. One of the explanations for this is the reputed connection between prostitution and drug use. Many female addicts turn to prostitution to support their habit. Women are arrested more often for prostitution than for more serious crimes. Women are also more likely than men to be jailed on drug charges.[119] Of all female inmates in 1986, 59 percent were sentenced for a nonviolent crime, and 12 percent were sentenced specifically for drug offenses.[120] It is also quite interesting that cocaine is by far the most commonly used drug among persons arrested, with marijuana a distant second choice.

According to a 1987 survey of juveniles in custody, 83 percent of youth in secure, state-operated institutions reported using an illegal drug in the past, and 63 percent reported using an illegal drug on a regular basis. Almost 40 percent of the incarcerated youth said that they were under the influence of drugs at the time of their offense. The most commonly mentioned illegal drugs were marijuana, cocaine, and amphetamines.[121] The alcohol and drug use of a cohort of juvenile offenders in a longitudinal study is summarized in Table 8.3. Of particular interest is the fact that in 1983, 82 percent of juveniles who committed sexual assaults reported alcohol use immediately before their crime was committed.[122]

An analysis of juvenile offenses in Florida reveals a 1,580 percent increase in the number of juvenile drug offenders sentenced to adult prisons on felony charges between 1983 and 1988.[123] During this same period the number of drug-related delinquency cases increased by about 85 percent.[124] It appears that juveniles arrested for drug offenses are being handled much more severely.

There is ample evidence that both juvenile and adult offenders are more likely than nonoffenders to use alcohol or illegal drugs, but does that mean that the drug use *caused* the crime? In a recent article, Huizinga and coworkers examined the temporal order of drug-alcohol use and other delinquent behavior and conclude that "other" delinquency generally precedes the use of alcohol or drugs. Therefore, alcohol and drug use cannot be the cause of other delinquent behavior. However, the same study concludes that there may be causal relationships *within* the arena of drug law violations:

1. The onset of alcohol use precedes the onset of either marijuana or polydrug use in 95 percent of all ascertainable cases; among those who never use alcohol, no more than 3 percent initiate marijuana use and no more than 1 percent initiate polydrug use.
2. Marijuana use precedes the onset of polydrug use in 95 percent of ascertainable cases.[125]

It should be stressed that this (and earlier) studies of the drugs–juvenile delinquency relationship were concerned more with alcohol and the "soft" drugs than with "hard" drugs such as heroin. Remember our earlier caveat regarding the nature of the drug having an impact on its connection with criminal behavior. Heroin and cocaine both produce a much more powerful physical craving in the addicted person than drugs such as marijuana, and the price is much more expensive than alcohol. The alcoholic and the regular marijuana user can ordinarily maintain their life-style through regular employment.

Research in Maryland (Baltimore), California, and New York (Harlem) indicates that criminal activity increases with higher levels of heroin use. Ball, Shaffer, and Nurco found that over a nine-year period, the crime rate of 354 heroin addicts dropped with less

TABLE 8.2 Any Drug Use by Male and Female Arrestees[1]

Any Drug Use by Male and Female Arrestees[1]

City	% Positive Any Drug	% Positive by Age 15-20	21-25	26-30	31-35	36+	% Positive by Race Black	White	Hispanic	Other
Birmingham (Males)	72	58	75	86	69	62	74	69	2	2
Birmingham (Females)	65	2	2	2	2	2	58	75	2	2
Chicago (Males)	80	70	83	84	88	74	82	71	72	2
Chicago (Females)	77	2	84	82	2	2	77	2	2	2
Cleveland (Males)	68	55	76	76	76	58	71	60	2	2
Cleveland (Females)	No data for females	—	—	—	—	—	—	—	—	—
Dallas (Males)	66	57	66	77	77	52	69	53	49	2
Dallas (Females)	65	66	61	76	60	55	63	68	2	2
Detroit (Males)	68	63	68	69	65	75	70	57	2	2
Detroit (Females)	81	2	84	82	2	2	81	82	2	2
Ft. Lauderdale (Males)	62	58	82	64	63	49	72	54	2	2
Ft. Lauderdale (Females)	No data for females	—	—	—	—	—	—	—	—	—
Houston (Males)	65	54	76	79	76	41	71	56	60	2
Houston (Females)	No data for females	—	—	—	—	—	—	—	—	—
Indianapolis (Males)	54	65	50	62	2	33	47	61	2	2
Indianapolis (Females)	No data for females	—	—	—	—	—	—	—	—	—
Kansas City (Males)	54	41	66	59	62	2	61	42	2	2
Kansas City (Females)	70	2	67	2	2	2	74	2	2	2
Los Angeles (Males)	75	65	74	83	80	72	82	72	74	24
Los Angeles (Females)	76	67	75	84	78	69	88	77	59	2
Miami (Males)	75	76	78	69	89	68	77	67	77	2
Miami (Females)	No data for females	—	—	—	—	—	—	—	—	—
New Orleans (Males)	70	66	76	78	74	58	73	54	2	2
New Orleans (Females)	55	32	53	65	71	48	54	59	2	2
New York (Males)	83	70	87	93	86	74	86	82	81	2
New York (Females)	80	70	80	83	85	77	83	79	74	2
Omaha (Males)	56	2	54	73	2	2	59	57	2	2
Omaha (Females)	No data for females	—	—	—	—	—	—	—	—	—
Philadelphia (Males)	81	82	83	85	90	59	82	69	87	2
Philadelphia (Females)	79	2	76	90	85	68	80	85	2	2
Phoenix (Males)	63	74	68	67	67	41	75	60	64	47
Phoenix (Females)	60	57	58	71	69	40	84	60	49	45
Portland (Males)	74	75	80	77	78	63	83	70	74	66
Portland (Females)	78	69	80	79	88	71	86	75	2	70
St. Louis (Males)	56	41	62	70	57	48	55	56	2	2
St. Louis (Females)	44	2	2	2	2	28	56	21	2	2
San Antonio (Males)	63	58	73	64	60	58	62	53	68	2
San Antonio (Females)	51	2	2	63	2	36	2	58	38	2
San Diego (Males)	82	72	86	86	86	72	85	83	79	2
San Diego (Females)	79	88	89	78	84	55	89	78	62	2

Source: National Institute of Justice, "Drug Use Forecasting Program," March 1990, p. 4.

Males
Females

[1] Positive urinalysis, January through December 1988.

[2] Fewer than 20 cases.

184

TABLE 8.3 Percentages of Most Recent Offenses Involving Alcohol or Drug Use Immediately Before the Commission of the Offense, 1979 Versus 1983, by Juvenile Offenders

Year	Offense	Alcohol or Drug Use Immediately Before Commission of Most Recent Offenses (percentage)			Mean Alcohol or Drug Use per Day (average percentage of days of year on which alcohol or drugs were used)	
		Alcohol Only	Drugs Only	Both Alcohol and Drugs	Alcohol	Drugs
1979	(Most recent offense)					
	Sexual assault	NA	NA	NA	NA	NA
	Aggravated assault (incl. gang fights)	23	1	9	36	33
	Robbery	10	10	6	32	44
	Burglary	14	2	12	34	33
	Larceny > $50	16	7	5	42	62
	Motor vehicle theft	20	5	15	46	84
1983	(Three most recent offenses)					
	Sexual assault	82	0	0	26	42
	Aggravated assault (incl. gang fights)	19	1	13	31	51
	Robbery	0	0	0	10	4
	Burglary	22	4	8	36	51
	Larceny > $50	10	2	16	45	58
	Motor vehicle theft	0	38	13	45	110

NA – not available.

Source: David Huizinga, Scott Menard, and Delbert Elliott, "Delinquency and Drug Use: Temporal and Developmental Patterns," *Justice Quarterly,* Vol. 6, No. 3 (September, 1989), p. 441.

narcotics use and rose 400 to 600 percent with increased use.[126] An earlier paper on the Baltimore study estimated that male opiate addicts commit crimes on an average of 178 days per year.[127] Johnson and colleagues revealed in a study of Harlem heroin users that daily users committed about five times as many robberies and burglaries as irregular users, an average of 209 per year.[128] Obviously, they are apprehended for only a tiny fraction of these crimes.

Statistics in Florida indicate that at least half of all street crime is directly related to the use, sale, or possession of illicit drugs. Reports from that same state also reveal that intense law enforcement "crackdowns" are effective in reducing drug-related crimes for a short time period and in specific geographic areas, but at the cost of increasing crime in adjacent neighborhoods.[129]

Almost everyone is familiar with the situation in Washington, DC. The tremendous growth in Washington's homicide rate and its connection to the sale and use of crack co-

caine has been well documented. Since 1981 Washington has ranked number one or number two in the nation both in murder and drug arrest rates.[130]

The balance of the evidence strongly supports the case for a causal relationship between illegal drug use and crime. This relationship is summarized by the Bureau of Justice Assistance:

The link between drug use and crime has been firmly established, making it difficult to discuss one to the exclusion of the other. Localities experiencing high rates of illicit drug usage also experience high rates of criminal activity. Property crimes are not the only class of offense showing increases. More and more frequently, drug users, traffickers and distributors are resorting to violence as a means of obtaining drugs and protecting their territories. Crack is a drug whose presence is often accompanied by violence. Nationwide, cities are reporting that anywhere from a third to a half of their homicides are drug-related. Intravenous drug use is posing an additional challenge for the criminal justice system as it struggles to deal with increasing numbers of abusers who are at higher risk for contracting the Acquired Immune Deficiency Syndrome (AIDS) virus. . . . The relationship between drug use and criminal activity is a generally accepted notion. . . . [131]

DRUG USE BY VICTIMS

There is evidence that drinking alcohol or using drugs *by the victim* also precipitates crime. According to the life-style/exposure theory, routines or life-styles involving alcohol or drug use may facilitate the spatial and temporal union of victims and criminals.[132] Ask any police officer about hanging around bars drinking or going into inner-city crack houses to buy and/or use drugs. These are both regarded as very high-risk activities.

A recent study of over six thousand cases in England strongly supports the contention that drinking at night away from home greatly increases the prospects of the drinker's suffering a personal attack or injury. For young male respondents, the probability of enduring a serious personal injury as a result of such a life-style was even greater.[133] Persons who use drugs or alcohol away from home are frequently in an environment unfamiliar to them, surrounded by persons who are involved in all types of criminal activities, and suffer from a diminished capacity for flight or self-protection.

DOMESTIC VIOLENCE

There seems to be a high degree of family violence in America, as well as an unwillingness to look too closely at the serious incidents of physical abuse that are occurring in many homes. Shame, guilt, fear of reprisal, and lack of appropriate community responses prevent many victims from reporting these crimes. In just a few years, however, official reports of child abuse have mushroomed—from 5,993 in 1967[134] to over 2 million in 1986.[135] As long ago as 1977, national surveys estimated at least 6 million incidents of *serious* physical abuse of spouses each year.[136] The general

picture emerging from the research literature is that women and children are usually the victims of domestic violence, and men are the perpetrators.[137] The one exception is in the case of spousal homicide, in which men are almost as likely as women to be victims. Women who murder their husbands usually cite constant, long-term physical abuse as their motivation, however.[138] It should also be recognized that couples who are not married have rates of domestic violence that are just as high or higher than married couples.[139]

Public opinion has long held that the wifebeater or child abuser is a "lower class, beer-drinking, undershirt-wearing Stanley Kowalski brute."[140] Family violence is not confined to any social, geographic, economic, or racial group, but it *is* strongly connected to the use of alcohol and drugs. Two decades ago Dr. Henry Kempe estimated that alcohol plays a role in about a third of all cases of child abuse.[141] A study conducted at an Arkansas alcoholism treatment center indicated that more than half of the parents being treated were also child abusers.[142] Another study in New York found that the husband's alcohol or drug abuse was an underlying factor in over 80 percent of wifebeating cases.[143] More recently, research in Indianapolis showed that more serious physical abuse is likely to be committed by men with an alcohol or drug problem.[144]

According to Cohen, violence among alcohol and drug users may occur because human aggression may be increased through drug use, and this propensity is dose related. Some of the possible explanations for this phenomenon are:

1. The drug might diminish ego controls over comportment, releasing submerged anger that can come forth as directed or diffuse outbursts.

2. It may impair judgment and psychomotor performance, making the individual dangerous to himself and to others.

3. It might induce restlessness, irritability, and impulsivity, causing hostile combativeness.

4. The drug could produce a paranoid thought disorder with a misreading of reality. False ideas of suspicion or persecution may bring

forth assaultive acts against the imagined tormentors.

5. The craving to obtain and use the drug can result in a variety of criminal behaviors, some of them assaultive.
6. An intoxicated or delirial state may result in combativeness and outbursts of poorly directed hyperactivity and violence.
7. Drug-induced feelings of bravado or omnipotence may obliterate one's ordinary sense of caution and prudence causing harm to one's self or others.
8. An amnesic or fugue state may occur during which unpredictable and irrational assaults may take place.[145]

In the case of certain drugs such as "ice," there is an almost certain direct link between drug use and violent or aggressive behavior. With alcohol, however, this relationship is somewhat more indirect. In fact, the most widely accepted viewpoint is that alcohol abuse is a disavowal technique used by abusive husbands. Some men may drink heavily prior to beating their wives or children because they know that by being drunk they will be released from responsibility both by their spouses and by the rest of society. In other words, drunkenness can provide a "time-out" period when the norms regarding appropriate behavior can be disregarded. Individuals may not become violent because they are drunk, but get drunk so that they may become violent—and be excused.[146]

DRUG/CRIME TRENDS IN THE 1990s

In addition to the dramatic increase in illicit drug use that has been observed during the past decade, some other disturbing trends are developing that merit special attention.

Drug Trafficking

The massive problem of illicit drug use in the United States is not the result of independent manufacturers, growers, and "pushers." It takes a great deal of *organized* effort to bring cocaine from Peru, heroin from Pak-

istan, and cannabis from Mexico into this country in a sufficient volume to satisfy current demand. Law enforcement officials' intelligence on drug distribution networks indicates that a number of well-organized, large, highly competitive regional organizations as well as hundreds of small, independent dealers are involved in the illicit drug trade. Traditional organized crime syndicates, small ethnic groups, street gangs, and motorcycle gangs are all involved in the importation, manufacture, distribution, and sale of illegal drugs.[147]

The growth of nontraditional organized crime is one of the most recent phenomena in illicit drug trafficking. Outlaw motorcycle gangs have been deeply involved in Oklahoma (Outlaws), Wyoming (Sons of Silence, Bandidos), Texas (Bandidos, Scorpions, Banshees, Ghostriders, Freewheelers, and Conquistadors), and several other states. These groups generally were once synonymous with the manufacture and distribution of amphetamines, but have expanded to include cocaine, heroin, and marijuana.

Los Angeles gangs, primarily the Crips and the Bloods, have developed far-reaching illicit drug networks that operate in Oregon, Washington, Missouri, Maryland, Texas, Colorado, and New York. In some communities such as Seattle, Tacoma, and Denver, they dominate the trade in crack cocaine.

In upstate New York markets have become more organized along ethnic lines. Jamaican and Hispanic groups seem to be controlling the distribution of larger quantities of drugs and have access to suppliers in the southeastern United States. In New York City, a major source for the importation and distribution of both domestic and international drugs, Chinese and Pakistani groups have become the main heroin traffickers. Most of the heroin originates in Southeast Asia. The federal Drug Enforcement Administration's New York City office reports that the city's most powerful cocaine trafficking organization has its roots in Cali, Colombia.

Maryland reports that the state's supply of illegal drugs is plentiful and the sources varied, with no single group maintaining control over the market. A recent development is the distribution of crack in rural areas of the state by Haitian migrant workers. Texas also reports a multitude of organized networks involved both in the manufacture and distribution of drugs. Traditional organized crime, border drug czars, Latin American organized crime, outlaw motorcycle gangs, and ethnic drug gangs are all involved in the Texas drug market.[148]

In California the Bureau of Organized Crime and Criminal Intelligence reports that criminal activities of street gangs exploded in 1987, with narcotics trafficking contributing heavily to the increased violence. Some of the gangs, especially the Crips and the Bloods, have transformed themselves into well-organized and sophisticated drug distribution networks. Competition between these gangs may explain a large portion of the seemingly "random" violence that occurs on their turf, and it is undoubtedly a major factor in the uneasy "truce" agreed upon shortly after the 1992 Los Angeles riots. California also has witnessed the involvement of outlaw motorcycle gangs, prison gangs, and three important international drug cartels: the Medellin cartel based in Colombia, the Triads based in Hong Kong, and the Yakuza based in Japan. In addition to heroin and cocaine trafficking, the cartels are also involved in real estate, business investment, and money laundering.[149]

Two New England states have become important links in the drug distribution pipeline. Canadian law enforcement authorities have verified that large quantities of both heroin and hashish are smuggled through Canada and Vermont to major metropolitan areas in the northeastern United States. Large quantities of cocaine imported through Florida also pass through Vermont on the way to Montreal. Rhode Island has become an important cocaine and heroin distribution center for New England, Canada, and the Midwest. Its proximity to New York and Boston make it a choice distribution center for several Colombian trafficking groups known as clans.[150]

Drugs, Crime, and Prison

In April 1988 the National Council on Crime and Delinquency issued its first national prison population forecast, based on the prison population projections of nine states. At that time it was estimated that those states would increase their prison populations by 21 percent during the next five years. By December 1989 the estimate for the five-year increase had risen to 68 percent. The earlier forecast had not taken into account the impact of the current "war on drugs," which threatens to overwhelm the nation's correctional system.[151]

This expansion of the prison population is due largely to increases in admissions for drug offenses. In 1985 about 15 percent of prison admissions were for drug crimes. By the end of 1988 that percentage had increased to over 35 percent, and over 80 percent of drug prison sentences were for cocaine (43.5 percent for sale and 37.9 percent for possession).[152] Between July 1, 1986, and June 30, 1989, drug offense prison admissions increased by 136 percent in Virginia and 201 percent in Michigan.[153] Similar increases were noted in most other states.

One of the reasons for this dramatic growth in drug-related prison admissions is parole failure and revocation. Increased emphasis on drug testing and the intensive surveillance of parolees has resulted in sharp increases in the number of drug offenders who are committed to prison. Approximately one of three prison admissions are people who have failed to complete their parole satisfactorily, and the primary reason for parole failure is the use or possession of drugs.[154] In California, prison admissions for parole violations now exceed prison admissions for new court sentences.[155]

The already high incarceration rate for minorities has exploded with the "get-tough" policies of the War on Drugs. Drug enforcement has somewhat narrowly focused on crack, a favorite illicit drug among the poor, who are also disproportionately black and Hispanic. In Virginia new drug commitments of whites *fell* from 62 percent of total drug commitments in 1983 to 34 percent in 1989, with minority commitments rising from 38 percent to 66 percent. In Florida, 73.3 percent of all drug offenders committed to prison are black.[156] There seems to be reasonable evidence that institutional racism has influenced drug law enforcement.

The projected 68 percent increase in our prison population translates into an additional $35 billion to build and operate new prisons from 1989 through 1994. By 1991 California became the first state to exceed 100,000 inmates, and by 1994 it will have over 136,000 inmates in prison. It will cost California approximately $4 billion annually to operate its prison system in 1994. Florida has experienced the fastest growth rate in its prison system, with a remarkable 180 percent increase between 1983 and 1989. Its prison population will reach 100,000 by 1994, perhaps earlier if it implements a plan for increased drug testing and intense surveillance of parolees and probationers.[157]

Treating Substance-Abusing Offenders

Law enforcement and corrections administrators have responded to the growing number of alcohol- and drug-involved arrests by increasing the enrollment of offenders in diversion, jail-based, probation, and prison drug treatment programs. In 1979 an estimated 4.4 percent of inmates in state correctional systems were in treatment.[158] By 1987 this figure had grown to 11.1 percent.[159] Despite this huge increase, however, the number of drug-using inmates far exceeds the enrollment level.

The most common types of treatment programs in jails and state prisons are Alcoholics Anonymous, Narcotics Anonymous, or other twelve-step approaches modeled closely after AA and NA. While over 80 percent of residential programs for noncriminal offenders incorporate family therapy or family counseling, less than 41 percent of prison programs provide these services. While the great majority of residential programs provide referral

and aftercare follow-up, fewer than 65 percent of prison programs provide referral, and less than 27 percent follow up.[160] Over half of all prison inmates were regularly involved in using drugs before their last arrest but were receiving no programmatic help while incarcerated. When released from prison without effective treatment, we can expect a high rate of crime to continue for these persons.

Professionals outside the correctional system might assume that treatment routinely would be provided to chemically dependent inmates. After all, it makes little sense to incarcerate a cocaine-abusing offender for a period of years and then send him back to the community without treatment! However, we have to consider the barriers to providing treatment within a prison such as constraints on resources, changes in priorities for specific types of programs, staff resistance, and inmate resistance.[161] Prisons and jails are first and foremost institutions designed for control and punishment of criminal offenders. Rehabilitative programming for inmates never has been a high priority. The American public generally has a punitive, nonrehabilitative approach toward crime, and support for rehabilitation has steadily and precipitously declined since the late 1960s.[162]

The literature on treatment of chemically dependent offenders presents a somewhat confusing picture. Some recent evaluations of treatment programs sometimes indicate little or no effect,[163] while others show that treatment decreased subsequent criminal activity and "normalized" the life-styles of offenders.[164] Very little of the research followed offenders for a sufficiently long posttreatment phase to generate much confidence in findings of "success."

There is somewhat more optimism regarding the use of civil commitment procedures to require treatment of probationers and parolees. Anglin's twenty-one-year study of the nation's first true civil commitment program, the California Civil Addict Program, resulted in consistently lower posttreatment drug use rates for clients receiving treatment.[165] Other long-term studies of clients of the Lexington, Kentucky, and Ft. Worth, Texas, Public Health Service Hospitals indicated that addicts treated under legal coercion had better outcomes than noncoerced clients.[166]

A typical model of the civil commitment procedure for criminal offenders is the Treatment Alternatives to Street Crime (TASC) Program. TASC programs have been developed with federal funds under local administration to identify drug abusers who come into contact with the criminal justice system, refer those who are eligible for appropriate treatment, monitor their progress in treatment, and return violators to the criminal justice system. A five-year follow-up of both outpatient and residential programs revealed that TASC clients referred from the criminal justice system did as well or better than other clients.[167]

Historically, methadone maintenance programs have been a major treatment modality for drug-involved criminal offenders. Studies of such programs in New York City since the 1950s indicate that methadone maintenance may be the most cost-effective outpatient treatment for the majority of opiate addicts under probation or parole supervision.[168] Unfortunately, many patients maintained on methadone also have serious alcohol and/or cocaine addictions. In such cases, a choice of other treatment alternatives should also be available.

Therapeutic communities (TCs) have a long history of providing treatment to criminally involved drug addicts. From 1965 until 1975 drug abusers were sent to TCs under civil commitment procedures by both federal and state courts. Since 1975 the civil commitment procedures have been gradually replaced with "legal referrals," which are equally coercive. Some TCs serve criminal justice clients almost exclusively. Clients in a therapeutic community are isolated from the outside world. Their philosophy is that there is no "cure," just control. Addicts are kept away from the neighborhood, friends, and situations that have been a part of their addiction. The TC's aim sounds surprisingly similar to the early moralistic treatments: to restructure an immature, addiction-prone individual into a strong, self-reliant person who no longer needs a drug.[169] A recent review of the research indicates that TCs are equally effective with legally coerced clients as with other clients.[170]

There are obvious explanations for many of the higher success rates claimed by treatment programs that work with legally coerced clients. First, residential programs such as TCs may require clients to be in residence for a year or more, and they are under constant scrutiny by staff and other residents. The risk of detection under such circumstances is quite high, and more successful outcomes are related to longer periods of treatment.[171] Second, clients in both residential and nonresidential programs may be on long-term parole or probation. Such clients may be routinely monitored either by treatment staff or by probation/parole officers for possible drug use, including unannounced urine analysis. Finally, the threat of legal coercion may simply have a deterrant effect.

Whatever one may think of the appropriateness of the "coerced treatment" approach, since passage of the Anti-Drug Abuse Act of 1988, the majority of illicit drug users in treatment in most communities have been treated through the justice system. Without this approach, there would be little treatment of any kind for criminal offenders available within the community.[172]

SUMMARY

Public policy regarding the use of drugs in the United States has been shaped by our culture, our historical inheritance, economic forces, and world affairs. Like most other industrialized Western nations, we have chosen to sanction, regulate, and tax two major drugs—alcohol and tobacco. Our policies regarding the regulation of these drugs are internally inconsistent, however. We spend millions of dollars on scientific research to show tobacco growers how to increase their yield, and we offer price supports to stabilize the tobacco industry. In the past our government has been dependent on tax revenues from tobacco and alcohol sales for a major portion of its budget. At the same time, other governmental offices issue periodic reports decrying the dangers of using either alcohol or tobacco, both strongly addicting drugs that together are responsible for approximately one-half million deaths each year in the United States. Our policies regarding these drugs seem diametrically opposed to policies regarding illicit drugs.

Since the Harrison Act, our policy toward most other illicit psychoactive drugs has been one of official prohibition. It is a policy that has been, at best, a dismal failure. Some even blame the prohibition approach for the worst of our social ills—increasing crime, despair in the inner city, disrespect for law and the political system, and the gradual decline of moral and ethical standards throughout the society. For these reasons, as well as the ever-increasing cost of the war on drugs, we must face the possibility of changing our policy to allow the legalization or decriminalization of at least some illicit drugs.

That criminals are heavier drug and alcohol users than other citizens is beyond dispute. How much crime is directly attributable to drug and alcohol use is another question. In some cases the user's physiological response to a drug might be aggressive behavior that results in a criminal act. For some individuals illicit drug use simply may be another aspect of their criminality that coexists along with certain other criminal activities. Their drug use and their stealing both may be due to the influences of life in an impoverished ghetto, rife with crime. Illicit drug use and other criminal activities may be mutually reinforcing; it is easier to locate and obtain certain drugs if one is already a member of a deviant subculture. If one is a "junkie," that status frequently provides easier access to various forms of criminal enterprise.

According to a recovering heroin addict, "You have put yourself on the wrong side of the law and your original framework for interaction becomes shaky. You find that people you know are stealing, kiting cheques, or doing insurance jobs. The process of osmosis

into this world is slow and gradual. By the time you realize what is going on, you have ceased to be shocked."[173]

For drugs such as marijuana, perhaps the major connection with crime is the secondary deviance that comes from being caught and officially labeled as a criminal. This is especially important for juveniles, since marijuana is the primary illicit drug used by our children. Official court processing and referral of these cases to agencies of the juvenile justice system are not likely to curtail further delinquent acts. In fact, just the opposite is likely to occur. The deeper a youthful drug offender is immersed in the system, the *more* likely we are to see subsequent delinquent behavior.[174]

It seems obvious that the answer to the nation's drug problem is not law enforcement. Law enforcement should be a vital component of any rational plan to stem the manufacture, sale, and use of illicit drugs, but as a primary strategy, it has failed us miserably. At the current rate of imprisonment for drug offenses, it is doubtful that either our economy or our political system can support such high rates of incarceration much longer.

ENDNOTES

1. Phillip Bean, *The Social Control of Drugs* (London: Martin Robertson, 1974).
2. Jason M. White, *Drug Dependence* (Englewood Cliffs, NJ: Prentice Hall, 1991), p. 166.
3. Ibid., p. 165.
4. Vera Rubin, *Cannabis and Culture* (The Hague: Mouton, 1975).
5. Ibid.
6. White, *Drug Dependence*, p. 167.
7. Mark H. Moore and Dean R. Gerstein (eds.), *Alcohol and Public Policy: Beyond the Shadow of Prohibition* (Washington, DC: National Academy Press, 1981).
8. This is the author's assessment of the situation after spending a sabbatical in Dublin, teaching at University College and working with the Irish National Council on Alcoholism.
9. White, *Drug Dependence*, p. 185.
10. U.S. Congress, Hearing Before the Select Committee

on Narcotics Abuse and Control, House of Representatives, 100th Cong., 2d sess., September 30, 1988, p. 61.

11. John F. Galliher, James L. McCartney, and Barbara E. Baum, "Nebraska's Marijuana Law: A Case of Unexpected Legislative Innovation," *Law and Society Review,* Vol. 8 (1974), pp. 441–455.

12. Howard Wayne Morgan, *Drugs in America: A Social History 1800–1900* (Syracuse, NY: Syracuse University Press), 1981.

13. Moore and Gerstein, *Alcohol and Public Policy: Beyond the Shadow of Prohibition,* p. 68.

14. William A. McKim, *Drugs and Behavior,* 2nd ed. (Englewood Cliffs, NJ: Prentice Hall, 1991), p. 278.

15. Moore and Gerstein, *Alcohol and Public Policy,* pp. 68–73.

16. Stanley I. Ornstein, "The Control of Alcohol Consumption Through Price Increases," *Journal of Studies on Alcohol,* Vol. 41 (1980), pp. 807–818.

17. David A. Richards, *Sex, Drugs, Death, and the Law* (Totowa, NJ: Rowman and Littlefield, 1982).

18. White, *Drug Dependence,* p. 191.

19. Moore and Gerstein, *Alcohol and Public Policy,* p. 62.

20. Clark Warburton, *Economic Results of Prohibition* (New York: Columbia University Press, 1932).

21. Steve Olson and Dean R. Gerstein, *Alcohol in America: Taking Action to Prevent Abuse* (Washington, DC: National Academy Press, 1985), p. 49.

22. Moore and Gerstein, *Alcohol and Public Policy,* pp. 63–64.

23. Robin Room and James Mosher, "Out of the Shadow of Treatment: A Role for Regulatory Agencies in the Prevention of Alcohol Problems," *Alcohol Health & Research World,* Vol. 4, No. 2 (1979–80), p. 11.

24. Moore and Gerstein, *Alcohol and Public Policy,* p. 65.

25. Olson and Gerstein, *Alcohol in America,* p. 59.

26. Philip J. Cook, "Increasing the Federal Alcohol Excise Tax," in Dean R. Gerstein (ed.), *Toward the Prevention of Alcohol Problems: Government, Business, and Community Action* (Washington, DC: National Academy Press, 1984), pp. 24–56.

27. Philip J. Cook, "The Effect of Liquor Taxes on Drinking, Cirrhosis, and Auto Accidents," in Moore and Gerstein, *Alcohol and Public Policy,* pp. 255–285.

28. Robert E. Popham, Wolfgang Schmidt, and Jan DeLint, "The Effects of Legal Restraint on Drinking," in Benjamin Kissin and Henri Begleiter (eds.), *The Biology of Alcoholism,* Volume 4, *Social Aspects of Alcoholism* (New York: Plenum Press, 1976), pp. 579–625.

29. Sully Ledermann, *Alcool-Alcoolisme-Alcoolisation,* Don-

nees Scientifiques de caractere physiologique, economique et social, Institut National d'Etudes Demographiques, Travaux et Documents, Cahier No. 29 (Paris: Presses Universitaires de France, 1956).

30. Ole-Jorgen Skog, *Alkoholkonsumets fordeling i befolkningen.* (Oslo: National Institute for Alcohol Research, 1971).

31. Olson and Gerstein, *Alcohol in America,* pp. 53–54.

32. Gerstein, *Toward the Prevention,* pp. 43–44.

33. Robert E. Popham, W. Schmidt, and J. DeLint, "Government Control Measures to Prevent Hazardous Drinking," in John A. Ewing and Beatrice A. Rouse (eds.), *Drinking* (Chicago: Nelson-Hall, 1978).

34. Popham et al., "The Effects of Legal Restraint," pp. 579–625.

35. Reginald G. Smart, "The Relationship of Availability of Alcoholic Beverages to Per Capita Consumption and Alcoholism Rates," *Journal of Studies on Alcohol,* Vol. 38, No. 5 (1977), pp. 891–896.

36. White, *Drug Dependence,* p. 186.

37. Popham et al., "The Effects of Legal Restraint," pp. 579–625.

38. J. Hoadley, B. Fuchs, and H. Holder, "The Effect of Alcohol Beverage Restrictions on Consumption: A 25-Year Longitudinal Analysis," *American Journal of Drug and Alcohol Abuse,* Vol. 10 (1984), pp. 375–401.

39. J. Blose and H. Holder, "Liquor-by-the-Drink and Alcohol-Related Traffic Crashes: A Natural Experiment Using Time-Series Analysis," *Journal of Studies on Alcohol,* Vol. 48 (1987), pp. 52–60.

40. S. MacDonald, *The Impact of Increased Availability of Wine in Grocery Stores on Consumption: Four Case Histories* (Toronto: Addiction Research Foundation, 1985).

41. Olson and Gerstein, *Alcohol in America,* p. 57.

42. Ibid., p. 73.

43. Public Health Service, Alcohol, Drug Abuse, and Mental Health Administration, National Institute on Alcohol Abuse and Alcoholism, *Sixth Special Report to the Congress on Alcohol and Health,* DHHS Publication No. (ADM) 87-1519 (Washington, DC: U.S. Department of Health and Human Services, 1987), p. 103.

44. P. Cook and G. Tauchen, "The Effect of Minimum Drinking Age Legislation on Youthful Auto Fatalities, 1970–1977," *Journal of Legal Studies,* Vol. 13 (1984), pp. 169–190.

45. Robert D. Arnold, *Effect of Raising the Legal Drinking Age on Driver Involvement in Fatal Crashes: The Experience of Thirteen States,* NHTSA Technical Report, DOT HS 806 902 (Washington, DC: U.S. Government Printing Office, 1985).

46. A. Williams, P. Zador, and R. Karpf, "The Effect of

Raising the Legal Minimum Drinking Age on Involvement in Fatal Crashes," *Journal of Legal Studies,* Vol. 12 (1983), pp. 169–179.

47. Reginald G. Smart, "Changes in Alcoholic Beverage Sales After Reduction in the Legal Drinking Age," *American Journal of Drug and Alcohol Abuse,* Vol. 4, No. 1 (1977), pp. 101–108.

48. USDOJ, Bureau of Justice Statistics, *Report to the Nation on Crime and Justice, 2nd ed.,* Report NCJ–105506, June, 1988, p. 7.

49. Dean R. Gerstein, "Alcohol Use and Consequences," in Moore and Gerstein, *Alcohol and Public Policy,* p. 212.

50. Moore and Gerstein, *Alcohol and Public Policy,* p. 83.

51. American Bar Association, Criminal Justice Section, *Drunk Driving Laws & Enforcement: An Assessment of Effectiveness* (New York: Sage Foundation, 1986), p. 31.

52. H. Laurence Ross, "Law, Science, and Accidents: The British Road Safety Act of 1967," *The Journal of Legal Studies,* Vol. 2, No. 1 (1973), pp. 1–78.

53. Paul Levy, Robert Voas, Penelope Johnson, and Terry M. Klein, "An Evaluation of the Department of Transportation's Alcohol Safety Action Projects," *Journal of Safety Research,* Vol. 10, No. 1 (1978), pp. 162–176.

54. Florida Department of Law Enforcement, unpublished report. (Tallahassee, August 1990).

55. ABA, *Drunk Driving Laws,* p. 101.

56. Ibid., p. 105.

57. Ibid., pp. 3–6.

58. *People* v. *Bartley,* No. 60593 (Ill. Sup. Ct., Nov. 21, 1985); *State* v. *Deskins,* 234 Kan. 529, 647 P.2d 1174 (1983); and *People* v. *Scott,* 63 N.Y. 2d 518, 473 N.E. 2d 1, 483 N.R.S. 2d 649 (1984).

59. USDOJ, *Report to the Nation,* p. 7.

60. U.S. Department of Justice (USDOJ), Bureau of Justice Statistics, *Special Report: Drunk Driving,* Report NCJ-109945, February 1988.

61. C. Aaron McNeece, "The Impact of Minimum Age Legislation on Alcohol-Related Juvenile Offenses," paper presented at the annual meeting of the Academy of Criminal Justice Sciences, San Francisco, 1988.

62. National Highway Traffic Safety Administration, *A Digest of State Alcohol Highway Safety Related Legislation, (1983–87)* (Washington, DC: The Administration, 1988).

63. BJS, *Drunk Driving,* pp. 2–3.

64. ABA, *Drunk Driving Laws,* p. 107.

65. *Rappaport* v. *Nichols,* 31 N.J. 188, 156 A.2d 1 (1959).

66. *Kelly* v. *Gwinnell,* 96 N.J. 538, 476 A.2d 1219 (1984).

67. ABA, *Drunk Driving Laws,* p. 108.

68. Olson and Gerstein, *Alcohol in America,* p. 67.

69. Michael Massing, "What Ever Happened to the War on Drugs?" *New York Review of Books,* Vol. 39, No. 11 (June 11, 1992), pp. 42–46.

70. Clarence Lusane and Dennis Desmond, *Pipe Dream Blues: Racism and the War on Drugs* (Boston: South End Press, 1992).

71. Michael Massing, "What Ever Happened to the War on Drugs?" p. 42.

72. Inciardi, "Editor's Introduction," p. 237.

73. Franklin E. Zimring and Gordon Hawkins, *The Search for Rational Drug Control* (Cambridge: Cambridge University Press, 1992).

74. U.S. General Accounting Office, *Controlling Drug Abuse: A Status Report,* Special Report from the Comptroller General of the United States (Washington, DC: U.S. Government Printing Office, March 1, 1988), p. 2.

75. U.S. Congress, Hearings, p. 137.

76. Ibid., p. 59.

77. Ibid., p. 27.

78. Jon Gettman, "Decriminalizing Marijuana," *American Behavioral Scientist,* Vol. 32, No. 3 (1989), pp. 243–247.

79. Karst J. Besteman, "War Is Not the Answer," *American Behavioral Scientist,* Vol. 32, No. 3 (1989), pp. 290–293.

80. James A. Inciardi, "Editor's Introduction: Debating the Legalization of Drugs," *American Behavioral Scientist,* Vol. 32, No. 3 (1989), pp. 233–241.

81. Nora S. Gustavson, "The War Metaphor: A Threat to Vulnerable Populations," *Social Work,* Vol. 36, No. 4 (July 1991), pp. 277–278.

82. Elaine Shannon, "A Losing Battle," *Time,* December 3, 1990, p. 44.

83. Inciardi, "Editor's Introduction," p. 239.

84. Shannon, "A Losing Battle," p. 44.

85. Florida Department of Corrections, unpublished report. Tallahassee, July 1991.

86. Inciardi, "Editor's Introduction," p. 238.

87. Richard J. Dennis, "The Economics of Legalizing Drugs," *The Atlantic Monthly,* November, 1990, p. 129.

88. Dennis, "The Economics of Legalizing Drugs," p. 126.

89. Ibid., p. 130.

194 *Regulating Drugs and Their Consequences*

90. Ibid.

91. Ralph A. Weisheit, "Declaring a Civil War on Drugs," in Ralph A. Weisheit (ed.), *Drugs, Crime, and the Criminal Justice System* (Cincinnati, OH: Anderson and the Academy of Criminal Justice Sciences, 1990), pp. 1–10.

92. James A. Inciardi and Duane C. McBride, "Legalization: A High-Risk Alternative in the War on Drugs," *American Behavioral Scientist*, Vol. 32, No. 3 (1989), pp. 259–289.

93. Jerald G. Bachman, Lloyd D. Johnston, and Patrick M. O'Malley, *Monitoring the Future: Questionnaire Responses from the Nation's High School Seniors* (Ann Arbor: University of Michigan, Institute for Social Research, 1987).

94. Massing, "What Ever Happened to the War on Drugs," p. 42.

95. Office on Smoking and Health, *The Health Consequences of Smoking: Nicotine Addiction* (Rockville, MD: The Office, 1988).

96. E. A. Nadelmann, "The Case for Legalization," *Public Interest*, Vol. 92, No. 3 (1988).

97. Steven Jonas, "Is the Drug Problem Soluble?" *American Behavioral Scientist*, Vol. 32, No. 3 (1989), pp. 295–315.

98. A. M. Bradley, "A Capsule Review of the State of the Art: the Sixth Special Report to the U.S. Congress on Alcohol and Health," *Alcohol Health & Research World*, Vol. 4 (Summer 1987).

99. Mark A. R. Kleiman, *Against Excess: Drug Policy for Results* (New York: Basic Books, 1992).

100. David W. Rasmussen and Bruce L. Benson, *Drug Offenders in Florida* (Tallahassee: Policy Sciences Program, Florida State University, July 1990), p. 3.

101. U.S. Department of Justice (USDOJ), Office of Justice Programs, National Institute of Justice, *1988 Drug Use Forecasting Annual Report,* March 1990.

102. Edwin Lemert, *Social Pathology: A Systematic Approach to the Theory of Sociopathic Behavior* (New York: McGraw-Hill, 1966).

103. Paul Tappan, *Crime, Justice, and Correction* (New York: McGraw-Hill, 1960).

104. Fred Goldman, "Drug Abuse, Crime and Economics: The Dismal Limits of Social Choice," in James A. Inciardi (ed.), *The Drugs-Crime Connection* (Beverly Hills, CA: Sage Publications, 1981), pp. 155–181.

105. Roger Langley and Richard C. Levy, *Wife Beating: The Silent Crisis* (New York: E. P. Dutton, 1977).

106. Natalie Shainess, "Psychological Aspects of Wifebattering," in M. Roy (ed.), *Battered Women* (New York: Van Nostrand Reinhold, 1977).

107. Albert R. Roberts, "Psychosocial Characteristics of Batterers: A Study of 234 Men Charged with Domestic Violence Offenses," *Journal of Family Violence*, Vol. 2, No. 1 (1987), pp. 81–93.

108. Albert R. Roberts, "Substance Abuse Among Men Who Batter Their Mates," *Journal of Substance Abuse Treatment*, Vol. 5 (1988), pp. 83–87.

109. Jason M. White, *Drug Dependence* (Englewood Cliffs, NJ: Prentice Hall, 1991), p. 143.

110. Janet Wright, "Domestic Violence and Substance Abuse: A Cooperative Approach Toward Working with Dually Affected Families," in Edith M. Freeman (ed.), *Social Work Practice with Clients Who Have Alcohol Problems* (Springfield, IL: Charles C Thomas, 1985), pp. 25–39.

111. Steven Belenko, "The Impact of Drug Offenders on the Criminal Justice System," in Ralph Weisheit (ed.), *Drugs, Crime and the Criminal Justice System* (Cincinnati, OH: Anderson, 1990), p. 27.

112. U.S. Department of Justice (USDOJ), Bureau of Justice Statistics, *Report to the Nation on Crime and Justice,* 2nd ed., Report No.NCJ-105506, March 1988, p. 14.

113. U.S. Department of Justice, Bureau of Justice Statistics, *Drug Law Violators, 1980–1986,* Report No. NCJ-111763, June 1988.

114. Juvenile Court Statistics, 1985.

115. USDOJ, Bureau of Justice Statistics, *Prisoners in 1988,* No. NCJ-116315, April, 1988, p. 7.

116. USDOJ, *Report to the Nation*, p. 51.

117. Thomas Mieczkowski, "The Accuracy of Self-Reported Drug Use: An Evaluation and Analysis of New Data," in Weisheit, *Drugs, Crime, and the Criminal Justice System,* pp. 275–302.

118. U.S. Department of Justice, Bureau of Justice Statistics, *Profile of State Prison Inmates,* Report No. NCJ-109926, January 1988.

119. U.S. Department of Justice, Office of Justice Programs, Bureau of Justice Statistics, *National Update,* Vol. 1, No. 1 (July 1991), p. 8.

120. Ibid., p. 10.

121. U.S. Department of Justice, Bureau of Justice Statistics, *Survey of Youth in Custody, 1987,* Report NCJ-113365, September 1988.

122. David H. Huizinga, Scott Menard, and Delbert S. Elliott, "Delinquency and Drug Use: Temporal and Developmental Patterns," *Justice Quarterly*, Vol. 6, No. 3 (September 1989), pp. 420–455.

123. Florida Department of Health and Rehabilitative

Services, Children Youth and Families Program Office, *Preliminary Data Report: Florida Offenders Under the Age of 18 Sentenced to Adult Prisons* (Tallahassee: The Department, 1989).

124. Department of Health and Rehabilitative Services, Children, Youth and Family Services, *Delinquents Charged with Drug Offenses in Florida* (Tallahassee: The Department, 1989).

125. Huizinga et al., "Delinquency and Drug Use," p. 448.

126. John C. Ball, J. W. Shaffer, and D. N. Nurco, "Day to Day Criminality of Heroin Addicts in Baltimore—A Study in the Continuity of Offense Rates," *Drug and Alcohol Dependence*, Vol. 12, (1983), pp. 119–142.

127. John C. Ball, Lawrence Rosen, John A. Flueck, and David N. Nurco, "Lifetime Criminality of Heroin Addicts in the United States," *Journal of Drug Issues* (Summer 1982), pp. 225–238.

128. B. Johnson, P. Goldstein, E. Preble, J. Schmeidler, D. Lipton, B. Spunt, and T. Miller, *Taking Care of Business: The Economics of Crime by Heroin Abusers* (Lexington, MA: Lexington Books, 1985).

129. Crime Prevention and Law Enforcement Study Commission, *Master Planning for Florida's Criminal Justice System*, Tallahassee, January 1, 1990.

130. *U.S. News & World Report*, July 30, 1990, p. 23.

131. U.S. Department of Justice, Office of Justice Programs, Bureau of Justice Assistance, *FY 1988 Report on Drug Control*, 1988.

132. Michael J. Hindelang, Michael R. Gottfredson, and James Garofalo, *Victims of Personal Crime: An Empirical Foundation for a Theory of Personal Victimization* (Cambridge, MA: Ballinger, 1978).

133. James R. Lasley, "Drinking Routines/Lifestyles and Predatory Victimization: A Causal Analysis," *Justice Quarterly*, Vol. 6, No. 4 (December 1989), pp. 529–542.

134. David Gil, *Violence Against Children* (Cambridge, MA: Harvard University Press, 1970).

135. American Humane Association, *Highlights of Official Child Neglect and Abuse Reporting* (Denver, CO: American Humane Association, 1988).

136. Murray A. Straus, "A Sociological Perspective on the Prevention and Treatment of Wifebeating," in M. Roy (ed.), *Battered Women* (New York: Van Nostrand Reinhold, 1977).

137. Margaret H. Hindman, "Family Violence," *Alcohol Health & Research World* (Fall 1979), pp. 2–11.

138. C. Y. McCormick, "Battered Women—The Last Resort," survey by Cook County Department of Corrections, Chicago, 1977.

139. Murray A. Straus, "Causes, Treatment and Research Needs," in U.S. Commission on Civil Rights, *Battered Women: Issue of Public Policy* (Washington, DC: The Commission, 1978).

140. Langley and Levy, *Wife Beating*, 1977.

141. Henry Kempe and Ray E. Helfer, *Helping the Battered Child and His Family* (New York: Lippincott, 1972).

142. Gisela Spieker, "Family Violence and Alcohol Abuse," paper presented at the 24th International Institute on Prevention and Treatment of Alcoholism, Zurich, 1978.

143. Maria Roy, "Current Survey of 150 Cases," in Roy, *Battered Women*.

144. Albert R. Roberts, "Substance Abuse Among Men Who Batter Their Mates," *Journal of Substance Abuse Treatment*, Vol. 5 (1988), pp. 83–87.

145. Sidney Cohen, *The Substance Abuse Problems* (New York: Haworth Press, 1981), pp. 358–359.

146. D. H. Coleman and M. A. Straus, "Alcohol Abuse and Family Violence," paper presented at the American Sociological Association Annual Meeting, 1979.

147. USDOJ, *FY 1988 Report*, p. 13.

148. Ibid.

149. Ibid., p. 14.

150. Ibid., p. 15.

151. James Austin and Aaron D. McVey, "The 1989 NCCD Prison Population Forecast: The Impact of the War on Drugs," *NCCD Focus* (December 1989), p. 1.

152. Criminal Justice Estimating Conference, *Final Report of the Florida Consensus*, February 23, 1989.

153. Austin and McVey, "1989 Forecast," p. 3.

154. Ibid.

155. James Austin and William Elms, *Parole Outcome in California: The Consequences of Determinate Sentencing, Punishment, and Incapacitation on Parole Performance* (San Francisco: NCCD, 1989).

156. Criminal Justice Estimating Conference, *Final Report*.

157. Ibid.

158. National Institute on Drug Abuse, *Drug Abuse Treatment in Prisons*, Treatment Research Reports (Rockville, MD: The Institute, 1981).

159. Marcia R. Chaiken, "Prison Programs for Drug-Involved Offenders," National Institute of Justice, *Research in Action* (October 1989), p. 1.

160. Ibid., p. 2.

161. Marcia R. Chaiken, *In-Prison Programs for Drug-Involved Offenders*, U.S. Department of Justice, National Institute of Justice, Office of Communica-

tion and Research Utilization (Washington, DC: The Department, July 1989).

162. Francis T. Cullen and Paul Gendreau, "The Effectiveness of Correctional Rehabilitation: Reconsidering the 'Nothing Works' Debate," in Lynne Goodstein and Doris Layton MacKenzie (eds.), *The American Prison: Issues in Research and Policy* (New York: Plenum Press, 1989), pp. 35–36.

163. Gennaro F. Vito, "The Kentucky Substance Abuse Program: A Private Program to Treat Probationers and Parolees," *Federal Probation,* Vol. 15, No. 1 (March 1989), pp. 65–72.

164. Gary Field, "The Effects of Intensive Treatment on Reducing the Criminal Recidivism of Addicted Offenders," *Federal Probation,* Vol. 53, No. 4 (December 1989), pp. 51–56.

165. M. Douglas Anglin, "The Efficacy of Civil Commitment in Treating Narcotic Addiction," *Compulsory Treatment of Drug Abuse: Research and Clinical Practice,* National Institute on Drug Abuse, Research Monograph Series No. 86 (Rockville, MD: The Institute, 1988), pp. 8–34.

166. James F. Maddux, "Clinical Experience with Civil Commitment," *Compulsory Treatment of Drug Abuse,* pp. 35–56.

167. Robert L. Hubbard, James J. Collins, J. Valley Rachal, and Elizabeth R. Cavanaugh, *Compulsory Treatment of Drug Abuse,* pp. 57–98.

168. Herman Joseph, "The Criminal Justice System and Opiate Addiction: A Historical Perspective," *Compulsory Treatment of Drug Abuse,* pp. 106–125.

169. William A. McKim, *Drugs and Behavior: An Introduction to Behavioral Pharmacology,* 2nd ed. (Englewood Cliffs, NJ: Prentice Hall, 1990), p. 245.

170. George De Leon, "Legal Pressure in Therapeutic Communities," *Compulsory Treatment of Drug Abuse,* pp. 160–177.

171. Gerstein and Harwood, *Treating Drug Problems.*

172. C. Aaron McNeece, *Substance Abuse Treatment Program Evaluation Project* (Tallahassee: Florida State University, Institute for Health and Human Services, December 1991).

173. Tam Stewart, *The Heroin Users* (London: Pandora, 1987), p. 77.

174. Twentieth Century Fund Task Force on Sentencing Policy toward Young Offenders, *Confronting Youth Crime* (New York: Holmes & Meier, 1978).

III

CHEMICAL DEPENDENCY IN SPECIAL POPULATIONS

Part Three addresses chemical dependency in several special population groups. We begin by discussing alcohol and drug problems among children and adolescents in Chapter 9. Most young people continue to experiment with alcohol, although an encouraging trend is that the percentages of high school students using other drugs, such as marijuana, may be decreasing. However, concern remains that drugs are readily available on school campuses and that much serious use probably occurs among youth who are school dropouts or who are in institutions. These young people are not included in the large surveys of drug use which generally rely on samples of students in regular school classes. Consistent with the systems approach of this book, Chapter 10 discusses substance abuse from a family systems perspective. Other views of chemical dependency, which focus more on the individual with alcohol or drug problems as part of a family constellation, are also presented. Given the large number of substance abusers in the United States, many family members (both in traditional and nontraditional families) are affected by these problems. We also call attention to some of the newer concepts that have emerged in the chemical dependency field such as "codependency" and "adult children of alcoholics."

The focus in Chapters 11, 12, and 13 is on groups that have experienced considerable oppression or isolation, the use of chemicals among these groups, and related problems. Chapter 11 concerns ethnicity. Since it is impossible to describe every ethnic group found in the United States, we consider those that are represented in the greatest numbers. There is considerable ethnic variation in the use of alcohol and other drugs, and ethnic and cultural factors also have implications for prevention, intervention, and treatment. The issue of the rights of gay men and lesbians has received increased attention in all sectors of society, from housing and employment to the church and the military. We devote Chapter 12 to the subject of chemical dependency among these groups with a particular emphasis on the defenses used by gay men and lesbians for psychological protection and with the issue of whether treatment with or separate from heterosexuals should be promoted. Chapter 13 is concerned with substance abuse and dependency among people with a variety of other physical and mental disabilities. The Americans with Disabilities Act of 1990 has increased awareness of individuals with disabilities. For at least the last decade, chemical dependency professionals and rehabilitation professionals have been concerned with the combination of substance disorders and other disabilities and with efforts to promote integrated treatment of these conditions.

Older persons are the subject of Chapter 14. In general, alcohol and illicit drug use remit with age, and those with serious alcohol and drug problems often fail to live to a ripe old age. But a number of alcoholics and addicts defy the odds and live a long life. In other cases, problems with alcohol and drugs can emerge during the later phases of the life cycle due to physical, psychological, or social changes. Finally, Chapter 15 is concerned with gender. Similarities and differences in chemical use and abuse between men and women are discussed since it cannot be assumed that theory, research, and practice pertaining to persons of one gender can be applied to those of the other gender. Particular attention is paid to the special needs of women since they have often been ignored.

Each of the seven chapters in Part Three focuses on specific groups, but common threads run through each chapter. First, we address the incidence and prevalence of substance abuse and dependence in each group to the extent that the empirical literature allows. In some cases, such as for men and women, considerable research has been done to identify the extent of alcohol and drug problems. Although methodological problems taint studies of most groups, it has been especially difficult to get a good picture of the substance abuse among some groups, such as gay men and lesbians. A second theme is the emphasis we have placed on research about the various aspects of chemical dependency—incidence, prevalence, characteristics of abusers, prevention, treatment, and so forth. Sound theory is the basis of good practice, and theory that has been empirically tested is especially useful. Many topics we have covered, important as they may be, have not been subjected to much empirical testing. We suggest that readers critically evaluate all the material provided, including empirical studies which frequently suffer from methodological problems such as poor controls for internal validity and limited generalizability. A third theme that deserves mention is the practical concerns of professionals that we have tried to address. Suggestions for prevention, intervention, treatment, aftercare, and follow-up are sprinkled throughout the chapters. Much more creativity is needed, however, and we hope that these pages might spur readers to think about fresh alternatives. Fourth, our concern about the practical has also led us to provide not only extensive lists of references to which readers may wish to refer, but also information on resources in various parts of the country that might prove helpful, that is, places where professionals might call and talk with others, share experiences, and obtain suggestions. A fifth common thread among these chapters is the use of case examples. Individual cases are not always easily generalized to the clients or practice situations of readers, but they are an attempt to illustrate the real-life complexities faced by clients and professionals in the chemical dependency field. The case illustrations are also designed to provide better integration of the theoretical and empirical material provided in the chapters.

9

Treating chemically dependent children and adolescents

There are no simple explanations of why children and adolescents use licit and illicit drugs.[1] Nor is it clear that most drug-using children and adolescents meet diagnostic criteria to justify diagnoses of alcohol dependency and drug dependency. In general, current use of illicit drugs among adolescents has decreased, dropping from 25 percent to 21 percent between 1979 and 1985.[2] In fact, only 6 to 10 percent of adolescents meet criteria that would justify a diagnosis of drug dependency.[3] Thus social workers should guard against the casual acceptance of diagnoses in children and adolescents. In part, the problem is one of definition. As was discussed in earlier chapters, serious defini-

tional problems exist in assessing substance abuse and dependency. However, with children and adolescents, giving and accepting diagnoses may become a prophecy of lifetime difficulties. On the other hand, to ignore symptoms of a child's substance abuse difficulties constitutes negligence. This chapter's intention is to provide a primer on walking the fine line between an uncritical acceptance of unwarranted labels and negligent practice. To accomplish this goal, this chapter will examine chemical dependency treatment for children and adolescents from the perspective of developmental and contextual factors and the perspective of treatment modality.

DEVELOPMENTAL AND CONTEXTUAL FACTORS

Because children and adolescents are experiencing rapid physiological, sociocultural, and psychological development, treatment strategies traditionally designed for adults must be adapted with developmental concerns in mind. There are critical legal, social, psychological, and cultural systems to consider when treating children and adolescents for alcohol and drug problems. Failure to assess any one of the systems accurately can result in ineffective treatment that leaves the child or adolescent vulnerable to increased alcohol and drug use and the family angered by insensitive practice.

Viewing presenting symptoms by a substance-abusing child or adolescent from a developmental framework provides a more inclusive perspective for social workers who are searching for an appropriate treatment strategy. The first developmental question is: "What level of medical risk does the substance use have for a child or adolescent?" The second developmental question is: "What meaning does the child or adolescent ascribe to the substance use?" After a discussion of the medical context of substance abuse, the second question is discussed in terms of its legal, social, and educational implications.

Medical and Psychiatric Context. The full extent of medical risk to a child's development caused by substance abuse cannot be easily assessed. Although catastrophic outcomes for children are frequently predicted when they use different addictive substances, conclusive studies for all drugs are not available. For example, Kandel, Davies, Karus, and Yamaguchi found that different drugs had different constellations of consequences for adolescents.[4] In general, substance abuse represents one of many risk factors that influence a child's physiological development. Other risk factors like poor nutrition, lack of sleep, and inadequate exercise also can adversely affect development.[5] Yet another area of risk factors is in family functioning. For example, having alcoholic parents presents a significant risk factor associated with the offspring's development of alcohol dependency.[6,7] Balanced against these risk factors is a child's resiliency. Resiliency represents a child's ability to overcome adverse events in his or her life.[8] Although resiliency in children is not well understood, it helps explain why some children can overcome adversity and seemingly live normal lives, while other children succumb.

Among the more serious consequences for chemically dependent children and adolescents is a rise in emotional difficulties.[9] The co-occurrence of severe emotional difficulties and drug abuse is not a coincidence. Adolescents may use drugs as a means of coping with the tribulations that they experience. For other youth, drug use exacerbates serious emotional disorders. Studies suggest a prominent role for substance use in the etiology and prognosis of psychiatric disorders such as affective disorders, conduct disorders and antisocial personality disorders, attention-deficit hyperactivity disorders, and anxiety disorders. Psychiatric disorders also appear to play a crucial role in the etiology of and vulnerability to substance use problems in youth.[10] Thus the presence of substance abuse and dependency in youth may be a harbinger of serious emotional difficulties; treatment will need to address both conditions concurrently.

A recent ominous risk factor is the possibility of human immunodeficiency virus (HIV) infection and subsequent development of AIDS.[11,12] Experimentation has always been a defining characteristic in the normative development of children and adolescents. The spread of the HIV has made such experimentation increasingly dangerous. Children and adolescents who use intravenous drugs and who are active sexually place themselves at a high risk to contract the HIV. Although drug use and promiscuity have typically been part of what has been labeled as "problem behavior" complex or syndrome, the level of medical risk for enacting such behaviors has risen dramatically in the last several decades.[13]

The implication of ideas like risk factors and resiliency is that no simple formula exists that can predict the effects of drug use on children. Not all drugs will affect all children in any predictable way. However, it cannot be disputed that reducing risk factors and increasing resiliency are beneficial for children. Efforts to ensure that children receive nutritious meals, are fully rested, exercise properly, and avoid harmful substances will assist them develop to their fullest potential.

Legal Context. It is a truism that the threat of litigation significantly affects practice decisions. The litigious stance of clients is complex and not easily analyzed. It is sufficient to note that social workers today, more so than ever before, must be cognizant of clients' expectations and up-to-date practice wisdom.

When children and adolescents are brought into a social worker's office, parents frequently expect social workers to employ professional methods to remedy the social, psychological, and familial problems brought on by substance abuse. Such an expectation is unfortunate because social workers do not have any single intervention that can dramatically "cure" children's or adolescents' substance use and abuse. Because alcohol and drug treatments in the United States are heavily influenced by twelve-step programs that sometimes make dramatic claims of success, social workers should carefully explain the limitations of available treatment. Otherwise, parents may expect dramatic and lasting results from treatment and may be angered by failure.[14]

Further, if parents do not understand their role in treatment, it is not surprising that they become increasingly vocal in their complaints about progress. To provide a partial remedy to these legal pitfalls, social workers must avoid endorsing treatment methods that run counter to published literature and practice wisdom. Unfortunately, published literature and practice wisdom do not always provide useful guidance in knowing what interventions to implement with troubled children and adolescents.

In any event, the child's or adolescent's legal standing must be considered when planning treatment. Although the age of consent varies from state to state, parents and guardians must give explicit consent before treatment can begin with minor children. Social workers should examine closely their agencies' guidelines on who can give informed consent for what procedures before undertaking treatment. Drug-abusing children's and adolescents' relationships with parents and/or guardians may be strained, providing fertile grounds for misunderstandings. By remembering that children and adolescents may in many cases be unable to give informed consent to proceed with treatment, social workers should from the very start incorporate parents into treatment planning and implementation.[15]

Although homilies about informed consent may seem elementary, such considerations are critical with substance-abusing adolescents. It may not always be clear if coercion has been used in placing the child or adolescent into treatment. The level of compliance with treatment directives may in part hinge on social workers' precise understanding of who initiated and who is maintaining interest in treatment. When parents initiate their children's or adolescents' entry into treatment, social workers will be faced with the uneviable task of gaining a child's or adolescent's cooperation without criticizing their parents.

Social Context. The meaning and function of drug use among children and adolescents are important considerations in planning and delivering treatment. Drug use and misuse can be seen as a disease, as a bad habit, as an indication of family dysfunction, or as a symptom of a mental disorder. Depending on how individuals construe drug dependency, reactions will differ to children and adolescents who are experiencing problems associated with drug use and misuse. Social workers must allow the afflicted child or adolescent, parents, friends, teachers, collaterals, and others to voice their understanding of drug abuse.

A child's or adolescent's misperceptions about how others perceive the drug use and misuse may pose a hindrance to successful treatment.[16] If, for example, a child or adolescent believes that others are morally critical of him or her, acrimonious arguments may ensue. On the other hand, if a child or adolescent thinks of the drug use and misuse as a disease, then it might eliminate some of the acrimonious arguments but encourage irresponsible, "I'm-not-responsible-because-I'm-sick" statements. In any event, understanding how the child or adolescent perceives others' evaluations of him or her may provide useful insights. Not surprisingly, treatment that incorporates the child's understanding of others' perceptions is most likely to avoid uncooperative and hostile attitudes.

In addition to assessing accurately the child or adolescent's understanding of others' perceptions, social workers should examine the meaning of the drug itself. The child's or adolescent's understanding or "relationship" to drugs can frequently assist social workers in planning treatment. We have discussed in Chapter 3 the impact of addicts' expectations regarding the effects of drugs. The reasoning is that using drugs will invariably have a specific effect. Such use in time creates a "relationship" between the child or adolescent and the drug. By expecting and receiving a specific effect when using drugs, children and adolescents may come to trust the drug and perceive it as a "friend." As a result, sadness is a natural consequence with the cessation of drug use. A child or adolescent who may not have other friends may consider a drug to be his or her "best friend." Treatment that focuses on resolution of the grief that follows a significant loss should be planned.

Educational Concerns. After homelife, a child's or adolescent's experiences in school help form the attitudes and provide the market that allows drug use. By its nature, the school provides a meeting place for children and adolescents who may engage in drug use as a social activity.[17,18] During childhood and adolescence, the importance of social activity among peers cannot be overemphasized. Children and adolescents observe, learn, and speak with each other, and by so doing become socialized into the common culture

of that school. Such intense activities that include drug use will interfere with educational activities in two ways. First, performance in the classroom will suffer. Documentation of the problems caused by drug use is widespread; attention, memory, and information processing are among the areas adversely affected by drug use.[19,20] Second, drug use is associated with conflict. Although conflicts are not inevitable with drug use, they occur with alarming frequency. Disputes over payment and extortion to secure payment for drugs can result in violent conflict that reduces confidence in the safety of school settings for all students.

Conclusion

The foremost rule that cannot be overemphasized is that the child or adolescent should not be viewed out of his or her legal, social, psychological, or cultural context. Such contexts provide social workers with the necessary background in undertaking drug and alcohol interventions. Although drugs have specific physiological effects, their use and meaning derive from their legal, social, and psychological contexts. From this perspective, it is not possible to understand chemical dependency in children and adolescents without considering the contexts in which use takes place.

Substance Abuse Treatment

Overview. The treatment modalities that will be discussed in this chapter are by no means the only ones available. In fact, it can be argued that social workers develop their own modality in accordance with their idiosyncratic abilities. Further, few treatment modalities provide a standard, reliable set of procedures that define its successful implementation. Treatment modalities are generally a loose compilation of interventive techniques, practice beliefs, and ontological assumptions. Because treatment modalities vary so widely in their implementation, it is difficult to state with any confidence that any one type of treatment will be effective.

In considering what type of treatment modality is best suited for preventing and remediating clients' problems, social workers should consider many issues in addition to reputed effectiveness. Issues such as cost, predicted compliance with treatment procedures, and level of family involvement are also important. The choice of treatment methods must take into account their degree of intrusiveness.

Thus primary *prevention* efforts that consist solely of educational efforts are the least intrusive, require the least involvement, and can be implemented in many settings. *Outpatient treatment and community self-help* groups (e.g., Alcoholics Anonymous) are the next level of treatment. A third level of treatment is *inpatient treatment,* usually in a hospital setting. The last and most intrusive level of treatment is *residential treatment and treatment communities.* Generally, the least intrusive treatment methods will cost less, require the least family involvement, and require the least disruption in day-to-day activities. More intrusive treatment methods are much more expensive and typically better suited when there is a medical risk, danger of suicide or homicide, or uncontrolled behavior that might result in harm to self or others.

Prevention

The current literature on treatment of drug use, misuse, and dependency emphasizes the complexity of preventing adolescent substance abuse. For example, Arkin discusses the need to differentiate among multiproblem youth, families, and environments in deciding prevention strategies.[21] Such recommendations, however, only highlight the conceptual quagmire of primary, secondary, and tertiary prevention strategies (see Chapter 7). Of the three strategies, only primary prevention is intended to prevent nonusing children and adolescents from beginning substance use. There is an increasing consensus that primary prevention efforts must ameliorate family and school environments to increase children's self-esteem and self-efficacy.[22,23] Secondary and tertiary prevention address

problems of children and adolescents that are caused by varying degrees of drug involvement. Both these types of prevention strategies focus on encouraging a cessation of drug use, remediating problems, and strengthening the children's and adolescents' resiliency.[24] However, prevention works best when there is a clear target for intensive efforts. Unfortunately, there is no clear profile for identifying the neediest children and adolescents at-risk for debilitating substance use.[25]

A related form of prevention efforts involves parent-led prevention programs. Such groups recommend four types of change: (1) changes in the home, (2) changes in the peer group, (3) changes in the schools, and (4) changes in the community.[26] Such groups are generally formed by grass-roots movements and have modest goals. Their expectations are to raise community awareness and to coordinate with community agencies. Overall, parent groups remain a small, albeit active, form of prevention programming.[27]

Drug Education. Traditionally, drug education has consisted of school- and districtwide teaching efforts. Drug education has been used with varying degrees of success for the last forty years.[28] Early drug education consisted of attempts to intimidate children and adolescents from any use of illicit drugs. In general, drug education consisted of didactic presentations that described the drug, its use, and consequences of its use. Such efforts were generally aimed at public school settings where public school teachers or other designated school staff were given a packet of materials to present to classes or to assemblies of students. Both the message and the presenter frequently presented a skewed picture of drug use and misuse. The drug's potency and consequences were described in terms that were often designed to scare students. In many circumstances, older students were well versed in the use of drugs and had not experienced significant consequences. Younger students were intrigued by the presentations and, in some cases, became more interested in drugs as a result of the drug education attempts.

In retrospect, one mistake was to rely on a didactic approach in a setting where teachers in all likelihood were not perceived as credible role models. Further, some of the teachers might have engaged in recreational use and were undoubtedly ambivalent about presenting materials that seemed incorrect. The lesson that became apparent by the beginning of the 1980s was that pure drug education campaigns needed revision both in terms of their content and their media.

The ineffectiveness of such drug education programs resulted in their becoming an object of derision in the 1960s and 1970s.[29] Thus one reason for their failure stemmed from promoting patently incorrect information. For example, marijuana was cited as causing psychotic decompensation, juvenile delinquency, and other catastrophic consequences. When children and adolescents experimented with marijuana and failed to experience dire consequences, the credibility of scare-oriented drug education became questionable. Traditional drug education also failed because messages were designed to scare passive participants into compliance. More recently, drug educators have enjoyed some success when they employed credible information sources, avoided "scare tactics," began drug education efforts in primary schools, and involved adolescents through the use of role plays and problem-solving paradigms.[30]

Outpatient and Community Self-help Approaches

As with many aspects of treatment for adolescent chemical dependency, there are sharp disagreements on the usefulness of outpatient and community self-help programs. Although some writers believe that outpatient treatment is ineffective,[31] others argue that it is a viable option for adolescents. For example, Semlitz and Gold outlined seven criteria that they believed would justify a recommendation for outpatient treatment:

1. Absence of acute psychiatric or medical difficulties
2. Absence of chronic medical difficulties

3. Willingness to abstain from all mood-altering drugs
4. Willingness to submit random urine screens
5. A history of successful outpatient treatment
6. Family investment and involvement in the treatment process
7. Evidence of self-motivation[32]

Some examples of outpatient treatment techniques for children and adolescents include cognitive-behavioral skills training interventions and abstinence-oriented self-help programs. Skills-training models of treatment rely on learning theories to organize practice techniques. Skills-training techniques presuppose that behaviors, whether desired or not, are learned in some social setting. By the same logic, a behavior that is once learned can subsequently be unlearned. Skills-training models emphasize that children and adolescents learn behaviors that would be incompatible with drug-using behaviors. Skills trainers construct curricula in which skills can be taught. Although some mention is made in passing about personal characteristics and how skills are taught, skills training has traditionally focused on *what* is taught, not *how* it is taught. Skills training typically includes some combination of teaching changes in behavior paired with information about the consequences of drug abuse. Skills-training interventions for drug-abusing adolescents typically consist of several components: drug education, social skills training, and problem solving (i.e., improving "faulty thinking").

Drug education has been discussed earlier. In outpatient settings, drug education is used to heighten a child or adolescent's awareness of the consequences of prolonged use. However, disseminating information to family members of drug-abusing youth is also a critical element of outpatient treatment. Such information can normalize family members' experience of stress and help prepare for the erratic behavior that is common among drug-dependent youth. A second component of cognitive interventions is problem-solving skills. Problem solving has been used in a number of settings in helping children and adolescents make informed decisions.

George Spivack, Jerome Platt, and Myrna Shure conducted studies in which problem-solving paradigms were examined.[33] Problem-solving protocols generally consist of a series of intuitively reasonable steps that should be taken in determining the solution to a problem. The first step is for a child or adolescent to slow down his or her decision making to allow the problem-solving sequence to begin. Basically, children and adolescents are taught to "stop" what they're doing. The second step is for a child or adolescent to consider what type of problem is confronting them. The third step is to generate alternates to the problem confronting the child or adolescent. Fourth, the alternatives are evaluated for their viability and their acceptability. Finally, the most promising alternate is chosen and enacted using newly learned social skills. Several investigators have applied variations of this problem-solving interventive method to a variety of drug-abusing populations.[34]

Skills-training interventions are found in inpatient and outpatient settings and are used extensively in prevention approaches. Because skills-training interventions follow a curriculum, they are relatively easy to plan, implement, and evaluate. Unfortunately, skills-training interventions may be difficult for children and adolescents to integrate. First, if children and adolescents are having difficulties at school, the intervention process may be a reminder of a disliked activity. Second, children and adolescents who are actively using drugs and alcohol may have problems learning the materials. Reasons for this difficulty stem from an inability to concentrate, lack of motivation to do well, conflict with authority figures, and thrill-seeking behaviors. However, these difficulties can be avoided in part if skills-training interventions comprise a primary prevention strategy aimed at elementary school children. Because these children are not usually experiencing difficulties from drug use, a primary prevention strategy does not encounter the resistance that is common among older children and adolescents.

Skills-training interventions are used in schools, clinics, and hospitals with children and adolescents who have varying degrees of drug and alcohol abuse. It is most effectively implemented in groups; these groups are most readily found in institutional settings such as the public schools.[35,36] The "Just Say No!" campaign popularized by Nancy Reagan is an example of a skill that could be taught to children and adolescents to help them avoid use. Skills training seeks to identify verbal and behavioral skills that enable children and adolescents to refuse offers of drug and alcohol use and to engage in prosocial behavioral repertoires.[37] Like cognitive-based interventions, skills-training is most efficiently conducted within institutional settings. Despite the burgeoning popularity of skills-training within institutional settings, its long-term effectiveness is unclear.[38]

One possible reason for the effectiveness of skills-training programs may lie in the use of peer-oriented treatment. Schinke, Orlandi, and Cole conducted an evaluation of the effectiveness of participatory substance abuse prevention programs in Boys and Girls Clubs (BGC) located in selected public housing projects. They found that public housing projects that received such prevention services through BGC had less drug-related activity, less damage to housing units, and increased parental involvement in youth activities.[39] This finding is in concert with school-based programs that have also found children and adolescents are able to benefit from school-based prevention and treatment programs that invite participation in their planning and delivery.[40]

Abstinence-Oriented Approaches. Treatment models that focus on abstinence as a treatment goal dominate programs in the United States. This model is most closely associated with Alcoholics Anonymous (AA). This model was originally designed for mature male alcoholics and may be difficult for most children and adolescents to understand, let alone embrace. Much as its name suggests, AA requires anonymity from its participants. Although AA is geared toward adults, some communities are making efforts to provide students with support groups. Abstinence models require that social workers under-stand the three parts of twelve-step programs: surrender steps, integrity steps, and serenity steps.[41] The surrender steps consist of treat-ment personnel persuading children or ado-lescents that they cannot control their use of drugs. Children or adolescents "surrender" their attempts to control drug use to a higher power. The "higher power" is not always intended to be synonymous with God or any similar deity, and the emphasis is on creating a spiritual defense against drug use. The integrity steps focus on an admission of the harm that has been caused; the direct admis-sion of responsibility to the harmed person enables children and adolescents to accept personal responsibility for conflicts precipi-tated by tension around drug and alcohol misuse.[42]

Integrity steps allow children and adoles-cents to apologize for difficulties that were caused by their drug and alcohol use. The last three steps in the twelve-step program, seren-ity steps, are concerned with maintaining a drug-free life-style. While the surrender steps assist chemically dependent children and adolescents to cease use, the integrity steps begin the task of rebuilding relationships through apologies, and the serenity steps focus on living a life without the presence of drugs and alcohol.

Despite the enormous popularity of the twelve-step programs throughout the United States, only one study examined their effec-tiveness with adolescents (a more thorough discussion of treatment effectiveness is found in Chapter 6). The data suggest that Alco-holics Anonymous benefited those adoles-cents who were able to understand and accept Alcoholics Anonymous principles and traditions.[43] Because there was no control group in the research project, it would be unwise to generalize the study's findings to all adolescents.

Family-Based Treatment. A truism in chem-ical dependency is that families are critical to consider in the treatment of chemical depen-dency of any family member. It is not surpris-ing that the role of the family system is considered so pivotal. Children's and adoles-cents' use of drugs often cause and are caused by family conflict.[44] Families are af-fected heavily by members' drug use and abuse. Not only do use and abuse cause prob-lems, but use may also be seen as a method of coping with family conflict.

One caveat, however, should be stressed. Because all families experience conflict, and not all children and adolescents experience drug dependency, social workers must be cau-tious in concluding that family conflict caused children or adolescents to abuse drugs. Severe family conflict creates a context for a child or adolescent in which the likelihood of abusive drug use increases dramatically. Because of peer influence, children in even the most "normal" families may experiment with or abuse drugs.[45] Adolescents, on the other hand, have begun to pull away from their fam-ilies in forming their own networks of friends and acquaintances. While a thorough family assessment generally should be conducted, clinical assessments of adolescents may also require that the network of friends be consid-ered when planning treatment.[46]

The most commonly used family treatment approach with substance abuse, structural-strategic family therapy, was developed by Sal-vador Minuchin and his associates.[47,48] Its popularity was due in part to its incorpora-tion of family development and a family sys-tems conceptual framework into its treatment procedures. Minuchin argued that intergen-erational "boundaries" should be maintained (i.e., children should respect and obey their parents) and that parents were indigenous allies in the treatment of children and adoles-cents. Structural approaches stressed that parents should be empowered to parent their children. Minuchin's assertions complement findings from surveys and studies of drug-abusing youth.[49]

Structural family therapy is used primarily with families in which one or more children are identified as having a problem. Although it is desirable to have the entire family involved to implement structural family ther-apy, some therapists will work with whoever is present.[50,51] The efficacy of structural family therapy with children and adolescents has been studied and positive results exist regarding its effectiveness with entire drug-abusing families.[52]

Inpatient Treatment

There is a common assumption that substance use, abuse, and dependency are progressive in their onset and in their severity, with use as least severe and dependency as most severe. However, as was discussed in Chapter 1, there are significant conceptual and definitional problems in differentiating abuse from dependency. The problem of measurement and diagnosis is reflected in lax admission policies of hospital wards targeting substance abuse and dependency in youth.[53]

To justify admission into an inpatient facility, children and adolescents should have a diagnosis that requires such action. As mentioned earlier in this chapter, children and adolescents should exhibit a high degree of medical risk, suicidal or homicidal threat, or a high likelihood of injury by neglect. Typically, however, diagnoses of substance dependency and conduct disorder are given for admission into inpatient treatment. Unfortunately, there are few hard signs of substance dependency, and it is often easy to misdiagnose to justify admission. Although some children and adolescents undoubtedly benefit from such treatment approaches, the increasing use of these alternatives reflects aggressive marketing by hospitals, parental fatigue, ineffective school environments, and the availability of funding (i.e., it is included in many insurance companies' coverage). By contrast, it is much more difficult for social workers to coordinate community resources, provide support to parents, get reimbursement for providing outpatient services for substance abuse, and advocate for better school environments. Community-based treatment that coordinates indigenous treatment resources lacks the glamor of a heroic treatment provider, but may be much more useful to adolescents in the long run. Currently, health care policy and the fragmentation of community-based service networks make inpatient treatment for children and adolescents an expensive and overused form of care.[54]

Inpatient treatment facilities typically use some variation of the twelve-step approach that is geared to a one-month time frame with extremely high costs (e.g., they can average about $25,000 per month). These one-month programs typically provide respite for parents, drug education, group encounters with peers, and individual treatment. Although inpatient treatment is prized by some experts for its ability to concentrate services in a short period of time, others point to the inefficiency of using a hospital setting to provide interventions that could be done much more inexpensively.[55]

Residential Treatment/Treatment Community

Longer inpatient programs for children and adolescents also exist. Treatment communities are one example of long-term inpatient care. Once admitted into such facilities, adolescents are encouraged to form close emotional ties with other patients. When successful, adolescents will perceive themselves as part of a group of peers who act as a support network.[56]

There is no evidence to suggest that inpatient treatment is any more effective with most children and adolescents than outpatient treatment.[57] However, for many parents who avail themselves of extended inpatient treatment for their children, the treatment period acts as a respite. Anecdotal reports suggest that the improvement that children and adolescents often demonstrate in inpatient settings is lost when they return to the home settings. For improvements to be maintained, critics of this approach suggest that children and adolescents need changes to occur while in their home settings. Changes that occur within an inpatient setting frequently occur within a vacuum; the typical frustrations and challenges that might encourage alcohol and drug use and abuse are absent in an inpatient setting. Thus improvements seen in the hospital don't necessarily extend to home settings.[58]

Friedman and Utada found that outpatient settings devoted more staff time to individual and family counseling than residential programs that had a heavier emphasis on art therapy, group counseling, vocational training, and medical services.[59] There is little doubt that extended residential communities are necessary for seriously disturbed children and adolescents. When children or adolescents are chronically endangering themselves with their drug and/or alcohol use, extended residential treatment may be the desired alternative because of its ability to provide twenty-four-hour monitoring of behavior.[60]

Case Example: Recovering Families

Family Service of Milwaukee instituted a new program entitled "Recovering Families." It was adopted because it allowed family members to receive a peer group experience that was coordinated with family therapy. Traditionally, family therapy and peer support/ treatment group (e.g., Alcoholics Anonymous) have not always been unified in their treatment philosophy, goals, or methods.[61] Recovering Families allowed all members of a family to be given an opportunity to receive a coordinated treatment experience with their peers and with their family members. The major difference between this case and the one described in Chapter 10 is that the structure of this time-limited program allowed *all* members of a family to be entered into groups formed around their peers and to be involved in family therapy. For example, it was common to have five groups: one group for chemically dependent family members, usually one of the parents; one group for spouses of a chemically dependent family member; one group for adolescents; one group for latency-aged children; and one group for young children. All family members agreed to abstain from alcohol use during the duration of treatment. Groups met at the same time, and family therapy was scheduled during other times during the week. In many instances, families had already begun family therapy before entering the Recovering Families program. All group leaders and therapists

were either Clinical Members of the American Association for Marriage and Family Therapy (AAMFT) or in training to become AAMFT Clinical Members. The program director was an AAMFT Clinical Member and certified as a drug and alcohol counselor. The family presented here was similar to many who went through the program.

Mr. and Mrs. W. had been married for eighteen years and had three children: Greg, 15 years, Susan, 10 years, and Betty, 6 years. They had sought treatment for family conflict stemming from Greg's angry behavior in school and at home. During the initial sessions with a family therapist, it was disclosed that Mr. W. was a binge drinker whose erratic behavior had increasingly become embarrassing for family members, especially for Greg and Susan. This discussion precipitated a crisis when Greg revealed that he was afraid that his alcohol use was getting out of control; he cited blackouts, episodes of fighting, and problems with concentrating on schoolwork. After explaining some of the potential health problems that can be caused by excessive drinking, the therapist requested that Mr. W. and Greg undergo diagnostic tests to ascertain the level of impairment, especially to their liver, cardiovascular system, and nervous system. The therapist believed that it was ethically necessary to rule out organic difficulties by qualified medical professionals before beginning alcohol treatment. This was crucial to understand which erratic behaviors, if any, were influenced by somatic difficulties. Further discussion with Mr. W.'s family history revealed that excessive drinking was common in several generations of his family. Mr. W. was a vigorous and professionally successful man whose achievements resulted from his competitive drive and understanding of his work environment. Mrs. W. worked outside the home as a successful real estate agent. Mrs. W.'s alcohol use did not appear excessive; typically, she had a glass of wine with dinner, but did not routinely use alcohol. This was confirmed by her husband and the children. Greg was an honors student with extensive extracurricular involvement in sports who had recently begun to do poorly in classes. Susan and Betty were also excellent students and popular among their peers.

During family therapy, family members discussed whether they would commit themselves to abstain from alcohol use for ten weeks. Strategically, it was important for family members to all agree that they would not use alcohol. The agreement to not use alcohol became a public contract with family members and an impartial witness concerning the family's commitment to sobriety. The therapist did not try to "persuade" the family that their alcohol use resulted in death. In keeping with contemporary family therapy treatment philosophies, the decision to cease had to be made by family members.[62] Forceful presentations by therapists on the problems associated with excessive alcohol use seldom persuade alcohol-dependent people to abstain from use.[63] The therapist took an approach in which she linked mishaps from the family's life to family members' use of alcohol, but left the ultimate decision to cease use to individual family members.

Mrs. W., Susan, and Betty immediately agreed not to use alcohol; Mr. W. and Greg were ambivalent about their commitment to abstain. The therapist did not immediately accept their wavering commitment and pressed them to make a firm choice with an understanding that relapse would be a constant temptation. Mr. W. and Greg eventually agreed unequivocally to abstain from any alcohol use during the ten weeks of the program.

Each family member entered into their respective peer groups, each with two group leaders; Mr. W. and Greg both went into the group for chemically dependent family members. Groups typically started with a review of the previous week and what was done to maintain sobriety. Focusing on relapse prevention helped empower family members. Throughout the discussion of what happened during the week, group members would also discuss the influence of alcohol misuse on family dynamics, whether from the perspective of an abuser or a family member. Greg proved to be valuable because he provided both abuser and family member perspectives. Although the group leaders originally were active in structuring the group discussion, group members increasingly assumed responsibility in supporting and challenging each others' statements and beliefs. Because this occurred for all family members, family therapy became a time to share new insights and to challenge each other. Although most W. family members found the groups to be stressful, they also stated that they realized the value of the intense ninety-minute sessions. Not unexpectedly, family members also sought out and attended psychoeducational presentations on alcohol misuse sponsored by the agency.

The challenge for Greg was to separate his anger toward his father's erratic behavior from his own problems caused by excessive use. Mr. W. was originally resistant to group members' comments but became increasingly willing to listen to his son during group and family therapy sessions. Mrs. W.'s attitudes toward drinking alcohol in general and binge drinking in particular took on an increasingly firm stance. Although her stance made clear that she was unwilling to subject herself and her family to the vagaries of her husband's alcohol abuse, she also risked demoralizing his uncertain progress toward sobriety. Family therapy sessions were increasingly devoted toward outlining what a drug-free family environment would look like.

At school, Greg's behavior had improved markedly and his grades were improving. Greg received additional counseling from a school social worker who was knowledgeable about teenage drug abuse. The focus of those sessions was to reconsider his peer group. Although Greg received support from some of his friends, other friends heavily used alcohol and other drugs. The latter group of friends were ambivalent about Greg's decision to abstain from alcohol use, although they did not explicitly criticize his choice. However, the school social worker was worried that substance-using friends were not diligent about schoolwork or attending class. In addition, they were often involved in verbal and physical fights with other students. Greg's father proved to be a valuable ally in helping Greg finally decide to not associate with his substance-using friends. Greg was impressed with his father's slow but seemingly successful fight to remain sober; Mr. W.'s newly found credibility was instrumental in Greg's decision.

Although the groups ended, family therapy continued. The family therapist cautioned against overconfidence; she was emphatic that both Mr. W. and Greg were vulnerable to relapses. In addition, family therapy also continued to help Mr. and Mrs. W. strengthen their marital relationship. The family therapist encouraged Mr. and Mrs. W. to attend Alcoholics Anonymous and Al-Anon, which provided continued support for both parents. Greg continued meeting informally with the school social worker; she proved invaluable in providing information and daily support.

Mr. and Mrs. W. relocated to another state and contact was lost. However, before leaving, the W. family expressed their gratitude to staff members in Recovering Families for their able stewardship of the treatment process. Although W. family members made all the decisions to become and stay sober, the staff members helped provide opportunities during which those choices could be made.

Conclusion

Many professionals claim to have developed treatment approaches that will positively affect children's and adolescents' drug and alcohol problems. Unfortunately, no one single treatment has been tested that is consistently effective with children's and adolescents' substance abuse. It can be argued that professionals who rely on only one untested treatment methodology are unethical. However, the research literature does not provide much guidance. It suggests that most treatments are somewhat effective sometimes and that the one of the few common features of successful treatment efforts is an empathic relationship with clients. Despite the claims of hospitals and clinics, no "cure" exists for children's and adolescents' drug and alcohol dependency.

Social workers, with their tradition of case management, are likely to be more useful in working with these clients than technically proficient therapists.[64] Because families with drug- and alcohol-dependent children and adolescents encounter a multitude of problems, social workers should strive to empower families and to find community resources. Furthermore, because financial considerations are increasingly critical in planning treatment strategies, social workers must consider the cost of treatment. As Smith argued, social workers should concentrate on clinical case management in assisting chemically dependent clients.[65] Rather than rely on the thin reed of therapy, social workers should also use their knowledge of the community to find more tangible resources for parents and their offspring.

ENDNOTES

1. Martha A. Morrison and Quentin T. Smith, "Psychiatric Issues of Adolescent Drug Dependence," *Pediatric Clinics of North America,* Vol. 34 (1987), pp. 461–480.

2. Lloyd D. Johnson, Patrick M. O'Malley, and Gerald G. Bachman, "Illicit Drug Use, Smoking, and Drinking by America's High School Students and Young Adults: 1975–1985," *National Institute on Drug Abuse,* (Rockville, MD: NIDA 1988).

3. Kirk Wheeler and Jeffrey Malmquist, "Treatment Approaches to Adolescent Chemical Dependency," *Pediatric Clinics of North America,* Vol. 34 (1987), pp. 437–447.

4. Denise Kandel, M. Davies, D. Karus, and K. Yamaguchi, "The Consequences in Young Adulthood of Adolescent Drug Involvement," *Archives of General Psychiatry,* Vol. 142 (1986), pp. 746–754.

5. George E. Obermeier and Paul B. Henry, "Adolescent Inpatient Treatment," *Journal of Chemical Dependency* Vol. 2, No. 1 (1988–89), pp. 163–182.

6. Thomas McKenna and Roy Pickens, "Alcoholic Children of Alcoholics," *Journal of Studies on Alcohol;* Vol. 42 (1981), pp. 1021–1029.

7. Victor J. Callan and Debra Jackson, "Children of Alcoholic Fathers and Recovered Alcoholic Fathers: Personal and Family Functioning," *Journal of Studies on Alcohol,* Vol. 47 (1986), pp. 180–182.

8. Emmy E. Werner, "Resilient Offspring of Alcoholics: A Longitudinal Study," *Journal of Studies on Alcohol,* Vol. 47 (1986), pp. 34–40.

9. Ann M. Downey, "The Impact of Drug Abuse upon Adolescent Suicide," *Omega Journal of Death and Dying*, Vol. 22, No. 4 (1990–91), pp. 261–275.

10. Oscar G. Bukstein, David A. Brent, and Yifrah Kaminar, "Comorbidity of Substance Abuse and Other Psychiatric Disorders in Adolescents," *American Journal of Psychiatry*, Vol. 146 (September 1989), pp. 1131–1141.

11. Harold A. Pincus, "AIDS, Drug Abuse, and Mental Health," *Public Health Reports*, Vol. 99 (1984), pp. 106–108.

12. James H. Price, "AIDS, the Schools, and Policy Issues," *Journal of School Health*, Vol. 56 (1986), pp. 137–140.

13. J. A. Robertson and H. A. Plant, "Alcohol, Sex and Risks of HIV Infection," *Drug and Alcohol Dependence*, Vol. 22 (1988), pp. 75–78.

14. Benjamin M. Schutz, *Legal Liability in Psychotherapy* (San Francisco: Jossey-Bass, 1982).

15. Douglas J. Besharov, *The Vulnerable Social Worker* (Silver Spring, MD: National Association of Social Workers, 1985).

16. Bruce A. Christiansen, Mark S. Goldman, and Andres Inn, "Development of Alcohol-Related Expectancies in Adolescents: Separating Pharmacological from Social-Learning Influences," *Journal of Consulting and Clinical Psychology*, Vol. 50 (1982), pp. 336–344.

17. Thomas E. Smith, Jeffrey Koob, and Thomas Wirtz, "Ecology of Adolescent Marijuana Abusers," *International Journal of the Addictions*, Vol. 20 (1985), pp. 1421–1428.

18. Tong Won Kim, *Social Factors and Marijuana Addiction: A Causal Structural Model,* unpublished doctoral dissertation, Florida State University, Tallahassee, 1991.

19. National Institute on Drug Abuse, *Marijuana Research Findings: 1980* (Rockville, MD: U.S. Government Printing Office, 1981).

20. ADAMHA; *Sixth Special Report to the U.S. Congress on Alcohol and Health* (Rockville, MD: U.S. Government Printing Office, 1987).

21. E. Arkin (ed.), *Communicating About Alcohol and Other Drugs: Strategies for Reaching Populations at Risk* (Rockville, MD: Office of Substance Abuse Prevention, 1991).

22. D. Schaffer, I. Phillips, N. B. Enzer, M. M. Silverman, and V. Anthony, *Prevention of Mental Disorders, Alcohol, and Other Drug Use in Children and Adolescents,* OSAP Prevention Monograph No. 2 (Rockville, MD: DHHS Publication No. 89-1646, 1989).

23. Karol L. Kumpfer and Charles W. Turner, "The Social Ecology Model of Adolescent Substance Abuse: Implications for Prevention," *The International Journal of the Addictions*, Vol. 25, No. 4A (1990–1991), pp. 435–463.

24. Schaffer et al., *Prevention of Mental Disorders.*

25. Jeannette L. Johnson, "Preventive Interventions for Children at Risk: An Introduction," *The International Journal of the Addictions*, Vol. 25 (1990–1991), pp. 429–434.

26. Marsha Mannatt, "Parents, Peers, and Pot," National Institute on Drug Abuse (Rockville, MD: U.S. Government Printing Office, 1979).

27. Michael Klitzner and Elizabeth Bamberger, "The Assessment of Parent-Led Prevention Programs: A National Descriptive Study," *Journal of Drug Education*, Vol. 20, No. 2 (1990), pp. 111–125.

28. Bill Kinder, Nancy E. Pape, and Steven Walfish, "Drug and Alcohol Education Programs: A Review of Outcome Studies," *International Journal of the Addictions*, Vol. 15 (1980).

29. Thomas E. Smith, "Reviewing Adolescent Marijuana Abuse," *Social Work*, Vol. 29 (January/February 1984), pp. 17–21.

30. Thomas E. Smith, "Reducing Adolescents' Marijuana Abuse," *Social Work*, Vol. 9 (Fall 1983), pp. 33–44.

31. Kirk Wheeler and Jeffrey Malmquist, "Treatment Approaches in Adolescent Chemical Dependency," *Pediatric Clinics of North America*, Vol. 34 (1987), pp. 437–447.

32. Linda Semlitz and Mark S. Gold, "Adolescent Drug Abuse," *Psychiatric Clinics of North America*, Vol. 9 (1986), pp. 455–473.

33. George Spivack, Jerome J. Platt, and Myrna B. Shure, *The Problem-Solving Approach to Adjustment* (San Francisco: Jossey-Bass, 1976).

34. Steven P. Schinke, Michael S. Moncher, Josephine Palleja, Luis H. Zayas, and Robert F. Schilling, "Hispanic Youth, Substance Abuse, and Stress: Implications For Prevention Research," *The International Journal of the Addictions*, Vol. 23, No. 8 (1988), pp. 809–826.

35. Thomas E. Smith, "Groupwork with Adolescent Drug Abusers," *Social Work with Groups*, Vol. 8 (1985), pp. 55–64.

36. Ibid.

37. David Smith, Stephen J. Levy, and Diane E. Striar, "Treatment Services for Youthful Drug Users," in George M. Beschner and Alfred S. Friedman (eds.), *Youth Drug Abuse: Problems, Issues, and Treatment* (Lexington, MA: Lexington Books, 1981).

38. Jeffrey Jenson, Elizabeth Wells, R. D. Plotnick, J. David Hawkins, and Rick Catalano, "The Effects of

Skills and Intentions to Use Drugs on Posttreatment Drug Use of Adolescents," *American Journal of Drug and Alcohol Abuse* (in press).

39. Steven P. Schinke, Mario A. Orlandi, and Kristin C. Cole, "Boys & Girls Clubs in Public Housing Developments: Prevention Services for Youth at Risk," *Journal of Community Psychology,* OSAP Special Issue (1992), pp. 118–128.

40. Smith et al., "Groupwork with Adolescent Drug Abusers."

41. Victoria Brundage, "Gregory Bateson, Alcoholics Anonymous, and Stoicism" *Psychiatry,* Vol. 48 (1985), pp. 40–51.

42. Marcia D. Brown-Standridge, "Creating Therapeutic Realities via Responsibility Messages," *American Journal of Family Therapy,* Vol. 12 (1987), pp. 206–224.

43. G. S. Alford, R. A. Koehler, and J. Leonard, "Alcoholics Anonymous-Narcotics Anonymous Model Inpatient Treatment of Chemically Dependent Adolescents: A Two-Year Outcome Study," *Journal of Studies on Alcohol,* Vol. 52 (1991), pp. 118–126.

44. Murray Bowen, "A Family Systems Approach to Alcoholism," *Addictions,* Vol. 21 (1974), pp. 3–11.

45. Kim, *"Social Factors and Marijuana Addiction: A Structural Model."*

46. Smith et al., "Groupwork with Adolescent Drug Abusers."

47. Salvador Minuchin, *Families and Family Therapy* (Cambridge, MA: Harvard University Press, 1974).

48. Salvador Minuchin and H. Charles Fishman, *Family Therapy Techniques* (Cambridge, MA: Harvard University Press, 1981).

49. Denise B. Kandel, "Inter- and Intragenerational Influences on Adolescent Marijuana Use," *Journal of Social Issues,* Vol. 30 (1974), pp. 107–135.

50. Jose Szapocznik, William M. Kurtines, Franklin H. Foote, Angel Perez-Vidal, and Olga Hervis, "Conjoint Versus One-Person Family Therapy: Some Evidence For The Effectiveness Of Conducting Family Therapy Through One Person with Drug-Abusing Adolescents," *Journal of Consulting and Clinical Psychology,* Vol. 51 (1983), pp. 990–999.

51. Jose Szapocznik, William M. Kurtines, Franklin H. Foote, Angel Perez-Vidal, and Olga Hervis, "Conjoint Versus One-Person Family Therapy: Further Evidence for the Effectiveness of Conducting Family Therapy Through One Person with Drug-Abusing Adolescents," *Journal of Consulting and Clinical Psychology,* Vol. 54 (1986), pp. 395–397.

52. Ibid. (1983, 1986); H. Charles Fishman, M. Duncan Stanton, and Bernice Rosman, "Treating Families of

Adolescent Drug Abusers," in M. Duncan Stanton, Thomas C. Todd, and Associates (eds.), *The Family Therapy of Drug Abuse and Addiction* (New York: Guilford Press, 1982).

53. See, for example, the discussion by Ira Strumwasser, Nitin V. Paranjpe, Marianne Udow, and David Share et al., "Appropriateness of Psychiatric and Substance Abuse Hospitalization: Implications for Payment and Utilization Management," *Medical-Care,* Vol. 29, No. 8 (August 1991), pp. 77–90.

54. Ira Schwartz, "Hospitalization of Adolescents for Psychiatric and Substance Abuse Treatment: Legal and Ethical Issues," *Journal of Adolescent Health Care,* Vol. 10, No. 6 (November 1989), pp. 473–478.

55. Strumwasser et al., "Appropriateness of Psychiatric and Substance Abuse Hospitalization," William R. Miller and Reid K. Hester, "Inpatient Alcoholism Treatment," *American Psychologist,* Vol. 41 (July 1986), pp. 794–803.

56. George E. Obermeier and Paul B. Henry, "Adolescent Inpatient Treatment" *Journal of Chemical Dependency,* Vol. 2, No. 1 (1988–1989), pp. 163–182.

57. A. Thomas McLellan, Lester Luborsky, Charles O'Brien, George E. Woody, and Keith A. Druley, "Is Treatment for Substance Abuse Effective?" *Journal of the American Medical Association,* Vol. 247 (1982), pp. 1423–1428.

58. Harvey Joanning, B. Gawinski, J. Morris, and William Quinn, "Organizing a Social Ecology to Treat Adolescent Drug Abuse," *Journal of Strategic and Systemic Therapies,* Vol. 5 (1986), pp. 55–66.

59. Alfred S. Friedman, and Arlene Utada, "High School Drug Use," *Clinical Research Notes* (Washington, DC: U.S. Government Printing Office, National Institute on Drug Abuse, 1983).

60. Downey, "The Impact of Drug Abuse upon Adolescent Suicide."

61. For a discussion of some of the tensions between family therapists and Alcoholics Anonymous, and a beginning rapprochement, see Sandra A. Zygarlicki and Thomas Edward Smith, "Alcoholism Treatment and Marriage and Family Therapists: An Empirical Study," *Contemporary Family Therapy,* Vol. 14 (1992), pp. 75–88.

62. Thomas E. Smith, "Alcohol and Misuse: A Systemic Conceptualization for Practitioners," in E. W. Nunnally, C. S. Chilman, and F. M. Cox (eds.), *Mental Illness, Delinquency, Addictions and Neglect,* Vol. 4 (1988), pp. 69–87.

63. Gregory Bateson argued that individuals who misuse alcohol are caught in an escalatory conflict with people who attempt to mandate sobriety. He argued per-

suasively that forceful attempts to end someone's alcohol use was similar to an arms race in which both parties vied for primacy; see Gregory Bateson, "The Cybernetics of 'Self': A Theory of Alcoholism," *Psychiatry,* Vol. 34, No. 1 (1971), pp. 1–18.

64. There are no studies that have systematically studied the issue of case management versus therapy. However, the multiple problems encountered by adolescents are not often amenable to a single-treatment provider no matter how skilled that provider may be. For a more thorough discussion, readers are referred to E. M. Freeman, *The Addiction Process: Effective Social Work Process* (New York: Longman, 1992).

65. See Smith, "Alcohol and Misuse," for a discussion of how alcohol misuse affects family members.

10

Family systems and chemical dependency

Previous chapters indicate that alcoholism and other drug addictions frequently impair an individual's physical, psychological, and social functioning. There is also recognition and acceptance that alcoholism and other drug addictions adversely affect the individual's marital and family relationships. According to a survey by the Gallup Organization, "alcoholism affects approximately one-third of all American families."[1] A 1985 report by the Children of Alcoholics Foundation estimates that one out of every eight Americans is the child or adult child of an alcoholic.[2]

Defining alcoholism at the family level lacks specificity, despite its intuitive appeal. Many terms in the literature attempt to cap-

ture this phenomenon, such as "family disease," "alcoholic family," "addicted or chemically dependent family," "alcohol impaired family," or "family with an alcoholic member." By necessity, an understanding of the family dynamics associated with alcoholism or other drug addiction cannot be reduced to a single definition but must entail descriptions of interactive processes which occur throughout the life cycle of the family. This chapter reviews some of the more noteworthy efforts to specify the etiology and treatment of the family processes associated with chemical dependency. Although most literature to date is about alcoholism, it is reasonable to assume that much of it can be generalized to other drug addiction.[3] For the purposes of this chapter, "alcoholism" will be used since this is consistent with the literature, but the reader should keep in mind that, theoretically, this may also include other forms of drug addiction. In addition, "family" is a term that is no longer clearly defined in our society. The material presented in this chapter applies to all forms of families, including nuclear, extended, single-parent, communal, and gay/lesbian.[4]

This chapter reviews the literature on a family perspective of chemical dependency, including the theory, research, and treatment of alcoholism and other drug addiction in families. Three dominant theoretical approaches—stress coping, behavioral, and family systems—are presented. The constructs of codependency, children of alcoholics, and adult children of alcoholics are also discussed as they relate to family dynamics. The ways in which theory shapes practice with chemically dependent family systems are addressed along with more specific treatment information for working with chemically dependent families. Finally, a case example is presented which illustrates some of the main concepts discussed in this chapter.

A FAMILY PERSPECTIVE IN THEORY, RESEARCH, AND TREATMENT

During the early decades of this century, a scientific tradition emerged in the social sciences. The study of alcoholism, however, was restrained by the moral overtones attached to the problem, which led to the belief that alcoholism was not amenable to scientific inquiry. The growing temperance movement culminated in the Prohibition amendment in 1919. Attempts at treatment of alcoholism (which were almost exclusively directed at men) consisted largely of removing the individual to a residential program for detoxification and some therapy, known euphemistically as "the cure." In *Alcoholics Anonymous*, Bill W., a founder of AA, describes his "rehabilitation" as belladonna treatment, hydrotherapy, and mild exercise.[5]

In the 1930s, the disease or biological model of alcoholism began to gain acceptance. AA, founded in 1935, embraced this model. While AA was originally oriented toward men, wives would hold meetings modeled after AA to discuss the effects of alcoholism on their lives (Lois W., Bill W.'s wife, is credited with organizing the first meeting). At this same time, psychoanalysis was also growing in popularity, and it explained alcoholism in terms of psychopathology. Both these models were limited to an examination of the etiology of alcoholism in the individual. Psychoanalysts acknowledged the impact of family dynamics on psychopathology, and they had some interest in the family aspects of alcoholism, but they looked at psychopathology in terms of each individual partner rather than their interaction.[6] Psychoanalytic practice wisdom prohibited the involvement of family members in therapy with the alcoholic as this was believed to contaminate the therapeutic transference. Another development of the 1930s was the emergence of the fields of marital therapy and child guidance, with their focus on interpersonal relationships. However, early practitioners used a "collaborative approach" in which separate therapists would meet with family members and then the therapists would consult with each other on their treatment sessions.[7]

Theory and research on alcoholism grew through the 1940s and 1950s but continued to be limited to a study of its physiological and emotional effects on the individual (predominantly middle-aged Anglo males), such as the seminal work by Jellinek.[8] Even the conceptualizations of alcoholism in the marital dyad maintained an individual focus.[9] For example, the "distressed personality" model, rooted in psychoanalysis, held that underlying psychopathology in the wife led to the development and maintenance of a drinking problem in the husband.[10] Alternatively, the "stress personality" model, which applied to both genders, viewed personality disturbance in the spouse as resulting from the chronic stress in the home generated by the alcoholic.[11]

In the 1940s, the "concurrent approach" to marital and family therapy began to emerge. In this model, one counselor would work with a couple but would meet with them separately.[12] One of the first attempts to include families in treatment involved concurrent group therapy for alcoholics and their wives.[13] These early programs demonstrated that involving spouses increased the completion rate of treatment and expanded the criteria of successful outcome to include both partners' psychosocial functioning as well as abstinence by the alcoholic.[14] By 1948, the support groups organized by the wives of AA members had become a formal network called Al-Anon Family Groups (now targeting spouses of both genders), and, in 1957, Alateen was formed for teenage children of alcoholics. Later, Alatot groups were developed for younger children. By the late 1950s, the "conjoint approach" to marital and family therapy was introduced in which one counselor would meet with couples and families as a unit.[15]

In the 1960s, as social science moved away from a strictly individual perspective and began to consider the influences of the environment, a third model for conceptualizing alcoholism in the marital dyad emerged. The "psychosocial" model integrated the distressed personality and stress personality models.[16] It focused on the consequences of the alcoholic's drinking behavior and the spouse's coping style on *both* the marital partners. Through the 1960s, the rise of systems theory and behavioral theory led to a broader perspective that focused on the interactive, reciprocal nature of family processes. Although conjoint family therapy developed during this time, family treatment for alcoholism continued to consist of a concurrent program for nonalcoholic spouses (i.e., wives). This was attributed to the general ignorance of alcoholism by family therapists, who often failed to identify this problem or considered it secondary to other problems. When alcoholism was recognized as a problem, family therapists frequently referred these families to alcoholism treatment programs, where alcoholism was viewed as an individual disease.[17] Alcoholism counselors reportedly avoided a family perspective due

to lack of training or a belief that it was incompatible with the disease model.[18]

This situation gradually changed during the 1970s and 1980s, and now some type of family involvement is part of most alcoholism treatment programs. The current literature includes studies in which the alcoholic is a parent, spouse, or child (although research on female alcoholics and addicts is still limited). In addition, there has been a self-help and clinical movement which has recognized that family members have problems in their own right due to the dynamics of alcoholism. This has led to such concepts as codependency,[19] children of alcoholics,[20] and adult children of alcoholics.[21] According to Seilhamer and Jacob, Western cultures have long recognized the detrimental impact of parental alcoholism on children.[22] However, they point out that there was little interest in these children until quite recently, when the first publications[23] identifying the clinical implications of being reared by an alcoholic parent began to appear. This was soon followed by an awareness of the impact of parental alcoholism on the adult functioning of offspring (the Adult Children of Alcoholics or ACOA movement). There is growing recognition that being the child of an ACOA (i.e., grandchild of an alcoholic), whether the parent is alcoholic or not, can have a potentially negative impact since alcoholism can affect families for several generations.[24] As a result, self-help and advocacy groups (such as the National Association for Children of Alcoholics) have emerged. ACOA support groups originally began in the 1970s under the auspices of Al-Anon. Over the next few years, independent ACOA groups developed,[25] and Co-dependents Anonymous (CODA) groups were also established.

THEORIES ON ALCOHOLISM AND THE FAMILY

Chapter 2 covered many theories regarding the etiology and treatment of alcoholism. At one extreme is a strict medical model, also known as the disease model, focused on individual biological factors with virtually no consideration of familial, social, or psychological variables. On the other extreme, there is a strict family systems model, focused on the family as a unit, with virtually no recognition of the individual apart from the family. In the middle are theories which address, to varying degrees, both the individual and the familial aspects of dysfunction. The difference between these theories can be quite confusing, even to a person familiar with the chemical dependency field. This section of the chapter is concerned with social and psychological aspects of chemical dependency. It introduces three predominant models which address alcoholism at the family level (behavioral, stress coping, and family systems) with an emphasis on the points which distinguish them. According to the continuum, the behavioral and stress-coping models fall in the midrange, while the family systems model falls toward the extreme.

Family systems theory evolved in the 1950s as an outgrowth of general systems theory, which emerged in biology in the 1940s. This theory represented an epistemological shift from a reductionist, linear (cause and effect) way of thinking to one that formulated circular causality, process orientation, and the interrelatedness of parts. The crux of systems theory, as applied to people, holds that addiction, like any other human behavior, exists in a larger context. However, the family is viewed not merely as the context for an individual's behavior, but as an entity unto itself. Rather than expressing individual pathology, the presence of problematic behavior (such as alcoholism) by a family member is considered a symptom of underlying dysfunction in the system. This alcoholic is referred to as the "identified patient" to indicate that it is the system itself which is dysfunctional. Rather than identifying the effects of alcoholism on the individual members of the family, a family systems approach focuses on the individuals *and* the interactions between them. The structure and dynamics of the family are assessed, and intervention planned, through applying systems concepts such as homeostasis, boundaries, triangles, and feedback.[26]

The behavioral and stress-coping models first developed as theories of individual behavior but now incorporate a systems perspective, recognizing that relationships among the family members are interrelated and reciprocal and that the individual both influences and is influenced by other family members. In turn, the family exists as part of the larger social system which affects both individual and family functioning. However, these models differ from family systems theory in that the family is generally seen more as a context for individual behavior than as an entity unto itself. While all three theories share a systems orientation, the term "family systems" will be used here in reference to that particular theoretical orientation even though the term is often used more broadly in the literature. Further, it should be noted that most family "systems" therapists actually treat the family as a closed system.

FAMILY SYSTEMS THEORY OF ALCOHOLISM AND THE FAMILY

Our attention in this section is on family systems theory. We are concerned with three areas of the current family systems literature on alcoholism: rituals and routines, shame, and rules and roles. A discussion of the behavioral and stress-coping models is presented later in the section on assessment and treatment.

Before proceeding, however, two criticisms of family systems theory should be noted. First, Steinglass noted that it is too descriptive and lacks scientific rigor. Critics claim that it is "commonsensical," imprecise, and virtually untestable.[27] However, its defenders consider this irrelevant since the main value of systems theory is not as a traditional scientific model but as a fundamentally different approach to the conceptualization of clinical problems and therapeutic interventions. Second, feminists contend that there is a gender bias in family systems theory. Goldner argues that the central tenet of "context," defined as a theoretical boundary which can be drawn around a family thereby making it a distinct entity, disregards the social forces that influence the family.[28] Another central tenet, *circularity,* assumes an equal distribution of power when, in fact, women are often subordinate to men within families just as they are within the larger society. She warns that ignoring the impact of the social context can lead to theorists and practitioners "blaming the victim" and "rationalizing the status quo" rather than challenging oppressive sex role arrangements in family life.

Rituals and Routines. Steinglass and his colleagues distinguish between an *alcoholic family,* which is tantamount to an *alcoholic system,* and a "family with an alcoholic member."[29] This distinction is made by applying three core concepts of family systems theory: (1) organization, (2) morphostasis or internal regulation, and (3) morphogenesis or controlled growth.

In the "alcoholic family," chronic alcoholism has become its central, organizing theme. "In these families, alcoholism is no longer a condition of an individual family member. Instead, it has become a family condition that has inserted itself into virtually every aspect of family life."[30] In these families, the erratic and unpredictable behavior of the alcoholic, over time, often elicits a characteristic response from other family members. Their behavior becomes impaired and contributes to the perpetuation of the drinking behavior, thus establishing a circular, reciprocal pattern within the family. The functioning of a family organized around alcoholism can be further understood by applying other principles of family systems theory, such as wholeness (the whole is greater than the sum of its parts), boundaries, and hierarchies.[31]

This organization occurs through a process in which the family regulatory behaviors (morphostasis) are altered to make them more compatible with avoiding the stress and conflict associated with alcoholism. The family accommodates to alcohol-related behaviors in an effort to achieve short-term stability (the process of morphostasis is also called *homeostasis*). However, this increases the likelihood that the drinking will continue because the system has (inadvertently) been organized to maintain it. According to Steinglass and his colleagues, family rituals offer the clearest opportunity to investigate this developmental process since they are considered to be the most meaningful shared activity.[32]

Rituals, encompassing cultural traditions, family celebrations, and daily routines, are symbolic events repeated in a systematic fashion over time which convey a sense of belonging among family members. Cultural traditions include religious and secular events which are generally observed by the larger society, such as Christmas, Thanksgiving, or Independence Day. Family celebrations, such as birthdays, graduations, weddings, vacations, and reunions, are special events that, although perhaps shared with the larger society, are practiced in unique ways by each family. Daily routines are the most distinctive form of activity and vary widely across families. Routines reveal how the family relates in terms of time and space, for example, at dinnertime, at bedtime, or during leisure time. "The one construct that more clearly encapsulates the notion of the Alcoholic Family (a family organized around alcoholism) [is the] invasion of family regulatory behaviors by alcoholism."[33] For example, the family may stop having meals together if the mother drinks in the evening and does not prepare them.

The family's long-term growth and development (morphogenesis) entails three major tasks that determine the family's identity: defining boundaries, establishing a family theme, and choosing shared values. Although greatly simplified in the present discussion, families accomplish these tasks as they move through a common developmental pathway encompassing early, middle, and late phases. During each developmental phase, the alcoholic family makes crucial, usually unconscious, decisions to either challenge or accommodate the drinking behavior of a family member and, thus, shapes family identity. In the early phase, the family initiates its identity. A key variable is how closely a couple links with their respective families of origin (which may also be alcoholic), since this will influence how the family responds to emerging drinking behavior. If the drinking behavior is not resolved, the middle phase for alcoholic families is characterized by maintaining this established identity. For alcoholic families, this means organizing around alcohol-related behaviors (i.e., invasion of rituals by alcoholism). In the later phase, the family consolidates and defends its alcoholic identity and, if the drinking is not successfully confronted, transmits this identity to future generations. Thus, according to this model, the etiology of an alcoholic family is rooted in the sacrifice of morphogenesis (long-term growth) for morphostasis (short-term stability).

Shame. The role of ritual invasion in the development and maintenance of alcoholism in a family has been shown to be important through numerous research studies.[34] Another construct associated with alcoholic systems (which is clinically derived but lacks adequate empirical validation) is "shame." While it is acknowledged that "normative shame" is necessary for an individual to be socially functional, shame-bound families are thought to engage in pathological patterns of communication and interaction which instill a sense of "toxic shame" in their offspring. The theoretical and clinical literature on the relationship between shame and chemical dependency at both the individual and family level is growing rapidly.[35]

Fossom and Mason define shame as "an inner sense of being completely diminished or insufficient as a person. . . . [It] is the ongoing premise that one is fundamentally bad, inadequate, defective, unworthy, or not fully valid as a human being."[36] Shame differs from guilt in that the latter comprises a painful feeling of regret for one's actions while the former is an acutely painful feeling about one's self as a person. Guilt offers the opportunity to reaffirm personal values, repair damage, and grow from the experience. Shame, however, is more likely to foreclose the possibility of growth, since it reasserts one's self-identity as unworthy. Although

shame is experienced as an intrapsychic process, its development occurs primarily through the interactions of the family. A shame-bound family operates according to a

set of rules and injunctions demanding control, perfectionism, blame, and denial. The pattern inhibits or defeats the development of authentic intimate relationships, promotes secrets and vague personal boundaries, unconsciously instills shame in the family members, as well as chaos in their lives, and binds them to perpetuate the shame in themselves and their kin. It does so regardless of the good intentions, wishes, and love which may also be a part of the system.[37]

Shame-bound systems can be addictive, compulsive, abusive, or phobic or exhibit some combination of these behaviors. Alcoholic families are susceptible to shame in at least two ways. First, members often construct elaborate networks for hiding the alcoholism from each other and from the community. Second, alcoholism is frequently associated with emotional, physical, or sexual abuse. Such abuse, as well as neglect, is usually cloaked in secrecy. Secrets maintain the equilibrium of the system by inhibiting family members from changing their behaviors. Thus secrets serve to perpetuate the addiction as well as the shame of the people involved.

Kaufman provides an explanation of how shame is transmitted from the family level to the individual.[38] He theorizes that a single developmental process is involved which takes different pathways, either to a healthy self or to a shame-bound self. The outcome depends upon the prevailing affect encountered by the child over time in his or her interactions with adults, primarily the parents. If the child's basic needs (physical and emotional) are understood and acknowledged on a consistent and predictable basis over time, the child acquires an inner sense of trust and competence in his or her ability to get needs met. Ultimately, this child develops healthy self-esteem. However, if the parent fails to meet the child's needs, the child attributes this as personal failure and feels deficient. If this pattern is repeated consistently, the normative experience of shame (which occurs when our needs are not met) evolves into the person's inner experience or identity. A shame-bound self is governed by feelings of being diminished, lonely, worthless, and alienated. Given the complexity of any family system over time, a child is likely to experience a combination of enhancing and diminishing responses. Parents can replace a shame-inducing reaction in a child with an affirming one by accepting and explaining the parent's own responsibility for the interaction. Thus they free the child from the sense that he or she failed to elicit the needed response from the parent. Unfortunately, many alcoholic or codependent parents frequently fail to take this corrective step.

Rules and Roles. Wegscheider discusses family interactive processes in terms of "self-worth."[39] Self-worth is reciprocal in that both the alcoholic and other family members suffer from very low self-worth and reinforce it in each other. Thus the family system does not encourage the health and wholeness of its members, nor do members encourage the health and wholeness of the family. All families, over time, establish rules and roles which determine the values and goals of the family, regulate power and authority, specify how the family will deal with change, and establish patterns of communication. These rules are seldom recognized consciously. "Alcoholic families are governed by rules that are inhuman, rigid, and designed to keep the system closed—unhealthy rules. They grow out of the alcoholic's personal goals, which are to maintain his [sic] access to alcohol, avoid pain, protect his [sic] defenses, and finally deny that any of these goals exist."[40] Wegscheider uses the analogy of a mobile, with family members suspended and held together by strings, which represent rules. An action by the alcoholic reverberates throughout the system. While the family's reactions are intended to bring stability, they actually produce long-term adaptation to alcoholism since "there is no healthy way to adapt to alcoholism."[41]

Families also adjust to alcoholism through the process of establishing roles (i.e., outward behavior patterns). All families function through roles (such as parent, child, etc.), but roles in alcoholic families take on an added dimension. Although there is little empirical study on the subject, it is theorized that these roles are a way of maintaining stability, but they fail to confront the problem of alcoholism, which threatens the system. Thus the family may preserve its identity, but at a high price of which it is seldom aware. There are six typical family roles: dependent (the alcoholic), enabler (the powerless spouse or partner), hero (the overachieving child), scapegoat (the delinquent child), lost child (the isolated child), and mascot (the immature child).[42] This is only a schema, since, in small families, one person may assume more than one role and, in large families, one role may be played by several people. Further, roles may shift over time. Although these roles may appear in all families at some time, "in alcoholic families the roles are more rigidly fixed and are played with greater intensity, compulsion, and delusion."[43]

CODEPENDENCY AND RELATED CONSTRUCTS

As discussed, alcoholism can be viewed at both the individual and familial level: an alcoholic suffers from personal impairment *and* contributes to the impairment of his or her family. Likewise, other family members can develop individual impairment *and* contribute to familial impairment. In turn, family dysfunction can exacerbate each individual family member's problems (i.e., the processes are reciprocal). The impairment of nonalcoholic family members can encompass the three related constructs of codependency, children of alcoholics, and adult children of alcoholics.

Codependency. There are several definitional issues that need to be considered in a discussion of codependency. It is a ubiquitous concept in the fields of chemical dependency and mental health, yet there is no general agreement as to its meaning. The concept is clinically derived, and to date, has received limited empirical attention. Despite its intuitive appeal, this ambiguity has led to much confusion and controversy in the appropriate use of this concept in assessment and treatment.

The concept originated when CD counselors first turned their attention to the spouse (i.e., wife) of the alcoholic. They used the term "enabler" since it was observed that the behavior of the spouse often served to support the alcoholic's drinking. Another early term was *coalcoholic,* which implied that the spouse also suffered from the disease through her relationship with the alcoholic. By the late 1970s, coalcoholic was replaced by *codependent* as the term *chemically dependent* to describe alcoholics and other addicts gained popularity. Mendenhall notes ongoing confusion over the term "coalcoholic" and contends that it should only refer to any family member who is also alcoholic.[44]

Codependency was a useful framework for explaining some of the dysfunctional behaviors observed in the wives of alcoholics. In their efforts to cope with the stressors brought on by their spouse's drinking, they eventually became a part of the problem by "enabling" it to continue through their own dependence on the relationship with the alcoholic. This concept was also useful in treatment, since it provided a framework for spouses regarding their own "recovery" from the effects of alcoholism. Mendenhall proposes that the term "codependent" can be used in reference to any person living in an ongoing committed relationship with an alcoholic or addict, whether spouse, parent, child, or grandparent.[45] The concept is often applied more broadly to describe individuals who engage in ongoing dysfunctional relationships, whether chemical dependency is present or not. While these definitions imply that the individual is codependent in relationship to an alcoholic or other person, current use holds that the individual is engaged in a disease process of dependency in his or her own right.[46] Codependent characteristics are thought to emerge from childhood abuse experienced in one's own family of origin.[47] Hence there is a clinically derived, theoretical relationship between the constructs of shame and codependency.

The concept of codependency seems to defy precision and various authors have defined it with their own constellation of attitudes and behaviors. Two representative definitions that capture the gist of this concept are offered here. Black states that it can refer to anyone "whose behavior is characterized by the numbing of feelings, by denial, low self-worth, and compulsive behavior. It manifests itself in relationships when you give another person power over your self-esteem."[48] Whitfield defines it as "any suffering and/or dysfunction that is associated with or results from focusing on the needs and behavior of others . . . [so] that they neglect their true self—who they really are."[49] Cermack argues for the inclusion of a "Co-dependent Personality Disorder" in the DSM-III-R and recommends criteria for a standardized definition.[50] Because the construct is so comprehensive and encompasses such diverse characteristics, Cermack identifies five types of codependency: the martyr, the prosecutor, the coconspirator, the drinking (or drugging) partner, and the apathetic codependent.[51,52]

Codependency purportedly develops when individuals learn to "repress their self-awareness, which means that these individuals do not get their needs met or feelings acknowledged."[53] The prevailing explanation is that this first occurs when children grow up in shaming family systems. They lose the ability to distinguish between their needs and the needs of others, and they do not develop a firm sense of self.[54] In adulthood, such individuals have difficulty managing stress, engaging in mature relationships, are at increased risk for alcoholism, and are particularly vulnerable to becoming involved with an alcoholic or prealcoholic partner. Further, in the absence of some sort of treatment, these individuals will likely perpetuate this cycle with their own children. A term often used in the clinical literature to convey this concept is "adult child," which implies that "within each of these adult-age individuals there is a child who has difficulty experiencing a healthy life until . . . recognition and healing of the past occur."[55] Interestingly, however, the literature on codependency and shame do not necessarily overlap. This is perhaps because codependency originated as a self-help movement while conceptualizations of shame are more theoretically derived; however, knowledgeable practitioners link the two concepts.

Kitchens identifies two contrasting models of codependency.[56] The "addict-centered" *model* emerged from the chemical dependency field. In this model, the codependent person reacts to the behavior of an addicted person, who is the center of the family. The addiction can be alcoholism, rigid religiosity, workaholism, or other dysfunctional behavior. "Regardless of the problem around which the family is centered, the fundamental element of the model has remained intact: A troubled individual, usually a parent, stands at the center of the problem and the other family members react to that person in self-defeating ways."[57] Alternatively, in the "faulty family" model, which arose from the mental health field, the family itself is viewed as the core problem. In essence, family members are not regarded as reacting to an addicted individual. Rather, the addict, along with other family members, belongs to a system in which all family members have developed dysfunctional patterns of coping with each other. Codependent families "have trouble predominantly in the areas of flexibility, boundaries, parent-child coalitions, blaming, poor communication, discounting, and unhealthy rules."[58] Such patterns have been discussed throughout this chapter, although other authors have used other terms, such as "shame-bound families" or "alcoholic families."[59]

Although "codependency" is used irrespective of gender, it has been described as more prevalent in women[60] and seems to be used most frequently in reference to women. However, there is a growing critique regarding sexism in this concept. According to this view, the term "codependency" implies both individual psychopathology in the woman as well as shared responsibility for dysfunction in a relationship. However, this ignores societal attitudes that foster the oppression of women and patterns of gender socialization that encourage the development of stereotypical female attitudes of passivity, dependence, and self-sacrifice.[61] Still others question the utility of attaching a label to women and assisting them to "recover" from what many view as essentially desirable female (or human) qualities. This debate is related to emerging theories on women's psychological development[62] which critique "male" models of human development as essentially based on separation and autonomy and propose a "female" model based on interdependence. The topic of codependency could certainly benefit from empirical investigation and perhaps reconceptualization.

Children of Alcoholics. A related issue to codependency is the concept of children of alcoholics (COAs). Of the estimated 28.6 million children of alcoholics in the United States, about 6.5 million are under the age of 18 and currently reside in homes where at least one parent is alcoholic.[63] In such alcoholic families, there is not a free flow of emotional expression and open communication. Black coined a phrase which captures the powerful injunctions regarding behavioral and emotional expression in these families: "don't talk, don't trust, don't feel."[64]

There is considerable clinical and empirical literature which indicates the detrimental effects of parental alcoholism on children. Being the child of an alcoholic places an individual at greater risk for alcoholism than children of nonalcoholics.[65] A precise risk has not been established due to methodological differences in prevalence studies, but it is estimated that the child of an alcoholic parent is one and one-half to three times as likely to develop alcoholism as the child of a nonalcoholic.[66] While there may be a genetic component to this risk,[67] several studies indicate that family environment is also a contributing factor.[68]

In addition to elevating the risk for alcoholism, children reared by alcoholic parents are thought to be more vulnerable to psychosocial impairment than other children. Hibbard reports that reviews of the research on COAs indicate that "they are probably at greater risk for conduct disorders, hyperactivity and attention-deficit disorder, somatic problems, substance abuse, truancy and delinquency, lower intelligence, more neuropsychological problems, lower scholastic achievement, and more interpersonal difficulties than other children."[69] Russell, Henderson, and Blume,[70] as reported by Seilhamer and Jacob, state that COAs are "over-represented in the caseloads of medical, psychiatric, and child guidance clinics; in the juvenile justice system; and in cases of child abuse."[71] It should be noted, however, that certain children of alcoholics show remarkable resiliency to the potentially damaging effects of parental alcoholism and often grow into fully functional adults despite these known risk factors. In fact, Seilhamer and Jacob conclude that the research on COA outcome is equivocal.[72]

Adult Children of Alcoholics. The psychosocial difficulties experienced by children and adolescents living with an alcoholic parent do not necessarily end as the individual matures. There is increasing evidence that the vulnerability of many COAs extends into adulthood. Of the estimated 28.6 million children of alcoholics in the United States, about 22 million are adults over the age of 18.[73] Parental alcoholism can be related to adult impairment, in particular, the so-called "adult children of alcoholics syndrome" proposed by chemical dependency counselors. This syndrome refers to a behavioral and emotional pattern displayed by some individuals from families with a history of parental alcoholism and codependency characterized by a restricted range of affect and extreme distrust of intimacy.[74] Although widely accepted in the chemical dependency field, the ACOA syndrome has not been validated through empirical research. There are only a few studies which have attempted to specify the individual or family characteristics associated with the ACOA syndrome.[75]

There is a lack of specificity in the literature regarding the etiology of the ACOA syn-

drome. A number of authors assert that an internalized sense of shame is linked to the dysfunctional behaviors of many adults, including those who display the ACOA syndrome (and who may or may not be alcoholic as well). Individuals who grew up in "shame-bound" families, whether characterized by alcoholism or other pathology, are thought to often experience impairment in adulthood. However, coming from a family with parental alcoholism or other pathology is not sufficient for the development of characteristics of the ACOA syndrome. According to G. Kaufman, current theory on the development of shame does not predict a particular pathogenic family process (i.e., alcoholism, incest, mental illness, etc.).[76] It is surmised that the model of a "shame-based" identity can only be applied to adults since it is presumed that children (less than age 18) have not fully developed a stable identity, healthy or otherwise.

Pathogenic processes in the family of origin are hypothesized to increase the risk of adult offspring establishing pathogenic family processes in their family of procreation. The findings of several studies suggest that the way in which rituals and routines are practiced in the family of origin may have either a detrimental or a protective influence on the development of alcoholism in offspring.[77] In essence, the authors found evidence that families that had a breakdown of rituals were associated with lower levels of functioning in young offspring, higher levels of alcoholism in adult offspring, and lower levels of ritual practices by adult offspring in their family of procreation. Thus a cross-generational pattern is established which perpetuates alcoholism and its related problems.

To conclude, definitional issues complicate an understanding of the emotional and behavioral patterns of alcoholism, codependency, COA, ACOA, and shame. These terms (and the constructs that they represent) are not only poorly defined, but they are also interrelated, and, therefore, it can be difficult to distinguish them from each other. Some authors contend that all alcoholics are also codependent, although this position is not universally accepted in the chemical dependency field.[78] Others use the terms "adult child," "ACOA," and "codependent" interchangeably. However, not all ACOAs meet the profile of codependency, nor are all "codependents" from alcoholic families. In an effort to be more inclusive of alcoholism and other forms of chemical dependency, the term "adult children of addicted families" is used by some authors.[79] Yet, since not all people displaying ACOA-like characteristics are from addicted families, the phrase "adult children of dysfunctional families" is becoming more common, especially since the process of recovery that has been helpful to ACOAs appears to be helpful to other people as well.[80] Such a trend is viewed by many practitioners and researchers as *too* inclusive. A phrase often repeated in the increasing overlapping fields of chemical dependency and mental health is that 90 percent of Americans are codependent; if so, this is normative! This phrase illustrates the struggle which exists to establish both compassionate and credible parameters around these concepts.

ASSESSMENT AND TREATMENT OF ALCOHOLIC FAMILIES

There are many reasons for including the family in treating what has traditionally been viewed as an individual problem. Wegscheider identifies several ways that involving the family can benefit the alcoholic in his or her individual treatment: they can provide useful information about the patient, they may be alcoholic or emotionally disturbed themselves (and negatively affect the patient if they are not treated, too), and they are likely to continue to enable the patient's dependency if they do not receive help.[81] Further, "family treatment may be our best hope for preventing alcoholism and drug dependency in the next generation."[82]

There are also reasons for focusing treatment on the family itself. According to Lawson and coworkers, it is unproductive to treat an individual separate from the system if he or she will be returning to live with the family,

family members are also under stress and probably in need of help, and only through participating together in treatment can the family truly understand its dynamics and develop new behaviors.[83] There is some evidence that alcoholics show a better response to treatment when it includes family members (especially the spouse).[84] In addition, such an approach allows the family to share a common goal and, even if problems continue, to perhaps experience some success in nondrinking areas of communication and interaction.[85]

A family may enter treatment through several routes. Lawson and coworkers classify alcoholic families using five categories.[86] First, a family may seek therapy with the undesirable behavior of a child as the presenting problem, when there is actually hidden alcoholism or drug addiction in one or both of the parents. Second, a family may acknowledge a problem with parental or spousal drinking, but it is not chronic and seems secondary to other problems in the family, although they probably may be interrelated (as is often the case in abuse or neglect). A third type of family presents with alcoholism as the major problem. These families are organized around the alcoholism, and it is a source of severe conflict. In the fourth type, an alcoholic family may seek help after the drinking individual has entered recovery and the family's equilibrium is disturbed. Finally, the identified patient may be an adolescent in a family without parental drinking, hidden parental drinking, or parents in recovery. Elkin contends that alcoholic families usually enter treatment in one of three ways: problems encountered by the children, the wife seeks treatment for herself, or the family experiences a crisis.[87]

Thus families may enter treatment with or without the goal of directly addressing alcoholism in a spouse, parent, or child. Depending upon the nature of the treatment they receive, the alcoholism may or may not be addressed. Since alcoholic families are quite adept at keeping their "secret" hidden, alcoholism may not surface unless the therapist looks for it. If the family acknowledges the problem but the alcoholic or addict doesn't, a process called *intervention* may help.[88]

Intervention is based on the premise that alcoholics who are in denial will resist any attempt to be engaged in treatment. Therefore, presenting them with the need for help must be done in a way that they can accept. Conducted in conjunction with a specially trained professional, an "intervention" is a carefully planned and rehearsed procedure. In a nonjudgmental tone, significant persons in the alcoholic's life (such as family members, friends, employer, doctor, etc.) confront him or her with firsthand, specific, behavioral feedback regarding how the alcoholic's drinking has affected them. Once the alcoholic's denial has been weakened by the reality of his or her behavior, the interveners present acceptable treatment options to the alcoholic, permitting him or her some input in the decision making. The alcoholic's excuses for avoiding treatment have been anticipated, so they are less likely to be successful.

In family treatment, the goal of therapy is not only sobriety for the identified alcoholic, but also improvement in family functioning. Wegscheider identifies three broad goals for treatment: (1) education about alcoholism as a family disease and how each member is contributing to it, (2) assistance in making their system more open and flexible, and (3) fostering each family member's personal growth and self-worth.[89] Elkin identifies five goals: (1) stop the drinking and/or isolate the drinking member, (2) stop life-threatening or destructive behavior of family members, (3) disengage children from parental roles and alter inappropriate parent-child alliances, (4) help re-form the parental alliance and authority, and (5) support members in obtaining necessary resources outside of the family.[90] As noted earlier, Kitchens recommends targeting inflexibility, boundary confusion, parent-child coalitions, scapegoating, inadequate communication, discounting feelings, and unhealthy rules.[91]

It should be recognized that a family-oriented perspective in the treatment of alcoholism does not imply that the family *caused* the problem. In fact, as noted throughout this book, there is likely no single cause of chemical abuse or dependency. These problems may arise from and be maintained by a combination of biopsychosocial factors in both the individual and family. A family-oriented approach conceptualizes the problem in terms of family functioning and directs treatment at that level. Although differing theoretically, each of the models presented here recognizes that interactive patterns maintain the drinking and contribute to family dysfunction. Therefore, each advocates including the family in some aspect of treatment and contends that any changes will affect the system, not just individuals.

Behavioral Perspective

A behavioral approach to working with couples or families is based on principles of behavioral theory. Such principles can be used in behavioral therapy of families or as a model of family therapy which utilizes behavioral principles (see the next section). Regardless, according to Goldenberg and Goldenberg, "the unique contribution of the behavioral approach lies not in its conceptualization of psychopathology or adherence to a particular theory or underlying set of principles but in its insistence on a rigorous, data-based set of procedures and a regularly monitored scientific methodology."[92] Briefly stated, behavioral theory argues that virtually all behavior is learned (as opposed to inborn) and maintained (or conditioned) through environmental or social consequences, such as reinforcement. Social learning theory and cognitive-behavioral theory add to the conditioning theories by recognizing that cognitive processes, such as modeling, mediate between the individual and the environment.

How does behavioral therapy apply to chemically dependent families? These families often attempt intuitively to use positive reinforcement (reward drinking behavior through attention or caretaking), negative reinforcement (protect the chemically dependent individual from the negative consequences of drinking or drugging), or punishment (inflict a penalty on the person for drinking or drugging).[93] Unfortunately, each of these responses is considered to increase the likelihood of drinking. Behavioral therapy, on the other hand, attempts to apply the principles of reinforcement to achieve desirable results. "The guiding principle of the application of behavioral techniques in family treatment of alcohol abuse is to increase and reinforce positive behaviors/interactions among family members and to decrease negative behaviors/interactions related to drinking."[94] Another application of behavioral theory to family treatment is modeling. For example, the therapist can model more functional interaction with the alcoholic for family members, and the spouse can model more appropriate drinking behavior for a nonabstinent individual.[95]

Behaviorally oriented family treatment differs from systems-oriented family therapy in several important ways. Treatment begins with a behavioral assessment of family difficulties, which identifies specific areas to target for intervention, as well as a careful analysis of antecedent and consequent events. Assessment is an ongoing process; intervention is modified in response to changing behaviors. Treatment is directed at observable behavior, and there is no effort to address intrapsychic processes or interpersonal patterns (other than those specifically related to the target behavior). The causes and effects of the problem are seen as linear rather than circular, as is common in most family therapy models. Further, the behavioral approach tends to focus on dyadic interactions rather than triads. Families are often educated in the principles of behavior therapy so that they can monitor and modify their own behavior and interactions.[96]

Stress-Coping Perspective

The stress-coping and behavioral models are similar in many respects. Both were first used to address addiction in the individual, and both have been expanded to include marital and family relationships. Like the behavioral and systems perspectives, the stress-coping perspective recognizes the reciprocal nature of family interaction. However, this perspective differs from the family systems perspective since it does not view the family as a unit unto itself but, rather, the family is viewed as the context for the stress and coping of individual members. The stress-coping model, ". . . which focuses on stressful life circumstances, social resources, and individual coping responses, can shed light on both the processes of remission and relapse for alcoholics in family settings and the processes by which family members adapt to an alcoholic partner or parent."[97]

For the alcoholic, this theory contends that "substance use represents an habitual maladaptive coping response to temporarily decrease life stress and strain."[98] Stressors may or may not precipitate drinking; this depends upon a number of factors, including the individual's coping mechanisms, treatment experiences, and life context (including the family). "An alcoholic's life context can provide a supportive milieu for continued improvement, cushion the impact of stressors, or trigger a relapse."[99] For the spouse and children of an alcoholic, other factors in their lives besides the alcoholic's behavior must be considered, such as environmental factors, life stressors, and the functioning of the individual or other family members (for children, this particularly refers to the nonalcoholic parent).[100]

Treatment using the stress-coping approach can vary widely. Al-Anon can be viewed as using this model in that it emphasizes the development of skills for coping with the stress of dealing with an alcoholic spouse. Al-Anon members are encouraged to find satisfaction through their own pursuits. In addition to Al-Anon, family members can learn more adaptive coping through individual therapy. These individual efforts, in turn, can have the added effect of facilitating changes in the alcoholic, since change in one member affects the whole system. Marital or family-oriented treatment assists members in identifying personal and familial stressors that impede the recovery process and shows them how to develop more adaptive cognitive and behavioral coping mechanisms, communication patterns, and problem-solving skills. Wallace identifies five coping mechanism often employed by the wives of alcoholics which may actually encourage continued drinking: (1) withdrawal, (2) protection of the alcoholic, (3) attack, (4) safeguarding family interests, and (5) acting out.[101] Identifying more effective strategies can be a complex process since ". . . the effectiveness of a particular coping skill will vary, in all likelihood, with (1) the situation itself, (2) the individual alcoholic, (3) the characteristics of the spouse, and (4) the strength and cohesiveness of the marital bond."[102]

Family Therapy Perspective

Family therapy is defined as "a variety of different strategies and techniques, based on somewhat different theories, for the ultimate goal of realigning relationships in the family to achieve better adjustment of all individuals in the family."[103] Family therapy (including marital therapy) represents a shift from viewing people as individuals to viewing them through their relationships to others. There are three broad goals of family therapy: "(1) to facilitate communication of thoughts and feelings between family members, (2) to shift disturbed, inflexible roles and coalitions, and (3) to serve as role models, educators, and demythologizers, showing by example how best to deal with family conflict."[104] Models of family therapy have been classified using several different frameworks. Walsh, for example, typically identifies six models: psychodynamic, Bowenian, experiential, structural, strategic, and behavioral.[105] Other authors use other classifications such as systemic, communication, or existential. Although each model shares a family systems theoretical orientation, they differ in terms of conceptualization of the problem, specific goals of treatment, strategies and techniques, and role of the therapist.[106]

There is no model of family therapy designed specifically to address addiction. Rather, the philosophy, goals, and strategies of each model are applied to alcoholism as the "presenting problem" indicative of underlying dysfunction in the family system. While the behavioral or stress-coping perspectives focus directly on the alcohol-related behaviors of family members, family therapy focuses more on the nature of the relationships among family members, which may not be unique to alcoholism. As stated by Collins, research suggests that ". . . the specific nature of the individual's impairment may be a less potent contributor to family dysfunction than is the fact that the family contains an impaired member."[107] Several authors provide guidelines for family therapy with chemically dependent families, although they have not been scientifically validated.[108]

Steinglass and his colleagues emphasize that alcoholic families are highly heterogeneous (as are families with an alcoholic member). They believe that "it is no more credible to propose that a single treatment approach will make sense for each and every alcoholic family than it is to assume that all alcoholic families follow comparable developmental courses or manifest the same personality features."[109] However, they do provide some guidelines, briefly highlighted here, for working with these families. It should also be noted that therapists are also heterogeneous. Therefore, as stated by E. Kaufman, ". . . each therapist should choose those systems of family therapy that best suits his or her personality, making use of those techniques that can be grafted onto one's own individual style and family background."[110]

The Steinglass team has outlined a four-stage sequence for working with alcoholic families.[111] The first stage is a careful assessment in which overall family functioning is evaluated (including the role of alcoholism) and the primary problem is identified and defined at the family level. The assessment, to determine if the system represents an alcoholic family or a family with an alcoholic member, can be accomplished through an interview focused on family rituals to ascertain the extent to which they have been invaded by alcoholism.[112] If the family has become organized around alcoholism,

> . . . a treatment program that leads to a cessation of drinking on the part of the family's alcoholic

member will, in such families, have profound implications at almost every level of family life. Thus, in such situations, overall treatment success is likely to depend not only on efforts aimed at alcoholism *per se*, but also on a comprehensive approach to dealing with the family-level implications of the cessation of drinking.[113]

The developmental phase of the family also needs to be ascertained since this has implications in terms of treatment goals and outcome criteria. Alcoholism may or may not be the presenting problem for a family. Families often seek help when they are in the midst of a developmental crisis. It is possible for a family to resolve their developmental crisis without eliminating the drinking. Steinglass and his colleagues describe a family making the transition to the later stage of its development.[114] At this stage, one of the family's developmental tasks is to launch adult children into age-appropriate roles. The family successfully achieved this goal even though the parents' drinking pattern remained unchanged.

The outcome of the assessment determines the course of treatment. For an alcoholic family, therapy must target the alcoholism first and then the presenting problem (if it remains after the alcoholism is addressed). For a family with an alcoholic member (i.e., not organized around alcohol), the problem as presented by the family becomes the focus of treatment and alcoholism may be addressed within this context, using traditional family therapy techniques.

If alcoholism is identified as the problem, the second stage is referred to as "family detoxification," which consists of "removing alcohol from the family system." The authors recommend that the therapist use a problem-solving approach, such as described by Haley.[115] This entails contracting with the alcoholic to stop drinking (including completing a medical detoxification regimen, if necessary) and identifying responsibilities for each family member. The alcoholic may refuse to acknowledge a problem and refuse to detoxify, yet the family may decide to continue treatment. If so, the alcoholic is ex-

cluded from the therapy. Examples of tasks in the contract are eliminating alcohol from the home and reinstating family routines. The therapist should anticipate difficulties in negotiating and implementing the contract, since the family is attempting to change instilled patterns.

Following successful completion of the diagnosis and detoxification stages, drinking is no longer considered the major issue. The next two stages address family interactional patterns, using any one of the models of family therapy. The third stage addresses the family's emotional instability which follows when drinking no longer occurs in a family that has been organized around alcohol. The task of this stage is to assist the family in tolerating this shift and in establishing new patterns that are not tied to alcohol. A psychoeducational approach explaining the difficulty of making these changes can be very helpful. The fourth stage, in which the family consolidates changes, can result in two possible outcomes. In the first, called *family stabilization*, the interactional patterns remain essentially unchanged, but the family no longer relies on drinking to regulate them. Alternatively, *family reorganization* occurs when the family fundamentally alters its interactional patterns.

The foregoing framework is a general guide since it is possible that a family will drop out of treatment at any stage. Further, a family may slip back into alcohol use at some point. In the latter instance, the therapist can renegotiate a *detox contract* and support the family in continuing to make changes. A family systems approach is not always the treatment of choice, since family members are not always available. In addition, family therapy does not eliminate the need to include individually oriented interventions in the treatment, such as AA or Al-Anon.

EFFECTIVENESS OF FAMILY TREATMENT

As discussed in Chapter 6, data on the effectiveness of treatment for alcoholism is often equivocal. This same pattern applies to studies that examine the effectiveness of family therapy of alcoholism. Collins reviewed outcome studies of family treatment using behavioral marital therapy, systems-oriented marital therapy, and Al-Anon groups.[116] She found inconclusive results, mainly attributable to methodological limitations of the studies. Steinglass, and coworkers interpret the literature as more supportive of the positive outcomes of family therapy.[117] Although acknowledging limitations of the data, they point out that no other treatment has been shown to be any more effective in producing desirable changes in behavior.

CASE EXAMPLE

The following case example illustrates some of the main points emphasized in the chapter, particularly regarding the family therapy perspective. It is a composite of several families with whom I have worked in my clinical practice. The names and significant characteristics have been altered to protect their identities. The reader should bear in mind that there is considerable variation among families, therapists, and modalities. This case represents only one possible approach and has been simplified for the sake of brevity.[118]

Presenting Problem. Emily is a white, 18-year-old high school senior. She was admitted to City Psychiatric Hospital in December following a suicide attempt. She had no history of prior psychiatric treatment or difficulties. She presents as an attractive, intelligent, and cooperative adolescent. Behavioral and emotional problems emerged one year ago and escalated rapidly: conflict with her parents over money, studying, household duties, and curfew; school failure and truancy; depression; and social isolation. If these problems persist, she will not graduate in May.

While in the hospital, Emily revealed extensive substance abuse, primarily alcohol, but occasional use of marijuana, cocaine, and "pills." She would use "whatever was available." She began drinking two years ago and reported that she "loved" alcohol, both the taste and the way it made her feel. Typical use consisted of daily drinking and binging on the weekend to the point of intoxication. She successfully hid her drinking from her parents. She described them as "preoccupied with their own problems." Emily feels that her father abuses alcohol. She claims that her suicide attempt, mixing alcohol with barbiturates, was an accident. It occurred after her boyfriend broke up with her and she felt lonely.

After being evaluated in the hospital, Emily was transferred to a thirty-day residential treatment program for adolescent substance abusers. She seems to have benefited from this treatment in that she now describes herself as "in recovery." She realizes that she must remain abstinent, and she attends several AA meetings a week. She meets regularly with the high school social worker and participates in a weekly peer support group. Although she feels that she is "turning her life around," conflict has continued with her parents. She and her family were referred to Mental Health Clinic for one hour per week outpatient family therapy following her discharge from the treatment program.

Family History. Other family members are the father, Jim, an accountant (age 42); Susan, a homemaker (age 42); and Jason, a high school freshman (age 15). They are a white, middle-class family. Both Jim and Susan described their family of origin as traditionally suburban middle class, with a breadwinner father and homemaker mother. They met in college, married immediately upon graduation, and had their first child two years later. Jim described his father as a steady drinker, who was frequently verbally abusive. In retrospect, Jim believes that his father drank heavily throughout his childhood and adolescence, although he believes that his mother protected him and his older brother from much of their father's alcoholic behavior. Susan reported that there was considerable conflict between her parents, who divorced when she was 16 years old. She rarely saw her father after the divorce. She reports no substance use by her parents.

The couple described their marriage as "average," although closer inspection reveals that they seldom interact. Jim, who is self-employed, has been quite focused on his business over the last few years. The struggling local economy had severely cut his income. Susan is actively involved in several charity organizations and social groups. They acknowledged having "drifted apart." In fact, there is little indication that the family as a whole has much interaction since they do not eat meals together and spend most of their time in separate rooms. Jim acknowledges that he has three to four drinks a night but does not see this as a problem. Susan confirms this intake and feels that Jim's drinking is a way for him to relax, given his work stress. Susan drinks socially on occasion. Jason denies any drinking or drug use, and his parents believe that this is an accurate report.

Assessment. According to a family systems perspective, Emily is the "identified patient" in this family. Although she clearly has an alcohol abuse problem in her own right, there appear to be underlying factors in the family which are contributing to her difficulty as well as to that of other family members. One pattern observed in this family is "triangulation." This concept can refer to the tendency of a marital dyad to maintain stability in their relationship by focusing their attention on a third person, usually a child. When a child experiences difficulties, the parents' attention is diverted away from addressing the problems in their relationship. From a systems perspective, all family members are participating in this pattern with the goal of reducing stress and conflict. Emily's problems could be seen as a way to keep her parents engaged with each other through their mutual concern for her. Thus they are spared from having to confront the lack of emotional support in their marriage. Developmentally, Emily is at an age when she should be starting to emancipate. This pattern may also serve to keep her in a nonadult role with her parents.

This family presents with at least three generations of active substance abuse. Jim is the adult child of an alcoholic father and a codependent mother and appears to be in denial regarding his own alcohol abuse problem. One could hypothesize that he learned the "don't talk, don't trust, don't feel" rules that are often encountered in these families. It is not surprising that he is having difficulties with intimacy in his marriage and with his children. Susan suffered a severe blow to her sense of security when her parents divorced and her father became distant. She may not recognize the potential for a similar outcome in her own marriage. They have evolved into a classic male alcoholic, female codependent pattern in which both minimize the extent of problems which alcohol is causing in their family. They are locked in behavioral patterns that are self-defeating and are actively training their children into these roles as well. It appears that alcoholism accounts for the lack of shared rituals and routines in their daily life, and therefore, they can be described as an "alcoholic family."

Treatment. From a systems perspective, the focus of therapy will be on improving family functioning (communication and interaction) for the benefit of all family members. [See specific treatment goals discussed on p. 225.] Since there is apparent active alcohol abuse in two family members (Emily and Jim), this will be the initial focus of treatment. Although Emily is engaged in a recovery program, the presence of alcohol in the home, her father's unwillingness to admit to his own alcohol abuse, conflict with her parents, and the general lack of emotional support in the family place her sobriety in jeopardy as well as the well-being of other family members, including Jim. Therefore, the therapy should begin with the immediate goal of cessation of Jim's drinking. Once this is addressed, the goal will become to assist the family in developing patterns of interaction and communication which foster the growth of all family members. The therapy will be conducted following the four-stage model outlined earlier in the chapter.

The first stage is diagnosing alcoholism and labeling it as a family problem. In the initial session, the therapist assesses the family functioning by questioning each family member. She wants to gain information as well as to establish a therapeutic relationship with them. Jim and Susan adamantly insist that Emily's oppositional behavior is the source of their family's current problems. They feel that otherwise they would be "normal" and cite their previous successful functioning (prior to Emily's difficulties) as evidence of their position. Emily remains noticeably sullen throughout the session. Jason seems to make every effort to appear invisible and grudgingly agrees with his parents when asked for his perspective by the therapist.

In the next session, Emily becomes more vocal. She had met with her school social worker who urged her to share her concerns about her father's drinking and her mother's acquiescence in family therapy. She defiantly reports that her father is an alcoholic and that "I should know." She and Jim immediately become entangled in a conflict. He denies that he had a problem and accuses her of trying to shift the blame for her behavior. Susan and Jason watch in silence, with evident discomfort. When questioned by the therapist, Susan expresses concerns for Jim's health, revealing her fear that he will have a heart attack due to the stress of their financial situation. She apparently attempts to deflect the focus back to Emily by adding that their daughter's difficulties have exacerbated his stress. When questioned again about Jim's drinking, she seems to minimize it by stating that he "needs to drink to relax." (Thus focusing on Emily also serves to avoid having to deal with the pressing economic problems of the family as well as their marital problems.)

The family is in a stand-off, and it is crucial for the therapist to address this issue openly. She presses Jason for his opinion (the "silent" member of a family is often the most valuable source of information). With reluctance, he agrees with both Emily's and Susan's concerns: he thinks his father drinks too much and also worries about his health. With Jason's revelation, Susan's resolve to "protect" Jim in his denial weakens. Although she continues to waver, with further probing by the

therapist, she and the children gradually align in their concern about Jim's drinking. They identify the following problems: embarrassment when he is drunk in public, anxiety when he wants to drive while intoxicated, fear of his rageful outbursts, sadness over his emotional unavailability, and concerns regarding his poor health and the financial instability of the family.

Jim becomes increasing defensive and, in an effort to keep him engaged in the therapy, the therapist reframes this feedback in terms of his family's honesty: although painful, it is an indication of their love for him. She commends him for having developed such a sense of trust with his family that they were willing to be so honest. (It should be noted that the therapist is not labeling him as alcoholic at this point. Rather, she is keeping the focus on this topic and facilitating the family members in their efforts to state directly how his drinking is causing problems in their family. This avoids the possibility that the father will "attack" the therapist, be supported by family members, and manage to avoid this issue.) The session concludes by the therapist clearly identifying that Jim's drinking appears to be a major problem for the family.

On the third session, the family comes in with a crisis: Jason had gotten into a fight at school and was suspended. (Some crisis was almost to be expected, since the family homeostasis had been disrupted last week. One could hypothesize that Jason was assisting Emily in maintaining the family's familiar patterns, particularly in terms of keeping the focus off Jim's drinking.) The therapist quickly moves to counteract this attempt to regain stability by using a psychoeducational approach with the family. She explains the idea of "family system" and how the behavior of each member affects the family as a whole. She observes that the last session disrupted their usual patterns and notes how distressing this can be. This shows that she is empathic with their situation, places this crisis in a larger context, neutralizes the diversion, and enables her to return the focus to Jim's drinking.

A long silence is broken by Jim's query as to whether the therapist thinks that he has a drinking problem. Aware of the importance of this juncture, she responds that this certainly seems to be the case, based on behavioral indicators, but primarily because she has heard the concerns of his family and cannot disregard them. Since his attendance at this session indicates how strongly he is committed to his family, she is sure that he has heard their concerns as well. (This response puts Jim in a bind, since to disagree with the therapist would suggest that he is disregarding the concerns of his family and would call into question his commitment to them.)

Jim does not respond and is obviously distressed by his predicament. Susan tries to "rescue" him by stating her concern about the problems involving Emily and Jason. The therapist explains that she has not forgotten this, but her experience and the clinical literature indicate that, when present, alcoholism must be addressed first if the family is to resolve other problems successfully. Since Emily is engaged in treatment, Jim's alcoholism must be addressed. Her goal is to keep the topic before the family despite their obvious discomfort. However, they seem reluctant to confront him further. Rather than engage in a power struggle with the family around this reluctance, she wonders aloud at the "power" that alcohol seemed to have over this family. Jim breaks the silence, saying that alcohol has no power over him. She asks why his family is so threatened by the topic (in this way, she highlights the process of alcoholism in the family, not Jim's alcoholism, per se). This provides a less threatening avenue for Susan, Emily, and Jason to once again talk to Jim about his alcohol abuse and the effect it has on them.

In the next session, Jim indicates the effect that his family's disclosure had on him. He was quite withdrawn during the ensuing week. He attempted to prove them wrong by showing that he could quit drinking whenever he wanted. However, in the face of his family's feedback and the unexpected struggle he had in avoiding alcohol, Jim reluctantly agrees that he might have a problem. At this point, several significant events have transpired in the therapy: Jim's denial regarding his alcohol abuse has been broken and his problem has been placed within the larger context of the family. The therapy enters stage 2: removal of alcohol from the family system.

The family and therapist agree to work together to help Jim stop drinking. The next step is to develop a detoxification contract with the entire family since this is now regarded as a family problem. Since hospitalization is not indicated, the therapist recommends an eight-week outpatient program (only a therapist adequately trained in assessment should make treatment recommendations). Jim will make an appointment with this agency for an evaluation prior to the next session. He will also remove all alcohol from the home (a request made by Emily). Jim asks that the family spend more time together and feels that this will assist him in not drinking. He becomes tearful as he talks about how he feels uninvolved in his children's lives (the therapist notes that he did not include Susan in this sentiment). They decide to have dinner together in the evenings. The therapist praises the family for their courage in confronting this problem together, provides some "reality testing" on the difficulty of their task, but reassures them that they can succeed in making desired changes.

The therapist begins the fifth session by reviewing the family's implementation of the detox contract. Jim has removed all the alcohol from the house, enrolled in an outpatient treatment program, and abstained for the full week. Family members confirm that he has not appeared to drink. However, they did not share any meals together. Susan, although expressing her relief over Jim's adherence to the contract, feels that he has become more "moody." Jim admits to feeling unsupported by the family, particularly since Susan has not organized any meals. Susan feels that there were too many different schedules among them to plan a specific time for dinner. The therapist anticipated problems with the contract, since the family is attempting to change entrenched patterns. She empathizes regarding the difficulty of their task, commends them for their successes, and assists them to negotiate a better plan. After considerable negotiation, all members agree to adjust their schedule to have dinner together at least three times in the coming week. In addition, they will participate in the family component of Jim's outpatient program. (It is important to recognize that the process of assisting them to develop new skills for problem solving, such as negotiation, is as important to the therapy as the product, the new contract. The therapist also notes the weakness of unity and authority in the parental dyad since they all negotiated equally and independently. Thus she is continually engaged in assessment, gathering information which will be useful when they begin to address nonalcohol-specific family patterns.)

The next week, Jim enters treatment. In the next six weeks, he indicates that he is clearly engaged in his treatment program. He is feeling a sense of comaraderie with other males that he has not enjoyed since being in the military. Nevertheless, he is finding it difficult not to drink and relies heavily on AA meetings and his sponsor for guidance. The family is actively involved in the family component of his treatment program. Emily is particularly enthusiastic, given her previous positive experience with treatment. She and her father have fewer conflicts as they support each other in their recovery efforts. Jim becomes more involved in Jason's sports activities. The children have developed a habit of "checking in" with Jim at least once per day. Jim frequently expresses a regret that he was not more available to them due to his drinking. The family is managing to have three evening meals together a week and is trying to share one activity together on the weekend.

As Jim continues to maintain sobriety, the therapy shifts into stage 3: the emotional desert. Jim is six weeks into his treatment and has been sober for two months. The focus of therapy is to support the family as they adjust to the absence of alcohol in the family system and to tolerate these changes. For years, they have slowly altered their behavior to accommodate Jim's drinking. In turn, family members have developed maladaptive behavior,

such as Emily's drinking, Susan's codependence, and Jason's social withdrawal. They must learn new patterns of interaction and communication. Since Jim drank excessively for a number of years, the shift from a "wet" to a "dry" state is quite stressful. The therapist expects this transition to be difficult and uses a psychoeducational framework to help them understand the nature of these changes.

Susan appears to experience the most difficult adjustment. She expresses a sense of unfamiliarity with Jim and discomfort with his new behavior. Toward the end of his treatment program, she begins to express anger toward him for now being the "perfect father," despite years of being essentially absent. Although pleased that the family is growing closer, she feels that an unfair burden has been placed on her to prepare meals and provide emotional support while Jim gets to "have fun" with the children or be self-absorbed in his recovery. Susan reveals that she has not been attending Al-Anon meetings or reading about codependency. The therapist discusses with the family, focusing on Susan, how she and Jason, although nonalcoholics, nevertheless must also work on their recovery.

The therapy is now concentrating on non-alcohol-specific areas of family functioning. Susan's concerns have touched on core problems of intimacy in the couple's relationship. To reinforce an appropriate boundary between the parental and child subsystems (that is, to avoid discussing private marital issues in the presence of the children), the therapist requests a meeting with Susan and Jim alone. (Although marital therapy seems indicated in this case, this change in format is not always necessary.) The goal of this marital therapy is to assist them in sharing their feelings and to problem solve through the use of traditional marital therapy techniques. An early task is to set guidelines for fair fighting as they express mutual feelings of bitterness and regret. The state of "disorganization" in the relationship is punctuated by joint statements regarding the possibility of divorce. Yet both partners indicate their commitment to each other and their desire to improve the marriage. After several conflictual sessions, the therapist is effective in helping each partner to take responsibility for his or her contribution to the breakdown of their marriage and to work toward conflict resolution.

The prospect of divorce is unsettling to both of them. This crisis unveils deep fears in Susan stemming from her parents' divorce, and she gains insight into the origins of her codependency. She realizes that she assumed a "childlike" position in the marriage and was avoiding many aspects of being a wife and mother, such as giving Jim full authority over financial matters and not monitoring the activities of her children. This appears to be the source of many of her complaints about changes in the family (i.e., being forced into a more mature role). She held the irrational belief that being more assertive and independent would cause him to leave her. For his part, Jim acknowledges that he encouraged her dependence, since this was the model he observed in his family of origin. However, this same upbringing left him with strong unmet needs and weak coping skills. Therefore, he was equally dependent on Susan and fearful of abandonment by her. He was overwhelmed by his perceived sole responsibility for the financial well-being of the family. Rather than turn to his wife for assistance, alcohol became a way of coping with his fears and anxieties. Once they identified these feelings, they were able to view each other's behavior in a more positive light. They began to build trust in their relationship, based on active choices rather than passivity.

The therapist meets with Jim and Susan for six weeks. At the conclusion of the marital sessions, the family had been in therapy for approximately four months. Jim has completed his eight-week treatment and has been participating in the weekly follow-up program for one month. He has been sober for over three months. Emily continues to attend follow-up at her treatment program and has been sober for almost six months. As Jim and Susan address their marital problems directly and change their relational patterns, the family entered stage 4: resolution. The goal of this stage is to help the family in their reorga-

nization since their basic patterns of functioning have undergone significant change. (If Jim had maintained sobriety but their interactional patterns had gone unchanged, the goal would have been family restabilization.) The role of the therapist is to assist them in developing more functional patterns through the application of traditional family therapy techniques.

A new stability in the marriage leads to overall improved functioning in the family. They remain in family therapy for two more months. As Susan and Jim continue to work on achieving mutuality in their relationship, their parenting improves. They make joint decisions regarding the children and feel more comfortable in asserting their authority. Thus rules and expectations become more clear, and as a result, Emily and Jason show more age-appropriate behavior. Jason begins to explore an unexpressed artistic ability. In the past, Jim had tried to push him into athletic pursuits, for which he was not temperamentally suited. Now they are looking for areas of common interest. While problems still arise, they offer opportunities for the family to build and practice skills for problem solving and conflict resolution. The family interacts more and eats together on a regular basis, with Jim sharing parental responsibility with Susan. They develop skills for more effective communication, particularly pertaining to emotional expression. All family members attend support groups to address their individual needs. Jim and Susan jointly sought advice for addressing their financial problems and are implementing a plan.

Breaking old patterns and consolidating new ones is a trial and error process that transpires over the course of their therapy. Yet this process will continue even after therapy is completed. One of the last issues discussed is Emily's impending graduation and her plans to attend college in the fall. She wants to begin working this summer so she can save her money and offset some of the expenses, since the family's financial situation remains uncertain. Jim's business has shown slow improvement since he quit drinking, and Susan is considering part-time employment.

At the final session, when we are reviewing treatment gains and looking forward to the future, they seem to realize that the end of therapy is really a beginning. Jim voices their commitment to break the cycle of alcoholism and codependence in their family. He states that, although his recovery will take a lifetime, he now understands that, for his family, it will take several generations. From Emily's attempt at death, the family has begun a new life.

SUMMARY

An overview of the history of a family perspective on the theory, research, and treatment of alcoholism indicates that this perspective is widely acknowledged and accepted in the field, although there is no general agreement as to practice. Family treatment can consist of viewing the family as the context for individual behavior as well as viewing the family as a system unto itself (a family systems approach). The related constructs of codependency, children of alcoholics, and adult children of alcoholics have gained a great deal of attention by professionals as well as the public, but these concepts lack empirical investigation that might make them more valuable in affecting positive treatment outcomes for family members. Three predominant models of family assessment and treatment are behavioral, stress-coping, and family systems therapy. There is no model of family intervention designed specifically to address addiction. These models share general principles but differ in specific guidelines for intervention. Although outcome studies are inconclusive, it appears that family therapy is equally effective in bringing about desired changes as other treatment modalities.

ENDNOTES

1. Michael Liepman, Ted Nirenbert, Richard Doolittle, Ann Begin, Thomas Broffman, and Mark Babich, "Family Functioning of Male Alcoholics and Their Female Partners During Periods of Drinking and Abstinence," *Family Process,* Vol. 28, No. 2 (June 1989), pp. 239–249.

2. Migs Woodside, "Research on Children of Alcoholics: Past and Future," *British Journal of Addiction,* Vol. 83, No. 7 (July 1988), pp. 785–792.

3. Saul Shiffman and Thomas Wills, *Coping and Substance Abuse* (Orlando, FL: Academic Press, 1985).

4. Randall Collins, *Sociology of Marriage and the Family: Gender, Love, and Property* (Chicago: Nelson-Hall, 1985).

5. *Alcoholics Anonymous* (New York: Alcoholics Anonymous World Services, 1939), p. 7.

6. Marion Lewis, "Alcoholism and Family Casework," *Social Casework,* Vol. 35, No. 18 (April 1937), pp. 39–44.

7. Irene Goldenberg and Herbert Goldenberg, *Family Therapy: An Overview* (Monterey, CA: Brooks/Cole, 1985).

8. Elvin Jellinek, *The Disease Concept of Alcoholism* (New Haven, CT: Hill House Press, 1960).

9. Andrew Billings, Marc Kessler, Christopher Gomberg, and Sheldon Weiner, "Marital Conflict Resolution of Alcoholic and Nonalcoholic Couples During Drinking and Nondrinking Sessions," *Journal of Studies on Alcohol,* Vol. 40, No. 3 (March 1979), pp. 183–195, and John Finney, Rudolph Moos, Ruth Cronkite, and Wendy Gamble, "A Conceptual Model of the Functioning of Married Persons with Impaired Partners: Spouses of Alcoholic Partners," *Journal of Marriage and the Family,* Vol. 55, No. 45 (February 1983), pp. 23–34.

10. Samuel Futterman, "Personality Trends in Wives of Alcoholics," *Journal of Psychiatric Social Work,* Vol. 23, No. 1 (October 1953), pp. 37–41; Marion Kalashian, "Working with Wives of Alcoholics in an Outpatient Clinical Setting," *Marriage and the Family,* Vol. 21, No. 2 (May 1959), pp. 130–133; and Gladys Price, "A Study of the Wives of Twenty Alcoholics," *Quarterly Journal of Studies on Alcohol,* Vol. 5 (March 1945), pp. 620–627.

11. Joan Jackson, "The Adjustment of the Family to the Crisis of Alcoholism," *Quarterly Journal of Studies on Alcohol,* Vol. 15, No. 4 (December 1954), pp. 562–568.

12. Goldenberg and Goldenberg, *Family Therapy.*

13. Lester Gliedman, David Rosenthal, Jerome Frank, and Helen Nash, "Group Therapy of Alcoholics with Concurrent Group Meetings of Their Wives," *Quarterly Journal on Studies of Alcoholism,* Vol. 17, No. 4 (December 1956), pp. 655–670, and John Ewing, Virginia Long, and Gustave Wenzel, "Concurrent Group

Therapy of Alcoholic Patients and Their Wives," *International Journal of Group Psychotherapy*, Vol. 11, No. 3 (July 1961), pp. 329–338.

14. Peter Steinglass, Linda Bennett, Steven Wolin, and David Reiss, *The Alcoholic Family* (New York: Basic Books, 1987).

15. Goldenberg and Goldenberg, *Family Therapy*.

16. Margaret Bailey, "Alcoholism and Marriage: A Review of Research and Professional Literature," *Quarterly Journal of Studies on Alcohol*, Vol. 22, No. 1 (March 1961), pp. 81–97.

17. Peter Steinglass, "A Systems View of Family Interaction and Psychopathology" in Theodore Jacobs (ed.), *Family Interaction and Psychopathology: Theories, Methods, and Findings* (New York: Plenum Press, 1987).

18. Gary Lawson, James Peterson, and Ann Lawson, *Alcoholism and the Family*, (Rockville, MD: Aspen Publications, 1983).

19. Timmen Cermack, *Diagnosing and Treating Co-dependency* (Minneapolis: Johnson Institute, 1986).

20. Robert Ackerman, *Children of Alcoholics: Bibliography and Resource Guide* (Pompano Beach, FL: Health Communications Press, 1983), and Robert Ackerman (ed.), *Growing in the Shadow* (Pompano Beach, FL: Health Communications Press, 1986).

21. Claudia Black, *It Will Never Happen to Me* (Denver: MAC, 1981), and Janet Woititz, *Adult Children of Alcoholics* (Deerfield Beach, FL: Health Communications Press, 1983).

22. Ruth Seilhamer and Theodore Jacob, "Family Factors and Adjustment of Children of Alcoholics," in Michael Windle and John Searles (eds.), *Children of Alcoholics: Critical Perspectives* (New York: Guilford Press, 1990).

23. Margaret Cork, *The Forgotten Child: A Study of Children with Alcoholic Parents* (Toronto: Alcoholism and Drug Addiction Research Foundation of Ontario, 1969); W. Bosma, "Children of Alcoholics—A Hidden Tragedy," *Maryland State Medical Journal*, Vol. 21, No. 1 (1972), pp. 31–36; and Sharon Slobada, "The Children of Alcoholics: A Neglected Problem," *Hospital and Community Psychiatry*, Vol. 25, No. 9 (September 1974), pp. 605–606.

24. Ann Smith, *Grandchildren of Alcoholics* (Pompano Beach, FL: Health Communications Press, 1988).

25. Claudia Black, *Double Duty* (New York: Ballantine Books, 1990).

26. A discussion of the basic tenets of family therapy can be found in any introductory family therapy text, such as Goldenberg and Goldenberg, *Family Therapy: An Overview*, or Michael Nichols and Richard Schwartz, *Family Therapy: Concepts and Methods* (Englewood Cliffs, NJ: Prentice Hall, 1991).

27. Peter Steinglass, "A Systems View of Family Interaction and Psychopathology," in Theodore Jacobs (ed.), *Family Interaction and Psychopathology: Theories, Methods, and Findings* (New York: Plenum Press, 1987).

28. Virginia Goldner, "Feminism and Family Therapy," *Family Process*, Vol. 24, No. 1 (March 1985), p. 33.

29. Steinglass et al., *The Alcoholic Family*.

30. Ibid., p. xiii.

31. Steinglass, "A Systems View of Family Interaction and Psychopathology."

32. Steinglass et al., *The Alcoholic Family*.

33. Ibid., p. 72.

34. Ibid., and Steven Wolin, Linda Bennett, and Theodore Jacobs, "Assessing Family Rituals in Alcoholic Families," in Evan Imber-Black, Janine Roberts, and Richard Whiting (eds.), *Rituals in Families and Family Therapy* (New York: W. W. Norton, 1988).

35. Recommended books on shame include Gershen Kaufman, *Shame: The Power of Caring* (Cambridge, MA: Schenkman Books, 1985); Gershen Kaufman, *The Psychology of Shame* (New York: Springer Publishing Company, 1985), used by permission. Merle Fossom and Marilyn Mason, *Facing the Shame: Families in Recovery* (New York: W. W. Norton, 1986); Ronald Potter-Efron and Patricia Potter-Efron (eds.), *The Treatment of Shame and Guilt in Alcoholism Counseling* (New York: Haworth Press, 1988); and Ronald Potter-Efron, *Shame, Guilt, and Alcoholism* (New York: Haworth Press, 1989).

36. Fossom and Mason, *Facing the Shame: Families in Recovery*, p. 5.

37. Ibid., p. 8.

38. Kaufman, *The Psychology of Shame*.

39. Sharon Wegscheider, *Another Chance: Hope and Health for the Alcoholic Family* (Palo Alto, CA: Science and Behavior Books, 1981), p. 81. Reprinted by permission of the author and publisher, Virginia Satir, Conjoint Family Therapy, Science and Behavior Books, Inc., P.O. Box 60519, Palo Alto, CA 94306 1-415-965-0954.

40. Ibid., p. 81.

41. Ibid., p. 76.

42. Ibid., p. 85.

43. Ibid., p. 85.

44. Warner Mendenhall, "Co-dependency Definitions and Dynamics," in Bruce Carruth and Warner Mendenhall (eds.), *Co-dependency: Issues in Treatment and Recovery* (New York: Haworth Press, 1989).

45. Ibid.

46. Anne Schaef, *Co-dependence: Misunderstood—Mistreated* (San Francisco: Harper & Row, 1986), and Warner Mendenhall, "Co-dependency Definitions and Dynamics."

47. James Morgan, "What Is Codependency?" *Journal of Clinical Psychology,* Vol. 47, No. 5 (September 1991), pp. 720–729.

48. Black, *Double Duty,* p. 6.

49. Charles Whitfield, "Co-dependence: Our Most Common Addiction—Some Physical, Mental, Emotional, and Spiritual Perspectives," in Carruth and Mendenhall, (eds.), *Co-dependency: Issues in Treatment and Recovery,* p. 19.

50. Cermack, *Diagnosing and Treating Co-dependency.*

51. Ibid.

52. For a more thorough clinical discussion of co-dependency, see Cermack, *Diagnosing and Treating Co-dependency;* Schaef, *Co-dependence: Misunderstood—Mistreated;* Melodie Beattie, *Codependent No More* (Center City, MN: Hazelden, 1987); Carruth and Mendenhall, *Co-dependency: Issues in Treatment and Recovery;* and James Kitchens, *Understanding and Treating Co-dependency* (Englewood Cliffs, N.J.: Prentice-Hall, 1991).

53. Mendenhall, "Co-dependency Definitions and Dynamics."

54. Kaufman, *Shame: The Power of Caring.*

55. Black, *Double Duty,* p. 3.

56. Kitchens, *Understanding and Treating Co-dependency.*

57. Ibid., p. 5.

58. Ibid., p. 139.

59. See Kitchens, *Understanding and Treating Co-dependency,* for a discussion of intervention techniques for working with individuals and families around the issue of codependency.

60. David Roth and Jeffrey Klein, "Eating Disorder and Addictions: Diagnostic Considerations," *The Counselor* (November/December 1990), pp. 28–33.

61. See, for example, Claudia Bepko, "Disorders of Power: Women and Addiction in the Family," in Monica McGoldrick, Carol Anderson, and Froma Walsh (eds.), *Women in Families: A Framework for Family Therapy* (New York: W. W. Norton, 1989), and Phyllis Frank and Gail Golden, "Blaming by Naming: Battered Women and the Epidemic of Co-dependence," *Social Work,* Vol. 37, No. 1 (January 1992), pp. 5–6.

62. Carol Gilligan, *In a Different Voice* (Cambridge, MA: Harvard University Press, 1982), and Judith Jordan, Alexandra Kaplan, Jean Miller, Irene Stiver, and Janet Surrey (eds.), *Women's Growth in Connection* (New York: Guilford Press, 1991).

63. Woodside, "Research on Children of Alcoholics."

64. Black, *It Will Never Happen to Me.*

65. Remi Cadoret, "Genetics of Alcoholism," in Lorraine Collins, Kenneth Leonard, and John Searles (eds.), *Alcohol and the Family: Research and Clinical Perspectives* (New York: Guilford Press, 1990).

66. Marcia Russell, "Prevalence of Alcoholism Among Children of Alcoholics," in Michael Windle and John Searles (eds.), *Children of Alcoholics: Critical Perspectives* (New York: Guilford Press, 1990).

67. Cadoret, "Genetics of Alcoholism."

68. Ruth Ann Seilhamer and Theodore Jacob, "Family Factors and Adjustment of Children of Alcoholics," in Windle and Searles, *Children of Alcoholics: Critical Perspectives,* and William Cook and John Goethe, "The Effects of Being Reared with an Alcoholic Half-sibling: A Classic Study Reanalyzed," *Family Process,* Vol. 29, No. 1 (March 1990), pp. 87–93.

69. Stephen Hibbard, "Personality and Object Relational Pathology in Young Adult Children of Alcoholics," *Psychotherapy,* Vol. 26, No. 4 (Winter 1989), p. 504.

70. Marcia Russell, Cynthia Henderson, and Sheila Blume (eds.), *Children of Alcoholics: A Review of the Literature* (New York: Children of Alcoholics Foundation, 1984).

71. Seilhamer and Jacob, "Family Factors and Adjustment of Children of Alcoholics," p. 169.

72. Ibid.

73. Woodside, "Research of Children of Alcoholics."

74. Black, *It Will Never Happen to Me;* Black, *Double Duty;* Wegscheider, *Another Chance;* and Woititz, *Adult Children of Alcoholics.*

75. Raymond Hawkins II, "The Adult Children of Alcoholics Test: Validation of a Self-Report Measure of the 'Don't Talk, Don't Trust, Don't Feel' Syndrome," paper presented at the Annual Conference of the National Association for Adult Children of Alcoholics, 1988, New Orleans, LA, and Catherine Hawkins, "Pathogenic Family Relations, Adult Children of Alcoholics Syndrome, and Shame Dynamics in Alcoholics, Depressives, and Normal Controls," unpublished dissertation, The University of Texas at Austin, 1992.

76. Kaufman, *Shame: The Power of Caring.*

77. Linda Bennett, Stephen Wolin, David Reiss, and Martha Teitelbaum, "Couples at Risk for Transmission of Alcoholism: Protective Influences," *Family Process,* Vol. 26, No. 1 (March 1987), pp. 111–129; Linda Bennett, Stephen Wolin, and David Reiss, "Deliberate Family Process: A Strategy for Protecting Children of Alcoholics," *British Journal of Addiction,*

Vol. 83, No. 7 (July 1988), pp. 821–829; Stephen Wolin, Linda Bennett, Denise Noonan, and Martha Teitelbaum, "Disrupted Family Rituals: A Factor in the Intergenerational Transmission of Alcoholism," *Journal of Studies on Alcohol*, Vol. 41, No. 3 (March 1980), pp. 200–214; and Stephen Wolin and Linda Bennett, "Family Rituals," *Family Process*, Vol. 23, No. 3 (September 1984), pp. 401–420.

78. Cermack, *Diagnosing and Treating Co-dependency*.

79. Black, *Double Duty*.

80. Ibid.

81. Wegscheider, *Another Chance*, p. 30.

82. Ibid., p. 31.

83. Gary Lawson, James Peterson, and Ann Lawson, *Alcoholism and the Family* (Rockville, MD: Aspen Publications, 1983), p. x.

84. Lorraine Collins, "Family Treatment of Alcohol Abuse: Behavioral and Systems Perspectives," in Collins, Leonard, and Searles, *Alcohol and the Family: Research and Clinical Perspectives*, pp. 285–308.

85. Lawson et al., *Alcoholism and the Family*, p. 286.

86. Ibid.

87. Michael Elkin, *Families Under the Influence: Changing Alcoholic Patterns* (New York: W. W. Norton, 1984).

88. Vernon Johnson, *I'll Quit Tomorrow* (San Francisco: Harper & Row, 1980), and Vernon Johnson, *Intervention: How to Help Someone Who Doesn't Want Help* (Minneapolis: Johnson Institute, 1986).

89. Wegscheider, *Another Chance*.

90. Elkin, *Families Under the Influence*, p. 80.

91. Kitchens, *Understanding and Treating Codependency*.

92. Goldenberg and Goldenberg, *Family Therapy*, p. 204.

93. Barbara McCrady, "The Family in the Change Process," in William Miller and Reid Hester (eds.), *Treating Addictive Behaviors* (New York: Plenum Press, 1986), p. 310.

94. Collins, "Family Treatment of Alcohol Abuse," p. 288.

95. See Timothy O'Farrell and Kathleen Cowles, "Marital and Family Therapy," in Reid Hester and William Miller (eds.), *Handbook of Alcoholism Treatment Approaches* (New York: Pergamon Press, 1989).

96. For a framework of a behavioral therapy approach for working with couples and families, see Ray Thomlison, "Behavioral Therapy in Social Work Practice," in Francis Turner (ed.), *Social Work Treatment: Interlocking Theoretical Approaches* (New York: The Free Press, 1986), p. 142.

97. Ruth Cronkite, John Finney, Jamie Nekich, and Rudolph Moos, "Remission Among Alcoholic Patients and Family Adaptation to Alcoholism: A Stress and Coping Perspective," in Collins, Leonard, and Searles, *Alcohol and the Family: Research and Clinical Perspectives*, p. 309.

98. Raymond Hawkins II, "Substance Abuse and Stress-Coping Resources: A Life Contextual Viewpoint" in Barbara Wallace (ed.), *The Chemically Dependent: Phases of Treatment and Recovery* (New York: Brunner/Mazel, 1992), p. 161.

99. Cronkite, Finney, Nekich, and Moos, "Remission Among Alcoholic Patients and Family Adaptation to Alcoholism," p. 310.

100. For a further discussion of this perspective, see Shiffman and Wills, *Coping and Substance Abuse;* Peter Monti, David Abrams, Ronald Kadden and Ned Cooney, *Treating Alcohol Dependence: A Coping Skills Training Guide* (New York: Guilford Press, 1989); Cronkite, Finney, Nekich and Moos, "Remission Among Alcoholic Patients and Family Adaptation to Alcoholism"; Thomas Wills, "Stress and Coping Factors in the Epidemology of Substance Use," in Lynn Kozlowski (ed.), *Research Advances in Alcohol and Drug Problems* (New York: Plenum Press, 1990).

101. John Wallace, *Alcoholism: New Light on the Disease* (Newport, RI: Edgehill, 1985).

102. Robert Rychtarik, "Assessment and Implications for Treatment," in Collins, Leonard, and Searles, *Alcohol and the Family: Research and Clinical Perspectives*, p. 357.

103. Vincent Foley, "Family Therapy," in Raymond Corsini (ed.), *Current Psychotherapies* (Itasca, IL: F. E. Peacock, 1984), pp. 447–490.

104. Goldenberg and Goldenberg, *Family Therapy*, p. 250.

105. Froma Walsh, "Family Therapy: A Systemic Orientation to Treatment," in Aaron Rosenblatt and Diana Waldfogel (eds.), *Handbook of Clinical Social Work* (San Francisco: Jossey-Bass, 1983), pp. 466–489.

106. A more thorough discussion of the different models of family therapy can be found in any basic family therapy text, as noted above.

107. Collins, "Family Treatment of Alcohol Abuse," p. 304.

108. Duncan Stanton and Thomas Todd (eds.), *The Family Therapy of Drug Abuse and Addiction* (New York: Guilford Press, 1982); Lawson, Peterson, and Lawson, *Alcoholism and the Family;* Elkin, *Families Under the Influence;* Edward Kaufman, "The Application of the Basic Principles of Family Therapy to the Treatment of Drug and Alcohol Abusers," in Edward Kaufman and Pauline Kaufman (eds.), *Family Therapy of Drug and Alcohol Abuse* (Boston: Allyn & Bacon, 1992); Steinglass, Ben-

nett, Wolin, and Reiss, *The Alcoholic Family;* and O'Far-rell and Cowles, "Marital and Family Therapy."

109. Steinglass, Bennett, Wolin, and Reiss, *The Alcoholic Family,* p. 364.

110. E. Kaufman, "The Application of the Basic Princi-ples of Family Therapy to the Treatment of Drug and Alcohol Abusers," p. 287.

111. Steinglass et al., *The Alcoholic Family.*

112. For an example of a family ritual interview, see Wolin, Bennett, and Jacobs, "Assessing Family Rituals in Alcoholic Families," in Imber-Black, Roberts, and Whiting, *Rituals in Families and Family Therapy* (New York: Norton, 1988).

113. Steinglass et al., *The Alcoholic Family,* p. 333.

114. Ibid.

115. Jay Haley, *Problem-Solving Therapy* (San Francisco: Jossey-Bass, 1976).

116. Collins, "Family Treatment of Alcohol Abuse."

117. Steinglass et al., *The Alcoholic Family.*

118. Additional case studies can be found in Peggy Papp (ed.), *Family Therapy: Full Length Case Studies* (New York: Gardner Press, 1977); Stanton and Todd, *The Family Therapy of Drug Abuse and Addiction;* Elkin, *Fami-lies Under the Influence;* Edward Kaufman (ed.), *Power to Change: Family Case Studies in the Treatment of Alcoholism* (Boston: Allyn & Bacon, 1984); Donald Davis, *Alco-holism Treatment: An Integrative Family and Individual Approach* (New York: Gardner Press, 1987); Steinglass et al., *The Alcoholic Family;* Kitchens, *Understanding and Treating Codependency;* and Kaufman and Kaufman, *Family Therapy of Alcohol and Drug Abuse.*

11

Ethnicity, culture, and substance abuse

Ethnicity and culture are social systems that influence the attitudes and behaviors of individuals and groups with respect to alcohol and drug use.[1] These systems have been called "the strongest determinants of drinking patterns in a society."[2] This chapter addresses the substance use and abuse of Americans whose ethnic roots are in many different countries. We consider Native Americans, African Americans, and Hispanic Americans; like Anglo Americans, they have considerable levels of alcohol and drug use.[3] Anglos, however, are less likely than members of these ethnic groups to encounter alcohol- and drug-related health problems (like cirrhosis) and social problems (like arrests). We consider

Asian Americans and Jewish Americans. They also comprise ethnic groups in the United States. While many of them use alcohol, they have fewer chemical dependency problems than most other ethnic groups. We briefly review information on alcohol use among the Irish, Italians, and the French, because many people in the United States are influenced by these cultural heritages.

One outcome of the proliferation of social and economic ties across the globe has been increased awareness of alcohol and drug use almost everywhere. The scholarly literature as well as accounts in the popular media indicate concerns in countries from Asia to the Commonwealth of Independent States to

Mexico.[4] Historically, there has been considerable interest in the drinking patterns of Europeans, primarily the French and Italians, and among the Irish and the Jews. As described in Chapter 2, the French and Irish have much higher rates of alcoholism than do the Italians and Jews. Various sociocultural explanations may account for these differences, such as the Italians' habit of drinking wine moderately with meals, while the French reportedly drink more distilled spirits in addition to wine and do more drinking apart from meals. Jews drink moderately, primarily in conjunction with religious ceremonies and at home, while the Irish drink to socialize, frequently outside the home in pubs. The Netherlands, the Scandinavian countries, Great Britain, Germany, the Mediterranean countries, and India all have their unique histories, customs, and laws that govern alcohol and drug use.[5] Also introduced in Chapter 2 and explored further in this chapter is that cultures with little ambivalence about chemical use and norms which promote moderation and integration of alcohol and even drug consumption within the society tend to have lower rates of chemical dependency problems than do countries like the United States in which the norms and attitudes associated with alcohol and drug use differ widely. While Americans have banned together in their concern about tobacco use, there is less consensus on many other mind-altering chemicals.

In the United States, substance abuse is primarily defined by the majority, because most incidence and prevalence studies have been conducted by whites on samples largely composed of whites.[6] Little attention has been paid to the conceptualizations of these issues by other ethnic groups. As we will see in this chapter, accounts of drinking and drug use among ethnic groups and among Americans as a whole can vary considerably depending on who wrote them.

Although there is controversy about the need for separate, culturally specific, chemical dependency programs,[7] an understanding of human service work with individuals from various cultures is necessary to function adequately in the field. The reported resistance of some clients to chemical dependency services offered by mainstream providers[8] is not surprising given the previous insensitive treatment of many ethnic groups. According to Weibel, "The appreciation of alcoholism or problem drinking as a culturally relative concept may prepare alcoholism counselors to deal more empathetically with their clients and allows for a more meaningful exchange of experience and new knowledge."[9]

A number of volumes have been written on culturally sensitive practice in the human service professions,[10] some specific to substance abuse prevention and treatment.[11] Models of practice with clients of different ethnic backgrounds generally emphasize the need to understand the history of the cultural group, particularly the group's experiences of oppression.[12] In the chemical dependency field, it is important to note the ways in which alcohol and other drugs have (or have not) been used by the group and the ways in which the group has come to define alcohol and other drug problems. The cultural values of the group, the group's expectations of its members, and the group's use of its native language are also very important in developing relevant prevention, assessment, and treatment strategies. While it is impossible to cover the many fine points of service provision to members of different ethnic groups in this chapter, it is important for chemical dependency professionals to develop a working knowledge of this material.

Before discussing various ethnic groups, three caveats about this chapter deserve mention. First, the material presented is largely illustrative generalizations of what is known about each of the groups discussed. For example, there are several hundred Native American and Alaskan Native tribes, each with many distinctive cultural features, including drinking and drug use, that cannot be captured in a few pages. The same holds true for the many cultural groups that fall under the categories of Hispanic, Asian, and so forth. Second, the cultural experiences of members of an ethnic group or subgroup are not identical.[13] For example, some Americans of German, Mexican, or Japanese background have little connection to their ancestors' heritage, while others practice traditions closely tied to their ancestors' homelands. The region of the United States or community in which one lives may also influence ethnic identification and cultural practices. Third, each person's experiences vary, regardless of their ethnic background. Even individuals who grew up in the same family may make different choices about how strongly they will identify with their cultural heritage. When human service professionals talk about differential diagnosis and treatment or individual treatment plans, they are reflecting the need to see the client as a unique human being and not to rely on generalizations. As Chapman notes, we want to avoid "treating the alcoholism rather than the client who happens to have alcoholism."[14] With these thoughts in mind, we present some information on what is known about chemical dependency among some of the major ethnic groups in the United States.

CHEMICAL USE AMONG NATIVE AMERICANS AND ALASKAN NATIVES

It is common knowledge, mostly as the result of Western movies, that American Indians were introduced to alcohol, or "firewater" as it was called, by the "white man."[15] While use of alcohol is recorded in the Bible and in ancient mythology and has been used by various groups for thousands of years, the history of most Native Americans' use of alcohol has been only a few centuries long. A small number of tribes in what is now the southwestern United States had a history of making alcohol for use in ceremonial and religious purposes, but most American Indians learned of alcohol from contact with explorers in the sixteenth and seventeenth centuries.[16] These early experiences[17] remain important in understanding Native Americans' contemporary use of alcohol, because in addition to learning about alcohol from the white man,

they also learned about drunkenness from him.[18] While whites initially offered Indians alcohol to form alliances,[19] alcohol was also used as a means of getting Indians drunk and taking advantage of them in trading and other transactions.[20]

It is also written that Indians were unprepared for the use of alcohol, and as a result, they experienced negative consequences following its introduction.[21] Such has not been the case with peyote, a hallucinogenic drug that has been used by Native Americans with few negative consequences.[22] According to MacAndrew and Edgerton, it is noteworthy that early accounts of Indian drunkenness were written by white men and "that the facts of the matter require that such talk be taken with a rather large grain of salt, for it is indisputably the case that not all North American Indians were irresistibly drawn to alcohol, nor did they, even if they drank it, always become uncontrollable as a consequence."[23]

Leland studied the "firewater myth" that Indians have an inordinate susceptibility to alcohol abuse, and the "reverse firewater myth," that Indians are less prone to alcohol abuse.[24] While she came to no definite conclusion about either, alcohol problems became a concern to some Indian leaders. With their encouragement, a federal law was passed in 1832 that prohibited distilled liquor on reservations; later, ale, beer, and wine were included.[25] Excessive drinking continued, however, as bootleggers and smugglers saw to it that alcohol remained available.[26] Indian prohibition may have inadvertently encouraged practices such as gulping and bingeing, since it was illegal to be caught with alcohol. The 1832 law became regarded as discriminatory, but it was not abolished until twenty years after the repeal of national Prohibition.[27] States and tribal councils are now responsible for alcoholic beverage control policies on their lands.[28] May reports that 69 percent of reservations currently prohibit alcohol, but this practice may continue to exacerbate some alcohol-related problems such as arrests for drunken driving and auto accidents when Indians travel to other areas to buy alcohol.[29]

Given both the historical and contempo-rary oppression of American Indians, one explanation of their alcohol and other drug use is that they are outlets for frustration or ways of coping with poverty; high levels of welfare dependence; lack of access to educa-tion, jobs, and other resources; and social alienation as a result of being cut off from reservation and tribal life and trying to recon-cile one's own culture with that of the major-ity.[30] Weibel-Orlando gives one picture of this devastation:

The Sioux called liquor "mni wakon" or "sacred water" in reference to its power to induce states of euphoria and to reduce pain and sadness. In the late 19th century, when the farms and the railroads of white pioneers displaced the Sioux and drastically altered their nomadic, big game-hunting way of life, they were forced to accept a lifestyle that lacks meaning for them. Alcohol, like the Vision Quest ritual, may help to fill psy-chological gaps left by the Sioux's loss of cultural integrity, perception of personal worth, and sense of self-esteem.[31]

The Native American population is now about equally divided between those who continue to live on reservations and those who live in urban areas.[32] To escape extreme poverty on the reservations wrought by gov-ernment intervention (for example, denial of mineral, oil, and land rights), some Indians migrated to cities, but those who have not acculturated have often seen their problems mount, and these problems include alcohol or other forms of drug abuse.[33] Although many Indians apparently remain caught between two worlds with conflicting values and expectations,[34] Heath cautions that the state of research on Native American accul-turation is such that the only broad general-ization that can currently be made is "to warn against the popular presumption that accul-turation invariably results in stress, which in turn prompts heavy drinking."[35] Oetting and his colleagues also describe the difficulties of trying to interpret findings from studies on cultural identification, but their research sug-gests that Native American children who see themselves as bicultural use alcohol and

drugs least and those who least identify with Indian culture use drugs most.[36]

Cultural Issues and Chemical Abuse Among American Indians and Alaskan Natives

Cultural values which may impact chemical abuse and its treatment among Native Ameri-cans include Indians' tendency to avoid inter-fering in the decisions made by others, and their preference for not giving direct advice or telling others what to do.[37] This is part of the Indian tradition, but it may be perceived as apathy by the majority culture.[38] While Lurie says that many whites find it difficult "to keep their noses out of other people's busi-ness,"[39] others suggest that Indians' fatalistic views of illness may contribute to a pattern in which chemically dependent individuals get into treatment late.[40] Furthermore, there seems to be an absence of shame attached to drunkenness and a lack of community sanc-tions against alcohol misuse among some Native Americans.[41] Like others, Native Amer-icans have been accused of enabling: "It appears to have been common experience for family members, for example, grandparents, to excuse unacceptable behavior and even fa-cilitate it by paying bills, including bail, and placing responsibility on others rather than the alcohol abuser themselves."[42]

Among Native Americans (as well as other groups), drinking is a very social activity and "is part of group membership and accep-tance."[43] It may be considered discourteous to refuse a drink and "bottle sharing" is com-mon.[44] Several authors have described events called "Indian drinking parties" at which cheap alcohol is consumed rapidly until there is none left or the imbibers become uncon-scious.[45] For many Native Americans, drink-ing alone is what is considered aberrant.[46] Lurie describes an interesting view of Native American alcohol use and abuse: "Getting drunk remains a very Indian thing to do when all else fails to maintain the Indian-white boundary."[47] She adds that "thus, before giving vent to aggressive inclinations, you get drunk or convince yourself and others you are drunk, in order that no one mistakes you for acting like a white man."[48] According to Weibel, the picture of the Indian who drinks excessively and behaves aggressively "contrasts with the Indian's typically quiet, low-affect social demeanor when sober."[49] And Oetting and his colleagues also note that substance abuse is antithetical to the Indian way of life because it destroys harmony and unity: "Recreational drugs destroy this harmony with nature and damage the ability of the mind, body, and spirit to work together. They are clearly counter to the Indian Way."[50] Great Indian leaders such as Tecumseh, Crazy Horse, and Sitting Bull did not condone drinking.[51] As Leland concludes, "Given the widespread use of liquor by the dominant society, a case certainly could be made that the best way for Native Americans to distinguish themselves from Whites would be to leave liquor alone."[52]

Substance Abuse Problems Among American Indians and Alaskan Natives

Alcoholism among American Indians and Alaskan Natives is a major health and social concern.[53] It is frequently referred to as their number one problem. Interest in the subject is reflected in an annotated bibliography published in 1980 by Mail and McDonald, which contained 969 references on alcohol use and abuse among Native Americans.[54] Mail noted that more than 450 articles suggested explanations for alcoholism among American Indians.[55] Similar to the etiological categories of alcoholism described in Chapter 2, she divided the theories into three groups and found that 15 articles discussed biological theories (such as possible genetic susceptibility to alcohol), while 157 discussed psychological theories, and 295 reported on sociocultural theories. Littman believes that there are many reasons for alcoholism among Native Americans but suggests that four explanations typify the literature on this subject: (1) relief from anxiety due to extreme poverty and other hardships, (2) the psychodynamic explanation of the need to release repressed anger (sometimes regarded as an outlet which prevents the development of psychiatric problems), (3) relief from pressures resulting from forced acculturation, and (4) promotion of group solidarity through a shared, social activity.[56]

Littman dismissed biological or genetic explanations specific to American Indians due to the lack of any convincing evidence, and Lewis describes American Indians as a social rather than a biological group, because many have a mixed racial background.[57] Lemert also noted little support for "racially induced vulnerability to the effects of alcohol,"[58] even though this explanation was used to justify laws prohibiting Indians from drinking.[59]

Weibel-Orlando notes that alcohol abuse is sometimes blamed on the carry-over of historical binge drinking.[60] Ablon earlier suggested that "widespread drinking problems found among Indians in the city appear to be carried from the reservations rather than being any new response to anxieties caused by the urbanization experience."[61]

Lewis adds to the list of possible causative factors suggesting that Indians themselves think they drink as an expression of defiance against the white man, and also as a response to boredom and despair.[62] And in explaining drinking among Native Alaskans in particular, Knisely suggested that "climate, daylight hours, the forceful introduction of modern technology (post–World War II), and the dramatic urbanization, with new leisure time, that replaced a subsistence way of life" might all be factors.[63]

Despite many criticisms of the methodologies that have been used to study substance abuse among native groups (e.g., the bias that may result from participant observation studies) and despite the problems in conducting research in this area (e.g., data collection is difficult due to the large number of tribes),[64] the literature is clear that Native American mortality is closely associated with alcoholism. For example, deaths from alcohol dependence syndrome, alcoholic psychoses, and chronic liver disease due to alcoholism are estimated to be more than four times higher than for the general population.[65] Liver disease alone constitutes the fifth leading cause of death among Indians: "for Indians ages 15 to 24 it is the ninth leading cause of death; for Indians ages 25 to 44, it is the second leading cause of death, with a rate of 31.6 per 100,000 compared with 5.9 per 100,000 for the general population in that age group."[66]

While alcoholism-related mortality rates for these indigenous groups are very high, Rhoades and his colleagues point to a less known fact—there has been a substantial reduction in the death rates directly attributable to alcoholism for both the general population and for native groups.[67] Rates for the general population declined from 8.1 in 1978 to 6.2 in 1985, and for indigenous groups, from 54.5 to 26.1 for the same years. While rates remain substantially higher for native groups, there is hope for continued progress with greater emphasis on ethnic-sensitive prevention, intervention, and treatment approaches. Also noteworthy are the differences in alcohol-related mortality rates reported for Native Americans and Native Alaskans by area, ranging from 32.7 in Alaska to 136.9 in Billings, Montana,[68] indicating the considerable variation among tribal groups in alcohol use and its consequences.[69] Some Indian tribes, like the Cherokee, have lower rates of alcohol consumption than the general population. Lemert notes that there is a smaller proportion of drinkers among Indians than in the general population, but while there are more abstainers, there are also more heavy drinkers.[70]

Interpretation of the available data on Native American drinking is also complicated by various anomalies. For example, Heath reports that most Hopis do not drink even though their reservation is surrounded by the Navajo Reservation where heavy drinking is practiced; the Hopis, however, have a much higher cirrhosis death rate than the Navajo.[71] Heath attributes this to Navajo binge drinking which gives the liver time to mend, while Hopi drinkers are ostracized and live in their own isolated skid row. (It should be noted, however, that a pattern of binge drinking may also cause serious physical damage.)

Stratton and his colleagues suggested a possible historical explanation for the differential rates of alcoholism among various tribes:

Tribes having a hunting-gathering tradition have more serious drinking problems than do tribes having an agricultural tradition emphasizing communal values and ceremonies. Furthermore, the western tribes that have preserved ceremonies and values reminiscent of their hunting gathering tradition have more serious alcohol problems than do tribes that have been more acculturated.[72]

They note that high rates of alcohol-related problems tend to be found among tribes in western Oklahoma (the Cheyenne-Arapaho, Anadarko, Wichita, and Caddo) compared with much lower rates among eastern tribes (the Chickasaw, Creek, Seminole, and Cherokee). The western tribes were hunters who lost their means of survival when the federal government prevented buffalo hunting. These tribes reportedly had more loosely integrated social structures and were introduced to alcohol much later than members of the eastern tribes who were primarily farmers and had more developed social and political structures. Although the eastern tribes also suffered displacement, they were able to reestablish their farms and communities.

After studying Navajos in the Denver area, Graves found "no convincing empirical evidence that there is something unique about the way Indians use alcoholic beverages, or that people in similar circumstances would not behave in a similar fashion."[73] Nofz also warns that high rates of alcohol problems are not an indication that an excessively large number of Indians drink or have drinking problems, but it does mean that for those Indians who drink, the consequences may be severe.[74]

In addition to liver disease, three of the other ten major causes of death among Native Americans—accidents, suicides, and homicides—are often alcohol related. They are the second, eighth, and ninth leading causes of death, respectively, among native groups.[75] High arrest rates for alcohol-related crimes are another concern.[76] These rates may reflect the tendency to drink in public, thereby increasing the likelihood of exposure to arrest.[77]

While Native Americans are slightly less than 1 percent of the general population, in 1987 reports showed that they comprised 3.6 percent of clients in state-supported alcoholism treatment programs.[78] The high rates of alcoholism among Native Americans are apparently reflected in these admission data.

Figures on drug use among Native American adults are scarce. Information from the Client Oriented Data Acquisition Process (CODAP) from twenty-three states, Washington DC, and U.S. territories in 1983 indicates that Native Americans were more likely than whites to report a problem with heroin, marijuana, PCP, and inhalants,[79] and they were twice as likely to receive drug treatment.[80]

May's review of the research indicates that drinking is more prevalent among Native American youth than youth in the general population.[81] After ten years of studying alcohol and other drug use among American Indian adolescents on reservations, Oetting and Beauvais concur that Indian youth drink more than other youth; while they experience their first episode of drunkenness at about the same age, Indian youth subsequently get drunk more often.[82] Compared with other youth, Native Americans have "higher use rates for nearly every category of drug," but they initially try drugs about a year later.[83] Weibel-Orlando's review of the literature on alcohol and drug use found that Indian youth drink more beer and use inhalants and marijuana more but have similar usage of other street drugs.[84] Inhalant abuse has been cited as a particular problem among ethnic groups such as Native Americans[85] because of the accessibility of products like gasoline, paint, and glue, even if one has little money. Oetting and Beauvais attribute alcohol and drug use on reservations to boredom, and they attribute increased drug use to the lack of availability of alcohol on many reservations.[86] Chemical dependency problems among Native American youth have been associated with role models who also abuse drugs and to reverence of elders, even

if they abuse alcohol.[87] Traditional, laissez-faire child rearing practices among some tribes such as the Ogala Sioux are another reason suggested.[88]

As for drinking among Indian women, May says:

As in the rest of the United States, fewer Indian women drink than Indian men. In some tribes in the Southwest (Pueblo and Navajo) it is rare and quite unacceptable for any woman to drink at all once they have passed their mid-20s and have done some experimentation. In other tribes, such as the Plains and Basin tribes, more women are drinkers at all ages and drinking is somewhat more acceptable. Women in these tribes are not as prone to negative sanctions.[89]

An analysis of data from several studies, representing several tribes, also showed substantially less drinking among Native American women than men, with Native American women in rural areas reporting more drinking than women in urban areas.[90] Among the Sioux, however, rural women reported *more* frequent drinking than rural men. As explanations for this anomaly among the Sioux, Weibel-Orlando suggests that high unemployment and welfare dependence may be contributing factors. Additionally, children are often cared for by other family members which may give parents (particularly mothers) more opportunity to drink. Similar to women in the general population, American Indian women drink less than their male counterparts but are at greater risk for alcohol-related health problems. Women account for almost half of cirrhosis-related deaths among Native Americans and Alaska Natives,[91] and the cirrhosis death rate for Indian women is six times higher than that for white women.[92] High rates of fetal alcohol syndrome have been reported among some tribes but not others (see Chapter 15).

Chemical Dependency Services for American Indians and Alaskan Natives

Few studies have investigated the treatment modalities that best serve Native Americans.[93] In 1975, an evaluation of treatment services for Native Americans was conducted based on chart reviews.[94] The disappointing results were that few cases included a treatment plan, a follow-up, and an evaluation of services, but there was no evidence that the situation was any better for alcohol abusers from other ethnic backgrounds.

The first major federal government initiative to develop alcoholism treatment services specifically for American Indians came as a result of the Comprehensive Alcohol Abuse and Alcoholism Prevention, Treatment, and Rehabilitation Act of 1970.[95] In 1978 the NIAAA began the transfer of its 156 alcoholism and drug abuse programs for indigenous groups to the Indian Health Service (IHS). The IHS is now the agency primarily responsible for federal government activities designed to prevent and treat alcohol and other drug problems among Native Americans and Alaskan Natives. A task force on Indian alcoholism was convened in 1986 by the Secretary of the U.S. Department of Health and Human Services, and the Anti-Drug Abuse Act of 1986 has also helped to increase the services available to Native Americans such as special treatment centers for Native American youth. As of 1988, the IHS reported that there were about 300 programs offering a variety of services to American Indians and Alaskan Natives.

The Western Region Indian Alcoholism Training Center at the University of Utah was established to educate Native Americans to become paraprofessionals in the chemical dependency field.[96] The National Center for American Indian and Alaska Native Mental Health Research at the University of Colorado also addresses alcohol and drug problems among native groups.[97] Other efforts include the development of culturally appropriate instruments for diagnosing alcohol and drug problems among Native Americans.[98]

But when the question is asked, "What should be done about alcohol and drug abuse among native groups?" the most pervasive answer is tribal involvement rather than government intervention.[99] Examples of tribal involvement include the Standing Rock Sioux's "over-all program to ameliorate alcoholism and problem drinking on the Reservation."[100] The Council of the Cheyenne River Sioux Tribe has declared that it will be alcohol and drug free by the year 2000.[101] Another example comes from the Alkali Lake community in the British Columbia province of Canada. The story of this small community is portrayed in the video "The Honour of All."[102] The group's efforts to eliminate alcoholism came when one couple in the community recovered from alcoholism and patiently waited for others to join them.[103] The community then mobilized to prevent alcohol abuse. Some tribes are requiring that persons elected to tribal office be sober.[104]

Willie presents a contrasting view of tribal involvement:

In the past, many Tribal Councils expected Alcoholism workers to turn out sober Indians as if they were on an assembly line, inputting alcoholics on one end and producing recovered alcoholics on the other; and yet the tribal leaders continued to approve liquor licenses and continued to promote fund raising events that were many times based on liquor sales.[105]

While the right type of tribal involvement is certainly thought to be important, a survey of seventy-one Native American alcoholism counselors who were also recovering alcoholics identified factors they thought most important in achieving sobriety.[106] They rated "internal" factors like recognition and acceptance of their drinking problem, Alcoholics Anonymous, meaningful activities, spiritual factors, and Indian pride as more helpful in attaining sobriety than "external factors" such as involvement with traditional Indian people, tribal activities, and Indian and non-Indian alcoholism programs.

Service providers should recognize that the Indian family model fosters mutual obligation or interdependence among relatives rather than independence from them.[107] Service providers have been advised to utilize this extended family and tribal network,[108] not only by involving families in treatment, but also in AA groups, which are usually reserved for alcoholics or addicts.[109] However, others note that Indians may not have family members on whom to rely[110] and that other family members may also be chemically dependent.[111] Thus different strategies may be needed to develop social support systems necessary to recovery. The story of the Two Arrows family that follows was written some time ago, but remains relevant in describing alcoholism in a Native American family.

Many Native Americans believe that substance abuse is externally caused, and personal responsibility for chemical abuse is often not recognized.[112] Confrontation and intervention with the individual that is advocated in much of the mainstream writing about substance abuse is, therefore, culturally incongruent for many Indians. When Indians are referred to treatment programs, education about confrontation prior to admission is suggested to prevent treatment dropouts.[113] This approach is used at Thunder Child, a chemical dependency treatment program for Native Americans, located in Wyoming, which is largely based on the Minnesota model. The Minnesota model has come to stand for traditional, inpatient alcoholism treatment comprised of education, group treatment with some individual sessions, and the introduction of the twelve-step programs (also see Chapter 6). Such programs have been adapted for Native Americans.

Traditional, Native American concepts of spirituality and religion have also been incorporated into treatment and self-help groups. Spiritual practices of Indians are used to gain harmony with the world. Moss and his colleagues recommend that treatment programs have medicine men (we assume the use of medicine women or other spiritual advisors is also appropriate) "on call" and that they should conduct regular spiritual meetings; the sanction of treatment programs by native leaders is also important.[114] The St. Cloud Minnesota Veterans Hospital has begun to utilize the traditional sweat lodge, a purification ritual in which Native Americans usually enter a small, tentlike structure heated by rocks. Indians may spend hours in the structure chanting Native songs, confessing, and seeking spiritual renewal.[115] The vision quest,

another ritual which may be helpful with alcohol or drug abuse, is used to find answers to personal problems or to seek the right path. The use of dances, ceremonies, and prayers is also important, but since these may be sacred activities, professionals who are not members of the tribal group may be excluded from participation.[116]

Incorporation of Indian spiritual and cultural practices into mainstream chemical dependency programs may be useful, but approaches that are uniquely or solely Indian may deserve more consideration from professionals. Take, for example, the use of peyote in treating alcoholism. Most chemical dependency professionals would probably have a difficult time endorsing the use of an hallucinogenic drug in the treatment of alcoholism or other drug addiction, yet this has been done successfully by the peyote religion or Native American Church (NAC).[117] The peyote ceremony is highly structured. Albaugh and Anderson "do not propose that either the pharmacological effects of peyote or the NAC by itself is a cure for alcoholism," but they do indicate that "others have reported success in the treatment of alcoholism in Indian populations by the NAC alone."[118] According to Karl Menninger:

Peyote is not harmful to these people; it is beneficial, comforting, inspiring, and appears to be spiritually nourishing. It is a better antidote to alcohol than anything the missionaries, the white man, the American Medical Association, and the public health services have come up with. It is understandable that these organizations should be a bit envious of the success of this primitive natural native remedy.[119]

In 1991 the Supreme Court ruled in *Employment Division of Oregon* v. *Smith* that the First Amendment does not protect those using peyote for religious purposes from prosecution under state drug laws. Twenty-four states do permit the use of peyote in religious ceremonies, and the American Civil Liberties Union has supported this aspect of religious freedom.[120]

The traditional, Christian overtones in regular AA groups, may be objectionable to

Native Americans,[121] but the religious preference of Native Americans should not be presumed. Some have been converted to Christianity by Protestant and Catholic missionaries and espouse these religions.[122] Traditional AA may be more appealing to highly acculturated Indians,[123] although this depends on the tribe's customs. Jilek-Aall writes that unlike many other tribes, the Coastal Salish Indians who reside in British Columbia and Washington State have a tradition of confession similar to the personal disclosure that takes place in AA.[124] She points to the usefulness of AA but also to the need for separate Indian AA groups due to distrust of whites who have been a source of conflict in Indians' lives, Indian men's concern about Indian women's relationships with white men at AA, the concept of anonymity that may conflict with the Indian's principle of openness, and Indians' discomfort in speaking in front of whites. In addition, the format of Indian AA meetings may differ from other AA meetings. There is less concern about beginning and ending on time. Cultural customs resembling the Indian potlatch (giveaway) feast are sometimes incorporated at AA "birthday" meetings.

Various helping professionals have attempted to develop treatment modalities specific to Native Americans. In the social work tradition, Nofz[125] describes a task-centered group approach (based on the work of Reid and Epstein[126]) that has proven useful with those who identify with elements of both Indian and non-Indian cultures. In keeping with Native American values, "the group is organized around specific tasks in managing sobriety, with special emphasis on adapting to those situations in which different values impose conflicting behavioral expectations. Thus alcohol abuse is not framed as an 'individual problem' and introspection into group members' personalities is avoided."[127] The group identifies the problems and the tasks to be addressed since Nofz believes that Indians often prefer a "doing" rather than an introspective approach. This approach also emphasizes Native American values of "self-determination" and of placing group welfare over individual welfare. Nofz suggests that the social worker develop a "'low key,' participatory [leadership] style" and act as a "group facilitator rather than therapist."[128] Treatment may take longer than is typical with the task-centered approach, because more time may be needed to develop rapport with the Indian participants. Confession within the groups and personal stories in AA may be replaced with the Indian tradition of storytelling. These stories "contain metaphorical descriptions of everyday problems, along with practical and moral advice," and they take direct attention off the individual.[129]

According to May, given the youthful age and short life span of many Indians, prevention of alcohol and drug problems among young people is critical.[130] He suggests several approaches for prevention and treatment among Native Americans:

1. The need for social and economic roles which are both meaningful and consonant with Indian values and roles
2. Education and other techniques that clarify that problems like chemical dependency can be reduced
3. More programs to limit alcohol morbidity and mortality among younger people
4. Innovative programs for chronic abusers that reflect contemporary and traditional Indian cultural approaches.

The approach to prevention among youth suggested by Oetting and Beauvais focuses on peer resistance, strengthening family relationships and cultural identification, improving economic well-being, and encouraging school success.[131] The Indian Health Service has placed emphasis on prevention of chemical dependency problems among youth and adults; efforts with children begin early in Head Start programs.[132] Weibel found that "events that are urban, sacred, indoors, public, of short duration, and include many non-Indians exhibit lower levels of drinking and aberrant subsequent behavior than do events that are rural, secular, outdoors, private, Indian, and not time bound."[133] To prevent excessive drinking among adults in social contexts, these factors may need to be taken into account.

Illustration: Charlie and Rhoda Two Arrows: Turmoil and Withdrawal

Rhoda and Charlie Two Arrows,* both full-blood Teton Dakota, were in their early thirties during their six years in San Francisco. Rhoda was one of four children who grew up in a family where traditional values and discipline were honored. She went to reservation day and boarding schools until the completion of the twelfth grade, after which she moved to a nearby town to live with a sister and work as a waitress. There she first met Charlie Two Arrows.

Charlie grew up on the periphery of the reservation and was exposed to a traditional but disorganized early home life. His mother died when he was young, and his father remarried a woman who joined him in a pattern of continual drinking that soon depleted the money from the lands of his first wife. Charlie attended a public school until the sixth grade and then began the round of hard farm work that has characterized his life to the present.

After their marriage, Rhoda and Charlie lived with Charlie's father. It was a hard life for Rhoda because her father-in-law drank heavily, and she had farm chores to do besides taking care of the household and a growing family of three children. The Two Arrows decided on an impulse to relocate to "sunny California" because they heard there was eternally good weather there and because it was the farthest relocation area from the reservation that they could choose. They planned to save up enough money to buy some land and cattle and then return.

Charlie came to San Francisco with no special skills, but the Bureau of Indian Affairs got him a job in a factory as a machinist. He was reputed to be one of the top workers in the factory, even though he soon initiated a pattern of going on a week's binge every two or three months. He was always careful to call in as ill to cover himself at work and so never got into serious employment difficulties because of his continued drinking. He did, however,

lose money for those days missed, since he did not receive sufficient benefits to cover those periods.

The Two Arrows lived in three apartments during their stay in San Francisco. Two years before they returned to the reservation, they moved into the public housing project in which they lived during the twelve months of interviews with them.

Rhoda had two more children in San Francisco and experienced three periods of acute illness during which she was hospitalized. At these times Charlie would often drink heavily, and welfare officials were called in several times, much to Charlie's later chagrin, because of his drunkenness or his "abandoning" the children. On the reservation, grandparents, aunts and uncles, or cousins are ready sources of short- or long-term babysitting, and most Indian women sorely miss such family support.

This couple lived almost completely in an Indian universe despite the immensely diverse population around them and the many cumbersome new rules of white society that dictated their daily life. Rhoda was active for a time in a local Indian Center, but she noticed that the more active her participation the more inclined Charlie was to drink, so she lessened her activities. Charlie did not care to go to Indian gatherings, because he feared that in a group situation pressure to drink would be brought upon him by other Indians.

The Two Arrows' three school-age children had considerable difficulty in the San Francisco school system. They could not understand the teachers' urgings to apply themselves to materials that had little relevance to their lives. . . . They seemed to withdraw almost totally from the situation. They did not read well and, as the years went by and their alienation from the total school experience deepened, found themselves further and further below the class reading level.

The Two-Arrows' contacts with the Bureau of Indian Affairs were frequent and

---

*The names used are fictitious.

involved. The Bureau was called in repeatedly when Rhoda was in the hospital and Charlie was having problems with his drinking and coping with the care of the children. During the last years, Rhoda called the Bureau office only occasionally to say that things were going well and that she would be eternally grateful that the Bureau had brought them out here. Although not liking the bustle and red tape of urban living, she felt it was all worth it to get away from her father-in-law and to have such conveniences as running water, a washing machine, and easy heating.

The facts of personal and family disorganization among the Sioux are well documented in the anthropological literature. Macgregor* has noted that the Sioux man particularly has suffered from the loss of the meaningful economic and social roles that he enjoyed in the dramatic Sioux life style of old. The woman now may be thrown into the position of the key family figure, causing additional psychological and social difficulties for the man. Rhoda and Charlie exhibited very different personalities and the general pattern of their family roles and behavior typifies this problem of contemporary Sioux. Rhoda was a handsome woman who bore herself with great pride, was gregarious, and enjoyed many kinds of activities. It was her strength and determination that held her family together throughout their many crises in San Francisco.

Charlie, on the other hand, was a very shy person, sensitive about his Indian identity and quick to take offense at imagined criticisms of Indians. He referred frequently to his lack of education. He was able to support his family; however, he was beset with many insecurities about himself and his worth. Charlie seldom spoke and appeared to loosen up only when in the presence of certain known Sioux or when drunk. Beneath his quiet exterior was the latent drinking problem that could surface

---

*G. Macgregor, "Community Development and Social Adaptation," *Human Organization,* Vol. 20 (1961– 62), p. 238.

any day, usually a Friday payday, when he just would not come home from work.

When Charlie returned from a drinking period, he was very remorseful. Because the Two Arrows were nominal Catholics, Rhoda twice attempted to send Charlie to a priest for counseling after his shamefaced return. On both occasions the priest did not have time to see him until a week or more had passed, and by then Charlie refused to talk to anyone about his problem. Once, in the middle of the night, Rhoda called the well-liked minister of a local Indian Protestant church. He came over immediately and talked to Charlie. This minister once said that every man in his congregation had had at one time a drinking problem, so he was well accustomed to this sort of counseling. He felt that one reason many white ministers are unable to reach Indians is that they are afraid to counsel persons with serious drinking problems, and this sort of interaction is frequently an essential one with Indian parishioners.

Charlie, and, to a lesser degree, Rhoda, held strongly to the important Sioux value placed on sharing and the giving of hospitality, which was difficult, given Charlie's salary. His father came out to stay with them almost every winter, and a variety of other relatives and friends would also drop in and remain for weeks at a time. These houseguests did little but drink and watch television during their prolonged stays, and rarely did any of them contribute to the grocery bill.

Life for the Two Arrows in San Francisco seemed to be an almost continual round of crises caused by unexpected expenses and family illness, by their impulsive, erratic behavior, and by their inability to meet the demands of white society.

Charlie finally found himself seriously involved in what seemed to him to be an incomprehensible maze of traffic offenses. While drunk one night he was picked up and booked on drunk driving and hit-and-run charges. When he sobered up the next day, he did not remember committing any of the crimes with which he was charged.

Charlie was released pending trial, and when he got home he informed Rhoda that all this was too much for him; he had decided they would go home. On the federal reservation area he would be safe from state reprisals. In the next few hours they packed the most essential of their belongings, crowded the children into the car, and left. Their flight to San Francisco from the reservation had not freed them from economic or psychological struggles. They had lived in the land of promise six years, and

returned without the money they had come to save. Moreover, Charlie was a wanted man. At present they are resettled with Charlie's father on his lands and Charlie is doing wage labor where he can find it. Rhoda harbors in her heart the hope of another relocation, but it is doubtful that Charlie could be roused to leave the reservation again.

Source: Joan Ablon, "Cultural Conflict in Urban Indians," *Mental Hygiene,* Vol. 55, No. 2 (April 1971), pp. 201–203.

AFRICAN AMERICANS AND CHEMICAL DEPENDENCY

Africans have a long history of alcohol consumption dating to the use of beer and palm wine in precolonial West Africa; use was ceremonial, medicinal, and social.[134]

In traditional African cultures, as in most of the rest of the world, alcohol was widely used. Palm wine was a regular part of the diet, an important part of community celebrations, and a medicinal substance believed to be particularly effective against measles and dysentery. It was used as a medium of exchange as well. Natural substances such as Kola nuts or guinea corn were used as intoxicants or stimulants.[135]

Intoxication, however, was disapproved, and excessive drinking and related problems were apparently uncommon.[136]

Harper and others have described the history of alcohol use by African Americans dating to the seventeenth century in which alcohol was provided to slaves to promote compliance and to prevent escapes; permission to imbibe heavily on weekends and holidays supposedly pacified the slaves and provided a respite from their oppressive existence.[137] Genovese's account is that even though slaves had easy access to cheap liquor, alcohol excess was less common among them than among the slaveholders and that "the general sobriety of

the slaves speaks well for their community strength and resistance to demoralization."[138]

Some accounts indicate that once slavery ended, African Americans were anxious to test their new found freedoms, including drinking alcohol at will.[139] Similar to the situation with American Indians, many whites tried to prevent African Americans from drinking, which they blamed for inciting problems such as violence and crime.[140] Herd's analysis is that drunkenness and alcohol-related mortality among African Americans in the nineteenth century were insignificant.[141] The early American temperance movement was closely associated with the antislavery movement, and abstinence was thought to be important to freedom and equality.[142] But African Americans withdrew from the temperance movement when southern prohibitionists were joined by groups such as the Ku Klux Klan and adopted their racist attitudes. As African Americans migrated from the South to northern cities to seek employment and other opportunities, they became familiar with nightclubs, speakeasies, and other sources of alcohol. Bootlegging became a ready source of income, and alcohol abuse eventually became a problem. During the 1950s, cirrhosis among African Americans grew to epidemic proportions. Herd questions whether urbanization alone would have led to such high rates of alcohol-related problems among African

Americans if the prohibitionists had not gone to such efforts to thwart black equality.

Contemporary Explanations of Substance Abuse Among African Americans

Harper offers four explanations for contemporary drinking patterns among African Americans:[143]

1. *The historical patterns of alcohol use and nonuse by Blacks have played a significant part in influencing their current drinking practices and their current attitudes toward drinking.* According to this explanation, some African Americans drink heavily on weekends after a hard week's work, reminiscent of the days when slaves were rewarded with alcohol and of the early days of freedom. Others, primarily women, do not drink at all due to early prohibitions against African Americans' drinking and to religious beliefs, role expectations, and family responsibilities. There are substantially different attitudes toward drinking among African Americans.

2. *Many Blacks choose to drink because (a) liquor stores and liquor dealers are readily accessible and (b) Black peer groups often expect one to drink and at times to drink heavily.* In white communities liquor stores and bars are generally located in commercial areas; these establishments are more prevalent in African-American residential neighborhoods. There is easy access to alcohol, and drinking is highly visible. Especially among men there may be pressure to drink. There is also a lack of sanctions against chemical abuse in some black communities.[144]

3. *Many Blacks, especially men, drink heavily due to the economic frustration of not being able to get a job or not being able to fulfill financial responsibilities.* Unemployment and economic deprivation may contribute to excessive drinking among African Americans. Although this chapter does not allow for a discussion of the complex issues surrounding the position of black men in the United States or of the issues surrounding the relationships between African-American men and women, Harper writes that the inability to fulfill the role of breadwinner is particularly problematic for men.

4. *Numerous emotions and motivations influence heavy drinking among Black Americans in their attempt to escape unpleasant feelings or to fulfill psychological needs.* The pain associated with the African-

American experience may be mitigated, at least temporarily, by using alcohol for social and recreational purposes. Dozier, also notes that "alcoholism is often tolerated as a stress reducer for many African Americans."[145]

Similar explanations may apply to drug use. Drugs can be easily obtained in many low-income communities and also provide temporary relief from frustration and discrimination. In addition, the drug trade can provide the kind of income unparalleled by most other work. Young people may be influenced by drug dealers' easy access to money and material possessions, despite the danger of their work.

Herd, however, believes that stress and racism fail to explain the relatively recent increase of problems like cirrhosis among Blacks.[146] She also discusses explanations for drinking among African Americans based on social disorganization (i.e., individual and family pathology) and on structural interpretations (i.e., social and economic marginality) that include the roles of political, legal, and economic institutions.[147] She is critical of the social disorganization literature which takes African-American drinking out of its social context and which is often based on studies with small samples of individuals that are not representative of larger African-American communities. She calls for greater study of social and economic conditions such as unemployment and discrimination in the criminal justice system that might contribute to substance abuse.

Watts and Wright say that of all the possible physiological, psychological, sociocultural, environmental, and ecological contributors, it remains unclear which "specific factors, at what times, contribute to the development of alcoholism" among African Americans.[148] African Americans are diverse in socioeconomic status and have origins in many countries (Africa, the West Indies, South and Central America, the Caribbean, and so forth). Each area has a unique history of alcohol and drug use. Even within the United States, the experiences of African Americans vary based on the region of the country in which they reside, but some experiences such as slavery and racism are pervasive influences for virtually all African-American individuals.[149]

Chemical Dependency Problems Among African Americans

African Americans suffer from poorer health than whites. Although the life expectancies for all Americans have increased, African Americans continue to die earlier than whites. The Task Force on Black and Minority Health appointed by the Secretary of Health and Human Services in 1984 reported that chemical dependency was one of the six leading contributors to the lower life expectancies of ethnic minorities.[150] The other five major contributors were cancer, heart disease and stroke, diabetes, homicides and accidents, and infant mortality. Many deaths associated with these causes are also related to alcohol and other drug consumption. The task force was particularly alarmed that rates of alcohol-related problems (such as fatty liver, cirrhosis, heart disease, cancers of the mouth and esophagus, accidents, and homicide) among African Americans, which had been lower than or similar to rates for whites, have increased dramatically since World War II. African-American death rates for cirrhosis are now twice the rate for whites. Robins, however, found no overall difference in rates of lifetime or current alcohol-related psychiatric disorders among blacks and whites based on data from the Epidemiological Catchment Area Program, even after controlling for age and gender.[151]

The 1984 National Alcohol Survey was the first major study of drinking which incorporated a representative (multistage area probability) sample of African Americans.[152] Earlier studies of African Americans have more serious methodological problems but have provided information consistent with at least some of the findings of the 1984 study.[153] Herd conducted initial analyses of data from the 1984 National Alcohol Survey, and combined with other current information, she found that:[154]

1. What might be considered an epidemic level of alcohol-related health problems for African Americans may be associated with a later onset of heavy drinking and more prolonged heavy drinking compared with whites.

2. African Americans' arrest rates for drunkenness are still higher than for whites, but have decreased faster than whites' since the 1960s. Current levels of arrests for liquor law violations and driving under the influence (DUI) are similar, perhaps due to more equitable application of drunk driving laws.

3. African Americans are now overrepresented in alcohol treatment programs, particularly programs for public inebriates, but also in more voluntary treatment (such as employee assistance programs).

4. While the drinking patterns of African-American and white men are generally similar (proportions of abstainers, infrequent drinkers, heavy drinkers, etc.), African-American men have more alcohol-related problems of all types. Among white men there is more heavy drinking and more alcohol-related problems in the 18- to 29-year age group; among African Americans these problems are more likely to occur in the 30- to 39-year-old group. While heavy drinking increases as income increases for white men, heavy drinking decreases as income increases for African-American men. White men drink more heavily in the North, Midwest, and in urban areas than in other parts of the country. This pattern was also true of African-American men, but the 1984 study indicates they now drink more heavily in the South and nonurban areas. This may indicate an increase in alcohol consumption by African-American men in some areas of the country, especially the South. African-American males report more problematic drinking patterns, including binge drinking, and more alcohol-related health problems than do white men. There are fewer differences with respect to the social and interpersonal problems reported.[155]

5. Compared with white women, the 1984 study showed that African-American women abstain more, drink less frequently, and report fewer alcohol-related problems, except health problems. These findings conflict with earlier studies which indicated more frequent heavy drinking as well as more abstention among African-American women. This may be due to the inclusion of more southern women in the 1984 study and more northern women in earlier studies

(the South has traditionally been known as a "drier" area than the North). Among younger women, African Americans are considerably less likely to drink than whites, but heavy frequent drinkers are represented in nearly equal proportions in both groups. For both groups, increased income is associated with less abstention and more frequent drinking.[156]

Also of interest is that African-American adolescents drink and use drugs less than their white peers,[157] but caution in interpreting findings from a number of studies is warranted because samples may exclude school dropouts or institutionalized youth. The 1988

National Household Survey on Drug Abuse Conducted by the National Institute on Drug Abuse showed that 14 percent of African-American adolescents (ages 12 to 17 years) have tried marijuana compared with 18 percent of whites and 17 percent of Hispanics (see Table 11.1). Inhalants have been tried by about half as many blacks as whites and Hispanics in this age group. Crack, thought to be especially prevalent in poor, inner-city communities, has been tried by no more African-American adolescents than white or Hispanic. One possible explanation for lower levels of alcohol and drug use among African-Ameri-

TABLE 11.1   Percent Surveyed Reporting Drug Use, 1988 by Race: U.S.Civilian Non-institutionalized Population

	White		Black		Hispanic	
	12–17 Years	18–25 Years	12–17 Years	18–25 Years	12–17 Years	18–25 Years
Drug						
			Used Past Month			
Marijuana	6.8	15.7	4.4	15.0	5.2	13.8
Cocaine/crack	1.3	4.2	[1]	4.3	1.3	6.7
Crack	[1]	[1]	[1]	[1]	[1]	[1]
Inhalants	2.4	2.2	[1]	[1]	1.4	[1]
Hallucinogens	1.1	2.4	[1]	[1]	0.5	[1]
Stimulants	1.5	2.6	[1]	[1]	0.6	2.5
Tranquilizers	0.3	1.2	[1]	[1]	[1]	[1]
Any	10.0	18.0	6.2	16.9	7.3	16.8
			Used Past Year			
Marijuana	13.0	29.2	9.1	23.5	12.8	22.1
Cocaine/crack	3.2	12.6	1.4	8.1	3.6	12.6
Crack	0.7	1.7	[1]	[1]	0.9	3.5
Inhalants	4.7	5.2	1.6	[1]	2.4	1.5
Hallucinogens	3.6	6.5	[1]	[1]	1.7	5.1
Stimulants	3.4	6.8	0.8	3.5	1.4	5.7
Tranquilizers	1.9	5.5	0.6	[1]	[1]	3.8
Any	26.0	33.1	12.1	25.9	16.3	28.7
			Ever Used			
Marijuana	18.2	60.4	13.5	45.3	16.9	42.0
Cocaine/crack	3.6	21.2	2.1	10.4	4.6	18.7
Crack	0.9	3.3	0.9	2.8	1.3	5.4
Inhalants	9.9	14.7	4.5	3.3	7.2	7.3
Hallucinogens	4.3	16.2	[1]	3.9	3.3	8.2
Stimulants	5.2	12.9	0.8	3.9	2.0	8.5
Tranquilizers	2.5	9.4	0.6	[1]	1.2	4.4
Any	26.0	62.5	18.7	47.0	24.3	47.6

[1] Low precisions; no estimates reported.

Source: National Institute on Drug Abuse, *National Household Survey on Drug Abuse: Population Estimates 1988,* Department of Health and Human Services Pub. No. (ADM) 89-1636 (Rockville, MD: NIDA, 1989).

can youth is that many have fundamentalist Protestant upbringings.[158] They are also likely to grow up in female-headed households with greater exposure to female relatives who have high levels of abstention.[159] One study found that the following factors were related to *increased* drinking among a sample of 1,177 African-American youth in grades 6, 8, 10, and 12: living with *both* parents; having parents who drink, but more important, having peers who drink; having greater knowledge about alcohol; and having more liberal attitudes toward alcohol use.[160] Urban or rural residence and mother's work status were not related to youth's drinking.

Findings from the 1990 National Household Survey on Drug Abuse revealed very similar levels of heavy alcohol use in the last month for white and black individuals age 12 and older, 5.0 percent for whites and 5.1 percent for blacks. Percentages of any illicit drug use in the past year were 13.1 for whites and 14.9 for blacks; for lifetime heroin use they were 0.7 percent for whites and 1.7 percent for blacks.[161] Evidence from a utilization study of state-supported alcoholism treatment programs indicates that 15.6 percent of clients were black, somewhat higher than the 12 percent of blacks in the general population.[162] Information from the National Drug and Alcoholism Treatment Utilization Survey and the Drug Abuse Warning Network indicate that African Americans have more illicit drug involvement and are three times more likely to receive drug abuse treatment than whites, and that cocaine-related deaths for African Americans tripled from 1982 to 1984 (they doubled for whites).[163] Additionally, blacks comprised 20.7 percent of admissions to state-supported drug treatment programs in 1987.[164]

Blacks (and Hispanics) are disproportionately treated for heroin addiction.[165] Estimates indicate that many as 40 percent of narcotics users in the United States are African American.[166] The risks of contracting AIDS through use of dirty needles or through sexual intercourse with intravenous drug users have been well publicized. Of all AIDS cases among heterosexuals associated with intravenous drug use that were reported between 1981 and 1988 in the United States, 54 percent were among African Americans and 26 percent were among Hispanics.[167] Among heterosexual men with a history of intravenous drug abuse (IVDA), 20 percent of AIDS cases were white, 51 percent were black, and 29 percent were Hispanic; among all women with IVDA, 23 percent were white, 60 percent were black, and 16 percent were Hispanic; among children with AIDS whose mothers had a history of intravenous drug use, 13 percent were white, 62 percent were black, and 25 percent were Hispanic; of children with AIDS whose mother's sexual partner was an intravenous drug user, 16 percent were white, 56 percent were black, and 28 percent were Hispanic.

Some of the important questions now being asked in the chemical dependency field are why African Americans, primarily men, experience much more serious consequences from drinking, especially health risks, when their drinking patterns are similar to whites; why African-American men's drinking- and alcohol-related problems increase later in life when they drink less in adolescence and early adulthood; and why African-American men and women in alcoholism treatment are much younger than whites when they drink less in younger age groups.[168] There are similar concerns about the increased risks of drug use for African Americans. Unemployment, poverty, and other factors related to deprived living environments likely exacerbate the effects of alcohol and drug use among this ethnic group.[169]

Chemical Dependency Treatment for African Americans

Although the importance of ethnic-specific services in gaining sobriety has been debated,[170] Beverly has argued that African Americans need these services because their life experiences differ from whites, and social service agencies controlled by whites are by definition racist.[171] Burks and Johnson also note that treatment theories which emphasize the "here and now" deny African Americans' historical experiences of discrimination.[172] They emphasize that African Americans know what is best for them, and they resent the idea that they should conform to white society rather than change it. As with other ethnic groups, a sense of ownership of services is important.

While chemical dependency services originated around the needs of white males, individuals who blame racism alone for inadequate services or who reject the idea that those of other ethnic backgrounds can help them in recovery may also be shortsighted.[173] Bell and Evans have discussed ways to make the therapeutic relationship between clients and counselors of differing ethnic backgrounds more productive in the field of chemical dependency.[174] This includes an understanding of the different personal experiences and counseling styles that black and white treatment providers may bring to their work, especially their views of their own ethnicity and that of others. Black clients may prefer different counseling styles depending on their experiences and identity.[175] For example, black clients described by Bell and Evans as "traditional" may be uncomfortable with the self-disclosure typically expected in chemical dependency treatment programs; black clients whose lives are largely separate from those of whites may prefer or insist on a counselor of the same ethnic background, while those who function more comfortably in both cultures may accept a black or white counselor.[176]

There is a lack of research-tested models for assisting black alcoholics,[177] but Ziter[178] believes that empowerment (techniques to prevent societal victimization and to increase self-esteem),[179] bicultural counseling (helping clients to negotiate the majority culture while supporting the positives of their own culture),[180] and the dual perspective (a method for comparing clients' values and behaviors and those relevant to their immediate social systems with that of the larger society)[181] are important elements in the effective treatment of African Americans.

The literature on African Americans also emphasizes the need for a strengths rather than a deficit perspective in treatment, capitalizing on the positive attributes of clients and their significant others rather than blaming the victim by focusing on presumed weaknesses or deficiencies.[182] In addition, use of an ecological systems perspective, focusing not only on the individual but on relationships with family and other social systems that might reinforce sobriety, has been recommended.[183] In addition to the nuclear family, the extended family of African Americans may include nonblood relatives such as close neighbors and friends who are referred to as "auntie" or "uncle"; these individuals can be sources of material as well as emotional support and may be helpful in treatment.[184]

According to McGee and Johnson, the "superwoman myth" is very strong among African Americans as is the idea that women can endure inordinate amounts of pain when other family members are chemically dependent.[185] They stress the need for codependency services as well as chemical dependency services in promoting recovery of the family.

Additional suggestions to increase the effectiveness of services for African Americans include addressing "racial pain," low self-concept and expectations, perceptions of physical unattractiveness, negative stereotypes, stereotypical role expectations, the necessity of operating in black and white cultures, and views of whites as being more competent professionals than blacks.[186] Other suggestions are to "reduce social distance between staff and clients, reduce paperwork required of clients, ask fewer questions unrelated to treatment, and do a better job to inform the black community of the purpose of the agency."[187]

Attempts have been made to identify differences between black and white women alcoholics that might improve treatment.[188] In one study, black women entering treatment reported fewer financial resources but higher self-esteem and more supportive social networks.[189] Small sample sizes in the studies that have been conducted prevent drawing firm conclusions. Chemical dependency treatment providers and researchers are still struggling with how to best match clients with treatment. Lamenting the paucity of research on the treatment of alcoholism among blacks, Winbush and Henderson entitled their 1983 chapter "'We May As Well Try This': Some Reflections on Alcoholism Services Research in the African-American Community."[190]

Cooperation with churches, core institutions in African-American communities, is repeatedly acknowledged as necessary for reaching many alcoholics and addicts.[191] Spiritual and religious convictions can be a "wellspring of hope and strength" in recovery.[192] The African Methodist Episcopal (AME) church in particular has taken an active role in addressing alcoholism, including recognition of the disease concept.[193] McGee and Johnson note that while churches in African-American communities can be very helpful, some deny the problems of alcohol and other drug abuse and oppose nonreligious treatment approaches.[194] Developing a relationship with church elders, deacons, and ministers and helping to educate them and other church members about chemical dependency are important steps in gaining allies in prevention and treatment. Such education may be necessary to avoid moralistic explanations of alcohol and other drug abuse,[195] as well as ideas that accepting Jesus Christ and prayer are the only requirements for the faithful to overcome these problems.

Other resources which can help address chemical dependency problems are physicians, other health care providers, and members of the business community, as well as civic groups and fraternities and sororities to which many African Americans belong. A resource for identifying problems and making referrals that appears unique to the chemical dependency literature on African Americans is barbers and beauticians.[196] Some innovative approaches have included showing films on chemical dependency in barber and beauty shops. Spiritualists, an indigenous resource used by some African Americans, might also be helpful.[197]

Self-help groups have had an impact in African-American communities, although there has been debate about their usefulness and sensitivity. Hudson traced the beginning of Alcoholics Anonymous in African-American communities to 1945 when Dr. Jim S., a black physician recovering from alcoholism,

began a group in Washington, DC.[198] According to Hudson's research, Dr. Jim's sobriety came when Ms. Ella G., a black friend of Dr. Jim's family, asked a white AA member to help him. Ms. Ella G. had learned about AA as a result of her church work and her brother's alcoholism. Alcoholics Anonymous received many requests for information from African Americans, and other early groups were formed by blacks in St. Louis, Greenwich Village, and Harlem. The AA office in New York, citing the policy that it took no political stands, left it to local groups to address African Americans seeking help. Rather than discriminatory or racist, Hudson defends this position as consistent with AA's view that the only requirement for membership is a desire to stop drinking and that the twelve steps and twelve traditions provide the guidance necessary to help others in need, regardless of their ethnic background.

Hudson also rejects claims that AA is not effective with African Americans because it reflects primarily white, middle-class values and it fails to address the deprivation and discrimination incurred by African Americans. He believes that Alcoholics Anonymous has been successful in African-American communities because its spiritual base is familiar, its fellowship is needed, and its traditional values appeal to members of most ethnic groups. Caldwell also believes that AA is well suited to African Americans because it is consonant with the value they place on interpersonal relationships and also with their appreciation of language, metaphors, and imagery.[199] He believes that there is nothing in the program itself that makes it inherently unsuitable for blacks. However, the question arises as to whether certain aspects of self-help groups such as admitting one's powerlessness might conflict with empowerment and strength approaches and avoidance of the deficits perspective suggested by other authors.

Prevention in African-American Communities

According to McRoy and Shorkey, "just as the problem and consequences of black alcoholism have been largely ignored in the research literature, historically black Americans and the black community have also tended to ignore this issue."[200] To prevent alcohol and drug problems among African Americans, the Chemical Dependency Subcommittee of the Task Force on Black and Minority Health made the following recommendations: improve data collection on alcohol and other drug abuse among ethnic minority groups, promote positive coping skills among youth, use school-based peer groups to encourage resistance to drug use, conduct research to learn how cirrhosis develops in minority populations, conduct research to better understand the role of alcohol use as a contributor to other causes of excess mortality such as the use of alcohol by those with hypertension and the role of alcohol in infant mortality, develop programs to prevent deaths and accidents related to chemical dependency, and educate health care professionals about alcohol and other drug abuse.[201] The task force also encouraged the private sector to educate minority researchers and health care providers about chemical dependency. The Cork Institute on Black Alcohol and Drug Abuse at the Morehouse School of Medicine in Atlanta has a program to incorporate more elective chemical dependency education into the clinical education of third- and fourth-year medical students.[202]

Also recommended are broad strategies which not only focus on substance abuse, but include "a large-scale ecological, environmental, systems-oriented approach" addressing social problems such as unemployment, failure to complete schooling,[203] crime, health, and welfare.[204] There should be an emphasis on the "will to" address the problem of chemical abuse[205] and on the collective responsibility of African-American communities to act.[206] Among African Americans there has been a renewed call to use mutual self-help efforts to address social problems.[207] Bell has emphasized the need for African-American communities to communicate rules, values, and sanctions regarding chemical use,[208] and Amuleru-Marshall urges "blacks to develop a stronger sense of community and a consensus

on acceptable versus unacceptable behavior based on 'Afro-centric' values."[209]

Rites of passage programs emphasizing positive achievements are currently being used as alternatives to the rites of drug use and incarceration.[210] Instilling black pride appears as an important theme in prevention and treatment. Special attention has been paid to alcohol advertising (billboards, magazines, etc.) directed toward blacks (see also Chapter 8).[211] Blacks apparently prefer Scotch and cognac (more expensive liquors) and advertising has taken advantage of this.[212] There has also been an outcry against alcoholic beverages developed to appeal to youth. Rather than alcohol advertising using African Americans, more emphasis is needed on African-American role models who promote sobriety and recovery. An important resource in the prevention and treatment of chemical abuse among African Americans has been the Institute on Black Chemical Abuse with offices in Minneapolis and St. Paul, Minnesota. According to a pamphlet published by the Institute:

The black community must itself determine under what circumstances and at what times alcohol or other drug use is appropriate. Black people must set their *own* agenda on this issue. That means, for instance, formal and regulatory control on beverage control boards and zoning commissions that determine the hours, places, and location for alcohol sale. Community residents must challenge current zoning practices allowing a high density of liquor stores and advertisements in their neighborhoods.[213]

HISPANIC AMERICANS AND SUBSTANCE ABUSE

So many different cultural and ethnic groups fall under the term Hispanic that discussions of substance use and abuse frequently obscure important differences between those whose roots are in Mexico, Cuba, Puerto Rico, Central American, South America, Spain, and other areas. McQuade notes that "there is no 'typical Hispanic.' Representing combinations of European, African and

Native American blood, each of these racial and national backgrounds influence a particular temperament and pre-disposition towards the use of alcohol and drugs."[214] Hispanic Americans are also quite diverse with respect to important factors such as education and living environment,[215] but they are younger than the U.S. population in general and are its fastest-growing segment[216] (now about 9 percent; Hispanics may be of any race). Among Hispanics, Mexican Americans are the largest and fastest-growing group.[217] Some projections are that the number of Hispanic Americans will surpass the number of African Americans during the 1990s.[218] Other important demographic factors about Hispanics are that their poverty rate is substantially higher than that of Anglos; in 1990 28.1 percent and 10.7 percent, respectively,[219] and compared to the general population, they have fewer married couples and more female-headed, single-parent households.[220] Given that McQuade also notes that, "however diversified, common language, religion and tradition have molded certain recurring patterns [among Hispanics],"[221] we consider both similarities and differences among Hispanics groups as they relate to substance use and abuse.

Incidence of Substance Use and Abuse Among Hispanic Americans

Heavy drinking and alcohol-related problems among Hispanic-American men *in general* seem to be at levels higher than for the population overall,[222] although some studies indicate that white men and Latin men report similar levels of abstainers as well as those consuming three or more drinks per day.[223] The most comprehensive look at Hispanic drinking in the United States is the 1984 National Alcohol Survey funded by the National Institute on Alcohol Abuse and Alcoholism, which contains a probability sample of 1,453 Hispanics. From this study, Caetano found that the rate of frequent, heavy drinkers among Hispanic men (those who consumed the most and did so most frequently in this study) is approximately 17 percent for those 18 to 29

years of age, 26 percent for those 30 to 39, 11 percent for those 40 to 49, 12 percent for those 50 to 59, and 3 percent for those age 60 and over, indicating the need for particular attention to those in the 30- to 39-year-old group.[224] This pattern is similar to that of African-American men reported in the previous section of this chapter and different from the general population where the proportion of heavy drinkers continues to decline from younger to older age groups.

Caetano combined the frequent, heavy drinkers with the frequent high maximum drinkers (the two heaviest drinking categories) in the 1984 survey and found that 44 percent of Mexican-American men fell into these categories compared with 24 percent of Puerto Rican Americans and 6 percent of Cuban Americans.[225] In general, the Hispanic men who were single, college educated, and had annual incomes over $30,000 drank more.

More Mexican-American men (22 percent) reported having at least one alcohol-related problem compared with 8 percent of Puerto Ricans and 4 percent of Cubans, but using a more stringent criteria of four or more problems, the rates were 7 percent, 5 percent, and 2 percent, respectively.[226] These figures can be slippery. As Caetano and others have noted, the numbers reported can change depending on how drinking categories and drinking problems are defined.[227] Other reports also indicate fewer problems among Cuban Americans, although there have been reports of Cuban immigrants' abusing substances to cope with the stresses of acculturation.[228] Alcocer also suggests that information on Cuban Americans may be incomplete since they have not been studied as thoroughly as some other Hispanic groups.[229]

A small, clinical study found that some alcoholic men of Puerto Rican origin had more cognitive impairment than did blacks or whites and that they drank more often, consumed more alcohol, and were of lower socioeconomic status.[230] A literature review by Gordon also raises concerns about the severity of alcoholism and drug use problems among Puerto Ricans in the United States.[231]

Caetano reports that compared with Puerto Rican and Cuban Americans, Mexican-American men and women fall more frequently into both the categories of abstainers and heavy drinkers.[232] He found more Mexican-American women (14 percent) in the two heaviest drinking categories than Cubans (7 percent) or Puerto Ricans (5 percent). Gordon found no more than isolated reports of drinking problems among Puerto Rican women, and he says that Dominican men in the United States drink moderately and Dominican women drink very little.[233]

Hispanic-American women have considerably higher proportions of abstainers and have apparently fewer alcohol problems than do American women in general. While Burman found that Mexican-American men had a higher prevalence of alcohol disorders than white men based on data from the Los Angeles Epidemiological Catchment Area Study, Mexican-American women had lower rates than white women.[234] Klatsky and his colleagues report that twice as many Latin as white women are abstainers and that half as many Latin as white women consume three or more drinks per day.[235] Caetano's analysis shows that about half of Hispanic women abstain and about one-fifth drink infrequently; 3 percent of Hispanic women are heavy drinkers compared with 17 percent of Hispanic men; however, 20 percent of Hispanic women in the 50 to 59 age bracket reported frequent, high maximum drinking.[236] Since heavy drinking among both men and women generally decreases with age, Caetano says a possible explanation for more drinking among women in the 50 to 59 age group is that they are mostly U.S. born and acculturated, and evidence suggests that with acculturation, more women of Hispanic origin may become drinkers.[237]

Data from the Hispanic Health and Nutrition Examination Survey (H-HANES) obtained from 1982 to 1984 on 4,912 Mexican Americans is generally consistent with other studies.[238] Forty-four percent of respondents were lifelong abstainers (which includes very light drinking), and another 4 percent of former drinkers currently abstain. Considerably more males than females drink, but drinking is more common among acculturated women; as education and income increase so does the likelihood of being a drinker. Also of interest from the H-HANES is information that gender differences are less pronounced among younger Hispanics than older and that the smallest gender differences were among young Puerto Ricans.[239]

Information from the 1990 National Household Survey on Drug Abuse indicates that 14.8 percent of Hispanics reported some use of an illicit drug in the past year compared with 14.9 percent of blacks and 13.1 percent of whites; figures for any cocaine use in the last year were 5.2 percent for Hispanics, 2.8 percent for whites, and 4.0 percent for blacks.[240] For lifetime heroin use, figures were 1.2 percent for Hispanics compared with 1.7 percent for blacks and 0.7 percent for whites. The H-HANES compared drug use among Mexican Americans, Puerto Ricans, and Cuban Americans ages 12 to 44 from 1982 to 1984 and found less use among Cuban Americans.[241] In the Southwest United States, 12.3 percent of Mexican Americans had used marijuana in the past month and 41.6 percent had used it at some time in their lives, compared with 15.1 percent and 42.7 percent, respectively, of Puerto Ricans in the New York City area, and 5.3 percent and 20.1 percent, respectively, of Cuban Americans in Dade County, Florida. Cocaine use for the Mexican Americans was 2.4 percent in the past month compared with 11.1 percent who had ever used it. Comparable figures for cocaine use among Puerto Ricans were 8.9 percent and 21.5 percent, respectively, and for Cuban Americans were 3.8 percent and 9.2 percent, respectively.

Sanchez-Dirks reported that in a 1974 study which included 1,509 Spanish (Hispanic)-American adolescents, more of the Hispanic male and female youth reported being abstainers and slightly more reported being infrequent drinkers than Anglo youth, while more Anglo youth reported being low-, medium-, or high-level drinkers.[242] Hispanic girls reported the lowest levels of consumption. Alcocer reviewed literature on the alcohol use of Hispanic-American youth in 1982 and found that they used less or that their use did not differ from white youth.[243] Although there is evidence that Hispanic youth drink less than whites, Wallace and Bachman's 1991 review of previous research indicates that youths' use by ethnic group is highest to lowest in the following order: Native American, white and Hispanic, black and Asian, and "that drug use [cigarette, alcohol, marijuana, and cocaine] is not disproportionately high among youth in most racial/ethnic minority groups."[244] Their analysis also indicates that differences between ethnic groups that were found can be explained primarily by background (parents' education, family structure, etc.) and life-style factors (religious views, college plans, etc.). However, studies of alcohol and drug use among youth tend to rely on school samples, and Hispanic Americans, Native Americans, and African Americans have high dropout rates.[245] The white dropout rate is also considerable in many areas. If dropouts use drugs more extensively than those who remain in school, these surveys are likely to underestimate drug use.

Historical and Cultural Perspectives on Substance Use and Abuse Among Hispanic Americans

In addition to the possible influences of acculturation on increased alcohol consumption,[246] poverty and discrimination may be contributing factors. According to Caetano, "heavy drinking and alcohol problems do not appear in a contextual vacuum, but are linked to the status of Hispanics as an underprivileged ethnic minority in the U.S."[247] Poverty is associated with less political power and may help explain reports of the large numbers of alcohol outlets in Hispanic[248] and African-American residential communities.[249]

Cultural-bound definitions of substance abuse among Hispanics are also tied to recognition of these problems. Chemical dependency is often not seen as an illness. Instead, Hispanics may view chemical dependency as a moral weakness and rely on God or divine intervention rather than professional help to solve the problem.[250] Comas-Díaz discusses Puerto Rican "folk beliefs encouraging externalization, passivity and fatalism regarding the problem of drinking" with alcoholism among Puerto Ricans sometimes thought to be caused by bad spirits, reinforcing denial of these problems.[251] Some authors have taken exception to the idea that denial of substance abuse problems among Hispanics is especially strong. In writing about Mexican Americans in particular, Gilbert and Cervantes say that the little data available suggest that they are as likely as others to be referred to treatment by themselves or by family members,[252] and González-Ramos has called resistance to services by Hispanics a myth.[253]

La familia (the family) is of central importance to Hispanics, but ethnic families can be a source of conflict as well as strength.[254] Since *confianza* (interdependence and trust) is an important value held by Hispanic families, both nuclear and extended, several authors have discussed the necessity of treating the family as a unit rather than treating members individually.[255] Among specific Hispanic cultures, familial relationship patterns differ. "For example, the relationship between mother and son is exceptionally close and dependent among Mexicans and Cubans. And Peruvians and Bolivians experience a stronger commitment to parents and siblings than to their spouses and children."[256] Maternal and sibling relationships are also very important in Puerto Rican families.[257] Traditional chemical dependency treatment programs have been known to stress getting into treatment for one's self, but other approaches might be needed with Hispanics clients.

Hispanic families often prefer to solve problems within their own boundaries. For many families this is culturally normative and adaptive,[258] but is sometimes misconstrued by professionals as dysfunctional. As with Native Americans, "concepts like assertiveness, detachment, and independence, commonly effective tools when working with many alcoholics and their families, will rarely, if ever, be understood, much less accepted, by Hispanic clients, because those concepts are seen as a direct threat to the family."[259]

The shame (*verguenza*) that results from drug use may isolate Hispanic alcoholics and addicts (particularly women) from their families. Melus recommends appealing to Hispanics to enter treatment because family unity is threatened,[260] and Gilbert recommends appealing to chemically dependent Hispanic mothers based on improving the lives of their children.[261]

McQuade discusses the extremes of female and male behavior among Hispanics; at one end of the continuum is the passive woman and at the other end is the authoritarian man.[262] The man may wish to be thought of as the *parrandero* (carefree reveler), but it is disgraceful to be the *borrachero* (staggering drunk).[263] Many men do not want to seek help publicly, and many women do not dare to do so.[264] Public disclosure of personal problems is generally unacceptable for Hispanic men and can result in feelings of emasculation or powerlessness.[265] Melus says that "attitudes and perceptions must be changed in the community to make treatment and prevention of alcoholism more successful."[266]

Differences in gender norms or the "double drinking standard"[267] in Hispanic cultures also contribute to a lack of recognition of substance abuse problems. Heavy drinking may be an acceptable practice among men, and it may even be justified as part of *machismo*. However, there is confusion about the meaning of this term. Machismo has been used to describe male virility, but it has also been defined as honor, respect, and fulfilling family obligations.[268] There is a notion that if a man "works hard and is a good family provider one then has the 'right' to drink without criticism from others."[269] As a result, men may excuse their heavy drinking and women may also deny that men drink excessively. Women may view their partner's substance abuse as a behavior to be tolerated rather than changed.[270] Anecdotal evidence indicates that Hispanic women tend to be the victims of alcohol-related problems as the result of men's heavy drinking.[271]

Gordon, however, denies any empirical support for the "widely accepted popular belief that Hispanic drinking is characterized by macho, aggressive drinking (more so than in other ethnic groups)."[272] Neff and his colleagues actually developed a scale to measure machismo and used it with a probability sample of 481 men in San Antonio, Texas.[273] While Mexican Americans and blacks had higher scores than Anglos, multivariate analysis failed to show that the heavier drinking reported by Mexican American than Anglo or black males was due to machismo.

The cultural mandate for Hispanic women is that they should avoid any appearance of intoxication or other drug-related problems. Like women in general (see Chapter 15), Hispanic women who are substance abusers reportedly face more stigmatization and rejection than their male counterparts.[274] A study of Anglo and Chicano (Mexican-American) narcotics addicts demonstrated that the women, particularly the Chicanas, were more likely to be living with an addicted partner and that the men, particularly the Chicanos, were less likely to reside with an addicted partner.[275]

While Hispanic-American women have relatively low rates of alcoholism, the needs of those who do develop chemical dependency problems should not be obscured. Comas-Díaz speculates that "Hispanic women cope with specific stresses that may lead to drinking. Such stresses include alcoholic significant others, cultural values discouraging direct expression of assertiveness and aggressiveness, a subordinated role in their society, [heading a] single household, plus the pressure of migration and acculturation."[276] The strongly held belief among many Hispanics that women should not drink much or exhibit substance abuse problems may prompt families to deny even the possibility of chemical abuse among their female members (see also Chapter 5 regarding denial). Anglin and his colleagues refer to Chicana narcotic addicts as "more deviant" than their Anglo counterparts and as individuals marginal to both the Chicano community and the larger society.[277] They reported that although the Chicanas entered addiction later than the Anglo women and used fewer drugs and engaged in less prostitution, they experienced more unemployment and more arrests (for all types of crimes).

Chemical Dependency Services for Hispanic Americans

Hispanic Americans are reported to under-utilize health and mental health services.[278] While the same has apparently been assumed about alcoholism services, Gilbert and Cervantes's analysis indicates that Mexican Americans utilize alcoholism services at rates higher than their representation in the population, but that more of their admissions to treatment are involuntary than is the case for the general population.[279] Data on utilization of state-supported treatment facilities in 1987 indicate that Hispanics constituted 5.5 percent of clients in alcoholism treatment and 9.8 percent of clients in drug treatment.[280] Compared with their representation in the population (now 9 percent and growing), these figures indicate that Hispanics are underrepresented in alcoholism treatment and slightly overrepresented in drug treatment. However, given the variation in alcoholism rates and drug use among Hispanic groups, it is difficult to tell how well these figures actually represent those in need of treatment.

There were a reported 602 specialized chemical dependency treatment programs for Hispanics in 1984 representing about 9 percent of all treatment programs in the United States,[281] but there is no particular definition of what constitutes a culturally specific or culturally sensitive treatment program. Having bilingual staff is important but may be insufficient to address competently cultural aspects of chemical dependency.

Quinones and Doyle describe efforts to develop a culturally relevant therapeutic community (TC) and outpatient treatment program for drug addicts in Newark, New Jersey, called CURA. The staff is Hispanic, and the program incorporates cultural values of *dignidad* (dignity), *respeto* (respect), and *ma-*

chismo rather than traditional TC methods of punishment (such as haircuts and wearing signs).[282] There is a need to educate more Hispanics to work in the chemical dependency field and to develop more culturally appropriate programs.[283]

Other recommendations for making services more useful to Hispanics are to target specific age groups and to use interventions appropriate to each of the groups that comprise the Hispanic population.[284] Advice about how to use social services[285] and client advocacy[286] may also increase service utilization. Concrete services, such as transportation to appointments, have also been suggested and can be especially important for low-income individuals from all ethnic groups.[287]

Since cultural norms regarding women's alcohol and drug use differ from men's, women are likely to require some different treatment strategies. Melus has recommended "more sensitive and cautious" treatment approaches as a result of the physical and verbal abuse that Hispanic women may incur from their families.[288] Comas-Díaz describes a group treatment approach with Puerto Rican women who are alcoholics based on literature which suggests that Hispanic women may feel isolated and alienated and on literature which recommends women's only groups as a forum for expressing anger and other feelings that cannot be vented directly toward family members.[289] However, she notes that the women enrolled in the group did not attend sessions regularly and had difficulty maintaining abstinence.

Aguilar and her colleagues suggest psychoeducational groups as a promising intervention strategy with Hispanics, particularly women, to address chemical dependency and codependency.[290] The groups they describe are for adult family members and are open to men and women, making them less suspect than women's-only groups, which men may perceive as threats to family cohesion. Education, group discussion, experiental exercises, and "homework" are used to educate members about chemical dependency. The majority of participants have been women. The program described by Comas-Díaz for Puerto Rican women also appears to be psychoeducational in nature since it incorporates education about alcoholism along with group psychotherapy.[291]

Many Hispanics are Catholic, and often the first person outside the family to whom they turn for help with a problem is a priest or nun. The clergy's support of chemical dependency treatment can facilitate recovery as can holding self-help group meetings at churches. The spiritual aspects of recovery for Hispanic substance abusers and their family members must also be addressed. Hispanic women are encouraged to emulate the Virgin Mary through self-sacrifice and acceptance of suffering, but this can cause one's own well-being to suffer. With careful reframing, Mary can be discussed in a more feminist light that emphasizes her strengths and independent characteristics.[292] Membership in fundamentalist churches has grown in Hispanic communities, and some of these churches have developed their own alcohol recovery programs.[293]

Hispanics may consult indigenous folk helpers such as *curanderos* and *curanderas* for help with chemical dependency problems, and this should not be summarily dismissed by professionals. The extent to which folk healers are used in recovery is not known,[294] but there are some indications that they are consulted frequently about such problems.[295] "Other indigenous Hispanic recovery models are based on spiritual systems that date back to the Native American and African roots of many of the Latin American subcultures. These traditions incorporate a long cultural history of attempting to help alcoholics through a combination of herbal medicine, enlisting the aid of spirits, and faith healing."[296] One treatment, *haba de San Ignacio,* is prepared from a seed and results in nausea and vomiting if taken with alcohol.[297]

Little has been written about self-help groups with respect to Hispanic populations. There are reportedly several hundred AA groups conducted in Spanish in the United States.[298] "As Hoffman noted, it is unclear whether transcultural adaptation of A.A. involves simple translation of A.A. doctrine or actual changes in content and emphasis of the A.A. program itself."[299] Aguilar and her colleagues recommend preparation to participate in groups such as Alcoholics Anonymous and Al-Anon, particularly when there are few other Hispanic members.[300] One of their suggestions is to describe "working the steps" of these programs as taking on responsibilities and as a means of gaining respect for one's self and from others.

Although detailed descriptions of culturally relevant treatment programs are few in the literature, there is some helpful information about culturally relevant prevention approaches. An important aspect of prevention for many Hispanics is *la comunidad* (community), since "Hispanics tend to live together, work together, and spend free time together."[301] Celebrations or fiestas are important in many Hispanic communities, but the use of alcohol during these occasions is common. McQuade describes fiestas as "compensation for life's suffering."[302] Fiestas without the use of alcohol are being incorporated into the prevention and treatment of alcoholism among Hispanics.[303]

Contact with gatekeepers in ethnic, social, civic, religious, neighborhood, and church organizations, as well as PTAs and other community groups, is recommended if prevention efforts are to be successful in Hispanic-American communities.[304] Gordon emphasizes community health centers or clinics as an important point of identification of substance abuse problems, especially for women and children, although in many cases the medical personnel either do not have the time or do not take the time to intervene.[305] These suggestions are similar for most communities. The key is in developing relationships with those in the target communities of interest and learning about the cultural norms that guide their work. Unfortunately, lack of coordination of community services often presents an obstacle in intervening in substance abuse problems.[306] Mutual education in which professionals learn about the community from its leaders and residents and, in turn, educate community leaders and groups about the dynamics of chemical abuse are necessary steps in initiating all types of chemical dependency services.[307]

The need for culturally appropriate prevention, education, and treatment in both English and Spanish has been stressed; for those whose first language is Spanish, their "native tongue is needed to express the deepest feelings and longings endemic to the recovery process."[308] With regard to prevention among men, the idea of the right to drink may require emphasis on responsible drinking.[309] One California prevention program featured the family with the mother as the central figure, as it often is in Hispanic family life. Use of the Spanish language media (newspapers, magazines, TV, etc.), developing community newsletters, and designing "foto-novelas" to prevent alcohol and drug abuse and to promote recovery are other suggestions.

In reaching out to children of alcoholics, one community health center in Washington, DC, has used *tardes infantil* (afternoons for children) to educate them about alcohol abuse.[310] Painting, movies, and dramatizations are used to help the children express their feelings about family issues; local theater groups have assisted with these activities. The Los Niños program in San Antonio, Texas, utilizes various prevention approaches with children including puppets.[311] An *abuelita* (grandmother) puppet is a central figure in this approach, because grandmothers are very important in Mexican-American life. Given the growth of the Hispanic population in the United States, it is likely that considerably more attention will be devoted to their integration into American society, including addressing problems associated with alcohol and drug use.

ASIAN AMERICANS

According to Kitano there are more than 20 Asian nationalities.[312] The largest groups of Asians in the United States are of Chinese and Filipino origin, but there are also Japa-nese, Asian Indians, Koreans, Vietnamese, and those of many other Asian nationalities.[313] Pacific Islanders are often included as part of the Asian population, but many take exception to placing so many diverse groups under a single classification. Asian Americans and Pacific Islanders constitute nearly 3 percent of the total U.S. population and many reside in Hawaii and on the Pacific Coast.[314]

Alcohol has been used for centuries in the Far East. Stoil traced references to *sake*, Japan's traditional alcoholic drink, to the fifth century; to wine in the Chinese literature of the eighth century; and to social drinking in the classical literature of Vietnam and the Korea.[315] There are few references to problematic use of alcohol in most Asian countries.[316] Singer's description of drinking in Hong Kong gives clues to possible explanations for the low prevalence of alcohol-related problems:

> The Chinese in Hong Kong traditionally drink at meals and banquets and not without food. Drinking is incidental to eating and drinking-centered institutions [e.g., bars] and groups are absent. The main aims of drinking are to promote conviviality and improve health. Moderate drinking is sanctioned on defined occasions, drunkenness especially in public strongly disapproved.[317]

Singer notes that while alcoholism may not be common among the Chinese people, it may be more prevalent than thought, with alcoholic psychosis accounting for an increasing proportion of first admissions to psychiatric hospitals in Hong Kong.[318] In China and some other Asian countries, the more significant problem has been narcotic addiction as a result of opium's availability.[319]

Differences in the cultural and social backgrounds of Asian groups reportedly affect attitudes toward alcohol use. The Moslem background of Indonesians and Malaysians prohibits drinking; the Confucianist and Taoist backgrounds of the Chinese emphasize that moderation (the "golden mean") be practiced in all aspects of life, including the use of alcohol; Buddhist, Shintoi, and Chinese philosophies influence the Japanese, but today's Japanese drinking practices reflect a more permissive, business-oriented, urban style; Filipinos' drinking has been influenced by Moslem, Spanish, American, and Japanese colonists.[320]

Hsu wrote that the Chinese prefer opium to other types of drugs because it promotes withdrawal or retreatist behavior and is more consistent with the concept of harmony with the environment (an important component of Taoism); he also wrote that Americans are attracted to drugs like marijuana and alcohol that disinhibit behavior and result in acting out and conflict with the environment, which is more typical of Americans' self-centered, aggressive nature.[321] Although everyone will not agree with Hsu's depiction, Singer adds that the Chinese abhor loss of self control and value intellectual control.[322] However, Singer and Hsu also note that even when intoxicated, Asians do not tend to act out (such as becoming violent or engaging in behavior that might prompt an arrest). This suggests the strong influence of cultural mores on behavior even when consuming alcohol.[323] Other sociocultural factors offered as possible explanations for narcotics use in China are the high degree of social disorganization typified by political upheaval, modernization, illiteracy, poverty, and poor health care, with opium rather than alcohol offering the cheapest, most readily available means of escape over the years.[324] We turn now to a consideration of alcohol and other drug use among Asian Americans.

Alcohol and Drug Use Among Asian Americans

Like Asians, Asian Americans apparently have relatively low levels of alcohol use, other drug use, and substance abuse problems compared to the general U.S. population, but (1) few epidemiological studies of alcohol and other drug use have included Asian Americans, (2) the use of probability samples in identifying substance use and abuse among Asians has been limited, and (3) few studies have identified Asian Americans by subgroup.[325] These observations led Matsushima

and his colleagues to suggest that it may be the *perception* rather than the *reality* that Asians Americans have few alcohol problems,[326] and Sue and his colleagues refer to alcoholism as "a problem of growing concern among Asian-Americans."[327] The 1977 Health Interview Survey (a household survey conducted by the National Center for Health Statistics) did show relatively low alcohol use in the 256 Asian/Pacific-American subjects who participated.[328] While this sample is small, 32 percent reported never drinking alcohol, 52 percent drank occasionally, 9 percent drank once or twice a week, and 8 percent drank three or more times a week. Klatsky and his colleagues studied records of nearly 60,000 individuals who had routine health examinations from 1978 to 1980 in Oakland, California, and found that both oriental men and oriental women reported much less drinking than those of other ethnic groups.[329] The study included 1,960 Chinese, 1,151 Filipinos, 702 Japanese, and 364 members of other oriental groups. In each of the ethnic groups they studied, men drank more than women, but the gender differences were least pronounced in whites and blacks, and, in ascending order, were more pronounced in Filipinos, Japanese, Latinos, and Chinese.

Another study, reported by Kitano and Chi, compared 298 Chinese, 295 Japanese, 280 Koreans, and 230 Filipinos from the Los Angeles area and found variation between the groups.[330] Most subjects were identified using Asian surnames from telephone directories, but Filipinos, who often have names similar to Hispanics, were identified through community agencies and snowball sampling techniques. Of men in the study, Koreans were most likely to be abstainers (46 percent), while about one-third of men in the other ethnic groups abstained (see Table 11.2). Chinese men were the most likely to be moderate drinkers (55 percent) and Korean men the least likely to fall in this category (28 percent), while slightly more than one-third of Japanese and Filipino men drank moderately. The Chinese men were least likely to be heavy drinkers (14 percent), while reports for Japanese and Filipino men were both 29 percent and for Korean men, 26 percent. The women in the study were substantially more likely than men to be abstainers in every ethnic group except the Japanese, where the proportion of male and female abstainers was nearly identical at about 33 percent. Japanese women were the least likely to abstain. The highest proportions of female abstainers were among the Koreans (82 percent) and the Filipinos (80 percent), while 69 percent of Chinese women abstained. Moderate drinking among the women was lowest among Filipinos (16 percent), followed by Koreans (18 percent), Chinese (31 percent), and Japanese (55 percent). Japanese women had the highest proportion of heavy drinkers (12 percent), while rates for all the other groups were lower (4 percent of the Filipino, 1 percent of the Korean, and none of the Chinese women). Despite differences in drinking patterns among the groups, few instances of alcohol-related problems were reported. Those most likely to drink were men under age 45 of higher socioeconomic status who had permissive attitudes toward alcohol use.

Ahern surveyed the literature on alcohol use among ethnic groups in Hawaii.[331] There are some differences in estimates, but, in general, Caucasians and Native Hawaiians' use is highest followed by the Japanese; Filipinos and Chinese drink the least. A 1984 study of 2,503 households in Hawaii presents a somewhat different picture.[332] The Japanese reported the highest rate of abstention (58.5 percent), followed by Filipinos (53.0 percent), Native Hawaiians (40.7 percent), and Caucasians (31.0 percent). Conversely, the highest percentage of heavy drinkers were Caucasians (13.6 percent), followed by Native Hawaiians (11.0 percent), Filipinos (6.7 percent), and Japanese (5.2 percent). Caucasians also reported the highest rates of lifetime prevalence of drug use followed by Native Hawaiians with fewer Japanese and Filipinos reporting drug use.

In a study of 141 patients 50 years and older receiving services through the Chinese-American Service League in Chicago, the number who abstained from alcohol decreased with age (as compared with the gen-

TABLE 11.2 Alcohol Consumption Patterns by Sex of Chinese, Japanese, Koreans, and Filipinos in Los Angeles (in percent)

QFV [1]	Chinese	Japanese	Korean	Filipino
Male				
Abstainer	31.2	32.8	45.8	34.5
Moderate	54.6	38.3	28.3	36.6
Heavy	14.2	28.9	25.8	29.0
	N-(218)	(235)	(155)	(145)
Female				
Abstainer	68.8	33.3	81.6	80.0
Moderate	31.3	55.0	17.6	16.5
Heavy	0	11.7	.8	3.5
	N-(80)	(60)	(125)	(85)
Total				
Abstainer	41.3	32.9	61.8	51.3
Moderate	48.3	41.7	23.6	29.1
Heavy	10.4	25.4	14.6	19.6
	N-(298)	(295)	(280)	(230)

1. Quantity, frequency, and variability of alcohol consumption.

Source: Harry H.L. Kitano and Iris Chi, "Asian Americans and Alcohol: The Chinese, Japanese, Koreans, and Filipinos in Los Angeles," in National Institute on Alcohol Abuse and Alcoholism, *Alcohol Use Among U.S. Ethnic Minorities*, DHHS Publication No. (ADM) 89-1435 (Rockville, MD: U.S. Department of Health and Human Services, September 1985), p. 376.

eral population in which abstinence increases with age).[333] The authors suggest that some Chinese begin drinking later in life because it is viewed as acceptable for health reasons. (Chinese herb medicines may contain substantial amounts of alcohol.)[334] However, health reasons were also cited as reasons for abstaining from alcohol.

In terms of problem indicators, data from the National Center for Health Statistics from 1979 to 1980 show that Chinese Americans have much lower age-adjusted death rates from cirrhosis than do whites or African Americans, 1.2, 4.7, and 10.5 per 100,000 members of the population, respectively.[335] While arrests rates of Japanese and Chinese Americans are lower than those for other groups, Kitano noted that a substantial portion of arrests among these ethnic groups were alcohol related.[336]

Data on drug use among Asian Americans are limited, but a study of 1,337 Asian Americans who received drug abuse treatment indicated that the primary drug of abuse was heroin (similar to the whites in the study) but that twice as many whites as Asians received methadone maintenance.[337] The Asians had considerably more primary and secondary barbiturate abuse, but the whites had more secondary use of all other drugs.

Studies are generally consistent in their reports that Asian-American youth drink and use other drugs less frequently than other youth. While Asian youth are more likely to abstain, some findings indicate that those who drink consume more than their counterparts of other ethnic backgrounds.[338]

Cultural and Genetic Influences in Substance Use Among Asian Americans

Discussions of Asian American drinking and drug use have largely been concerned with explaining why the incidence of chemcal abuse is lower than among other population groups. Genetic and sociocultural explanations have both received attention. There is evidence on both sides, with many more questions to be answered. We begin by discussing sociocultural factors, then genetic factors,

and summarizing with a synthesis of evidence on these perspectives.

Sociocultural Influences. In addition to the various philosophical and religious traditions that influence Asian Americans (Confucianist, Taoist, Moslem, and so forth), acculturation may also play a part in Asian American drinking.[339] Phin and Phillips note that "peripheral studies of Chinese who have sought treatment for narcotic abuse and Japanese who have sought treatment for barbiturate abuse have linked abuse to problems with acculturation."[340] In 1968 Wang predicted that alcoholism among Chinese Americans would increase as they move "from the old pattern of domination by father and husband to the new pattern of the increasing power for mother and wife, and from the Chinese pattern of loyalty to personal and familial authority figures, to the American pattern of allegiance to impersonal and abstract ideals."[341] Matsushima and his colleagues also believe that as with other immigrant groups facing the pressures of acculturation, *"an increase in alcohol consumption, alcohol abuse and alcoholism is something to be expected rather than to be speculated about."*[342] The Japanese-American and Chinese-American students studied by Sue and his colleagues at the University of Washington in Seattle drank less than their Caucasian-American counterparts, but greater acculturation (as measured by less fluency in Japanese or Chinese and a greater number of generations of family that had resided in the United States) was related to increased alcohol consumption.[343] The researchers reported that the Asian-American students had more negative attitudes toward alcohol, as did their parents, but they were less likely than Caucasian students to report that alcohol harms the body.

However, analyses by Clark and Hesselbrock of data from a joint U.S. and Japanese research endeavor indicate that the effects of acculturation are not clear.[344] For example, they found that Japanese men in Japan consumed more alcohol and had more alcohol-related problems than did Japanese Americans residing in California and Hawaii and Caucasians residing in California. Sue recently concluded that among both Asians in Asia and in America, frequency and amount of drinking are on the rise.[345] Further information confounding interpretation of the acculturation explanation comes from Lubben and his colleagues.[346] They found only partial support for acculturation as a current explanation of drinking practices among Filipino-American men and women. Their nonprobability sample of 230 Filipinos may not be representative of the population (for example, 90 percent reported having at least some college education and men reported attending church somewhat more often than women). Male drinking was interpreted to be influenced more by Western practices and female drinking by traditional Asian practices, giving support to an acculturation explanation for men but not for women. The best predictor of women's drinking was church attendance (more frequent attendance was associated with less drinking); education was also important (greater education was associated with more drinking). Women who were younger and who were Catholic drank more, but age and religion were less important predictors of their drinking than church attendance and education. Predictors of male drinking were different than for the females. For men, the most important predictors of increased drinking were lower income and having friends who drank, followed by less frequent church attendance. Neither age, education, nor Catholicism were significant for men but were for women. In addition to acculturation, gender role explanations are likely to account for a substantial amount of the variance in men's and women's drinking.

Other cultural factors also reportedly affect drinking and drug use and identification of substance abuse problems. Asians attach considerable shame to these problems and families generally try to conceal them. For example, Coleman reported that Asian-American "families had a tendency to be permissive about allowing junkies to be high or to crash at home," apparently to prevent embarrassment.[347] The desire to "save face" and to show respect to family members, particularly elders, may also result in concealing a problem until it escalates.

Genetic Influences. Evidence that Asians may metabolize alcohol more rapidly than whites, led to speculation about the role of the flushing response (also called the flushing reflex or reaction) in inhibiting alcohol use among this population.[348] "This physiological reaction is characterized by facial flushing, which is often accompanied by headaches, dizziness, rapid heart rate, itching, or other symptoms of discomfort."[349] Both Stoil and Sue discuss the scientific literature on the flushing response beginning with Wolff's work in 1972.[350] Shortly after, Goedde and colleagues found that the Japanese subjects they studied tended to lack an enzyme called aldehyde dehydrogenase (ALDH) 1, but they had ALDH 2, while nearly all Japanese alcoholics and all the German subjects studied had both ALDH 1 and 2; additional research also suggests that flushing may help protect against drinking.[351] As described by Stoil, a byproduct of alcohol metabolism, acetaldehyde, is a highly toxic substance. If not converted into a nontoxic form, it causes the discomfort associated with the flushing response (which has been likened to an Antabuse reaction). Without ALDH 1, the body does not dispose of acetaldehyde quickly enough to prevent flushing.

The flushing response may help protect against alcohol abuse and alcoholism, but apparently it does not fully explain why Asians have a lower rate of alcoholism. Kitano concluded that "the results of research comparing Asians with whites generally support the hypothesis that there are racial differences in toxic responses to alcohol. However, it should be noted that not all Asians exhibit the flushing response and that there may not necessarily be a cause-effect relationship between the toxic response, the consumption of alcohol, and problem behavior."[352] Towle, for example, reported that about three quarters of the Japanese Americans he studied who flushed could continue to drink after the onset of this response.[353] Johnson's extensive study of the subject indicates that "contrary to popular beliefs, flushing is only marginally related to reduced alcohol use."[354] John Ewing has noted that contemporary social, cultural, and psychological factors may also limit the ability of the flushing response to continue to act as a protective factor.[355] While groups such as Eskimos and Native Americans have some Asian ancestry, a substantial number have serious alcohol problems, also failing to support flushing as a sufficient, protective factor.[356]

Sue and his colleagues suggest that while the flushing response alone may be insufficient to prevent excessive drinking, interaction effects may be present in which cultural prohibitions against drunkenness arise as a result of adverse physiological responses to alcohol consumption, and cultural taboos on drinking may cause individuals to report negative physical consequences from drinking.[357] In summary, cultural and genetic influences may have reciprocal effects, and it is difficult to separate the effects of one set of these factors from the other in explaining chemical use by Asians and Asian Americans.

Substance Abuse Services for Asian Americans

The lack of special chemical dependency services for Asian Americans is likely related to two factors: Asians comprise only a small percentage of the U.S. population, and they apparently have a low incidence of chemical dependency problems. Asians' preference for not attracting attention to themselves may also inhibit the development of special services to meet their needs.[358] Asian Americans reportedly underutilize chemical dependency treatment services.[359] Just 0.2 percent of those admitted to state-sponsored alcohol treatment programs in 1987 were of Asian or Pacific Island heritage.[360] Kitano reported that Asian Americans say that they would prefer to receive services from an ethnic agency, but specialized services for problems may not

be available, causing them to turn to religious leaders, doctors, or family and friends for help.[361]

Underutilization of substance abuse treatment services by Asian Americans has been blamed on inaccessibility and cultural values.[362] Inaccessibility may be due to language barriers, insensitivity to Asian cultures, Asians' distrust of other cultures, and limited outreach to Asian Americans.[363] Cultural factors that may inhibit treatment use are lack of identification of substance abuse as a problem, lack of familiarity with social service agencies, pride in handling one's problems alone, preference for handling problems within the family or one's immediate community, and the stigma associated with drinking problems that would bring shame on one's self and on one's family.[364] To improve treatment and prevention, Matsushima and his colleagues recommend extensive outreach efforts, education about substance abuse, and bilingual and bicultural services.[365]

A statewide survey in Hawaii attempted to identify barriers to seeking professional help among Caucasians, Native Hawaiians, Japanese, and Filipinos.[366] "Personal embarrassment" was rated slightly higher by Japanese than Native Hawaiians or Filipinos and was rated lowest by Caucasians, but most individuals said they would not be embarrassed to seek treatment. Likewise, among all ethnic groups, most said that they would not "be ashamed or embarrassed if my family or friends knew." However, of all the items on the list, personal and family embarrassment were identified as the most substantial, potential barriers to seeking treatment. More Filipinos than Japanese and Native Hawaiians did not know where to go for help, while Caucasians were most likely to report knowing where to seek assistance.

Coleman indicated that despite family interconnectedness, therapists tend to treat Asian-American family members separately from addicts in order to "sever unhealthy supports."[367] The suggestions that Phin and Phillip describe for treating Asian-American drug abusers include support of traditional values and cultural identification; use of Asian-American staff; emphasis on commonalties among Asian groups rather than on unique cultural factors; involvement with the larger Asian community; family therapy; and for women, consciousness raising and identity building.[368] Little has been written on self-help groups with Asians. Some groups in the United States conduct their meetings in Japanese, and there is a version of Alcoholics Anonymous in Japan called *Danshukai*.[369]

Some general suggestions from the literature on the help-seeking behavior of Asian Americans are also in order.[370] The multiservice model, in which agencies locate together, or a single agency offers multiple services, may make services more appealing. Asian Americans who are hesitant to seek mental health services may be more willing to go to an agency which also offers other social services. As is true for all ethnic and cultural groups, sanction from respected members of the ethnic community is useful in encouraging service utilization. Agencies may garner support by including board members who are representative of the Asian-American groups to be served and by gaining the backing of Asian-American organizations and churches.

Chemical dependency professionals can also make individual attempts to better serve Asian-American clients. For example, those who are aware of values such as filial piety (respect of children for their parents) will likely be more effective in helping clients develop solutions to problems that are consistent with their culture. Likewise, social service providers can better assist clients if they understand how Asian Americans view problems. The most frequent explanations of personal or behavioral problems are organic. Holistic medicine views the mind and body as functioning together, not separately, as is often the case in Western cultures. A Westerner may consider a particular problem as purely psychological, while those from Asian and Pacific cultures may view the problem as having a biological basis, thus relieving the individual and family of personal blame. Kitano's study of mental illness among Japanese and Japanese Americans found that fam-

ilies tended to see these problems as moral issues, such as laziness, indicating the need for education about these problems and for preparing families to utilize services.[371]

Like many Native Americans, Asian Americans may have great hesitation about self-disclosure, because they have been taught to be stoic and endure problems without complaining. Suggestions for making Asian and Asian-American clients feel more comfortable include taking a personal approach, since they may construe professional demeanor as disinterest. Other suggestions are to speak to the client in a quiet, respectful tone of voice and to use indirect rather than direct questions. Older clients should be shown special respect. Treatment providers should also be aware that Asian-American clients may say what they think the professional would like to hear as a sign of respect.

JEWS AND CHEMICAL DEPENDENCY

Cultural factors associated with low rates of alcohol problems among Jews were noted by Immanuel Kant two hundred years ago.[372] Keller notes that the Bible contains a number of accounts of Jewish drinking and drunkenness, but he suggests three reasons why alcoholism did not become a problem for the Jews: (1) they denounced pagan gods who had been worshipped with orgiastic drinking, (2) they developed a religious culture with a focus on the Torah and with worship and education taking place at synagogues, and (3) they confined drinking to rituals practiced at the synagogue and at home.[373] Weiss calls Judaism "permissive in matters concerning alcohol use."[374] In Israel, alcohol is readily available and its use in rituals remains common. But in recent years, the country's concerns about alcoholism have begun to mount.[375] The 1980s marked the first time that Israel had enough alcoholics to be included in international rankings on rates of alcoholism.[376] Two percent of the Israeli adult population is reportedly alcoholic.[377] Drinking and alcohol-related problems have been blamed on "adoption of foreign norms" that encourage drinking "for pleasure and fun."[378] Other explanations concern the adjustment problems of Holocaust survivors and the difficulties that immigrants have experienced earning a living and finding a place in the society.[379]

The literature on alcohol use, alcohol problems, and prevention and treatment efforts in Israel is growing rapidly.[380] Concern about the need to prevent excessive drinking in Israel has resulted in the establishment of organizations such as the Israeli Department of Prevention and Treatment of Alcoholism and the Israeli Society for the Prevention of Alcoholism.[381] Israel's official state policy is that alcoholism is a disease, and the number of treatment centers in the country has grown.[382] But Jews live in many places besides Israel. We now turn our attention to Jews in the United States.

Extent of Alcohol and Other Drug Use Among Jewish Americans

A major U.S. study published in 1968 reported that 92 percent of Jews, a greater proportion than any other major religious group, drank alcohol.[383] A 1984 study also shows that a large percentage of Jews drink alcohol.[384] But despite high rates of drinkers, Jews continue to be known for their low rates of alcoholism.[385] Glatt noted that it is curious that Jews, who have been exposed to many strains and stressors and who exhibit at least as much neuroticism as the rest of the population, tend not to develop alcohol problems.[386] In contrast, he mentioned some anecdotal reports of overrepresentation of Jews among drug abusers and noted that, unlike alcohol, there were no proscriptions against drug use in the Jewish culture.[387] A more recent article in the *Jewish Exponent* indicated an acceptance of medication use among Jews and "heavy use . . . of diet pills, tranquilizers and mood-altering drugs."[388] Teller noted information in *Psychiatric News* indicating significant numbers of Jewish alcoholics and addicts and the possibility of cross-addiction among this group.[389]

There are a few empirical investigations of drug use among Jewish college students. One study, published in 1980, is based on a sample of 278 undergraduate psychology students, about equally divided between men and women, 84 of whom were Jewish.[390] The researchers found support for earlier studies that indicated that Jews, rather than Catholics or Protestants, and that men, rather than women, use marijuana more frequently, but length of marijuana use was not related to religious affiliation or gender. Among the males, Jews used marijuana an average of 5.77 times per month, compared with 2.50 for Catholics, and 0.91 for Protestants; among females, use was 1.20 for Jews compared with 1.71 for Catholics, and 0.97 for Protestants. Students who rated highest on measures of creativity, adventuresomeness, and some aspects of novelty seeking used marijuana more frequently. Although not statistically significant, there was a trend for more frequent marijuana users to be less authoritarian. The authors attributed their findings about marijuana use to explanations that "traditionally in our society, adventuresomeness has been encouraged in the male and discouraged in the female, and Jews repeatedly have been found to be less authoritarian than Catholics or Protestants."[391]

Another survey, using data collected in 1980, based on 704 male students and staff ages 18 to 25 at the University of California at San Diego, 110 of whom were Jewish and the remainder Christian (i.e., Catholic or Protestant), indicated no differences in average quantity and frequency of alcohol consumption.[392] The Christian men did report more heavy drinking and more drinking problems and had more first-degree relatives and some second-degree relatives with histories of alcoholism. The authors say these findings support descriptions of Jews as nonproblem drinkers. The same study found no statistically significant differences in lifetime drug use or related problems and no substantial pattern of differences in drug use between the two groups. Although random sampling was used and there was a 70 percent response rate, the relatively small number of Jews and the fact that all subjects were males at a college limits the study's generalizability.

While Jews apparently have low rates of alcoholism, Flasher and Maisto emphasize that being Jewish does not provide total immunity from alcoholism or other drug abuse, and they question whether rates of alcoholism among Jews are really so low.[393] In 1958 Snyder found that Jews may underreport their drinking, perhaps due to the need to maintain their image as sober people,[394] although in 1980 researchers studying Jewish alcoholics indicated that they had no problem in identifying subjects.[395] Given the current state of research on Jews, it is not possible to report with confidence the extent of their substance abuse or whether substance abuse has increased among this group.[396]

Explanations of Low Rates of Alcoholism Among Jewish Americans

Jews reportedly have much lower rates of alcoholism than many other religious groups, but Jews are also a cultural group. Many individuals have a strong Jewish identity but do not participate in Judaism on a religious level.[397] The reportedly lower rates of alcoholism among those who identify themselves as Jewish (in the religious sense, the cultural sense, or both), combined with information that many Jews use alcohol, has resulted in a good deal of attention paid to what might be viewed as these contradictory circumstances. Various authors have noted cultural norms that suggest that drunkenness is a behavior of Gentiles (Christians or other non-Jews), not Jews, and that drunkenness, especially among Jewish women, is strongly condemned.[398] Disapproval of drunkenness along with factors such as the well-defined role of alcohol in religious ceremonies and holidays[399] and "the importance of moderation in all life activities"[400] may provide Jews with a degree of insularity from alcoholism.

Early, notable studies of differences in drinking between Jewish Americans and other groups were conducted by Glad[401] and by Snyder.[402] Glad reviewed the state of knowledge at the time and found six potential

explanations for these differences. First were biological determinants. Despite interest in this topic,[403] Glad discounted this explanation, because Jews do not constitute a separate race. In his own research, Glad defined Jews as those who had a "Jewish self-consciousness." A second explanation Glad encountered was that of "group protection"—the idea that Jews are sober because this behavior protects them from further endangerment and further condemnation by others, a position espoused by Immanuel Kant in the 1700s.[404] This is also referred to as the "in-group, out-group factor." The third hypothesis Glad encountered was religious sanctions against alcohol use, often expressed in the "drunkenness is not Jewish" idea. The fourth hypothesis he discerned was that drinking among Jews was ritualized or sacred. Bales also suggested this explanation in his frequently cited article on cultural factors affecting drinking.[405] Snyder emphasized these third and fourth points as well as the importance of adherence to Jewish religious orthodoxy in encouraging sobriety. In Snyder's words, "through the ceremonial use of beverage alcohol religious Jews learn how to drink in a controlled manner; but through constant reference to the hedonism of outsiders, in association with a broader pattern of religious and ethnocentric ideas and sentiments, Jews also learn how not to drink."[406] A fifth hypothesis Glad considered concerned family solidarity, the idea that a strong and secure family life among Jews provided insulation from alcoholism. Many years earlier, Emile Durkheim, in his classic work on suicide, described the protection that social solidarity offers against deviant behavior.[407] The final hypothesis Glad outlined was that a preference for wine, rather than distilled spirits, resulted in less inebriety among Jews.

Glad's empirical investigation concerned 49 male adolescents from each of three groups: American Jews, American Irish-Catholics, and a "control group" of third-generation Americans of central and north European descent. He did not find support for the group protection hypothesis, and he found evidence about familial (parental) influences on drinking inconclusive. He did find that Jewish adolescents drank in a more matter-of-fact manner, but contrary to expectations, Jewish adolescents were more likely to associate drinking with independence and maturity. Jews did prefer wine, but he thought this evidence insufficient to provide an explanation for lower rates of inebriety. Like Bales and Snyder, Glad concluded "that the rates of inebriety in the adult Jewish and Irish cultures in America are explainable in terms of (a) the Jewish tendency to drink for socially and symbolically instrumental results, and (b) the Irish tendency to use alcohol for personally and socially affective consequences."[408]

Snyder's comparison of Jewish subgroups found the lowest to highest frequency of intoxication in the following order: Orthodox, Conservative, Reform, and secular Jews.[409] (Later work by Snyder and his colleagues in Israel also indicates that the more Orthodox Ashkenasi Jews experience less alcoholism than the Sephardi and Oriental Jews but that other factors such as economic status and cultural stress might also influence these rates.[410]) After reviewing subsequent studies related to Snyder's belief that religious Orthodoxy promotes sobriety, Flasher and Maisto concluded that some studies support this view and others do not. They suggest investigating whether members of other religious groups who had moved away from their religious traditions also have higher rates of drinking and alcoholism.[411] However, increased acculturation with a concomitant move away from traditional Jewish life and religious practices continues to be offered as one possible explanation for increased alcohol problems among Jews.[412]

In a continuation of efforts to investigate religious and cultural issues in alcoholism among Jews, Glassner and Berg conducted a qualitative study of eighty-eight Jews in central New York state using a randomly selected stratified sample.[413] They found that Orthodox Jews drank as part of rituals, did not know heavy drinkers, defined alcoholism as a disease, and were fearful of alcoholics. Reform and "nonpracticing" Jews more closely resembled each other. They drank

more as part of regular socialization, were more likely to know alcoholics, defined alcoholism as a psychological dependence, and were more likely to view alcoholism with condemnation and blame. Conservative Jews (who incorporate both aspects of Orthodoxy and Reformism) were less clear in their views of alcoholism, but many considered it a habit. Conservatives were more likely than Orthodox Jews, but less likely than Reform and nonpracticing Jews, to know alcoholics. Glassner and Berg identified four factors which they believe taken together continue to help Jews avoid alcohol problems: (1) Jews continue to believe that they are not susceptible to alcohol problems; (2) even with a trend away from religious Orthodoxy, Jews continue to practice ritualistic drinking during events like religious observances; they drink moderately, mostly while eating, and they continue to teach these practices to their children; (3) the bulk of Jews' social relationships are with others (primarily Jews) who drink moderately and do not have alcohol problems; (4) rather than rationalize excessive drinking, Jews avoid drinking too much by practices such as nursing a single drink at a party.[414] These explanations are in keeping with Ullman's earlier discussion of the protective nature of drinking customs that are well integrated within the cultures of Orthodox Jews, Italians, and Chinese.[415]

The literature may give the impression of homogeneity among Jews in the United States, but Sanua says that Jews are heterogeneous with respect to sociodemographic characteristics and religious differences.[416] He suggests that the available studies are inadequate to provide a comprehensive picture of alcoholism and drug abuse among this population. Weiss and Eldar call for cross-cultural studies comparing Jews in Israel and in other countries to isolate factors in the development of alcoholism among Jews.[417]

Prevention and Treatment of Chemical Dependency Among Jewish Americans

There are indications that Jews voluntarily use mental health services more than others,[418] but the same has not been said of chemical dependency treatment. Denial and lack of recognition of alcoholism (and perhaps other drug abuse) by substance abusers, their families, and professionals are considered significant barriers to chemical dependency treatment among Jews.[419] Or as one rabbi put it, "The general impression is that there are no Jewish alcoholics, so in addition to the low self-esteem that is often attached to alcoholism, there is the additional feeling of failure as a Jew. The way you deal with that is to deny your Jewishness. 'If I were really Jewish, I wouldn't be an alcoholic.'"[420] Thus, there is concern that "the failure to seek treatment may be especially common among Jewish alcoholics."[421] Rabbis' understanding of the problem is considered particularly important, but they have been known to accept the stereotype that Jews do not become alcoholics.[422] One suggestion for assisting Jews with chemical dependency problems is to hold self-help group meetings in synagogue facilities.[423]

Two organizations of particular interest to Jews are the JACS Foundation, whose central office is in New York City, and the Alcohol and Drug Action Program (ADAP) of the Jewish Family Services of Los Angeles.[424] JACS assists Jews with chemical dependency problems and their significant others and incorporates Jewish content in recovery. In addition to offering mainstream or traditional alcoholism services, ADAP also helps Jews who would benefit from the incorporation of their religious beliefs in their recovery. Rabbinic counseling and L'Chaim workshops are some of ADAP's innovative services. L'Chaim (the Yiddish word for health) workshops emphasize the compatibility of twelve-step programs with Judaism and act as a bridge to participation in these groups. The workshops also help participants with issues such as maintaining sobriety during September, the time of the major Jewish religious holidays (just as other groups help Christians in December).[425] While Alcoholics Anonymous might be viewed as having a Christian orientation, the literature indicates that Jews can become comfortable with AA and have successfully used the program.[426] Master notes that Rabbi Daniel Grossman emphasizes that powerlessness in AA need not be associated with the Holocaust and that surrender is to God and to one's self.[427] Other suggestions for better serving Jews include such obvious but often overlooked practices as making Kosher food available during inpatient treatment.[428]

SUMMARY

We close our discussion by reviewing a number of themes that emerge from our consideration of ethnic systems and substance abuse:

1. There is considerable variation in alcohol and drug use and related problems among ethnic groups in the United States.
2. The research on ethnicity and substance abuse is inadequate. The methodology of epidemiological studies has improved in many cases, but few studies have tested culturally specific treatment approaches or the effects of special prevention programs for ethnic minority groups.
3. Acculturation is often mentioned as a factor that tends to increase alcohol and drug consumption. Definitions of acculturation vary, as do the research findings on this topic. Studies are needed to clarify the relationship of acculturation to substance use and abuse.
4. Among all ethnic groups, women use alcohol and drugs less than men, but as discussed in Chapter 15, whether this will remain the case is uncertain. Women substance abusers are more stigmatized among all ethnic groups than men.
5. Discrimination and deprivation are thought to be related to substance abuse problems, particularly to the more severe health and social consequences experienced by members of certain ethnic groups, even when their patterns of use are similar to the majority.
6. Genetic explanations have thus far not explained the differences in alcohol consumption and its consequences among ethnic groups.
7. Ethnic minority youth generally report less alcohol and drug use than white youth, but methodological problems in studies of youth (such as exclusion of the large number of school dropouts) may cloud the true picture of use across groups.

8. Strong family ties are important among most ethnic groups, but even well-meaning families can present obstacles to recovery. Education of family members and incorporation of them in treatment are universally suggested.

9. A consistent theme in the prevention literature is that ethnic communities must take an active role in defining social norms and promoting responsibility in alcohol and drug use.

10. Community gatekeepers (such as members of ethnic, religious, business, and educational organizations and institutions) should be recruited and educated to provide pathways to prevention and treatment (also see Chapter 7).

11. Indigenous helpers (medicine men, cuanderas, etc.) should be considered potentially viable helping resources by professionals.

12. Development of model programs is needed for prevention and treatment of substance abuse among ethnic groups along with funding to support their implementation.

13. There is a need for greater understanding of those factors that protect members of ethnic groups from alcohol and drug problems.

14. Ethnic sensitivity and competence are necessary to function effectively as a professional in the field of chemical dependency.

ENDNOTES

1. The terms "ethnicity" and "culture" are used in this chapter rather than "race." Race is thought to be a politically divisive term, while ethnicity and culture are thought to better reflect the richness of the experience of the groups discussed here. See James W. Green, *Cultural Awareness in the Human Services* (Englewood Cliffs, NJ: Prentice Hall, 1982).

2. Arthur L. Klatsky, Abraham B. Siegelaub, Cynthia Landy, and Gary B. Friedman, "Racial Patterns of Alcoholic Beverage Use," *Alcoholism: Clinical and Experimental Research,* Vol. 7, No. 4 (Fall 1983), p. 372.

3. The terms Native American, American Indian, and Indian are used interchangeably in this chapter, as are the terms African American and black, and Hispanic American and Latino.

4. Leslie Brody, "Asia's Drug Problems Appear to Be Getting Worse," *Honolulu Star-Bulletin,* September 18, 1986, p. F–4; Laura Castaneda, "Mexicans Turn to Inhalants; Nation Fears Rise in Addiction," *Austin American-Statesman,* October 13, 1990, p. A32; and Oleg Romaniouk, "Vodka's Stranglehold on Russia," *Cape Cod Times,* June 30, 1992, p. A11.

5. Information on the history of alcohol use and policies regarding alcoholic beverages in over two dozen countries is found in Gunno Armyr, Åke Elmér, and Ulrich Herz, *Alcohol in the World of the 80s* (Stockholm: Sober Förlags AB, 1982).

6. James M. Schaefer, "Ethnic and Racial Variations in Alcohol Use and Abuse," *Alcohol and Health Monograph 4, Special Population Issues,* DHHS Publication No. (ADM) 82–1193, (Rockville, MD: National Institute on Alcohol Abuse and Alcoholism, 1982), pp. 293–294.

7. Donald E. Maypole and Ruth E. Anderson, "Alcoholism Programs Serving Minorities," *Alcohol Health & Research World* (Winter 1986–87), pp. 62–65.

8. See Arleen Rogan, "Recovery from Alcoholism, Issues for Black and Native American Alcoholics," *Alcohol Health & Research World* (Fall 1986), pp. 42–44.

9. Joan Crofut Weibel, "American Indians, Urbanization and Alcohol: A Developing Urban Indian Drinking Ethos," in National Institute on Alcohol Abuse and Alcoholism (NIAAA), *Alcohol and Health Monograph 4, Special Population Issues,*

10. Some of them are Wynetta Devore and Elfriede Schlesinger, *Ethnic-Sensitive Social Work Practice,* 2nd ed. (Columbus, OH: Charles E. Merrill, 1987); James W. Green, *Cultural Awareness in the Human Services* (Englewood Cliffs, NJ: Prentice Hall, 1982); and Sadye M. L. Logan, Edith M. Freeman, and Ruth G. McRoy, *Social Work Practice with Black Families, A Culturally Specific Perspective* (New York: Longman, 1990).

11. See, for example, Frederick D. Harper (ed.), *Alcohol Abuse and Black America* (Alexandria, VA: Douglass Publishers, 1976); NIAAA, *Alcohol and Health Monograph No. 4, Special Population Issues;* M. Jean Gilbert and Richard C. Cervantes, *Mexican Americans and Alcohol,* Monograph 11 (Los Angeles: Spanish Speaking Mental Health Research Center, University of California, 1987); Thomas D. Watts and Roosevelt Wright, Jr. (eds.), *Black Alcoholism: Toward A Comprehensive Understanding* (Springfield, IL: Charles C Thomas, 1983); and S. G. Levy and Sheila B. Blume (eds.), *Addictions in the Jewish Community* (New York: Commission on Synagogue Relations, 1986).

12. Devore and Schlesinger, *Ethnic Sensitive Social Work Practice.*

13. See Green, *Cultural Awareness in the Human Services,* for an elaboration of points in the remainder of this paragraph.

14. Robert Jacque Chapman, "Cultural Bias in Alcoholism Counseling," *Alcoholism Treatment Quarterly,* Vol. 5, Nos. 1/2, (1988), p. 106.

15. See Allan M. Winkler, "Drinking on the American Frontier," *Quarterly Journal of Studies on Alcohol,* Vol. 29 (1968), pp. 413–445.

16. Indian Health Service, *Alcoholism: A High Priority Health Problem, A Report of the Indian Health Service Task Force on Alcoholism,* Department of Health Education and Welfare, Pub. No. (HSA) 77–1001 (Washington, DC: Indian Health Service, 1977); Edwin M. Lemert, "Drinking Among American Indians," in Edith Lisansky Gomberg, Helene Raskin White, and John A. Carpenter (eds.), *Alcohol, Science and Society Revisited* (Ann Arbor: University of Michigan Press, and New Jersey: Rutgers Center for Alcohol Studies, 1982), pp. 80–95; and Terry Beartusk cited in Kathy Brown Ramsperger, "Salvation for an Invisible People," *The Counselor* (May/June 1989), pp. 21–23.

17. For some interesting early accounts of Native American drinking, see R. C. Dailey, "The Role of Alcohol Among North American Indian Tribes as Reprinted in *The Jesuit Relations,*" in Mac Marshall (ed.), *Beliefs, Behaviors, & Alcoholic Beverages, A Cross-Cultural Survey* (Ann Arbor: University of Michigan Press, 1979), pp. 116–127.

18. Craig MacAndrew and Robert B. Edgerton, *Drunken Comportment: A Social Explanation* (Chicago: Aldine, 1969), see especially Chapter 7; also see Dennis Kelso and William Dubay, "Alaskan Natives and Alcohol: A Sociocultural and Epidemiological Review," in National Institute on Alcohol Abuse and Alcoholism, *Alcohol Use Among U.S. Ethnic Minorities, Research Monograph No. 18* (Rockville, MD: U.S. Department of Health and Human Services, 1985), pp. 223–238.

19. Indian Health Service, *Alcoholism: A High Priority Health Problem.*

20. Winkler, "Drinking on the American Frontier."

21. Ibid., Ramsperger, "Salvation for an Invisible People;" and Lemert, "Drinking Among American Indians."

22. Robert L. Bergman, "Navajo Peyote Use: Its Apparent Safety," *American Journal of Psychiatry,* Vol. 128, No. 6 (December 1971), pp. 695–699.

23. MacAndrew and Edgerton, *Drunken Comportment,* p. 123.

24. Joy Leland, *Firewater Myths, North American Indian Drinking and Alcohol Addiction* (New Brunswick, NJ: Rutgers Center of Alcohol Studies, 1976).

25. Indian Health Service, *Alcoholism: A High Priority Health Problem;* also see Winkler, "Drinking on the American Frontier."

26. Indian Health Service, *Alcoholism: A High Priority Health Problem.*

27. Ibid.

28. Philip A. May, "Substance Abuse and American Indians: Prevalence and Susceptibility," *The International Journal of the Addictions,* Vol. 17, No. 7 (1982), pp. 1185–1209; also see Weibel, "American Indians, Urbanization and Alcohol."

29. May, "Substance Abuse and American Indians."

30. See Gerard Littman, "Alcoholism, Illness, and Social Pathology Among American Indians in Transition," *American Journal of Public Health,* Vol. 60, No. 9 (1970), pp. 1769–1787 © American Public Health Association; Weibel, "American Indians, Urbanization and Alcohol."

31. Joan C. Weibel-Orlando, "Drinking Patterns of Urban and Rural American Indians," *Alcohol Health & Research World* (Winter 1986/87), p. 8.

32. Ibid.

33. Weibel, "American Indians, Urbanization and Alcohol."

34. Michael P. Nofz, "Alcohol Abuse and Culturally Marginal American Indians," *Social Casework* (February 1988), p. 68; and Littman, "Alcoholism, Illness, and Social Pathology."

35. Dwight B. Heath, "American Indians and Alcohol: Epidemiological and Sociocultural Relevance," in National Institute on Alcohol Abuse and Alcoholism, *Alcohol Use Among U.S. Ethnic Minorities,* p. 216.

36. E. R. Oetting, Fred Beauvais, and George S. Goldstein, *Drug Abuse Among Native American Youth: Summary of Findings (1975–1981)* (Fort Collins: Colorado State University, 1982).

37. Littman, "Alcoholism, Illness and Social Pathology"; Everett R. Rhoades, Russell D. Mason, Phyllis Eddy, Eva M. Smith, and Thomas R. Burns, "The Indian Health Service Approach to Alcoholism Among American Indians and Alaska Natives," *Public Health Reports,* Vol. 103, No. 6, (November–December 1988), pp. 621–627; and Audry Hill, "Treatment and Prevention Of Alcoholism in the Native American Family," in Gary W. Lawson and Ann W. Lawson (eds.), *Alcoholism & Substance Abuse in Special Populations* (Rockville, MD: Aspen Publishers, 1989), see pp. 262–265, 268.

38. Rhoades et al., "The Indian Health Service Approach."

39. Nancy Oestreich Lurie, "The World's Oldest On-Going Protest Demonstration: North American Indian Drinking Patterns," in Marshall, *Beliefs, Behaviors, & Alcoholic Beverages,* p. 135.

40. See Littman, "Alcoholism, Illness, and Social Pathology."

41. Ibid.; also see Rhoades et al., "The Indian Health Service Approach," p. 626.

42. Rhoades et al., "The Indian Health Service Approach," p. 626.

43. Weibel, "American Indians, Urbanization and Alcohol," p. 337; also see Merwyn S. Garbarino, "Life in

the City: Chicago," in Jack O. Waddell and O. Michael Watson (eds.), *The American Indian in Urban Society* (Boston: Little, Brown, 1971), pp. 193–196; and Peter Z. Snyder, "The Social Environment of the Urban Indian," p. 237, in the same book. Much of the literature in this paragraph is also cited in National Institute on Alcohol Abuse and Alcoholism (NIAAA), "Alcohol Topics: Research Review, Alcohol and Native Americans" (Rockville MD: The Institute, 1985).

44. M. Burns, J. M. Daily, and H. Moskowitz, *Drinking Practices and Problems of Urban American Indians in Los Angeles, Part 1, Study Description and Findings. Preliminary Report* (Santa Monica, CA: Planning Analysis and Research Institute, 1974), cited in Weibel, "American Indians, Urbanization and Alcohol."

45. See, for example, Weibel-Orlando, "Drinking Patterns of Urban and Rural American Indians;" Lemert, "Drinking Among American Indians."

46. J. C. Weibel and T. Weisner, *An Ethnography of Urban Indian Drinking Patterns in California* (Los Angeles: The Alcohol Research Center, The Neuropsychiatric Institute, University of California, 1980), cited in Weibel, "American Indians, Urbanization and Alcohol."

47. Lurie, "The World's Oldest On-going Protest Demonstration," p. 138; also see Ronald G. Lewis, "Alcoholism and the Native Americans—A Review of the Literature," in National Institute on Alcohol Abuse and Alcoholism (NIAAA), *Alcohol and Health Monograph 4, Special Population Issues*, p. 320.

48. Lurie, "The World's Oldest On-going Protest Demonstration," p. 133.

49. Weibel, "American Indians, Urbanization and Alcohol," p. 338.

50. Oetting et al., *Drug Abuse Among Native American Youth*, p. 35.

51. Lewis, "Alcoholism and the Native Americans," p. 320.

52. Joy H. Leland, "Native American Alcohol Use: A Review of the Literature," in Patricia D. Mail and David R. McDonald, *Tulapai to Tokay: A Bibliography of Alcohol Use and Abuse Among Native Americans of North America,* (New Haven: HRAF Press, 1980), p. 38.

53. See for example, Theodore G. Graves, "Drinking and Drunkenness Among Urban Indians," in Waddell and Watson, *The American Indian in Urban Society,* pp. 274–311; and Heath, "American Indians and Alcohol."

54. Mail and McDonald, *Tulapai to Tokay.*

55. P. Mail, "American Indian Alcoholism: What Is Not Being Done?" *The IHS Primary Care Provider,* Vol. 9,

No. 3 (March 1984), pp. 1–5, cited in NIAAA, "Alcohol Topics: Research Review, Alcohol and Native Americans," p. 3.

56. Littman, "Alcoholism, Illness, and Social Pathology."

57. Lewis, "Alcoholism and the Native Americans," p. 319; May, "Substance Abuse and American Indians."

58. Lemert, "Drinking Among American Indians," p. 87.

59. Kelso and Dubay, "Alaskan Natives and Alcohol," pp. 223–238.

60. Weibel-Orlando, "Drinking Patterns of Urban and Rural American Indians."

61. Joan Ablon, "Cultural Conflict in Urban Indians," *Mental Hygiene,* Vol. 55, No. 2 (April 1971), p. 204.

62. Lewis, "Alcoholism and the Native Americans," pp. 319–320.

63. E. R. Knisley, "Native Alaskan Indians, Eskimos and Aleuts and Their Drinking Habits," paper presented at the 30th International Congress on Alcoholism and Drug Dependence, 1972; cited in Lewis, "Alcoholism and the Native American," p. 324.

64. Lewis, "Alcoholism and the Native Americans," pp. 315–328; Nofz, "Alcohol Abuse and Culturally Marginal American Indians"; and Heath, "American Indians and Alcohol."

65. The remainder of this paragraph relies on Rhoades et al., "The Indian Health Service Approach."

66. Rhoades et al., "The Indian Health Service Approach," p. 622, based on data from *Indian Health Service Chart Series Book* (Rockville, MD: Indian Health Service, April 1988).

67. Much of this paragraph relies on Rhoades et al., "The Indian Health Service Approach."

68. Rhoades et al., "The Indian Health Service Approach"; these figures are based on data from 1981 to 1983.

69. Heath, "American Indians and Alcohol."

70. Lemert, "Drinking Among American Indians."

71. Heath, "American Indians and Alcohol."

72. Ray Stratton, Arthur Zeiner, and Alfonso Paredes, "Tribal Affiliation and Prevalence of Alcohol Problems," *Journal of Studies on Alcohol,* Vol. 39, No. 7 (1978), p. 1175.

73. Graves, "Drinking and Drunkenness Among Urban Indians," pp. 305–306.

74. Nofz, "Alcohol Abuse and Culturally Marginal American Indians"; also see Weibel, "American Indians, Urbanization and Alcohol," p. 339.

75. Rhoades et al., "The Indian Health Service Approach," p. 622.

76. Lewis, "Alcoholism and the Native Americans," and Weibel, "American Indians, Urbanization and Alcohol."

77. Littman, "Alcoholism, Illness, and Social Pathology"; Lewis, "Alcoholism and the Native Americans"; and Weibel, "American Indians, Urbanization and Alcohol."

78. William Butynski and Diane M. Canova, "Alcohol Problem Resources and Services in State Supported Programs, FY 1987," *Public Health Reports,* Vol. 103, No. 6 (November–December 1988), pp. 611–620.

79. U.S. Department of Health and Human Services, *Report of the Secretary's Task Force on Black & Minority Health, Volume 1, Executive Summary,* p. 138.

80. Data from the National Institute on Drug Abuse cited in *Report of the Secretary's Task Force on Black Minority Health,* Volume 1, p. 137.

81. May, "Substance Abuse and American Indians."

82. E. R. Oetting and Fred Beauvais, "Epidemiology and Correlates of Alcohol Use Among Indian Adolescents Living on Reservations," in National Institute on Alcohol Abuse and Alcoholism, *Alcohol Use Among U.S. Ethnic Minorities,* pp. 239–267.

83. Ibid.

84. Joan C. Weibel-Orlando, "Pass the Bottle, Bro!: A Comparison of Urban and Rural Indian Drinking Patterns," in National Institute on Alcohol and Alcoholism, *Alcohol Use Among U.S. Ethnic Minorities,* pp. 269–289.

85. Ibid.

86. Oetting and Beauvais, "Epidemiology and Correlates of Alcohol Use."

87. G. Trimble, "Drug Abuse Prevention Research Needs Among American Indians and Alaska Natives," *White Cloud Journal of American Indian Mental Health,* Vol. 3, No. 3 (1984), pp. 32–34, cited in NIAAA, "Alcohol Topics: Research Review, Alcohol and Native Americans."

88. R. Wax, "The Warrior Dropouts," *Transactions,* Vol. 4, pp. 40–46, cited in Joan Weibel-Orlando, "Substance Abuse Among American Indian Youth: A Continuing Crisis," *Journal of Drug Issues,* Vol. 14, (1984), pp. 313–335.

89. May, "Substance Abuse and American Indians," p. 1191.

90. Weibel-Orlando, "Drinking Patterns of Rural and Urban American Indians," and Weibel-Orlando, "Pass the Bottle, Bro!"

91. Indian Health Service, *Indian Health Service Chart Series Book,* DHHS Pub. No. 1988 0-218-547: QL3 (Washington, DC: Superintendent of Documents,

U.S. Government Printing Office, 1988), cited in National Institute on Alcohol Abuse and Alcoholism, *Seventh Special Report to the U.S. Congress on Alcohol and Health* (Rockville, MD: U.S. Department of Health and Human Services, January 1990), p. 36.

92. NIAA, *Alcohol Use Among U.S. Ethnic Minorities,* p. xxi.

93. Lewis, "Alcoholism and the Native Americans."

94. Sheldon I. Miller, Edward Helmick, Lawrence Berg, Paul Nutting, and Gregory Schorr, "An Evaluation of Alcoholism Treatment Services for Alaskan Natives," *Hospital and Community Psychiatry,* Vol. 26, No. 12 (December 1975), pp. 829–831.

95. This paragraph relies on Rhoades et al., "The Indian Health Service Approach."

96. E. Daniel Edwards, "A Description and Evaluation of American Indian Social Work Training Programs," unpublished doctoral dissertation, University of Utah, 1976, cited in Fenton Moss, E. Daniel Edwards, Margie E. Edwards, Fred V. Janzen, and George Howell, "Sobriety and American Indian Problem Drinkers," *Alcoholism Treatment Quarterly,* Vol. 2, No. 2 (Summer 1985), pp. 81–96.

97. Deborah Goodman, "Mental and Addictive Disorders in American Indians/Alaska Natives Studied," *ADAMHA News,* Vol. 18, No. 2 (March–April 1992), pp. 14–15.

98. Spero M. Manson, James H. Shore, Joseph D. Bloom, George Keepers, and Gordon Neligh, "Alcohol Abuse and Major Affective Disorders: Advances in Epidemiologic Research Among American Indians," in NIAAA, *Alcohol Use Among U.S. Ethnic Minorities,* pp. 291–300; and Goodman, "Mental and Addictive Disorders."

99. Lewis, "Alcoholism and the Native Americans," p. 323; also see Rhoades et al., "The Indian Health Service Approach;" NIAAA, "Alcohol Topics: Research Review, Alcohol and Native Americans"; Littman, "Alcoholism, Illness, and Social Pathology," and Louise Jilek-Aall, "Acculturation, Alcoholism, and Indian-Style Alcoholics Anonymous," *Journal of Studies on Alcohol,* Supplement No. 9 (1981), pp. 143–158.

100. James O. Whittaker, "Alcohol and the Standing Rock Sioux Tribe, II. Psychodynamic and Cultural Factors in Drinking," *Quarterly Journal of Studies on Alcohol,* Vol. 24 (1963), pp. 80–90.

101. Rhoades et al., "The Indian Health Service Approach."

102. The film is available from Alkali Lake Indian Band, P.O. Box 4479, Williams Lake, B.C., Canada V2G 2V5 or contact the Bureau of Indian Affairs.

103. Elvin Willie, "The Story of Alakali Lake: Anomaly of Community Recovery or National Trend in Indian

Country?" *Alcoholism Treatment Quarterly*, Vol. 6, Nos. 3/4" (1989), pp. 167–173, and Veronica Taylor, "The Triumph of the Alkali Lake Indian Band," *Alcohol Health & Research World*, Vol. 12, No. 1 (Fall 1987), p. 57.

104. Rhoades et al., "The Indian Health Service Approach."

105. Willie, "The Story of Alkali Lake," p. 168.

106. Moss et al., "Sobriety and American Indian Problem Drinkers."

107. See, for example, John G. Red Horse, "Family Structure and Value Orientation in American Indians," *Social Casework*, Vol. 61, No. 8 (October 1980), pp. 462–467.

108. Ramsperger, "Salvation for an Invisible People."

109. Littman, "Alcoholism, Illness, and Social Pathology," p. 1782; also see Jilek-Aall, "Acculturation, Alcoholism, and Indian-Style Alcoholics Anonymous."

110. J. F. Merker "Indians of the Great Plains: Issues in Counseling and Family Therapy," paper presented at the National Council on Alcoholism Forum, New Orleans, LA, April 1981, cited in NIAAA, "Alcoholic Topics: Research Review, Alcohol and Native Americans."

111. A. Whiting, personal communication, June 1985, cited in NIAAA, "Alcohol Topics: Research Review, Alcohol and Native Americans."

112. Nofz, "Alcohol Abuse and Culturally Marginal American Indians," p. 70.

113. The remainder of this paragraph relies on Ramsperger, "Salvation for an Invisible People."

114. Moss et al., "Sobriety and American Indian Problem Drinkers."

115. "VA Hospital Calls in 'Medicine Man' to Help Indians Beat Alcoholism," *Austin American-Statesman*, August 25, 1991, p. D28.

116. Nofz, "Alcohol Abuse and Culturally Marginal American Indians."

117. Bergman, "Navajo Peyote Use," and Bernard J. Albaugh and Philip O. Anderson, "Peyote in the Treatment of Alcoholism Among American Indians," *American Journal of Psychiatry*, Vol. 131, No. 11 (November 1974), pp. 1247–1250.

118. Albaugh and Anderson, "Treatment of Alcoholism Among Native Americans," p. 1249.

119. Karl A. Menninger, "Discussion," following Bergman, "Navajo Peyote Use," p. 699.

120. David Fidanque, "Religious Freedom Makes Comeback in Oregon, with Passage of Peyote Bill," *Civil Liberties*, 1992, p. 5.

121. Littman, "Alcoholism, Illness, and Social Pathology."

122. Jilek-Aall, "Acculturation, Alcoholism, and Indian-Style Alcoholics Anonymous."

123. Lewis, "Alcoholism and the Native Americans," p. 323.

124. The remainder of this paragraph relies on Jilek-Aall, "Acculturation, Alcoholism and Indian Style Alcoholics Anonymous."

125. This paragraph relies on Nofz, "Alcohol Abuse and Culturally Marginal American Indians."

126. See William J. Reid and Laura Epstein, *Task-Centered Casework* (New York: Columbia Press, 1972), and Laura Epstein, *Helping People: The Task-Centered Approach* (St. Louis, MO: C. V. Mosby, 1980).

127. Nofz, "Alcohol Abuse and Culturally Marginal American Indians," p. 70.

128. Ibid., p. 71.

129. Ibid.

130. May, "Substance Abuse Among American Indians."

131. Oetting and Beauvais, "Epidemiology and Correlates of Alcohol Use."

132. "Indian Health Service School/Community-Based Alcoholism Substance Abuse Prevention Survey" (Rockville, MD: Indian Health Service, 1987), cited in Rhoades et al., "The Indian Health Service Approach," pp. 625–626.

133. Weibel, "American Indians, Urbanization and Alcohol," p. 344.

134. For an account, see Denise Herd, "Ambiguity in Black Drinking Norms, An Ethnohistorical Interpretation," in Linda A. Bennett and Genevieve M. Ames (eds.), *The American Experience with Alcohol: Contrasting Cultural Perspectives* (New York: Plenum Press, 1985), pp. 149–170.

135. Vivian Rouson Gossett, "Alcohol and Drug Abuse in Black America, A Guide for Community Action" (Minneapolis: Institute on Black Chemical Abuse, 1988), p. 2.

136. Herd, "Ambiguity in Black Drinking Norms," and Gossett, "Alcohol and Drug Abuse in Black America."

137. Frederick D. Harper, "Research and Treatment with Black Alcoholics," *Alcohol Health & Research World*, Vol. 4, No. 4, pp. 10–16; Frederick D. Harper, "Etiology: Why Do Blacks Drink?" in Harper, *Alcohol Abuse and Black America*, pp. 27–37; also see Eugene D. Genovese, *Roll, Jordan, Roll, The World the Slaves Made* (New York: Pantheon Books, 1974).

138. Genovese, *Roll, Jordan, Roll*, p. 644; also see Gossett, "Alcohol and Drug Use in Black America."

139. Gossett, "Alcohol and Drug Use in Black America."

140. Denise Herd, "Migration, Cultural Transformation and the Rise of Black Liver Cirrhosis Mortality," *British Journal of Addiction,* Vol. 80 (1985), pp. 397–410.

141. John Koren, *Economic Aspects of the Liquor Problem* (Boston: Houghton Mifflin, 1899), and U.S. Census Bureau Office, *Tenth Census: 1880, Volume II, Vital Statistics of the United States* (Washington, DC: U.S. Government Printing Office, 1886), cited in Herd, "Migration, Cultural Transformation and the Rise of Black of Liver Cirrhosis Mortality"; also see Denise Herd, "The Epidemiology of Drinking Patterns and Alcohol-Related Problems Among U.S. Blacks," in National Institute on Alcohol Abuse and Alcoholism, *Alcohol Use Among U.S. Ethnic Minorities,* pp. 3–50.

142. The remainder of this paragraph relies primarily on Herd, "Migration, Cultural Transformation and the Rise of Black Liver Cirrhosis Mortality"; Herd, "Ambiguity in Black Drinking Norms." Also see the account in Gossett, "Alcohol and Drug Abuse in Black America."

143. Harper, "Etiology: Why Do Blacks Drink?"; italicized material is quoted verbatim.

144. Also see Gossett, "Alcohol and Drug Abuse in Black America," p. 18.

145. Cheryl Davenport Dozier, "The African-American and Alcoholism, Roadblocks to Treatment," *The Counselor* (May/June 1989), p. 33.

146. Herd, "Ambiguity in Black Drinking Norms."

147. Herd, "Editorial, Rethinking Black Drinking," *British Journal of Addiction,* Vol. 82 (1987), pp. 219–223.

148. "Prevention of Alcohol Abuse Among Black Americans," an interview with Thomas D. Watts and Roosevelt Wright, Jr., *Alcohol Health & Research World* (Winter 1986/87), pp. 40–41, 65.

149. Ibid.; see also Dozier, "The African-American and Alcoholism."

150. U.S. Department of Health and Human Services, *Report of the Secretary's Task Force on Black and Minority Health,* p. 138.

151. Lee N. Robins, "Alcohol Abuse in Blacks and Whites as Indicated in the Epidemiological Catchment Area Program," in National Institute on Alcohol Abuse and Alcoholism, *Alcohol Use Among U.S. Ethnic Minorities,* pp. 63–73.

152. Denise Herd, "Drinking Patterns in the Black Population," in Walter B. Clark and Michael E. Hilton (eds.), *Alcohol in America, Drinking Practices and Problems* (Albany: State University of New York Press, 1991), pp. 308–328, adapted from Herd, 'The Epidemiology of Drinking Patterns and Alcohol-Related Problems among U.S. Blacks."

153. For discussions of earlier studies see Klatsky et al., "Racial Patterns of Alcoholic Beverage Use," and Barbara W. Lex, "Review of Alcohol Problems in Ethnic Minority Groups," *Journal of Consulting and Clinical Psychology,* Vol. 55, No. 3 (1987), pp. 293–300.

154. Herd, "Drinking Patterns in the Black Population"; also see Herd, "The Epidemiology of Drinking Patterns and Alcohol-Related Problems Among U.S. Blacks."

155. For another analyses of these data comparing African-American and white men, see Herd, "Subgroup Differences in Drinking Patterns Among Black and White Men: Results from a National Survey," *Journal of Studies on Alcohol,* Vol. 51, No. 3 (1990), pp. 221–232.

156. Also see Marsha Lillie-Blanton, Ellen MacKenzie, and James C. Anthony, "Black-White Differences in Alcohol Use by Women: Baltimore Survey Findings," *Public Health Reports,* Vol. 106, No. 2 (1991), pp. 124–133, who report that their findings based on data collected in 1981 from the Baltimore Epidemiologic Catchment Area household survey are similar to the 1984 national survey. Lillie-Blanton et al. concluded that "after controlling for differences in sociodemographic characteristics, black women were found to be at no greater risk than whites for heavy drinking or for suffering from alcohol abuse or dependence" (p. 124).

157. Laura Ronan, "Alcohol-Related Health Risks Among Black Americans, Highlights of the Secretary's Task Force Report on Black and Minority Health," *Alcohol Health & Research World* (Winter 1986/87), pp. 36–39, 65; also see Denise Herd, "Editorial, Rethinking Black Drinking"; Herd, "The Epidemiology of Drinking Patterns and Alcohol-Related Problems Among U.S. Blacks"; and Thomas Harford and Cherry Lowman, "Alcohol Use Among Black and White Teenagers," in National Institute on Alcohol Abuse and Alcoholism, *Alcohol Use Among U.S. Ethnic Minorities,* pp. 51–61. Results of surveys are also summarized in Office for Substance Abuse Prevention, "The Fact Is Alcohol and Other Drug Use Is a Special Concern for African American Families and Communities" (Rockville, MD: August 1990).

158. Thomas C. Harford, "Drinking Patterns Among Black and Nonblack Adolescents: Results of a National Survey," in Roosevelt Wright Jr., and Thomas D. Watts, *Prevention of Black Alcoholism, Issues and Strategies,* (Springfield, IL: Charles C. Thomas, 1985), pp. 122–139.

159. Herd, "Subgroup Differences in Drinking Patterns Among Black and White Men."

160. Mary Ann Forney, Paul D. Forney, and William K. Ripley, "Alcohol Use Among Black Adolescents: Parental and Peer Influences," *Journal of Alcohol and Drug Education*, Vol. 36, No. 3 (1991), p. 36–45.

161. National Institute on Drug Abuse (NIDA), *National Household Survey on Drug Abuse: Main Findings, 1990* (Rockville, MD: U.S. Department of Health and Human Services, 1991), pp. 32, 70, and 95.

162. Butynski and Canova, "Alcohol Problem Resources and Services in State Supported Programs, FY 1987."

163. *Report of the Secretary's Task Force on Black and Minority Health*, p. 136.

164. Butynski and Canova, "Alcohol Problem Resources and Services in State Supported Programs, FY 1987."

165. National Institute on Drug Abuse, "SMSA Statistics 1981: Data from the Client Oriented Data Acquisition Process (CODAP): Statistical Series E, Administrative Report" (Rockville, MD: National Institute on Drug Abuse, 1983), cited in Richard M. Selik, Kenneth G. Castro, and Marguerite Pappaioanou, "Distribution of AIDS Cases, by Racial/Ethnic Group and Exposure Category, United States, June 1, 1981–July 4, 1988," *MMWR Surveillance Summaries*, Vol. 37, No. SS-3, pp. 29–37.

166. Gossett, "Alcohol And Drug Abuse in Black America."

167. The remainder of this paragraph is based on Selik et al., "Distribution of AIDS Cases."

168. Herd, "Drinking Patterns in the Black Population," and Lillie-Blanton et al., "Black-White Differences in Alcohol Use by Women."

169. See "An Interview with Peter Bell," *Alcohol Health & Research World* (Winter 1986/87), pp. 24, 50–51, and Julia A. Lee, Brian E. Mavis, and Bertram E. Stoffelmayr, "A Comparison of Problems-of-Life for Blacks and Whites Entering Substance Abuse Treatment Programs," *Journal of Psychoactive Drugs*, Vol. 23, No. 3, 1991, pp. 233–239.

170. See, for example, Moss et al., "Sobriety and American Indian Problem Drinkers."

171. Creigs C. Beverly, "Toward a Model for Counseling Black Alcoholics," *Journal of Non-White Concerns* (July 1975), pp. 169–176.

172. Ethel B. Burks and Tyron S. Johnson, "The Black Drug Abuser: The Lack of Utilization of Treatment Services," in Arnold G. Schecter, (ed.), *Drug Dependence and Alcoholism, Vol. 2, Social and Behavioral Issues* (New York: Plenum Press, 1981), pp. 113–120.

173. For a discussion of this issue also see Peter Bell and Jimmy Evans, "Counseling the Black Alcoholic Client," in Watts and Wright, *Black Alcoholism*, pp. 100–121, and Gossett, "Alcohol and Drug Abuse in Black America."

174. See, for example, Bell and Evans, "Counseling the Black Alcoholic Client."

175. Bell and Evans, "Counseling the Black Alcoholic Client"; also see William H. Wheeler, *Counseling from a Cultural Perspective*, 1977, © William H. Wheeler (A. L. Nellums and Associates, Atlanta, GA).

176. Bell and Evans, "Counseling the Black Alcoholic Client."

177. Beverly, "Toward a Model for Counseling Black Alcoholics"; see also Raymond A. Winbush and Pamela S. Henderson, "'We May as Well Try This': Some Reflections on Alcoholism Services Research in the African-American Community," in Watts and Wright, *Black Alcoholism*, pp. 198–205.

178. Mary Lou Politi Ziter, "Culturally Sensitive Treatment of Black Alcoholic Families," *Social Work* (March–April 1987), pp. 130–135.

179. Barbara Bryant Solomon, *Black Empowerment: Social Work in Oppressed Communities* (New York: Columbia University Press, 1976).

180. Beverly, "Toward a Model for Counseling Black Alcoholics."

181. Delores G. Norton, *The Dual Perspective: Inclusion of Ethnic Minority Content in the Social Work Curriculum* (New York: Council on Social Work Education, 1978).

182. Roosevelt Wright, Jr., Barbara Lynn Kail, and Robert F. Creecy, "Culturally Sensitive Social Work Practice with Black Alcoholics and Their Families," in Sadye M. L. Logan, Edith M. Freeman, and Ruth G. McRoy, *Social Work Practice with Black Families* (New York: Longman, 1990), pp. 203–222.

183. Ibid.

184. Frieda Brown and Joan Tooley, "Alcoholism in the Black Community," in Lawson and Lawson, *Alcoholism & Substance Abuse in Special Populations*, pp. 115–130.

185. Gloria McGee and Leola Johnson, "Black, Beautiful and Recovering" (Center City, MN: Hazelden, 1985).

186. Ibid.

187. John Nickens, "Black Outreach Alcoholism Program of Brevard County, Results and Evaluations," 1972, cited in Burks and Johnson, "The Black Drug Abuser," p. 117.

188. Marvin P. Dawkins and Frederick D. Harper, "Alcoholism Among Women: A Comparison of Black and White Problem Drinkers," *The International Journal of the Addictions*, Vol. 18, No. 3 (1983), pp. 333–349.

189. Hortensia Amaro, Linda J. Beckman, and Vickie M. Mays, "A Comparison of Black and White Women

Entering Alcoholism Treatment," *Journal of Studies on Alcohol,* Vol. 48, No. 3 (1987), pp. 220–228.

190. Winbush and Henderson, "'We May as Well Try This.'"

191. See, for example, Carolyn F. Swift and Sethard Beverly, "The Utilization of Ministers as Alcohol Counselors and Educators: Increasing Prevention and Treatment Resources in the Black Community," in Wright and Watts, *Prevention of Black Alcoholism,* pp. 182–198.

192. Thomas Prugh, "The Black Church: A Foundation of Recovery," *Alcohol Health and Research World* (Winter 1986/87), pp. 52–54; also see Dorothy Headley Knox, "Spirituality: A Tool in the Assessment and Treatment of Black Alcoholics and Their Families," *Alcoholism Treatment Quarterly,* Vol. 2, Nos. 3/4 (Fall 1985/Winter 1985–86), pp. 31–44.

193. Prugh, "The Black Church: A Foundation of Recovery."

194. McGee and Johnson, "Black, Beautiful and Recovering."

195. Prugh, "The Black Church: A Foundation of Recovery."

196. Dozier, "The African-American and Alcoholism," and Wright et al., "Culturally Sensitive Social Work Practice."

197. Prugh, "The Black Church: A Foundation of Recovery."

198. This paragraph relies on Henry L. Hudson, "How and Why Alcoholics Anonymous Works for Blacks," *Alcoholism Treatment Quarterly,* Vol. 2, Nos. 3–4 (Fall 1985–Winter 1985/86), pp. 11–30.

199. Fulton J. Caldwell, "Alcoholics Anonymous As a Viable Treatment Resource for Black Alcoholics," in Watts and Wright, *Black Alcoholism, Toward a Comprehensive Understanding,* pp. 85–99.

200. Ruth G. McRoy and Clayton T. Shorkey, "Alcohol Use and Abuse Among Blacks," in Edith Freeman (ed.), *Social Work Practice with Clients with Alcohol Problems* (Springfield, IL: Charles C Thomas, 1985), pp. 202–213.

201. Ronan, "Alcohol-Related Health Risks Among Black Americans."

202. "An Interview with O. Amuleru-Marshall," *Alcohol Health & Research World* (Winter 1986/87), pp. 25, 51.

203. "Prevention of Alcohol Abuse Among Black Americans."

204. David Grant and BoisSan Moore, "MIBCA-Sponsored Conference, Groundwork for Future Action," *Alcohol Health & Research World* (Winter 1986/87), pp. 18–23.

205. "Prevention of Alcohol Abuse Among Black Americans."

206. Grant and Moore, "MIBCA-Sponsored Conference."

207. See, for example, Glenn C. Loury, "The Moral Quandry of the Black Community," *Public Interest,* No. 79 (Spring 1985), pp. 9–22.

208. "An Interview with Peter Bell."

209. Cited in Grant and Moore, "MIBCA-Sponsored Conference," p. 18.

210. Gossett, "Alcohol and Drug Use in Black America."

211. Herd, "Editorial, Rethinking Black Drinking."

212. See, for example, Gossett, "Alcohol Abuse in Black America," and Harper, "Research and Treatment with Black Alcoholics."

213. Gossett, "Alcohol and Drug Abuse in Black America," p. 6.

214. Francis X. McQuade, "Treatment and Recovery Issues for the Addicted Hispanic," *The Counselor* (May/June 1989), p. 29.

215. Anthony M. Alcocer, "Alcohol Use and Abuse Among the Hispanic American Population," in NIAAA, *Alcohol and Health Monograph No. 4, Special Population Issues,* pp. 361–382, and Raul Caetano, "Responding to Alcohol-Related Problems Among Hispanics," *Contemporary Drug Problems,* Fall 1988, pp. 335–363.

216. Also see Elaine Bratic Arkin and Judith E. Funkhouser, "Reaching Hispanic/Latino Youth," in Elaine Bratic Arkin and Judith E. Funkhouser (eds.), *Communicating About Alcohol and Other Drugs: Strategies for Reaching Populations at Risk, OSAP Prevention Monograph 5* (Rockville, MD: Office for Substance Abuse Prevention, 1990), Chapter 3.

217. Alcocer, "Alcohol Use and Abuse Among the Hispanic American Population."

218. Michael J. Stoil, "Special Populations," *Alcohol Health & Research World,* Vol. 13, No. 2 (1989), p. 176.

219. U.S. Bureau of the Census, *Statistical Abstract of the United States, 1992* (Washington, DC: U.S. Government Printing Office, 1992), p. 456.

220. Arkin and Funkhouser, "Reaching Hispanic/Latino Youth."

221. McQuade, "Treatment and Recovery Issues," p. 29.

222. See Alcocer, "Alcohol Use and Abuse Among the Hispanic American Population"; Lex, "Review of Alcohol Problems in Ethnic Minority Groups"; and M. Jean Gilbert and Richard C. Cervantes, *Mexican Americans and Alcohol, Monograph 11* (Los Angeles: Spanish Speaking Mental Health Research Center, 1987).

223. Arthur L. Klatsky, Abraham Siegelaub, Cynthia Landy, and Gary D. Friedman, "Racial Patterns of Alcoholic Beverage Use," *Alcoholism Clinical and Experimental Research* (Fall 1983), pp. 372–377.

224. Raul Caetano, "Drinking Patterns and Alcohol Problems in a National Sample of U.S. Hispanics," in *Alcohol Use Among U.S. Ethnic Minorities,* pp. 147–162; Raul Caetano, "Findings from the 1984 National Survey of Alcohol Use Among U.S. Hispanics," in Clark and Hilton, *Alcohol in America,* pp. 293–307; and Caetano, "Responding to Alcohol-Related Problems Among Hispanics."

225. Caetano, "Responding to Alcohol-Related Problems Among Hispanics."

226. Caetano, "Findings from the 1984 National Survey of Alcohol Use Among U.S. Hispanics."

227. Caetano, "Responding to Alcohol-Related Problems Among Hispanics."

228. See J. Bryan Page, Lucy Rio, Jacqueline Sweeney and Carolyn McKay, "Alcohol and Adaption to Exile in Miami's Cuban Population," in Bennett and Ames, *The American Experience with Alcohol,* pp. 315–332, and M. A. Scopetta, O. E. King, and J. Szapocnick, "Relationship of Acculturation, Incidence of Drug Abuse and Effective Treatment for Cuban Americans" (Washington, DC: National Institute on Drug Abuse, 1977), Research Contract No. 271-75-4136, cited in Lillian Comas-Díaz, "Puerto Rican Alcoholic Women: Treatment Considerations," *Alcoholism Treatment Quarterly,* Vol. 3, No. 1 (Spring 1986), pp. 47–57.

229. Alcocer, "Alcohol Use and Abuse Among the Hispanic American Population."

230. Ricardo Castaneda and Marc Galanter, "Ethnic Differences in Drinking Practice and Cognitive Impairment Among Detoxifying Alcoholics," *Journal of Studies on Alcoholic,* Vol. 49, No. 4 (1988), pp. 335–339.

231. Andrew J. Gordon, "State-of-the-Art Review: Caribbean Hispanics and Their Alcohol Use," in *Alcohol Use Among U.S. Among U.S. Ethnic Minorities,* pp. 135–146.

232. Raul Caetano, "Drinking Patterns and Alcohol Problems in a National Sample of U.S. Hispanics."

233. Gordon, "State-of-the-Art Review."

234. M. Audrey Burnam, "Prevalence of Alcohol Abuse and Dependence Among Mexican Americans and Non-Hispanic Whites in the Community," in *Alcohol Use Among U.S. Ethnic Minorities,* pp. 163–177.

235. Klatsky et al., "Racial Patterns of Alcoholic Beverage Use."

236. Caetano, "Drinking Patterns and Alcohol Problems in a National Sample of U.S. Hispanics," and Caetano, "Responding to Alcohol-Related Problems Among Hispanics."

237. Caetano, "Responding to Alcohol-Related Problems Among Hispanics"; also see "Alcocer, Alcohol Use and Abuse Among the Hispanic American Population," pp. 366–367, for a discussion of acculturation, and Paul W. Haberman, "Alcoholism Treatment Indicators Among Hispanics in New York City," *Alcoholism Treatment Quarterly,* Vol. 4, No. 4 (1987), p. 79.

238. Charles M. Christian, Terry S. Zobeck, Henry J. Malin, and Dale C. Hitchcock, "Self-Reported Alcohol Use and Abuse Among Mexican Americans: Preliminary Findings from the Hispanic Health and Nutrition Examination Survey Adult Sample Person Supplement, in *Alcohol Use Among U.S. Ethnic Minorities,* pp. 425–438.

239. H. Amaro, personal communication, August 1988, cited in Arkin and Funkhouser, "Reaching Hispanic/Latino Youth," p. 182.

240. NIDA, *National Household Survey on Drug Abuse: Main Findings, 1990,* pp. 32, 53, and 70.

241. National Institute on Drug Abuse (NIDA), *Use of Selected Drugs Among Hispanics: Mexican Americans, Puerto Ricans, Cuban Americans, Findings from the Hispanic Health and Nutrition Examination Survey* (Rockville, MD: U.S. Department of Health and Human Services, 1987).

242. Ruth Sanchez-Dirks, "Drinking Practices Among Hispanic Youth," *Alcohol Health & Research World,* Winter 1978, pp. 21–27.

243. Alcocer, "Alcohol Use and Abuse Among the Hispanic American Population."

244. John M. Wallace and Jerald G. Bachman, "Explaining Racial/Ethnic Differences in Adolescent Drug Use: The Impact of Background and Lifestyle," *Social Problems,* Vol. 38, No. 3 (August 1991), pp. 333–357.

245. This and other methodological problems in studying alcohol use among youth are discussed in M. Jean Gilbert and Anthony M. Alcocer, "Alcohol Use and Hispanic Youth: An Overview," *The Journal of Drug Issues,* Vol. 18, No. 1 (1988), pp. 33–48.

246. See M. Jean Gilbert, "Alcohol-Related Practices, Problems, and Norms Among Mexican Americans: An Overview" in *Alcohol Use Among U.S. Ethnic Minorities,* pp. 115–134 for a discussion of studies on acculturation and the complexity of studying the issue.

247. Caetano, "Responding to Alcohol-Related Problems Among Hispanics," p. 356.

248. Marcelline Burns, "The Alcohol Problem in Los Angeles," *Abstracts and Reviews in Alcohol and Driving,* Vol. 4 (1983), pp. 9–15.

249. For a discussion see Harper, "Research and Treatment with Black Alcoholics."

250. McQuade, "Treatment and Recovery Issues"; also see Marian A. Aguilar, Diana M. DiNitto, Cynthia Franklin, and Becky Lopez-Pilkinton, "Mexican-American Families: A Psychoeducational Approach for Addressing Chemical Dependency and Codependency," *Child and Adolescent Social Work Journal,* Vol. 8, No. 4 (1991), pp. 309–326.

251. Comas-Díaz, "Puerto Rican Alcoholic Women."

252. M. Jean Gilbert and Richard C. Cervantes, "Alcohol Services for Mexican Americans: A Review of Utilization Patterns, Treatment Considerations and Prevention Activities," in Gilbert and Cervantes, *Mexican Americans and Alcohol,* pp. 61–93.

253. Gladys González-Ramos, "Examining the Myth of Hispanic Families' Resistance to Treatment: Using the School as a Site for Services," *Social Work in Education,* Vol. 12, No. 4 (1990), pp. 261–274.

254. Devore and Schlesinger, *Ethnic-Sensitive Social Work Practice,* and McQuade, "Treatment and Recovery Issues."

255. Antonio Melus, "Culture and Language in the Treatment of Alcoholism," *Alcohol Health & Research World,* Summer 1980, pp. 19–20; Aguilar et al., "Mexican-American Families"; and Comas-Diaz, "Puerto Rican Women."

256. Melus, "Culture and Language," pp. 19–20.

257. Comas-Díaz, "Puerto Rican Alcoholic Women."

258. Robert B. Hampson, W. Robert Beavers, and Yosaf Hulgus, "Cross-Ethnic Family Differences: Interactional Assessment of White, Black, and Mexican-American Families," *Journal of Marital and Family Therapy,* Vol. 16, No. 3 (1990), pp. 307–319.

259. Melus, "Culture and Language," p. 20.

260. Ibid.

261. M. Jean Gilbert, "Programmatic Approaches to the Alcohol-Related Needs of Mexican Americans, in Gilbert and Cervantes, *Mexican Americans and Alcohol,* pp. 95–107.

262. McQuade, "Treatment and Recovery Issues."

263. Ibid.

264. Ibid., and Aguilar et al., "Mexican American Families."

265. Ronald Figueroa and Philip Oliver-Diaz, "Hispanic Alcoholics' Children Need Extra Help," *Alcohol Health & Research World* (Winter 1986/87), pp. 66–67.

266. Melus, "Culture and Language," p. 20.

267. Gilbert, "Alcohol-Related Practices, Problems, and Norms Among Mexican Americans: An Overview."

268. Gordon, "State-of-the-Art Review."

269. Caetano, "Responding to Alcohol-Related Problems Among Hispanics," p. 343, refers to M. Jean Gilbert, "Mexican-Americans in California: Intracultural Variation in Attitudes and Behavior Related to Alcohol," in Bennett and Ames, *The American Experience with Alcohol,* p. 268.

270. Aguilar et al., "Mexican-American Families"; and McQuade, "Treatment and Recovery Issues."

271. Caetano, "Responding to Alcohol-Related Problems Among Hispanics."

272. Gordon, "State-of-the-Art Review."

273. James Alan Neff, Thomas J. Prihoda, and Sue Keir Hoppe, "'Machismo,' Self-Esteem, Education and High Maximum Drinking Among Anglo, Black and Mexican-American Male Drinkers," *Journal of Studies on Alcohol,* Vol. 52, No. 5 (1991), pp. 458–463.

274. Melus, "Culture and Language."

275. M. Douglas Anglin, May W. Booth, Timothy M. Ryan, and Yih-Ing Hser, "Ethnic Differences in Narcotics Addiction. II. Chicano and Anglo Addiction Career Patterns," *The International Journal of the Addictions,* Vol. 23, No. 10 (1988), pp. 1011–1027.

276. Comas-Díaz, "Puerto Rican Women," p. 48.

277. Anglin et al., "Ethnic Differences in Narcotics Addiction, II."

278. See Alcocer, "Alcohol Use and Abuse Among the Hispanic American Population."

279. For a discussion, see Gilbert and Cervantes, "Alcohol Services for Mexican-Americans."

280. Butynski and Canova, "Alcohol Problem Resources and Services in State Supported Programs, FY 1987."

281. P. G. Reed and D. S. Sanchez, "Characteristics of Alcoholism Services in the United States—1984" (Rockville, MD: National Institute on Alcohol Abuse and Alcoholism, 1986), cited in Caetano, "Responding to Alcohol-Related Problems Among Hispanics."

282. Mark A. Quinones and Kathleen M. Doyle, "Cultural Variables and the Hispanic Drug Abuser," in Schecter, *Drug Dependence and Alcoholism, Volume 2,* pp. 1–9.

283. Caetano, "Responding to Alcohol-Related Problems Among Hispanics"; also see Gilbert and Cervantes, "Alcohol Services for Mexican Americans."

284. Caetano, "Responding to Alcohol-Related Problems Among Hispanics."

285. Comas-Díaz, "Puerto Rican Alcoholic Women."

286. Melus, "Culture and Language."

287. Comas-Díaz, "Puerto Rican Alcoholic Women"; and Aguilar et al., "Mexican-American Families."

288. Melus, "Culture and Language."

289. Comas-Díaz, "Puerto Rican Alcoholic Women."

290. Aguilar et al., "Mexican-American Families."

291. Comas-Díaz, "Puerto Rican Alcoholic Women."

292. Aguilar et al., "Mexican-American Families."

293. Figueroa and Oliver-Diaz, "Hispanic Alcoholics' Children," and Andrew J. Gordon, "Alcoholism Treatment Services to Hispanics: An Ethnographic Examination of a Community's Services," *Family and Community Health*, Vol. 13, No. 4 (1991), pp. 12–24.

294. Caetano, "Responding to Alcohol-Related Problems Among Hispanics."

295. R. C. Trotter and J. A. Chavira, "Discovering New Models for Alcohol, Counseling in Minority Groups," in B. Velimirov (ed.), *Modern Medicine and Medical Anthropology in the United States-Mexico Border Population* (Washington, DC: Pan American Health Organization, 1978), pp. 164–171, cited in Gilbert and Cervantes, "Alcohol Services for Mexican Americans," pp. 78–79.

296. Figueroa and Oliver-Diaz, "Hispanic Alcoholics' Children," p. 66.

297. Trotter and Chavira, "Discovering New Models," cited in Gilbert and Cervantes, *"Alcohol Services for Mexican Americans,"* p. 79.

298. Milton A. Maxwell, "Alcoholics Anonymous," in Gomberg et al. (eds)., *Alcohol, Science and Society Revisited*, p. 297; Gilbert and Cervantes, "Alcohol Services for Mexican Americans."

299. F. A. Hoffman, "Mexican American Participation in Alcoholics Anonymous," unpublished proposal submitted to the National Institute on Alcohol Abuse and Alcoholism, 1984, referred to in Gilbert and Cervantes, "Alcohol Services for Mexican Americans," p. 76.

300. Aguilar et al., "Mexican-American Families."

301. Melus, "Culture and Language"; also see Comas-Díaz, "Puerto Rican Alcoholic Women."

302. McQuade, "Treatment and Recovery Issues," p. 30.

303. Aguilar et al., "Mexican-American Families"; McQuade, "Treatment and Recovery Issues"; and Comas-Díaz, "Puerto Rican Alcoholic Women."

304. Caetano, "Responding to Alcohol-Related Problems Among Hispanics."

305. Gordon, "Alcoholism Treatment Services to Hispanics."

306. Ibid.

307. Caetano, "Responding to Alcohol-Related Problems Among Hispanics."

308. McQuade, "Treatment and Recovery Issues," p. 30.

309. The remainder of this paragraph relies on Caetano, "Responding to Alcohol-Related Problems."

310. Melus, "Culture and Language."

311. Sylvia Rodriguez-Andrew, "Los Niños: Intervention Efforts with Mexican-American Families," *Focus on Family and Chemical Dependency* (March/April 1984), pp. 8, 20.

312. Harry H. L. Kitano, "Alcohol Drinking Patterns: The Asian Americans," in NIAAA, *Alcohol and Health Monograph 4, Special Population Issues*, pp. 411–430.

313. U.S. Bureau of the census, press release CB91-216 cited in U.S. Bureau of the Census, *Statistical Abstract of the United States, 1992* (112th edition), (Washington DC: U.S. Government Printing Office, 1992), p. 17.

314. U.S. Bureau of the Census, press release CB91-215 cited in U.S. Bureau of the Census, *Statistical Abstract of the United States, 1992*, pp. 24–25.

315. Michael J. Stoil, "The Case of the Missing Gene, Hereditary Protection Against Alcoholism," *Alcohol Health & Research World* (Winter 1987/88), pp. 130–136.

316. Ibid.; Richard P. Wang, "A Study of Alcoholism in Chinatown," *International Journal of Social Psychiatry*, Vol. 14 (1968), pp. 260–267; and David Sue, "Use and Abuse of Alcohol by Asian Americans," *Journal of Psychoactive Drugs*, Vol. 19, No. 1 (January–March 1987), pp. 57–66.

317. K. Singer, "Drinking Patterns and Alcoholism in the Chinese," *British Journal of Addiction*, Vol. 67 (1972), p. 13.

318. Ibid.

319. Singer, "Drinking Patterns and Alcoholism in the Chinese," and K. Singer, "The Choice of Intoxicant Among the Chinese," *British Journal of Addiction*, Vol. 69 (1974), pp. 257–268.

320. Kitano, "Alcohol Drinking Patterns: The Asian Americans"; also see "'Old Country' Values Influence Asian-American Drinking," *Alcohol Health and Research World* (Winter 1986/87), p. 47; see Singer, "Drinking Patterns and Alcoholism in the Chinese," on the subject of alcoholism and Confucian philosophy; on Confucianism and Taoism, see Wang, "A Study of Alcoholism in Chinatown," and Singer, "The Choice of Intoxicant among the Chinese"; and on Western influences on Filipinos see James E. Lubben, Iris Chi, and Harry H. L. Kitano, "Exploring Filipino American Drinking Behavior," *Journal of Studies on Alcohol*, Vol. 49, No. 1 (1988), pp. 26–29.

321. See Francis L. K. Hsu, *Americans and Chinese* (London: Cresset Press, 1955); for additional discussion of Hsu's work and this point, see Singer, "The Choice of

Intoxicant Among the Chinese"; Wang, "A Study of Alcoholism in Chinatown"; and Sue, "Use and Abuse of Alcohol by Asian Americans."

322. Singer, "The Choice of Intoxicant Among the Chinese."

323. Sue, "Use and Abuse of Alcohol by Asian Americans."

324. Singer, "The Choice of Intoxicant Among the Chinese."

325. Bob Matsushima, Carlos Gonzalez, Curtiss Brown, and Emily Gibson, "Do Pacific/Asians Have Alcohol Problems? A Preliminary Report," in Schecter, *Drug Dependence and Alcoholism*, Vol. 2, pp. 39–46.

326. Matsushima et al., "Do Pacific/Asians Have Alcohol Problems?"

327. Stanley Sue, Nolan Zane, and Joanne Ito, "Alcohol Drinking Patterns Among Asian and Caucasian Americans," *Journal of Cross-Cultural Psychology*, Vol. 10, No. 1 (March 1979), p. 54.

328. E. K. Yu, W. T. Liu, and P. Kurzeja, "Physical and Mental Health Status Indicators for Asian/Pacific Americans, Report to the Task Force on Black and Minority Health" (Bethesda, MD: National Institutes of Health, 1984), cited in Elena S. H. Yu and William T. Liu, "Alcohol Use and Abuse Among Chinese-Americans, Epidemiologic Data," *Alcohol Health & Research World* (Winter 1986/87), pp. 14–17, 60–61.

329. Klatsky et al., Racial Patterns of Alcoholic Beverage Use."

330. Harry H. L. Kitano and Iris Chi, "Asian-Americans and Alcohol Use: Exploring Cultural Differences in Las Angeles," *Alcohol Health & Research World* (Winter 1986/87), pp. 42–47); and Harry H. L. Kitano, and Iris Chi, "Asian-Americans and Alcohol: The Chinese, Japanese, Koreans, and Filipinos in Los Angeles," in *Alcohol Use Among U.S. Ethnic Minorities*, pp. 373–382.

331. Frank M. Ahern, "Alcohol Use and Abuse Among Four Ethnic Groups in Hawaii: Native Hawaiians, Japanese, Filipinos, and Caucasians," in *Alcohol Use Among U.S. Ethnic Minorities*, pp. 315–328.

332. Sharon R. Murakami, "An Epidemiological Survey of Alcohol, Drug, and Mental Health Problems in Hawaii: A Comparison of Four Ethnic Groups," in *Alcohol Use Among U.S. Ethnic Minorities*, pp. 343–353.

333. Yu and Liu, "Alcohol Use and Abuse Among Chinese-Americans."

334. Wang, "A Study of Alcoholism in Chinatown."

335. Yu and Liu, "Alcohol Use and Abuse Among Chinese-Americans."

336. Kitano, "Alcohol Drinking Patterns: The Asian Americans."

337. Matsushima et al., "Do Pacific/Asians Have Alcohol Problems?" also see John G. Phin and Paul Phillips, "Drug Treatment Entry Patterns and Socioeconomic Characteristics of Asian American, Native American, and Puerto Rican Clients," in Schecter, *Drug Dependence and Alcoholism*, Volume 2, pp. 803–818.

338. For a discussion see Sue, "Use and Abuse of Alcohol by Asian Americans."

339. Matsushima et al., "Do Pacific/Asians Have Alcohol Problems?"; also see Kitano, "Alcohol Drinking Patterns: The Asian Americans," and Kitano and Chi, "Asian-Americans and Alcohol Use, Exploring Cultural Differences in Los Angeles."

340. Phin and Phillips, "Drug Treatment Entry Patterns," p. 808.

341. Wang, "A Study of Alcoholism in Chinatown," p. 26.

342. Matsushima, "Do Pacific/Asians Have Alcohol Problems?" p. 45; also see Kitano, "Alcohol Drinking Patterns: The Asian Americans," and Wang, "A Study of Alcoholism in Chinatown."

343. Sue et al., "Alcohol Drinking Patterns Among Asian and Caucasian Americans."

344. Walter B. Clark and Michie Hesselbrock, "A Comparative Analysis of U.S. and Japanese Drinking Patterns," in National Institute on Alcohol Abuse and Alcoholism, *Alcohol Use Patterns Among Populations of Different Cultures* (Washington, DC: U.S. Government Printing Office, 1988), pp. 79–98.

345. Sue, "Use and Abuse of Alcohol by Asian Americans."

346. Lubben et al., "Exploring Filipino American Drinking Behavior"; this is apparently the same Filipino American sample discussed in Kitano and Chi, "Asian-Americans and Alcohol Use."

347. Sandra B. Coleman, "Cross-Cultural Approaches to Working with Addict Families," in Schecter, *Drug Dependence and Alcoholism*, Vol.2, pp. 941–948.

348. Sue, "Use and Abuse of Alcohol by Asian Americans."

349. National Institute on Alcohol Abuse and Alcoholism, *Seventh Special Report to the U.S. Congress on Alcohol and Health* (Rockville, MD: U.S. Department of Health and Human Services, January 1990), p. 35.

350. Peter H. Wolff, "Ethnic Differences in Alcohol Sensitivity," *Science*, Vol. 175 (1972), pp. 449–450; see Stoil, "The Case of the Missing Gene;" and Sue, "Use and Abuse of Alcohol by Asian Americans" for a discussion of research on flushing.

351. The work of H. W. Goledde, S. Harada, and D. P. Agarwal, "Racial Differences in Alcohol Sensitivity: A New Hypothesis," *Human Genetics,* Vol. 51 (1979), pp. 331–334 and later research developments on flushing are also traced in Stoil, "The Case of the Missing Gene."

352. Kitano, "Alcohol Drinking Patterns: The Asian Americans," p. 414; also see Stoil, "The Case of the Missing Gene;" and Sue, "Use and Abuse of Alcohol by Asian Americans."

353. Leland H. Towle, "Japanese-American Drinking, Some Results from the Joint Japanese-U.S. Alcohol Epidemiology Project," *Alcohol Health & Research World,* Vol. 12, No. 3 (1988), pp. 216–223 and Vol. 12, No. 4 (1988), pp. 314–315.

354. Ronald C. Johnson, "The Flushing Response and Alcohol Use," in NIAAA, *Alcohol Use Among U.S. Ethnic Minorities,* p. 383.

355. J. A. Ewing, "Explaining Alcoholism: What Does Research Tell Us and Where Does It Need to Go?" *Japanese Journal of Studies on Alcohol,* Vol. 15 (1980), pp. 268–283, cited in Stoil, "The Case of the Missing Gene."

356. See Sue, "Use and Abuse of Alcohol by Asian Americans;" and Shaefer, "Ethnic and Racial Variations" for a discussion of this point and related research.

357. Sue et al., "Alcohol Drinking Patterns Among Asian and Caucasian Americans."

358. Kitano, "Alcohol Drinking Patterns: The Asian Americans."

359. Sue, "Use and Abuse of Alcohol by Asian Americans," and Matsushima et al., "Do Pacific/Asians Have Alcohol Problem?"

360. Butynski and Canova, "Alcohol Problem Resources and Services in State Supported Programs, FY 1987."

361. H. H. Kitano, "Social Service Needs of Asian Americans in the West Los Angeles Area," paper presented to the United Way of Los Angeles, 1980, cited in Kitano, "Alcohol Drinking Patterns: The Asian Americans."

362. Kitano, "Alcohol Drinking Patterns: The Asian Americans."

363. Phin and Phillips, "Drug Treatment Entry Patterns."

364. Phin and Phillips, "Drug Treatment Entry Patterns."

365. Matsushima et al., "Do Pacific/Asians Have Alcohol Problems?"

366. Murakami, "An Epidemiological Survey of Alcohol, Drug, and Mental Health Problems in Hawaii."

367. Coleman, "Cross Cultural Approaches to Working with Addict Families."

368. Phin and Phillips, "Drug Treatment Entry Patterns."

369. Kitano, "Alcohol Drinking Patterns: The Asian Americans."

370. The remaining paragraphs in this section rely primarily on Hideki A. Ishisaka and Calvin Y. Takagi, "Social Work with Asian and Pacific Americans," in Green, *Cultural Awareness in the Human Services,* pp. 122–156.

371. Harry H. Kitano, "Mental Illness in Four Cultures," *Journal of Social Psychology,* Vol. 80 (1970), pp. 112–134, cited in Kitano, "Alcohol Drinking Patterns: The Asian Americans."

372. E. M. Jellinek, "Immanuel Kant on Drinking," *Quarterly Journal of Studies on Alcohol,* Vol. 1, (1941), pp. 777–778.

373. Mark Keller, "The Great Jewish Drink Mystery," in Marshall, *Beliefs, Behaviors, & Alcoholic Beverages,* pp. 404–414.

374. Shoshana Weiss, "Primary Prevention of Excessive Drinking and the Jewish Culture-Preventive Efforts in Israel 1984–1985," *Journal of Primary Prevention,* Vol. 8, No. 4 (1988), p. 218.

375. Weiss, "Primary Prevention of Excessive Drinking and the Jewish Culture"; Shoshana Weiss and Penina Eldar, "Alcohol and Alcohol Problems Research 14. Israel," *British Journal of Addiction,* Vol. 82 (1987), pp. 227–235; Charles R. Snyder, Phyllis Palgi, Pnina Eldar, and Beatrice Elian, "Alcoholism Among the Jews in Israel: A Pilot Study, I. Research Rationale and a Look at the Ethnic Factor," *Journal of Studies on Alcohol,* Vol. 43, No. 7 (1982), pp. 623–654; and Marinel Sagiv, "The Problem of Alcohol in Israel," *Archives of International Medicine,* Vol. 139 (March 1979), pp. 280–281.

376. Weiss, "Primary Prevention of Excessive Drinking and the Jewish Culture," and Weiss and Eldar, "Alcohol and Alcohol Problems Research 14. Israel."

377. H. Bar, "Drinking Patterns of the Israeli Public" (second research) [Hebrew-text] (Jerusalem, The Israel Institute of Applied Social Research, 1984), cited in Weiss, "Primary Prevention of Excessive Drinking and the Jewish Culture," and Weiss and Eldar, "Alcohol and Alcohol Problems Research 14. Israel."

378. Weiss, "Primary Prevention of Excessive Drinking and the Jewish Culture," p. 220; also see Weiss and Eldar, "Alcohol and Alcohol Problems Research 14. Israel."

379. Weiss and Eldar, "Alcohol and Alcohol Problems Research 14. Israel."

380. Ibid.

381. Weiss, "Primary Prevention of Excessive Drinking and the Jewish Culture."

382. Weiss and Eldar, "Alcohol and Alcohol Problems Research 14. Israel."

383. Donald Cahalan and Ira Cisin, "American Drinking Practices: Summary of Findings from a National Probability Sample. I. Extent of Drinking by Population Subgroups," *Quarterly Journal of Studies on Alcohol,* Vol. 29 (1968), pp. 130–151.

384. Michael E. Hilton, "The Demographic Distribution of Drinking Patterns in 1984," in Clark and Hilton (eds.), *Alcohol in America,* pp. 73–86, reprinted from *Drug and Alcohol Dependence,* Vol. 22, (1988), pp. 37–47 © Elsevier Science Publishing Co., Inc., Limerick, Ireland.

385. M. M. Glatt, "Alcoholism and Drug Dependence Amongst Jews," *British Journal of Addiction,* Vol. 64 (1970), pp. 297–304, and Barry Glassner and Bruce Berg, "How Jews Avoid Alcohol Problems," *American Sociological Review,* Vol. 45 (August 1980), pp. 647–664.

386. Glatt, "Alcoholism and Drug Dependence Amongst Jews."

387. Ibid.

388. Sissy Carpey, "Alcoholism, New Expressions of Jewish Concern Create Climate of Hope," *Jewish Exponent,* June 7, 1985, p. 48.

389. Barbara Teller, "Chemical Dependency in the Jewish Community," *The Counselor,* (May/June 1989), pp. 27–28.

390. Russell Eisenman, Jan Carl Grossman, and Ronald Goldstein, "Undergraduate Marijuana Use as Related to Internal Sensation Novelty Seeking and Openness to Experience," *Journal of Clinical Psychology* Vol. 36, No. 4 (October 1980), pp. 1013–1019.

391. Ibid., p. 1018.

392. Maristela G. Monteiro and Marc A. Schuckit, "Alcohol, Drug, and Mental Health Problems Among Jewish and Christian Men at a University," *American Journal of Drug and Alcohol Abuse,* Vol. 15, No. 4 (1989), pp. 403–412.

393. Lydia V. Flasher and Stephen A. Maisto, "A Review of Theory and Research on Drinking Patterns Among Jews," *The Journal of Nervous and Mental Disease,* Vol. 172, No. 10 (1984), pp. 596–603.

394. Charles R. Snyder, *Alcohol and the Jews, A Cultural Study of Drinking and Sobriety* (Glencoe, IL: The Free Press, 1958).

395. Sheila Blume, Dee Dropkin, and Lloyd Sokolow, "The Jewish Alcoholic: A Descriptive Study," *Alcohol Health and Research World,* Summer 1980, pp. 21–26.

396. Flasher and Maisto, "A Review of Theory and Research on Drinking Patterns Among Jews;" Monteiro and Schuckit, "Alcohol, Drug, and Mental Health Problems Among Jewish and Christian Men at a University."

397. Teller, "Chemical Dependency in the Jewish Community."

398. See, for example, Blume et al., "The Jewish Alcoholic: A Descriptive Study."

399. Robert Freed Bales, Cultural Differences in Rates of Alcoholism, *Quarterly Journal of Studies on Alcoholism,* Vol. 6 (1946), pp. 480–499.

400. Teller, "Chemical Dependency in the Jewish Community."

401. Donald Davison Glad, "Attitudes and Experiences of American-Jewish and American-Irish Male Youth as Related to Differences in Adult Rates of Inebriety," *Quarterly Journal of Studies on Alcohol,* Vol. 8 (1947), pp. 406–472.

402. Snyder, *Alcohol and the Jews.*

403. Mark Keller, "The Great Jewish Drink Mystery," in Marshall, *Beliefs, Behavior, & Alcoholic Beverages,* pp. 404–414, and L. Cheinisse, "La Race Juive Jouit-elle d'une Immunité a l'égard de l'alcoholisme," *Semaine Medicale* Vol. 28, (1908), pp. 613–615, cited in Snyder et al., "Alcoholism Among the Jews in Israel."

404. See Jellinek, "Immanuel Kant on Drinking."

405. Bales, Cultural Differences in Rates of Alcoholism."

406. Snyder, *Alcohol and the Jews,* p. 182.

407. Emile Durkheim, *Le Suicide* (Paris: Felix Alcan, 1897).

408. Glad, "Attitudes and Experiences of American-Jewish and American-Irish Male Youth," p. 462.

409. Snyder, *Alcohol and the Jews,* p. 101.

410. Snyder et al., "Alcoholism Among the Jews in Israel."

411. Flasher and Maisto, "A Review of Theory and Research on Drinking Patterns Among Jews," p. 599.

412. Blume et al., "The Jewish Alcoholic," and Teller, "Chemical Dependency in the Jewish Community."

413. Barry Glassner and Bruce Berg, "Social Locations and Interpretations: How Jews Define Alcoholism," *Journal of Studies on Alcohol,* Vol. 45, No. 1 (1984), pp. 16–25.

414. Glassner and Berg, "How Jews Avoid Alcohol Problems."

415. Albert D. Ullman, "Sociocultural Backgrounds of Alcoholism," *Annals of the American Academy of Political and Social Science,* Vol. 315 (1958), pp. 48–54.

416. Victor D. Sanua, "Psychopathology and Social Deviance Among Jews," *Journal of Jewish Communal Service*, Vol. 58, No. 1 (1981), pp. 12–23.

417. Weiss and Eldar, "Alcohol and Alcohol Problems Research 14. Israel."

418. See Montiero and Schuckit, "Alcohol, Drug, and Mental Health Problems."

419. Flasher and Maisto, "A Review of Theory and Research on Drinking Patterns Among Jews," p. 601.

420. Carpey, "Alcoholism," p. 47.

421. Flasher and Maisto, "A Review of Theory and Research on Drinking Patterns Among Jews," p. 601.

422. Blume et al., "The Jewish Alcoholic," and Teller, "Chemical Dependency in the Jewish Community."

423. Blume et al., "The Jewish Alcoholic," and Carpey, "Alcoholism."

424. Some of this paragraph relies on Teller, "Chemical Dependency in the Jewish Community"; also see Carpey, "Alcoholism."

425. Teller, "Chemical Dependency in the Jewish Community."

426. Lisa Master, "Jewish Experience of Alcoholics Anonymous," *Smith College Studies in Social Work*, Vol. 59, No. 2 (1989), pp. 183–199.

427. Master, "Jewish Experience of Alcoholics Anonymous."

428. Teller, "Chemical Dependency in the Jewish Community."

12

Gay men, lesbians, and chemical dependency

Like alcoholism and other forms of drug abuse, homosexuality[1] has variously been called a crime, a sin, and an illness or disease.[2] Human service professionals generally refer to neither chemical dependency nor homosexuality as a crime or as a sin, but many individuals have fought for the treatment of chemical dependency using a disease or illness perspective, while also fighting to eliminate the definition of homosexuality as a crime or disease. In 1973 the American Psychiatric Association removed homosexuality from its *Diagnostic and Statistical Manual of Mental Disorders*. The American Psychological Association concurred with this decision. However, certain acts between members of the same gender remain crimes in some states. Ziebold comments that many still consider the terms alcoholic and homosexual "odious,"[3] and gay men and lesbians with chemical dependency problems may face added stigma that compounds their lack of access to good health and mental health care.[4]

This chapter explores alcohol and drug use among gay men and lesbians. The focus is largely on alcohol abuse, since it is discussed more widely in the literature on these populations. Gay men and lesbians function in the social systems of the majority culture, but many are also integrally involved in the social systems or subcultures of gay and lesbian communities. While it is beyond the scope of this volume to discuss many aspects of the life-styles of lesbians and gay men, the diversity among them, and the many myths surrounding them, such knowledge is important in helping the reader integrate the material presented here. There is also a considerable clinical literature addressing mental health issues with gay men and lesbians of value to chemical dependency professionals.

SUBSTANCE ABUSE AMONG LESBIANS AND GAY MEN

Since Kinsey's research in the 1940s, many have assumed that the incidence of homosexuality in the general population is 10 percent and that a higher percentage of individuals have had some homosexual experience.[5] While recent reports suggest that these figures may be overestimates,[6] the literature generally indicates similar levels of social adjustment and similar incidences of social or psychological problems for gay men and lesbians compared with heterosexual men and women.[7] The incidences of substance abuse and of suicide *may*, however, be higher for gay men and lesbians,[8] and a strong association between alcohol use, alcoholism, and suicide in the general population has been documented.[9]

In 1978 the President's Commission on Mental Health recognized gay male and lesbian alcoholics as an "at-risk" group "that has been inadequately or inappropriately served."[10] They shared this concern with many gay men and lesbians. The advent of the human immunodeficiency virus (HIV) has further raised concerns about substance abuse among gay men and lesbians as it has among most segments of the population. There is concern not only about the transmission of HIV through sexual activity and through intravenous drug use, but also about alcohol's deleterious effect on the immune system and on judgment that may play a part in the transmission of the virus.[11]

Several studies provide evidence of higher rates of substance abuse among gay men and particularly lesbians compared with men and women in the general population. A study by Fifield conducted in Los Angeles and published in 1975 has been cited frequently.[12] She estimated that nearly one-third of the gay and lesbian population drank excessively. Weinberg and Williams conducted a study of gay men which included a question on alcohol.[13] Of the 1,057 U.S. respondents, 29.4 percent said they "drank more than they should many times" and another 31.3 percent said they did so "sometimes." Lohrenz and his colleagues found that 29 percent of the 145 gay men in their study recruited from four urban areas in Kansas scored as alcoholics on the Michigan Alcoholism Screening Test.[14] In an in-depth study of gay men and lesbians, Saghir and Robins generally found more heavy drinking, alcohol-related problems, and nonprescription drug use in a gay and lesbian sample compared with heterosexual men and women, but their nonprobability sample was also relatively small (89 gay men, 57 lesbians, 35 heterosexual men, and 44 heterosexual women).[15] The differences they found between the heterosexual and lesbian women were substantial, while the differences between the gay and straight men were much smaller. The lesbians drank considerably more than the heterosexual women; their drinking was more similar to that of the gay and heterosexual men. In a further analysis of these data, 28 percent of the lesbians met the criteria the authors described for alcoholism, compared with 5 percent of the heterosexual women; another 33 percent of the lesbians were considered heavy drinkers or "questionable" alcoholics compared with 7 percent of the heterosexuals.[16]

Despite similarities in their findings, most of the studies conducted to date have serious methodological limitations such as the use of convenience samples rather than general population surveys.[17] Some samples have been obtained from gay and lesbian organizations, while others have included subjects identified in gay bars or other social settings where those with drinking problems may be overrepresented. Reports have been criticized for inflating estimates.[18]

McKirnan and Peterson tried to obtain a broader sample by widely dispersing 21,000 surveys through various channels in Chicago's gay community including newspapers, community organizations, bars, and so forth.[19] About 16 percent (3,400) were returned. They compared their results for alcohol use with the widely cited Clark and Midanik general population survey[20] and for other drug use with a study by Clayton et al.[21] Comparisons indicated that gay men and lesbians were less likely to abstain from alcohol (14 percent of the respondents were abstainers compared to 29 percent of the general population), more likely to be moderate drinkers (71 percent and 57 percent, respectively), and were similar in terms of the percentage of heavy drinkers (15 percent and 14 percent, respectively). Thirteen percent of the gay male respondents and 14 percent of the lesbians were abstainers, while abstention rates among the general population are not only higher but are more disparate between genders (23 percent for men and 34 percent for women). Seventeen percent of the gay men and 9 percent of the lesbians were heavy drinkers compared with 21 percent of men and 7 percent of women in the general population. Higher rates of alcohol problems were reported for lesbians and gay men than for the general population (23 percent and 12 percent, respectively). Similar to Saghir and Robins's study, the gay men and lesbians were relatively similar in terms of drinking problems, while in the general population, men report substantially higher rates of problems than women. In the younger age groups, the level of alcohol-related problems among gay men and men in the general population was about the same, but after age 30 problems declined for heterosexual men, while they remained relatively constant for gay men. Among the gay men and lesbians, 56 percent had used marijuana in the previous year compared with 20 percent of men and women in the general population, while the figures for cocaine use in the past year were 23 percent and 8.5 percent, respectively, and for frequent cocaine use 2.3 percent and 0.7 percent, respectively. Figures for frequent marijuana

users were more alike at 11 percent and 9 percent, respectively. Like the findings for alcohol, there was less of a difference in drug use between lesbians and gay men than between men and women in the general population, and there was more drug use among older gay men and lesbians than their counterparts in the general population. McKirnan and Peterson conclude that "there is . . . some cause for concern about substance abuse among homosexuals, although we did not find the very heavy alcohol and drug use that has often been ascribed to homosexual populations."[22]

Stall and Wiley were able to obtain information on the drinking and drug use of 1,034 gay and heterosexual men in San Francisco as part of a larger epidemiological study of AIDS.[23] This study did use random sampling (multistage cluster), although participation was, of course, voluntary. After controlling for age, the researchers found few differences in the quantity and frequency of alcohol consumption. Like some of McKirnan and Peterson's findings, the gay men's drinking tended to be consistent across age groups, while it declined with age among the heterosexuals. However, the gay men, particularly the younger ones, were more likely to be abstainers than their heterosexual counterparts, but they were also more likely to be heavier drinkers. The gay men were more likely to use marijuana, MDA, psychedelics, barbiturates, ethyl chloride, and amphetamines, but the greatest difference was in the use of "poppers." Most of the drug use was among the younger gay men, but in general, drug use for the gay sample was not frequent.

While some studies paint a picture of alcohol use and alcohol problems among gay men and lesbians that is two or three times greater than in the general population,[24] the more recent studies suggest that these differences may not be as dramatic as thought. The McKirnan and Peterson and the Stall and Wiley studies were conducted about 15 years after the Fifield and Saghir and Robins studies. Much has changed since that time. AIDS has arrived; there is a greater awareness of health-risk factors, and chemical dependence has become known as a treatable disease.

Hastings suggests that the gay rights and women's rights movements, greater openness about gay or lesbian identity, greater opportunities for socialization outside bars, and specialized substance abuse education and treatment for gay men and lesbians may have helped to mitigate drinking.[25] Due to the number of other available drugs and the difficulty in quantifying them by amount and frequency of use, it is especially difficult to interpret findings about this aspect of chemical dependency.[26] Studies suggest greater drug use, but much of it may be experimental. Additional exploration is needed to determine the extent of alcohol and drug-related problems among gay men and lesbians.

In addition to concerns about substance abuse among gay men and lesbians, Small and Leach noted that nearly one-third of the men they saw in their clinical alcoholism practice were "concerned about homosexuality."[27] This suggests that not only is knowledge of substance abuse among helping professionals working with gay men and lesbians a prerequisite, but that chemical dependency professionals need knowledge of gay men and lesbians.

SUBSTANCE ABUSE: CAUSES AND CONNECTIONS

At one time, the excessive use of alcohol to cope with fears of homosexuality or latent homosexuality was advanced as a cause of alcoholism.[28] In discussing this literature, Small and Leach noted that "it might be inferred that overt homosexuality averts alcoholism, or that no one can manifest both alcoholism and overt homosexuality."[29] Presumably this suggested that when one stops covering up his or her gayness, there is no need to drink excessively. Other individuals espoused the position that by "treating" homosexuality and converting the client to heterosexism, substance abuse problems would remit.[30]

Recent literature takes the position that chemical abuse and homosexuality are not causally linked, despite evidence of poten-

tially higher rates of alcohol and other drug use among lesbians and gay men.[31] As Israelstam states, "Present day authors working with the alcohol problems of homosexuals believe it is not homosexuality (physical acts or emotional attachments), but rather homophobia (guilt and/or negative attitudes) in both homosexuals and heterosexuals that causes the stress and denial that may lead to alcohol and drug problems in the homosexual group."[32] This position appears consistent with the view of lesbian feminists. They offer a political explanation of alcohol and other drug abuse in which the majority group sees that alcohol and drugs are available as a means of rendering minority groups more powerless[33] (also see Chapter 11 on substance abuse in ethnic minority communities).

Brandsma and Pattison summarize four explanations for alcohol abuse problems among lesbians and gay men: (1) Alcohol may assist members of this oppressed group cope with the shame, isolation, guilt, and other negative feelings. (2) The view of homosexuality as deviant may contribute to the development of other socially identified forms of deviance such as alcoholism. (3) Gay men and lesbians have had few outlets for socialization except gay bars and parties where drinking is a part of the environment. (4) Alcohol can reduce anxieties associated with identifying and accepting one's self as a gay man or as a lesbian, including initiation of sexual relationships with persons of the same gender.[34] Additional comments from the descriptive literature on substance abuse among gay men and lesbians affirm these views:

Gay people drink and party to hide from the world, to escape their feelings of being different, and all too many never manage to take off the mask. Shallowness and narcissistic self-indulgence are then interpreted and given public currency as the evidence of the "homosexual personality," not as evidence of societal confinement. Accepting this view of themselves, the victims accumulate more guilt and more of an urge to escape into drinking.[35]

A high level of psychic stress, polarization towards bars and cocktail parties as the primary basis for social interaction, and a closing off of alternative modes of relief in everyday living: these are the forces of oppression, and alcoholism is one of the resulting symptoms.[36]

Others point out that lack of access to roles in marriage, child rearing, and mainstream occupations may exacerbate drinking and drug use.[37] As in the general population, there are probably many explanations for chemical abuse and dependency among gay men and lesbians.[38]

Kus has challenged some of these explanations for substance abuse among gay men and lesbians, especially what he terms "gay bar ethnotheory."[39] Ziebold earlier reviewed evidence that "most homosexuals do not spend much time in bars"; however, the literature abounds with discussion of these bars, especially their importance in the initial socialization to gay life-styles.[40] Kus acknowledges the effects of oppression in the lives of gay men and lesbians, but he offers a "gay non-acceptance theory," attributing substance abuse to unresolved issues at each stage of the "coming out" process. The various stages of this process (and the different labels given to them) have been discussed by many authors.[41] As described by Kus, during the first stage, which he calls *identification,* the individual recognizes that he or she is homosexual. In the second stage, which he calls *cognitive changes,* the individual addresses homophobia (a term coined by Weinberg)[42] by learning about gay and lesbian lifestyles. In stage 3, *acceptance,* individuals free themselves from the shame and guilt that society attaches to homosexuality. The fourth stage, *action,* involves positive acceptance of a gay life-style and often involves disclosure to others. According to Kus, homosexuality oriented individuals may develop substance abuse problems because they are unable to acknowledge and accept their homosexuality in a positive light.

Kus attempted to validate his theory by studying twenty homosexual men in recovery from substance abuse. Based on their recall, all the men had developed drinking problems before they began going to gay bars, evidence that Kus cites as discrediting the gay bar ethnotheory. One of Kus's hypotheses was that accepting being gay would lead to sobriety, but evidence showed that it was becoming sober that led the respondents to accept themselves as gay. This seems logical given that clarity of thinking and the ability to address problems rationally comes after one is sober. (In the clinical literature, Zehner and Lewis and Glaus have discussed the need to make sobriety the first step in assisting gay men and lesbians who are chemically dependent.[43]) Earlier, Small and Leach indicated that in seven of ten cases they reported, the alcoholic men "who were able to accept and live comfortably with the need for abstinence seemed also most likely to achieve relatively successful sexual function"; however, the other three "patients who had come to terms with their homosexuality seemed to find it easier to accept the diagnosis of alcoholism and the need for abstinence."[44] Small and Leach also concluded that "recovery from pathological drinking seemed to be within reach almost as soon as the patient could view alcoholism as a condition independent of homosexuality."[45]

An analysis by Lewis and coworkers provides equivocal information on whether gay bar ethnotheory may explain the drinking behavior of lesbians.[46] The lesbians in their study described as "nonsocial drinkers" began having "homosexual psychological responses" at an average age of 13, followed by their "first significant homosexual experiences" at an average age of 21, while heavy drinking started somewhat later, at an average age of 24. Although the age at which the lesbians began going to gay bars was not indicated, after controlling for frequency of bar attendance, there was still a higher rate of alcoholism and heavy drinking among the lesbians than the heterosexual women they studied. However, half the lesbians did not go to gay bars, and the drinking of the lesbians who did and did not go to bars was similar.

Do lesbians and gay men believe that their sexual orientation influences their drinking? Hawkins interviewed thirty lesbian alcoholics, twenty-two of whom "clearly" believed that their lesbianism had not contributed to their alcoholism.[47] In their sample containing gay men and lesbians with a range of drinking behaviors, Saghir and Robins reported that 90 percent of the lesbians they interviewed saw no connection between their drinking behavior and their sexual orientation compared with 62 percent of the gay men. The remaining lesbians and gay men saw a connection between their affectional preference and their drinking, largely as a result of socialization in gay bars.[48]

Some additional studies of lesbians are of interest here, since much of the literature on homosexuality has been written about gay men with the often erroneous assumption that it applies to lesbians. In the mid-1970s, Hawkins found no "scientific" studies on substance abuse among lesbians, only "source material" written by Lillene Fifield for the Gay Community Services Center in Los Angeles, California.[49] Shortly after, Diamond and Wilsnack interviewed ten lesbians who drank excessively.[50] While their discussion of the high level of dependency needs (and other theories of alcoholism) among lesbians is interesting, they warn that their research only suggests further avenues of study. In a more recent study, fifteen lesbians who were not alcoholic were compared with fifteen lesbians who were alcoholic; the alcoholics reported more unhappiness in childhood, more loneliness, and fewer individuals in whom they could currently confide.[51] While differences were not found in their relationships with their mothers, the alcoholics were more likely to report poor relationships with their fathers and indicated that their fathers also had drinking problems. The only significant difference with respect to involvement in group activities was that the alcoholic women were more involved with religious groups. The authors conclude that the lesbian alcoholics had more social supports than anticipated, but this may have been due to the fact that these women were in recovery and were participating in groups such as Alcoholics Anonymous.

All these studies are interesting, but the issue of genetic transmission of chemical dependency has been given minimal consideration in the literature on gay men and lesbians. Lewis and associates found no statistically significant difference in the proportion of lesbian and heterosexual women with alcoholic parents in their small sample, suggesting that there may be equal genetic risk of alcoholism between the groups.[52] Kus notes that little is known about whether there are general biological differences between gay men and men with other affectional preferences.[53] Most alcoholic men in his study reported drinking "abusively" from their first drink.[54] This may indicate that a genetic predisposition is a precursor of alcoholism in at least some gay men as it may be in the general population. Family social history and other environmental factors have also only been touched upon in the substance abuse research literature on gay men and lesbians. The oppression or unresolved coming out issues faced by gay men and lesbians may interact with genetic and environmental factors to produce higher rates of substance abuse among them. Ziebold adds another interesting caveat to this literature when he "wonder[ed] whether the many studies on homosexuals are not reflecting much alcoholic thinking and feeling, and thus whether we will get a true picture of the mental health of homosexual persons until studies begin to distinguish between alcoholic and nonalcoholic subjects."[55]

A neglected population in the substance abuse literature is gay male and lesbian adolescents. Wellisch and his colleagues matched fourteen gay male and lesbian adolescents who were substance abusers with fourteen adolescent, heterosexual substance abusers.[56] All were clients of the same treatment program. They found that both groups received the same number of therapy sessions; however, sexuality was more often discussed in the therapy sessions of the gay and lesbian than heterosexual adolescents. The gay and lesbian adolescents were more likely to discuss sexual identity in their individual than group sessions. In fact, for the gay, lesbian, and heterosexual adolescents there was more focus on substantive issues in individual rather than group sessions, suggesting that further study be done to determine the most effective treatment modalities for these young clients.

Gay men and lesbians from African-American, Hispanic-American, and other cultural backgrounds are also overlooked in the literature. Icard and Traunstein have discussed black, gay, alcoholic men, the multiple sources of discrimination they face, and the need for attention to the interactions of substance abuse, ethnicity and culture, sexual preference, and reference groups in developing treatment plans for them.[57]

PREVENTION ISSUES

Opportunities for socialization and other activities—political, civic, religious, and so on—have proliferated in gay and lesbian communities. These activities, which raise awareness of issues affecting gay men and lesbians and promote "gay pride," provide alternatives to the bars and may help avert substance abuse.[58] More than a decade ago, Mongeon and Ziebold offered a model for preventing alcohol abuse in gay communities.[59] Since there is so much distrust of traditional or mainstream society, they asserted that prevention can be successful only if it is a self-help effort among gay men and lesbians. Their optimism about such an approach is based on the success of similar approaches that have already been used for controlling venereal diseases. (These approaches are also being used to contain the spread of the human immunodeficiency virus.) While it has been suggested that a contributing factor to alcoholism in gay and lesbian communities may be greater tolerance and encouragement of excessive drinking,[60] Mongeon and Ziebold believe that the gay community is acutely aware of its drinking and drug problems.

Like many prevention models, Mongeon and Ziebold's focuses on both change in the individual and change in the environment. The focus on the individual would involve an early intervention program "to increase self-esteem and coping skills."[61] (Similar approaches have been used with women and other oppressed groups.) There would also be an outreach program to change the environmental context in which drinking takes

place. In bars they recommend "separate space where alcohol is not served," "hours during which alcoholic drinks will not be served," and promoting nonalcoholic beverages that also produce a good profit,[62] but Israelstam points out that gay bar owners may be more supportive of antidrug campaigns than alcohol prevention and education on their premises.[63] Since venereal disease and human immunodeficiency virus testing have been done in bars, it may also be logical to use these establishments as sites for substance abuse screening. Finnegan and Cook believe that since the gay bar remains a central place for socialization, "to flatly tell gay/lesbian clients to stay out of bars is not always the most therapeutic move."[64] They agree that changing socialization within the bar may be a reasonable alternative. However, the emphasis on socialization in bars may be giving way to other alternatives, and any good professional can identify other social outlets for clients.[65] This is particularly important if the client is an alcohol or drug abuser. An overarching concern in the gay literature is that, ultimately, it is the integration of gay men and lesbians into the broader society and reduction of both culturally reinforced and internalized homophobia that will help to prevent substance abuse.[66]

TREATMENT ISSUES

The empirical literature on chemical dependency treatment of gay men and lesbians is scarce, but a number of issues are raised in the clinical literature. They include denial and defensiveness, inclusion of significant others, and whether gay and lesbian clients are better treated in separate programs.

Denial and Defensiveness

Denial is the defense mechanism most often discussed in the chemical dependency literature (see Chapter 5). It also operates in the process of identifying as a gay man or lesbian. "As children born and raised primarily by heterosexual parents in a homophobic culture, gay men and lesbians learn by osmosis to be homophobic."[67] Given the serious consequences of self-hatred that arise from internalized homophobia, excessive use of alcohol and other drugs may not be surprising.[68] It has also been noted that gay men and lesbians may use their sexual orientation and oppressed status as an "excuse" or rationalization for drug or alcohol use or as a means of averting attention away from sobriety,[69] but this should not automatically be assumed.[70] Several suggestions have been made for addressing a client's sexual orientation. According to Finnegan and Cook:

In order to treat their gay and lesbian clients in constructive and health-enhancing ways, counselors must be able to determine when to focus on their clients' alcoholism and basically ignore their sexual orientation and when to attend closely to client's sexual orientation and the interplay between it and the alcoholism. Although the counselor needs always to be sensitive to sexual orientation, there are times when it must be directly addressed if it is creating problems for the client.[71]

Ziebold stresses that "for the homosexual alcoholic, sexual identity will be paramount among his or her concerns and must be handled openly and without bias,"[72] although other professionals note that the lesbian clients they have served are more comfortable discussing their sexual orientation than their chemical dependency.[73] While confronting clients about what their affectional preference is can be destructive, exploration of a client's relationships and sexual history is important.[74] Colcher advises professionals to approach sexual orientation as they would other client characteristics such as age or ethnicity and to present themselves "in a warm, nonjudgemental way regarding homosexuality."[75] The illustration entitled "Lesbian Chemical Dependency—A Composite Case" illustrates the importance of the professional's recognition and acceptance of a client's sexual identity.

Chemical dependency can be as stigmatizing in gay communities as it is in straight communities,[76] and some believe that treating alcoholics who are gay or lesbian is a particu-larly difficult challenge because of their strong defense systems. "Every gay and lesbian person develops defenses to deal with the forces and stresses of oppression" and "the gay/lesbian alcoholic's defenses attain extra strength because the defenses against the disease of alcoholism and the disease of homophobia intertwine."[77] For gay men who are chemically dependent, there is a double stigma.[78] For lesbians, there may be a triple stigma, since chemically dependent women generally face more social disapproval than their male counterparts.[79] Members of ethnic minority groups may face added stigma.[80] Finnegan and Cook caution that chemical dependency professionals "need to be mindful of distinguishing between confronting defenses that protect alcoholism and respecting defenses that serve as survival mechanisms."[81]

In addition to denial, other defenses may subvert treatment. When the professional treating the chemically dependent gay male or lesbian is heterosexual, the client may complain that he or she cannot relate to a straight counselor or that the counselor cannot effectively assist someone whose sexual orientation he or she does not share.[82] Similar scenarios occur when clients complain that a nonalcoholic professional cannot understand their problems. Well-educated professionals anticipate these behaviors and usually addresses them by refocusing on the client's chemical dependency and restating their desire to assist the client. However, a client's desire for another counselor is not always resistance. It may be an accurate perception that the counselor is not accepting of gay and lesbian clients and is uncomfortable working with them.[83] Of the 145 gay men surveyed by Lohrenz and his colleagues, 55 percent said they would prefer a therapist of the same sexual orientation if they needed assistance, and 42 percent said the therapist's sexual orientation was not a concern.[84] Israelstam describes a "bill of rights" for clients developed by San Francisco's Department of Health that includes the right to be treated by a professional sensitive to gay life-styles, including a professional of the same sexual preference.[85]

Lesbian Chemical Dependency—A Composite Case

by Louise Warren, MSSW, CSW-ACP

Leslie was 23 the first time she sought help for her dual addiction to alcohol and amphetamines. She began drinking at age 16. Leslie was living in a midsized Texas city with her parents and two older brothers. She knew at age 14 that she was attracted to girls. When her friends at school talked about boys, she felt vaguely disinterested. She knew that her relationships with girl friends were emotionally very important to her, and she began to feel sexually drawn to girls as well.

In her midteens Leslie would surreptitiously read lesbian literature, which was not difficult to obtain in her city. What *was* difficult was finding a person with whom to talk about her feelings or a place to do this. At age 16, she built up her courage and asked a sales clerk at a woman's book store where she might find "someone like me" to talk to. The woman suggested a popular lesbian bar.

Leslie described herself as "incredibly nervous" when she went to her first lesbian bar. Easily passing for 18, alcohol quickly addressed her anxiety. Leslie's father and grandfather also drank heavily. Within two weeks, Leslie met her first girlfriend, Paula. Paula and Leslie had a social life that revolved around meeting at the bar, shooting pool, and getting drunk. The relationship quickly became sexual. Although spending more and more time around lesbians and in environments heavily populated by lesbians felt rather comfortable for Leslie, becoming sexual was much more difficult. Paula, who was 20, noticed how difficult it was for Leslie to relax, and suggested that they do a line of cocaine on top of the alcohol. This created a pleasant psychological mixture of arousal and relaxation.

A pattern was thus created for Leslie. As with many lesbians, her social life revolved around the bar. Sexual experiences were accompanied by use of alcohol or alcohol and some type of stimulant.

Leslie finished high school with poor grades, made half-hearted attempts at going to a local community college, and eventually began working full-time for the family business.

Between the ages of 20 and 23, several significant events happened that underscored Leslie's worsening addictive disease. She received two DWIs and incurred serious financial debt in a effort to pay the consequent fines. Leslie had also begun shooting speed regularly, and as a result she developed three serious infections, one of which required a hospitalization. Leslie also watched her brother go to prison on several drug charges.

Leslie first sought help after her brother's conviction. John had been both her closest ally in her family, as well as her primary drug source. She sought help at a women's addiction referral agency. Through the use of the Johns Hopkins Questionnaire, as well as information gathered through her social history, Leslie was told that she showed signs of being dually addicted to alcohol and speed. She was not particularly surprised and accepted several referrals for help. Leslie never told her counselor that she was lesbian, and the counselor never asked any questions that might have elicited this information. Leslie felt "it was none of her [the counselor's] business," and did not see any connection between her sexual identity and her chemical dependency.

She attempted to follow through on the suggested referrals, which included attending self-help meetings and seeing a counselor who specialized in alcohol and drug abuse issues. Roadblocks quickly presented themselves—all her lesbian friends drank heavily, and she had no idea where to meet other women. She did not feel comfortable in self-help meetings. Anything she might have shared seemed to include coming out as a lesbian, and she thought she would be laughed at and not taken seriously. Besides, she thought, how were these straight people going to understand *her?* For the first time in her life, during these first few sober days, she began to feel ashamed of her sexuality.

Leslie got drunk seventy-two hours after seeking help, and stayed drunk for another two years. During this time, her brother was both released from jail, and then returned on new drug-related offenses. After visiting him in prison, she once again sought help from the women's addiction referral agency.

Leslie saw a new counselor, who utilized the same assessment tools as before, but who also picked up on subtle cues provided by the client. Leslie talked about "them" in reference to significant others. She also talked about "the bar" in ways that indicated it was at least equally a social club as it was a place to drink alcohol. The counselor used the same pronouns as Leslie, thereby not assuming that Leslie was heterosexual, and asked Leslie if she knew of places to meet people in addition to the bar. After a few moments of silence, Leslie told the counselor she was lesbian. The counselor told Leslie that she, too, was lesbian, and was a recovering alcoholic.

With this barrier down, Leslie was able for the first time to fully discuss her chemical dependency. She stated she knew she needed help, she just had no idea how to be sober and still be able to have a fulfilling social, emotional, and sexual life. The counselor used appropriate self-disclosure to provide Leslie with enough hope so that she could begin to seriously consider sobriety. This time Leslie was referred to gay and lesbian self-help meetings and to a treatment center with an openly lesbian counselor. Treatment lectures included content on internal and social homophobia.

At this writing, Leslie has nine years of sobriety, is in a seven-year relationship, and runs the family business. She states that had she remained closeted, she would have died from her addiction.

Significant Others

Scant attention has been given to including the partners of gay men and lesbians in substance abuse treatment.[86] Correcting these oversights includes changing policies such as "permitting visits from lovers in a detoxification hospital if the policy is 'family' only,"[87] but the issue can be far more complex. "Given the limited size and scope of the lesbian community, it would not be surprising that the nonalcoholic lesbian might be reticent to alienate a friend or lover by confronting that person about her substance abuse."[88] Whitney writes that gay or lesbian co-alcoholics may be particularly prone to adopt the victim role, because they are already demeaned in a homophobic society,[89] and Finnegan and McNally say that "being gay or lesbian . . . is perfect training for codependence."[90] (Codependency is also discussed in Chapter 10.) Like other codependents, gay men and lesbians may be desperately trying to keep their partner because of their low self-esteem. Whitney recommends group treatment for these individuals. The lack of role models for gay men and lesbians makes it difficult to know what a healthy and happy intimate relationship is, and the disruption caused by chemical abuse makes it more difficult to achieve a fulfilling relationship.[91] Gay Al-Anon can be very helpful to gay and lesbian partners of chemically dependent individuals. Anderson and Henderson call "couples and family therapy . . . the treatment of choice when significant others are aiding in the maintenance of alcoholic drinking" by lesbians, (and they suggest group treatment for substance abusers when significant others are not involved in their recovery).[92] In addition, gay men and lesbians may have alcoholic parents and may benefit from Gay Adult Children of Alcoholics groups which are also available in some communities.

The inclusion of parents and siblings in the chemical dependency treatment of gay men and lesbians has also received little attention. Exposing one's chemical abuse is generally difficult enough, but if coming out to family members is also involved, the process can be especially stressful for everyone concerned. The client is likely to be concerned about being rejected on both counts, and parents may "focus on their own perceived failures in raising not only an alcoholic [or drug abuser] but also a homosexual."[93] At the Pride Institute, an inpatient chemical dependency treatment facility for gay men and lesbians, "some patients invite their families to participate in the [family portion of the] program specifically so they can come out."[94]

Intervention can be an important step in getting substance abusers into treatment, but Ziebold notes that gays may not have family or even close friends to intervene; gays also reportedly have less job stability than other alcoholics, and therefore, are less likely to have an employer to do this.[95] In the absence of other supports, acquaintances in the gay community may be the only ones available to intervene.[96] Unfortunately, there is a lack of programs and facilities designed to treat gay male and lesbian alcoholics, especially halfway houses,[97] which can be critical when family or significant others are not involved.[98]

Treatment: Together or Apart

Considerable debate exists as to whether chemical dependency treatment programs should be established for gay and lesbian clients separate from heterosexual clients.[99] Similar questions arise over whether women should be treated separately from men, and the logical extension is whether lesbians should be treated separately from gay men. Hawkins reported that of thirty lesbians that were alcoholic, twenty-one responded "not necessarily" or "no" when asked "Should alcoholism programs be solely operated by, for, and within the lesbian community."[100] While

some chemical dependency treatment programs provide special services for women, most do not provide any special accommodations for gay male and lesbian clients.[101] There are apparently no studies comparing the effectiveness of separate programs for gay men and lesbians with programs in which these clients are treated with heterosexual clients.

Over one hundred specialized chemical dependency programs for gay men and lesbians in the United States have been identified.[102] According to Vourakis, many gay and lesbian clients do well in separate programs, because the staff at these programs may be particularly adept at addressing chemical dependency and helping clients with concerns they may have about their sexual identity.[103] In this type of program, clients need not fear ostracism if they reveal their affectional preference. In fact, a goal of these programs is to affirm gay and lesbian lifestyles and to foster gay pride.[104] Gay men and lesbians have a long-standing distrust of traditional social service agencies due to misdiagnosis of their problems or well-founded fears that providers were more interested in helping them change their sexual preference than treating their presenting problem.[105]

However, separate programs may reinforce homophobia in heterosexual professionals and contribute to alienation of gay men and lesbians from the rest of society.[106] Additionally, Hellman and his colleagues note that programs that treat clients sensitively regardless of their sexual preference are needed by those unsure of their sexual identity and for those who are concerned about exposure of their gay or lesbian identity.[107] Smith and Schneider report on the usefulness of gay alcoholic clients receiving social approval from straight as well as gay individuals.[108] Additional arguments for "integrated" treatment are that it "offers a richness of experience, maintains a proper focus on alcoholism as the primary disease, and facilitates adjustment to the real world after treatment."[109] If treatment programs were more sensitive to the needs of gays and lesbians, separate programs may not be needed.[110] Blume believes that rather than separate programs, "the solution really lies in changing existing agencies so that everyone can be served."[111]

Vourakis recommends the use of heterosexual and openly homosexual staff in treatment programs and adds that gay treatment staff, both recovering and nonalcoholic, can serve as important role models for gay men and lesbians who are newly "clean" and sober.[112] However, she notes that gay and lesbian counselors often do not come out to the professional community, because they are unsure of their colleagues' views on homosexuality or because they have reason to believe their colleagues would not be accepting. This deprives gay male and lesbian clients of important role models.[113] Clearly, closer association between gay and lesbian communities and the chemical dependency treatment community would be beneficial.

Vourakis also believes that clients should not necessarily be in the same treatment group solely because they are gay or lesbian; there is a great deal of diversity among gay men and lesbians requiring that individual characteristics and preferences be taken into account. The difficulty in identifying enough gay or lesbian clients in some areas to form a group is also an obstacle to separate treatment, and adequate funding to support separate programs is another. Nicoloff and Stiglitz suggest offering special services for gay and lesbian clients within alcohol and drug abuse programs, but they acknowledge that administrators may fear that client referrals and funding might be jeopardized if the agency becomes "gay identified."[114] Colcher recommends incorporating alcoholism professionals in agencies that specialize in providing health care services to gay men and lesbians.[115] Ziebold urges gay communities to offer substance abuse intervention services through gay-identified agencies.[116] Kus also encourages the gay community to reach out and assist alcohol treatment centers.[117]

When programs reach out to gay, lesbian, bisexual, and heterosexual clients, the homophobia of heterosexual clients often needs to be addressed. For example, heterosexual clients may misinterpret a gay man or lesbian's social interaction with them as "coming on."[118] While the question of separate or mutual services remains unresolved, the principle of client self-determination indicates that the professional's responsibility is to help the client explore all the treatment options, and the client's responsibility is to select from among the available options.

CHEMICAL DEPENDENCY PROFESSIONALS

Individuals working in the field of chemical dependency may harbor their own prejudices toward gay men and lesbians. Blume believes that paraprofessionals in the field "sometimes hold very traditional values, values that have not been challenged through professional training or supervision."[119] Freudenberger provided an account of the very negative attitudes of staff of a therapeutic community toward gay men and lesbians that were conveyed to addicts, and he emphasized the need for consciousness-raising groups to address homophobia.[120] Staff education about gay and lesbian life-styles and culture is also needed.[121] Gaining credibility in gay and lesbian communities requires that chemical dependency professionals, especially those who are heterosexual, network with individuals serving gay male and lesbian clients in health care, counseling, and other agencies. Building relationships with civic groups and other organizations in the gay community such as the Metropolitan Community Church, social clubs, and political groups is also necessary. Developing contacts within Gay AA and attending meetings of Gay AA (as appropriate) is recommended, as is displaying gay- and lesbian-sensitive literature in one's office.[122] Clinicians who find that they are unable to overcome their discomfort with homosexuality have an obligation to refer gay male and lesbian clients to therapists who can better treat them.[123] In addition to addressing one's own homophobia, professionals need to become comfortable with discussing sexuality with clients, regardless of their own affectional preference.[124]

Hellman and his colleagues[125] and Israelstam[126] have studied the attitudes and knowledge of chemical dependency service providers concerning lesbians and gay men. The 164 professionals in New York City who responded to the Hellman survey felt that their education about gay male and lesbian life-styles was inadequate, that clinical supervision in this area was lacking, and that they had limited knowledge about referral resources for these clients. The therapists' academic degrees and years of practice were not related to their knowledge of working with gay male and lesbian alcoholics, but as might be expected, gay male and lesbian professionals reported being most prepared to work with this clientele. There was an awareness among most respondents that gay men and lesbians have unique treatment needs, and many also thought that achieving sobriety was as difficult, if not more difficult, for these individuals compared with heterosexuals. In spite of their reported lack of knowledge, 82 percent of the professionals indicated that they were comfortable working with gay men and lesbians, and 79 percent said they would treat them rather than refer them elsewhere.

Israelstam's study included responses from eighty-five substance abuse professionals in Ontario, Canada. Respondents indicated that they were most comfortable working with heterosexual clients and least comfortable with clients trying to hide their homosexuality; comfort level with openly gay men or lesbians fell in between. Three quarters of the respondents believed that it was important to take sexual orientation into account when treating alcoholism, but they were divided on the issue of whether gay men and lesbians needed specialized treatment for their drinking problems. Few of the respondents had any specialized education in working with gay men or lesbians. Fifield's earlier survey found that very few substance abuse programs reached out to gay men and lesbians and less than a quarter provided staff training in this area.[127]

SELF-HELP GROUPS

Although there is really no way of knowing, Bittle believes that gay men and lesbians are underrepresented in AA,[128] but there appears to be substantial support for the position that twelve-step programs such as Alcoholics Anonymous can be important resources for gay men and lesbians.[129] In an effort to encourage participation in self-help programs and to help explore aspects of chemical dependency specific to them, groups for gays and lesbians have emerged. Gay Alcoholics Anonymous is the best known, and Israelstam calls it "the largest of A.A.'s splinter groups."[130] Some groups are for gay men only or lesbians only. There is also Alcoholics Together, which began in Los Angeles in 1970 to meet the needs of gay men and lesbian alcoholics.[131] Israelstam believes that the self-help movement has been more responsive to drinking problems among gays than professionals have been.

While the only requirement for membership in AA is a desire for sobriety, some members may hold stereotypical beliefs about gay men and lesbians.[132] Bittle offers a number of other reasons for his perception that Alcoholics Anonymous may be "experienced by gay people as hostile or unattractive:"[133]

1. AA emphasizes the similarities rather than the differences among members, but gay men and lesbian members are likely to feel that their sexual or affectional preference is a difference that cannot be ignored.
2. The feeling that many members are not comfortable with issues of homosexuality causes gay men and lesbians to hide their sexual or affectional preference, which is harmful to their well-being. This conflicts with AA's emphasis on honesty.[134]
3. While the fellowship of AA encourages members to develop a program of recovery unique to their life-style, individual members may offer their own approach as the preferred method. As a result, the program often appears to be orthodox and rigid to gay men and lesbians (as it can to heterosexuals).
4. In the early stages of recovery, the idea of sexual abstinence is often promoted to members as is

putting sexual issues on the "back burner" until more stable sobriety is achieved, yet the issues of sexuality and alcohol abuse are often inextricably linked for the gay man or lesbian and likely need to addressed together. (This may also be true for heterosexuals.)

5. Gay men and lesbian members (as well as heterosexuals) often encounter difficulty with the concepts of God, a higher power, and spirituality, since traditional religious groups have often condemned their sexual orientation and practices (and perhaps their alcoholism). However, the spiritual dimension of recovery, which may be interpreted quite broadly, can be important and should not be overlooked.[135]

There is some disagreement over the role AA and NA might play in the life of a recovering gay man or lesbian. Ziebold writes that in spite of their usefulness, AA and Gay AA "do not provide a social setting to substitute for gay bar life, nor do they offer the more intense short-term therapy required by many alcoholics to get firmly started into successful recovery."[136] But Warren notes that many lesbians do find social fulfillment in these groups.[137] Obstacles to utilizing self-help groups may reflect the individual's interpretation of these programs. They are not an answer for everyone, but professionals as well as AA, NA, and Gay AA members can help gay and lesbian newcomers appreciate their usefulness.

To use AA more effectively, Bittle encourages gay men and lesbians to obtain a gay or lesbian sponsor or one who is knowledgeable about and comfortable with these life-styles, and he recommends they use additional support groups to address issues not regularly discussed in AA meetings.[138] He also encourages them to foster education within AA about gay men and lesbians once they have achieved solid sobriety and comfort with their sexual or affectional preference.

In his study of the etiology of chemical dependency in homosexual men, Kus discovered four elements of participation in AA that were important in helping the respondents accept their homosexuality:[139]

1. Just as AA members accept that they are powerless over alcohol, it may be helpful to accept that individuals are powerless over their affectional preference or sexual orientation (i.e., it cannot be changed).

2. In making one's moral inventory during the fourth step of the AA program, acknowledging anger and resentment about being gay can help eliminate these feelings. In working on this step, homophobia, self-hatred, and other negative feelings can also be addressed. The sixth and seventh steps addressing "character defects" and shortcomings can also be used to help remove these self-defeating feelings.

3. Recognizing that continued sobriety requires coming to peace with other issues (such as sexual identity and family issues) may result in acceptance of one's self as gay.

4. Associating with gays in AA and attending other self-help groups for gay alcoholics and addicts can also facilitate acceptance through positive role models.

Kus urges urban AA groups to provide a "loner" network for rural gays who do not have the benefit of Gay AA. This can be done with letters, phone calls, and visits.[140] Kus also reminds gays in rural areas that it only takes two to make a meeting, and he encourages travel to communities with Gay AA whenever possible.

Israelstam discusses the various perspectives on whether AA or Gay AA is best suited for gay men and lesbians.[141] The opinions vary, with some saying that Gay AA allows more freedom in discussing gay issues[142] and others indicating that at AA there is less "sex talk" and that members generally have longer sobriety and help more with the spiritual aspects of the program.[143] In his study of twenty-eight gay men and one lesbian who were recovering alcoholics, Saunders found that most currently attended AA, and most attended both general and gay meetings.[144] Kus and others encourage attendance at AA as well as Gay AA, since AA helps gay men and lesbians recognize the similarities that they do share with other alcoholics.[145] Lesbians may also benefit from women's AA groups and from Women for Sobriety (see Chapter 15).

RESOURCES

We conclude this chapter with information on some of the resources that can be helpful in serving lesbians and gay men with chemical abuse and dependency problems. The National Association of Lesbian and Gay Alcoholism Professionals (NALGAP, 204 W. 20th St., New York, NY 10011; 212/713-5074), formerly the National Association of Gay Alcoholism Professionals, was established in 1979 to address the problem of chemical dependency in the gay and lesbian community. NALGAP has four major goals: (1) to encourage support and communication among professionals in the field, (2) to educate those working with gay men or lesbians who are chemically dependent, (3) to raise the consciousness about alcoholism and other drug abuse in gay and lesbian communities in order to overcome denial, and (4) to advocate for improved treatment of alcoholics and other drug abusers who are gay or lesbian.[146] The organization publishes a quarterly newsletter and maintains a directory of chemical dependency services and educational materials for gay men and lesbians. NALGAP works with other groups concerned about gay men and lesbians and with groups concerned about chemical dependency.

The National Lesbian and Gay Health Foundation (P.O. Box 65472, Washington, DC 20035) provides information on substance abuse and other health issues.[147] The New York State Division of Substance Abuse Services, Narcotic and Drug Research, Inc., Bureau of Training and Resource Development (2 World Trade Center, Room 6701, 67th Floor, New York, NY 10047; 212/488-3662) has offered a three-day course called Gays in Treatment. The Homosexuality Education and Linkage Program (H.E.L.P.) by E. Sue Blume, CSW (P.O. Box 7167 Garden City, NY 11530), also includes material on substance abuse. The Gayellow Pages (P.O. Box 292, Village Station, New York, NY 10014; 212/674-0120) lists services and resources of many types.

A number of outpatient and inpatient programs that specialize in treating gay men and lesbians with substance abuse problems have assisted professionals interested in working with this clientele. Two of them are the Whitman-Walker Clinic located in Washington, DC, and the Pride Institute (411 Waverly Oaks Drive, Waltham, MA 01254).

SUMMARY

While additional evidence is needed to determine whether chemical dependency is more prevalent among lesbians and gay men than among heterosexuals, the use of alcohol and drugs to excess remains an issue for gay and lesbian communities. The specific etiologies of substance abuse in the general population remain unclear, but there is concern that the oppression faced by gay men and lesbians may contribute to increased use of alcohol and other drugs. Many human service professionals lack the depth of understanding of gay and lesbian lifestyles that may improve services to these groups. Prominent among the treatment issues raised by substance abuse among lesbians and gay men are the strong defense mechanisms used to protect both their sexual identity and their substance abuse. Another issue is the inclusion of family members in the treatment of gay male and lesbian alcoholics which can be difficult because family members may not recognize that the individual is gay or lesbian. Although it should go without saying, it is also essential that the partners of gay men and lesbians be included in treatment, especially because many of these individuals have not had the opportunity to observe healthy relationships among gay or lesbian couples. There is considerable debate about whether the preferred method of treating gay men and lesbians is within mainstream treatment programs or whether both gay men and lesbians should be treated separately. Some believe that societal homophobia requires that treatment be separate, because professional service providers as well as heterosexual clients may also harbor these negative feelings. Others believe that such separatism reinforces homophobia and fails to contribute to a more just society. The self-help movement also figures prominently in the recovery of lesbians and gay men with chemical dependency. Gay AA and Alcoholics Together typify the self help groups addressed especially to these populations. Other organizations, especially the National Association of Lesbian and Gay Alcoholism Professionals, are also important resources in helping to better serve this clientele.

ENDNOTES

1. Language is an important aspect of all cultures; so too is it important among gay men and lesbians. The word "homosexual" means a preference for sexual and affectional partners of the same gender; see Raymond M. Berger, "Homosexuality: Gay Men," in Anne Minahan (ed.), *Encyclopedia of Social Work*, Volume 1, 18th ed. (Silver Spring, MD: National Association of Social Workers, 1987), pp. 795–805; and A. Elfin Moses and Robert O. Hawkins, Jr., *Counseling Lesbian Women and Gay Men: A Life-Issues Approach* (St. Louis, MO: C.V. Mosby, 1982). While the term homosexual continues to be used in the literature, many consider it not only passe but unacceptable; see Robert J. Kus, "Alcoholism and Non-Acceptance of Gay Self: The Critical Link," *Journal of Homosexuality*, Vol. 15, Nos. 1–2 (1988), note 1, p. 39; also see Sophie Freud Loewenstein, "Understanding Lesbian Women," *Social Casework*, Vol. 61, No. 1 (January 1980), p. 29. Some individuals reject any labeling at all; see James L. Hawkins, "Lesbianism and Alcoholism," in Milton Greenblatt and Marc A. Schuckit (eds.), *Alcoholism Problems in Women and Children* (New York: Grune & Stratton, 1976), pp. 137–153. In this chapter, the terms "lesbian" and "gay men" are used, except in some references to other authors' works which utilize the term homosexual.

2. Sandra C. Anderson and Donna C. Henderson, "Working with Lesbian Alcoholics," *Social Work*, Vol. 30, No. 6 (1985), pp. 518–525, and Lowenstein, "Understanding Lesbian Women."

3. Thomas O. Ziebold, "Alcoholism and Recovery: Gays Helping Gays," *Christopher Street*, Vol. 3, No. 6 (January 1979), p. 36.

4. Thomas O. Ziebold and John E. Mongeon, "Introduction: Alcoholism and the Homosexual Community," *Journal of Homosexuality*, Vol. 7, No. 4 (1982), pp. 3–7; Herbert J. Freudenberger, "The Gay Addict in a Drug and Alcohol Abuse Therapeutic Community," *Homosexual Counseling Journal*, Vol. 3, No. 1 (1976), pp.

34–45; and Sandee Potter, "Social Work, Traditional Health Care Systems and Lesbian Invisibility," *Journal of Social Work and Human Sexuality*, Vol. 3, No 2-3 (1984–1985), pp. 59–68.

5. Alfred C. Kinsey, Wardell B. Pomeroy, and Clyde E. Martin, *Sexual Behavior in the Human Male* (Philadelphia: W.B. Saunders, 1948), and Alan P. Bell and Martin S. Weinberg, *Homosexualities: A Study of Diversity Among Men and Women* (New York: Simon & Schuster, 1978).

6. John O. G. Billy, Koray Tanfer, William R. Grady, and Daniel H. Klepinger, "The Sexual Behavior of Men in the United States," Family Planning Perspectives, Vol. 25, No. 2 (1993), pp. 52–60.

7. See, for example, Marcel T. Saghir and Eli Robins, *Male and Female Homosexuality: A Comprehensive Investigation* (Baltimore: Williams and Wilkins, 1973); Edward J. Small, Jr. and Barry Leach, "Counseling Homosexual Alcoholics: Ten Case Histories," *Journal of Studies on Alcohol*, Vol. 38, No. 11 (1977), pp. 2077–2086; and Anderson and Henderson, "Working with Lesbian Alcoholics."

8. Judith M. Saunders and S. M. Valente, "Suicide Risk Among Gay Men and Lesbians: A Review," *Death Studies*, Vol. 11 (1987), pp. 1–23; Marcel T. Saghir, Eli Robins, Bonnie Walbran, and Kathye A. Gentry, "Homosexuality. IV. Psychiatric Disorders and Disability in the Female Homosexual," *American Journal of Psychiatry*, Vol. 127, No. 2 (August, 1970), pp. 147–154; and Marcel T. Saghir, Eli Robins, Bonnie Walbran, and Kathye A. Gentry, "Homosexuality: III. Psychiatric Disorders and Disability in the Male Homosexual," *American Journal of Psychiatry*, Vol. 126, No. 8 (February 1970), pp. 1079–1086.

9. See National Institute on Alcohol Abuse and Alcoholism, *Sixth Special Report to the U.S. Congress, On Alcohol and Health* (Rockville, MD: U.S. Department of Health and Human Services, 1987), pp. 11–12; also see Saunders and Valente, "Suicide Risk Among Gay Men and Lesbians: A Review."

10. See Ziebold and Mongeon, "Introduction: Alcoholism and the Homosexual Community."

11. See, for example, Craig A. Molgaard, Chester Nakamura, Melbourne Hovell, and John P. Elder, "Assessing Alcoholism as a Risk Factor for Acquired Immunodeficiency Syndrome (AIDS)," *Social Science & Medicine*, Vol. 27, No. 11 (1988), pp. 1147–1152, and Ron Stall and James Wiley, "A Comparison of Alcohol and Drug Use Patterns of Homosexual and Heterosexual Men: The San Francisco Men's Health Study," *Drug and Alcohol Dependence*, Vol. 22 (1988), pp. 63–73.

12. Lillene Fifield, *On My Way to Nowhere: Alienated, Isolated, Drunk* (Los Angeles: Gay Community Services

Center & Department of Health Services, 1975), cited in Kus, "Alcoholism and Non-Acceptance of Gay Self"; Hawkins, "Lesbianism and Alcoholism"; and Molgaard et al., "Assessing Alcoholism as a Risk Factor."

13. Martin S. Weinberg and Colin J. Williams, *Male Homosexuals: Their Problems and Adaptations* (New York: Oxford University Press, 1974), p. 116.

14. Leander J. Lohrenz, John C. Connelly, Lolafaye Coyne, and Keith E. Spare, "Alcohol Problems in Several Midwestern Homosexual Communities," *Journal of Studies on Alcohol,* Vol. 39, No. 11 (1978), pp. 1959–1963.

15. Saghir and Robins, *Male and Female Homosexuality;* also see Saghir et al., "Homosexuality IV. Psychiatric Disorders and Disability in the Female Homosexual," and Saghir et al., "Homosexuality III. Psychiatric Disorders and Disability in the Male Homosexual."

16. Collins E. Lewis, Marcel T. Saghir, and Eli Robins, "Drinking Patterns in Homosexual and Heterosexual Women," *Journal of Clinical Psychiatry,* Vol. 43, No. 7 (1982), pp. 277–279.

17. Joseph H. Neisen and Hilary Sandall, "Alcohol and Other Drug Abuse in a Gay/Lesbian Population: Related to Victimization?" *Journal of Psychology and Human Sexuality,* Vol. 3, No. 1 (1990), pp. 151–168; also see David J. McKirnan and Peggy L. Peterson, "Alcohol and Drug Use Among Homosexual Men and Women: Epidemiology and Population Characteristics," *Addictive Behaviors,* Vol. 14 (1989), pp. 545–553, and Stall and Wiley, "A Comparison of Alcohol and Drug Use Patterns of Homosexual and Heterosexual Men."

18. Potter, "Social Work, Traditional Health Care Systems and Lesbian Invisibility," p. 62.

19. Reprinted from *Addictive Behaviors,* Volume 14, David J. McKirnan and Peggy L. Peterson, "Alcohol and Drug Use Among Homosexual Men and Women: Epidemiology and Population Characteristics," pp. 545–553, Copyright 1989, with kind permission from Pergamon Press Ltd, Headington Hill Hall, Oxford OX3 OBW, UK.

20. Walter B. Clark and Lorraine Midanik, "Alcohol Use and Alcohol Problems Among U.S. Adults: Results of the 1979 National Survey," in National Institute of Alcohol Abuse and Alcoholism, *Alcohol and Health: Alcohol Consumption and Related Problems,* Monograph No. 1 (Rockville, MD: U.S. Dept. of Health and Human Services) (1982).

21. Richard R. Clayton, Harwin L. Voss, Cynthia Robbins, and William F. Skinner, "Gender Differences in Drug Use: An Epidemiological Perspective," in Barbara A. Ray and Monique C. Braude (eds.), *Women*

and Drugs: A New Era for Research, NIDA Research Monograph 65 (Washington, DC: U.S. Government Printing Office, 1986), pp. 80–99.

22. McKirnan and Peterson, "Alcohol and Drug Use Among Homosexual Men and Women," p. 552.

23. Stall and Wiley, "A Comparison of Alcohol and Drug Use Patterns."

24. Ziebold and Mongeon, "Introduction: Alcoholism and the Homosexual Community;" and William E. Bittle, "Alcoholics Anonymous and the Gay Alcoholic," *Journal of Homosexuality,* Vol. 7, No. 4 (1982), pp. 81–88.

25. P. Hastings, "Alcohol and the Lesbian Community: Changing Patterns of Awareness," *Surveyor,* Vol. 18 (1982), pp. 3–7, cited in Stephen Israelstam and Sylvia Lambert, "Homosexuals Who Indulge in Excessive Use of Alcohol and Drugs: Psychosocial Factors to Be Taken into Account by Community and Intervention Workers," *Journal of Alcohol and Drug Education,* Vol. 34, No. 3 (1989), pp. 54–69.

26. Stall and Wiley, "A Comparison of Alcohol and Drug Use Patterns."

27. Small and Leach, "Counseling Homosexual Alcoholics," p. 2077.

28. For a review of the literature supporting and refuting a causal relationship between alcoholism and homosexuality, see S. Israelstam and S. Lambert, "Homosexuality as a Cause of Alcoholism: A Historical Review," *The International Journal of the Addictions,* Vol. 18, No. 8 (1983), pp. 1085–1107.

29. Small and Leach, "Counseling Homosexual Alcoholics," p. 2078.

30. See Stephen Israelstam, "Alcohol and Drug Problems of Gay Males and Lesbians: Therapy, Counselling and Prevention Issues," *The Journal of Drug Issues,* Vol. 16, No. 3 (1986), pp. 443–461.

31. Small and Leach, "Counseling Homosexual Alcoholics"; Peter M. Nardi, "Alcoholism and Homosexuality: A Theoretical Perspective," *Journal of Homosexuality,* Vol. 7, No. 4 (1982), pp. 9–25, and Ziebold and Mongeon, "Introduction."

32. Israelstam, "Alcohol and Drug Problems of Gay Males and Lesbians," p. 455.

33. Lee K. Nicoloff and Eloise A. Stiglitz, "Lesbian Alcoholism: Etiology, Treatment, and Recovery," in Boston Lesbian Psychologies Collective (ed.), *Lesbian Psychologies* (Urbana and Chicago: University of Illinois Press, 1987), pp. 283–293.

34. Jeffrey M. Brandsma and E. Mansell Pattison, "Homosexuality and Alcoholism," in E. Mansell Pattison and Edward Kaufman (eds.), *Encyclopedic Hand-*

book of Alcoholism (New York: Gardner Press, 1982), pp. 736–741.

35. Ziebold and Mongeon, "Introduction," pp. 5–6, offer this comment referring to Merle Miller, *On Being Different* (New York: Random House, 1971).

36. Ziebold, "Alcoholism and Recovery," p. 40.

37. McKirnan and Peterson, Alcohol and Drug Use Among Homosexual Men and Women," p. 552.

38. Neisen and Sandall, "Alcohol and Other Drug Abuse in a Gay/Lesbian Population."

39. Kus, "Alcoholism and Non-Acceptance of Gay Self."

40. See Ziebold, "Alcoholism and Recovery," p. 38, for a discussion.

41. See, for example, Moses and Hawkins, *Counseling Lesbian Women and Gay Men: A Life-Issues Approach;* Marta Ann Zehner and Joyce Lewis, "Homosexuality and Alcoholism: Social and Developmental Perspectives," in Robert Schoenberg and Richard S. Goldberg (eds.), *With Compassion Toward Some, Homosexuality and Social Work in America* (New York: Harrington Park Press, 1985), pp. 75–89; and Cassandra Diamond-Friedman, "A Multivariant Model of Alcoholism Specific to Gay-Lesbian Populations," *Alcoholism Treatment Quarterly*, Vol. 7, No. 2 (1990), pp. 111–117.

42. George Weinberg, *Society and the Healthy Homosexual* (Garden City, NY: Anchor/Doubleday, 1972).

43. Zehner and Lewis, "Homosexuality and Alcoholism: Social and Developmental Perspectives," and Kathleen O'Halleran Glaus, "Alcoholism, Chemical Dependency and the Lesbian Client," *Women and Therapy*, Vol. 8, Nos. 1–2 (1988), pp. 131–144.

44. Small and Leach, "Counseling Homosexual Alcoholics," p. 2084.

45. Ibid.

46. Lewis et al., "Drinking Patterns in Homosexual and Heterosexual Women."

47. Hawkins, "Lesbianism and Alcoholism."

48. Saghir and Robins, *Male and Female Homosexuality.*

49. Hawkins, "Lesbianism and Alcoholism."

50. Deborah L. Diamond and Sharon C. Wilsnack, "Alcohol Abuse Among Lesbians: A Descriptive Study," *Journal of Homosexuality*, Vol. 4, No. 2 (Winter 1978), pp. 123–142.

51. Rebecca Schilit, W. Mark Clark, and Elizabeth Ann Shallenberger, "Social Supports and Lesbian Alcoholics," *Affilia*, Vol. 3, No. 2 (Summer 1988), p. 37.

52. Lewis et al., "Drinking Patterns in Homosexual and Heterosexual Women."

53. Robert J. Kus, "Alcoholics Anonymous and Gay American Men," *Journal of Homosexuality*, Vol. 14, Nos. 1–2 (1987), pp. 253–276; also see Nardi, "Alcoholism and Homosexuality: A Theoretical Perspective."

54. Kus, "Alcoholism and Non-Acceptance of Gay Self," pp. 31–32.

55. Ziebold, "Alcoholism and Recovery," p. 38.

56. David K. Wellisch, G. G. DeAngelis, and Carl Paternite, "A Study of Therapy of Homosexual Adolescent Drug Users in a Residential Treatment Setting," *Adolescence*, Vol. 16, No. 63 (Fall 1981), pp. 689–700.

57. Larry Icard and Donald M. Traunstein, "Black, Gay, Alcoholic Men: Their Character and Treatment," *Social Casework* (May 1987), pp. 267–272.

58. Ziebold, "Alcoholism and Recovery."

59. John E. Mongeon and Thomas O. Ziebold, "Preventing Alcohol Abuse in the Gay Community: Toward a Theory and Model," *Journal of Homosexuality*, Vol. 7, No. 4 (1982), pp. 89–99.

60. Peter M. Nardi, "Alcohol Treatment and the Non-Traditional 'Family' Structures of Gays and Lesbians," *Journal of Alcohol and Drug Education*, Vol. 27 (Winter 1982), pp. 83–89; also see Diamond and Wilsnack, "Alcohol Abuse among Lesbians."

61. Mongeon and Ziebold, "Preventing Alcohol Abuse in the Gay Community," p. 94; also see Kus, "Alcoholism and Non-Acceptance of Gay Self," for a discussion of the need to increase self-esteem.

62. Mongeon and Ziebold, "Preventing Alcohol Abuse in the Gay Community," p. 96.

63. Israelstam, "Alcohol and Drug Problems of Gay Males and Lesbians," p. 454.

64. Dana G. Finnegan and David Cook, "Special Issues Affecting the Treatment of Gay Male and Lesbian Alcoholics," *Alcoholism Treatment Quarterly*, Vol. 3 (1984), p. 97.

65. Personal communication with Louise Warren, and Glaus, "Alcoholism, Chemical Dependency and the Lesbian Client."

66. Israelstam, "Alcohol and Drug Problems of Gay Males and Lesbians," p. 455; also see Kus, "Alcoholism and Non-Acceptance of Gay Self."

67. Finnegan and Cook, "Special Issues," p. 88.

68. Ibid.

69. Small and Leach, "Counseling Homosexual Alcoholics"; also see Anderson and Henderson, "Working with Lesbian Alcoholics," and Tom Mills Smith, "Specific Approaches and Techniques in the Treatment of Gay Male Alcohol Abusers," *Journal of Homosexuality*, Vol. 7, No. 4 (1982), pp. 53–69.

70. Anderson and Henderson, "Working with Lesbian Alcoholics," p. 521.

71. Finnegan and Cook, "Special Issues," p. 85; also see Smith, "Specific Approaches."

72. Ziebold, "Alcoholism and Recovery," p. 41.

73. Personal communication with Louise Warren.

74. Finnegan and Cook, "Special Issues," p. 90; also see Smith, "Specific Approaches."

75. Ronnie W. Colcher, "Counseling the Homosexual Alcoholic," *Journal of Homosexuality*, Vol. 7, No. 4 (1982), p. 48.

76. Colcher, "Counseling the Homosexual Alcoholic," p. 49; also see C. A. Polo, "Common Sense Approach to Working with Gay Alcoholics," Alcohol and Drug Problems Association Meeting, New Orleans, LA, 1976, cited in Israelstam, "Alcohol and Drug Problems of Gay Males and Lesbians," p. 452.

77. Finnegan and Cook, "Special Issues," p. 89.

78. Christine Vourakis, "Homosexuals in Substance Abuse Treatment," in Gerald Bennett, Christine Vourakis, and Donna S. Woolf (eds.), *Substance Abuse: Pharmacologic, Developmental and Clinical Perspectives* (New York: John Wiley and Sons, 1983), pp. 400–419; also see Finnegan and Cook, "Special Issues."

79. Anderson and Henderson, "Working with Lesbian Alcoholics."

80. Finnegan and Cook, "Special Issues," p. 89.

81. Ibid.

82. E. Sue Blume, "Substance Abuse (Of Being Queer, Magic Pills, and Social Lubricants)," in Hilda Hidalgo, Travis L. Peterson, and Natalie Jane Woodman (eds.), *Lesbian and Gay Issues: A Resource Manual for Social Workers* (Silver Spring, MD: National Association of Social Workers, 1985), pp. 79–87.

83. Personal communication with Louise Warren.

84. Lohrenz et al., "Alcohol Problems in Several Midwestern Communities."

85. Israelstam, "Alcohol and Drug Problems of Gay Males and Lesbians"; also see Raymond M. Berger, "Health Care for Lesbians and Gays: What Social Workers Should Know," *Journal of Social Work & Human Sexuality*, Vol. 1, No. 3 (Spring 1983), pp. 59–73.

86. Nardi, "Alcohol Treatment and the Non-Traditional 'Family' Structures of Gays and Lesbians"; Ziebold and Mongeon, "Introduction;" Blume, "Substance Abuse"; and Scott Whitney, "The Ties That Bind": Strategies for Counseling the Gay Male Co-Alcoholic," *Journal of Homosexuality*, Vol. 7, No. 4 (Summer 1982), pp. 37–41.

87. Blume, "Substance Abuse," p. 85; also see Nicoloff and Stiglitz, "Lesbian Alcoholism."

88. Schilit et al., "Social Supports," p. 37.

89. Whitney, "The Ties That Bind."

90. Dana G. Finnegan and Emily B. McNally, "The Lonely Journey: Lesbians and Gay Men Who Are Co-dependent," *Alcoholism Treatment Quarterly*, Vol. 6, No. 1 (1989), p. 125.

91. Nardi, "Alcohol Treatment and the Non-Traditional 'Family' Structures."

92. Anderson and Henderson, "Working with Lesbian Alcoholics," p. 522.

93. Nardi, "Alcohol Treatment and the Non-Traditional 'Family' Structures," p. 87.

94. Ellen Ratner, "A Model for the Treatment of Lesbian and Gay Alcohol Abusers," *Alcoholism Treatment Quarterly*, Vol. 5, No. 1/2 (1988), p. 42.

95. Ziebold, "Alcoholism and Recovery."

96. Ibid.

97. Rosanne Driscoll, "A Gay-Identified Alcohol Treatment Program: A Follow-Up Study," *Journal of Homosexuality*, Vol. 7, No. 4 (1982), pp. 71–80.

98. Israelstam, "Alcoholism and Drug Problems of Gay Males and Lesbians."

99. For a discussion of this issue, see Vourakis, "Homosexuals in Substance Abuse Treatment"; Israelstam, "Alcohol Problems of Gay Males and Lesbians"; and Nicoloff and Stiglitz, "Lesbian Alcoholism."

100. Hawkins, "Lesbianism and Alcoholism," p. 147.

101. Blume, "Substance Abuse."

102. See Diamond-Friedman, "A Multivariant Model of Alcoholism Specific to Gay-Lesbian Populations," p. 112.

103. Vourakis, "Homosexuals in Substance Abuse Treatment."

104. Ratner, "A Model for the Treatment."

105. Driscoll, "A Gay-Identified Alcohol Treatment Program"; and Nicoloff and Stiglitz, "Lesbian Alcoholism."

106. Tricia A. Zigrang, "Who Should Be Doing What About the Gay Alcoholic?" *Journal of Homosexuality*, Vol. 7, No. 4 (1982), pp. 27–35.

107. Ronald E. Hellman, Michael Stanton, Jacalyn Lee, Alex Tytun, and Ron Vachon, "Treatment of Homosexual Alcoholics in Government-Funded Agencies: Provider Training and Attitudes," *Hospital and Community Psychiatry*, Vol. 40, No. 11 (November 1989), pp. 1163–1168.

108. S. B. Smith and M. A. Schneider, "Treatment of Gays in a Straight Environment," National Drug Abuse Conference, 1978, cited in Israelstam, "Alcohol and Drug Problems of Gay Males and Lesbians."

109. Nicoloff and Stiglitz, "Lesbian Alcoholism," p. 288.

110. Vourakis, "Homosexuals in Substance Abuse Treatment"; also see Freudenberger, "The Gay Addict in a Drug Abuse Therapeutic Community."

111. Blume, "Substance Abuse," p. 83.

112. Vourakis, "Homosexuals in Substance Abuse Treatment."

113. Blume, "Substance Abuse," p. 86; also see Ratner, "A Model for the Treatment."

114. Nicoloff and Stiglitz, "Lesbian Alcoholism."

115. Colcher, "Counseling the Homosexual Alcoholic."

116. Ziebold, "Alcoholism and Recovery."

117. Kus, "Alcoholism and Non-Acceptance of Gay Self."

118. Nicoloff and Stiglitz, "Lesbian Alcoholism."

119. Blume, "Substance Abuse," p. 82.

120. Freudenberger, "The Gay Addict in a Drug and Alcohol Abuse Therapeutic Community."

121. Glaus, "Alcoholism, Chemical Dependency and the Lesbian Client."

122. Finnegan and Cook, "Special Issues."

123. Kus, "Alcoholism and Non-Acceptance of Gay Self"; also see Colcher, "Counseling the Homosexual Alcoholic," and Finnegan and Cook, "Special Issues."

124. Ziebold, "Alcoholism and Recovery."

125. Hellman et al., "Treatment of Homosexual Alcoholics."

126. Stephen Israelstam, "Knowledge and Opinions of Alcohol Intervention Workers in Ontario, Canada, Regarding Issues Affecting Male Gays and Lesbians: Parts I and II," *The International Journal of the Addictions,* Vol. 23, No. 3 (1988), pp. 227–252.

127. Fifield, "On My Way to Nowhere," cited in Hawkins, "Alcoholism and Lesbianism."

128. Bittle, "Alcoholics Anonymous and the Gay Alcoholic."

129. Colcher, "Counseling the Homosexual Alcoholic."

130. Israelstam, "Alcohol and Drug Problems of Gay Males and Lesbians," p. 447.

131. Hawkins, "Alcoholism and Lesbianism."

132. Colcher, "Counseling the Homosexual Alcoholic," and Nicoloff and Stiglitz, "Lesbian Alcoholism."

133. Bittle, "Alcoholics Anonymous," p. 81.

134. Also see Hawkins, "Lesbianism and Alcoholism."

135. Also see Ratner, "A Model for the Treatment."

136. Ziebold, "Alcoholism and Recovery," p. 44.

137. Personal communication with Louise Warren.

138. Bittle, "Alcoholics Anonymous and the Gay Alcoholic."

139. See Kus, "Alcoholism and Non-Acceptance of Gay Self," and Robert J. Kus, "Alcoholics Anonymous and Gay American Men," *Journal of Homosexuality,* Vol. 14, No. 1–2 (1987), pp. 253–276.

140. Also see Colcher, "Counseling the Homosexual Alcoholic."

141. Israelstam, "Alcohol and Drug Problems of Gay Males and Lesbians."

142. Colcher, "Counseling the Homosexual Alcoholic."

143. K. A. Jones, J. D. Latham, and M. D. Jenner, "Social Environment Within Conventional Alcoholism Treatment Agencies as Perceived by Gay and Non-Gay Recovering Alcoholics: A Preliminary Report" (Seattle: National Council on Alcoholism Convention, 1980), cited in Israelstam, "Alcohol and Drug Problems of Gay Males and Lesbians," p. 448.

144. Edward J. Saunders, "Homosexual Recovering Alcoholics: A Descriptive Study," *Alcohol Health and Research World* (Winter 1983–84), pp. 18–22.

145. Kus, "Alcoholics Anonymous," and Ratner, "A Model for the Treatment."

146. This paragraph relies on Emily B. McNally and Dana G. Finnegan, "Working Together: The National Association of Gay Alcoholism Professionals," *Journal of Homosexuality,* Vol. 7, No. 4 (1982), pp. 101–103.

147. For information on these and other resources see Blume, "Substance Abuse;" and Wisconsin Clearinghouse for Alcohol and Other Drug Information, "Lesbians, Gay Men and Their Alcohol and Other Drug Use: Resources," (Madison, WI: University of Wisconsin System, 1980 rev. ed).

13

Compounding the problem: substance abuse and other disabilities

The relatively brief history of professional treatment of substance abuse and dependency has been a time of learning how to improve services to alcoholics and addicts. During this period, substance abusers with other major physical or mental disabilities have been underserved by chemical dependency treatment programs. In its Winter 1980/81 issue of *Alcohol Health & Research World*, the National Institute on Alcohol Abuse and Alcoholism (NIAAA) began to raise the consciousness of chemical dependency professionals about those with multiple disabilities. The professional literature of other health and social service professionals has also begun to reflect a growing concern about the combination of substance abuse and other disabilities.

Until recently, a good deal of finger pointing occurred between professional groups that come into contact with multidisabled clients. Those in the chemical dependency field accused professionals in the fields of mental illness and physical disabilities of overlooking or even tacitly condoning alcohol and drug misuse in their clientele.[1] Likewise, chemical dependency specialists were blamed for being uninformed about other disabilities and insensitive to the special treatment needs of multidisabled clients. As late as 1989,

Alexander Boros, one of the first to assist chemically dependent persons with additional disabilities, wrote that "persons with physical impairments have not benefited fully from . . . gains achieved in the addiction field. With few exceptions, intensive inpatient treatment programs do not meet the needs of physically impaired clients."[2] Physical barriers have prevented acceptance of those with mobility impairments; interpreters for those who are deaf have rarely been employed; few programs have designed or redesigned materials useful to those with visual impairments, brain injury, mental retardation, or other disabling conditions. While insufficient funding for chemical dependency services has contributed to the lack of attention to those with multiple disabilities, a greater attitude of cooperation among professionals is emerging along with more "cross-training" to ensure a knowledgeable cadre of specialists to serve multidisabled individuals. Debate continues, however, over the incidence of substance abuse problems among those with other disabilities, who should treat the substance abuse problems of multidisabled individuals, the optimum settings for treatment, and the treatment techniques and modalities that might produce the best results. These topics are the concern of this chapter.

Several terms have been used to describe those with more than one disability. NIAAA sometimes uses the term "multidisabled."[3] The National Institute of Mental Health (NIMH) uses "comorbid," despite its unpleasant sound.[4] Social workers frequently use "dually diagnosed."[5] Other terms are concurrent or coexisting disabilities. All these terms can be confusing, because they do not specify the particular disabilities involved. Mental disorders in conjunction with substance disorders have received the most attention. Other disabilities on which some literature is available are spinal cord injury, traumatic brain injury, hearing and visual impairments, mental retardation, epilepsy, and diabetes.

Estimates are that forty-three million Americans have a physical or mental disability.[6] In a study using 1985 data, "alcohol-related [hospital] discharge rates were dramatically higher for the disabled than for the general population."[7] Although the number of dually diagnosed individuals has not been determined, those with some types of disabilities, such as mental disorders, are apparently at greater risk for alcohol and drug problems than the general population.[8]

There is agreement that those with multiple disabilities are likely to need some special services to help them in their recovery from substance abuse. Groups such as Addiction Intervention with the Disabled (located at Kent State University), and the Institute on Alcohol, Drugs and Disabilities (located in San Mateo, California),[9] are pressing for chemical dependency treatment adapted or designed specifically for multidisabled clients.

Section V of the Rehabilitation Act of 1973 prohibits discrimination against those with disabilities, including alcohol and drug disorders, by health care and other service agencies that receive federal assistance. The Americans with Disabilities Act (ADA), which passed with overwhelming congressional and presidential support in 1990, puts further pressure on public and private facilities to serve those with disabilities. The act defines a disabled individual as one who has "a physical impairment that substantially limits one or more major life activities, a record of such impairment, or being regarded as having such an impairment."[10] It prohibits health care providers from discriminating against illegal drug users who are otherwise eligible for services. The act's employment discrimination provisions do not protect employees or applicants for employment who are currently using illegal drugs; however, these employment provisions do not exclude individuals with other disabilities if they use or are addicted to drugs. Substance abusers who have been rehabilitated and no longer use illegal drugs may be considered disabled under these employment provisions. De Miranda notes that the controversies over the passage of ADA reflect ambivalence "about whether to view alcoholism/addiction as a 'real' disability."[11]

MENTAL ILLNESS AND SUBSTANCE ABUSE[12]

Interest in the co-occurence of mental illness and substance abuse or dependence by treatment providers and researchers in the fields of mental health and chemical dependency has surged in recent years.[13] Using criteria found in the *Diagnostic and Statistical Manual of Mental Disorders—III—Revised,*[14] Sciacca distinguishes two groups of clients who have mental illness and substance disorders.[15] Mentally ill and chemically abusing or addicted (MICAA) clients are those with serious axis I mental disorders (such as schizophrenia or bipolar disorder) in addition to axis I substance abuse or dependence disorders. These individuals are distinguished from chemically abusing mentally ill persons (CAMI) who have no freestanding axis I disorder of severe mental illness, but who have an axis I substance abuse or dependency disorder in combination with an axis II mental disorder (such as borderline personality disorder).

Just how prevalent is comorbidity of mental and substance disorders? The studies surveyed by Kofoed and his colleagues indicate that 25 to 40 percent of all psychiatric patients also have substance abuse problems.[16] Similarly, Bauer reported that "it is common to see prevalence rates of substance abuse ranging between 20–50% of any psychiatric population."[17] However, Minkoff believes that 50 to 70 percent of mentally ill young adults have serious substance abuse problems.[18]

The most definitive information on comorbidity in the general population comes from the NIMH Epidemiologic Catchment Area (ECA) studies:

Analyses of ECA lifetime prevalence data indicate that for an adult with a primary mental disorder diagnosis, the chance of having an alcohol or drug abuse disorder at some point is nearly one in 3; for the alcoholic, the likelihood of suffering a mental disorder or drug abuse disorder is nearly half; for the individual with a diagnosed drug disorder, lifetime probability of a mental disorder or alcohol abuse disorder is 7 in 10.[19]

Although mental disorders and psychoactive substance abuse disorders may have separate etiologies and courses,[20] evidence from the Epidemiologic Catchment Area studies "seems to support the hypothesis that mental illness and substance abuse occur together more frequently than chance would predict."[21]

Some of the variation in estimates of comorbidity may be explained by the differences in problem definition and population groups studied. For example, Minkoff believes that any use of particular drugs by those with serious mental disorders should be considered abuse,[22] while others use more restrictive definitions.[23] Since younger rather than older mentally ill clients are more likely to have experienced substance abuse,[24] those working with young adult chronic clients report higher estimates. Others on the front lines of service to clients with mental illness across the age spectrum note that approximately 50 percent exhibit serious problems with substance use or abuse.[25] For many mentally ill individuals, virtually any use of nonprescribed psychoactive drugs, including alcohol, can lead to problems in functioning.[26] Ryglewicz and Pepper refer to such clients as "substance-vulnerable."[27] If criteria for dual diagnoses are modified to include these clients, the number of MICAA individuals increases substantially.

Other difficulties in obtaining accurate data on the incidence and prevalence of comorbidity have been the tendencies of mental health professionals to overlook substance use and abuse problems ("everyone drinks")[28] and of substance abuse professionals to minimize mental health problems ("they will clear up with sobriety").[29] Reporting accurate diagnoses, especially during emergencies, can be difficult, because the effects produced by some abused drugs appear very similar to the manifestations of psychoses.[30] Administrative rules and regulations, some related to the requirements of different funding sources, can also prevent accurate reporting. "Many [psychiatric treatment] units are unable to record two primary diagnoses because of computerized systems that allow for the recording of only one major diagnosis."[31] As a result, the number of dual-diagnosis patients is underreported.

Making Accurate Diagnoses

Since patients with substance-induced psychoses may be misdiagnosed as having an acute exacerbation of a severe mental illness by staff at psychiatric emergency screening units, urine toxicologies can help to reveal the extent and types of substance use. However, they are seldom utilized. The treatment regimen used by physicians responding to psychiatric emergencies may differ depending on whether the patient's psychoses was induced by substance abuse, by mental illness, or by a combination of the two. In many cases, a drug-induced psychosis will clear within a few days following abstinence. However, for those with serious mental illnesses, abstinence from nonprescribed drugs is often not enough to remedy the situation. Psychotropic medications may be necessary to address symptoms of mental illness. A detailed patient history (see Chapter 5) may be needed to confirm a diagnosis. Self-reports of clients should generally be supplemented by interviews with family members or other colaterals, as well as close reading of previous inpatient and outpatient treatment records, court records, school records, and so forth, to obtain information that the client may not be able or willing to provide. Identification of any temporal relationships between substance use or abuse and exacerbation of mental illness symptoms is necessary in developing a long-range treatment plan. Mee-Lee suggests using thorough histories to determine whether clients have exhibited mental disorders when not abusing drugs and to determine if mental problems predated drug use.[32] The opportunity to observe a client when totally drug free can be instrumental in determining whether a single diagnosis of substance abuse or dependency is appropriate or if dual diagnoses should be made. However, if the individual's records clearly show beneficial results from psychotropic medication, they are usually not withheld.

Helping professionals are generally aware that substance abuse can exacerbate mental disorders. There is less awareness that many individuals with mental disorders have such fragile brain chemistry that "social" use can also cause psychotic episodes. Take the case of a young man who had three mental hospital admissions in one year. All his mental health workers assumed it was noncompliance with medications that precipitated his episodes, but none had asked about his alcohol use. Prior to each hospital admission, he had drank up to a six-pack of beer. When the client independently recognized the association between his drinking and his psychotic episodes, and decided to quit drinking altogether, he was not hospitalized for several years. In another example, a caseworker was asked at a staffing about a female client with whom she had worked closely for three years. The client had had multiple psychiatric hospitalizations. The caseworker gave a long list of observations about the client's daily behaviors but none indicated intoxication or addiction. Subsequently, the client met with the mental health team and was asked what symptoms she had noticed before admissions. Much to her caseworker's surprise, the client replied that every time she drank even one beer, the next thing she knew, she was in the hospital. Her use of alcohol was so minimal that it had gone undetected, but its effects were powerful enough to precipitate rehospitalization. These examples demonstrate the need to screen clients with mental disorders for substance use as well as abuse.

Since problematic drug use may be missed by professionals, standard screening instruments (see Chapter 5) are recommended as a part of routine client assessment. The Michigan Alcoholism Screening Test (MAST)[33] or one of its shorter forms or the CAGE questionnaire[34] may be useful with dually diagnosed clients. Covert drug use, however, may go unnoticed without the aid of lab work.[35]

Relationships Between Abused Drugs and Mental Disorders

The nonprescribed psychoactive drugs used by dually diagnosed individuals may be related to their particular mental disorder.

For example, Treffert addresses the propensity of persons with paranoid schizophrenia to use marijuana,[36] a phenomenon Khantzian calls nonrandom, self-medication.[37] Schneier and Siris reviewed a number of studies and found that "schizophrenic groups' use of amphetamines and cocaine, cannabis, hallucinogens, inhalants, caffeine, and tobacco was significantly greater than or equal to use by control groups consisting of other psychiatric patients or normal subjects" and that their "use of alcohol, opiates, and sedative hypnotics was significantly less than or equal to use by controls"; they agree that these patterns are selective.[38] McLellan and his colleagues report that among psychiatric patients, amphetamines or hallucinogens were preferred by persons with paranoid schizophrenia but were less likely to be used by depressed patients, whereas barbiturates were more likely to be preferred by depressed rather than schizophrenic patients.[39] Furthermore, they found that stimulant and polydrug users showed greater psychiatric symptomatology (especially schizophrenia, psychasthenia, and paranoia) than did other drug abusers, whereas opiate users had less psychiatric symptomatology, except for depression and psychopathy.

The McLellan group considered both "self-medication" and "causative" explanations for their findings. The causative view suggests that chronic drug use causes mental illness by producing biological changes in the individual. The self-medication explanation, which has engendered considerable discussion among mental health and substance abuse professionals,[40] suggests that depressed individuals are drawn to barbiturate, benzodiazepine, and sedative-hypnotic use because these drugs help alleviate distressful symptoms (although over the long run, they may exacerbate depression). The self-medication explanation is less clear with respect to paranoid schizophrenics' use of hallucinogens and amphetamines, because these drugs increase dysphoria by exacerbating hallucinations, confusion, and suspiciousness. However, some effects of amphetamines may be pleasing, such as greater awareness, energy,

and feelings of power. Additional research is beginning to clarify the relationship between the problems of mental illness and the choice of abused substances. For example, Glassman recently reviewed evidence suggesting that nicotine may augment the release of dopamine and that this "could be especially appealing to psychiatric patients in whom these systems are defective."[41]

Professionals who treat individuals with psychiatric disorders encourage them to comply with their psychotropic medication regimen. They also educate clients about potential side effects of these prescribed drugs. Education about the potential adverse effects of using alcohol and nonprescribed should also be clear and consistent: (1) use or abuse of alcohol, street drugs, and/or other nonprescribed drugs can adversely affect mental stability, and (2) the interactions of nonprescribed and prescribed drugs can be harmful or lethal. However, slogans such as "just say no to drugs" and "only sick people use drugs" can confuse some mentally ill clients. Treatment staff must continually differentiate between "medications" (drugs prescribed by the psychiatrist or primary health care physician and used as prescribed) and "street drugs," alcohol, and improperly used over-the-counter and prescription drugs.[42]

Treatment

Consensus has not been reached on the optimal psychotherapeutic treatments for clients with mental and substance abuse disorders. Comprehensive models for their treatment are lacking,[43] but some diagnostic distinctions seem to be important in determining the course of treatment for MICAA and CAMI clients. For example, Sciacca believes that CAMI clients can be appropriately treated in traditional chemical dependency programs, because they can tolerate the confrontation that has traditionally been a part of these programs.[44] For MICAA clients she recommends more supportive treatment, because too much confrontation may cause seriously mentally ill clients to regress, withdraw, or become delusional.[45] In any event, substance abuse must cease before mental disorders can be successfully treated.

Unfortunately, programs for those with mental illness or chemical dependency often do not allow for much treatment individualization. When psychopathology is apparent following detoxification, comorbid clients may be denied alcohol and drug treatment services for reasons such as "lack of motivation" or "inability to benefit from treatment." While some clients may be too fragile or too confused to benefit from substance abuse services,[46] many are capable of understanding the dynamics of substance abuse and recovery. Most are simply offered standard mental health services at outpatient clinics,[47] but they may be precluded from participating in other programs designed for seriously mentally ill clients due to fears that they will cause disruption or introduce other clients to psychoactive substance abuse. Overall, MICAA clients do not fit easily into unmodified traditional treatment settings for chemical abusers or for those with severe mental illness.[48] Most continue to encounter serious gaps in services.[49]

Simultaneous Treatment. Some initial attempts to treat dually diagnosed clients involved joint treatment by a chemical dependency professional and a mental health professional. Another variation has been to treat these patients in psychiatric programs and to invite chemical dependency professionals to provide education and to conduct groups as "add-ons" to mental health treatment.[50] Newer models are emerging using simultaneous treatments for mental illness and substance abuse problems.[51] In these models, mental disorders and substance disorders are generally considered similar or parallel illnesses. Minkoff describes the following similarities between the two disorders: both are primary illnesses, both are chronic, both have multifactor etiology, and both involve denial as well as loss of control and powerlessness.[52] Bricker offers twelve parallels such as, "The risk of relapse in either disease is always high, and will inevitably trigger a relapse in the other."[53] Bak-

dash emphasizes the cyclical nature of these problems in that substance use or abuse produces mental distress which increases drug use which in turn creates more mental distress, and so forth.[54] These descriptions suggest a rationale for treating both illnesses simultaneously.

In addition to presenting mental disorders and substance disorders as similar or parallel types of problems, integrated programs focus on the unique problems of clients who experience both problems concurrently. For example, the cyclical nature and interplay of substance abuse and mental illness can be addressed in these programs without concern that the time of clients with a diagnosis of substance abuse or mental disorder could be put to better use. The treatment modalities used in special programs for dually diagnosed clients are similar to those used in inpatient psychiatric and substance abuse programs and may include education, group therapy, individual therapy, family education, family therapy, and an introduction to self-help programs.

Specialized psychoeducational groups for dually diagnosed individuals have been gaining momentum as important complements to other treatment modalities. Using the analogy of a railroad track, Pepper depicts the "cognitive rail" of treatment as psychoeducation and the "emotional rail" as psychotherapy.[55] Attending an educational, cognitive support group can be a positive experience that evokes little psychological resistance. A number of programs are now using psychoeducational groups for MICAA and CAMI clients.[56] For example, Webb's psychoeducational, group therapy program, called Good Chemistry, is being used throughout Texas by dually diagnosed individuals as an alternative or supplement to twelve-step group attendance.[57] Good Chemistry teaches MICAA clients to utilize self-help groups better, provides them with an opportunity to discuss both illnesses in a supportive atmosphere, and reinforces the benefits of staying mentally stable (which often includes the need for psychotropic medications) as well as staying sober and clean. This comprehensive perspective is important for dually diagnosed clients and helps keep them from becoming confused by some recovering substance abusers who oppose the use of any medications.

Psychoeducation may be most useful when it begins with a definition of substance abuse that clients can understand and appreciate. Based on Atkinson's work, Kofoed and Keys suggest the following brief definition of substance abuse problems for use with clients: "A loss of consistent control over substance use."[58] Another is the use of substances that results in serious life problems, including family, social, psychological, job, and legal problems.[59] These definitions can be used to achieve one of the most important outcomes of treatment—helping mentally ill clients discover a repeated cycle of substance use before mental illness exacerbations occur[60] or a pattern in which increases in psychiatric symptoms (such as may occur when clients take their medication differently than prescribed, refuse to take it at all, or run out of medication) result in the use of nonprescribed, psychoactive drugs. Kofoed and Keys describe the use of their therapy group, the Substance Abuse Group Experience (SAGE), with psychiatric inpatients to help persuade them to "acknowledge their drug addiction and to seek continued substance abuse treatment."[61] SAGE was initiated at a general VA hospital for patients who also had drug or alcohol problems. Peer group discussions are used to address denial and to encourage outpatient follow-up after discharge.

Detoxification. Dually diagnosed clients may present special management problems in community-based detoxification programs (also see Chapter 6). Unless a patient's history is known at the time of admission, detoxification program staff may be unable to determine whether the client has a serious mental disorder until withdrawal progresses. Many community (social setting) detoxification programs are not equipped to assist those with severe mental illnesses. When these problems are detected, the client is likely to be transferred to a psychiatric program. Detoxification in psychiatric hospitals, especially those

in which substance abuse and mental disorders are treated simultaneously, may be preferable for many dually diagnosed clients.

Homeless Shelters. Mentally ill persons, substance abusers, and clients with both these problems often spend time in public, not-for-profit, or church-sponsored missions and shelters such as the Salvation Army when they have nowhere else to go. There are a growing number of shelters for homeless individuals around the country. Persons who are "high" on drugs, intoxicated, or currently experiencing serious mental health problems are neither welcomed nor well served in many of these programs because of their unmet medical and mental health needs. The difficulties in serving those who are homeless, mentally ill, and chemically abusing or dependent[62] are matched only by their tremendous need for services. Patience and understanding are necessary to engage these individuals in relationships with service providers.

Meeting survival needs is their highest priority. After helping them obtain food, shelter, and health care, it is possible to encourage them to obtain mental health and substance abuse treatment. This process can begin with psychoeducational, therapy groups, such as modified Good Chemistry meetings, held at shelters and soup kitchens.[63] These groups focus on the identification of the symptoms of mental illness and substance abuse or dependence and encouragement to accept services. The next steps are treatment in detoxification units and substance abuse programs or crisis stabilization units, often followed by involvement in residential programs which promote independent living skills and help the client obtain a regular source of income, and later, assistance in obtaining permanent housing. A smooth transition through this continuum of care promotes the chances of long-term, successful outcomes for homeless individuals with severe mental health and substance abuse problems.

Inpatient Treatment. Dually diagnosed clients with private mental health care coverage may soon exhaust their benefits or lose them if they can no longer hold a job. Those without financial means who seek inpatient treatment voluntarily in publicly supported programs usually face long waits, but dually diagnosed clients generally cannot wait. When inpatient treatment or other supportive living arrangements are not available, clients may be forced onto the streets, where it is difficult to maintain abstinence or control symptoms of mental illness. Caton and her colleagues emphasize that clients dually diagnosed with mental and substance disorders "cannot be managed on an outpatient or brief inpatient basis. Long-term hospital care is often required."[64]

It may seem that a reasonable approach to inpatient care for these dually diagnosed clients lies in their attending traditional inpatient substance abuse programs and traditional inpatient psychiatric programs in tandem, but this strategy has not proven very successful.[65] Patients often receive conflicting information about drug use and mental illness when treatment is not integrated. Interactions between dual-diagnosis and single-diagnosis clients may also be problematic. Chemically dependent clients may be uncomfortable with individuals also struggling to control symptoms of mental illness (such as hallucinations or other thought disorders) and who may need more concrete approaches to substance abuse education and group therapy. As a result, dually diagnosed clients may be inhibited from talking about their psychiatric problems or attempt to deny them. On the other hand, dually diagnosed clients treated in psychiatric programs may succeed at minimizing their drug abuse because other clients are unaware of the need to address this behavior.

Since programs that offer simultaneous, parallel, or integrated treatment for mental illness and substance abuse remain scarce, some substance abuse programs are responding to the increase of dually diagnosed clients on their caseloads by hiring professional staff who are acquainted with both illnesses. Lawlor and Sciacca, however, believe that these clients are best served in psychiatric settings where the expertise to treat mental health problems with therapeutic interventions, including psychotropic medications, is available.[66] Staff in these programs must, of course, be educated about substance abuse. Lawlor implores mental health professionals to stop "passing the buck" and to take responsibility for treating these individuals.[67]

Supervised Living Arrangements. As Daley and his associates suggest, clients with mental and substance disorders who lack supportive social networks may find residential treatment programs such as halfway houses particularly beneficial.[68] An increasing number of halfway houses for mentally ill clients accept residents who also have substance abuse problems. Residents of these programs typically participate in individual and group therapy, psychiatric services, educational classes, and social and recreational activities geared to promote their social functioning and to develop their independent living skills. Before referring dually diagnosed clients to these programs, clinicians are wise to ensure that abstinence from alcohol and other nonprescribed drugs is part of the treatment regimen. Other halfway houses are designed for substance abusers; they may accept dually diagnosed clients, especially if their mental illnesses are in remission. Before making referrals to these programs, it is necessary to determine whether clients taking psychotropic medications are admitted.

A growing number of residential programs are responding to the special needs of those with coexisting mental and substance disorders. Programs in which length of stay is based on individual need are particularly desirable, since the length of treatment required by dually diagnosed clients may exceed that needed by singly diagnosed clients or permitted by halfway houses that serve substance abusers or mentally ill persons. In communities without specialized programs, professionals are left with piecing together services for dually diagnosed clients.

Day Treatment. If a client has a "clean" (drug-free) environment in which to live, such as with a supportive and enlightened relative or in a community support residential program, day treatment may be an alternative to traditional inpatient treatment. Sciacca and

Aliesan and Firth describe model day treatment programs for dually diagnosed clients that incorporate many of the principles mentioned in this chapter such as "nonconfrontational" approaches and assistance in helping clients identify the relationship between their drug use and their mental illness.[69]

Outpatient Treatment. In many communities, outpatient services for mentally ill clients and services for substance abusers are administered by two separate agencies, complicating coordination of services for dually diagnosed clients. In other communities, the same agency (typically a community mental health center) is responsible for services for mentally ill clients and substance abusers, but services to these client groups are provided by separate programs or treatment teams. In this situation, one team may monitor a dually diagnosed client's psychiatric symptoms, psychotropic medications and their side effects, and compliance with medications, while the other team is concerned with the client's sobriety, relapse prevention plan, and participation in self-help programs. Ongoing communication and collaboration between program staff are necessary to successfully assist dually diagnosed clients assigned to two programs or treatment teams. But in these programs, which are typically overburdened with large caseloads, the amount of staff contact and the quality of interaction with each client are often far less than desirable. Assessments are often hurried and not comprehensive; treatment plans are not as fleshed out or creative or as individualized as they could be. A better approach is for one team with expertise in both areas to provide client services. Many community mental health outpatient centers are developing these teams, but the demand for their services also threatens to limit the time available for interaction with clients. Intensive case management is another important component of outpatient treatment for dually diagnosed clients that has been utilized to help ensure continuity of services.

Developing Independent Living and Social Skills. While many singly diagnosed clients have functioned well in the past, many mentally ill substance-abusing individuals, especially those who have been living on the streets, need help with independent living skills. These skills are generally taught through training and educational programs that use "showing" and "doing" rather than lecturing. In addition, at the Homestead Supervised Apartment Program operated by the Austin-Travis County MHMR Center in Austin, Texas, staff help clients practice social skills weekly for an hour and a half in the context of the "Lunch Bunch." Lunch and conversation are used to focus attention on pleasantries instead of problems and crises. Alumni members and prospective referrals are also welcomed. The only restriction on clients' participation is that they cannot attend if intoxicated or "high." This activity models ways to enjoy life without drinking and "drugging." Participation in these groups can lead to the development of a network of sober peers. Without sober peers with whom to identify and socialize, many clients find it difficult to stay sober.

Family Involvement. The family of a mentally ill client can be the most important ally a treatment team has. Families are often knowledgeable about the most subtle nuances of behavioral changes in the client. They can provide invaluable information for the construction of an accurate social history, and they can be taught to recognize early warning signs of relapse.[70] This sort of partnership with families is particularly vital with dually diagnosed clients. Family members who understand and help create treatment goals can also share the task of reinforcing accomplishments. For instance, family members can learn the values of being consistent, practicing "tough love," giving positive reinforcement, shaping and extinguishing behaviors, and not "enabling."

Family members often feel alone when facing the mental illness and substance abuse of a loved one. The stigma of these conditions often keeps them from sharing their fears with others. Family support groups such as Al-Anon for those with alcoholic loved ones and Naranon for those with drug-addicted loved ones can offer tremendous relief through acceptance, understanding, and fellowship. Support groups for family members of those with mental illness have been developed through the National Alliance for the Mentally Ill (NAMI). Another group, developed by Kathleen Sciacca, called MICAA-Non, focuses on concerns unique to families with a dually diagnosed member. These groups are currently led by professionals; eventually it is expected that they will be co-led by family members.

A useful source of information for young adults with serious mental health problems and their families, as well as professionals, is The Information Exchange, Inc. (TIE), 20 Squadron Blvd., Suite 400, New City, New York, 19056. "TIE-Lines" is its reasonably priced publication. Each issue contains information on young adults with dual diagnoses of mental illness and substance abuse. Other helpful resources are Daley and Campbell's *Coping with Dual Disorders: Chemical Dependency and Mental Illness*, Daley and Sinberg's *Taking Care of Yourself: When a Family Member Has Dual Disorders*, and Evans and Sullivan's *Dual Diagnosis: Counseling the Mentally Ill Substance Abuser.*[71]

Self-Help Programs. Just as many alcoholics benefit from Alcoholics Anonymous, adaptations of AA are now used to help those with other types of problems. For example, many mentally ill individuals benefit from Emotions Anonymous (EA). These groups are also a useful adjunct to professional services for those with mental illness and substance abuse. Bricker and his associates have been using a support group for individuals with schizophrenia and chemical abuse problems since 1984. Officially called Support Together for Emotional and Mental Serenity and Sobriety (STEMSS), it is informally known as "Double Trouble."[72] The program utilizes six steps which refer to mental illness and substance dependence adapted by J. Thomas Erickson and Michael Bricker from the original twelve steps of AA. Double Trouble meetings are held weekly and focus on chemical dependency and mental illness as parallel disorders. The meetings offer direction and social inter-

action for those with dual problems. Similar groups are developing across the United States. For example, in 1987, the Eisenhower Circle Group, a closed-discussion AA meeting, was started so that "alcoholics and addicts who are also mental health consumers would feel comfortable sharing their experiences and find support in their dual recovery process."[73]

Special support groups are often needed for those with mental and substance disorders because some members of traditional self-help groups do not understand severe mental illness. We have all heard stories of mentally ill substance abusers being advised by a well-meaning individual to go off medications, which they lump together with all other "drugs." In 1984, a group of physicians who are members of AA published *The A.A. Member—Medications and Other Drugs.*[74] It includes examples of people who use medications properly and improperly and clearly admonishes that "No AA Member Plays Doctor." This message will not reach everyone, but professionals who make referrals to AA and NA can help by preparing clients for misguided advice. Since many communities lack a sufficient number of meetings of special self-help groups in which dually diagnosed clients can participate as often as they may need, Minkoff suggests that these clients be coached on how to participate in regular AA groups.[75] Professionals can also assist clients in selecting those community AA meetings most appropriate for them. Modified step study can also be very helpful for those with dual diagnoses. Evans and Sullivan have published a workbook for sponsors (and professional helpers) called *Step Study Counseling with the Dual Disordered Client.*[76]

MENTAL RETARDATION

According to PL 95-602, The Rehabilitation, Comprehensive Services and Developmental Disabilities Amendment of 1978, developmental disabilities are physical and mental impairments that are manifest before age 22, that are not likely to remit, and that impair one's functioning such as the ability to live independently. The law indicates that developmentally disabled individuals are likely to require an array of services to ensure that they are able to function at the highest level possible. Mental retardation is prominent among these developmental disabilities. The levels of intellectual functioning of persons with mental retardation vary from mild (an IQ of 50 to 70) to profound (an IQ of 0 to 20).[77] We are concerned primarily with those who fall in the mild range, because they are most likely to reside in the community and have access to alcohol and nonprescribed drugs. Fetal alcohol syndrome (see Chapters 4 and 15) is one of the primary causes of mental retardation, but our interest here is in the drinking and drug-taking behavior of those with mental retardation.

Discussions of the drinking of mentally retarded persons began early in this century.[78] Later, in 1956, Wallin indicated that there did not seem to be an excess of alcoholics among persons with mental retardation,[79] but in the 1960s Tredgold and Soddy wrote that mentally retarded individuals had a particular susceptibility to alcohol,[80] and Davies noted a close association between mental retardation and inebriety.[81] During the next two decades there was "a long silence on this topic."[82] One explanation for this lack of attention was that it seemed unlikely that many mentally retarded people would drink alcohol or use illicit drugs. Mentally retarded individuals who lived in the community were often protected by their families from exposure to psychoactive substances, and many mentally retarded individuals lived in institutions where access to these substances was limited. Deinstitutionalization has changed this. Many mildly mentally retarded individuals now live rather independently in the community with less protection from families and professionals. They have greater access to alcohol as well as to nonprescribed psychoactive drugs. Studies indicate that many have used alcohol and, to a lesser extent, other drugs.[83]

Recent interest in the problems that mentally retarded individuals might experience when confronted with the use of alcohol or other drugs seems to have been aroused primarily by Wenc and Selan.[84] In the chemical dependency literature and at conferences, they addressed the isolation of those with mental retardation, their need for socialization, and the possible connection of these factors with substance use and abuse. Mentally retarded individuals recognize that they are different, but they want to fit in with the rest of the community. Wenc indicated that mentally retarded individuals tend to frequent the same spots—restaurants, stores, and even bars—and to be known by the proprietors.[85] According to Selan, "like the other estimated 70 million Americans who drink, retarded persons experience that alcohol performs important psychological and social functions."[86] In the words of some of her clients, here is why they drink: "When I am drunk, I am just like everybody else," "It's what everyone else is doing," "The people in the bar are not handicapped," "Bars are always warm and friendly," and "I am less lonely; there is always someone to talk with."[87]

Selan also reported that her client's became more intellectually and emotionally vulnerable when drinking or intoxicated, and some had terrible experiences such as being physically abused and robbed.[88] These events also occur in the general population, but the cognitive deficits of mentally retarded individuals may further imperil them. According to Sengstock, Vergason, and Sullivan, "textbooks dealing with the nature of the mentally retarded stress the fact that the retarded are easily misled, exploited and abused."[89] However, textbooks on mental retardation ignore substance abuse, and substance abuse texts ignore mental retardation.[90]

Is There a Problem?

There are no good estimates of the number of mentally retarded individuals who have drinking or drug problems. Attempts to extrapolate from general population figures can be misleading, since mentally retarded persons may not experience these problems at the same rate as others. Current information has been gleaned from a handful of studies with different types of subjects, different sampling and data gathering techniques, and varying sample sizes.[91] These studies fall into two categories—those that attempt to determine the extent of alcohol and drug use and related problems among mentally retarded persons and those that focus on mentally retarded persons with substance abuse problems. The limited available evidence generally suggests that mentally retarded individuals are less likely to use alcohol and drugs and to experience substance abuse problems.

Among efforts to determine the extent of alcohol consumption among mentally retarded individuals is Huang's study which compared 190 educable mentally retarded junior and senior high school students with 187 other students and found less drinking by the mentally retarded students.[92] Thirty-two percent of the mentally retarded students reported drinking at least twice during a twelve-month period compared with 59 percent of the other students. However, among those who drank, the mentally retarded students claimed they drank more often than the other students. There was also evidence of greater peer pressure to drink among the students with mental retardation or that they were more easily led to drink.

Using ethnographic techniques, Edgerton studied alcohol and drug use across four different samples of persons with mental retardation: (1) 48 "candidates for normalization," (2) 40 adults living independently, (3) 45 inner-city blacks, and (4) 48 deinstitutionalized adults.[93] Edgerton is vehement that despite ample opportunity to drink and use other drugs, these individuals were less likely to do so and less likely to develop alcohol- and drug-related problems than their families and friends. Few of the subjects who used alcohol or other drugs became dependent on them, and they did not engage in socially inappropriate behavior when using them. Concerns that mentally retarded individuals may be especially susceptible to these substances were not borne out by this investigation despite the many problems they faced, such as social rejection and low socioeconomic status. Reiss found that just 2 percent of 205 mentally retarded individuals participating in commu-

nity-based day programs had drug or alcohol abuse problems.[94] A study by Halpern involved several hundred mentally retarded adults living semi-independently.[95] Fifty-six percent reported some level of alcohol consumption and 3 percent some marijuana use. Halpern's figures are also lower than for the general population and problems related to use appeared to be infrequent.

DiNitto and Krishef used survey methodology and asked staff of Associations for Retarded Citizens and group care facilities to administer a brief instrument to clients to determine whether they drank and the consequences they experienced from drinking.[96] Twenty-four programs assisted and responses were obtained from 214 mentally retarded individuals. Fifty-two percent of those respondents had drunk alcohol at some point in their lives with 7 percent reporting daily drinking, 33 percent drinking at least once a week, and 47 percent drinking at least once a month. About half usually drank in their own homes and about a third in a bar. Ninety-two percent of the individuals had a paid job, and of them, one-third said they had been absent from work due to feeling sick after drinking. Four had received substance abuse services (AA, detox, counseling, or services from a church-sponsored program). This study indicates somewhat more cause for concern about drinking among persons with mental retardation.

Myers reported that she did not find evidence of alcohol or drug abuse in a sample of 113 developmentally disabled individuals ages 10 to 21 whom she saw for psychiatric consultation.[97] She speculated on two reasons for this finding: close supervision by parents and the youths' unwillingness to report use. Other reasons have also been offered to explain findings of less substance abuse among those with mental retardation.[98]

1. Mentally retarded individuals may not wish to emulate those they know who have alcohol and other drug problems.[99]
2. Parents and professionals have taught mentally retarded persons not to drink alcohol and to use prescribed drugs only.[100]

3. Many mentally retarded individuals have limited incomes and the expense of alcohol and other drugs may act as a deterrent.[101]
4. Some belong to religious groups that negatively sanction alcohol and drug use.[102]

In addition, studies that rely on samples of mentally retarded persons living in supervised facilities may be biased toward findings of less alcohol and drug use than may be present among mentally retarded persons living independently in the community. Supervised programs often prohibit drinking, or they may not accept individuals who use psychoactive substances, especially when problematic use is indicated.[103]

Studies that focus on mentally retarded persons with drinking problems are scarce, but Krishef and DiNitto engaged the participation of Associations for Retarded Citizens (ARCs) and Alcohol Treatment Programs (ATPs) to investigate this subject.[104] The fifty-four ARCs and fifty ATPs that responded were able to identify 414 clients whom they believed to be dually diagnosed with mental retardation and alcohol abuse or alcoholism. Eighty-two percent were males. The alcohol-related problems that these individuals experienced were quite similar to the problems of those with alcohol abuse or dependency in the general population and included employment problems (such as absenteeism) and legal offenses (such as public intoxication as well as more serious crimes). Family and social conflicts, including hostile and aggressive behavior, were the most frequently reported problems.

Westermeyer and his colleagues also studied substance abuse problems by identifying forty mentally retarded individuals with DSM-III diagnoses of substance disorders from various types of programs (a chemical dependency treatment program, an AA group for individuals with mental retardation, and residential facilities for those with mental retardation).[105] They matched these subjects with forty mentally retarded persons not known to have alcohol or drug problems. As might be expected, the substance abusers began drinking earlier, had more frequent lifetime use of alcohol and other drugs, had more of some childhood acting out behaviors (but not the most serious types), and were more likely to report substance-related problems (psychological, family, social, and employment). An added note is that during the study, five of the control group members were also identified as having had substance abuse problems. Like Krishef and DiNitto, Westermeyer and coworkers believe that the substance abuse problems of mentally retarded persons are similar to those of the general population. They were also concerned that mentally retarded substance abusers experienced problems at lower doses of alcohol and other drugs than individuals in the general population. Even so, their concluding remarks may seem somewhat paternalistic:

Licit use (e.g., alcohol) should be at least restricted and monitored. In cases of mentally retarded persons at risk, licit use should be delayed or avoided altogether. Mentally retarded persons (like children, adolescents, prisoners, the mentally ill, and other vulnerable persons) should be protected against any exposure to illicit drugs. Agencies and families serving mentally retarded persons should recognize their special obligation to protect mentally retarded persons against substance abuse.[106]

Russian researchers studied drinking among 122 mentally retarded male youths, most of whom were between 14 and 18 years of age, and found extensive problems.[107] Compared to youths with normal intellectual functioning, the "mentally retarded youths developed a very unique clinical picture of early alcoholism, the principal symptoms developed more rapidly (three to four times more rapidly) than in the youth population at large, and were accompanied by more marked personality changes."[108] The descriptions of exacerbation of reduced mental functioning among these mentally retarded persons and their conflicts with others were of particular concern. Although it may be risky to make cross-cultural comparisons, the evidence provided by Rychkova lends support to the recommendations expressed by Westermeyer and coworkers.

Treating Mentally Retarded Substance Abusers

What is the most appropriate treatment for persons with diagnoses of mental retardation and substance abuse or dependency? The Krishef and DiNitto study indicated that a number of alcoholism treatment programs modified their services to meet the needs of this group of clients.[109] Examples were longer treatment periods, using more supportive and directive techniques and less confrontation, greater emphasis on alcohol education, simplification and more repetition of concepts, use of more concrete goals over shorter time frames, use of more behavioral treatment, working closely with the client's family, being more patient, and use of more individual and less group treatment. Wenc recommends use of a multidisciplinary service team to ensure that the client receives comprehensive services.[110] Since detoxification centers are a likely entry point into substance abuse treatment, he also recommends that each center designate a staff liaison to the developmentally disabled community.

A significant aide in assisting mentally retarded persons with alcohol or drug problems is a publication called *The Maine Approach: A Treatment Model for the Intellectually Limited Substance Abuser*.[111] It is a practical, comprehensive, model program for assisting mentally retarded persons with alcohol and drug problems which relies heavily on the use of behavioral techniques and contracting. The *Maine Approach* describes assessment interviewing, the treatment process, aftercare, and the administrative arrangements used to establish the program. The manual provides many useful tools such as interviewing formats, informed consent forms, and sample treatment plans. A brief case illustration along with treatment considerations from *The Maine Approach* is reproduced in the accompanying box.

The Maine Approach recommends the use of AA by mentally retarded substance abusers who are intellectually capable of participating and encourages assisting clients in locating a sponsor who will actively work with them. Wenc also discussed the use of AA by these dually diagnosed individuals, and emphasized the need for making special efforts to accompany them to group meetings rather than simply referring them.[112] Wenc believes that the socialization aspects of these groups are especially beneficial for mentally retarded persons.

While traditional AA groups are an option, mentally retarded individuals report that they are sometimes uncomfortable in these groups, maybe because they feel that some members are not comfortable with mental retardation.[113] Like other multiply diagnosed populations, something special seemed to be needed for mentally retarded persons with alcohol or drug use problems. An early publication on this topic was a brief article on Emotions Anonymous (EA) founded by Jim Voytilla in Minnesota.[114] As with some of the other new, self-help groups for dually diagnosed individuals, professional involvement was an important element in organizing Emotions Anonymous. Voytilla combined elements of Alcoholics Anonymous with education and relaxation techniques to form a long-term approach to outpatient treatment. The term "emotions" is substituted for the word alcohol in the twelve steps of AA because of the severe anxieties and tensions that mentally retarded persons face. EA members set goals for themselves each week and report back to the group. The behavioral technique of social reinforcement is used to provide ample reward for goal achievement.

MOBILITY IMPAIRMENTS

Spinal cord injuries (SCI) are often the result of alcohol- or other drug-related accidents.[115] A number of SCI patients abused psychoactive drugs prior to becoming disabled, and alcohol or other drugs may have directly contributed to their accident. Less frequently, psychoactive drug abuse seems to be initiated as a reaction to a spinal cord injury.

O'Donnell and his colleagues studied forty-seven SCI patients (thirty-nine men and eight women) admitted over a six-month period to a state-operated hospital and found

Case Study
Jerry: A 24-year-old Client of the Bureau of Mental Retardation

I. HISTORY

A. **Mental Retardation**—Jerry is diagnosed as having moderate mental retardation (MR). His reported degree of MR, however, is not reflected in his presentation of himself or his conceptual understanding. He is streetwise and relatively high-functioning. Jerry learned at an early age that doing well on his tests would mean that he would "lose his money" [Supplemental Security Income (SSI)].

B. **Family**—Mother died when he was very young which left his alcoholic father alone to raise six children. His older brother, Patrick, was the first to introduce Jerry to alcohol and Valium. One sister is a continuous heavy user of Valium and her husband is also an alcoholic. Only one sister has been willing or able to provide a clean, healthy chemical-free living environment. This sister has been supportive of Jerry, but is also very soft-hearted and nonconfrontive. Jerry has taken advantage of this and overrun her household, causing many problems within her family unit.

C. **Medical**—Jerry has had many hospital admissions associated with his drinking, both medical and psychiatric. Many times he would feel the need to "dry out" so he would call the ambulance and tell them he had also taken drugs. This ploy was necessary for him to be admitted. Jerry also had been diagnosed as having problems with his "nerves" and was prescribed Valium by a local doctor. Despite all this and his poor eating habits (associated with his drinking) Jerry has maintained relatively good health.

D. **Arrests**—His arrests include drunk and disorderly, shoplifting (usually steals vanilla or aftershave when alcohol is not available), and one incident of property damage. Many of his charges (well over twenty) have not been prosecuted or Jerry is released with only a fine to pay, because Jerry will often use his mental retardation to pretend he doesn't understand the police or the judge.

E. **Substance Abuse Treatment**—Outpatient: Jerry has had outpatient counseling off and on for the past four years, his sobriety is sporadic. Residential treatment: Jerry has two previous admissions to residential treatment. The information there was at a level which was too high for him, yet he maintained sobriety for six months following treatment. Shelter: He has had numerous admittances, also a halfway house and group home for alcoholics.

One thing that has been an outstanding problem with Jerry is his manipulative behavior. He knows systems and he knows how to use them—BMR [Bureau of Mental Retardation], alcoholism rehabilitation programs, SSI, hospitals, and the courts.

II. CASE PLANNING

A. **Joint Planning**—The Mental Retardation Alcoholism Project became involved with Jerry's case in August 1982. At that time, Jerry was moving back and forth from Aroostook County to Bangor. A team meeting was called to discuss his case. BMR staff from Aroostook County and Bangor, the project coordinator, and Jerry met to plan for his treatment. (Representatives from local substance abuse treatment providers were unable to attend but were informed of the team's decisions.) These meetings have provided an opportunity for the team to discuss case management. It also gave Jerry a chance to get consistent messages from all care providers. Although he has continued at times to try to play one person against another, these manipulation attempts were unsuccessful.

B. **Locate a Supportive Environment**—Jerry was an individual who clearly wanted independence. At the same time, it was just as clear to providers that, in order to maintain sobriety, Jerry would need a supportive and somewhat structured environment. The team decided that a group home for alcoholics would offer him that support (access to AA meetings, his own room, shared transportation and nonmentally retarded peers). Jerry agreed to this plan but stated that he would like to live on his own when things got better. A plan was set up to assist Jerry in getting an apartment if he was able to maintain sobriety on his own for one year.

C. **Integration into AA**—There were two ways that Jerry could become familiar with AA. He attended meetings at the shelter (the staff were very willing to help Jerry become used to the meetings). He also had the support and encouragement to go to meetings at the group home.

D. **Set up a Reward System**—BMR, as representative payee for Jerry, knew that money was very important to him. It became clear to the team that, although Jerry had maintained sobriety for awhile, an incentive program was necessary to help him stay that way. Jerry agreed to a plan that would give him extra spending money if he attended his AA and treatment regularly.

E. **Group Therapy**—Jerry was used to dealing with people on the streets and could communicate verbally quite well. Therefore, his participation in group therapy was fairly good. This was supplemented by shelter staff who worked with him individually to deal with the scapegoating by others and to understand the information which was at a level too difficult for him.

F. **Involve in a Meaningful Task**—The team recognized the need for Jerry to become involved in a meaningful task but had difficulty in locating something that was appropriate for his needs. He was too high functioning for sheltered workshops for the mentally retarded and lower-skill jobs were very difficult to come by. Jerry, however, solved this problem on his own and became a volunteer at the halfway house.

III. FOLLOW-UP

Things went relatively smooth for Jerry and he was able to maintain sobriety for nearly eight months. At that time, he began playing his old games and soon after began drinking. The team continued to meet and plan for his case. (Jerry stopped coming to the meetings.) The team decided that an assessment of his "enabling" systems was necessary. The following plan was set up:

A. **Contract**—BMR set up a contract with the client. He would be dealt with in their office only if he came in sober. This included the times when he would come in for his SSI check. Jerry agreed.

B. **Work with the Courts**—Jerry again was being arrested and then given a fine for his actions. This meant very little to him since BMR was his representative payee and, therefore, budgeted his money and helped pay his bills. Since substance abuse treatment providers often dealt with the courts, the shelter agreed to make recommendations to them, including the need for treatment, the next time he got caught.

C. **SSI**—Jerry abuses this system just as he does many others. When Jerry began drinking, his money went for booze, not a place to live or food. Social Security has a rule that, in order to receive benefits, the individual must have a permanent residence. Jerry, who usually lives "on the streets" when he's drinking, was told that SSI would be contacted if he did not have a room.

D. **The Double Bind**—One problem that we have not been able to solve is a double bind in the system and how Jerry is very wise to this fact. BMR must manage his case to assure that he has money for food and shelter. Jerry knows where he can get free shelter and free food, so his money can be spent on booze. He knows that he will always be taken care of.

We have continued to work with Jerry's case, within our limits. He made considerable progress during his seven and a half months of sobriety, and we have continued to confront his drinking and drinking behavior in hopes that he will again try chemically-free living.

Source: *The Maine Approach: A Treatment Model for the Intellectually Limited Substance Abuser* (Augusta: The Maine Department of Mental Health and Mental Retardation; and Waterville, ME: The Kennebec Valley Regional Health Agency, 1984), pp. 22–25.

that 62 percent had alcohol- or other drug-related injuries.[116] Forty-one patients had a prior history of alcohol or drug abuse and 32 apparently resumed use following injury. Heinemann and his colleagues found that 43 percent of the seventy-five spinal cord injury subjects they studied were intoxicated at the time of injury, including twenty-seven of forty-nine patients who were identified as having drinking problems before injury, one of four who developed problems postinjury, and three of the twenty who reportedly had no alcohol problem.[117] Drinking behaviors generally declined after SCI, but two-thirds of study participants were drinking eighteen months later with a median frequency of "four drinks one to two times each week." Only 11 percent of the sample had ever received alcohol treatment (7 percent preinjury and 4 percent postinjury). Several individuals who thought they needed treatment immediately following their injury later changed their mind.

In a study of 137 SCI patients, Frisbie and Tun found that prior to paralysis, 94 were drinkers (i.e., they drank an average of at least one drink per day for at least a year).[118] Thirty-nine had been drinking on the day of their injury. Following the injury, 33 became abstainers, 12 reduced consumption, 8 increased consumption, and 7 became drinkers.

Studies of youthful rehabilitation clients and college students with various physical disabilities have produced inconsistent findings about alcohol and drug use. Some suggest higher use and abuse figures than the general population,[119] while others indicate little or no differences.[120] Comparisons may be difficult to make due to the confounding effects of various types of disabilities. One study focused on fifty-seven college students with orthopedic impairments who relied on wheelchairs. Of interest were the findings that "abuse of mood-altering drugs, including alcohol, appears to have predated disability for the most problematic cohort in this study. A trauma related disability correlated with greater likelihood of alcohol or other drug abuse during college than did a congenital disability."[121] The authors were particularly concerned about the number of participants who were taking prescription medications but who lacked knowledge about the adverse interactions their medications might have with alcohol or other drugs. The Chemical Dependency/Physical Disability Program at Abbott Northwestern Hospital/Sister Kenny Institute in Minneapolis, Minnesota, reported that seventy-two of the first eighty-eight clients admitted with onset of disability after their tenth birthday had chemical dependency problems prior to incurring the disability.[122]

There is interest in whether SCI patients, as well as patients who have suffered other injuries such as traumatic brain injury (TBI), have certain personality types. Some SCI patients appear to be thrill seekers who have shunned intellectual interests and pursued behaviors more likely to result in self-destruction.[123] Their inability to pursue previous physical activities increases their frustration during rehabilitation.

The crisis caused by SCI or other serious injury can provide a prime opportunity for intervening in a substance abuse problem.[124] Frisbie and Tun noted that those who reduced alcohol consumption or stopped drinking in their study did so primarily for health-related reasons often in response to advice from loved ones or a physician.[125] But there are barriers to the general rehabilitation of SCI patients. Some SCI patients become comfortable in the institutional setting and fail to make progress because of fears of independent living.[126] Successful rehabilitation may result in a termination of Social Security benefits, public assistance payments, or Veterans Administration benefits. These benefits might exceed what can be earned from employment. Disability payment systems which fail to reward the patient's progress have long been criticized as encouraging dependency.

As the rehabilitation process progresses, patients may resume alcohol and drug use.[127] Family, friends, and even professional caregivers may offer these substances to promote enjoyment and normalcy. Family members may be angry that the individual was responsible for the behavior that caused the injury and that has left everyone overburdened. At the same time, they may be feeling guilty over their resentment toward the disabled person. Loved ones are trying to cope with their caregiving responsibilities and wish they could do more. The strains caused by the disability may make opening a beer or rolling a joint for the disabled individual easier than engaging in hostile encounters.

O'Donnell and his colleagues warn of the problems that those with spinal cord injuries (paraplegia and quadriplegia) encounter from the use or abuse of alcohol or other drugs.[128] For example, depressant drugs exacerbate depressed mood and impede motor activity; lack of movement contributes to other physical problems such as pulmonary, joint, and urinary. In addition, the amount of urine produced by drinking beverages like beer can cause unnecessary dependence on catheterization when bladder control has already been diminished. Clues that SCI patients may be suffering from chemical dependency are lack of attention to health care, nutrition, and hygiene and the development of "severe decubitis ulcers (bed sores) aggravated by sitting in a wheelchair for days while they are stoned or drunk."[129]

Some suggestions for screening male SCI patients for substance abuse have emerged in the literature. Rohe and Basford present evidence that the MacAndrew Alcoholism Scale (see Chapter 5) may successfully predict which SCI patients had injuries related to their alcohol use.[130] Earlier detection may promote rehabilitation of those with alcohol abuse and dependency problems and help to deter life-altering SCI accidents. For example, scales such as the MacAndrew may identify young medical patients who have not experienced such serious consequences as SCI but whose alcohol and drug use puts them at risk for such injuries. Most accidents that result in SCI are preventable.

One of the first substance abuse treatment programs for SCI patients was developed at the Veterans Administration Spinal Cord Injury Service in Long Beach, California, following drug raids there by federal marshals.[131] It is an integrated service program simultaneously addressing substance abuse and SCI using a therapeutic community model. The Veterans Administration already had treatment programs for alcoholics and addicts, and its SCI units offered the advantages of physical accessibility and the staff and equipment needed for inpatient care. The staff structured the program specifically for this clientele. For example, since it may take a quadriplegic patient two to four hours to accomplish morning hygiene and grooming routines, even with assistance, treatment activities begin later in the day than is the norm in most inpatient chemical dependency programs. The program offers a wide range of services including education for independent living, assertiveness training, vocational rehabilitation, spiritual awareness, and participation in self-help groups. Schaschl and Straw describe another type of chemical dependency program that incorporates physically impaired individuals (the major physical impairment of clients served by the program is spinal cord injury) with able-bodied patients.[132] There are special group sessions for physically disabled persons to address their unique problems, and special services are also provided to family members.

TRAUMATIC HEAD AND BRAIN INJURY

Like SCI, a link between traumatic head injury or traumatic brain injury (TBI) and substance use, abuse, or dependency seems apparent. Many people believe that an intoxicated individual is more likely to be in an accident, but some also believe that the likelihood of suffering a traumatic injury is reduced, because alcohol is a depressant that relaxes the body.[133] While evidence supports the first of these assumptions, Sparadeo and Gill counter the second.[134] They also report that head trauma patients admitted with a positive blood-alcohol level (BAL), especially those at 0.10 percent or above, experience a more difficult medical course. These patients stayed in the hospital longer, had a longer period of agitation, and had lower cognitive status at the time of discharge. A positive BAL at the time of injury is a problem because "there is an increase in the volume of blood, increasing brain bleeding and agitation."[135] An accurate diagnosis is difficult to make because it may be unclear whether the patient's symptoms are due to intoxication, a head injury, or both.[136] Alcohol also reduces the "ability to marshall an appropriate response to hemorrhage and shock" and "poses a major anesthesia risk for those requiring emergency surgery"; however, it is not clear whether it is intoxication at the time of injury or a history of alcohol abuse and its related problems that cause a poorer cognitive outcome.[137]

Literature reviews implicate alcohol in more than half of all traumatic head injuries with 29 to 58 percent of head injured individuals legally intoxicated at the time the trauma occurred; studies also report that 25 to 68 percent of TBI patients have histories indicative of addiction.[138] Conversely, Hillbom and Holm found that "traumatic head injuries seem to be about two to four times more prevalent in the histories of alcoholics than in the histories of the general population."[139] Alcohol is by far the drug most frequently associated with traumatic brain injury, followed by hashish.[140] Some cocaine use has

been reported, although far less frequently; data on other drug use are lacking.[141]

As with many other disabilities, substance use or abuse may precede TBI or vice versa. It has been suggested that chemical use following trauma may be prompted by alienation by peers, a change in behavior of family members, a desire to assert independence, or most often—just plain boredom.[142] However, Kreutzer and his associates found that, in general, drinkers curtailed their use of alcohol following traumatic brain injury.[143] According to Sparadeo, the most severely injured do not return to drinking, but of those with moderate or minor injuries, 30 percent and 50 percent respectively, return to drinking.[144] The belief among head injury professionals is that substantial numbers of patients do continue to use alcohol and other drugs, and this warrants concern.[145] Alcohol and drug consumption may interfere with cognitive functioning already impaired by the brain trauma. Alcohol use may also be contraindicated due to physical problems and medications taken as a result of brain injury. In addition, there is a high likelihood of a subsequent head injury for those who return to drinking.[146] There may also be an association between substance abuse, antisocial personality (ASP) disorder, and the likelihood of sustaining a traumatic brain injury.[147] Those with ASP tend to act out, and alcohol may contribute to this behavior, resulting in a serious accident. A recent study indicates that the most frequent post-injury arrests for patients following TBI were alcohol and drug related.[148]

Professionals in the head injury field seem to agree that assessment for substance abuse and dependency problems should be routine, but apparently only a portion of programs do this.[149] Since an accurate assessment may be hampered when the patient's memory has been impaired by TBI,[150] Kreutzer and his associates recommend the use of multiple assessment tools, including standardized questionnaires, records, and interviews with patients and collaterals in the home setting.[151] They have used three standardized instruments with TBI patients, the Brief MAST (see Chapter 5), the General Health and History

Questionnaire (developed by Kreutzer and colleagues), and the Quantity, Frequency, Variability Index (QFVI).[152] Along with neuropsychological and rehabilitation evaluations, Jones recommends the CAGE Questionnaire (also see Chapter 5), because it is brief and minimizes the use of abstract or complex concepts.[153] The CAGE has also been recommended for use with patients who experienced trauma resulting in other types of injuries.[154]

Henry and Jones discuss the behavioral and psychological problems that head injury patients face in recovery.[155] The number and intensity of these problems vary depending on the individual and the injury. Henry notes six problem areas: attention, memory, language, reasoning and judgment, executive functions (abilities of initiation, organization, direction, monitoring, and self-evaluation), and emotion. For example, head injuries may result in a diminuation of cause and effect reasoning, of the ability to make inferences, of problem-solving skills, and of determining appropriate behavior. Confabulation to hide memory deficits may be mistaken as intentional dishonesty. Common behaviors among those with TBI such as giggling at inappropriate times (e.g., during group therapy or self-help meetings) or making inappropriate remarks may be misunderstood by others who may then ostracize the brain-injured individual. In order to help the head-injured person, Henry suggests that it is often appropriate for professionals and self-help group sponsors to openly address these behaviors with the individual, discuss specific examples of these behaviors, and give advice gently but firmly for making modifications in behavior.

Similar to those with dual diagnoses of mental and substance disorders, those with TBI or SCI and substance disorders often find that appropriate treatment alternatives are scarce. The refrain has become familiar—rehabilitation centers for those recovering from traumatic brain injury may feel ill equipped to treat problems of chemical dependency, and chemical dependency programs may feel inadequate to respond to the unique aspects of treating those with TBI. Sparadeo and his colleagues believe that in-surance companies may be exacerbating the problem by arguing over which problem should be treated first, or patients find themselves in chemical dependency treatment without comprehensive head injury rehabilitation, because substance abuse treatment is the less costly of the two.[156]

According to Strauss, "we are not dealing with a simple dual diagnosis, but with a truly integrated problem"; therefore, an integrated program of treatment for both the head injury and the substance abuse is recommended.[157] Model programs are being implemented but have yet to be evaluated.[158] Behavioral techniques are often used in these programs,[159] because deficits experienced by brain-injured patients are likely to make insight-oriented, psychodynamic approaches unsuitable.[160] These behavioral approaches help clients achieve successes by working on long-term goals in small steps.[161] TBI patients with cognitive deficits benefit when material is repeated and presented more slowly than may be done in traditional chemical dependency programs. A longer time period is often needed to engage clients with TBI in overcoming denial, to help them accept a goal of abstinence, and to provide treatment.[162] Since the problems of TBI patients vary so widely, individualization of treatment must be the rule. The case of a patient who received integrated treatment is found in the accompanying box. The National Head Injury Foundation located in Washington, DC, and its Task Force on Chemical Dependency are good sources of information on the combination of TBI and substance disorders and their treatment.

With regard to self-help groups, concepts used in AA, such as "higher power," may be too abstract for those with severe cognitive impairments to grasp.[163] Repetition of the twelve steps and making concepts as concrete as possible are suggested.[164] Peterman has reworded the twelve steps of Alcoholics Anonymous so that they can be more readily understood by those with head injuries.[165] Regular AA or NA meetings can be followed with sessions for TBI clients so that they can benefit from additional explanation.[166]

Case Study: A Search for the Right Mix*

Profile

Sex: male/**Age:** 31
Family status: married, daughter, 3 years old
Occupation: machinist
Education: high school graduate

At age 16, Tom began to use alcohol; he drank moderately. At 19, he was involved in a motor vehicle accident in which he was pushed out the car door. He was unconscious for a short period of time, hospitalized briefly, then released. No changes in behavior were reported following his accident.

In 1985, at age 25, Tom married. Cycles of drinking and sobriety continued for three years, often precipitated by work-related stress and problems with relatives. He drank at home, alone, in the garage, basement, or woods, hiding it from his wife.

In January 1988, following a severe dispute with his family, Tom began to drink heavily. He never lightened up. What followed were 15 months of intoxication, a second head injury, behavioral changes, and strong suicide rumination before Tom found the right mix—an integrated head injury and substance abuse treatment program.

March 16, 1988 • Tom began one-on-one alcohol counseling once a week; he continued to drink almost every night.

June 1988 • Tom was promoted from a day-shift machinist to the night-shift lead foreman. Due to increased pressures at work and an inability to acclimate his sleep pattern, Tom began to drink on the job. Coworkers noted incidences of drinking; however, supervisors were unaware.

Tom was intoxicated 75 percent of each day; he was emotional, soppy, disappointed in himself, and continually promised to stop.

August 11, 1988 • Tom crashed his motorcycle on his way home from work.

Upon admission to the hospital, diagnoses revealed bifrontal contusions, left occipital lobe contusions, and a blood alcohol level positive for intoxication. He was unconscious for six hours. Confused and severely agitated, Tom was restrained and heavily sedated.

September 2, 1988 • Tom was transferred to an acute rehabilitation unit for occupational, cognitive, and behavioral therapies. He made rapid progress.

September 9, 1988 • Once home, Tom began outpatient cognitive and vocational therapy and one-on-one alcohol counseling three times per week.

Three weeks later, Tom began drinking. He was no longer emotional and apologetic, rather he was verbally aggressive to others and physically self-abusive, running his head into the wall and refrigerator. His wife reported seizure-like temper tantrums during which he was beyond reason.

Soon after, Tom was arrested following a fight with a store clerk.

October 23, 1988 • Tom was admitted to an inpatient alcohol treatment center for two weeks. The program's schedule was active and group-oriented. Tom found that he was often mentally fatigued and distracted. Counseling did not compensate for Tom's injury-related cognitive deficits such as perseveration, impaired memory, and decreased ability to organize and orally express information. The level of language communicated in group sessions was higher than Tom's comprehension level.

November 5, 1988 • Upon discharge, Tom resumed outpatient therapies and alcohol counseling. Drinking binges continued every few weeks. Relatives and police were called to intervene during drinking episodes.

December 1988 • Tom returned to work on a trial basis with his previous employer. Three days later, he was arrested for DWI and lost his driver's license. Tom's wife, therapists, and employer determined he was not ready to return to work. Drinking incidents continued every few weeks. He became depressed and frustrated.

January 1989 • Tom began to talk of committing suicide. His wife repeatedly found him with guns in the house. She removed the guns. Suicide ideation was more prominent when Tom was intoxicated.

February 22, 1989 • "Kill myself" was at the top of Tom's list of things to do; he began drinking. He met with his alcohol counselor. The counselor insisted that Tom admit himself into an inpatient program; he feared that Tom was a serious threat to himself.

• Tom was unwillingly admitted to the inpatient alcohol treatment program for another two-week stay. For the first time, Tom admitted he had an alcohol problem.

March 16, 1989 • Tom was admitted to an inpatient program which offered integrated head injury and substance abuse treatment. A comprehensive assessment revealed an impaired ability to organize and express information, perseverances, a low frustration tolerance, and premorbid reading and writing difficulties—a problem diagnosed in his childhood. It also found Tom was able to attend to a task in a structured environment, was highly motivated, and was aware of his deficits.

Tom signed a substance abuse contract agreeing not to use alcohol. The potential loss of privileges acted as an incentive to maintain abstinence. In individual alcohol counseling sessions, Tom identified "drinking triggers" and developed relapse prevention strategies to avoid them. These were reinforced in situation-specific role-play scenarios. Tom attended a weekly substance abuse education group for people with head injuries. With his wife, he participated in couples' counseling. Toward discharge, Tom attended carefully selected AA meetings, accompanied by his alcohol counselor who acted as another listener.

Tom participated in a highly structured regimen of physical, occupational, cognitive, and vocational therapies. All members of the treatment team worked with Tom on maintaining sobriety. To reduce anxiety, Tom learned progressive muscle relaxation, biofeedback, and visualization techniques. Tom progressed rapidly in all therapy areas.

Tom had three drinking relapses during his six-month stay.

September 22, 1989 • Tom was discharged home. One week later, he returned to work as a machinist with his former employer.

October 19, 1989 • Tom drank heavily on the job and was taken home.

November 4, 1989 • Tom got drunk again. On his wife's insistence, he moved out. Tom continued to work.

December 16, 1989 • Tom moved back home. He said he was serious about working things out and taking responsibility for his life. He began counseling with his minister and started going to church.

He stayed sober for six months.

1990 • Tom used alcohol three times; all were minor incidences in which he was able to admit he was drinking and stop immediately.

Tom regained confidence in himself and his relationships with his wife and daughter. He pursued recreational activities which occupied his free time and increased his feelings of accomplishment. On his own, Tom enrolled in a literacy program.

He continues to work as a machinist with his former employer.

1991 • Tom remains alcohol-free.

*This case study was compiled from reports from the client's case file and interviews with his wife. The client's name was changed in this case study to protect his privacy.

Source: Meg Batson, "Case Study: A Search for the Right Mix," *Headlines,* Summer, 1991, pp. 14–15.

SENSORY DISABILITIES

The sensory impairments we discuss are hearing and visual. Although information on these impairments in combination with substance abuse is scarce, the lack of information on visual disabilities is especially striking.

Hearing Impairments

McCrone[167] reports that "the major causes of deafness include premature birth, rubella, meningitis, heredity and Rh incompatibility" and that many deaf clients being treated for substance abuse today have hearing loss as a result of the rubella epidemic ("rubella bubble") of 1964–1965.[168] In one of the few studies of alcohol use among persons who are deaf, Isaacs concluded that "no significant differences were found between the deaf and hearing samples on patterns of drinking or other parameters of alcohol use."[169] His sample was admittedly small, but it was an attempt to bring empirical investigation to this area. Locke and Johnson studied substance use among students at a senior high school for deaf individuals.[170] Twenty-six of the 46 respondents reported regular alcohol use and 6 reported occasional use. Some drunkenness was reported. Five students had had alcohol-related traffic violations. Fifteen were currently using other drugs and 12 others had tried them. Four respondents had been arrested for disorderly conduct or theft while using drugs. Fulton reported that "one third to one half of the client caseloads in our Counseling and Placement Center at Gallaudet [College] are substance abuse related."[171]

In 1982, McCrone used population estimates of deafness and substance abuse and figured that among persons with deafness, there might be 73,000 alcoholics, 8,500 heroin users, and 14,700 cocaine users.[172] In 1984, Steitler provided estimates of more than 1 million persons with both deafness and substance abuse or dependency.[173] More recent estimates are apparently not available, and it is really not known whether rates of substance use, abuse, or dependency among deaf persons differ from those of the general population. Dixon expressed surprise that estimates of substance abuse among deaf persons are not higher given the misconceptions about deafness and the poor treatment of deaf persons by the public.[174]

The life experiences of those who are prelingually deaf is substantially different from those who became deaf postlingually, and the degree to which hearing impaired individuals relate to the deaf and hearing communities varies.[175] Families are often overprotective of their deaf members, and the deaf community tends to be close knit and mistrustful of hearing individuals.[176] Within the culture of deaf persons, substance abuse education, including knowledge about professional treatment resources and self-help groups, is often lacking.[177] As a result, chemical dependency is still often viewed in moralistic terms.[178] According to Boros, members of the deaf community "deny alcoholism among their own, fearful that a dual stigma will be imposed upon them—'deaf and drunk.'"[179] In addition, "the deaf community tends to be very insular, with its own clubs and social life which revolves around alcohol use. An extensive 'grapevine' militates against persons coming forward to discuss and treat their problem."[180] Deaf clients often report that a hearing sibling introduced them to drug use.[181]

Assisting substance abusers with hearing impairments requires familiarity with their communication styles. Since the degree of hearing loss varies, some individuals benefit from devices that amplify sound. Among deaf individuals, American Sign Language (ASL) is used most frequently, but it is not the only language: "Variations include spoken English, a mixture of signed and spoken English, manual codes for English, finger-spelled English, unique and privately-developed 'homesigns,' and various regional dialects of American Sign Language."[182] The level of language proficiency also varies. Chemical dependency professionals who rely on "talk therapies" are challenged by gestural languages, since these languages often do not have translations for the jargon of treatment programs and self-help groups.[183] Gestures and other movements used by deaf persons are often misinterpreted by hearing individuals. "For example, a subtle twitching of the nose signifies 'yeah-I-know,' and a furrowed brow may represent a question"; waving an arm is an attempt to get another's attention, but may be interpreted as abnormal by outsiders and result in misdiagnosis.[184] Determining a hearing impaired client's preferred mode of communication is important, but an appropriate interpreter may not be available. Chemical dependency professionals who can communicate directly with deaf individuals are the best choice but are difficult to find. As a result, many hearing impaired substance abusers are underserved.

The first published material on the dual disability of alcoholism and hearing impairment that Boros could find is an article entitled "A.A. and the Deaf Mute,"[185] which appeared in *The Grapevine* (AA's newsletter) in December 1968. Special treatment programs did not emerge until the middle of the 1970s. Boros recounts the development of professional services for this population beginning with a program of multiple services (no longer in existence) offered by the Hearing Society of the San Francisco Bay Area. Other programs are the St. Paul-Ramsey Hospital Program for Deaf Alcoholics; the Hurley Medical Center in Flint, Michigan, in conjunction with the area's affiliate of the National Council on Alcoholism and Drug Dependence; and Alcoholism Intervention for the Deaf (AID), which began as a volunteer effort and later became Addiction Intervention with the Disabled.[186] According to Boros, initial opposition to AID came from the deaf community, which claimed that the program "singled out deaf people from other disabled persons as having drinking problems."[187] Considerable groundwork was done in both the hearing impaired and professional chemical dependency communities to initiate the AID program. In 1979, NIAAA funded a demonstration project for deaf alcoholics at the Cape Cod Alcoholism Intervention and Rehabilitation Unit (CCAIRU) in Massachusetts. This program developed as the result of Paul Rothfeld's friendship with a young man, Stephen Miller, who had dual diagnoses of deafness and substance abuse.[188] No special services for hearing impaired alcoholics were available to Miller. He struggled with his disabilities and eventually took his own life. The facility for hearing impaired clients at CCAIRU is named for him.

The lack of chemical dependency professionals knowledgable about hearing impairments and the even smaller number who can communicate fully with hearing impaired clients[189] translates into unresponsiveness toward the deaf community.[190] Professionals can learn to work with an interpreter, but this requires preparation[191] and is not as useful as direct communication. The level of ability of interpreters varies and certified interpreters are usually needed to ensure accurate communication. Professional interpreters subscribe to a code of ethics that includes standards for confidentiality and objectiveness, but clients may still hesitate to reveal confidences with the interpreter present.[192] In crises, interpreters may not be readily available. Family and friends may be able to communicate well with the deaf individual, but the client may not wish to share certain information with them. Another barrier to treatment is the tendency for some hearing impaired persons to agree passively with professionals rather than express their own opinions.[193] More must be done to foster the participation of hearing impaired persons in substance abuse treatment and to prepare chemical dependency professionals to treat hearing impaired clients.

Many chemical dependency programs rely on the use of standardized questionnaires and written materials to assess and treat clients. However, many deaf clients do not read at a level that allows them to understand these materials fully.[194] There is a need for validation of diagnostic instruments and development of educational materials for use with deaf individuals.[195] Some visual aides such as pictorial prevention and treatment materials are available.[196]

With regard to treatment, it has not been determined whether mainstream or separate programs are preferable.[197] However, in mainstream programs, it is not possible to interpret all the interaction for clients with severe hearing impairments.[198] Rothfeld recommends separate programs,[199] while the program at the Rochester Institute of Technology has brought together members of the hearing and hearing impaired communities to promote mainstreaming of deaf persons in chemical dependency treatment programs.[200] There is often a need to simplify materials to correspond to clients' reading levels and to slow the pace of presentations since the material is often new to the client.[201] Fatigue may become a factor since the demands of absorbing new material are substantial and gesturing requires additional energy.[202] Longer periods of treatment, especially in inpatient settings, may be needed to compensate for these factors.[203] While there are some opportunities for inpatient treatment nationwide, outpatient services and aftercare for hearing impaired clients are sorely lacking.[204] Help may not just be a phone call away for the hearing impaired alcoholic.[205] Both treatment programs and deaf clients must have Telecommunications Devices for the Deaf (TDD) or at least have access to communication relay services to facilitate calls in times of crisis or at other times when support is needed.[206] There are few halfway houses for substance abusers who are deaf,[207] but this is beginning to change. With the advent of the ADA more efforts are being made to accommodate individuals with disabilities.

Some self-help groups are conducted in sign language, but the frequency of meetings may be insufficient to adequately assist those who are deaf and chemically dependent.[208] Most self-help groups do not employ interpreters on a regular basis, and bringing one's own interpreter can be expensive and may draw unwanted attention.[209] Interpreting meetings may not be as effective as conducting them entirely in ASL. Few recovering role models who are deaf and alcoholic are available to serve as sponsors.[210] The Stephen Miller House version of the twelve steps of Alcoholics Anonymous for persons who are deaf is available from the National Head Injury Foundation.[211] Another version of the

steps for hearing impaired individuals is found in an article by Hetherington.[212]

A few articles address strategies to assist hearing impaired adolescents who abuse alcohol and other drugs. Reality therapy has been recommended because of its straightforward approach, focus on client strengths, and orientation to the present.[213] Gallaudet College has developed a program for students that incorporates education, prevention, intervention, and treatment and makes use of peer advisors and professionals.[214]

A listing of accessible chemical dependency services is available in national mental health service directories for those with hearing impairments.[215] Sylvester also provides a list of resources,[216] and Alcoholics Anonymous offers literature for hearing impaired alcoholics.[217] Signs of Sobriety (S.O.S.), located in New Jersey, is an advocacy group pressing for legislative reforms in the treatment of deaf chemical abusers.[218]

Visual Impairments

The major cause of vision loss in the United States is diabetes, and diabetes can be aggravated by alcohol or other drug abuse.[219] Other causes of visual problems are cataracts, glaucoma, vascular disease, trauma, and heredity, but the etiology of one-third of the cases is unknown.[220] Approximately 2 million Americans are totally blind or have severe visual impairments.

According to de Miranda, "without doubt the group of people whose alcohol or other drug problems have been the most ignored . . . are those who are blind or visually impaired."[221] In 1983, Peterson and Nelipovich published a brief article with basic information about alcohol abuse and alcoholism to assist rehabilitation counselors in identifying these problems among their visually impaired clientele and in referring them to treatment programs and self-help groups.[222] In 1981, Glass described the general course of rehabilitation for individuals with visual handicaps to help acquaint chemical dependency personnel with this process.[223] Recognizing the gap in the literature, Burns and de Miranda[224] and the Addiction Research Foundation[225] have recently developed materials to assist chemical dependency professionals in reaching out to those with visual impairments.

Isolation and unemployment are major problems for those with visual impairments.[226] One study investigated the response of state rehabilitation counselors to their work with visually impaired substance abusers. Of the 32 respondents, half reported no success in helping these clients secure gainful employment and that the client's substance abuse presented a greater obstacle than their visual impairment.[227] The counselors wanted more education in working with these dually disabled clients.

To learn more about substance use among individuals with visual impairments, the Wisconsin Bureau of Community Program's Office for Persons with Physical Disabilities and Alcohol and Other Drug Abuse surveyed clients of the state's vocational rehabilitation program and centers for independent living.[228] Of the respondents, 271 were blind or visually impaired. While the representativeness of the sample is not certain, more of these respondents were heavy drinkers than in the general population (21 percent versus 12 percent, respectively). In addition, drinking was greater among those who lived with other family members than it was among those living alone, suggesting that enabling may play a part in drinking among those with physical disabilities. Also of note was that those who were blind or visually impaired, those with orthopedic impairments, and those with spinal cord injuries were more often heavy drinkers or moderate drinkers than those with other disabilities.

Glass describes two types of problem drinkers among the visually impaired.[229] Type A had a drinking problem prior to the onset of their visual impairment. They lack adequate coping skills and require specific alcoholism treatment. Type B develop alcohol problems after the onset of visual impairments (or another disabling condition). Their chemical abuse may remit following adequate adjustment to the visual disability. Nelipovich and Buss believe that it is important to recognize which disability came first:[230]

If the visual impairment is of long standing and if an appropriate level of acceptance of and adjustment to this impairment has been reached before alcohol abuse begins, then treatment should be geared to addressing the alcohol abuse. If the visual impairment has been more recent, then treatment should focus on helping the client to accept and adjust to the visual impairment first, and then on treating the alcohol abuse.

They add that the greatest challenge is to assist those who have accepted neither of their disabilities. To assess the dual disabilities of substance abuse and visual disability, Nelipovich and Buss suggest that professionals employ the "ASK" approach by determining the client's level of *a*cceptance of each disability, the client's *s*kills for coping with these disabilities, and the clients *k*nowledge about these disabilities.[231]

Helping professionals are encouraged to remember some basic aspects of interacting with individuals who are visually impaired.[232] For example, communicate directly with the individual rather than deferring to those who might accompany the client to the treatment center. Speak in a normal tone of voice and at a normal speed. Identify yourself to the client and let him or her know when you are entering and leaving the room. Ask individuals how they prefer to acquaint themselves with new surroundings and then help orient them to the physical environment of the treatment setting. In intensive treatment programs, appoint a guide for the first few days to allow the individual time to learn to move about the facility independently. Recreational and social activities might require obtaining Braille playing cards, games, and leisure reading materials.

Treatment facilities can use large-print materials or have magnification devices and other optical aides available so that clients with sufficient vision can utilize educational materials independently without relying on readers. For others, materials in Braille (including admission and consent forms) are useful, but only about 10 percent of those who are blind read Braille. Audiotapes and reading material aloud are also needed. Since most chemical dependency programs are not currently able to provide all the services needed by visually impaired clients (such as the latest technological equipment), cooperation with agencies that specialize in serving this clientele are needed.[233]

Self-help groups are also recommended for visually impaired substance abusers. It is especially helpful to have a member welcome the newcomer and introduce him or her to others. In addition, members can offer transportation to visually impaired individuals, especially in communities where public transportation is lacking. The Big Book and some other AA materials are available in Braille and on audiocassette and can be ordered from AA's General Service Office.

OTHER PHYSICAL DISABILITIES

Alcohol or drug abuse may be an obvious cause of physically disabling conditions such as liver disease or mental disorders such as organic brain syndrome, but many individuals are unaware of other conditions associated with alcohol abuse. For example, "it is less widely recognized that chronic alcohol abuse may be a predisposing factor of several varieties of arthritis," such as gout.[234]

In many cases there is a clear indication that use of alcohol or other drugs can exacerbate another disability. For example, although many diabetics are able to accommodate modest amounts of alcohol in their diets, drinking is contraindicated for others.[235] The numbers of individuals who are both diabetic and alcoholic is not thought to be large, but diabetics who drink may incur consequences as severe as brain damage or death.[236] Accurate diagnosis of a diabetic's situation in emergencies can be complicated by the difficulty in distinguishing many of the symptoms of hypoglycemia from those of intoxication.[237] There is evidence that alcohol can make an individual with epilepsy more prone to seizures.[238] The exact relationship among alcohol consumption, epilepsy, and seizures is a subject of controversy in the medical community, but according to Stoil, "epileptics who drink to intoxication encounter high risks, in part because of the indirect effects of alcohol consumption on management of their condition."[239] At a minimum, he advises that those with epilepsy be informed of these risks and that patients should be monitored for symptoms of substance abuse to prevent serious negative consequences. Individuals with epilepsy who have not been drinking and not been taking nonprescribed drugs are sometimes mistaken as intoxicated due to the disorientation and lack of coordination that follows a seizure. Likewise, even in the absence of alcohol and other drug use, seizures can be problems for those with mental retardation or traumatic brain injury. Law enforcement officers working the streets must take care not to make an erroneous arrest for public intoxication or an inappropriate referral to a detoxification center. Medical personnel are certainly aware of the need to make this distinction. It should also be remembered that alcohol and drug abuse can cause seizures in individuals who do not have other disabilities.

In many cases, some of the psychoactive drugs discussed in this book are prescribed to bring relief to an individual suffering a severe injury or illness despite the potential for addiction. For example, individuals with back injuries or other conditions may be prescribed analgesics for pain. More controversial is the experimental use of marijuana with glaucoma patients to reduce pressure in the eye and with cancer patients to reduce nausea and vomiting from chemotherapy.[240] Although there are some indications that marijuana may have therapeutic value, additional research will help clarify its usefulness in treatment. But many individuals use alcohol and other drugs in ways that are not therapeutic and that can result in dependence or cause or aggravate other conditions. Clearly, the interactions of substance abuse and other disabilities can be quite complex—as complex as the individual who has them.

RESOURCES

A number of resources are available to assist those interested in substance disorders and other physical or mental impairments. Some of those specific to particular disabilities have been referred to earlier in this chapter. Others address a broad range of disabilities. One of the oldest is Addiction Intervention with the Disabled, which continues to operate under the direction of Alexander Boros at Kent State University. Another resource is the Institute on Alcohol, Drugs and Disability (IADD), formerly the Coalition on Disability and Chemical Dependency, located in San Mateo, California. Its newsletter, *The Seed,* and other materials are available including an extensive bibliography.[241] The federal government's National Clearinghouse for Alcohol and Drug Information (NCADI) located in Rockville, Maryland, is another source of information. The National Center for Youth with Disabilities located in Minneapolis, Minnesota, is also concerned with multiple disabilities. Its newsletter is called *Connections* and it has published a special issue of *CYD-LINE Reviews* entitled "Substance Abuse by Youth with Disabilities and Chronic Illnesses."[242] One of the newest resources in the field is the Resource Center on Substance Abuse Prevention and Disability, located in Washington, DC, and funded by the U.S. Department of Health and Human Services.

SUMMARY

This chapter reviewed information on the combination of psychoactive substance disorders and other disabilities, including the systems that respond to these problems. Any physical or mental disability may coexist with substance abuse. Substance abuse may predate or precipitate another disability as is often the case with spinal cord injury, traumatic brain injury, or other tragic accidents. Coping with a physical or mental disability may also result in the abuse of alcohol or nonprescribed drugs to diminish psychological anguish or physical pain or to produce euphoric affects. Yet multiple disabilities do not necessarily occur in a cause-effect relationship. An individual's visual impairment, for example, may be unrelated to his or her alcohol or drug abuse. Those interested in the combination of chemical dependency and other disabilities will continue to investigate and debate statistics on prevalence rates and question the nature of the relationship between substance disorders and other disabilities. For prevention specialists and treatment providers, the most pressing concern is that multidisabled individuals need help now. The combination of disabling conditions presents a challenge to those with multiple diagnoses, their loved ones, and the professionals who work with them. While there are some helpful suggestions from those in the field, few cookbook-style solutions or tested approaches are available. The development of more innovative programs for substance abusers with other disabilities and studies of their effectiveness would be particularly helpful. Meanwhile, a resourceful professional who is continually willing to be informed remains a tremendous asset to rehabilitation, second only to the tenacity of clients and their loved ones in overcoming these adversities.

ENDNOTES

1. See, for example, Bobby G. Greer, "Substance Abuse Among People with Disabilities: A Problem of Too Much Accessibility," *Journal of Rehabilitation,* Vol. 52, No. 1 (1986), pp. 34–38, and M. Nelipovich and E. Buss, "Investigating Alcohol Abuse Among Persons Who Are Blind," *Journal of Visual Impairment and Blindness* (October 1991), pp. 343–345.

2. Alexander Boros, "Facing the Challenge," *Alcohol Health & Research World,* Vol. 13, No. 2 (1989), p. 103.

3. Margaret H. Hindman, "The Multidisabled: Emerging Responses," *Alcohol Health & Research World* (Winter 1980–81), pp. 4–10.

4. "Comorbidity: Mental and Addictive Disorders," *ADAMHA NEWS,* Fifteenth Anniversary Issue (March–April 1989), p. 13, and Frederick K. Goodwin, "From the Alcohol, Drug Abuse, and Mental Health Administration," *Journal of the American Medical Association,* (June 23/30, 1989), p. 3517.

5. Lial Kofoed and Alison Keys, "Using Group Therapy to Persuade Dual-Diagnosis Patients to Seek Substance Abuse Treatment," *Hospital and Community Psychiatry,* Vol. 39, No. 11 (1988), pp. 1209–1211.

6. "Senate-Passed Bill Prohibits Bias Against the Disabled," *Congressional Quarterly Weekly Report,* September 16, 1989, p. 2417.

7. Mary C. Dufour, Daryl Bertolucci, Carol Cowell, Frederick S. Stinson, and John Noble, "Alcohol-Related Morbidity Among the Disabled, The Medicare Experience 1985," *Alcohol Health & Research World* (Winter 1989), pp. 158–161.

8. "Comorbidity: Mental and Addictive Disorders," and Hindman, "The Multidisabled."

9. John de Miranda and Linda Cherry, "California Responds: Changing Treatment Systems Through Advocacy for the Disabled," *Alcohol Health & Research World* (Winter 1989), pp. 154–157.

10. "Senate-Passed Bill Prohibits Bias," p. 2417.

11. John de Miranda, "The Common Ground: Alcoholism, Addiction and Disability," *Addiction & Recovery* (August 1990), pp. 42–45.

12. An earlier version of this section appears in Deborah K. Webb and Diana M. DiNitto, "Clinical Practice with Clients Having Dual Diagnoses: Mental Illness and Substance Abuse," in Roberta G. Sands, *Clinical Social Work Practice in Community Mental Health* (New York: Macmillan, 1991), pp. 291–332, by prior agreement.

13. See, for example, Dennis C. Daley, Howard Moss, and Frances Campbell, *Dual Disorders: Counseling Clients with Chemical Dependency and Mental Illness* (Center City, MN: Hazelden Foundation, 1987).

14. American Psychiatric Association, *Diagnostic and Statistical Manual of Mental Disorders,* 3rd ed., rev. (Washington, DC: The Association, 1987).

15. Kathleen Sciacca, "Workshop on the Dually Diagnosed," Big Spring, TX, October 1989.

16. Lial Kofoed, Joyce Kania, Thomas Walsh, and Roland M. Atkinson, "Outpatient Treatment of Patients with Substance Abuse and Coexisting Psychiatric Disorders," *American Journal of Psychiatry,* Vol. 143, No. 7, pp. 867–872.

17. Anne Bauer, "Dual Diagnosis Patients: The State of the Problem, *TIE-LINES,* Vol. 4, No. 3 (1987), p. 1; also see Daniel J. Safer, "Substance Abuse by Young Adult Chronic Patients," *Hospital and Community Psychiatry,* Vol. 38, No. 5 (1987), pp. 511–514; Gregory B. Teague, Carolyn Mercer-McFadden, and Robert E. Drake, "Problems of Dually Diagnosed Individuals," *TIE-Lines,* Vol. 4, No. 1 (1989), p. 1; Arthur I. Alterman, "Substance Abuse in Psychiatric Patients: Etiological, Developmental, and Treatment Considerations," in Arthur I. Alterman (ed.), *Substance Abuse and Psychopathology* (New York: Plenum Press, 1985), pp. 121–136; and Linda D. Menicucci, Laurie Wermuth, and James

Sorenson, "Treatment Providers' Assessment of Dual-Prognosis Patients: Diagnosis, Treatment, Referral, and Family Involvement," *The International Journal of the Addictions,* Vol. 23, No. 6 (1988), pp. 617–622.

18. Kenneth Minkoff, "Beyond Deinstitutionalization: A New Ideology for the Postinstitutional Era," *Hospital and Community Psychiatry,* Vol. 38, No. 9, (1987), pp. 945–950; also see Helen E. Ross, Frederick B. Glaser, and Teresa Germanson, "The Prevalence of Psychiatric Disorders in Patients with Alcohol and Other Drug Problems," *Archives of General Psychiatry,* Vol. 45 (1988), pp. 1023–1031.

19. "Comorbidity: Mental and Addictive Disorders."

20. Alterman, "Substance Abuse in Psychiatric Patients."

21. Anthony F. Lehman, C. K. Patrick Myers, and Eric Corty, "Assessment and Classification of Patients with Psychiatric and Substance Abuse Syndromes," *Hospital and Community Psychiatry,* Vol. 40, No. 10 (1989), pp. 1019–1025.

22. Kenneth Minkoff, "Dual Diagnosis Workshop," Texas Department of Mental Health and Mental Retardation, Austin, May 1990.

23. Marc Schuckit, "Alcoholic Patients with Secondary Depression," *American Journal of Psychiatry,* Vol. 140, No. 6 (1983), pp. 711–714.

24. Bauer, "Dual Diagnosis Patients"; Minkoff, "Beyond Deinstitutionalization"; and Bert Pepper, and Hilary Ryglewicz, "Schizophrenia: A Constant Brain Disorder in a Changing World," Presentation at the 140th Annual Meeting of the American Psychiatric Association, Chicago, IL (New York: TIE-Lines, 1987).

25. Deborah K. Webb, data from the Homestead Supervised Apartment Program, Austin-Travis County MHMR (1990).

26. Minkoff, "Dual Diagnosis Workshop," and Bert Pepper, "Dual Disorders," presentation Houston, TX, September 1990.

27. Hilary Ryglewicz and Bert Pepper, *Alcohol, Drugs, and Mental/Emotional Problems: What You Need to Know to Help Your Dual-Disorder Client* (New York: The Information Exchange, 1990), p. 39.

28. Ibid.

29. Roger D. Weiss and Steven M. Mirin, "The Dual Diagnosis Alcoholic: Evaluation and Treatment," *Psychiatric Annals,* Vol. 19, No. 5 (1989), pp. 261–265; Siegfried H. Soika, "Mental Illness and Alcoholism: Implications for Treatment," in David Cook, Christine Fewell, and John Riolo, *Social Work Treatment of Alcohol Problems* (Rutgers, NH: Rutgers Center of Alcohol Studies, 1983), pp. 88–108; William D. Clark, "Alcoholism: Blocks to Diagnosis and Treatment," *The*

American Journal of Medicine, Vol. 71 (1981), pp. 275–286; and A. Scott Winter, "Dual Diagnosis = Double Trouble," *The Counselor,* (January/February 1991), pp. 9 and 34.

30. Winston M. Turner and Ming T. Tsuang, "Impact of Substance Abuse on the Course and Outcome of Schizophrenia," *Schizophrenia Bulletin,* Vol. 16, No. 1 (1990), pp. 87–95.

31. Menicucci, Wermuth, and Sorrenson, "Treatment Providers' Assessment," p. 619.

32. David Mee-Lee, "Diagnostic Dilemmas in Working with Dually Diagnosed Clients," *The Counselor* (January/February 1991), pp. 10–12.

33. Melvin L. Selzer, "The Michigan Alcoholism Screening Test: The Quest for a New Diagnostic Instrument," *American Journal of Psychiatry,* Vol. 127 (1971), pp. 1653–1658.

34. John A. Ewing, "Detecting Alcoholism, The CAGE Questionnaire," *Journal of the American Medical Association,* Vol. 252, No. 14 (1984), pp. 1905–1907; and Booker Bush, Sheila Shaw, Paul Cleary, Thomas L. Delbanco, and Mark A. Aronson, "Screening for Alcohol Abuse Using the CAGE Questionnaire," *The American Journal of Medicine,* Vol. 82 (1987), pp. 231–235.

35. Richard C. W. Hall, Michael K. Popkin, Sandra K. Stickney, and Earl R. Gardner, "Covert Outpatient Drug Abuse: Incidence and Therapist Recognition," *Journal of Nervous and Mental Disease,* Vol. 166, No. 5 (1978), pp. 343–348.

36. Darold A. Treffert, "Marijuana Use in Schizophrenia: A Clear Hazard," *American Journal of Psychiatry,* Vol. 135, No. 10 (1978), pp. 1213–1215.

37. Edward J. Khantzian, "The Self-Medication Hypothesis of Addictive Disorders: Focus on Heroin and Cocaine Dependence," *American Journal of Psychiatry,* Vol. 142, No. 11 (1985), pp. 1259–1264.

38. Franklin R. Schneier and Samuel G. Siris, "A Review of Psychoactive Substance Use and Abuse in Schizophrenia: Patterns of Choice," *The Journal of Nervous and Mental Disease,* Vol. 175, No. 11 (1987), p. 641.

39. A. Thomas McLellan, Anna Rose Childress, and George E. Woody, "Drug Abuse and Psychiatric Disorder: Role of Drug Choice," in Arthur I. Alterman (ed.), *Substance Abuse and Psychopathology* (New York: Plenum Press, 1985), pp. 137–172.

40. Also see Khantzian, "The Self-Medication Hypothesis"; Schneier and Siris, "A Review of Psychoactive Substance Use"; and Lisa Dixon, Gretchen Haas, Peter J. Weiden, John Sweeney, and Allen J. Frances, "Drug Abuse in Schizophrenic Patients: Clinical Correlates and Reasons for Use," *American Journal of Psychiatry,* Vol. 148, No. 2 (1991), pp. 224–230.

41. Alexander H. Glassman, "Cigarette Smoking: Implications for Psychiatric Illness," *American Journal of Psychiatry,* Vol. 150, No. 4 (1993), pp. 546–553; quote from p. 551.

42. Michael G. Bricker, *STEMSS, Support Together for Emotional and Mental Serenity and Sobriety* (West Bend, WI: © Michael G. Bricker 1989, 1991), and Bricker, *The Twelve Parallels Between Chemical Dependency and Mental Illness,* (West Bend, WI: © Michael G. Bricker 1989); also see Kathleen Sciacca, "New Initiatives in the Treatment of the Chronic Patient with Alcohol/Substance Use Problems," *TIE-Lines,* Vol. 4, No. 3 (July 1987), pp. 5–6.

43. Kate B. Carey, "Emerging Treatment Guidelines for Mentally Ill Chemical Abusers," *Hospital and Community Psychiatry,* Vol. 40, No. 4 (1989), pp. 341–349, and M. Susan Ridgely, Howard H. Goldman, and Mark Willenbring, "Barriers to the Care of Persons with Dual Diagnoses: Organizational and Financing Issues," *Schizophrenia Bulletin,* Vol. 16, No. 1 (1990), pp. 123–132.

44. Kathleen Sciacca, "Dual Diagnosis Workshop," Texas Department of Mental Health and Mental Retardation, Austin, May 1990.

45. Also see A. Thomas McLellan, Lester Luborsky, George E. Woody, Charles P. O'Brien, and Keith A. Druley, "Predicting Response to Alcohol and Drug Abuse Treatments," *Archives of General Psychiatry,* Vol. 40 (June 1983), pp. 620–625, and Katie Evans and Michael Sullivan, *Dual Diagnosis: Counseling the Mentally Ill Substance Abuser* (New York: Guilford Press, 1990).

46. Patricia Ann Harrison, Jodi A. Martin, Vincente B. Tuason, and Norman G. Hoffman, "Conjoint Treatment of Dual Disorders," in Alterman, *Substance Abuse and Psychopathology,* pp. 367–390.

47. Phyllis Solomon and Joseph Davis, "The Effects of Alcohol Abuse Among the New Chronically Mentally Ill," *Social Work in Health Care,* Vol. 11, No. 3 (1986), pp. 65–74.

48. Ryglewicz and Pepper, *Alcohol, Drugs, and Mental Emotional Problems,* and Webb and DiNitto, "Clinical Practice with Clients Having Dual Diagnoses: Mental Illness and Substance Abuse."

49. Daley, Moss, and Campbell, *Dual Disorders.*

50. Edward L. Hendrickson, "Treating the Dually Diagnosed (Mental Disorder/Substance Use) Client," *TIE-Lines,* Vol. 5, No. 4 (1988), pp. 1–4.

51. Michael G. Bricker, *STEMSS and 12 Step Recovery Programs: A Comparison* (West Bend, WI: © Michael G. Bricker, 1989); K. Minkoff, "An Integrated Treatment Model for Dual Diagnosis of Psychosis and Addic-

tion," *Hospital and Community Psychiatry*, Vol. 40, No. 10 (1989), pp. 1031–1036; Robert E. Drake, Gregory J. McHugo, Douglas L. Noordsy, "Treatment of Alcoholism Among Schizophrenic Outpatients: 4-Year Outcomes," *American Journal of Psychiatry*, Vol. 150, No. 2 (1993), pp. 328–329; and Stephen J. Bartels and Winfield N. Thomas, "Lessons from a Pilot Residential Treatment Program for People with Dual Diagnoses of Severe Mental Illness and Substance Use Disorder," *Psychosocial Rehabilitation Journal*, Vol. 15, No. 2 (1991), pp. 19–30.

52. Minkoff, "An Integrated Treatment Model."

53. Bricker, *The Twelve Parallels Between Chemical Dependency and Mental Illness.*

54. Diane P. Bakdash, "Psychiatric/Mental Health Nursing," in Gerald Bennett, Christine Vourakis, and Donna S. Woolf (eds.), *Substance Abuse: Pharmacologic, Developmental, and Clinical Perspectives* (New York: John Wiley and Sons, 1983), pp. 223–239.

55. Bert Pepper, "Some Experience with Psychoeducation Groups for Clients with Dual Disorders," *TIE-Lines*, Vol. 8, No. 2 (1991), p. 4.

56. See, for example, Kate Aliesan and Robert C. Firth, "A MICA Program: Outpatient Rehabilitation Services for Individuals with Concurrent Mental Illness and Chemical Abuse Disorders," *Journal of Applied Rehabilitation Counseling*, Vol. 21, No. 3 (1990), pp. 25–29; Kofoed and Keys, "Using Group Therapy"; and Fred C. Osher and Lial L. Kofoed, "Treatment of Patients with Psychiatric and Psychoactive Substance Abuse Disorders," *Hospital and Community Psychiatry*, Vol. 40, No. 10 (1989), pp. 1025–1030.

57. Deborah K. Webb, *Good Chemistry Co-Leader's Manual* (Austin, TX: © Deborah K. Webb 1992).

58. Kofoed and Keys, "Using Group Therapy," R. M. Atkinson, "Persuading Alcoholic Patients to Seek Treatment," *Comprehensive Therapy*, Vol. 11 (1985), pp. 16–24.

59. See, for example, Mark Keller, "Alcoholism: Nature and Extent of the Problem," in Seldon D. Bacon, *Understanding Alcoholism: Annals of the American Academy of Political and Social Science* (Philadelphia: The American Academy of Political and Social Science Society, 1958), pp. 1–11.

60. Sciacca, "New Initiatives," and Mark Schuckit, "Alcoholism and Other Psychiatric Disorders," *Hospital and Community Psychiatry*, Vol. 34, No. 11 (1983), pp. 1022–1026.

61. Kofoed and Keys, "Using Group Therapy," p. 1210; also see Osher and Kofoed, "Treatment of Patients."

62. H. Richard Lamb, "Will We Save the Homeless Mentally Ill?" *American Journal of Psychiatry*, Vol. 147, No. 5 (1990), pp. 649–651.

63. Webb, *Good Chemistry Co-Leader's Manual.*

64. Carol L. M. Caton, Alexander Gralnick, Stephen Bender, and Robert Simon, "Young Chronic Patients and Substance Abuse," *Hospital and Community Psychiatry*, Vol. 40, No. 10 (1989), p. 1039.

65. Osher and Kofoed, "Treatment of Patients with Psychiatric and Psychoactive Substance Abuse Disorders"; M. Susan Ridgely, Fred C. Osher, and John A. Talbott, *Chronic Mentally Ill Young Adults with Substance Abuse Problems: Treatment and Training Issues* (Baltimore: University of Maryland School of Medicine, October 1987); Minkoff, "An Integrated Treatment Model"; and Menicucci et al., "Treatment Providers' Assessment."

66. Larry Lawlor, "Re: The 3-D Client: Responsibility Abyss," *TIE-Lines*, Vol. 4, No. 3 (July 1987), p. 7, and Sciacca, "New Initiatives."

67. Lawlor, "Re: The 3-D Client"; also see Robert E. Drake, Gregory B. Teague, and S. Reid Warren III, "Dual Diagnosis: The New Hampshire Program," *Addiction and Recovery*, (June 1990), pp. 35–39.

68. Daley et al., *Dual Disorders.*

69. Sciacca, "New Initiatives," and Aliesan and Firth, "A MICA Program."

70. Terrence T. Gorski and Merlene Miller, *Staying Sober: A Guide for Relapse Prevention* (Independence, MO: Independence Press, 1986).

71. Dennis Daley and Frances Campbell, *Coping with Dual Disorders: Chemical Dependency and Mental Illness* (Center City, MN: Hazelden Foundation, 1989); Dennis Daley and Janet Sinberg, *Taking Care of Yourself: When a Family Member Has Dual Disorders* (Center City, MN: Hazelden Foundation, 1989); and Katie Evans and G. Michael Sullivan, *Dual Diagnosis: Counseling the Mentally Ill Substance Abuser* (New York: Guilford Press, 1990).

72. Bricker, *STEMSS and 12-Step Recovery Programs;* and Bricker, *STEMSS, Support Together.*

73. Informational materials from the Eisenhower Circle Group of Alcoholics Anonymous (Ypsilanti, MI).

74. Alcoholics Anonymous World Services, Inc., *The A.A. Member—Medications and Other Drugs* (New York: AA, 1984).

75. Minkoff, "An Integrated Treatment Model."

76. Katie Evans and J. Michael Sullivan, *Step Study Counseling with the Dual Disordered Client* (Center City, MN: Hazelden Foundation, 1990).

77. See Herbert J. Grossman (ed.), *Classification in Mental Retardation* (Washington, DC: American Association on Mental Deficiency, 1983).

78. See Henry Goddard, *The Kallikak Family, A Study in the Heredity of Feeble-Mindedness* (New York: Macmillan, 1912); W. N. East, "Mental Defectiveness and Alcohol and Drug Addiction," *British Journal of Inebriety,* Vol. 29 (1932), pp. 149–168, cited in Joseph Westermeyer, Thithiya Phaobtong, and John Neider, "Substance Use and Abuse Among Mentally Retarded Persons: A Comparison of Patients and a Survey Population," *American Journal of Drug and Alcohol Abuse,* Vol. 14, No. 1 (1988), pp. 109–123; and Ruth E. Fairbank, "The Subnormal Child-Seventeen Years After," *Mental Hygiene,* Vol. 17, No. 2 (1933), pp. 177–208.

79. J. E. Wallin, "Mental Deficiency in Relation to Problems of Genesis, Social Work and Occupational Consequences, Utilization, Control, and Prevention," *Journal of Clinical Psychology* (1956).

80. R. F. Tredgold and K. Soddy, *Textbook of Mental Deficiency (Subnormality),* 10th ed. (Baltimore: William and Wilkens, 1963).

81. S. P. Davies, *The Mentally Retarded in Society* (New York: Columbia University Press, 1964).

82. Westermeyer et al., "Substance Use and Abuse Among Mentally Retarded Persons"; also see Curtis H. Krishef and Diana M. DiNitto, "Alcohol Abuse Among Mentally Retarded Individuals," *Mental Retardation,* Vol. 19, No. 4 (1981), pp. 151–155.

83. Allen M. Huang, "The Drinking Behavior of the Educable Mentally Retarded and the Nonretarded Students," *Journal of Alcohol and Drug Education,* Vol. 26, No. 3 (1981), pp. 41–50; Krishef and DiNitto, "Alcohol Abuse Among Mentally Retarded Individuals"; Robert B. Edgerton, "Alcohol and Drug Use by Mentally Retarded Adults," *American Journal of Mental Deficiency,* Vol. 90, No. 6 (1986), pp. 602–609; and Andrew S. Halpern, Daniel W. Close, and Debra J. Nelson, *On My Own, The Impact of Semi-Independent Living Programs for Adults with Mental Retardation* (Baltimore: Paul H. Brookes, 1986).

84. Frank Wenc, "The Developmentally Disabled Substance Abuser," *Alcohol Health and Research World* (Winter 1980/81), pp. 42–46; and Bella H. Selan, "The Psychological Consequences of Alcohol Use or Abuse by Retarded Persons," paper presented at the American Association on Mental Deficiency, Annual Conference, Detroit, MI, May 26, 1981.

85. Wenc, "The Developmentally Disabled Substance Abuser."

86. Selan, "The Psychological Consequences of Alcohol Use or Abuse by Retarded Persons," p. 6.

87. Ibid., p. 5.

88. Also see Westermeyer et al., "Substance Use and Abuse Among Mentally Retarded Persons."

89. Wayne L. Sengstock, Glenn A. Vergason, and Margaret M. Sullivan, "Considerations and Issues in a Drug Abuse Program for the Mentally Retarded," *Education and Training of the Mentally Retarded,* Vol. 10 (October 1975), pp. 139–143.

90. Dawn Delaney and Alan Poling, "Drug Abuse Among Mentally Retarded People: An Overlooked Problem?" *Journal of Alcohol and Drug Education,* Vol. 35, No. 2 (1990), pp. 48–54.

91. Dennis Moore and Lewis Polsgrove, "Disabilities, Developmental Handicaps, and Substance Misuse: A Review," *The International Journal of the Addictions,* Vol. 26, No. 1 (1991), pp. 65–90.

92. Huang, "The Drinking Behavior of the Educable Mentally Retarded."

93. Edgerton, "Alcohol and Drug Use by Mentally Retarded Adults."

94. Steven Reiss, "Prevalence of Dual Diagnosis in Community-Based Day Programs in the Chicago Metropolitan Area," *American Journal on Mental Retardation,* Vol. 94, No. 6, (1990), pp. 578–585.

95. Halpern et al., *On My Own.*

96. Diana M. DiNitto and Curtis H. Krishef, "Drinking Patterns of Mentally Retarded Persons," *Alcohol Health & Research World* (Winter 1983/84), pp. 40–42.

97. Beverly A. Myers, "Psychiatric Problems in Adolescents with Developmental Disabilities," *Journal of the American Academy of Child and Adolescent Psychiatry,* Vol. 26, No. 1 (1987), pp. 74–79.

98. Also see Delaney and Poling, "Drug Abuse Among Mentally Retarded People," for a review of this literature on substance abuse and mental retardation.

99. Edgerton, "Alcohol and Drug Use by Mentally Retarded Adults"; also see Halpern et al., *On My Own.*

100. Edgerton, "Alcohol and Drug Use by Mentally Retarded Adults."

101. Ibid.

102. Halpern et al., *On My Own.*

103. Ibid., and Krishef and DiNitto, "Alcohol Abuse Among Mentally Retarded Individuals."

104. Krishef and DiNitto, "Alcohol Abuse Among Mentally Retarded Individuals," and Diana M. DiNitto and Curtis H. Krishef, "Family and Social Problems of Mentally Retarded Alcohol Users," *Social and Behavioral Science Documents,* Vol. 17, No. 1 (1987), p. 31.

105. Westermeyer et al., "Substance Use and Abuse Among Mentally Retarded Persons."

106. Ibid., p. 122.

107. L. S. Rychkova, "Clinical Characteristics of Early Alcoholism in Adolescents with Slight Mental Retar-

dation of Exogenous Etiology," *Soviet Neurology and Psychology* (Fall 1987), pp. 55–63.

108. Ibid., p. 62.

109. Krishef and DiNitto, "Alcohol Abuse Among Mentally Retarded Individuals."

110. Wenc, "The Developmentally Disabled Substance Abuser."

111. *The Maine Approach: A Treatment Model for the Intellectually Limited Substance Abuser* (Augusta: The Maine Department of Mental Health and Mental Retardation; and Waterville, ME: The Kennebec Valley Regional Health Agency, 1984).

112. Wenc, "The Developmentally Disabled Substance Abuser"; also see *The Maine Approach.*

113. John Small, "Emotions Anonymous: Counseling the Mentally Retarded Substance Abuser," *Alcohol Health & Research World* (Winter 1980/81), p. 46.

114. Ibid.

115. See, for example, James J. O'Donnell, Jonathan E. Cooper, John E. Gessner, Isabelle Shehan, and Judy Ashley, "Alcohol, Drugs, and Spinal Cord Injury, *Alcohol Health & Research World* (Winter, 1981/82), pp. 27–29; James H. Frisbie and Carlos G. Tun, "Drinking and Spinal Cord Injury," *Journal of the American Paraplegia Society,* Vol. 7 (1984), pp. 71–73; and Daniel E. Rohe and Jeffrey R. Basford, "Traumatic Spinal Cord Injury, Alcohol, and the Minnesota Multiphasic Personality Inventory," *Rehabilitation Psychology,* Vol. 34, No. 1 (1989), pp. 25–32.

116. O'Donnell et al., "Alcohol, Drugs, and Spinal Cord Injury," and Allen W. Heinemann, Matthew Doll, and Sidney Schnoll, "Treatment of Alcohol Abuse in Persons with Recent Spinal Cord Injuries," *Alcohol Health & Research World,* Vol. 13, No. 2 (1989), pp. 110–117.

117. Heinemann et al., "Treatment of Alcohol Abuse in Persons with Recent Spinal Cord Injuries."

118. Frisbie and Tun, "Drinking and Spinal Cord Injury."

119. Garry A. Rasmussen and Ronald P. De Boer, "Alcohol and Drug Use Among Clients at a Residential Vocational Rehabilitation Facility," *Alcohol Health & Research World,* (Winter 1980/81), pp. 48–56.

120. Dennis Moore and Harvey Siegal, "Alcohol and Other Drug Use Among Orthopedically Impaired College Students," *Alcohol Health & Research World,* Vol. 13, No. 2 (1989), pp. 118–123.

121. Ibid., p. 123.

122. Sharon Schaschl and Dennis Straw, "Results of a Model Intervention Program for Physically Impaired Persons," *Alcohol Health & Research World,* Vol. 13, No. 2 (1989), pp. 150–153.

123. O'Donnell et al., "Alcohol, Drugs, and Spinal Cord Injury."

124. Heinemann et al., "Treatment of Alcohol Abuse in Persons with Recent Spinal Cord Injuries," and Gregory A. Jones, "Alcohol Abuse and Traumatic Brain Injury," *Alcohol Health & Research World,* Vol. 13, No. 2 (1989), pp. 104–109.

125. Frisbie and Tun, "Drinking and Spinal Cord Injury."

126. Pete Anderson, "Alcoholism and the Spinal Cord Disabled: A Model Program," *Alcohol Health & Research World* (Winter 1980/81), pp. 37–41.

127. Much of this paragraph relies on O'Donnell et al., "Alcohol, Drugs, and Spinal Cord Injury."

128. Much of this paragraph relies on ibid.; also see Heinemann et al., "Treatment of Alcohol Abuse in Persons with Recent Spinal Cord Injuries"; and Schaschl and Straw, "Results of a Model Intervention Program."

129. Anderson, "Alcoholism and the Spinal Cord Disabled," p. 38.

130. Rohe and Basford, "Traumatic Spinal Cord Injury, Alcohol, and the Minnesota Multiphasic Personality Inventory."

131. Anderson, "Alcoholism and the Spinal Cord Disabled," p. 38.

132. Schaschl and Straw, "Results of a Model Intervention Program."

133. Francis R. Sparadeo and Daryl Gill, "Effects of Prior Alcohol Use on Head Injury Recovery," *Journal of Head Trauma Rehabilitation,* Vol. 4, No. 1 (1989), pp. 75–82.

134. Ibid.

135. Lisa Terry, "Treating the Head Injured Substance Abuser," *New Jersey Rehab* (no date).

136. Judith Mitiguy, "Alcohol and Head Trauma," *Headlines* (Summer 1991), pp. 3–4, 6–9, and James Wasco, "Attacking the Problem Before It Starts," *Headlines* (Summer 1991), p. 20.

137. Mitiguy, "Alcohol and Head Trauma," p. 6.

138. Sparadeo and Gill, "Effects of Prior Alcohol Use," and Francis R. Sparadeo, David Strauss, and Jeffrey T. Barth, "The Incidence, Impact, and Treatment of Substance Abuse in Head Trauma Rehabilitation," *Journal of Head Trauma Rehabilitation,* Vol. 5, No. 3 (1990), pp. 1–8.

139. Matti Hillbom and Lena Holm, "Contribution of Traumatic Head Injury to Neuropsychological Deficits in Alcoholics," *Journal of Neurology, Neurosurgery and Psychiatry,* Vol. 49, No. 12 (1986), pp. 1348–1353.

140. D. Gill, M. Stambrook, A. Moore, and L. Peters, "Legal and Illicit Drug Use After Head Injury," presented at the Annual Conference of the Canadian Psychological Association, June 8, 1989, Halifax, Nova Scotia, cited in Sparadeo, Strauss, and Barth, "The Incidence, Impact and Treatment of Substance Abuse."

141. Mitiguy, "Alcohol and Head Trauma," and Terry, "Treating the Head Injured Substance Abuser."

142. Sparadeo et al., "The Incidence, Impact, and Treatment of Substance Abuse," and Suzan Kaitz, "Integrated Treatment: Safety Net for Survival," *Headlines* (Summer 1991), pp. 11–12, 14, 16–17.

143. Jeffrey S. Kreutzer, Kathleen R. Doherty, Jennifer A. Harris, and Nathan D. Zasler, "Alcohol Use Among Persons with Traumatic Brain Injury," *Journal of Head Trauma Rehabilitation*, Vol. 5, No. 3 (1990), pp. 9–20.

144. Francis R. Sparadeo cited in Terry, "Treating the Head Injured Substance Abuser."

145. Sparadeo et al., "The Incidence, Impact and Treatment of Substance Abuse," and Kreutzer et al., "Alcohol Use Among Persons with Traumatic Brain Injury."

146. Sparadeo et al., "The Incidence, Impact and Treatment of Substance Abuse"; Mitiguy, "Alcohol and Head Trauma"; and Kaitz, "Integrated Treatment."

147. Paul Malloy, Nora Noel, Richard Longabaugh, and Martha Beattie, "Determinants of Neuropsychological Impairment in Antisocial Substance Abusers," *Addictive Behaviors*, Vol. 15 (1990), pp. 431–438.

148. Jeffrey S. Kreutzer et al., "Substance Abuse and Crime Patterns among Persons with Traumatic Brain Injury Referred for Supported Employment," Brain Injury, Vol. 5, No. 2 (1991), pp. 177–187.

149. Sparadeo et al., "The Incidence, Impact, and Treatment of Substance Abuse."

150. Jones, "Alcohol Abuse and Traumatic Brain Injury."

151. Kreutzer et al., "Alcohol Use Among Persons with Traumatic Brain Injury."

152. For information on the QFVI, see Don Cahalan and Ira H. Cissin, "American Drinking Practices: Summary of Findings from a National Probability Sample, I. Extent of Drinking by Population Subgroups," *Quarterly Journal of Studies on Alcohol*, Vol. 29 (1968), pp. 130–151.

153. Jones, "Alcohol Abuse and Traumatic Brain Injury."

154. R. Wayne Shipley, Stephen M. Taylor, and Donna R. Falvo, "Concurrent Evaluation and Rehabilitation of Alcohol Abuse and Trauma," *Journal of Applied Rehabilitation Counseling*, Vol. 21, No. 3 (1990), pp. 37–39.

155. Kevin Henry, *A Letter to Sponsors of Chemically Dependent Head Injured Persons* (Washington, DC: National Head Injury Foundation, April 1988); Jones, "Alcohol Abuse and Traumatic Brain Injury."

156. Sparadeo et al., "The Incidence, Impact, and Treatment of Substance Abuse."

157. David Strauss quoted in Kaitz, "Integrated Treatment," p. 11; also see *New Medico Head Injury System* (Lynn, MA: New Medico Associates, 1990).

158. Sparadeo et al., "The Incidence, Impact, and Treatment of Substance Abuse."

159. Ibid.

160. Jones, "Alcohol Abuse and Traumatic Brain Injury."

161. R. L. Wood, *Brain Injury Rehabilitation: A Neurobehavioral Approach* (Rockville, MD: Aspen Publishers, 1987), cited in Jones, "Alcohol Abuse and Traumatic Brain Injury."

162. David Strauss cited in Kaitz, "Integrated Treatment."

163. Kaitz, "Integrated Treatment."

164. Karen Feinberg, "Maintaining Gains Through AA," *Headlines* (Summer 1991), p. 16.

165. Bill Peterman, "TBI Explanation [of the original 12 steps of AA]," in Henry, *A Letter to Sponsors of Chemically Dependent Head Injured Persons.*

166. Terry, "Treating the Head Injured Substance Abuser."

167. William P. McCrone, "Serving the Deaf Substance Abuser," *Journal of Psychoactive Drugs*, Vol. 14, No. 3 (1982), p. 199.

168. Also see Rene A. Sylvester, "Treatment of the Deaf Alcoholic: A Review," *Alcoholism Treatment Quarterly*, Vol. 3, No. 4 (1986), pp. 1–23.

169. Morton Isaacs, "Patterns of Drinking Among the Deaf," *American Journal of Drug and Alcohol Abuse*, Vol. 6, No. 4 (1979), pp. 463–476.

170. Reginald Locke and Shirley Johnson, "A Descriptive Study of Drug Use Among the Hearing Impaired in a Senior High School for the Hearing Impaired," in Arnold J. Schecter (ed.), *Drug Dependence and Alcoholism*, Vol. 2, *Social and Behavioral Issues* (New York: Plenum Press, 1981), pp. 833–841.

171. Kay Fulton, "Alcohol and Drug Abuse Among the Deaf, Collaborative Programming for the Purposes of Prevention, Intervention and Treatment," in Douglas Watson and Bruce Heller (eds.), *Mental Health and Deafness: Strategic Perspectives* (Silver Spring, MD: American Deafness and Rehabilitation Association, 1983), p. 367.

172. McCrone, "Serving the Deaf Substance Abuser," pp. 199–203.

173. K. A. Steitler, "Substance Abuse and the Deaf Adolescent," in G. B. Anderson and D. Watson (eds.), *The Habilitation and Rehabilitation of Deaf Adolescents* (Little Rock: University of Arkansas Rehabilitation Research and Training Center on Deafness and Hearing-Impairments, 1984), cited in Annie Steinberg, "Issues in Providing Mental Health Services to Hearing-Impaired Persons," *Hospital and Community Psychiatry,* Vol. 42, No. 4 (1991), pp. 380–389.

174. Thomas L. Dixon, "Addiction Among the Hearing-Impaired," *EAP Digest* (January/February 1987), pp. 41–44 and 74.

175. Steinberg, "Issues in Providing Mental Health Services."

176. Sylvester, "Treatment of the Deaf Alcoholic," and Donald G. Jorgensen and Connie Russert, "An Outpatient Treatment Approach for Hearing-Impaired Alcoholics," *American Annals of the Deaf* (February 1982), pp. 41–44.

177. Alexander Boros, "Activating Solutions to Alcoholism Among the Hearing Impaired," in Arnold J. Schecter (ed.), *Drug Dependence and Alcoholism,* Volume 2, *Social and Behavioral Issues* (New York: Plenum Press, 1981), pp. 1007–1014; McCrone, "Serving the Deaf Substance Abuser"; and Fulton, "Alcohol and Drug Abuse Among the Deaf."

178. Steinberg, "Issues in Providing Mental Health Services"; Sylvester, "Treatment of the Deaf Alcoholic"; Dixon, "Addiction Among the Hearing Impaired"; and Boros, "Activating Solutions to Alcoholism."

179. Alexander Boros, "Alcoholism Intervention for the Deaf," *Alcohol Health & Research World* (Winter 1980/81), p. 28; also see Boros, "Activating Solutions to Alcoholism."

180. New York State Division of Alcoholism and Alcohol Abuse, "Alcoholism and the Hearing Impaired," *DAAA Focus,* Vol. 3, No. 3 (April 1988), p. 1; also see Fulton, "Alcohol and Drug Use Among the Deaf."

181. McCrone, "Serving the Deaf Substance Abuser."

182. Steinberg, "Issues in Providing Mental Health Services," p. 381; also see Dixon, "Addiction Among the Hearing Impaired"; Sylvester, "Treatment of the Deaf Alcoholic"; and Isaacs, "Patterns of Drinking Among the Deaf."

183. Jorgensen and Russert, "An Outpatient Treatment Approach."

184. Steinberg, "Issues in Providing Mental Health Services," p. 381.

185. Boros, "Alcoholism Intervention for the Deaf."

186. Ibid.

187. Ibid., p. 29.

188. Paul Rothfeld, "Alcoholism Treatment for the Deaf: Specialized Services for Special People," *Journal of Rehabilitation of the Deaf,* Vol. 14, No. 4 (1981), pp. 14–17.

189. Fulton, "Alcohol and Drug Abuse Among the Deaf"; Janet E. Dick, "Serving Hearing-Impaired Alcoholics," *Social Work* (November 1989), pp. 555–556; and Mary Ann Kelin and Pedro Acevedo, "Self-Help Groups for Deaf Adolescents: Problems of Drug and Alcohol Abuse," in Glenn B. Anderson and Douglas Watson (eds.), *Innovations in the Habilitation and Rehabilitation of Deaf Adolescents* (Little Rock, AR: University of Arkansas Press, 1987), pp. 325–330.

190. Boros, "Activating Solutions to Alcoholism."

191. Boros, "Alcoholism Intervention for the Deaf," and Steinberg, "Issues in Providing Mental Health Services."

192. Steinberg, "Issues in Providing Mental Health Services."

193. Thomas N. Grant, Carol A. Kramer, and Karen Nash, "Working with Deaf Alcoholics in a Vocational Training Program," *Journal of Rehabilitation of the Deaf,* Vol. 15, No. 4 (1982), pp. 14–20.

194. Dixon, "Addiction Among the Hearing Impaired"; New York State Division of Alcoholism and Alcohol Abuse (NYSDAAA), "Alcoholism and the Hearing-Impaired"; and Steinberg, "Issues in Providing Mental Health Services."

195. Sylvester, "Treatment of the Deaf Alcoholic."

196. *Addiction Intervention with the Disabled,* Kent State University: Kent, OH.

197. Boros, "Alcoholism Intervention for the Deaf," and Sylvester, "Treatment of the Deaf Alcoholic."

198. Ibid.; Rothfeld, "Alcoholism Treatment for the Deaf"; William Dore, "An Open Letter to Chemical Dependency Counselors," *The Counselor* (May/June, 1989), p. 26; Jorgensen and Russert, "An Outpatient Treatment Approach"; and Dick, "Serving Hearing-Impaired Alcoholics."

199. Rothfeld, "Alcoholism Treatment for the Deaf."

200. Dixon, "Addiction Among the Hearing Impaired."

201. Boros, "Alcoholism Intervention for the Deaf."

202. Ibid., and Gladys A. Kearns, "Hearing-Impaired Alcoholics—An Underserved Community," *Alcohol Health & Research World, 13,* No. 2 (1989), pp. 162–166.

203. NYSDAAA, "Alcoholism and the Hearing-Impaired," and Sylvester, "Treatment of the Deaf Alcoholic."

204. Steinberg, "Issues in Providing Mental Health Services."

205. Rothfeld, "Alcoholism Treatment for the Deaf."

206. Ibid., and McCrone, "Serving the Deaf Substance Abuser."

207. NYSDAAA, "Alcoholism and the Hearing-Impaired."

208. Boros, "Alcoholism Intervention for the Deaf," and Dick, "Serving Hearing-Impaired Alcoholics."

209. Steinberg, "Issues in Providing Mental Health Services."

210. Sylvester, "Treatment of the Deaf Alcoholic," and NYSDAAA, "Alcoholism and the Hearing-Impaired."

211. See Stephen Miller House Version [of the Twelve Steps of Alcoholics Anonymous for the deaf] in Henry, "A Letter to Sponsors."

212. Richard G. Hetherington, "Deafness and Alcoholism," *Journal of Rehabilitation of the Deaf*, Vol. 12, No. 4 (1979), pp. 9–12.

213. Jerry Edelwich and Pat Arre, "Reality Therapy as an Intervention for Deaf Adolescents Involved in Alcohol and Drug Use and Abuse," in Anderson and Watson, *Innovations in the Habilitation and Rehabilitation of Deaf Adolescents*, pp. 344–349. Reality therapy was developed by William Glasser; see his book *Reality Therapy* (New York: Harper Colophon, 1965).

214. John Mihall, Emily Smith, and Melanie Wilding, "Gallaudet's Student Development Approach to Substance Abuse Education and Identification/Treatment," in Anderson and Watson, *Innovations in the Habilitation and Rehabilitation of Deaf Adolescents*, pp. 331–343.

215. Steinberg, "Issues in Providing Mental Health Services."

216. Sylvester, "Treatment of the Deaf Alcoholic."

217. Alcoholics Anonymous World Services, New York, New York.

218. John L. Hulick, "S.O.S.," *The Counselor* (May/June 1989), p. 25.

219. Leonard F. Burns and John de Miranda, *Blindness and Visual Impairment: Drug and Alcohol Abuse Prevention & Treatment* (San Mateo, CA: Peninsula Health Concepts, August 1991).

220. The remainder of this paragraph relies on *A Look at Alcohol and Other Drug Abuse Prevention and . . . Blindness and Visual Impairments* (Washington, DC: Resource Center on Substance Abuse Prevention and Disability, no date).

221. John de Miranda, *California Alcohol, Drug and Disability Study: Literature Review and Bibliography* (San Mateo, CA: Institute on Alcohol, Drugs and Disability, 1990), p. 9; also see M. Nelipovich and E. Buss, "Investigating Alcohol Abuse Among Persons Who

are Blind," *Journal of Visual Impairment and Blindness* (October, 1991), pp. 343–345.

222. James Peterson and Michael Nelipovich, "Alcoholism and the Visually Impaired Client," *Journal of Visual Impairment and Blindness*, Vol. 77 (1983), pp. 345–348.

223. Edward J. Glass, "Problem Drinking Among the Blind and Visually Impaired," *Alcohol Health & Research World* (Winter 1980/81), pp. 20–25.

224. Burns and de Miranda, *Blindness and Visual Impairment.*

225. *Working with People with Visual Impairments* (Toronto: Addiction Research Foundation, no date).

226. Burns and de Miranda, *Blindness and Visual Impairment.*

227. Michael Nelipovich and Randy Parker, "The Visually Impaired Substance Abuser," *Journal of Visual Impairment and Blindness* (September 1981), p. 305.

228. Nelipovich and Buss, "Investigating Alcohol Abuse Among Persons Who Are Blind."

229. Glass, "Problem Drinking Among the Blind and Visually Impaired."

230. Michael Nelipovich and Elmer Buss, "Alcohol Abuse and Persons Who Are Blind, Treatment Considerations," *Alcohol Health & Research World*, Vol. 13, No. 2 (1989), p. 129.

231. Nelipovich and Buss, "Investigating Alcohol Abuse Among Persons Who Are Blind."

232. The remainder of this section relies primarily on Nelipovich and Buss, "Alcohol Abuse and Persons Who Are Blind"; also see *Working with People with Visual Impairments;* and *A Look at Alcohol and Other Drug Abuse Prevention and . . . Blindness and Visual Impairment.*

233. Burns and de Miranda, *Blindness and Visual Impairment.*

234. David J. Nashel, "Arthritic Disease and Alcohol Abuse," *Alcohol Health and Research World*, Vol. 13, No. 2 (1989), pp. 124–125.

235. Ronald A. Arky, "Alcohol Use and the Diabetic Patient," *Alcohol Health & Research World*, Vol. 8, No. 2 (1983/84), pp. 8–13.

236. Keith Ryan, "Alcohol and Blood Sugar Disorders, An Overview," *Alcohol Health & Research World*, Vol. 8, No. 2 (1983/84), pp. 3–7 and 15; also see Arky, "Alcohol Use and the Diabetic Patient."

237. Ryan, "Alcohol and Blood Sugar Disorders, An Overview."

238. For a discussion of this issue, see Ruth E. Little and James L. Gayle, "Epilepsy and Alcoholism," *Alcohol Health & Research World* (Winter 1980/81), pp. 31–36.

239. Michael J. Stoil, "Epilepsy, Seizures, and Alcohol," *Alcohol Health & Research World,* Vol. 13, No. 2 (1989), p. 141.

240. Weldon Winters and Peter Venturelli, *Drugs and Society,* 2nd ed. (Boston: Jones and Bartlett, 1988), pp. 136–137. © Boston: Jones and Bartlett Publishers. Reprinted by permission.

241. de Miranda, *California Alcohol, Drug and Disability Study.*

242. National Center for Youth with Disabilities, *CYDLINE Reviews: Substance Use by Youth with Disabilities and Chronic Illnesses* (Minneapolis: The Center, May 1990).

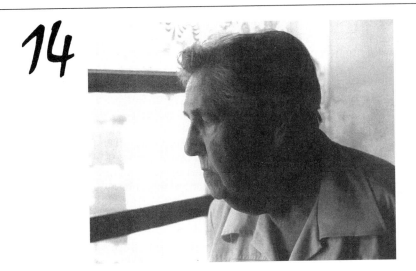

14

Alcohol and drug use among the elderly

INTRODUCTION

While the age demarcation is seen to vary, "elderly" generally refers to persons at least 60 or 65 years of age. The only group of persons in the United States today who were alive at the time of the Eighteenth Amendment to the Constitution which brought us Prohibition in 1920, as well as when it was repealed with the Twenty-first Amendment in 1933, are the elderly. Gilliland and James[1] state that from a social perspective, such legislation had much to say about what our society believed to be good or evil, and as young persons during this time, the elderly cut their eyeteeth on these messages.

This chapter focuses primarily on the elderly and their abuse of one particular substance—alcohol. Much more information is available on their use of alcohol than their use of illicit drugs. Whenever the population of interest is the elderly, writers begin by telling the demographic story. This is because America, like most other nations in the world, is aging. Life expectancy in the United States has increased from 47.3 years in 1900 to 75.0 years in 1987, and the oldest age segment is growing most rapidly. There were 29.8 million persons aged 65 and over in the United States in 1987 (12 percent of the total population), and this number is expected to increase to 34.9 million in the year 2000 (13 percent). The cohort aged 85 and over increased by 141 percent between 1960 and 1980, and Census Bureau projections indicate that an additional increase of 117 percent is expected between 1980 and 2000.[2]

A growing elderly population has gone hand in hand with a growing interest in alcohol abuse among older people. Graham[3] believes this concern stems from both humanitarian and economic interests. She asks, on the one hand, to what extent does alcohol abuse undermine elders' quality of life and, on the other hand, how much does alcohol use and abuse among the elderly contribute to growing health care costs?

PREVALENCE AND PATTERNS

No standardized methods have been utilized for estimating the prevalence of alcohol abuse among the elderly, and the domains typically included in alcohol abuse questionnaires are problematic in terms of older respondents.[4,5] For example, elders with memory loss may have difficulty remembering recent alcohol consumption, and a number of authors have suggested that denial of alcohol abuse and symptoms of drunkenness or dependence is greater among the elderly than other age groups. Another problem with using consumption as a measure is that studies at the National Institute on Aging have shown that the elderly have a decreased tolerance for alcohol and its effects.[6]

Measures have routinely been standardized on nonelderly men; thus they also lack recognition of the particular alcohol-related health, social, and legal problems of male and female elderly. Perhaps an even more fundamental issue with respect to the validity of the research in this area is that alcohol abuse has been variously defined and the concepts of alcohol abuse, alcohol dependence, problem drinking, heavy drinking, and alcoholism (chronic and acute) have been used and operationalized differently.

Keeping in mind these methodological limitations, there appears to be general agreement among researchers that prevalence rates are higher among younger than older persons and that elderly men abuse alcohol more often than do elderly women. Prevalency rates for alcohol abuse by the aged (also variously defined) have ranged anywhere from 4 percent to 14 percent.[7,8] Allowing for these variations, Bienenfeld[9] states that most surveys agree that at least 10 percent of persons aged 65 and over have some kind of drinking problem and that 8 percent in this same age group are alcohol dependent.

When DSM-III-R[10] criteria for alcoholism have been utilized, as in the case of the Epidemiologic Catchment Area Program (ECA), rates of alcohol abuse and dependence were seen to differ from most other prevalency studies. The ECA project was a combination of five interrelated epidemiologic research studies conducted in New Haven, Baltimore, St. Louis, Los Angeles, and Durham, North Carolina, and the surrounding counties. An instrument to collect information covering three diagnostic systems, including DSM-III-R, was specially designed for these studies. For men aged 65 and over, the lifetime prevalence rate of alcohol abuse was 14 percent, whereas for women in this same age group, the rate was 1.5 percent. Remission rates were seen to rise consistently with increasing age.[11]

Reasons for the low rate of alcohol abuse among older people when compared to rates for younger persons, include the fact that alcohol abusers have shorter life expectancy. While alcoholics can and do survive to old age, an undetermined number die earlier as a result of alcohol-related medical complications. Other explanations are that older Americans were influenced early in their lives by the Prohibition Era mentality, and consequently, the drinking mores of the older generation may be responsible for lower rates. Finally, some individuals who abuse alcohol may reduce their consumption because of disabilities or increased effects related to the ingestion of alcohol.[12,13]

As with younger populations, special groups of older persons are seen to have higher rates of alcoholism than the general population of elderly. While bearing in mind that clinical diagnoses of alcoholism tend to be underdiagnosed when compared with prevalency rates determined by population surveys, estimates for the prevalence of alcoholism in the general medical population of elderly range from 25 to 50 percent. Even higher rates—50 to 75 percent—have been reported for general psychiatric populations.[14,15] Others have noted a high rate of alcoholism among older male patients who are residents of veterans' hospitals and domiciliaries, and among the homeless population. Butler, Lewis, and Sunderland[16] caution, however, that only about 5 percent of alcoholics fit the stereotypic caricature of the inebriated individual who is seen sleeping on sidewalks or doorsteps. In a study conducted by the author of this chapter, competent yet self-neglectful elders were also seen to have a higher rate of alcohol abuse (15 percent) when compared with elders who were either abused or neglected by others (4 percent).[17]

In terms of duration, alcoholism among the elderly is of two types: early onset (Type I) and late-life onset (Type II, also labeled reactive or geriatric alcoholism). It is estimated that half of elderly alcoholics began drinking heavily prior to age 40 and about two-thirds began before age 60.[18] While it may change in the future due to higher use among young females, elderly women are more likely than elderly men to fall in the late-life-onset category.[19] This leaves a smaller but still sizable number of older persons who started to abuse alcohol late in life.

ANTECEDENTS AND CORRELATES

Although each has its shortcomings both conceptually and empirically, each of the models of addiction described in Chapter 2 suggests certain causations of alcoholism, which, in turn, relate to treatment approaches. Not all these models have received much attention in the literature on alcoholism among the aged, although a wide range of antecedent factors have been suggested. The determinants of alcohol abuse among the elderly which have been examined most extensively have been either sociocultural or psychologic/psychosocial in nature.

Sociocultural Models

Minnis[20] has proposed a sociological perspective for studying the determinants of alcoholism. Social control theory, as formulated by Hirschi,[21] assumes that deviance (e.g., alcoholism) results when an individual's bond with society is weak or broken. Based on this theory, Minnis has stated four hypotheses to explain alcohol abuse:

1. The greater the attachment to conventional others, the less likely is the elderly person to engage in alcohol abuse.
2. The greater the commitment to conventional goals or aspirations, the less likely is the elderly person to engage in alcohol abuse.
3. The greater the involvement in conventional activities, the less likely is the older person to engage in alcohol abuse.
4. The greater the beliefs in the moral validity of conventional norms, the less likely is the elderly person to engage in alcohol abuse.

To this author's knowledge, this model of alcohol abuse remains untested. Perhaps this is due to the difficulty that would be encountered in measuring some of the concepts employed in the hypotheses (e.g., attachment, commitment, involvement, moral validity, conventional activities, and norms).

The ECA Project looked at sociodemographic factors such as age, sex, race, marital status, education, employment, and study site as correlates of alcohol abuse or dependence. Being younger, male, separated or divorced, and poor and having less than a high school education were all found to be associated with a higher prevalence of alcoholism, regardless of age. Site, race, and employment status were not found, however, to have a relationship to the prevalence of alcoholism in the study sample.[22]

Gurnack and Thomas[23] have stated that little research exists which specifically focuses on late-onset alcohol abuse. They further question the validity of the term "late onset."

It appears, however, that a considerable number of studies exist that have contrasted the characteristics of early- and late-onset elderly alcoholics. It could be argued that there has actually been a disproportionate interest shown in the sociocultural and psychological determinants of late-onset alcoholism since estimates indicate that only one-third of elderly alcohol abusers fall into this group.

Psychologic or Psychosocial Models

Psychological factors are particularly problematic to investigate, although several authors have concluded that alcohol abuse in old age is less likely to be associated with "deep-seated" psychological problems or personality factors than excessive drinking among young persons.[24,25] Royce[26] more explicitly states that persons who began to drink at a late age were reported as having no evidence of severe antisocial behaviors or psychiatric problems and as having fewer life-style disruptions. In an empirical study by Atkinson, Tolson, and Turner[27] conducted at a Veterans Administration geriatric alcoholism outpatient program, late-onset problems were determined to be "milder" and more circumscribed than earlier onset and, further, were associated with less family alcoholism and greater overall psychological stability.

The psychosocial model of addiction proposes that an interrelated constellation of personal, environmental, behavioral, and health care system factors influence the onset, continuation, and termination of alcohol abuse.[28] While the model is a popular one due to its holistic approach, it is also difficult to test empirically because of its complex and multivariable nature. Most researchers view the psychosocial model as one of stress and coping or adaptation and use it to explain late-onset rather than early-onset alcoholism among elders. Accordingly, loneliness, losses, physical or emotional separation from children, poor health, and lack of purposeful activity can precipitate alcohol abuse.[29] Such factors are viewed as causing the elder to become less attached to or isolated from sources of social support such as his or her family, community, society, or peers, and he or she must rely on past coping skills to deal with feelings of grief, low self-esteem, and low status.

In a study conducted at the Mayo Clinic between 1972 and 1983, researchers found little difference in terms of demographics between early- and late-onset alcoholics.[30] The sample consisted of 216 primarily middle-class men and women aged 65 and older who were patients at the clinic. The outstanding finding was that the majority of patients had a favorable social status despite their alcoholism (67 percent lived at home with a spouse, and many continued to be active in their jobs). In this particular study, early-onset alcoholism was present in 59 percent of the men and 51 percent of the women, and late-onset was seen in 39 percent of the men and 46 percent of the women (undetermined for the rest).

A number of earlier studies suggested that retirement had the potential to be a serious life crisis for many aging persons, especially for elderly men. According to this body of research, retirement is associated with loss—loss of roles, status, income, and mobility, thus leading to loss of stability and self-worth. In a study conducted by Rosin and Glatt,[31] retirement was found to be a precipitating factor of excessive drinking among male professionals versus working class men in the sample. Retirement was also seen as an antecedent of drinking problems among older Californians.[32]

While their study examined alcohol use rather than abuse, Alexander and Duff[33] surveyed 260 residents aged 57 to 97 at three retirement communities. Their results showed that regular drinking was more common in these communities and the rate of abstinence was lower than in the general population of elders. These researchers argue that drinking was associated with social activity and that it was an integral part of the leisure subculture found in such communities.

More recent findings have also cast doubt on viewing retirement as a possible determinant of late-onset alcohol abuse. For example, Vejnoska[34] found that drinking decreased among rural Arizonians soon after retirement. Along the same lines, in a study by Gomberg,[35] men reported that they drank heavily in response to the stresses and frustrations associated with work and that when they retired, they moderated their consumption.

Ekerdt, deLabry, Glynn, and Davis[36] studied changes in drinking behaviors with retirement in 100 men aged 55 and over who had retired and 316 age-matched men who were employed. These researchers found no evidence that retirement was associated with shifts in alcohol consumption or drinking behaviors. What they did find, though, was that retirees were more likely to report the onset of periodic heavier drinking and problems with drinking than the controls.

In a study of Mayo Clinic patients being treated for alcoholism, the researchers found that patients with a late onset of the problem reported an association between a life event and problem drinking more frequently than the early-onset patients (81 percent versus 45 percent; $p < .001$).[37] Perhaps more notable is the fact that the groups did not differ in terms of all the other stressors that were examined, including retirement, death of a spouse or close relative, family conflict, physical health problems, employment stress, psychologic symptoms, and financial problems. Similarly, in their study of 1,410 elders in two retirement and two age-heterogeneous communities, LaGreca, Akers, and Dwyer[38] found no support for their hypothesis that higher frequency, greater quantity, or problem drinking occurs in response to significant life events. If anything, these authors point out, drinking appeared to decrease with the experience of life events.

Early research in the area suggested that declining health and accompanying anxiety are factors associated with alcohol abuse among the elderly. Giordano and Beckham[39] point out that physical health or the individual's perceived health status plays a role in determining older persons' energies and adaptive capacities. The flaw in much of this research, however, is that matched controls were not used nor were early- and late-onset alcohol abusers compared. Rather alcoholic elderly persons were asked if they had a medical or health problem, and the resulting percentage was deemed to be large.

Studies conducted during the 1980s disputed some of the earlier findings in terms of the relationship between health and alcohol abuse. Bainton[40] found there was a greater likelihood of drinking among older people in good health and Barnes[41] found poor health was associated with a decrease in drinking.

Loneliness, alienation, and boredom have been proposed as variables which are related to abuse of alcohol by the elderly. The disengagement theory of aging posits that older people become less engaged over time and become isolated from others. As a result of this separation from the mainstream of society and activity, an individual may drink to cope with or to dull the feelings associated with disengagement. In a survey of two hundred elders, Leigh[42] discovered that 50 percent of the women studied and 25 percent of the men cited loneliness as the reason for their use of alcohol and medication. When asked how they coped with feelings of loneliness and depression, 13 percent said they had a drink while 2 percent turned to drugs and alcohol.

As Gurnack and Thomas[43] point out, and is evidenced in the preceding discussion, the relationship between life stressors and the onset of alcohol abuse is still not clearly defined. There is also considerable disagreement about cause and effect when looking at factors purported to explain addiction. One can easily inquire as to which are the antecedents and which are the consequences of alcohol abuse among elders.

ALCOHOL AND DRUG ABUSE

The elderly are the largest users of legal drugs and on the average, take three prescription drugs and seven over-the-counter drugs on a regular basis.[44,45] There is little wonder that the major problem with drug abuse among the elderly is with licit rather than illicit drugs. The ECA study estimated that the lifetime prevalence rates for illicit drug dependence in the 60-plus age group was less than 1 percent as contrasted with 17 percent for the 18- to 29-year age group. Among the individuals in the sample who did not meet the DSM-III-R criteria for alcohol dependence, 3.5 percent received a diagnosis of illicit drug dependence. For those with a diagnosis of alcohol dependence, however, the rate was much greater (18 percent).[46]

The South Carolina Commission on Alcohol and Drug Abuse (SCCADA) also examined the prevalency and nature of alcohol and drug abuse by collecting data from its alcohol programs throughout the forty-five counties of the state. Client records were reviewed for the 1976 year to determine primary, secondary, and tertiary substances of concern. Of the 28,836 clients in the total population, 5,500 were aged 55 and over. Among this older group, 96 percent mentioned alcohol as a problem substance, but only 2.7 percent reported a second substance as being problematic. Sedatives led the list of both secondary and tertiary problem substances (0.8 percent and 0.3 percent, respectively).[47]

Mixing alcohol and prescription drugs is probably more common than the SCCADA study indicates, though, since clients were asked to self-report on their problem at the time of intake. In the study conducted at the Mayo Clinic on elderly inpatients who were receiving treatment for their alcoholism, 14 percent were assessed by the medical team as part of a comprehensive workup as having a drug abuse or dependence problem.[48]

Abrams and Alexopoulos[49] state that provider-initiated misuse or the failure of the prescription-writer to take into account the physiological (as well as psychosocial) aspects of aging, along with the elderly consumer's belief that over-the-counter drugs are not harmful, "may contribute to patterns of abuse or dependence." Approximately 80 percent of the elderly who take over-the-counter drugs regularly also use alcohol and/or prescription medications. Allergy, cold, and sleep medications which are sold without prescriptions contain antihistamines and anticholinergic drugs that can enhance the anticholinergic effects of antipsychotic and tricyclic antidepressant medications. Some nonprescription preparations also contain amounts of alcohol and caffeine which can lead to oversedation and a reduction in the therapeutic effects of commonly prescribed antihypertensive, antiarrhythmic, and anxiolytic medications. Lamy[50] reports that of the one hundred most frequently prescribed drugs, one-half interact with alcohol. Further, all of the ten most frequently prescribed drugs can interact with alcohol. Clearly, the interactive effects of alcohol and drugs pose a risk of harm for older persons or can even be life threatening.

It is interesting to note in a study by Folkman, Bernstein, and Lazarus[51] over a six-month period of 141 community-dwelling subjects aged 65 to 74 that misuse of substances (alcohol and prescription and over-the-counter drugs) was not found to be linked to low self-esteem or a low sense of mastery over the environment. The antecedent personality variables which were studied did not correlate with misuse as hypothesized. Instead, these authors suggest that misuse was related in part to the inadequate attention given to the patient's total pattern of drug and alcohol use by all those involved—physicians, pharmacists, and patients themselves.

In hearings before the House of Representatives Select Committee on Aging,[52] it was pointed out that fewer than 2 percent of U.S. medical students were required to take courses in geriatrics and most took only one course in pharmacology; hence, many physicians have only minimal knowledge about the aging process and how it affects drug tolerance and dependence. Other factors that were cited as contributing to the abuse and misuse of medication among the elderly included patient noncompliance (over one-half of the elderly have been found to not comply with their daily drug regimen), the high cost of prescription drugs, and the lack of formal Food and Drug Administration guidelines for premarket clinical testing of drugs for elderly consumers.

ASSESSMENT AND BIOPSYCHOSOCIAL EFFECTS

Assessment Strategies and Problems

There are numerous diagnostic instruments for the detection of alcoholism in clinical settings which relate to risk factors and biopsychosocial symptoms of alcoholism. As noted elsewhere, these can include the DSM-III-R, the Michigan Alcoholism Screening Test (MAST), CAGE questions, the Quantitative Inventory of Alcohol Disorders (QIAD), and the Structured Addictions Assessment Interview for Selecting Treatment (SAAST).[53,54] Physicians also use medical tests such as lean body mass and amount of alcohol consumed, but these measures are confounded by age effects, making them less useful in assessing alcoholism among the elderly. Bienenfeld[55] concludes that a person may even begin to experience alcohol-induced problems without changing the amount of alcohol consumed, simply by becoming older.

Most health professionals would likely agree that assessment of alcohol abuse needs to be comprehensive, interdisciplinary, and age and gender relevant. Along these lines, Graham[56] suggests that five overlapping areas need to be included in screening for alcohol abuse among the elderly: (1) quantity and frequency of alcohol consumption, (2) alcohol-related social and legal problems (e.g., housing problems, falls or accidents, poor nutrition, inadequate self- and home-care, lack of exercise, and social isolation), (3) alcohol-related health problems, (4) symptoms of drunkenness or dependence, and (5) self-recognition of alcohol-related problems. Beresford and coworkers[57] add that a series of neuropsychological tests should also be executed as a protocol. Measures of concept formation and abstraction, short- and long-term memory, motor strength, speed, and dexterity, visual-

motor coordination, attention, concentration, and vigilance, novel problem solving, language functions, and perceptual integrity need to be included according to these authors.

Graham and Beresford and coworkers, along with others, have noted particular difficulties in assessing elders for alcohol abuse using existing measures.[58,59,60] Self-report of alcohol consumption and dependence or drunkenness may be unreliable for several reasons. Denial, sense of stigma, social desirability effects, and memory loss can affect accurate recollection or admission of a alcohol problem among the elderly. And as cited, physical and cognitive changes due to aging itself or a disease process, confound consumption measures. The health problems and cognitive impairment that are related to alcohol abuse that have been used as markers have not been standardized for general elderly populations, and therefore are questionable when used to distinguish the elderly alcohol abuser.

Effects

What are the effects or consequences of alcohol abuse among the elderly? The problem with temporal ordering needs to be mentioned here again because determining which factors are antecedent and which are the effects of alcohol abuse is not a straightforward exercise. Nevertheless, it is generally agreed that there are interrelated biopsychosocial effects associated with alcoholism, some of which are age specific, and some of which are not.

Medical Complications

Miller and Gold[61] categorize the physiological effects from alcohol and drugs as cardiovascular, gastrointestinal, metabolic, and cerebrovascular. Alcohol itself, according to Hartford and Samorajski,[62] can lead to such things as hypertension, myocardial infarction, cardiac arrhythmias, stroke, peptic ulcer disease, immunosuppression, accidents, dehydration, and electrolyte abnormalities, among others.

Looking specifically at the effect of aging and alcohol on the liver, Scott and Mitchell[63] state that alcohol competes with other drugs for metabolic enzymes in the liver and impairs drug clearance if acutely ingested. Conversely, if chronically ingested, alcohol induces additional metabolic enzymes which can lead to increased drug clearance. These medical researchers conclude by saying that while routine liver tests change little with age, there may be less biochemical and metabolic reserve capacity in the older person's liver if it is stressed by diminished blood flow, infections, or exogenous drugs and toxins. As discussed earlier in the section on alcohol and drug abuse and misuse and reiterated by Scott and Mitchell, drug-alcohol and aging interactions are particularly complex and can lead to unpredictable medical problems.

Cognitive Impairment

Beresford and colleagues[64] state that, "it is misleading and even irresponsible to examine a patient on a very difficult measure, obtain errors or slowness, and then label such a patient as "brained damaged," and go on to note that this has been the case when looking at elderly alcoholic patients. These authors recommend that the issues of test coverage and difficulty level be examined and that age norms be considered since there is increasing evidence that decrements in test scores produced by chronic alcoholism and by abnormal aging are separate and additive at most.

Alcohol-related dementia has been described in the literature as a global cognitive impairment that mimics Alzheimer's disease but does not progress after the cessation of drinking. It has been estimated that at least 10 percent of persons presenting with dementia actually have alcohol-related brain disease. While this appears to be a consequence of alcohol abuse, it might also be suggested that excessive drinking occurs in response to the emotional symptoms of dementia or impaired mental functioning.[65,66] Studies of alcohol-related dementia have found that as age increases, there is a more severe decline in intellect among older alcoholics. Such findings have been confirmed with brain scans that reveal significant cerebral atrophy among alcoholics, especially older alcoholics.[67]

In a study which used older and younger and nonalcoholic control groups, and was therefore able to tease out the effects of alcohol abuse and aging, it was found that tactile discrimination accuracy for nonverbal information was disrupted by aging but that alcoholism alone does not have this effect. The researchers also reported that the combined effects of aging and alcohol abuse were seen only on tactile tasks that required identification of verbal items.[68]

Goldman[69] states there is reason for some optimism, however, in regard to cognitive impairment in chronic alcoholics. He reports that while many alcoholics continue to show impairment of cognitive functioning on both neuropsychological and intelligence tests (e.g., deficits in visual perception, learning, and memory and in problem solving), studies have shown that a considerable recovery of cognitive functioning can occur immediately after drinking ceases and slower improvements can be made thereafter.

Depression and Suicide

Do older persons drink because they are depressed or drink and become depressed or both? Depression is often referred to as the most common psychiatric problem seen in the elderly population and is viewed as a response to loss.[70] Normally the aging process involves losses—loss of a spouse or loved one, loss of health, loss of job and income, loss of social roles, and loss of status. We all grieve our losses, but depression can set in when we get stuck in the grieving process.

Depression is characterized by physical, emotional, cognitive, behavioral, and social disturbances. An individual suffering from depression might experience somatic difficulties; experience moods characterized by feelings of sadness, despondency, and hopelessness; have thoughts of death and feelings of worthlessness and self-reproach; be unable to experience pleasure; suffer changes in appetite, sleep habits, and level of energy; and lose interest in usual social and sexual activities.[71,72]

Alcohol itself is a depressant and alcohol abuse and depression have long been associated. While some authors contend that virtually all alcoholics are depressed, the comparison of reported prevalence rates of depression in elderly alcoholics is difficult due to problems with distinguishing depressive symptoms which are common in alcohol abusers, and evidence of a primary affective disorder. In looking at major depression in particular, however, using DSM-III-R criteria, Mayo Clinic researchers gave 8.3 percent of the alcoholics in their sample this diagnosis.[73] They contrasted this figure with a 3.7 percent rate determined in a study of a general elderly population in North Carolina and the 0.8 to 1.8 percent rates for the lifetime prevalence of major depressive episodes reported by Robins and coworkers.[74,75]

Alcohol abuse is considered a risk factor in suicide among the elderly.[76] Suicides in the older population represent a disproportionate amount of successful suicides when compared with the total population. Rich, Young, and Fowler[77] determined that overall for the population, males had a rate of 18.2 suicides per 100,000 while females had a rate of 7.9. For persons aged 65 and over, these rates jumped to 31.9 for males and 15.9 for females. Pfeiffer[78] has further noted that suicide rates steadily increase with age and a peak is reached at age 80–84, where the suicide rate for white males (who have higher rates at all ages than women and nonwhites) is 51.4 per 100,000. Rates of suicide for elderly alcohol abusers are suggested to be even higher than rates in the general population.[79,80]

CASE FINDING AND TREATMENT

There is consensus that alcohol abuse among the elderly is a hidden problem; therefore, case finding is a critical step which needs to be examined before issues of treatment can be discussed. Dupree[81] looked at the effectiveness of three case-finding strategies employed in Florida to locate elderly alcohol abusers. These approaches employed formal caregivers, the general public, and community health clinics. The author concludes that there was a general hesitancy among formal caregivers and community health clinic staff to label older persons as alcoholic and that periodic, consistent contact and on-site visits were needed to enhance and sustain the referral flow which was indicated at these sites. At the same time, referrals resulting from a public awareness campaign remained constant.

Graham and Romaniec[82] likewise report that case finding presented ethical dilemmas among outreach agency personnel. Outreach workers expressed concern for the elderly alcoholic client's right to privacy and felt that intervention could intrude on that privacy. In summary, they believed that no intervention should be attempted in cases of milder alcohol problems and that intervention was only warranted when drinking interfered with the client's health or medical treatment.

In a nationwide examination of alcoholism treatment programs serving twenty-six hundred persons aged 21 and over, Janik and Dunham[83] found few age-related differences among alcoholics in treatment. These authors concluded specialized alcoholism treatment programs for the elderly were perhaps unnecessary. This conclusion appears premature if one accepts Beresford and colleagues' statement, "if we know little about screening elderly populations with respect to alcoholism, we know considerably less about specific treatment strategies appropriate to this age group."[84] These authors go on to say that from a clinical perspective, complete abstinence from alcohol is the only practical treatment goal in light of the profound physical, psychological, and social effects older persons experience when they abuse alcohol.

As social workers rather than physicians, Rathbone-McCuan and Hashimi are also careful to include the client's wants and desires in treatment planning and delivery, which also may help to avoid some of the dilemmas cited earlier with respect to case finding. They believe that a framework to guide interventions "should explicate how alcohol abuse interferes with what older men and women are required, expected, or prefer to do in their daily lives."[85] According to this perspective, it is important to consider environmental, physical, and social behavioral factors from a causal and interventive point of view. Goals of treatment might include either total abstinence or controlled drinking, depending on what is most appropriate and attainable for individual elders, based on their history and circumstances.

While there are disproportionately few elderly persons receiving mental health services (which some believe reflects ageist attitudes whereby people believe that older persons cannot be helped given their age and declining health), there is evidence that older alcohol abusers are more likely to complete a treatment program.[86,87] Several authors have further reported that as a group, later-life-onset alcohol abusers were the most responsive to treatment.[88,89] Atkinson, Tolson, and Turner[90] found, though, that treatment program variables were better predictors of compliance than age of onset in their study conducted at a Veterans Administration geriatric alcoholism outpatient program.

Traditional treatment approaches to alcoholism have used multiple modalities such as detoxification; Alcoholics Anonymous; behavior modification; individual, family, or group therapy; and aversion therapy (hypoaversion, disulfiram/antabuse, condition reflex treatment). These approaches have been variously utilized and found to be effective with groups of elderly alcohol abusers. Carstensen, Rychtarik, and Prue[91] have indicated some success with a behavioral inpatient program which consisted of medical attention, individual counseling, alcohol education class, training in self-management and problem solving, vocational assistance, and marital therapy when appropriate. Participants aged 60 and over at time of treatment were contacted two to four years after discharge and results indicated that beneficial effects were maintained for 50 percent of the sample. An additional 12 percent reported significant modification of their drinking at follow-up.

In a study conducted at a Veterans Administration hospital of twenty-four male alcoholics treated in a mixed-age outpatient group (mean age = 58.8 years) and twenty-five male and female alcoholics treated in special peer groups (mean age = 60.2 years), Kofoed and coworkers[92] found that peer group patients remained in treatment significantly longer and were more likely to complete treatment than were mixed-age controls. These authors describe treatment as consisting of group therapy which tended to be active and to emphasize expression of feelings. Peer and staff confrontation was fairly frequent and policies regarding alcohol use (breathalyzer tests were given) and attendance were strictly enforced for the two groups.

As reported on by Felker,[93] a peer group approach was also utilized in Madison, Wisconsin, by a geriatric nurse practitioner and social worker who named their endeavor "Elderly Recovery Group." The program had minimal norms, rules, and structures, and the first thirty minutes of each weekly ninety-minute meeting was devoted to informal socializing. Next an inquiry was made about members who were not present, and members gave information about persons with whom they had had contact. A "Thought and Meditation for the Day" was then read by a member and discussion ensued either about the thought or members' current problems or experiences. Expression of feelings were reinforced and the group facilitators provided "on-the-spot" planning for dealing with age- and health-related issues. Two-thirds of the members were attending Alcoholics Anonymous at the same time they attended the Elderly Recovery Group. In terms of treatment effectiveness, of the fifteen members of the group who were active during the year being reported on, twelve, or 80 percent, remained sober and three continued to abuse alcohol.

Blake[94] emphasizes that sociopsychological approaches to alcoholism in the elderly relate more to the stress of aging than do traditional alcoholism treatment programs. He cites the work of Zimberg,[95] Mishara and Kastenbaum,[96] and the National Institute on Alco-

A Case Example

Mr. R. is a 71-year-old man who has a long history of heavy alcohol consumption. He was widowed last year and has two sons, both of whom live in distant states and have little contact with their father. Due to health problems and a recent hospitalization, Mr. R.'s 68-year-old sister, Ms. W., who lives nearby, has been visiting regularly. Ms. W. is concerned with Mr. R.'s heavy drinking since his return from the hospital. Upon finding him passed out on a recent occasion, she telephoned an agency in the aging network and was referred to a day treatment program for elderly alcoholics. While Mr. R. was initially angry that his sister had telephoned the program and had given them his name, he allowed an outreach worker from the program to visit him at his home while Ms. W. was present. The worker described the program, but Mr. R. explained that he needed only the help of his sister to get by. At that point, Ms. W. stated that her own health was failing and

that she could not keep up with the needs of her brother. Mr. R. was given a few days to consider all this information and then recontacted by the worker. Plans were made for Mr. R. to come to the day treatment program three days per week where he was first evaluated for needed health and social services and then assisted with developing a case plan. Transportation to the program was provided, and Mr. R. soon began to participate in such activities as playing cards and attending a group meeting of his peers who also experienced problems with drinking. Routine blood pressure checks were conducted, along with an exercise program. On the days that Mr. R. did not attend the treatment program, "meals on wheels" were provided to him in his home. Ms. W. continued to visit her brother in the evening and on weekends and telephoned his sons to report on his progress.

hol Abuse and Alcoholism,[97] which all recommend such sociotherapeutic approaches and consider "senior services and home care treatment to be proper directions for treatment to follow." The National Institute on Alcohol Abuse and Alcoholism has further urged that the range of services employed in community-based approaches to alcohol abuse among the elderly be coordinated.

Keeping in mind that sociotherapy typically consists of building informal social support networks, Alcoholics Anonymous, peer groups, and involvement with other self-help organizations,[98] along with the physical health and nutritional needs of the elderly, Rathbone-McCuan and Hashimi[99] have proposed an ideal treatment model for older alcoholics. They state that such a model would have both health and social components which would differ from day treatment for younger alcoholics. Under the health component, activities would include regular

health screening, physical and occupational rehabilitation, linkages to nursing homes or other inpatient settings for short-term admissions along with accessible hospital-based services, and nutrition and pharmacy input. On the social side, individuals would be involved in Alcoholics Anonymous and be encouraged to participate in social activities not focused on recovery as well. Participants in the program would receive intensive case management to coordinate needed housing, legal, and transportation services and employment and recreational activities counseling. Older recovering alcoholics would also be included on the treatment team and would have extensive outreach functions both in the community as well as within the program.

In the future, those who work in the medical and aging fields are likely to see an increasing number of female and male elderly alcoholics. It is hoped that these individuals will have at their disposal a growing body of information on the problem, its sufferers, and which outreach and treatment approaches seem to work or not work with the older population and special groups of elders. This means that the research and practice literature, along with the practitioner's own experiences, will serve as funds of knowledge for working in this area. The only way we can continue to draw from these wells is to continuously fill them with new scientific findings, along with our own insights derived from practice.

ENDNOTES

1. Burt E. Gilliland and Richard K. James, *Crisis Intervention Strategies* (Pacific Grove, CA: Brooks/Cole, 1988), p. 276.

2. U.S. Census Bureau, *An Aging World* (Washington, DC: U.S. Government Printing Office, 1987).

3. Kathryn Graham, "Identifying and Measuring Alcohol Abuse Among the Elderly: Serious Problems with Existing Instrumentation," *Journal of Studies on Alcohol*, Vol. 47, No. 4 (1986), pp. 322–326.

4. Dan G. Blazer and Margaret R. Pennybacker, "Epidemiology of Alcoholism in the Elderly," in James T. Hartford and T. Samorajski (eds.), *Alcoholism in the Elderly: Social and Biomedical Issues*, Aging Series Volume 25 (New York: Raven Press, 1984), pp. 25–33.

5. Graham, "Identifying and Measuring Alcohol Abuse Among the Elderly," p. 325.

6. Robert N. Butler, Myra Lewis, and Trey Sunderland, *Aging and Mental Health: Positive Psychosocial and Biomedical Approaches*, 4th ed. (New York: Macmillan, 1991), pp. 210–211.

7. Eloise Rathbone-McCuan and Joan Hashimi, *Isolated Elders* (Rockville, MD: Aspen Publishers, 1982), p. 212.

8. George J. Warheit and Joanne B. Auth, "The Mental Health and Social Correlates of Alcohol Use Among Differing Life Cycle Groups," in George Maddox, Lee N. Robins, and Nathan Rosenberg (eds.), *Nature and Extent of Alcohol Problems Among the Elderly* (New York: Springer, 1986), pp. 29–82.

9. David Bienenfeld, "Alcoholism in the Elderly," *American Family Physician*, Vol. 36, No. 2 (1987), pp. 163–169.

10. American Psychiatric Association, *Diagnostic and Statistical Manual of Mental Disorders*, 3rd ed. (Washington, DC: The Association, 1987).

11. Lee N. Robins, John E. Helzer, T. R. Przybeck, and D. A. Regier, "Alcohol Disorders in the Community: A Report from the Epidemiologic Catchment Area," in *Alcoholism: Origins and Outcomes* (New York: Raven Press, 1988).

12. Bienenfeld, "Alcoholism in the Elderly," pp. 164–165.

13. Graham, "Identifying and Measuring Alcohol Abuse in the Elderly," p. 322.

14. J. Randall Curtis, Gail Geller, Emma J. Stokes, David M. Levine, and R. D. Moore, "Characteristics, Diagnosis and Treatment of Alcoholism in Elderly Patients," *Journal of American Geriatrics Society*, Vol. 37 (1989), pp. 310–316.

15. Mark A. Schuckit, "A Clinical Review of Alcohol, Alcoholism, and the Elderly Patient," *Journal of Clinical Psychiatry*, Vol. 43 (1983), 396–399.

16. Butler, Lewis, and Sunderland, *Aging and Mental Health*, p. 211.

17. Linda Vinton, "An Exploratory Study of Self-Neglectful Elderly," *Journal of Gerontological Social Work*, Vol. 18, No. 1/2 (1991), pp. 55–67.

18. Roland Atkinson, John A. Turner, Lial L. Kofoed, and Robert L. Tolson, "Early Versus Late Onset Alcoholism in Older Persons: Preliminary Findings," *Alcoholism*, Vol. 9 (1985), pp. 513–515.

19. Charles E. Holzer, Jerome K. Myers, Myrna W. Weissman, Gary L. Tischler, Philip J. Leaf, James Anthony, and Philip B. Bednarski, "Antecedents and Correlates of Alcohol Abuse and Dependence in the Elderly," in George Maddox, Lee N. Robins, and Nathan Rosenberg, (eds.), *Nature and Extent of Alcohol Problems Among the Elderly*, (New York: Springer, 1986), pp. 217–244.

20. John R. Minnis, "Toward an Understanding of Alcohol Abuse Among the Elderly: A Sociological Perspective," *Journal of Alcohol and Drug Education*, Vol. 33, No. 3 (1988), pp. 32–40.

21. Travis Hirschi, *Causes of Delinquency* (Berkeley: University of California Press, 1969).

22. Holzer et al., "Antecedents and Correlates," pp. 217–244.

23. Anne M. Gurnack and Jeanne L. Thomas, "Behavioral Factors Related to Elderly Alcohol Abuse: Research and Policy Issues," *The International Journal of the Addictions*, Vol. 24, No. 7, pp. 641–654.

24. U.S. Department of Health and Human Services, "Nature and Extent of Alcohol Problems Among the Elderly," *Research Monograph 14* DHHS Pub. No. ADM 84-1321 (Washington, DC: U.S. Government Printing Office, 1984).

25. Meyer D. Glantz, "Predictions of Elderly Drug Abuse," *Journal of Psychoactive Drugs,* Vol. 13, No. 2 (1981), pp. 117–126.

26. James E. Royce, *Alcohol Problems and Alcoholism: A Comprehensive Survey* (New York: The Free Press, 1981).

27. Roland M. Atkinson, Robert L. Tolson, and John A. Turner, "Late Versus Early Onset Problem Drinking in Older Men," *Alcoholism Clinical and Experimental Research,* Vol. 14, No. 4 (July–August 1990), pp. 574–579.

28. Gilliland and James, *Crisis Intervention Strategies,* p. 282.

29. Jeffrey A. Giordano and Kathryn Beckham, "Alcohol Use and Abuse in Old Age: An Examination of Type II Alcoholism," *Journal of Gerontological Social Work,* Vol. 9, No. 1 (1985), pp. 65–83.

30. Richard E. Finlayson, Richard D. Hurt, Leo J. Davis, and Robert M. Morse, "Alcoholism in Elderly Persons: A Study of the Psychiatric and Psychosocial Features of 216 Inpatients," *Mayo Clinic Proceedings,* Vol. 63, pp. 761–768.

31. Arnold J. Rosin and M. M. Glatt, "The Older Alcoholic and the Family," *Quarterly Journal of Studies on Alcohol,* Vol. 32 (1971), pp. 53–59.

32. R. A. M. Downing, "Alcoholism and the Elderly: A Comparative Study of Coping Strategies Utilized by Alcoholics and Non-Alcoholics," unpublished thesis, California State University, Los Angeles, 1979.

33. Francesca Alexander and Robert W. Duff, "Social Interaction and Alcohol Use in Retirement Communities," *The Gerontologist,* Vol. 28, No. 5 (1988), pp. 632–636.

34. J. Vejnoska, "Arizona Group Studies Drinking of Elderly," *National Institute of Alcohol Abuse and Alcoholism Information and Feature Service,* 1982.

35. Edith L. Gomberg, "Alcohol Use and Alcohol Problems Among the Elderly," in National Institute on Alcohol Abuse and Alcoholism, *Alcohol and Health Monograph 4, Special Population Issues,* DHHS Pub. No. ADM 82-1193 (Washington, DC: U.S. Government Printing Office, 1982).

36. David J. Ekerdt, Lorraine O. deLabry, Robert J. Glynn, and Richard W. Davis, "Change in Drinking Behaviors with Retirement: Findings from the Normative Aging Study," *Journal of Studies on Alcohol,* Vol. 50, No. 4 (July 1989), pp. 347–353.

37. Finlayson et al., "Alcoholism in Elderly Persons," pp. 761–768.

38. Anthony J. LaGreca, Ronald L. Akers, and Jeffrey W. Dwyer, "Life Events and Alcohol Behavior Among Older Adults," *The Gerontologist,* Vol. 28, No. 4 (1988), pp. 552–558.

39. Giordano and Beckham, "Alcohol Use and Abuse in Old Age," p. 72.

40. Barry R. Bainton, "Drinking Patterns of the Rural Aged," in Christine L. Fry (ed.), *Dimensions: Aging, Culture, and Health,* (Brooklyn, NY: J. F. Bergin, 1981).

41. Grace M. Barnes, "Alcohol Use Among Older Persons: Findings from a Western New York State General Population Survey," *Journal of the American Geriatrics Society,* Vol. 27, No. 6 (1979), pp. 244–250.

42. D. H. Leigh, "Prevention Work Among the Elderly: A Workable Model," paper presented at the Annual Forum of the National Council on Alcoholism, Seattle, WA, 1980.

43. Gurnack and Thomas, "Behavioral Factors," p. 649.

44. F. T. Crews, "Factors Predisposing to Alcohol and Medication Abuse in the Elderly," part of handout from University of Florida Geriatric Education Center teleconference.

45. Patricia Bandy and Patricia A. President, "Recent Literature on Drug Abuse Prevention and Mass Media: Focusing on Youth, Parents, Women and the Elderly," *Journal of Drug Education,* Vol. 13, No. 3 (1983), pp. 255–271.

46. Robins et al., "Alcohol Disorders in the Community."

47. Larry G. Peppers and Ronald G. Stover, "The Elderly Abuser: A Challenge for the Future," *Journal of Drug Issues,* Vol. 9, No. 1 (1979), pp. 73–83.

48. Finlayson et al., "Alcoholism in Elderly Persons," p. 761.

49. Robert C. Abrams and George S. Alexopoulos, "Substance Abuse in the Elderly: Over-the-Counter and Illegal Drugs," *Hospital and Community Psychiatry,* Vol. 39, No. 8 (August 1988), pp. 822–823.

50. Peter P. Lamy, "Alcohol Misuse and Abuse Among the Elderly," *Drug Intelligence in Clinical Pharmacology,* Vol. 18 (1984), p. 649.

51. Susan Folkman, Linda Bernstein, and Richard S. Lazarus, "Stress Processes and the Misuse of Drugs in Older Adults," *Psychology and Aging,* Vol. 2, No. 4 (1987), pp. 366–374.

52. Hearing Before the House of Representatives Select Committee on Aging, *Drug Use and Misuse Among the Elderly* (Washington, DC: U.S. Government Printing Office, June 23, 1989).

53. Thomas P. Beresford, Frederic C. Blow, Kirk J. Brower, Kenneth M. Adams, and Richard C. W. Hall, "Alcoholism and Aging in the General Hospital," *Psychosomatics,* Vol. 29, No. 1 (Winter 1988), pp. 61–72.

54. Graham, "Identifying and Measuring," p. 323.

55. Bienenfeld, "Alcoholism in the Elderly," pp. 164–165.

56. Graham, "Identifying and Measuring," pp. 323–325.

57. Beresford et al., "Alcoholism and Aging," p. 69.

58. Graham, "Identifying and Measuring," p. 325.

59. Beresford et al., "Alcoholism and Aging," p. 69.

60. Rathbone-McCuan and Hashimi, *Isolated Elders,* pp. 220–223.

61. Norman S. Miller and Mark S. Gold, *Alcohol* (New York: Plenum Press, 1991), p. 242.

62. James T. Hartford and T. Samorajski, "Alcoholism in the Geriatric Population," *Journal of the American Geriatrics Society,* Vol. 30 (1982), p. 18.

63. Robert B. Scott and Mack C. Mitchell, "Aging, Alcohol, and the Liver," *Journal of the American Geriatrics Society,* Vol. 36, No. 3 (1988), pp. 255–265.

64. Beresford et al., "Alcoholism and Aging," p. 69.

65. Richard M. Atkinson (ed.), *Alcohol and Drug Abuse in Old Age* (Washington, DC: American Psychiatric Press, 1984).

66. O. Thienhaus and J. Hartford, "Alcoholism in the Elderly," *Psychiatric Medicine,* Vol. 2 (1984), pp. 27–41.

67. Hartford and Samorajski, "Alcoholism in the Geriatric Population," p. 18.

68. Marlene Oscar-Berman, Amy Weinstein, and Diane Wysocki, "Bimanual Tactual Discrimination in Aging Alcoholics," *Alcoholism Clinical and Experimental Research,* Vol. 7, No. 4 (Fall 1983), pp. 398–403.

69. Mark S. Goldman, "Cognitive Impairment in Chronic Alcoholics: Some Cause for Optimism," *American Psychologist,* Vol. 38, No. 10 (October 1983), pp. 1045–1054.

70. Butler, Lewis, and Sunderland, *Aging and Mental Health,* p. 125.

71. Rathbone-McCuan and Hashimi, *Isolated Elders,* p. 218.

72. G. K. Klerman and Myrna M. Weissman, "Depressions Among Women: Their Nature and Causes," in M. Guttentag, S. Salasin, and D. Belle (eds.), *The Mental Health of Women* (New York: Academic Press, 1980), pp. 57–92.

73. Finlayson et al., "Alcoholism in Elderly Persons," p. 766.

74. Dan Blazer and Candyce D. Williams, "Epidemiology of Dysphoria and Depression in an Elderly Population," *American Journal of Psychiatry,* Vol. 137 (1980), pp. 439–444.

75. Lee N. Robins, John E. Helzer, Myrna M. Weissman, H. Orvaschel, Ernest Gruenberg, Jack D. Burke, and Darrel A. Regier, "Lifetime Prevalence of Specific Psychiatric Disorders in Three Sites," *Archives of General Psychiatry,* Vol. 41 (1984), pp. 949–958.

76. Joseph Richman, *Suicide in the Elderly* (New York: Springer, 1992).

77. Charles L. Rich, Deborah Young, and Richard C. Fowler, "San Diego Suicide Study," *Archives of General Psychiatry,* Vol. 43 (1986), pp. 577–582.

78. Eric Pfeiffer, "Psychopathology and Social Pathology," in J. E. Birren and K. Warner Schaie (eds.), *Handbook of Psychology and Aging* (New York: Van Nostrand Reinhold, 1977).

79. Atkinson, Turner, Kofoed, and Tolson, "Early Versus Late Onset Alcoholism," pp. 513–515.

80. Hartford and Samorajski, "Alcoholism in the Geriatric Population," pp. 18–24.

81. Larry W. Dupree, "Comparison of Three Case-Finding Strategies Relative to Elderly Alcohol Abusers," *Journal of Applied Gerontology,* Vol. 8, No. 4 (December 1989), pp. 502–511.

82. Kathryn Graham and Jadzia Romaniec, "Case-Finding vs. Right to Privacy: A General Dilemma Emerging from a Study of the Elderly," *Journal of Drug Issues,* Vol. 16, No. 3 (Summer 1986), pp. 391–395.

83. Stephen W. Janik and Roger G. Dunham, "A Nationwide Examination of the Need for Specific Alcoholism Treatment Programs for the Elderly," *Journal of Studies on Alcohol,* Vol. 44, No. 2 (March 1983), pp. 307–317.

84. Beresford et al., "Alcoholism and Aging," p. 70.

85. Rathbone-McCuan and Hashimi, *Isolated Elders,* p. 223.

86. Laura L. Carstensen, Robert G. Rychtarik, and Donald M. Prue, "Behavioral Treatment of the Geriatric Alcohol Abuser: A Long-Term Follow-up Study," *Addictive Behaviors,* Vol. 10 (1985), pp. 307–311.

87. Mark A. Shuckit, "Geriatric Alcoholism and Drug Abuse," *The Gerontologist,* Vol. 17 (1977), pp. 168–174.

88. Roger G. Dunham, "Aging and Changing Patterns of Alcohol Use," *Journal of Psychoactive Drugs,* Vol. 13 (1981), pp. 143–151.

89. Larry N. Dupree, Helen Broskowski, and Lawrence I. Schonfeld, "The Gerontology Alcohol Project: A Behavioral Treatment Program for Elderly Alcohol Abusers," *The Gerontologist,* Vol. 24(5), (1984), pp. 510–516.

90. Atkinson, Tolson, and Turner, "Late Versus Early Onset Problem Drinking in Older Men," pp. 574–579.

91. Carstensen, Rychtarik, and Prue, "Behavioral Treatment of the Geriatric Alcohol Abuser," p. 307.

92. Lial L. Kofoed, Robert L. Tolson, Roland M. Atkinson, Rodger L. Toth, and John A. Turner, "Treatment Compliance of Older Alcoholics: An Elder-Specific Approach Is Superior to 'Mainstreaming,'" *Journal of Studies on Alcohol,* Vol. 48, No. 1 (1987), pp. 47–51.

93. Margaret P. Felker, "A Recovery Group for Elderly Alcoholics," *Geriatric Nursing* (March/April 1988), pp. 110–113.

94. Richard Blake, "Mental Health Counseling and Older Problem Drinkers," *Journal of Mental Health Counseling*, Vol. 12, No. 3 (July 1990), pp. 354–367.

95. Sheldon Zimberg, "Diagnosis and Treatment of Elderly Alcoholics," *Alcoholism: Clinical and Experimental Research*, Vol. 2, No. 1 (1978), pp. 27–29.

96. Brian L. Mishara and Robert Kastenbaum, *Alcoholism and Old Age* (Orlando, FL: Grune & Stratton, 1980).

97. National Institute on Alcohol Abuse and Alcoholism, *A Guide to Planning Alcoholism Treatment Programs,* DHHS Pub. No. ADM 86-1430 (Washington, DC: U.S. Government Printing Office, 1986).

98. Edith J. Gomberg, "Alcohol Use and Alcohol Problems Among the Elderly," in National Institute on Alcohol Abuse and Alcoholism, *Alcohol and Health Monograph No. 4, Special Population Issues* (Washington, DC: U.S. Government Printing Office), pp. 263–289. "Patterns of Alcohol Use and Abuse Among the Elderly," in National Institute on Alcohol Abuse and Alcoholism, *Alcohol and Health Monograph No. 4,* Special Population Issues (DHHS Pub. No. ADM 82-1193) (Rockville, MD) 1982.

99. Rathbone-McCuan and Hashimi, *Isolated Elders*, p. 233.

15

Gender and drugs: fact, fiction, and unanswered questions

Men and women operate in many of the same social systems, but these systems view substance disorders from a different perspective when the person using alcohol or drugs is a woman rather than a man. Chemically dependent women are typically considered more sick or deviant than men who abuse alcohol or other drugs in the same way.[1] Test this difference for yourself. Think of one of the hundreds of "drunk jokes" or one of the many cartoons that feature a male alcoholic (for example, the character Thirsty in the syndicated cartoon "Hi and Lois" by Greg and Brian Walker). Substitute a female alcoholic and the joke isn't so funny. The social systems of the family, the courts, the medical establishment, and so forth treat male and female drug abusers quite

differently. These differences and other social, physiological, and psychological factors that distinguish the psychoactive drug problems of men and women are the subjects of this chapter. More important, the implications of these differences for prevention and recovery are addressed. We begin with a woman's story that illustrates many of these issues.

SUSAN'S STORY*

Looking good was something Susan always knew how to do. She was a cheerleader, an

---

*Susan's story is based on the accounts of many alcoholic women in recovery, especially one woman who is well known to both authors.

honor student, and part of the "in crowd" all through junior high and high school, when those kinds of things really count. Even in college, she was active in lots of extracurricular activities and kept a 3.0 grade point average. Only if you looked very carefully would you see the cracks in her outwardly perfect facade. Mixing wine in her grape juice after school in junior high, sneaking bourbon out of her dad's liquor cabinet on a regular basis, the real reason she often stayed out all night during high school (she kept getting drunk and was afraid to come home), the time she showed up "blasted" at her Economics 301 final, the blackouts, her reputation for being able to hold her liquor, the time she woke up in the woods with a frat boy trying to take off her clothes. As with most women beginning their addiction to alcohol, nobody really noticed. Or if they did, they explained her behavior as "feisty, a little rebellious, going through a phase." And as Susan herself said, "It's no big deal."

Susan wasn't looking very closely at herself either. When she looked at her family, she saw a mother whose life revolved around her husband, and she saw a father whose life revolved around his job, wasn't everybody like that? When she saw her dad drinking every night and her mother covering up the many times he "had a few too many," it didn't even occur to her there might be a problem; after all, he always had a job of some kind and put food on the table for the family. When she looked at her older brother, she saw the one source of affection she had felt in her family; twenty years later she remembered the sexual abuse. Most of the time she didn't look at all.

Susan's first marriage started before she finished college because she got pregnant, but then that wasn't all that unusual. A second child soon after gave Susan the illusion that she had "settled down with a family," just like she thought she was supposed to do. Her drinking became more episodic, because she was very busy with two small children, and her husband did not really like to drink as she did. One time, however, she went overboard at her husband's company party. All the hidden anguish of her life erupted in a rage. She stomped out of the party and tried to hitch a ride, anywhere! She has no memory of how she got home the next day or what happened to her. Her husband made her go to an Alcoholics Anonymous meeting. She was 23 years old. It was perfectly clear to Susan that this was not the place for her. She was not an alcoholic. Besides, when she finally mentioned having "blackouts" to her physician, he said it was normal, and she should "cut down a little."

Susan became more careful with her drinking. When she and her husband divorced, drinking was not the issue (she thought). She saw nothing unusual in buying a bottle of Scotch her first day in her new apartment and drinking it until she passed out. She spent many nights drinking Scotch, always waiting until the kids were in bed to start drinking, and always "falling asleep" on the couch. Her new job kept her busy during the day. It was only after the kids were asleep and things got quiet that she would "reward herself." After all, it's a tough job being a single parent.

Soon the nights were taken up with a new acquaintance who liked to drink just as she did. He also had access to other drugs that she had never tried. The next year was spent "experimenting" with the finest: clearlight acid from San Francisco, peyote from Mexico, hashish, marijuana, and cocaine from the connection of a prominent businessman in town. A whole new world of "beautiful people" opened up and Susan felt like she'd walked through the looking glass, far away from the "straight" middle-class world where she had always felt like an outsider. Even so, she didn't quit her job or quite lose track of her children. Her lover became her new husband. When he tapered off drugs and switched to martinis, she did too. Like many women substance abusers, Susan's use mirrored her husband's.

Most of the time they didn't start drinking until 5 P.M. They always had lots to celebrate, or sometimes just a need to "take the edge off." Susan's job was becoming more stressful, and her husband's work was either feast or famine. The arguments seemed unfortunate, but they continued to forgive each other for having "a few too many." Even when he hit her, she understood. One time she threw an end table across the room at him and cut his face. Neither one remembered why the next day. The kids seemed to have grown up into a life of their own—they were teenagers and were gone a lot. Susan rarely saw any friends who didn't like to drink. Although she couldn't control her drinking anymore around her family, no one told her she had a problem. She once was advised by her mother to "cut down a little," and her dad told her to quit drinking brandy after dinner. The hangovers were becoming almost unendurable, but she forced herself to show up at work, even when she had the shakes. As the humiliations of covering for both herself and her husband piled up, Susan became more and more isolated (except from people who drank just as she did).

One day a drinking buddy of Susan's told her she had joined AA. Susan was stunned! Why would she want to do that? She drinks just like I do, she thought. A few months later when Susan had moved out of the house after a particularly abusive episode with her husband, this friend gave her a copy of the Big Book of Alcoholics Anonymous. "Have a nice life," was the way the friend inscribed the front page. Susan read the book, drinking martinis the whole time. Three years later, she sobered up. During those three years, "I tried everything to control my drinking—except quitting drinking." She tried marriage counseling, only drinking wine, individual therapy, vitamins, will power, AA, self-help books, leaving her husband, reconciling with her husband, and all she could put together was a few weeks of abstinence. It never occurred to her to enter "treatment," partly because no one suggested it, and partly because she didn't have the money or insurance to cover it. At least once, she celebrated her sobriety with a pitcher of martinis. Like other substance abusers, she was "on an endless cycle of 'I'll do better tomorrow' and of course I was always drunk again by 9 o'clock that night." Her husband continued to drink, because "he thought I was the one with the problem."

How did Susan finally get sober? Was it because she "hit bottom" and got "sick and tired of being sick and tired" as they say in AA? The answer according to Susan is a spiritual one—"but for the grace of God and her A.A. woman friend" she would still be drinking or dead. Academics, researchers, and practitioners want more concrete answers. Yet given the high rates of relapse from substance abuse, the road to recovery is still elusive.

Susan's story doesn't end with sobriety. She is now "recovering from recovery," a long painful process of facing the reality of her past alcohol abuse, lost dreams, and learning to live sober "one day at a time." She divorced her husband. She started her recovery with no job and no place to live. She now has a new job that she loves, but the salary is much lower. She is slowly repairing the relationship with her children. One of her children has already gone through her own addiction to drugs and into recovery. Susan goes to AA regularly and sponsors other women. She has been in therapy for a number of years dealing with her own shame and guilt, depression, family of origin issues, sexual abuse, and "trying to find out what's normal." Many times when Susan has disclosed to another person that she is a recovering alcoholic, they don't believe her. Her favorite response is "Baby, this is what an alcoholic looks like!" She still knows how to look good.

AN EQUALITY WOMEN DON'T WANT

Within every age group in the United States there are more men than women who drink alcohol, and within every age group, more men than women are classified as heavy drinkers. For instance, in 1985, about 14 percent of men were reported to be heavy drinkers compared with 3 percent of women.[2] While more women than men abstain from alcohol, the number of "heavy" drinkers among women may be underestimated. Definitions of heavy drinking differ among studies, but a typical definition includes five or more drinks at one sitting[3] or consumption of 1 ounce or more of pure alcohol per day.[4] These definitions, however, may fail to consider gender differences. For example, body weight, as well as water and fat content in the body, affect the metabolism of alcohol. When consumed, alcohol is dispersed or diluted throughout the water in the body. The concentration of alcohol is relative to the total amount of body water. On the average, women weigh less than men, and they have more body fat in relation to water content. Generally speaking, a 140-pound woman will have a higher blood-alcohol level after ingesting the same amount of alcohol over the same time period than a 140-pound man, and she will almost certainly have a higher blood-alcohol level than a 180-pound man. Yet studies of drinking behavior do not usually take these well-known facts into account. If adjustments for physiological factors are made, and measures of heavy drinking were adjusted accordingly, the percentage of women classified as heavy drinkers might increase substantially.

Although heavy drinking can be detrimental, it is not necessarily the same as alcoholism. In addition to estimates of heavy drinkers, we are also interested in differences in estimates of male and female alcoholics in the population. In recent years, estimates of the ratio of men to women with problems of alcohol abuse and alcoholism have changed. Edith Lisansky Gomberg, one of the earliest researchers on women and alcoholism, reviewed literature on this subject and reported that rates varied depending on the populations studied, such as rural versus urban or clinical samples versus general population samples.[5] In the 1950s, estimates indicated that there were as many as five or six male alcoholics for every female. In the 1960s and 1970s estimates were about 4 to 1. Today, reports indicate that approximately 12.5 percent of American men and just over 5 percent of American women meet the diagnostic criteria for alcohol abuse or dependence, a ratio of 2.4 to 1.[6] Of those who are treated, however, the estimates are closer to four males for every woman served.[7] While women have reduced the gap in reported rates of alcoholism, they apparently continue to be underserved by treatment providers. A variety of social factors, such as the additional stigma

and lack of social supports faced by chemically dependent women, discussed throughout this chapter, are thought to account for much of the variance in treatment rates. The number of women entering treatment is, however, growing, primarily in the younger age groups.[8]

The United States and other Western cultures are not alone in reports that men are at higher risk for alcoholism than women. Figures for Eastern countries like Korea and Taiwan paint a more dramatic picture of gender differences. Helzer and his colleagues conducted a cross-national study in St. Louis, Missouri; Edmonton, Canada; Puerto Rico; Taipei City, Taiwan; and South Korea.[9] The lifetime prevalence rates for alcoholism (i.e., anyone who at any time in their life had the symptoms of alcoholism) varied considerably across countries but were substantially higher for men than for women at all sites. Edmonton had the smallest current male to female ratio at 4:1, while Taiwan had the largest difference at a ratio of 18:1. South Korea had a ratio of 16:1 and for Puerto Rico it was 12:1. In St. Louis, the ratio was 7:1. The bad news for women is that as lifetime prevalence rates for the general population increased over the years in each of the countries, the prevalence rate for women not only rose, but it rose disproportionately. The authors of the study concluded that the general acceptance of alcohol in a society appears to influence rates of alcoholism among women. The exception to this trend was Korea where alcoholism among women remained very low. The authors suggested that male domination and strictly defined sex roles in Korea continue to mitigate against women's drinking.

In addition to alcohol, men are also more likely to report the use of almost all types of illicit drugs (marijuana, cocaine, crack, inhalants, and heroin). However, patterns of use vary by age group. For example, the 1990 Household Survey on Drug Use conducted in the United States indicates no differences between men and women in the 12- to 17-year age bracket in the use of alcohol or marijuana during their lifetime, in the past year, or during the past month, while in older age groups men generally used more.[10] Cocaine use was also more similar for teens of both genders than for men and women in older age brackets. Women age 12 to 17 are slightly more likely than young men to have ever used nonprescribed stimulants and sedatives, while in older age groups, men generally reported more use. Although women generally report less use of alcohol and drugs, one danger in making these comparisons is that the chemical dependency problems of women may be minimized, resulting in women continuing to be underserved by treatment providers. Other studies concerned with *polydrug* use in Canada indicate that alcoholic men and women are at similar risk for abusing other drugs.[11] The alcoholic women, however, continued to outnumber men in their abuse of barbiturates, sedatives, or minor tranquilizers, while the men continued to be more likely to abuse cannabis and tobacco.

Will rates of chemical abuse and dependency for men and women soon be equal in the United States? The evidence varies. The National Household Survey shows more similarities among young men and women in their drinking and drug use which may portend more problems for women. Other investigations, such as the cross-cultural study of Helzer and coworkers, also suggest that this may eventually happen. Gaps in rates of alcohol disorders and age of onset for men and women seem to be narrowing at the same time that rates are increasing for both genders.[12] The Wilsnacks and their colleagues, however, conducted a study that focused on women and found no evidence of a major increase in rates of alcohol consumption by women from 1971 to 1981.[13] Consistent with previous surveys, women remained predominantly abstainers (39 percent) or light drinkers (38 percent) with increasing abstinence in the age groups over 50. The percentage of drinkers increased among middle-aged women (35–64) and heavy drinking increased in the 35–49-year-old group. The proportion of heavy drinkers remained relatively low (6 percent). Although these findings are similar to earlier surveys, others have reported increased heavy drinking among younger women.[14] One alarming finding, according to Sharon Wilsnack, is that "Even if there were no increase in the rate of drinking, . . . population projections indicate that there will be 200,000 more women alcoholics by 1995 as the Baby Boomers age. And that is a major health problem."[15] Given the public's historical intolerance of female intoxication[16] it may be that male to female alcoholism ratios will not converge completely, at least not in the near future.

Erickson and Watson provide an interesting analysis of convergence with respect to the use of illicit drugs among men and women in younger age groups.[17] Their research review indicates that in the early 1970s, when drug use was on the rise, men's and women's usage rates were becoming more similar due to increases in women's drug use. More recently, they report that rates are converging slightly, because men's illicit drug use has declined, making them more similar to women.

A number of women—among them chemical dependency professionals and recovering alcoholics and addicts—think that the rates of chemical dependency problems have already converged.[18] Many feel certain that women are equal to men when it comes to the incidence of chemical dependency problems but that the research has failed to uncover this fact. While their concerns could be dismissed as unscientific, the methodological problems in the literature on gender differences warrant attention in a later section of this chapter. This review of research issues points to the need for healthy skepticism about the literature on substance disorders and gender differences. In the meantime, we turn our attention to some of the differences that have been studied.

BIOLOGICAL DIFFERENCES

The biological differences among male and female substance abusers that concern us fall into three categories. First is genetic factors that may influence the etiology of substance abuse in men and women. Second is a number of physiological differences, especially in the metabolism of alcohol and in the consequences of alcohol consumption and alcoholism for men and women. Third is sexual dysfunction, including the gynecological and obstetrical problems that chemically dependent women face.

Genetics and Etiology

The effects of heredity and environment have been given considerable attention in the search for the etiology of alcoholism and other drug problems. Chapter 2 covered etiological theories at length. Family, adoption, twin, and clinical studies provide evidence that a significant risk factor for the development of alcoholism is to have one or more first-degree relatives who are alcoholics.[19] Sons of alcoholics appear to be particularly vulnerable. Here we focus on possible gender differences in the familial etiology of substance abuse.

Cloninger, Bohman, and their associates have identified two types of alcoholics from studies of Swedish adoptees.[20] They studied individuals adopted early in life to differentiate genetic and environmental influences. Child welfare records and records of other governmental agencies were used to collect the data. The more common and milder type of alcoholism found in the adoptees was labeled "milieu limited" (or Type I) by the researchers, and it occurs in both men and women. Type I alcoholism is associated with the presence of *two* conditions: mild, untreated, adult-onset alcohol abuse in either the biological mother or father *and* low socioeconomic status of the adoptive father. Those with only one risk factor had no greater chance of becoming alcoholic than the rest of the population. The adoptive father's low socioeconomic status was the only environmental (milieu) factor that influenced the development of Type I alcoholism. Alcoholism in the adoptive parents did not lead to a greater occurrence of alcoholism among their children.

The other type of alcoholism they found is called "male limited" (Type II). It is the more severe form and accounted for 25 percent of alcoholism cases among men. Type II is associated with severe alcoholism in the biological father (but not the biological mother). These fathers developed alcoholism early in life and had several episodes of treatment. They were also more likely to have a history of criminal involvement. No factors in the adoptive home appeared to prevent the development of male-limited alcoholism, although many of the male adoptees had less severe alcoholism problems than their biological fathers. Daughters tended not to develop this type of alcoholism, but daughters of fathers with severe alcoholism had a greater frequency of medically unexplained complaints of pain or discomfort.

Although the Swedish adoption studies as well as similar findings in the United States by Gilligan and colleagues[21] indicate that daughters of alcoholics are far less susceptible to the more severe form of alcoholism, genetics does appear to play a substantial role in the development of alcoholism in both men and women.[22] But the fact that women are less susceptible to the more severe form remains an interesting issue. The Gilligan group suggests that the expression of alcoholism may also be related to personality characteristics and psychopathology, factors that may also be influenced by heredity and may be gender related. Gender socialization (i.e., environmental factors) may also continue to account for some of the difference, and it will be interesting to note the prevalence of these forms of alcoholism if gender norms continue to converge in the United States.

Also of note is that while sons of alcoholic fathers are at substantial risk for developing alcoholism, especially in its most serious form, women who become alcoholics may be more likely to have alcoholic parents than men. For example, in a study conducted by Glenn and Parsons, the rate of maternal alcoholism was 11.1 percent for men and 25 percent for women.[23] The rate of paternal alcoholism was 35.8 percent for men and 50 percent for women. Of the alcoholic men in this study, 6.17 percent had two alcoholic parents, while 16.7 percent of women reported that both their parents were alcoholics. The effects of heredity and environment are confounded in this study, but the findings raise concern about the susceptibility of women to parental alcoholism. In addition, there is some evidence that alcoholic women have higher rates of mental illness in their families of origin[24] and more disruptive early family lives than men.[25]

Is Biology Destiny?

At the beginning of this chapter, we noted that women generally reach higher blood-alcohol levels (BAL) or concentrations (BAC) than men of the same weight after drinking the same amount of alcohol. Men can also more consistently predict their blood-alcohol levels than women, because the menstrual cycle, which changes the balance of hormones in a women's body, may affect alcohol metabolism; women seem to achieve the highest blood alcohol levels in the days just before the menstrual flow begins.[26] In addition, oral contraceptives may inhibit alcohol metabolism,[27] so that women taking "the pill" are likely to become intoxicated faster and remain intoxicated longer than those not taking it.[28] Although McKim notes that women appear to eliminate alcohol faster than men,[29] there are some practical lessons to be learned from what is known about alcohol metabolism. First, women who try to "keep up" with men when drinking are likely to become more intoxicated, and; therefore, more impaired than their male counterparts. Second, the blood-alcohol charts that help people to approximate their level of intoxication by checking the number of drinks consumed and the amount of time elapsed are only approximations. A woman's BAL may be higher than what is suggested, also putting her at greater risk for alcohol-related traffic accidents or other mishaps.

Differences in alcohol metabolism may help to explain what is called the "telescoping effect" in which women apparently develop alcoholism more quickly than men once serious drinking is initiated.[30] It may also help to explain many of the physiological risks from

drinking that appear to be greater for women than they are for men. Women reportedly experience greater physiological impairment earlier in their drinking careers than men, even though they may consume less alcohol.[31] Hill, for example, summarizes the evidence on liver disease:

The female alcoholic appears to run a greater risk for developing liver disease at an earlier age, following a shorter duration of heavy drinking, and pre-sumably in association with a lower level of consumption than males. Once the liver has sustained injury, women appear to have the added risk of increased mortality over that of their male counterparts.[32]

Women alcoholics also have higher rates of other alcohol-related health problems such as accidents and circulatory disorders.[33]

There is confusion over whether women experience higher alcohol-related death rates than men. Some of the confusion is due to whether alcoholic women are compared to women in the general population or to male alcoholics.[34] Male alcoholics appear to have death rates at least twice as high as those reported for men in the general population, and alcoholic women are reported to have death rates that are nearly three times as high as women in the general population. If death rates for female and male alcoholics are compared, women alcoholics do not appear to have greater mortality than male alcoholics. But Hill has argued that female alcoholics should be compared with women in the general population and male alcoholics with men in the general population. If this is done, then women alcoholics experience higher mortality rates than do alcoholic men.

Given differences in alcohol and drug metabolism, women are also likely to "run a higher risk of alcohol and other drug overdoses at a lower level of consumption" than are men.[35] Data from the Drug Abuse Warning Network (DAWN) gathered from emergency room admissions show that about one-fourth of men and one-half of women attributed their drug overdose to an intent to commit suicide.[36] Consistent with general population data that women attempt but men complete suicide more frequently, the women in the DAWN analyses reportedly attempted suicide more often, but more of the men died as a result of a drug overdose. Confusion over whether suicide rates are higher among substance-abusing women also occurs because of the comparison group used, but Hill concludes that even using the more conservative estimates, women alcoholics die from suicide at a rate at least equal to alcoholic men.[37]

Sexual Dysfunction

Among nonalcoholics, the effects of alcohol consumption on the sexual performance of men is probably better recognized than it is among women. Despite alcohol's disinhibiting effects, many men can attest to difficulty in achieving an erection during an episode of heavy drinking. Women may also experience negative effects such as difficulty achieving orgasm.[38] Perhaps Shakespeare said it best: "Alcohol provoketh the desire but taketh away the performance."[39]

Problems of sexual dysfunction are frequently experienced by male and female alcoholics. Difficulty achieving erections, impotence, and premature ejaculation are found among male alcoholics,[40] and women may become anorgasmic.[41] Lack of sexual desire is often reported. Wilsnack notes that "rates of sexual inhibition, reduced sexual responsiveness, and orgasmic dysfunction in 13 samples of alcoholic women ranged from 28 to 100 percent."[42] There is hope, however, that these patterns of dysfunction may not be fixed or permanent, and will change when substance abusers begin to recover from their addictions. In a study of sixty-one recovering alcoholic women, Apter-Marsh reported that the rate of orgasm achieved with a partner and through masturbation increased over time.[43] Of interest is that prior to addiction, the subjects reported being orgasmic 47 percent of the time; during addiction they achieved orgasm 55 percent of the time, but following sobriety (a mean of 4.2 years for the sample), they were orgasmic 70 percent of the time. The lowest frequency of sexual activity

and orgasm occurred during the fragile period of the first three months of sobriety, when many of the women temporarily ceased sexual activity with both self and partners.

The effects of barbiturate use in sexual functioning are reported to be similar to alcohol since both fall into the class of sedative-hypnotic drugs.[44] Both male and female narcotics addicts are reported to have low levels of sexual desire and difficulty in achieving orgasm.[45] In the case of lower levels of cocaine use, sexual desire, excitement, and orgasm reportedly are enhanced, but high doses may result in impotence in men and may also take a toll on orgasms, especially in women.[46] Reports of pleasurable sexual responsiveness among cocaine users may be due to subjective expectations.[47] With amphetamine use, desire is reportedly enhanced at low doses and diminished with high doses; the effects on orgasm are similar to that of cocaine use.[48] There is evidence of sexual performance problems associated with benzodiazepine use in high doses.[49] While marijuana reportedly enhances sexual feelings, regular use may result in erectile difficulties in men, and it may also reduce their testosterone levels and affect sperm production, including impaired fertility.[50] A drug most popular in enhancing sexual pleasure among gay men is amyl nitrite, known as "poppers" or "snappers."

While there may well be a direct cause and effect relationship in which alcohol and other drug abuse results in sexual dysfunction, the relationship between these two factors may also be reciprocal or circular and reflect psychological and social issues.[51] For example, men and women may drink excessively as a means of coping with the psychological and sexual difficulties they experience. Wilsnack points out that a particularly high-risk subgroup for the development of both sexual dysfunction and alcoholism appears to be women who have experienced sexual abuse and rape, including those with histories of incest.[52] Klassen and Wilsnack also found that many women who drink, especially those classified as heavy drinkers, believe that alcohol not only reduces their sexual inhibitions but also increases their feelings of closeness to others.[53] Substance abuse, however, generally diminishes the ability to engage in healthy and satisfying emotional and sexual relationships, since it clouds one's ability to make rational judgments and to act in a manner consistent with one's feelings. Alcoholic women have also reported more guilt related to sexual activity than nonalcoholic women,[54] and women frequently become the targets of others' sexual aggression as a result of one or both parties' drinking.[55]

Gynecological and Reproductive Problems

Alcoholic women report gynecological and reproductive disorders more frequently than nonalcoholic women, including dysmenorrhea, irregular periods, hysterectomies, infertility, spontaneous abortions, still birth, premature birth, and birth defects.[56] Women who are chronic marijuana users may have abnormal periods and may not ovulate.[57] Cocaine can also suppress female hormones and affect the menstrual cycle.[58] In a review of drug use and premenstrual dysphoria, Mello concluded that:

In women who do not experience premenstrual dysphoria, there appears to be no consistent relationship between drug use and menstrual cycle phase. However, there is some evidence that women who do have premenstrual dysphoria may increase alcohol and/or marijuana use at the premenstrum. These data suggest that premenstrual dysphoria may be one proximal determinant of increased drug use by women.[59]

While there is speculation about a relationship between alcohol and other drug abuse and premenstrual distress, it remains unclear whether gynecological problems precede chemical abuse and are causative factors in the development of alcoholism or other drug abuse or whether gynecological problems are the results of excessive drinking and drug use.[60]

The topics of fetal alcohol syndrome (FAS) and fetal alcohol effects (FAE) have received considerable attention in recent editions of the *Special Report to the U.S. Congress on Alcohol and Health*. Almost every society has had some folk wisdom regarding alcohol use and pregnancy (see, for example, *The Old Testament,* "The Book of Judges," Chapter 13). Alcohol is a well-known teratogen (a substance that produces abnormal formations). FAS was first described in the American literature in 1973 by Jones and his colleagues.[61] It is defined as:

a distinct pattern of abnormalities found in children born to alcohol-abusing mothers. Criteria for defining FAS were standardized by the Fetal Alcohol Study Group of the Research Society on Alcoholism in 1980. The criteria include: prenatal and/or postnatal growth retardation; impairment of the central nervous system (neurological abnormalities, developmental delays, behavioral dysfunction, intellectual impairment, and skull or brain malformations); and facial abnormalities such as small eye openings, a thin upper lip, and an unusually long, flattened midface.[62]

The eleven children originally studied by Jones and his colleagues were followed up ten years later.[63] Two of the children had died and one was lost to follow-up, but in the remaining eight cases, many of the symptoms of the syndrome were permanent. Facial deformities had improved somewhat, and stable home environments had helped with social and emotional development, but some additional abnormalities (hearing, dental, and vision problems) had also become apparent.

FAS is a leading cause of mental retardation. The exact rate of FAS is not known, largely because of the difficulties in measuring previous alcohol consumption.[64] The NIAAA indicates that early estimates averaged 1.1 cases per 1,000 births, while retrospective studies now indicate an average of 2.2 cases per 1,000 births in North America.[65] Children with fewer of the symptoms have been labeled as having fetal alcohol effects, now referred to as "alcohol-related birth defects."[66] Estimates of FAE are thought to be about three times higher than FAS in the general population.[67] While FAS is generally associated with heavy drinking, no one yet knows if there is a level of alcohol consumption at which no such effects will be produced. Clarren and his associates write that "It is probable that there is no *single* dose-response relationship for ethanol teratogenesis, but rather that each abnormal outcome in brain structure or function, morphology, and growth has its own dose-response and gestational timing parameters."[68] In 1981 the Surgeon General encouraged women who are planning on conceiving or who know they are pregnant to abstain totally.[69] Many women apparently automatically reduce their alcohol consumption while pregnant. Alcohol may be less appealing during this time, probably because of nausea or other effects of pregnancy. As of late 1989, alcoholic beverage containers must contain warnings of alcohol's potential to cause birth defects (look carefully for the small print).

Sandmaier, in a pamphlet directed to pregnant women, describes the way in which alcohol affects the fetus:

When a pregnant women takes a drink, the alcohol readily crosses the placenta to the fetus. Moreover, the alcohol travels through the baby's bloodstream in the same concentration as that of the mother. So if the expectant mother becomes drunk at a party, her unborn baby becomes drunk as well. But, of course, the tiny, developing system of the fetus is not nearly as equipped to handle alcohol as the system of its adult mother. Among other things, the undeveloped liver of the unborn baby can burn up alcohol at less than half the rate of an adult liver, which means that alcohol remains in the fetal system longer than in the adult system.[70]

Since not all women who drink or who drink abusively during pregnancy give birth to children with FAE or FAS, it is important for researchers to isolate those factors which contribute to the development of these problems and those which mitigate against them.[71]

The rate of FAS seems to vary among different population groups. African Americans[72] and some Native American tribes[73] have been found to be at greater risk than the general population. A study by May and his colleagues of three Indian tribes indicated that while the Pueblo and the Navajo had rates similar to the rest of the population, the Plains Indians had the highest rate ever reported at almost one case in every one hundred births.[74] The authors suggest that social and cultural customs are possible explanations for the variance in rates. Although abusive drinking by women is not condoned among any of the tribes, the Plains Indians apparently demonstrate greater tolerance of women drinkers, while the Pueblos and Navajo more strongly ostracize them.

In addition to alcohol, infants who have been exposed to other drugs in utero are also of concern. The Alcohol, Drug Abuse, and Mental Health Administration (ADAMHA) estimated that "approximately 100,000 drug-exposed babies are born each year in the United States";[75] however, Chasnoff estimated that 375,000 babies (11 percent of all births) are born each year to mothers who had used an illicit drug.[76] The drugs used include crack, heroin, methadone, cocaine, amphetamines, PCP, and marijuana. Poor, inner-city neighborhoods seem to report the highest rates, as high as 50 percent according to NIDA.[77] The question of whether private hospitals in more affluent areas underreport the incidence of chemically exposed infants remains untested.[78] According to estimates from NIDA's household survey, of the 60.1 million women of child bearing age in the country, 4.8 million had used some illicit drug in the month previous to the survey.[79] While a number of negative outcomes for drug-exposed infants have been reported, such as premature birth, hypertension, visual abnormalities, and an abnormal brain, the effects of drug use have not been differentiated from other physical, social (including environmental), and psychological factors during pregnancy.[80]

Currently, there is good news and bad news with respect to assisting women whose pregnancies are threatened due to alcohol or other drug exposure. The good news is that some researchers and service providers believe that pregnancy may motivate women to receive treatment for chemical dependency.[81] The bad news is that recent criminal prosecutions of pregnant women who abuse drugs may act as a deterrent to seeking prenatal care and chemical dependency treatment. According to Gustavsson:

The war on drugs has become a war on pregnant women, particularly poor women of color. As attempts to reduce both the supply and demand for mood-altering chemicals by instituting harsh criminal sanctions fail, attention is being redirected toward a group that is easy to identify, dislike, and control. Pregnant women who use chemicals and give birth to infants suffering from a variety of health problems fit these three criteria.[82]

In some cases, children born to mothers who test positive for drugs have been removed and placed in the state's custody, and attempts are being made around the country to prosecute mothers of drug-exposed infants for child abuse or for other crimes such as manslaughter if the fetus or infant does not survive.[83] The verdict is still out on whether convictions will be upheld in higher courts. Many chemical dependency treatment programs will not admit a pregnant woman, but special treatment programs for pregnant women and women with children are being developed.[84] ADAMHA (now the Substance Abuse and Mental Health Services Administration) called the development of more of them an "urgent need."[85] While the outcomes of pregnancy are ideally a concern of both parents, the affects of fathers' drug use on pregnancy has not received much serious attention.

SOCIAL DIFFERENCES

In addition to experiencing more physical deterioration than men, women alcoholics are often reported to have more personally destructive drinking careers and to have suffered greater social and psychological deterioration prior to entering treatment.[86] Female narcotics addicts appear similar to their male counterparts in many aspects of their patterns of use and relapse, but both women alcoholics and addicts reportedly have shorter drinking and drug careers before entering treatment than men.[87] Some of the social differences between men and women

reported in the literature are not surprising. For example, alcoholic women may suffer more economic disadvantage than alcoholic men.[88] This is consistent with the financial disadvantages (more frequent unemployment, low-status jobs, and more dependency on welfare) of women compared to men in the general population. Additional social issues deserve attention in our consideration of women with chemical dependency problems. These include negative attitudes toward them, lack of social supports, and drug-related criminal activity.

Falling from the Pedestal

Until the 1970s, alcoholism and drug addiction were viewed almost exclusively as problems of men. The women substance abusers who were noticed were considered particularly deviant, and they tended to be scorned as unfeminine and promiscuous. Gomberg noted that the "universality of this attitude is such that both sexes and all social classes show the same negative attitude."[89] It appears that this picture has not changed substantially. Kagle refers to alcoholic women as a "discredited social group."[90] They seem to suffer from the "double whammy" of societal bias against alcoholics and against women. There is likely to be a "triple whammy" if the woman is also a member of an oppressed ethnic group. Ridlon believes that in spite of efforts to establish equality in social and economic spheres, women are expected to remain on a pedestal—above the problems of chemical abuse and dependency—due to their responsibilities as primary child rearers and as the keepers of marital and other familial relationships.[91] Women's chemically induced behavior is typically excused or rationalized. For example, women stopped for drunk driving are more likely to be escorted home by police, whereas men are more likely to be arrested for driving while intoxicated.[92] Women's depression may be explained as mental illness rather than a result of alcoholism or drug addiction. This "status insularity" impedes the recognition of psychoactive drug problems in women.[93]

Social Supports

Alcohol use varies by marital status.[94] Among women, widows are most likely to be abstainers followed by those who are married. Divorced, separated, and never married women are less likely to abstain, and cohabitating women are the least likely to abstain. Conversely, cohabitating women are most likely to be heavy drinkers, followed by married, divorced, or separated women. Widows are least likely to be heavy drinkers. Married men are more likely to abstain than are those who are divorced, separated, or never married, while divorced or separated men report more heavy drinking than married or never married men.

But male partners apparently play a significant role in women's chemical dependency. A consistent finding in the research on social factors is that women frequently engage in excessive drinking and drug use as a result of their relationships with male partners who are alcoholics or addicts rather than the other way around. Some researchers contend that a relationship with an addicted male is the greatest factor predisposing a woman's addiction.[95] In a series of studies of men and women in methadone maintenance programs, Hser, Anglin, and Booth found that:

it was much more likely that a woman's partner was an addict than a man's partner. For many women, spouses' or partners' use was the major reason for their own first addiction to and/or increased use of narcotics. As a related matter, the heroin habits of many women were often supported by others (including a spouse or partner).[96]

Evidence from other countries also supports this conclusion.[97]

Factors that seem to increase the risk of relapse for both men and women following treatment for alcoholism include interpersonal and marital conflict[98] and the lack of family supports.[99] Since women alcoholics are reportedly less likely to be married than men alcoholics when they enter treatment,[100] they may be at greater risk for relapse. Additional reports also suggest that alcoholic women have greater marital instability than alcoholic

men, but perhaps not more than women in the general population since they also experience high rates of divorce and separation.[101] But, a recent finding by Wilsnack and her colleagues from a longitudinal study of 143 problem drinking women and 157 nonproblem drinking women suggests that divorce and separation may actually be more of a "remedy" than a "risk."[102] Among the women problem drinkers identified in the early part of their study, those that became divorced or separated during the study period (1981–1986) had lower levels of subsequent alcohol dependence.

While women are more likely than men to become alcohol or drug dependent as a result of having a partner who has these problems, once in treatment, they are likely to have less social support than men. Lindbeck suggests that this may be due to the husband's especially strong denial of his wife's drinking.[103] This denial may result from the husband's own excessive use of alcohol or other drugs. In addition, professionals may have "excused" men from participation in their wives' treatment, because these husbands have been considered exceptional for staying with their alcohol or drug dependent wives.[104] Today's treatment programs are more likely to expect equal participation by both husbands and wives of alcoholics and addicts.

Not only do chemically dependent women receive less support for entering treatment, according to Beckman and Amaro, they are more likely to encounter opposition to entering treatment from family and friends.[105] Such opposition is almost unheard of among the families and friends of men. When women do get this support, it reportedly is more likely to come from children and parents, while men are more likely to be motivated to enter treatment by their spouses.[106] Although the sample used in her study was small (eighteen subjects), Robinson concurs that families rarely played a part in women's referrals to treatment and were often an actual barrier to treatment.[107] Saunders and his associates also found that women were less likely than their male counterparts to have been advised to stop or reduce their drinking by family members.[108] In a comparison of black and white women entering treatment, Amaro and her colleagues found that more black (68 percent) than white (49 percent) women had family or friends who suggested treatment, and fewer black (8 percent) than white (25 percent) women faced opposition from significant others to their entering treatment.[109]

Two examples from alcoholic women in recovery who were respondents in an exploratory study illustrate families' opposition to seeking help:

My parents didn't see that I had any drinking problem. Part of it was that they just didn't see a lot. They'd say, "if your husband would give you some money, you'd be O.K."

The rest of my family was just vaguely aware of what was going on, and they were counter-supportive. They talked about A.A. in a derogatory way.[110]

Another study confirms the weak social support structure and isolation of alcoholic women in treatment compared to nonalcoholic female controls.[111] The alcoholic women had significantly fewer friends and no close women friends, felt lonely some or most of the time, had more poor relationships with others, were more resentful toward their parents, and received less emotional support from them.

It does not take much study to note that mothers, even mothers with alcohol and other drug problems, are more likely to be the caretakers of their children than fathers. While these mothers are probably aware that chemical dependency treatment will benefit their children, the inability to secure safe child care can impede their entering treatment. Conversely, access to child care at chemical dependency programs encourages participation in treatment.[112]

There are also indications that other social systems such as health care and criminal justice systems are less likely to address the chemical dependency problems of women. Saunders compared men and women with alcohol-related liver disease and found that even in these life-threatening cases, women were still somewhat less likely to have been advised by a physician to curtail drinking or to have been referred to a hospital for alcoholism treatment; they were also less likely to have been convicted for alcohol-related offenses.[113] While women in this study more often received psychiatric treatment for non-alcoholic-related problems, few of the men or women were referred to alcoholism counseling or to Alcoholics Anonymous.

Crime

The relationship between drug use and crime is known to almost everyone (see Chapter 8). In an effort to determine the level of drug use among arrestees, the National Institute of Justice implemented the Drug Use Forecasting (DUF) program.[114] In 1990, twenty-three cities were participating. Among men arrested, the DUF indicated that from 57 to 80 percent tested positive for drugs, depending on the city, and among women arrested, the figures ranged from 44 to 88 percent. In the majority of cities, men and women were most likely to test positive for cocaine. Other research suggests that women in prison may actually be more likely than male inmates to have used heroin.[115] Rough estimates of the number of women incarcerated due to alcohol or other drug-related offenses are as high as 90 percent,[116] yet the hard evidence on this subject is inadequate to justify drug use as a primary, causative factor in the rise in the number of incarcerated women.

Like female alcoholics and addicts, female criminals are typically seen as more abnormal than their male counterparts. While the criminal activity of men has been described as motivated by economics, status, or a need for acceptance, female criminals are characterized as maladjusted, "doubly deviant,"[117] or the victim of biological, psychological, or personal imbalance.[118] In their extensive review of the literature on this topic, Erickson and Watson found that female addicts have most often been linked to the crime of prostitution, with the assumption that they became prostitutes to support their drug habit, or they became addicts to cope with the stress of prostitution.[119] They add that this simplistic and narrow view of the behavior of female drug users is the result of a lack of research on women by criminologists and addiction specialists, and the perception that addiction and crime are primarily male activities. In addition, prior to the criminalization of narcotics use, opiate addiction was greater for women than for men; following criminalization, the pattern was reversed, with male opiate addicts now outnumbering females.[120] Although previous studies have clearly reported less criminal involvement for women addicts,[121] Hser and colleagues found support for the position that many women turn to illegal activities just as men do after addiction to narcotics.[122] The major gender difference these researchers noted was the type of crime committed—both men and women reported theft; men reported burglary or robbery more than women, while women reported forgery and prostitution more often. Erickson and Watson report that the most common crimes of women drug users are drug offenses (especially drug dealing), while prostitution is the primary offense for a smaller group of women who use drugs (primarily narcotics addicts).[123]

Erickson and Watson do not deny an association between drug use and prostitution among women, but their review raises questions about the assumption that the need to support a drug habit is the factor that precedes prostitution. For example, the report of the Special Committee on Pornography and Prostitution in Canada states that many prostitutes do not use drugs and alcohol because of the dangers they face and the need to be alert; instead, prostitution results from the need to meet their everyday economic needs.[124] However, among female addicts, prostitution is common, and the frequency of these offenses may be increasing for some. Inciardi and Pottieger compared 153 women heroin users studied in 1977 and 1978 with 133 similar women studied in 1983 and 1984.[125] While the percentage involved in prostitution decreased from 71 to 54 percent, the incidence of this offense increased from 38 percent of their total crimes to 54 percent.

The later cohort also reverted more often to prostitution and drug sales than property offenses.

Past stereotypes that made illicit drug use by women synonymous with prostitution no longer seem adequate. More recent research suggests that female addicts engage in prostitution less frequently and engage in a greater variety of other criminal activities than was formerly assumed.[126] Criminology researchers are suggesting that gender-based theories of crime alone are inadequate to explain differences in criminal activity. The interaction of gender and class must be considered, since differences in level of criminal activity between the genders become less apparent as socioeconomic status declines.[127]

PSYCHOLOGICAL DIFFERENCES

Psychological issues that chemically dependent individuals face have also received considerable attention in the literature. They include a variety of symptoms often attributed not only to substance abusers but also to women in the general population, such as low self-esteem and depression. The high incidence of physical and sexual abuse reported by women substance abusers may also be a substantial factor contributing to their psychological distress.

Psychological Distress

Symptoms of psychological distress, such as depression[128] and low self-esteem,[129] as well as passivity, aggression, and conflict[130] are mentioned as especially problematic for alcoholic and alcohol-abusing women, while male alcoholics are more often reported to have sociopathy[131] and antisocial personality disorders.[132] There is some similar evidence for male and female cocaine abusers.[133] Since women in the general population are also described as having more psychological problems, it is unclear to what extent gender, substance abuse, or an interaction between these two factors explains psychopathology in chemically dependent women.[134] DeSoto et al. studied 163 men and 149 women members of Alcoholics Anonymous with varying lengths of abstinence and found no differences in symptomatology using raw scores, but when these scores were normed for gender, men were *more* symptomatic with respect to depression, anxiety, and phobic anxiety, and they also scored higher on overall symptomatology or pathology.[135] A follow-up study four years later with 233 of these same subjects showed the same course of recovery from severity of symptoms or pathology for both abstinent alcoholic men and women.[136] In the first six months of abstinence there typically was considerable distress (depression, obsessive-compulsive behavior, and interpersonal sensitivity), comparable to that seen in psychiatric inpatients. These symptoms dramatically decreased after three years of abstinence, with continuing improvement after ten or more years of abstinence, at which time symptomatology approached the norm for the general population. The *Seventh Special Report to the U.S. Congress on Alcohol and Health* cites a number of studies showing the decrease of depressive symptoms, anxiety, and cognitive impairment as alcoholics progress from drinking to abstinence, although an important etiological question remains unanswered: Which comes first—the psychological distress or the substance abuse?[137]

In spite of these hopeful indications that both men and women can recover fully from the psychological impairment associated with substance abuse, there is some evidence that women may experience a more difficult (or at least different) road in the recovery process because of additional psychological stressors they face. For example, alcoholic women are reported to have had more disruption in their families of origin than alcoholic men, such as mentally ill and alcoholic parents,[138] and they report more isolation and unhappiness in early life than nonalcoholic women.[139] More recently, the devastating effects of the physical and sexual abuse of women substance abusers are being acknowledged.

Physical and Sexual Abuse

Connections between physical abuse and alcoholism have become clearer in recent decades. For instance, research on battered women indicates a high degree of drinking problems in their battering husbands or partners. Lehmann and Krupp reported that of 1,500 calls about spouse abuse to a community hotline, 828 women callers (55 percent) reported that their husbands were abusive while drinking.[140] Since many alcoholic women have husbands and partners who also drink heavily, it may be reasonable to assume that a great many alcoholic women are physically abused. Additional research could also help to determine whether there is a difference in the risk of women (and men) being battered if both partners are alcoholics or addicts or if one partner is chemically dependent and the other is not. For example, a man (whether or not he is chemically dependent) may strike out at his wife, but if she is chemically dependent, she may be less able to defend herself from physical or psychological abuse. Given concerns about the incidence of alcohol and other drug problems reported among gay men and lesbians (see Chapter 12), similar studies of partners of the same gender would also be useful.

Women alcoholics apparently suffer from a high degree of sexual trauma in addition to other types of abuse. Wilsnack reports several studies that found a high incidence of incest and other sexual abuse, including rape, among alcoholic women.[141] For example, Covington found that rates appear higher than in the general population, ranging from 12 to 53 percent for incest or other childhood sexual abuse and as high as 74 percent for all types of sexual trauma combined.[142] Other reports indicate that the combined rates of incest, battering, child sexual abuse, and sexual assault for women in alcoholism treatment in various studies range from 40 to 74 percent[143] and that as many as 29 to 54 percent of women alcoholics in treatment have been raped at some point in their lives.[144] Covington notes that for the majority of women alcoholics, "this [abuse] has been part of their life experience, and it is part of the same guilt and degradation that contributes, along with the stigma of alcoholism, to their lower-self esteem."[145] Gomberg has also commented on the "internalized shame factor" (lack of self-worth and self-hatred; see also Chapter 10) "as an important, even necessary, condition" to alcoholism for women, although she concludes that it is not sufficient to explain chemical dependency in women.[146]

WOMEN, RECOVERY, AND TREATMENT

Vannicelli[147] traced the idea that women substance abusers are "sicker" than men substance abusers to Benjamin Karpman, who in 1948 suggested that these women had to be more abnormal than their male counterparts in order to violate the more restrictive social barriers against women developing alcoholism.[148] Assertions such as these led to a belief that women alcoholics were not only sicker than male alcoholics but that they were also more difficult to treat. Vanicelli investigated whether this was true by reviewing twenty-three studies that reported gender-related treatment outcomes.[149] Eighteen of the studies showed no significant difference in treatment outcomes between male and female alcoholics; four studies showed better outcomes for women, and one showed better outcomes for men. Hser and associates[150] and the Institute of Medicine[151] also agree that recovery rates following treatment are similar for men and women.

Interpretations of existing treatment effectiveness studies are often confounded due to high relapse rates for both men and women, lack of study of gender differences among treatment dropouts, and failure to study those lost to follow-up.[152] Each of these problems makes it difficult to discern just what aspects of treatment promote recovery and whether there are gender-related differences in the recovery process.[153] In spite of the differences in the drinking and drug abuse problems of men and women that have been identified, the research to date indicates that their recovery patterns are quite similar. De-Soto, O'Donnell, and DeSoto, for example, found that the course of recovery as measured by severity of psychological symptoms, work history, and probability of relapse was essentially the same for men and women.[154] The combined relapse rates for men and women were highest in the first six months of abstinence (46 percent). Between six months and two years, the percentage of relapse dropped to 24 percent. Relapse rates for both men and women tended to flatten to almost zero after the first five years of abstinence.

Treatment Matching

Do similarities in patterns of relapse and recovery for men and women imply that the treatments offered to them should be the same, or could treatment outcomes be improved by matching clients to treatment based on gender? Given that Anglin and his colleagues found that female addicts were more motivated for treatment than men, they were surprised to find that women did not surpass men in positive treatment outcomes.[155] Like many others, they believe that women's outcomes might be better if treatment addressed their specific needs. Few studies have examined topics such as whether various treatment modalities (individual, family, or group) or various theoretical perspectives (psychodynamic, behavioral, etc.) are superior for women, whether women do better in women's only or coed treatment programs, or whether having a male or female therapist makes a difference.[156] Annis characterizes the literature on these subjects as "dominated by rhetoric and speculation" as well as by "myth" and "cliches",[157] and Braiker describes the research as being "riddled with methodological problems, yielding equivocal and frequently contradictory results."[158] There is a critical need for more systematic studies designed to evaluate the response of female and male substance abusers to various types of treatment.

In one of the few research studies designed to address the question of whether co-ed treatment is better than all women's treatment, Swedish researchers Dalhgren and Willander suggest that an all-women's treatment approach offers more positive results.[159] Their two-year follow-up study involved two hundred alcohol-dependent women who were randomly assigned to either a specialized female outpatient unit or a mixed male and female unit. Women treated in the specialized female unit had significantly better social adjustment and consumed less alcohol following treatment. Sixty-seven percent of the female unit clients showed improvement after the first year and 59 percent after the second year, compared with 45 percent and 48 percent of the controls, respectively.

Dalhgren and Willander report that the unique treatment components of the all-women's unit included assistance for mothers from a child psychiatrist, an individualized treatment program for each client, relatives involvement in the treatment, and a focus on women's problems including the women's exchange of experiences with each other. These components are consistent with the clinical literature that indicates that factors such as attention to children's needs and a safe environment in which to discuss gender issues are important considerations in women's chemical dependency treatment. Unfortunately, many studies fail to describe adequately the treatment rendered to clients, making it difficult to replicate treatments.

It is also important to remember that women are not just like "peas in a pod." There is some evidence to indicate that treatment strategies should reflect the varying characteristics of women such as ethnic differences. The results of at least one study show that black and white women in alcoholism treatment differed on several dimensions that may have important implications for treatment.[160] Black women had more limited financial resources and less insurance coverage, and were significantly younger. Ethnic differences that may require differential treatment methods are explored further in Chapter 11.

Evidence also indicates that women of different generations may need different types of treatment that reflect their life experiences. The findings of Harrison and Belille, based on a sample of 1,776 adult women in chemical dependency treatment, show substantial differences between women who grew up in the 1940s and 1950s and those born later.[161] These differences were apparent with respect to substance abuse patterns, education and employment patterns, familial alcohol and other drug abuse, familial violence, and psychosocial dysfunction. Similar to prevalence studies done by NIDA, younger women were four to six times more likely to report marijuana, hallucinogen, and cocaine or other stimulant use, while the older women were twice as likely to report only alcohol use. Younger women were more likely to use in the company of others; older women tended to report solitary use. Older women were more often homemakers, and younger women more often reported poorer sociovocational functioning, including higher unemployment. Younger women were more likely to be high school dropouts and to have greater dependence on welfare. They also reported more drug use and more violence in their family of origin and in their present family constellation. The authors think that rather than age or maturational level, these differences reflect cohort or societal changes. This seems reasonable given that women who became teenagers in the late 1960s and in the 1970s were more likely to have been exposed to drug use other than alcohol and are more likely to come from nonintact families. These findings raise concerns that patterns of poly-drug use and more impaired psychosocial functioning among today's young women may present even greater challenges in treatment and recovery.

Self-Help Groups

Like the number of women seeking assistance from treatment programs, the number attending self-help programs is also increasing. Women used to be as rare in AA as they were in treatment programs, particularly public programs, but this has changed. AA membership among women has risen consistently. In 1989, women comprised an estimated 35 percent of members compared with 30 percent in 1983 and 22 percent in 1968.[162] The participation of women in AA is reflected in the growth of all-women's AA groups (men are also holding meetings of their own); women are featured in many more of the recovery stories in the Big Book of Alcoholics Anonymous; women are routinely invited as guest speakers at local meetings and at state and national AA conventions; and at some of the thousands of meetings held daily around the world, women are starting the "Lord's Prayer" with "Our Father and Mother."

The twelve steps of Alcoholics Anonymous have helped many men and women recover, but even with the emergence of AA groups for women only, not everyone has been satisfied with the program's gender sensitivity. Kasl claims that since "the steps were formulated by a white, middle-class male in the 1930s; not surprisingly, they work to break down an overinflated ego, and put reliance on an all-powerful male God."[163] She believes that most women need just the opposite—to strengthen their sense of self and affirm their own inner wisdom. Earlier, Jean Kirkpatrick expressed similar sentiments about women's identity. In 1975 she introduced a self-help program called Women for Sobriety (WFS).[164] While Kirkpatrick says that AA may be more effective in early sobriety, "if you can get 90 meetings in 90 days,"[165] WFS can be used alone or as a complement to AA or other programs.[166] Currently there are more than three hundred and fifty WFS groups.[167]

Rather than the twelve steps of AA (see Chapter 6), WFS uses Thirteen Statements of Acceptance. For example, "I am a competent woman and have much to give life."[168] At the heart of WFS is its "New Life Program." Kaskutas identifies four major themes of WFS: no drinking, positive thinking, believing one is competent, and growing spiritually and emotionally.[169] WFS meetings are led by certified moderators. During meetings, members focus on what happened to them during the previous week and on current topics posed for discussion. But unlike AA, members are discouraged from telling the stories of their drinking and from introducing themselves as alcoholics or addicts, because these are considered examples of negative rather than positive thinking. Kaskutas describes the WFS program as far less directive than AA. For example, members are not told to "keep coming back," to get a sponsor, or to work the steps. She also says the program is highly accepting with much more "cross-talk" than in AA. Kaskutas maintains that:

Sobriety is inside the mind for the WFS members; thus, their *decision* to affirm sobriety. *Sobriety is outside the self* for AA members; thus their *reliance* on meetings, on 12th-step activities, and on a power greater than themselves. In AA, members admit to a loss of control (surrender); in WFS, members strive to regain control (take charge).[170]

Others, of course, take exception to this description of AA. While the philosophies of AA and WFS apparently differ, some women take what they need from each program and make good use of both.

Kirkpatrick emphasizes proper nutrition for WFS members and advises limiting coffee intake, smoking, and candy.[171] Although not as prevalent as AA groups, Women for Sobriety and other self-help groups are options for women seeking recovery. Kasl has also offered an alternative set of steps to AA that she says emphasize "empowerment."[172] An example is: "We became willing to let go of our shame, guilt, and other behavior that prevents us from taking control of our lives and loving ourselves."

MURKY METHODOLOGICAL WATERS

Our review of the literature on women with alcohol and other drug problems leaves important questions unanswered. Are women at greater or lesser risk for substance abuse and its consequences than men? Can we expect rates of reported problems to converge? Is the etiology of chemical abuse and dependence in women different from that for men?

Is the course of treatment and recovery the same? Would women benefit from different treatment methods than men? There are several explanations for why there is inadequate research on these and other questions.

The Feminist Critique

Early feminist criticisms of social science research addressed two areas that are also particularly vulnerable in substance abuse studies: (1) the lack of research on women and (2) the inaccurate research "findings" that were produced. Speculation about men's drinking and findings from studies using only male subjects were often generalized to women or dubious conclusions were drawn about women based on research interest in men. It is likely that even the research community (largely composed of male researchers), dedicated to "objectivity," has been affected by the "status insularity" of women substance abusers previously described in this chapter. No doubt, this has contributed to an underrepresentation of women in the chemical dependency research literature. A brief history of some of the literature illustrates this point.[173]

In 1960, McCord and McCord attempted to explain the cause of alcoholism.[174] At the risk of oversimplifying their research, they used dependency theory to suggest that alcoholism develops in men as a result of their inability to express or fulfill dependency needs in our society. Women were not included in their study, but it was suggested that women were protected from excessive drinking because of society's acceptance of their dependence. The McCords also suggested that "role confusion" rather than "dependency conflict" might better explain women's alcoholism and that due to women's changing role in society, alcoholism rates among women would likely increase (as they have). In 1972 McClelland and his colleague in *The Drinking Man* attributed part of the variance in men's drinking to their need to increase feelings of power.[175] As the study's title implies, women were not included, and the authors suggested that the power theory may

not be applicable to them. Others commented that women's lower rates of alcoholism might be partially explained by their lack of interest in power. In the 1970s, Wilsnack explored the possibility that problems with sex role identification may help to explain alcoholism in women.[176] She attempted to test dependency, power, and sex role identification theories. Her findings did not support the power or dependency explanations, but she did find that drinking resulted in women feeling more feminine.

Meanwhile, the women's and feminist movements have changed many ideas about masculine and feminine characteristics and the appropriate behaviors of men and women. Scida and Vanicelli, for example, proposed a broader sex conflict explanation of women's drinking that was not limited to the need to enhance feelings of femininity.[177] Wilsnack[178] wrote that female alcoholics had not adequately integrated masculine and feminine characteristics, and Colman[179] also found that women who were problem drinkers or at risk for such problems lack flexibility in being both assertive and expressive. Integrating these ideas, Henderson and Boyd suggest a model of addiction in which:

Substance use is a choice that people often make in an attempt to integrate the polarities represented by the metaphors of masculine/feminine. For instance, individuals often describe their drug experience as supplying them with the qualities they believe they lack. These may be characteristics that are stereotypically labeled masculine or feminine such as feelings of warmth, sensuality, power, dependence, affiliation, peace, etc.[180]

Henderson and Boyd pose an interesting hypothesis, and additional studies in this area may improve our understanding of the causes of substance abuse in men and women.

While substance abuse and dependency researchers are taking greater care to describe the gender composition of participants in their studies, the proportion of female participants in alcohol and drug abuse and dependence research remains low. Emrick's 1974 analysis of 271 treatment evaluation studies revealed that only 4 (1.5 percent) solely involved women.[181] Vannicelli's 1984 review of 259 studies (which picks up after Emrick's review) found only 6 studies (2.3 percent) focused solely on women. In many cases, female and male subjects have been combined in data analyses as if this would make no difference. Even after a congressional mandate in the 1970s for increased attention to women's alcoholism problems, only 8 percent of research subjects in treatment outcome studies from 1972 to 1980 were women.[182]

Alcohol, Drugs, and Measurement

Lack of agreement on what constitutes alcoholism and other drug problems and lack of standard measures for assessing these problems continues to plague the substance abuse literature on both men and women. The issue of whether alcohol and drug problems should be measured differently in men and women has received particularly little attention. Although most screening measures were developed using primarily male subjects, there are now some screening instruments for women.[183]

While polydrug abuse is thought to be quite common among alcoholics and addicts, many studies investigate alcohol or other drug use, but not both. The establishment of two separate federal agencies in the 1970s, the National Institute on Alcohol Abuse and Alcoholism (NIAAA) and the National Institute on Drug Abuse (NIDA), has contributed to a pattern of funding studies on alcohol *or* on other drugs. This may obscure the patterns of substance use, abuse, and dependence in men and women. Corrigan's review of the epidemiological and survey evidence suggests that the higher rates of abuse of prescription and over-the-counter drugs by females needs to be considered in determining the dynamics of substance abuse among this group.[184]

In describing the differences between male and female substance abusers, little effort has been made to determine whether the problems they face are due to gender, substance abuse, or an interaction between the two. Davis tried to clarify differences between male and female vocational rehabilitation clients who showed evidence of substance abuse problems by comparing them with clients who did not report substance abuse.[185] She found that the vast majority of the problems these individuals reported were associated with gender *or* substance abuse, but not an interaction between the two. Women, regardless of whether or not they were substance abusers, felt more bothered by family problems, had more current medical problems, and had made more suicide attempts. Men did not score higher than women on any problem area. The substance abusers, regardless of their gender, had more current family problems, anxiety, and problems controlling violence. There was only one problem for which the interaction of substance abuse and gender was associated with more problems: women substance abusers had more psychiatric hospitalizations. According to these findings, women substance abusers are the more seriously disadvantaged group because they share the problems of both the women in the study and the substance abusers in the study.

As noted earlier, methodological problems are also pervasive in studies of the substance abuse treatment process and of treatment outcomes. In attempts to find better ways for investigating these phenomena, those concerned about psychoactive drug problems in women hope that researchers will be mindful of possible gender differences. For example, Leukefeld and Tims state that a basic need in the area of relapse research is "descriptive studies to pinpoint who relapses: These studies would provide a clearer understanding of sex, age, and drug types as these variables impact on relapse."[186]

Out of Sight, Out of Mind

Part of the unequal treatment of women in the substance abuse literature exists as a result of the inequality of men and women in treatment programs. Men have long outnumbered women in treatment programs, especially public and community-based, not-for-profit programs. A great deal of valuable research has been conducted on substance abusers treated at Veterans Administration hospitals and other public facilities where, to date, few patients have been women. The proportion of women treated in private programs is higher, but these programs have rarely been involved in the large-scale research supported by NIAAA and NIDA. Studies of both tiers (public and private) of the chemical dependency treatment system are needed, because the sociodemographic characteristics of clients served in these programs, and perhaps other treatment factors, differ.

In considering the research that has been done on male alcoholics, Braiker cautions against "throwing the baby out with the bathwater—simply because the baby is a boy rather than girl."[187] However, the field is far from making a determination about the extent to which gender should be considered in prevention and treatment services. Consideration of gender in selecting research samples and reporting results is improving according to some authors,[188] but others are not as optimistic. They continue to cite neglect from male researchers and the continued possibility of gender bias in the bulk of the research literature.[189]

SUSAN'S STORY REVISITED

Methodological problems of research studies and the lack of empirical evidence supporting all-women's treatment programs have sustained the controversy on whether or not there are real differences between male and female substance abusers. The argument continues to be made that "an alcoholic is an alcoholic is an alcoholic." However, this chapter describes many differences in the lives of substance-abusing women that a reasonable person would expect to impact recovery. Susan's story illustrates some of these differences:[190]

- The reluctance of women to identify their alcohol or other drug problems due to the social stigma involved and instead to seek help for mental, health, emotional, or family problems

- The propensity of health care professionals and the criminal justice system to fail to detect and address alcohol and other drug problems in women
- The higher incidence of substance abuse and psychiatric disorders in the families of origin of female alcoholics
- The alarming estimates of incest, child sexual abuse, and sexual assault in the histories of female substance abusers
- The influence of having a male partner who is an alcoholic or drug addict
- The greater child care responsibilities of women and the lack of child care services that would allow women to seek treatment
- The social isolation of chemically dependent women and the opposition of family and friends to women's entering treatment
- The higher rate of affective disorders in women
- The high rate of marital instability
- The lack of financial resources

Fortunately for Susan, she did not experience some of the physiological problems such as liver disease or the gynecological problems for which alcoholic women also have a greater propensity.

WHERE DO WE GO FROM HERE?

Identification

The telescoping effect of alcohol and other drug use among women makes it critical that their chemical abuse problems be recognized early. Unfortunately, many women effectively hide their problems, and, even when their work performance is poor[191] or when they have serious health problems,[192] women are less likely than men to be confronted with their substance abuse. Duckert recommends routine screening for substance abuse during a women's regular gynecological and prenatal care,[193] and Turnbull suggests further training of medical, mental health, and social service professionals so they can recognize the signs of substance abuse in women.[194] Perhaps a most important step in breaking the chain of shame and denial that surrounds women's substance abuse is the education of their family, friends, and coworkers (i.e., the American public).

Treatment

A major report by the Institute of Medicine recommends attention to several factors in treatment programs that may improve women's chances of recovery. These include:

- Offering child care options
- Assessment and treatment of psychiatric and medical disorders
- Assertiveness and other skills training and methods of building self-esteem
- Making staff available to educate and treat family and friends and to encourage their support
- Teaching coping strategies for dealing with stress[195]

Other clinicians have advocated all-women's groups in all phases of the recovery process, particularly in dealing with problems related to sexual abuse.[196] Although the effectiveness of all-women's programs has yet to be validated empirically in the United States, there is a compelling reason for treating women separately: the overwhelming majority of sexual abuse survivors are women and most perpetrators are male.[197] In addition, women in mixed groups tend to be supportive of the male members and neglect their own issues. For example, the results of a study by Aries suggested that in mixed groups, the women had minimal interactions with female group members and allowed men to dominate the discussions.[198] The need for long-term aftercare and the development of a sober support network is also important to women who often have less social support and may be more isolated than men.[199]

The Big Picture

Of prime importance is the continuing need to challenge the gaps in knowledge and communications among researchers, policy-makers, service providers, and the general public.[200] During the 1970s, NIAAA sponsored an initiative to increase the responsiveness of treatment programs to women. A number of programs were funded across the country to develop services especially for women. Emphasis was more on increasing services than on rigorous process and outcome evaluations. NIAAA was also concerned that women were underrepresented as referrals to employee assistance programs (EAPs). In the 1980s it funded several research projects to increase the number of women with substance abuse problems assisted through EAPs. These studies identified little in the way of especially promising techniques to assist women at work, although many interventions were tried, including special supervisory training, lunch-time education, and information included with paychecks.[201]

In the 1990s, the federal government is making mental and physical disorders in women a service and research priority.[202] Current NIAAA efforts include gender-specific research in a major, multisite study on matching clients to treatments for alcoholism, a ten-year follow-up study of problem drinking in women, increased research on maternal and fetal effects of alcohol, and a National Longitudinal Alcohol Epidemiological Survey which will provide information on arrests and barriers to treatment services, particularly among women. A similar research agenda is in place at NIDA that includes studies of drug abuse effects on reproduction, of women in clinical research on the pharmacotherapy of cocaine abuse, and of AIDS outreach programs targeting specific subgroups of women. In addition, the Office for Women's Services was established in 1992 under the new Substance Abuse and Mental Health Services Administration (SAMHSA). The office is concerned with mental health and substance abuse services for women, including mothers who are substance abusers and women from various cultural backgrounds. It will collect data on mental health and substance abuse problems among women and identify service gaps and recommend policy to promote better treatment of women.[203]

SUMMARY

The literature indicates a number of differences in substance problems among men and women. Men use alcohol and drugs more than women, and they have higher rates of alcohol and drug problems than women, although evidence indicates that these gender gaps have narrowed. Women metabolize alcohol and drugs differently than men, and they are especially susceptible to a number of alcohol-related physical problems as a result of excessive alcohol use. Women with substance abuse problems seem to lack some of the social supports that men have, and women often become involved with alcohol and other drugs as a result of involvement with a male partner who is an alcoholic or addict. Health, mental health, and criminal justice systems have been more reluctant to address alcohol and drug problems in women than men. Historically women substance abusers have been described as psychologically more impaired than male substance abusers, but whether this is true is questionable given that the patterns of relapse and recovery are similar for men and women with alcohol and drug problems.

The jury is still out on many other questions regarding gender and substance abuse such as whether alcohol and drug problems among men and women will converge and whether treatment matching by gender can substantially improve treatment outcomes. Greater attention to research with alcohol- and drug-abusing women may well lead to answers to these questions, and the federal government now seems more committed to addressing these issues. In the meantime, chemical dependency treatment providers must continue to reach out to women in all sociodemographic categories who are affected by alcohol and drug problems to assure that they receive the services that are currently available. Until definitive studies are completed, the authors join other clinicians and researchers in recommending that practical steps be taken to attend to some of the issues that can be reasonably expected to impact the recovery process of women.

ENDNOTES

1. See, for example, Jeanne C. Marsh, Mary Ellen Colten, and M. Belinda Tucker, "Women's Use of Drugs and Alcohol: New Perspectives" *Journal of Social Issues,* Vol. 38, No. 2 (1982) pp. 1–8; Jill Doner Kagle, "Women Who Drink: Changing Images, Changing Realities," *Journal of Social Work Education,* Vol. 23, No. 3 (1987), pp. 21–28.

2. See National Institute on Alcohol Abuse and Alcoholism (NIAAA), *Sixth Special Report to the United States Congress on Alcohol and Health* (Rockville, MD: The Institute, January 1987), p. 3; also see Henry Malin, Ronald Wilson, Gerald Williams, and Sherrie Aitken, "1983 Alcohol/Health Practices Supplement," *Alcohol Health & Research World* (Winter 1985/86), pp. 48–52.

3. See, for example, Don Cahalan and Ira H. Cisin, "American Drinking Practices: Summary of Findings from a National Probability Sample," *Journal of Studies on Alcohol,* Vol. 29 (1968), pp. 130–151.

4. See, for example, NIAAA, *Sixth Special Report to the United States Congress on Alcohol and Health,* p. 3.

5. Edith S. Gomberg, "The Female Alcoholic," in Ralph E. Tarter and A. Arthur Sugerman, *Alcoholism: Interdisciplinary Approaches to an Enduring Problem* (Reading, MA: Addison-Wesley, 1976), pp. 605–607.

6. See "Patterns in Mental and Addictive Disorders," *ADAMHA News Supplement* (July–August 1991), p. 2.

7. See Institute of Medicine, *Broadening the Base of Treatment for Alcohol Problems* (Washington, DC: National Academy Press, 1990), p. 356.

8. Ibid.

9. John E. Helzer, Glorisa J. Canino, Eng-Kung Yeh, Roger C. Bland, Chung Kyoon Lee, Hai-Gwo Hwu, and Stephen Newman, "Alcoholism—North America and Asia," *Archives of General Psychiatry,* Vol. 47 (April 1990), pp. 313–319.

10. National Institute on Drug Abuse (NIDA), *National Household Survey on Drug Abuse: Main Findings 1990,* DHHS Pub. No. (ADM) 91-1788 (Rockville MD: U.S. Department of Health and Human Services, 1991).

11. Helen E. Ross, "Alcohol and Drug Abuse in Treated Alcoholics: A Comparison of Men and Women," *Alcoholism: Clinical and Experimental Research,* Vol. 13, No. 6 (November–December 1989), pp. 810–816.

12. Lee N. Robins, John E. Helzer, Thomas R. Przybeck, and Darrell A. Regier, "Alcohol Disorders in the Community: A Report from the Epidemiologic Catchment Area," in Robert M. Rose and James E. Barrett (eds.) *Alcoholism: Origins and Outcome* (New York: Raven Press, 1988), pp. 15–29.

13. Richard W. Wilsnack, Sharon C. Wilsnack, and Albert D. Klassen, "Women's Drinking and Drinking Problems: Patterns from a 1981 National Survey," *American Journal of Public Health*, Vol. 74 (1984), pp. 1231–1238, and Sharon C. Wilsnack, Richard W. Wilsnack, and Albert D. Klassen, "Drinking and Drinking Problems Among Women in a U.S. National Survey," *Alcohol Health & Research World*, Vol. 9, No. 2 (1985), pp. 3–13.

14. Kaye Middleton Fillmore, "When Angels Fall: Women's Drinking as Cultural Preoccupation and as Reality," in Sharon C. Wilsnack and Linda J. Beckman (eds.), *Alcohol Problems in Women: Antecedents, Consequences, and Intervention* (New York: Guilford Press, 1984), pp. 7–36, and Michael E. Hilton, "Trends in U.S. Drinking Patterns: Further Evidence from the Past 20 Years," *British Journal of Addiction*, Vol. 83 (1988), pp. 269–278.

15. Cited in Susan S. Lang, "When Women Drink," *Parade Magazine*, January 20, 1991, p. 18.

16. Edith S. Lisansky Gomberg, "Historical and Political Perspective: Women and Drug Use," *Journal of Social Issues*, Vol. 38, No. 2 (1982), pp. 9–23.

17. See Patricia G. Erickson and Valerie A. Watson, "Women, Illicit Drugs, and Crime," in Lynn T. Kozlowski et al. (eds.), *Research Advances in Alcohol and Drug Problems*, Volume 10 (New York: Plenum Press, 1990), pp. 251–272; this analysis refers primarily to L. D. Johnston, P. M. O'Malley, and J. G. Bachman, *National Trends in Drug Use and Related Factors Among American High School Students and Young Adults, 1975–1986* (Rockville, MD: National Institute on Drug Abuse, 1987).

18. See, for example, Jean Kirkpatrick, *Turnabout: Help for a New Life* (Garden City, NY: Doubleday, 1978), p. 162.

19. See, for example, reviews of this literature by Donald W. Goodwin, "Is Alcoholism Hereditary? A Review and Critique," *Archives of General Psychiatry*, Vol. 25 (1971), pp. 545–549, and Nancy S. Cotton, "The Familial Incidence of Alcoholism: A Review," *Journal of Studies on Alcohol*, Vol. 40, No. 1 (1979), pp. 89–116.

20. C. Robert Cloninger, Michael Bohman, and Sören Sigvardsson, "Inheritance of Alcohol Abuse," *Archives of General Psychiatry*, Vol. 38 (August 1981), pp. 861–868; C. Robert Cloninger, "Genetic and Environmental Factors in the Development of Alcoholism," *Journal of Psychiatric Treatment and Evaluation*, Vol. 5 (1983), pp. 487–496; Michael Bohman, C. Robert Cloninger, Anne-Liis von Knorring, and Sören Sigvardsson, "An Adoption Study of Somatoform Disorders," *Archives of General Psychiatry*, Vol. 41 (September 1984) pp. 872–878; and Michael Bohman, Sören Sigvardsson, and C. Robert Cloninger, "Maternal Inheritance of Alcohol Abuse," *Archives of General Psychiatry*, Vol. 38 (1981), pp. 965–969. Also see NIAAA, *Sixth Special Report to the U.S. Congress*, Chapter II, for a review of this literature.

21. Sheila B. Gilligan, Theodore Reich, and C. Robert Cloninger, "Alcohol-related Symptoms in Heterogeneous Families of Hospitalized Alcoholics," *Alcoholism: Clinical and Experimental Research*, Vol. 12, No. 5 (1988), pp. 671–678.

22. Also see Kenneth S. Kendler, Andrew C. Heath, Michael C. Neale, Ronald C. Kessler, Lindon J. Eaves, "A Population-Based Twin Study of Alcoholism in Women," *Journal of the American Medical Association*, Vol. 268, No. 14 (1992) pp. 1877–1882.

23. Susan Wagner Glenn and Oscar A. Parsons, "Alcohol Abuse and Familial Alcoholism: Psychosocial Correlates in Men and Women," *Journal of Studies on Alcohol*, Vol. 50, No. 2 (1989), p. 123.

24. Joan Curlee, "A Comparison of Male and Female Patients at an Alcoholism Treatment Center," *The Journal of Psychology*, Vol. 74 (1970), pp. 239–247.

25. Edith Gomberg, "Risk Factors Related to Alcohol Problems Among Women: Proneness and Vulnerability," in National Institute on Alcohol Abuse and Alcoholism, *Research Monograph No. 1, Alcoholism and Alcohol Abuse Among Women: Research Issues*, DHEW Pub. No. (ADM) 80-835 (Rockville, MD: U.S. Department of Health, Education, and Welfare, 1980), pp. 83–106; also see Dorothy L. Hurley, "Women, Alcohol and Incest: An Analytical Review," *Journal of Studies on Alcohol*, Vol. 52, No. 3 (1991), pp. 253–268.

26. Ben Morgan Jones and Marilyn K. Jones, "Alcohol Effects in Women During the Menstrual Cycle," *Annals of the New York Academy of Sciences*, Vol. 273 (1976), pp. 576–587.

27. Ben Morgan Jones and Marilyn K. Jones, "Women and Alcohol: Intoxication, Metabolism and the Menstrual Cycle," in Milton Greenblatt and Marc A. Schuckit (eds.), *Alcoholism Problems in Women and Children* (New York: Grune & Stratton, 1976), pp. 103–136.

28. Also see James H. Winchester, "The Special Problems of Women Alcoholics," *The Reader's Digest* (March 1978), reprint.

29. William A. McKim, *Drugs and Behavior: An Introduction to Behavioral Pharmacology*, 2nd ed. (Englewood Cliffs, NJ: Prentice-Hall, 1991), p. 92.

30. Steven J. Wolin, "Introduction: The Psychosocial Consequences," in NIAAA, *Alcoholism and Alcohol Abuse Among Women*, pp. 63–72; and Camberwell Council on Alcoholism, *Women and Alcohol* (London: Tavistock Publications, 1980).

31. Paul M. Roman, *Women and Alcohol Use: A Review of the Research Literature* (Rockville, MD: U.S. Department of Health and Human Services, Public Health Service/Alcohol, Drug Abuse, and Mental Health Administration, 1988).

32. Shirley Y Hill, "Introduction: The Biological Consequences," in NIAAA, *Alcoholism and Alcohol Abuse Among Women,* p. 50; Shirley Y. Hill, "Biological Consequences of Alcoholism and Alcohol-Related Problems Among Women," in National Institute on Alcohol Abuse and Alcoholism, *Alcohol and Health Monograph 4, Special Population Issues,* DHHS Pub. No. (ADM) 82-1193 (Rockville, MD: U.S. Department of Health and Human Services, 1982), p. 53; also see Institute on Medicine, *Broadening the Base of Treatment for Alcohol Problems* (Washington, DC: National Academy Press, 1990).

33. Hill, "Biological Consequences of Alcoholism and Alcohol-Related Problems Among Women," pp. 44–48.

34. This paragraph relies on ibid.

35. Eileen M. Corrigan, "Gender Differences in Alcohol and Other Drug Use," *Addictive Behaviors,* Vol. 10 (1985), p. 315.

36. See Drug Abuse Warning Network, *Project DAWN Annual Report—1979; 1980* (Rockville, MD: National Institute on Drug Abuse, 1979; 1980) cited in ibid.

37. See Hill, "Biological Consequences of Alcoholism" for a discussion.

38. William H. Masters, Virginia E. Johnson, and Robert C. Kolodny, *Masters and Johnson on Sex and Human Loving* (Boston: Little, Brown, 1986), p. 521.

39. William Shakespeare, *The Tragedy of Macbeth* (New York: Washington Square Press, 1959), p. 29, Act 2, scene 3, line 34.

40. Masters, Johnson, and Kolodny, *Masters and Johnson on Sex and Human Loving,* p. 519, Helen Singer Kaplan, *Disorders of Sexual Desire* (New York: Simon & Schuster, 1979), p. 203.

41. M. J. Sholty, *Female Sexual Experience and Satisfaction as Related to Alcohol Consumption* (Baltimore: University of Maryland, Alcohol and Drug Abuse Program, 1979), cited in Roman, *Women and Alcohol Use: A Review of the Research Literature.*

42. Sharon C. Wilsnack, "Alcohol Abuse and Alcoholism in Women," in E. Mansell Pattison and Edward Kaufman (eds.), *Encyclopedia Handbook of Alcoholism* (New York: Gardner Press, 1982), p. 724.

43. Mildred Apter-Marsh, "The Sexual Behavior of Alcoholic Women While Drinking and During Sobriety," *Alcoholism Treatment Quarterly,* Vol. 1, No. 3 (1984), pp.

35–48; also see Mark S. Gold, "Alcohol, Drugs, and Sexual Dysfunction," *Alcoholism and Addiction* (December 1988), p. 13.

44. Kaplan, *Disorders of Sexual Desire,* p. 203.

45. Masters, Johnson and Kolodny, *Masters and Johnson on Sex and Human Loving,* pp. 521–522; also see Kaplan, *Disorders of Sexual Desire,* p. 204.

46. Ibid.

47. Masters, Johnson, and Kolodny, *Masters and Johnson on Sex and Human Loving,* p. 522; also see Mark S. Gold, "Sexual Dysfunction Challenges Today's Addiction Clinicians," *Alcoholism and Addiction* (July–August 1987), p. 11.

48. Ibid.; also see Mark S. Gold, "Alcohol, Drugs and Sexual Dysfunction."

49. Kaplan, *Disorders of Sexual Desire,* p. 203.

50. Ronald C. Bloodworth, "Medical Problems Associated with Marijuana Abuse," *Psychiatric Medicine,* Vol. 3, No. 3 (1987), pp. 173–184.

51. Albert D. Klassen and Sharon C. Wilsnack, "Sexual Experience and Drinking Among Women in a U.S. National Survey," *Archives of Sexual Behavior,* Vol. 15, No. 5 (1986), pp. 363–392; also see Paul M. Roman, "Biological Features of Women's Alcohol Use: A Review," *Public Health Reports,* Vol. 103, No. 6 (November–December 1988), pp. 628–637.

52. Sharon C. Wilsnack, "Drinking, Sexuality, and Sexual Dysfunction in Women," in Sharon C. Wilsnack and Linda J. Beckman (eds.), *Alcohol Problems in Women* (New York: Guilford Press, 1984), Chapter 7, pp. 189–227.

53. Klassen and Wilsnack, "Sexual Experience and Drinking Among Women in a U.S. National Survey."

54. Valerie Pinhas, "Sex Guilt and Sexual Control in Women Alcoholics in Early Sobriety," *Sexuality and Disability* (Winter 1980), pp. 256–272.

55. Klassen and Wilsnack, "Sexual Experience and Drinking Among Women in a U.S. National Survey."

56. Wilsnack, "Alcohol Abuse and Alcoholism in Women"; Edith S. Gomberg, "The Female Alcoholic"; and Roman, "Biological Features of Women's Alcohol Use: A Review."

57. See Bloodworth, "Medical Problems Associated with Marijuana Abuse."

58. *ADAMHA News Supplement* (July–August 1991), p. 3.

59. Nancy K. Mello, "Drug Use Patterns and Premenstrual Dysphoria," in Barbara A. Ray and Monique C. Braude, *Women and Drugs: A New Era for Research, NIDA Research Monograph 65* (Rockville, MD: National Institute on Drug Abuse, 1986), p. 44.

60. Gomberg, "The Female Alcoholic"; Marc A. Schuckit and Jane Duby, "Alcoholism in Women," in Benjamin Kissin and Henri Begleiter (eds.), *The Biology of Alcoholism*, Volume 6, *The Pathogensis of Alcoholism, Psychosocial Factors* (New York: Plenum Press, 1983), pp. 215–241; Roman, *Women and Alcohol Use: A Review of the Research Literature;* Wilsnack, "Alcohol Abuse and Alcoholism in Women"; and Mello, "Drug Use Patterns and Premenstural Dysphoria."

61. Kenneth L. Jones and David W. Smith, "Recognition of the Fetal Alcohol Syndrome in Early Infancy," *The Lancet* Vol. II, No. 7836 (November 3, 1973), pp. 999–1001, and Kenneth L. Jones, David W. Smith, Christy N. Ulleland, and Ann P. Streissguth, "Pattern of Malformation in Offspring of Chronic Alcoholic Mothers," *The Lancet* Vol. I, No. 7815 (June 9, 1973), pp. 1267–1271.

62. *ADAMHA News*, Vol. 17, No. 5 (September–October 1991), p. 9.

63. Ann Pytkowicz Streissguth, Sterling Keith Clarren, and Kenneth Lyons Jones, "Natural History of the Fetal Alcohol Syndrome: A 10-Year Follow-Up of Eleven Patients," *The Lancet* Vol. II, No. 8446 (July 13, 1985), pp. 85–91.

64. National Institute on Alcohol Abuse and Alcoholism (NIAAA), "Fetal Alcohol Syndrome and Other Effects of Alcohol on Pregnancy Outcome," *Seventh Special Report to the U.S. Congress on Alcohol and Health* (Rockville, MD: Department of Health and Human Services, January 1990), Chapter VI.

65. Ibid.

66. Sterling K. Clarren, Douglas M. Bowden, and Susan J. Astley, "Pregnancy Outcomes After Weekly Oral Administration of Ethanol During Gestation in the Pig-Tailed Macaque (Macaca nemestrina)," *Teratology*, Vol. 35 (1987), pp. 345–354.

67. Ernest L. Abel, *Fetal Alcohol Syndrome and Fetal Alcohol Effects* (New York: Plenum Press, 1984), see Chapter 6.

68. Clarren et al., "Pregnancy Outcomes After Weekly Oral Administration of Ethanol," p. 345.

69. NIAAA, *Seventh Special Report to the U.S. Congress on Alcohol and Health.*

70. Marian Sandmaier, *Alcohol and Your Unborn Baby*, a pamphlet distributed by The Texas Commission on Alcoholism, Austin, TX, no date.

71. NIAAA, *Sixth Special Report to the U.S. Congress on Alcohol and Health;* NIAAA, *Seventh Special Report to the U.S. Congress on Alcohol and Health;* and Robert J. Sokol, Joel Ager, Susan Martier, Sara Debanne, Claire Ernhart, Jan Kuzma, and Sheldon I. Miller, "Significant Determinants of Susceptibility to Alcohol Terato-

genicity," *Annals of the New York Academy of Sciences*, Vol. 477 (1986), pp. 87–102.

72. Sokol et al., "Significant Determinants of Susceptibility."

73. Philip A. May, Karen J. Hymbaugh, John M. Aase, and Jonathan M. Samet, "Epidemiology of Fetal Alcohol Syndrome Among American Indians of the Southwest," *Social Biology*, Vol. 30, No. 4 (1983), pp. 374–387.

74. Ibid.

75. *ADAMHA News*, Vol. 17, No. 5 (September–October 1991), p. 1.

76. Ira Chasnoff, "Drug Use and Women: Establishing a Standard of Care," in D. Hutchings (ed.), *Parental Abuse of Licit and Illicit Drugs* (New York: New York Academy of Sciences, 1989), pp. 208–210; see also Nora S. Gustavsson, "Pregnant Chemically Dependent Women: The New Criminals," *Affilia*, Vol. 6, No. 2 (Summer 1991), pp. 61–73.

77. "Prenatal Substance Abuse," *New View* (Newsletter of the Texas Commission on Alcohol and Drug Abuse), Vol. 1, No. 5 (May 1991), p. 1.

78. Gustavsson, "Pregnant Chemically Dependent Women: The New Criminals."

79. *ADAMHA News*, Vol. 17, No. 5 (September–October 1991), p. 1.

80. Gustavsson, "Pregnant Chemically Dependent Women: The New Criminals."

81. *ADAMHA News*, Vol. 17, No. 5, p. 2.

82. Gustavsson, "Pregnant Chemically Dependent Women: The New Criminals," p. 61.

83. See, for example, Andrea Sachs, "Here Come the Pregnancy Police," *Time*, May 22, 1989, pp. 104–105.

84. Wendy Jameson and Neal Halfon, "Treatment Programs for Drug-Dependent Women and Their Children," *Youth Law News* (Special Issue 1990), pp. 20–21.

85. *ADAMHA News*, Vol. 17, No. 5, pp. 1–2.

86. See Joan Curlee, "A Comparison of Male and Female Patients at an Alcoholism Treatment Center," *Journal of Psychology*, Vol. 74 (1970), pp. 239–247; Genevieve Knupfer, "Problems Associated with Drunkenness in Women: Some Research Issues," in NIAAA, *Alcohol and Health Monograph 4, Special Population Issues*, pp. 3–39; also see Wilsnack, "Alcohol Abuse and Alcoholism in Women," for a discussion.

87. Yih-Ing Hser, M. Douglas Anglin, and Mary W. Booth, "Sex Differences in Addict Careers. 3. Addiction," *American Journal of Drug and Alcohol Abuse*, Vol. 13, No. 3 (1987), pp. 231–251; M. Douglas Anglin,

Yih-Ing Hser, and Mary W. Booth, "Sex Differences in Addict Careers. 4. Treatment," *American Journal of Drug and Alcohol Abuse,* Vol. 13, No. 3 (1987), pp. 253–280.

88. Linda J. Beckman and Hortensia Amaro, "Personal and Social Difficulties Faced by Women and Men Entering Alcoholism Treatment," *Journal of Studies on Alcohol,* Vol. 47 (1986), pp. 135–145.

89. Edith S. Gomberg, "Women and Alcoholism," in Violet Franks and Vasanti Burtle (eds.), *Women in Therapy* (New York: Brunner/Mazel, 1974), p. 170.

90. Kagle, "Women Who Drink: Changing Images, Changing Realities."

91. Florence V. Ridlon, *A Fallen Angel: The Status Insularity of the Female Alcoholic* (London: Associated University Presses, 1988).

92. Sheila Blume, "Women and Alcohol: A Review," *Journal of the American Medical Association,* Vol. 256 (1986), pp. 1467–1470.

93. Ridlon, *A Fallen Angel: The Status Insularity of the Female Alcoholic.*

94. Wilsnack et al., "Drinking and Drinking Problems Among Women in a U.S. National Survey."

95. *ADAMHA News Supplement,* July–August, 1991; also see Walter R. Cuskey, Lisa H. Berger, and Judianne Densen-Gerber, "Issues in the Treatment of Female Addiction: A Review and Critique of the Literature," in Elizabeth Howell and Marjorie Bayes (eds.), *Women and Mental Health* (New York: Basic Books, 1981), pp. 269–295.

96. Hser, Anglin, and Booth, "Sex Differences in Addict Careers. 3. Addiction," p. 249.

97. Torild Hammer and Per Vaglum, "The Increase in Alcohol Consumption Among Women: A Phenomenon Related to Accessibility or Stress? A General Population Study," *British Journal of Addiction,* Vol. 84 (1989), pp. 767–775.

98. Rudolf H. Moos and Bernice S. Moos, "The Process of Recovery from Alcoholism: III. Comparing Functioning in Families of Alcoholics and Matched Control Families," *Journal of Studies on Alcohol,* Vol. 45, No. 2 (1984), pp. 111–118.

99. Andrew G. Billings and Rudolf H. Moos, "Social Support and Functioning Among Community and Clinical Groups: A Panel Model," *Journal of Behavioral Medicine,* Vol. 5, No. 3 (1982), pp. 295–311.

100. Curlee, "A Comparison of Male and Female Patients at an Alcoholism Treatment Center," and Gomberg, "The Female Alcoholic."

101. Geraldine Youcha, *Women and Alcohol* (New York: Crown Publishers, 1986).

102. Sharon C. Wilsnack, Albert D. Klassen, Brett E. Schur, and Richard W. Wilsnack, "Predicting Onset and Chronicity of Women's Problem Drinking: A Five-Year Longitudinal Analysis," *American Journal of Public Health,* Vol. 81, No. 3 (1991), pp. 305–317.

103. Vera L. Lindbeck, "The Woman Alcoholic: A Review of the Literature," *The International Journal of the Addictions,* Vol. 7, No. 3 (1972), pp. 567–580.

104. Ibid.

105. Beckman and Amaro, "Personal and Social Difficulties Faced by Women and Men Entering Alcoholism Treatment."

106. Ibid.

107. Sue Dobbs Robinson, "Women and Alcohol Abuse-Factors Involved in Successful Interventions," *International Journal of the Addictions,* Vol. 19, No. 6 (1984), pp. 601–611.

108. John B. Saunders, A. D. Wodak, and Roger Williams, "Past Experience of Advice and Treatment for Drinking Problems of Patients with Alcoholic Liver Disease," *British Journal of Addiction,* Vol. 80 (1985), pp. 51–56.

109. Hortensia Amaro, Linda J. Beckman, and Vickie M. Mays, "A Comparison of Black and White Women Entering Alcoholism Treatment," *Journal of Studies on Alcohol,* Vol. 48, No. 3 (1987), pp. 220–228.

110. Diane R. Davis, "Recovery Factors of Alcoholic Women: A Pilot Study," The University of Texas at Austin, School of Social Work, 1991.

111. Rebecca Schilit and Edith Lisansky Gromberg, "Social Support Structures of Women in Treatment for Alcoholism," *Health and Social Work* (Summer 1987), pp. 187–195.

112. Linda J. Beckman and Katherine M. Kocel, "The Treatment-Delivery System and Alcohol Abuse in Women: Social Policy Implications," *Journal of Social Issues,* Vol. 38, No. 2 (1982), pp. 139–151.

113. Saunders et al., "Past Experience of Advice."

114. National Institute of Justice, *Research in Action,* October 1990.

115. Joseph J. Senna and Larry J. Siegel, *Introduction to Criminal Justice,* 5th ed. (St. Paul, MN: West, 1990), p. 562.

116. Elaine DeCostanzo and Helen Scholes, "Women Behind Bars, Their Numbers Increase," *Corrections Today* (June 1988), pp. 104–108.

117. Erickson and Watson, "Women, Illicit Drugs, and Crime."

118. Douglas A. Smith and Raymond Paternoster, "The Gender Gap in Theories of Deviance," *Journal of*

Research in Crime and Delinquency, Vol. 24, No. 2 (May 1987), pp. 140–171.

119. Much of this section relies on Erickson and Watson, "Women, Illicit Drugs, and Crime;" see their work for the list of studies on which their conclusions are based.

120. See ibid. for a discussion of the analyses reported in W. R. Cuskey, T. Premkumar, and L. Sigel, "Survey of Opiate Addiction Among Females in the United States between 1850 and 1970," *Public Health Review,* Vol. 1 (1972), pp. 5–39 and R. G. Ferrence and P. C. Whitehead, "Sex Differences in Psychoactive Drug Use: Recent Epidemiology," in O. J. Kalant (ed.), *Alcohol and Drug Problems in Women* (New York: Plenum Press, 1980), pp. 125–201.

121. M. R. Burt, T. J. Glynn, and B. J. Sowder, *Psychosocial Characteristics of Drug-Abusing Women,* NIDA, Services Research Monograph Series (Bethesda, MD: Burt Associates, 1979), cited in Hser, Anglin, and Booth, "Sex Differences in Addict Careers. 3. *Addiction*"; also see Yih-Ing Hser, M. Douglas Anglin, and Chih-Ping Chou, "Narcotics Use and Crime Among Addicted Women: Longitudinal Patterns and Effects of Social Interventions," in Thomas Mieczkowski (ed.), *Drugs, Crime, and Social Policy: Research, Issues, and Concerns* (Boston: Allyn and Bacon, 1992), pp. 197–221.

122. Hser et al., "Sex Differences in Addict Careers. 3."

123. Erickson and Watson, "Women, Illicit Drugs, and Crime."

124. Special Committee on Pornography and Prostitution, *Pornography and Prostitution in Canada* (Ottawa: Department of Supply and Services, 1985), cited in Erickson and Watson, "Women, Illicit Drugs, and Crime."

125. James A. Inciardi and Anne E. Pottieger, "Drug Use and Crime Among Two Cohorts of Women Narcotics Users: An Empirical Assessment," *Journal of Drug Issues,* Vol. 16, No. 1 (1986), pp. 61–106.

126. Erickson and Watson, "Women, Illicit Drugs, and Crime."

127. John Hagan, A. R. Gillis, and John Simpson, "The Class Structure of Gender and Delinquency: Toward a Power-Control Theory of Common Delinquent Behavior," *American Journal of Sociology,* Vol. 90, No. 6 (1985), pp. 1151–1178.

128. See, for example, Beckman and Amaro, "Personal and Social Difficulties Faced by Women and Men Entering Alcoholism Treatment"; Hope R. Conte, Robert Plutchik, Susan Picard, Marc Galanter, and Jacob Jacoby, "Sex Differences in Personality Traits and Coping Styles of Hospitalized Alcoholics," *Journal of Studies on Alcohol,* Vol. 52, No. 1 (1991), pp. 26–32;

and Joanne E. Turnbull and Edith S. L. Gomberg, "Impact of Depressive Symptomatology on Alcohol Problems in Women," *Alcoholism: Clinical and Experimental Research,* Vol. 12, No. 3 (May–June 1988), pp. 374–381.

129. See, for example, Roman, *Women and Alcohol Use: A Review of the Research Literature,* and Linda J. Beckman, "Treatment Needs of Women Alcoholics," *Alcoholism Treatment Quarterly,* Vol. 1, No. 2 (Summer 1984), pp. 101–114.

130. Conte et al., "Sex Differences in Personality Traits and Coping Styles of Hospitalized Alcoholics."

131. Marc A. Schuckit and Elizabeth R. Morrissey, "Alcoholism in Women: Some Clinical and Social Perspectives with an Emphasis on Possible Subtypes," in Greenblatt and Schuckit (eds.), *Alcoholism Problems in Women and Children,* pp. 5–35, and Sharon C. Wilsnack, "Alcohol Abuse and Alcoholism in Women."

132. Ross, "Alcohol and Drug Abuse in Treated Alcoholics: A Comparison of Men and Women," and Michie N. Hesselbrock, Roger E. Meyer, and Janet J. Keener, "Psychopathology in Hospitalized Alcoholics," *Archives of General Psychiatry,* Vol. 42 (November 1985), pp. 1050–1055.

133. Margaret L. Griffin, Roger D. Weiss, Steven M. Mirin, and Ulrike Lange, "A Comparison of Male and Female Cocaine Abusers," *Archives of General Psychiatry,* Vol. 46 (February 1989), pp. 122–126.

134. Roman, *Women and Alcohol Use: A Review of the Research Literature,* and Elizabeth R. Morrissey and Marc A. Schuckit, "Stressful Life Events and Alcohol Problems Among Women Seen at a Detoxification Center," *Journal of Studies on Alcohol,* Vol. 39, No. 9 (1978), pp. 1559–1576.

135. Clinton B. De Soto, William E. O'Donnell, Linda J. Allred, and Cheryl E. Lopes, "Symptomatology in Alcoholics at Various Stages of Abstinence," *Alcoholism: Clinical and Experimental Research,* Vol. 9, No. 6 (November–December 1985), pp. 505–512.

136. Clinton B. De Soto, William E. O'Donnell, and Janet L. De Soto, "Long-Term Recovery in Alcoholics," *Alcoholism: Clinical and Experimental Research,* Vol. 13 (October 1989), pp. 693–697.

137. NIAAA, *Seventh Special Report.*

138. Curlee, "A Comparison of Male and Female Patients at an Alcoholism Treatment Center," and Glenn and Parsons, "Alcohol Abuse and Familial Alcoholism: Psychosocial Correlates in Men and Women."

139. Schilit and Gomberg, "Social Support Structures of Women in Treatment for Alcoholism."

140. Nannette Lehmann and Steven L. Krupp, "Incidence of Alcohol-Related Domestic Violence," *Alcohol Health and Research World* (Winter 1983/84), pp. 23–27 and 39.

141. Sharon C. Wilsnack, "Drinking, Sexuality, and Sexual Dysfunction in Women," in Wilsnack and Beckman, *Alcohol Problems in Women,* pp. 189–227; also see Hurley, "Women, Alcohol and Incest: An Analytical Review."

142. S.S. Covington, "Sexual Experience, Dysfunction and Abuse: A Comparative Study of Alcoholic and Non-Alcoholic Women, doctoral dissertation, Union Graduate School, 1982, cited in Wilsnack, "Drinking, Sexuality, and Sexual Dysfunction in Women," pp. 189–227.

143. S. Covington, "Sex and Violence: The Unmentionable in Alcoholism Treatment," paper presented at the National Alcoholism Forum, Washington, DC, 1982, cited in Brenda L. Underhill, "Issues Relevant to Aftercare Programs for Women," *Alcohol Health & Research World,* Fall 1986, p. 46.

144. Roman, *Women and Alcohol Use.*

145. Covington, "Sex and Violence," cited in Underhill, "Issues Relevant to Aftercare," pp. 46–47.

146. Edith S. Lisansky Gomberg, "Shame and Guilt Issues Among Women Alcoholics," *Alcoholism Treatment Quarterly,* Vol. 4, No. 2 (1987), pp. 139–155.

147. Marsha Vannicelli, ""Treatment Outcome of Alcoholic Women: The State of the Art in Relation to Sex Bias and Expectancy Effects," in Wilsnack and Beckman (eds.), *Alcohol Problems in Women,* Chapter 13, pp. 369–412, see especially p. 376.

148. Benjamin M. Karpman, *The Woman Alcoholic: Case Studies in the Psychodynamics of Alcoholism* (Washington, DC: Linacre, 1948).

149. Vannicelli, "Treatment Outcome of Alcoholic Women: The State of the Art in Relation to Sex Bias and Expectancy Effects," pp. 369–412.

150. Hser, Anglin, and Booth, "Sex Differences in Addict Careers. 3. Addiction."

151. Institute of Medicine, *Broadening the Base of Treatment for Alcohol Problems,* p. 356; also see Helen M. Annis and Carolyn B. Liban, "Alcoholism in Women: Treatment Modalities and Outcomes," in Oriana Josseau Kalant, *Alcohol and Drug Problems in Women: Research Advances in Alcohol and Drug Problems,* Volume 5 (New York: Plenum Press, 1980), pp. 385–422.

152. Institute of Medicine, *Broadening the Base of Treatment for Alcoholism.*

153. Richard Longabaugh and David C. Lewis, "Key Issues in Treatment Outcome Studies," *Alcohol Health and Research World,* Vol. 12, No. 3 (1988), pp. 168–175.

154. De Soto, O'Donnell, and DeSoto, "Long-Term Recovery in Alcoholics."

155. Anglin et al., "Sex Differences in Addict Careers. 4. Treatment."

156. Vannicelli, "Treatment Outcome of Alcoholic Women: The State of the Art in Relation to Sex Bias and Expectancy Effects," pp. 369–412; also see Institute of Medicine, *Broadening the Base of Treatment for Alcoholism.*

157. Helen M. Annis, "Treatment of Alcoholic Women," in Griffith Edwards and Marcus Grant (eds.), *Alcoholism Treatment in Transition* (London: Croom Helm, 1980), Chapter 8, p. 128.

158. Harriet B. Braiker, "Therapeutic Issues in the Treatment of Alcoholic Women," in Wilsnack and Beckman (eds.), *Alcohol Problems in Women,* Chp. 12, pp. 349–368, especially p. 349.

159. Lena Dahlgren and Anders Willander, "Are Special Treatment Facilities for Female Alcoholics Needed? A Controlled 2-Year Follow-up Study from a Specialized Female Unit (EWA) Versus a Mixed Male/Female Treatment Facility," *Alcoholism: Clinical and Experimental Research,* Vol. 13, No. 4 (July/August 1989), pp. 499–504.

160. Amaro, Beckman, and Mays, "A Comparison of Black and White Women Entering Alcoholism Treatment."

161. Patricia Ann Harrison and Carol A. Belille, "Women in Treatment: Beyond the Stereotype," *Journal of Studies on Alcohol,* Vol. 48, No. 6 (1987), pp. 574–578.

162. Alcoholics Anonymous World Services, *Alcoholics Anonymous Membership Survey* (New York: Alcoholics Anonymous World Services, 1989), and Chad D. Emrick, "Alcoholics Anonymous: Affiliation Processes and Effectiveness as Treatment," *Alcoholism: Clinical and Experimental Research,* Vol. 11, No. 5 (September/October 1987), pp. 416–423.

163. Charlotte Davis Kasl, "The Twelve Step Controversy," *Ms. Magazine* (November/December 1990), pp. 30–31.

164. Kirkpatrick, *Turnabout: Help for a New Life.*

165. J. S. Rudolf, "Jean Kirkpatrick," *Sober Times* (October 1990).

166. Women for Sobriety, "Who We Are" (Quakertown, PA: Author, 1976).

167. Rudolf, "Jean Kirkpatrick."

168. Women for Sobriety, "Overview" (Quakerstown, PA: Author, 1989).

169. The remainder of this paragraph relies on Lee Kaskutas, "Women for Sobriety: A Qualitative Analy-

sis," *Contemporary Drug Problems* (Summer 1989), pp. 177–200; also see Kirkpatrick, *Turnabout*, for a discussion of Women for Sobriety.

170. Kaskutas, "Women for Sobriety," p. 195.

171. Jean Kirkpatrick, "A Self-help Program for Women Alcoholics," *Alcohol Health & Research World* (Summer 1982), reprint.

172. Kasl, "The Twelve Step Controversy," p. 31.

173. This history is also recounted in Sharon C. Wilsnack, "The Impact of Sex Roles on Women's Alcohol Use and Abuse," in Greenblatt and Schuckit, *Alcoholism Problems in Women and Children*, pp. 37–63, and in Dorothy Henderson and Carol Boyd, "Masculinity, Femininity, and Addiction," in Mieczkowski (ed.), *Drugs, Crime, and Social Policy: Research, Issues and Concerns*, pp. 153–166.

174. William McCord and Joan McCord, *Origins of Alcoholism* (Stanford, CA: Stanford University Press, 1960), see especially pp. 162–164.

175. David C. McClelland, William N. Davis, Rudolf Kalin, and Eric Wanner, *The Drinking Man* (New York: The Free Press, 1972).

176. Sharon C. Wilsnack, "Sex Role Identity in Female Alcoholism," *Journal of Abnormal Psychology*, Vol. 82, No. 2 (1973), pp. 253–261 and Sharon C. Wilsnack, "Feminity by the Bottle," in Cristen C. Eddy and John L. Ford, *Alcoholism in Women* (Dubuque, IA: Kendall/Hunt, 1980), pp. 16–24.

177. Joan Scida and Marsha Vannicelli, "Sex-Role Conflict and Women's Drinking," *Journal of Studies on Alcohol*, Vol. 40, No. 1 (1979), pp. 28–44.

178. Wilsnack, "The Impact of Sex Roles on Women's Alcohol Use and Abuse."

179. C. J. Colman, "Problem Drinking Women: Aspects of Their Marital Interaction and Sex Role Style," unpublished doctoral dissertation, Howard University, 1975, cited in Wilsnack, "The Impact of Sex Roles on Women's Alcohol Use and Abuse," and in Henderson and Boyd, "Masculinity, Feminity, and Addiction."

180. This paragraph relies on Henderson and Boyd, "Masculinity, Feminity, and Addiction," p. 159.

181. These four studies were part of the original pool of studies discussed in Chad D. Emrick, "A Review of Psychologically Oriented Treatment of Alcoholism," *Quarterly Journal of Studies on Alcohol*, Vol. 35 (1974), pp. 523–549. Emrick did not discuss gender differences but made the data available to Marsha Vannicelli who discussed them in her article "Treatment Outcome of Alcoholic Women: The State of the Art in Relation to Sex Bias and Expectancy Effects," in Wilsnack and Beckman, *Alcohol Problems in Women*, pp. 369–412.

182. Vannicelli, "Treatment Outcome of Alcoholic Women: The State of the Art in Relation to Sex Bias and Expectancy Effects", pp. 369–412.

183. *ADAMHA News Supplement*, Vol. 17, No. 4 (July–August 1991).

184. Corrigan, "Gender Differences in Alcohol and Other Drug Use."

185. Diane R. Davis, "Gender Differences Among Substance Abusers: New Wine in an Old Vessel," dissertation, University of Texas at Austin, 1992.

186. Carl G. Leukefeld and Frank M. Tims, "Relapse and Recovery in Drug Abuse: Research and Practice," *The International Journal of the Addictions*, Vol. 24, No. 3 (1989), p. 197.

187. Braiker, "Therapeutic Issues in the Treatment of Alcoholic Women," pp. 349–368, especially p. 350.

188. Roman, *Women and Alcohol Use: A Review of the Research Literature*.

189. Fanny Duckert, "Recruitment into Treatment and Effects of Treatment for Female Problem Drinkers," *Addictive Behaviors*, Vol. 12 (1987), pp. 137–150.

190. Also see Institute of Medicine, *Broadening the Base of Treatment for Alcoholism*, p. 357.

191. Susan D. Solomon, "Women in the Workplace: An Overview of NIAAA's Occupational Alcoholism Demonstration Project," *Alcohol Health & Research World*, Vol. 7, No. 3 (Spring 1983), Special Focus: Women in the Workplace, pp. 3–5.

192. Saunders et al., "Past Experience of Advice and Treatment for Drinking Problems of Patients with Alcoholic Liver Disease."

193. Duckert, "Recruitment into Treatment and Effects of Treatment for Alcoholism."

194. Joanne E. Turnbull, "Treatment Issues for Alcoholic Women," *Social Casework*, Vol. 70, No. 6 (1989), pp. 364–369.

195. Institute of Medicine, *Broadening the Base of Treatment for Alcoholism*.

196. Underhill, "Issues Relevant to Aftercare Programs for Women."

197. Ibid.

198. Elizabeth Aries, "Interaction Patterns and Themes of Male, Female, and Mixed Groups," *Small Group Behavior*, Vol. 7, No. 1, (February 1976), pp. 7–18.

199. Underhill, "Issues Relevant to Aftercare Programs for Women."

200. Jan Waterson and Betsy Ettorre, "Providing Services for Women with Difficulties with Alcohol or Other Drugs: The Current U.K. Situation as Seen by Women Practitioners, Researchers and Policy Makers in the

Field," *Drug and Alcohol Dependence,* Vol. 24 (1989), p. 124.

201. See *Alcohol Health & Research World,* Vol. 7, No. 3 (Spring 1983), Special Focus: Women in the Workplace.

202. *ADMAHA News,* Vol. 17, No. 4 (July–August 1991).

203. "New Offices to Track Special Issues," *ADAMHA News,* Vol. 18, No. 4 (September–October 1992), p. 7.

IV
SUMMARY AND CONCLUSIONS

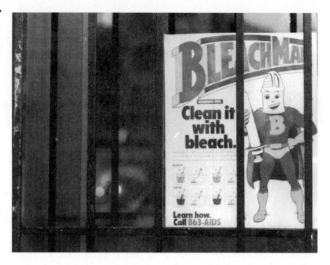

16

Chemical dependency: current issues and future prospects

We know a great deal about the phenomenon of drug use and abuse: unfortunately, much of that knowledge simply is not utilized in developing public policy and planning programs. One reason is that this is a highly charged emotional issue for many individuals and many politically powerful groups. For example, the legalization (or decriminalization) of any illicit drug faces a steep uphill battle as long as it is opposed by organized church groups and large factions of both major political parties. Nevertheless, it seems to us that the following observations should be made in this concluding chapter:

- *There have always been some people in just about every society who use drugs.* The type of drugs

used may vary, as well as the proportion of individuals using them, but drug use is one of the more common historical phenomena. This is not likely to change.

- *Society cannot prevent drug use: at most, it may control or regulate it.* Various efforts to prohibit drug use, especially in a civil rights–oriented democracy such as the United States, are doomed to failure. Furthermore, the side effects of prohibition efforts may be worse than the direct effects of drug use. Prohibition of beverage alcohol and the current "war on drugs" are examples of these policy failures.

- *Societal decisions about which drugs to allow or prohibit are essentially political decisions.* Some drugs with minimal (or nonexistent) benefits are frequently allowed and regulated, while others with comparatively safe risk levels are illegal. We have examined the case against both alcohol and tobacco at several other points in this book.

- *While other drugs many come and go, alcohol is the one great historical constant in drug use.* Undoubtedly, alcohol's popularity is related to its status as the only *legal* psychoactive drug that most people can use to get "high."

- *New drugs that are even more addicting than the current popular drugs will become major problems in the next century.* Only a decade ago, almost no one had heard of "ice." In some communities today, it rivals crack cocaine in popularity. As society advances in its technological capacity, the chemists who invent new psychoactive drugs will continue refining and "improving" their products.

- *We do not know how to effectively treat many drug abuse problems.* As we explained in Chapter 6, treatment programs for alcohol and drug abuse have had mixed results. Many persons who are chemically dependent are just as likely to recover without treatment as they are with treatment, and relapse rates for those who do "recover" are quite high.

- *Insurers and other organizations who finance treatment programs are demanding more for their money.* Despite some evidence that inpatient programs sometimes may be more effective than outpatient treatment programs, they are much more expensive. When they are used, insurance companies are insisting on shorter stays.

Based on these observations, several courses of action regarding research, policy change, and the delivery of services are outlined in the paragraphs that follow.

RESEARCH

Despite several excellent recent studies of treatment effectiveness, the state of knowledge in this field is still in its infancy. We know that most programs seem to have little or no effect, and we know that there is a moderately strong relationship between length of treatment and treatment effectiveness. We still do not know *why* most treatment is ineffective, and the most obvious reason is that the research methodologies used in evaluating treatment programs are simply not designed to answer this question. We strongly suspect that one of the reasons for this is that we are still ignorant about the etiology of alcohol and drug problems.

Furthermore, there is much concern about the appropriateness of viewing alcoholism or drug addiction as phenomena amenable to the medical model. There are, of course, many justifications for this point of view. First, it is much easier to find ways to finance treatment if chemical dependency is a medical problem. Second, many of the physiological *consequences* of alcohol or drug abuse are undeniably appropriate for medical treatment. However, social workers and other professionals working in the field of chemical dependency treatment may pay lip service to the disease concept, but they generally do not treat it with a medical model. Except for medical detoxification, most treatment consists of talk therapies and self-help programs.

Too much of the research on drug and alcohol abuse and treatment has been narrowly focused on specific subpopulations that may behave quite differently from other groups. At the risk of overgeneralizing, white male alcoholics have received a great deal more attention than most other groups. Women alcoholics and drug users have been underrepresented in chemical dependency research. Research on illicit drugs, especially opiates, has been conducted primarily on those who have been arrested and have become involved in the criminal justice system. Research on noncriminal substance abusers has concentrated on low-income groups and special populations such as Veterans Administration clients.

One avenue of research that has been largely ignored is the study of those persons who have recovered from chemical dependency without treatment. One recent study of 101 opiate addicts who recovered without the help of any formal treatment discovered a potentially useful pattern of recovery among these persons, rather than a "spontaneous remission." This pattern included forming a resolve, becoming abstinent, creating an alternative, dealing with the craving problem, and becoming "ordinary."[1] More research is needed on similar groups of persons dependent on other drugs, especially alcohol. The "natural history" model of alcoholism as described by Vaillant may be an appropriate place to begin.[2]

Given the apparently high degree of interest in the use of acupuncture as a treatment modality, especially in the criminal justice system, more research is needed on this approach. While some studies have documented higher program completion rates for alcoholism treatment,[3] the long-term effectiveness of acupuncture has not been thoroughly examined. Other recent studies have found acupuncture to be ineffective either in improving treatment completion rates or reducing recidivism rates.[4] Nevertheless, chemically dependent offenders in some jurisdictions are being *required* to undergo acupuncture treatment to participate in court-sponsored diversion programs, and the practice seems to be spreading rapidly.

No one can deny that new, innovative treatment methods are sorely needed. However, it would seem prudent to begin on a small scale and thoroughly evaluate the impact of new methods before allowing them to proliferate. Law enforcement and treatment professionals are so desperate for ways to deal with the growing problems of abuse and addiction that it is understandable why they might be willing to use nontraditional methods. After all, the more traditional approaches have been successful with relatively few clients.

POLICY CHANGE

We proposed a number of policy changes in Chapter 8 that we will not repeat here. We will remind the reader, however, that we think our national drug policy should be guided by the overall philosophy of minimizing risks both to the user and to the larger society. This does not necessarily mean that we should legalize or decriminalize illicit drugs, although that option certainly should be given serious consideration. It does mean that we should do things like expand methadone maintenance clinics and needle/syringe exchange programs. The AIDS crisis alone is enough to justify this change. On a less controversial level, why not require brewers and distillers to add vitamins and minerals to alcoholic beverages in order to prevent some of the nutritional problems associated with alcohol abuse?

Decriminalization should be seriously considered for another very practical reason. We run the risk of bankrupting ourselves as a nation if we continue to incarcerate drug offenders at the present rate. (For example, at the current rate of increase in drug-related prison admissions in Florida, everyone in the state will be incarcerated by the year 2021!) Not only is this an immense financial problem, but it is also responsible for an overall increase in criminality and disrespect for society and its institutions. Cocaine users who spend a year or two in prison are much more likely to become involved in other criminal activity once they are returned to the community. In many states persons convicted of murder, armed robbery, and rape are being released from prison early to make room for the dramatic increase in drug offenders.

While we are imprisoning so many people for illicit drug use, the federal government continues to provide subsidies and price supports to tobacco farmers and to benefit from tax revenues on both tobacco and alcohol sales. Remember that tobacco alone kills more people each year than all illicit drugs combined! It is no surprise that adolescents fail to see any rationality or fairness in our current policies.

PROVIDING SERVICES

In our view chemical dependency treatment services, especially those public programs available to low-income individuals, are woefully inadequate. The private tier of services are so expensive that they are generally unavailable to anyone except the wealthy or those fortunate enough to have adequate insurance. Current estimates indicate that as many as half of all Americans either have no health insurance or are seriously underinsured.[5] There does seem to be a widespread recognition that something must be done about the cost of services. One approach is to provide "managed care." To see how this concept evolved, however, we should first review the development of third-party coverage for chemical dependency.

Third-Party Coverage

Early in its existence the National Institute on Alcohol Abuse and Alcoholism (NIAAA) decided that health insurance for alcoholism was the best way to assure a stable funding base for treatment. State alcoholism agencies joined the effort, and by 1981, thirty-three states had mandated that group health insurance providers had to offer optional coverage for treatment. The federal Health Maintenance Organization Act of 1973 required all HMOs to provide alcoholism treatment services to qualify for federal subsidies.[6] By 1990 similar initiatives regarding drug abuse treatment had resulted in mandatory coverage laws in 18 states and the District of Columbia.[7] Growing numbers of employee assistance programs provided chemical dependency services. By 1988 about 140 million Americans had specifically defined coverage for drug treatment in their health insurance plans. About 74 percent of full-time employees of medium-sized and large firms had this type of insurance coverage, as well as 94 percent of public employees.[8]

In recent years, however, the high cost and the relative ineffectiveness of treatment for both alcohol and drug abuse have prompted insurers of all types to reconsider. It appears that the movement toward universal coverage of chemical dependency has leveled off or perhaps lost ground. Private coverage is likely to be optional, expensive, and more difficult to obtain. When private coverage is available, insurers are insisting on more effective and *cheaper* methods of treatment. Some third-party payors have strongly questioned the

value of treatment, and there is a movement to view drug and alcohol treatment as part of the nonmedical/surgical fringe of health coverage that may be differentially limited to trim increasing overall costs.[9]

Managed Care

During the last decade there were serious attempts by managed care companies to cut the costs of treating drug and alcohol abuse. Stimulated by the work of Miller and Hester[10] and Saxe and coworkers,[11] they attempted to direct all drug clients away from hospital-based inpatient programs toward outpatient services. The primary motivation for this movement was the evidence regarding the relative ineffectiveness and the greater expense of inpatient programs. (See Chapter 6.)

Managed care is generally provided in the context of a health maintenance organization (HMO), preferred provider organization (PPO), or independent practice association (IPA). Whatever the setting, the essence of managed care is attention to health care delivery and health care costs.[12]

The objective of managed care strategies is to accumulate information about accepted clinical practices, their costs, and their appropriateness as treatment strategies. They attempt to generate knowledge to be used as protocols for permitting or disallowing reimbursement for particular services. Managed care uses strategies such as prospective certification or preadmission review of hospital stays, utilization review during or after discharge, the use of preferred providers who cooperate on "planned treatment" approaches, and specialized case management directed at cost containment.[13] It is thought that if managed care strategies for drug and alcohol treatment are supported by adequate research on treatment effectiveness, they can ensure access to appropriate treatment while containing the costs.[14]

There are obviously many tensions between managed care organizations and insurers, on the one hand, and residential treatment organizations (especially hospital-based programs), on the other. As we discussed earlier, there is some evidence that treatment outcomes are related to length of treatment, and there is agreement that some clients need lengthy, inpatient services.[15] Legislation regarding managed care has focused primarily on cost containment and has not adequately dealt with its potential to compromise the quality of treatment.[16] Still, until service providers have evidence that the more expensive methods produce better outcomes, the cost containment philosophies of managed care organizations will be difficult to refute.

CONCLUDING THOUGHTS

The stakes in our "war on drugs" are enormously high. Generations of our young people are at risk, not just for addiction, but for all the associated problems that go hand in hand with drug and alcohol abuse under our current policies: AIDS, domestic violence, incarceration, and the inability to function economically and socially as normal citizens.

Our current approach to treating chemical dependency and substance abuse has not served us well. We believe that a large part of the problem is that we have *not* used a systemic perspective in planning treatment strategies. Too frequently we have considered drug or alcohol abuse as an *individual* problem amenable to a *clinical* solution. Even the use of family systems is much too narrow a perspective for a problem of such magnitude. If America has the most widespread abuse of alcohol and drugs of any modern industrial society, it seems likely to be related to factors at the *societal* level. Realistic solutions must be planned and executed at the same level.

In a recent address to the National Council of Governors, President Clinton encouraged the group to be creative in seeking innovative new solutions to the problems associated with welfare dependency and health care. At the same time, he admonished them to have the courage to change "if the new, innovative approaches don't work." The same principle should be applied to the problems of drug abuse and dependency. Even when new approaches have failed to

produce results ("weed and seed," acupuncture, expedited case management, etc.), they seem to proliferate and to become quickly entrenched. The new bureaucracies that are responsible for administering the funds and providing the services are reluctant to consider the implications of their failure to treat chemically dependent clients effectively. Once a treatment modality has been adopted, staff have been hired, and a program has been established, it is much easier to deal with the problem of program failure by making minor modifications than by starting over with a new approach.

However, the problems of drug abuse and dependency are of such a magnitude that new, dramatic intervention strategies are essential. The new strategies must use a *systemic* approach in dealing with these problems at the level of the client, the community, and the nation. We have reached the point where program failure is no longer acceptable. *No* new approach should be rejected out of hand. The future of our nation is at stake.

ENDNOTES

1. Patrick Biernacki, *Recovery from Opiate Addiction Without Treatment: A Summary*, Research Monograph 98 (Washington, DC: National Institute on Drug Abuse, 1990).

2. George E. Valliant, *The Natural History of Alcoholism: Causes, Patterns and Paths to Recovery* (Cambridge, MA: Harvard University Press, 1983).

3. Alex Brumbaugh, *Acute Care Program: First Year Report* (Santa Barbara, CA: Santa Barbara Council on Alcoholism and Drug Abuse, 1992).

4. T. M. Worner, B. Zeller, H. Schwarz, F. Zwas, and D. Lyon, "Acupuncture Fails to Improve Treatment Outcome in Alcoholics," *Drug and Alcohol Dependence,* Vol. 30 (1992), pp. 169–173.

5. Speech by former Surgeon General C. Everett Koop at Florida State University, Tallahassee, FL, November 19, 1991.

6. Constance Weisner and Robin Room, "Financing and Ideology in Alcohol Treatment," in Maureen E. Kelleher, Bruce K. MacMurray, and Thomas M. Shapiro, *Drugs and Society: A Critical Reader, 2nd ed.* (Dubuque, IA: Kendall/Hunt, 1988), pp. 360–378.

7. Dean R. Gerstein and Henrick R. Harwood (eds.),

Treating Drug Problems, Volume 1 (Washington, DC: National Academy Press, 1990).

8. Ibid., p. 289.

9. Ibid., p. 294.

10. William R. Miller and Reid K. Hester, "Inpatient Alcoholism Treatment: Who Benefits?" *American Psychologist,* Vol. 41 (1986), pp. 794–805.

11. Leonard M. Saxe, Denise M. Dougherty, K. Esty, and Michelle Fine, *The Effectiveness and Costs of Alcoholism Treatment,* Health Technology Case Study 22 (Washington, DC: Office of Technology Assessment, 1983).

12. Linda M. Richardson and Carol S. Austad, "Realities of Mental Health Practice in Managed-Care Settings,"

Professional Psychology: Research and Practice, Vol. 22, No. 1 (1991), pp. 52–59.

13. Lloyd I. Sederer and R. Lawrence St. Clair, "Quality Assurance and Managed Health Care," *Psychiatric Clinics of North America,* Vol. 13, No. 1 (March 1990), pp. 89–97.

14. Gerstein and Harwood, *Treating Drug Problems,* p. 286.

15. Ibid., p. 135.

16. Russ Newman and Patricia M. Bricklin, "Parameters of Managed Mental Health Care: Legal, Ethical, and Professional Guidelines," *Professional Psychology Research and Practice,* Vol. 22, No. 1 (February 1991), pp. 26–35.

Index